ORGANIZATIONAL BEHAVIOR

ORGANIZATIONAL BEHAVIOR

Robert Kreitner
Angelo Kinicki

both of Arizona State University

1989

BPI
IRWIN

Homewood, IL 60430
Boston, MA 02116

Cover photo: Michel Tcherevkoff/THE IMAGE BANK

Sponsoring editor: William R. Bayer
Project editor: Jean Roberts
Production manager: Bette Ittersagen
Designer: Jeanne Wolfgeher
Compositor: Arcata Graphics/Kingsport
Typeface: 10.5/12 Times Roman
Printer: R. R. Donnelley & Sons Company

LIBRARY OF CONGRESS
Library of Congress Cataloging-in-Publication Data

Kreitner, Robert.
    Organizational behavior/Robert J. Kreitner, Angelo J. Kinicki.
        p.   cm.
    Includes index.
    ISBN 0-256-03512-1
    1. Organizational behavior.   I. Kinicki, Angelo J.   II. Title.
HD58.7.K75 1989
658.3—dc 19   88–25848
                                                                    CIP

Printed in the United States of America
    2 3 4 5 6 7 8 9 0 DO 6 5 4 3 2 1 0 9

*Dedicated to the memory of
Donald A. Kolbe, Jr., a good
friend and a fine editor.
This book was his idea.*

R. K.

*Dedicated with love and
appreciation to Joyce Kinicki,
my wife and best friend.*

A. K.

Preface

This textbook is intended to help present and future managers learn more about people at work. It is the product of our combined 25 years of teaching and researching organizational behavior. Our colleagues and students have taught us many valuable lessons about textbooks. First and foremost, they desire a *balanced* exposure to the entire field, including up-to-date conceptual/ research insights and real-world applications. Regarding this latter feature, *Organizational Behavior* was researched and written with two classroom questions constantly in mind: So what? and Who cares? These seemingly simple questions kept us honest when it came to distinguishing relevant from irrelevant material, translating abstract theory and research results to straightforward and concise explanations, and integrating many real-world examples.

Additionally, today's students want an *interactive* textbook that encourages them to do more than passively read page after page. Toward that end, this book integrates 18 *self-assessment exercises* into the textual material. Readers will gain experiential insights about their motivation to manage, value system, attitudes toward female executives, need for achievement, job satisfaction, conflict-handling style, leadership style, creativity, and exposure to stress, among other things. Norms are provided for comparison purposes. The net result is a comprehensive but user-friendly introduction to organizational behavior.

The field of organizational behavior, which involves understanding and managing people at work, is exciting and endlessly challenging because it focuses on *the human factor*. Because this is a book about understanding and managing people at work, students will read about some intriguing people. In their own way, each provides instructive insights about what to do (or what not to do) in modern work organizations. For example, in Chapter 10 students will accompany Janet Long as she struggles to learn more about herself and group dynamics in the Wilderness Lab in the Colorado Rockies. In Chapter 16, readers will discover how two paramedics, Richard Awe and Joseph Pessolano, deal with stress as they race through the busy streets of New York City. Chapter 5 provides a rare, off-the-record account of job dissatisfaction from the people who wear Pluto, Goofy, and Winnie the Pooh costumes at Disney World. These and many other real people appearing in this book help promote greater understanding of why people at work behave as they do.

A key element of learning is *surprise*. We have included some instructive surprises to keep things lively. For example, readers will be surprised to learn that Hewelett-Packard gave one employee an award for contempt and defiance. Also surprising is the method Federal Express used to get its college-age cargo handlers to meet their performance goals. Even more surprising is Tampa

Electric Company's practice of giving its misbehaving employees a day off with full pay! In each of these cases, however, the supporting textual material provides a solid, research-based rationale for why such surprising organizational behavior tactics worked.

Organizational Behavior is designed to be a complete teaching and learning tool that captures the reader's interest and imparts useful knowledge. Important pedagogical features are described below.

- Classic and modern topics are given balanced treatment in terms of the latest and best available theoretical models, research results, and practical applications. Complete coverage of traditional topics such as communication, motivation, leadership, and organization structure/design is complemented by discussion of emerging topics. Among these modern topics are social information processing, social learning theory, behavioral self-management, information richness, communication competence, vertical dyad leadership, substitutes for leadership, the garbage can model of decision making, social support and hardiness as moderators of stress, coping with stress, organizational life cycles and effectiveness, and organizational cultures.

- Several concise learning objectives open each chapter to (1) focus the reader's attention and (2) serve as a comprehension check.

- Every chapter begins with a real-name, real-world case study to provide a context for the topics at hand. Each case is followed by a warm-up question to promote learning readiness. A "Back to the Opening Case" feature following each chapter offers questions to underscore the practical implications of what was just read.

- A stimulating art program including 136 figures, 103 application tables, and 69 technical tables makes the textual material come to life. Among the dozens of organizations discussed in the application tables are IBM, Exxon, Hewlett-Packard, Dana Corp., General Motors, B. F. Goodrich, the Internal Revenue Service, Westinghouse, Honeywell, Liz Claiborne, and the U.S. Navy.

- Hundreds of real-world examples have been woven into the textual material to make it interesting and relevant.

- Women play a prominent role throughout this text. Special effort has been devoted to uncovering research insights about relevant female-male differences.

- In keeping with the AACSB's call for broader international coverage, every chapter includes at least one application table discussing organizational behavior in a country other than the United States. A total of 20 international tables and two international figures are identified with a globe logo. Among the different nations and regions covered are Great Britain, South Korea, France, Japan, Europe, the U.S.S.R., China, West Germany, Australia, and Switzerland.

- A "Summary of Key Concepts" feature following each chapter concisely refamiliarizes the reader with the material just covered.

- Throughout the text, key terms are printed in boldface for emphasis and easy reference. A list of key terms for review purposes follows each chapter.
- Ten discussion questions at the end of every chapter challenge the reader to explore the personal and practical implications of what has just been covered.
- Hands-on exercises at the end of each chapter foster experiential learning. Although some of the exercises are best done in classroom groups, the vast majority can be completed by readers working alone.

Any book represents the fruit of many people's labor. Our colleagues at Arizona State University have been very supportive of this project. Peter Hom, in particular, has been a constant source of material, good ideas, and constructive feedback. Thanks Pete. Larry Penley, our department chairman, deserves our thanks for his helpful advice on organizational communication. Warmest thanks also to Maria Muto and Mike Morris for their skillful, dedicated, and quality work on the lecture supplement manual and test bank, respectively. Both of us sincerely appreciate the sage advice of our friend and colleague Keith Davis.

To the following reviewers of all or portions of the manuscript goes our sincerest appreciation. Their feedback was thoughtful, rigorous, and above all, extremely helpful:

(Ms.) Arnon Reichers, Ohio State University

Sandra Morgan, University of Hartford

Gene Bocialetti, University of New Hampshire

Margaret Neale, University of Arizona

Peter Hom, Arizona State University

Lewis A. Taylor III, University of Miami

Peter Yeager, Richmond, Virginia

Tony Mento, Loyola College, Maryland

Edward J. Conlon, University of Iowa

Gene Murkison, Georgia Southern College

Finally, we would like to thank our wives, Margaret and Joyce. They believe in us and what we do, and vice versa. Thanks in large measure to their moral and technical support, this project strengthened rather than strained our valued friendship.

We hope you enjoy this textbook. Best wishes for success and happiness!

Robert Kreitner
Angelo Kinicki

Contents

4 · Perception, Attributions, and Learning   106

5 · Motivation through Needs and Satisfaction   142

6 · Motivation through Equity, Expectancy, and Goal Setting   174

7 · Performance Appraisal, Feedback, and Rewards   210

Performance Appraisal: Definition and Components, **213** *Components of the Performance Appraisal Process. Recent Performance Appraisal Research Findings.* Alternative Performance Appraisal Techniques, **220** *Goal Setting/ Management by Objectives. Written Essays. Critical Incidents. Graphic Rating Scales. Weighted Checklists. Rankings. Behaviorally Anchored Rating Scales. Forced Distribution. Forced Choice. Paired Comparisons. Concluding Comment.* Feedback, **227** *Feedback Is a Control Mechanism. Conceptual Model of the Feedback Process. Practical Lessons from Feedback Research.* Organizational Reward Systems, **235** *Types of Rewards. Organizational Reward Norms. Reward Distribution Criteria. Desired Outcomes of the Reward System.* The Contingent Rewards Controversy, **239** *Pro: Performance-Contingent Rewards Enhance Motivation. Con: Performance-Contingent Rewards Erode Intrinsic Motivation. Practical Implications.* Summary of Key Concepts, **244** Key Terms, **245** Discussion Questions, **245** Exercise 7, **246**

8 · Behavior Modification and Self-Management   248

Principles of Behavior Modification, **252** *A-B-C Contingencies. Contingent Consequences. Schedules of Reinforcement. Behavior Shaping.* A Model for Modifying Job Behavior, **261** *Step 1: Identify Target Behavior. Step 2: Functionally Analyze the Situation. Step 3: Arrange Antecedents and Provide Consequences. Step 4: Evaluate Results.* B. Mod. in the Workplace: Research and Practical Implications, **269** *Recent Research Evidence. Some Practical Implications.* Behavioral Self-Management, **272** *Behavioral Self-Management and the Practice of Management. The Mechanics of Self-Regulation. Social Learning Model of Self-Management. Research and Managerial Implications.* Summary of Key Concepts, **279** Key Terms, **280** Discussion Questions, **280** Exercise 8, **281**

PART THREE
Understanding and Managing Group Processes   284

9 · Organizational Socialization   286

Social Facilitation, **289** *Research Insights. Implications for Studying and Managing Organizational Behavior.* Social Networks, **291** *Social Network Transactions. Social Network Functions. Prescribed and Emergent Clusters. Recent Social Network Research. The Practical Value of a Social Network Perspective.* Organizational Roles and Norms, **295** *Roles. Norms. Relevant Research Insights and Managerial Implica-*

PART FOUR
Understanding and Managing Organizational Processes and Problems   442

ORGANIZATIONAL BEHAVIOR

PART ONE

Organizational Behavior: Definition, Background, and Context

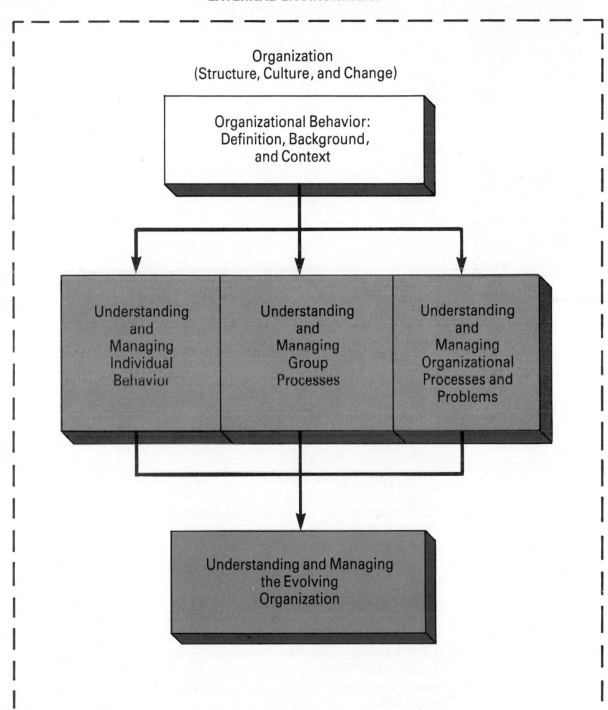

Chapter 1

Managing Organizational Behavior

LEARNING OBJECTIVES

When you finish studying the material in this chapter,
you should be able to:

- Explain how "people" can make or break both managers and organizations.
- Define the term *management.*
- Discuss what we have learned from Mintzberg's research on managerial roles.
- Identify the seven characteristics associated with motivation to manage.
- Summarize recent research about motivation to manage among college students.
- Define the term *organizational behavior* and explain how McGregor's Theory Y helped pave the way for this modern field of study.
- Explain how the contingency approach has influenced modern management thinking.
- Identify and briefly explain five sources and three uses of organizational behavior research.

OPENING CASE 1

She Worked Magic in a Dead-End Job

Pillsbury Co. executives used to refer sneeringly to the distribution department as an "elephant's graveyard." It was tantamount to corporate oblivion, involving little more than taking orders and shuffling invoices. But that was before Becky Roloff, 32, came along.

In her two years as distribution director, Roloff took 450 mostly uninspired employees and transformed them into a gung-ho group by rewarding them with recognition and reconceiving what was a bureaucratic task into a focused strategic mission. Now, when a job in distribution opens up, 30 or 40 people apply.

Corporate Humanist

After brief stints as a Cargill Inc. grain trader and in purchasing at Pillsbury, Roloff set out for Harvard business school. She graduated in the top 10% of her class. In 1984, Roloff headed a task force to deal with the pesticide-contamination crisis that engulfed the food industry. Last May [1986] she became Pillsbury's first female marketing director. Besides all that, she's a wife and a mother of an 18-month-old son.

ReBecca K. Roloff insists that she's unlike the "numbers jocks" with whom she trained at Harvard. She sees herself as a corporate humanist, an outgrowth perhaps of the prairie populism and strong, family-oriented German Catholic moralism of her upbringing in a small North Dakota town. Ask about the corporation's responsibilities, and she says: "How do you make money today and tomorrow so your employees can pay for the 30-year mortgages they have?"

Roloff credits her success to intuitive "people" skills—something that sets her apart from many contemporaries. "She believes that if you take care of people first, then you'll be taken care of, too," says her husband, Mark. Adds Warren G. Malkerson, a Pillsbury vice president: "Becky has the ability to make people more productive than they would ever expect themselves to be."

She proved that during her stint in distribution. There, she launched a program under which employees attempt to "catch each other in the act" of excellence. Those so caught are nominated for a special recognition. Just being nominated gets an employee a plaque. Big winners are brought to company headquarters to be feted, Roloff says, "as king or queen for a day."

Roloff was willing to break out of old molds. She defined distribution not merely as freight expediting but as a sales-support function for stores and distributors. She found that some 25% of sales could be tied to decisions by customers based on such things as timely and correct shipments. So she formulated new objectives that emphasized service and led to sales gains.

Outside of her 60-hour workweek, she juggles the demands of marriage and motherhood. It helps that her husband has quit the business world to help take care of their son, Luke, and to pursue a theology degree part

Someone once said the best place to begin is at the end. This practice meshes very nicely with management because management is a goal-oriented or "ends-oriented" endeavor. Relative to the content of this book, a worthy goal for future managers is to develop a progressive philosophy of management. Consider, for example, the enlightened philosophy behind Motorola's widely admired participative management program (PMP). Here is how Motorola's PMP corporate director explains the program:

> The participative management program is based on several underlying assumptions about people. First, every employee, regardless of his or her position within the company, is a valuable resource for ideas. Second, an individual's behavior is primarily the consequence of how he or she is treated. The supervisor who treats people with respect or dignity as involved, responsible employees will seldom be disappointed. Third, people expect to live and work in a rational world. If management decisions appear to be reasonable, people can and will work more effectively. And, finally, every employee's effectiveness depends on how aware he or she is of the company's goals, objectives, and performance.[1]

Aside from being an admirable goal for present and future managers, this philosophy pinpoints two key thrusts of this book. They are:

1. *A human resource development thrust.* Are employees a commodity to be hired and discarded depending on the short-run whims of the organization? Or are they a valuable resource to be nurtured and developed? Historically, the first assumption was the rule. More recently, however, foreign competition and a more demanding work force at home have encouraged American managers to adopt the latter human resource perspective. For example, the recently

---

[1] E. L. Simpson, "Motorola's Participative Management," *Management World*, July 1983, p. 20.

retired chief executive officer of Ford Motor Company explained the automaker's philosophy this way:

> The business community must bear the primary responsibility for tapping the full potential of the men and women whose lives and livelihoods are directly dependent upon its enterprises. Employers are uniquely positioned to nurture and develop the talents, skills, and abilities of employees.[2]

This progressive view is in keeping with the call for a long-term, strategic approach to management. Accordingly, this book firmly embraces the idea that people are valuable human resources requiring systematic nurturing and development.

2. *A managerial thrust.* Few would argue with the claim that we all should know more about why people behave as they do. After all, by better understanding others, we gain greater understanding of ourselves. But from a managerial standpoint, simply acquiring knowledge about organizational behavior is not enough. That knowledge needs to be put to work to get something accomplished. Hence, this book strives to help you both understand and manage organizational behavior by blending theory, research, and practical techniques.

The purpose of this chapter is to discuss people as the key to managerial and organizational success, explore the manager's job, define organizational behavior, and consider how we can learn more about organizational behavior. A topical model for the balance of the book also is introduced.

■ PEOPLE: THE KEY TO MANAGERIAL AND ORGANIZATIONAL SUCCESS

Given the high degree of complexity and rapid change managers face today, personal and organizational success can be elusive. Unforeseen economic, political, social, or technological changes can render even the best laid plans useless. More often than not, the success of individual managers and organizations pivots on such human factors as commitment, motivation, communication, leadership, and trust. Those who fail to appreciate the vital role *people* play in managerial and organizational success are destined to finish behind those who do.

People and Managerial Success

Why do some managers steadily move up through the ranks while others, who are similarly qualified, prematurely derail? A study conducted by researchers at the Center for Creative Leadership provides a revealing answer to this question. Interviewers asked top-level managers in several Fortune 500 companies to relate stories about two types of managers: (1) those who made it to top management positions and (2) those who did not. Stories about 20 successful managers were then compared with stories about 21 derailed managers.

---

[2] Philip Caldwell, "Cultivating Human Potential at Ford," *The Journal of Business Strategy,* Spring 1984, p. 75.

All 41 managers possessed significant strengths. However, "insensitivity to others was cited as a reason for derailment more often than any other flaw."[3] Managers in this study were considered to be insensitive if they intimidated co-workers with an abrasive and bullying style. In addition, managers who failed to make it to the top were perceived as more aloof and arrogant than their successful counterparts.

These research findings reinforce what enlightened managers have known all along. For instance, a General Electric Company executive recently told *Business Week:* "People don't fail due to lack of technical skills and energy. . . . They are most often derailed because of people problems."[4] Managers need to be able to work effectively with others if they are to make it to the top of the organizational pyramid.

People and Organizational Success

In recent years, many executives have said something along the lines of, "We're a good company because we have good people" (see Table 1–1). Critics generally view this type of statement as a hollow cliché or a public relations ploy. But there is mounting evidence that *successful* organizations treat *all* their employees with care and respect. Evidence of this connection between a "people orientation" and organizational success was uncovered by Peters and Waterman, the authors of the best-selling book *In Search of Excellence.*

After studying 43 consistently successful businesses, including IBM, Procter & Gamble, McDonald's, and Delta Air Lines, Inc., Peters and Waterman identified eight attributes of excellence. Important among the eight attributes of excellence is "productivity through people." Regarding this key contributor to corporate excellence, Peters and Waterman concluded that truly excellent organizations:

> Treat people as adults. Treat them as partners; treat them with dignity; treat them with respect. Treat *them*—not capital spending and automation—as the primary source of productivity gains. These are fundamental lessons from the excellent companies research. In other words, if you want productivity and the financial reward that goes with it, you must treat your workers as your most important asset.[5]

Although Peters and Waterman's research methodology has been criticized for not being rigorous enough,[6] their conclusion that a genuine concern for people and organizational success go hand in hand is a convincing one. As

[3] Morgan W. McCall, Jr., and Michael M. Lombardo, "What Makes a Top Executive?" *Psychology Today,* February 1983, pp. 26, 28.

[4] Teresa Carson, "Fast-Track Kids," *Business Week,* November 10, 1986, p. 92.

[5] Thomas J. Peters and Robert H. Waterman, Jr., *In Search of Excellence* (New York: Harper & Row, 1982), p. 238.

[6] Critical reviews of *In Search of Excellence* may be found in Daniel T. Carroll, "A Disappointing Search for Excellence," *Harvard Business Review,* November–December 1983, pp. 78–88; "Who's Excellent Now?" *Business Week,* November 5, 1984, pp. 76–78; and Michael A. Hitt and R. Duane Ireland, "Peters and Waterman Revisited: The Unended Quest for Excellence," *Academy of Management Executive,* May 1987, pp. 91–98.

■ **TABLE 1–1** People Count at IBM

> After a *Fortune* magazine survey ranked IBM as the most admired U.S. corporation for the second consecutive year, the highly successful computer company's chief executive officer said the following about IBM's key strengths:
>
>> A commitment to excellence and a commitment to customer service. The fundamental thing is that the people who work in the company make it a good company. That's really the secret: the people. It's our good fortune to have superior people who work hard and support each other. They have adapted to our set of basic beliefs—the standards we expect of one another—and follow those standards in dealing with one another and with people outside the company. I know it sounds corny, but it's true, and there's no point in trying to analyze it much more than that. Mr. Watson, Sr. [IBM founder Thomas J. Watson, Sr.], used to say, "You can take my factories, burn my buildings, but give me my people and I'll build the business right back again." And he was right. There really isn't much magic. It's not feathers and mirrors, it's human qualities that make our company strong.

an intuitive test of this proposition, can you think of an organization that treats its people with contempt, yet still has enjoyed long-term success? Probably not.

■ THE MANAGER'S JOB: GETTING THINGS DONE THROUGH OTHERS

For better or for worse, managers touch our lives in many ways. Schools, hospitals, government agencies, and large and small businesses all require systematic management. Formally defined, **management** is the process of working with and through others to achieve organizational objectives in an efficient manner. From the standpoint of organizational behavior, the central feature of this definition is "working with and through others" (see Table 1–2). Henry Mintzberg, a management scholar, observed: "No job is more vital to our society than that of the manager. It is the manager who determines whether our social institutions serve us well or whether they squander our talents and resources."[7] This reality is underscored by observational studies of managers at work and by research on motivation to manage.

Managerial Roles

By observing managers performing their regular duties, researchers provide insightful answers to the question, What do managers do? Until fairly recently, conventional wisdom was that managers perform *functions* such as planning,

---

[7] Henry Mintzberg, "The Manager's Job: Folklore and Fact," *Harvard Business Review*, July–August 1975, p. 61.

■ **TABLE 1–2** The Manager's Job: Two Views

According to a long-time manager and university professor:

    Managing, in my opinion, is like two other very important human activities: parenting and teaching. Like a parent or a teacher, a good manager's primary functions are to encourage people to work in some system in a way that allows them to make a substantial personal contribution, to recognize success, and to give new encouragement after failure. The workers' understanding of their work and their surroundings must be taken into account in the management of the system.

According to a management professor:

    The art of managing is to figure out what each person is capable of, and create assignments that are within their reach, or slightly above, so they can learn.

SOURCES: J. Herbert Hollomon, "Management and the Labor of Love," *Management Review,* January 1983, p. 12; and Allan Cohen, as quoted in Laurie Baum, "Delegating Your Way to Job Survival," *Business Week,* November 2, 1987, p. 206.

organizing, and controlling. However, observation of managers led Mintzberg to reject the traditional functional perspective of management. Mintzberg believes the functional approach to describing what managers do is vague, unrealistic, and obsolete.

According to Mintzberg, the functional approach characterizes the manager's job as much more rational and systematic than it is. Contrary to the impression created by the functional approach, the managers Mintzberg observed were not reflective and systematic planners. They were action-oriented individuals who preferred to communicate verbally. Observational studies by Mintzberg and others reveal the typical manager's day to be a fragmented collection of brief episodes. For example, in a replication of Mintzberg's original study, four top-level managers spent 63 percent of their time on activities lasting less than nine minutes each. Only 5 percent of the managers' time was devoted to activities lasting more than an hour.[8] A breakdown of the typical manager's day, according to this observational study, is presented in Figure 1–1.

To realistically capture the essence of management, Mintzberg identified three categories of managerial roles: interpersonal, informational, and decisional. He subdivided these three categories into 10 specific managerial roles (see Table 1–3). Mintzberg's 10 managerial roles reflect the need for a wide

---

[8] See Lance B. Kurke and Howard E. Aldrich, ''Mintzberg Was Right!: A Replication and Extension of *The Nature of Managerial Work*,'' *Management Science,* August 1983, pp. 975–84. A summary of Mintzberg's original study may be found in Henry Mintzberg, ''Managerial Work: Analysis from Observation,'' *Management Science,* October 1971, pp. B97–B110. For an instructive critique of the structured observation method, see Mark J. Martinko and William L. Gardner, ''Beyond Structured Observation: Methodological Issues and New Directions,'' *Academy of Management Review,* October 1985, pp. 676–95.

■ FIGURE 1-1 Observational Studies Reveal How Managers Spend Their Time

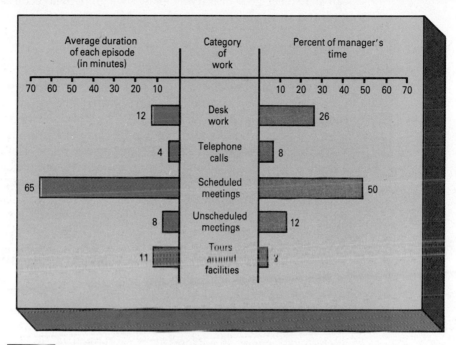

SOURCE: Based on data from Lance B. Kurke and Howard E. Aldrich, "Mintzberg Was Right!: A Replication and Extension of *The Nature of Managerial Work*," *Management Science*, August 1983, p. 979.

■ TABLE 1-3 Mintzberg's Managerial Roles

Category	Role	Description of Role
Interpersonal roles	1. Figurehead	Performing ceremonial duties (e.g., greeting visitors and signing documents)
	2. Leader	Hiring, training, and motivating subordinates to get the job done properly
	3. Liaison	Making contacts outside normal vertical chain of command
Informational roles	4. Monitor	Scanning environment for relevant information; receiving unsolicited information through personal contacts, gossip, and hearsay
	5. Disseminator	Passing along selected privileged information to subordinates
	6. Spokesperson	Transmitting selected information to people outside unit or organization (e.g., giving a public speech)
Decisional roles	7. Entrepreneur	Formulating and introducing changes; initiating new projects; looking for new ideas
	8. Disturbance handler	Responding involuntarily to pressures and nonroutine situations (e.g., strikes, boycotts)
	9. Resource allocator	Determining who will get what resources
	10. Negotiator	Participating in negotiating sessions with other parties (e.g., vendors, key personnel, unions) to make sure the organization's interests are adequately represented

range of interpersonal skills. A solid background in organizational behavior can help managers effectively play such important people-oriented roles as leader, disseminator, disturbance handler, and negotiator.

Motivation to Manage

Is there a formula for managerial success? Experience tells us it takes a combination of ability, desire, and opportunity. Of course, to some degree luck—such as being in the right place at the right time—plays a role in managerial success. Desire deserves special attention here because it often enables aspiring managers to translate ability, opportunities, and luck into success. Take Frederick W. Smith, founder of Federal Express, for example. He built his successful billion-dollar airfreight company from an idea he formulated in an economics term paper while studying at Yale University. Ironically, Smith's professor told him it was an ill-conceived idea and gave him a C.[9] Someone with less desire than Smith might have become discouraged and given up. But Smith, like many successful managers, forged ahead despite setbacks. Research on motivation to manage during the last couple of decades has advanced our understanding of desire and other contributors to managerial success.

By identifying personal traits positively correlated with both rapid movement up the career ladder and managerial effectiveness, John B. Miner developed a psychometric test for measuring **motivation to manage.** Miner's questionnaire assesses the strength of seven factors (see Table 1–4). Although Miner's complete questionnaire is not presented in Table 1–4, we have added scales so you can gauge the strength of your motivation to manage. (Arbitrary norms for comparison purposes are: Total score of 7–21 = Relatively low motivation to manage; 22–34 = Moderate; 35–49 = Relatively high.) How do you measure up? Remember, though, high motivation to manage is only part of the formula for managerial success. The right combination of ability and opportunity is also necessary.

Longitudinal research by Miner and others shows that the steady decline in motivation to manage among college students during the 1960s and 1970s has stopped. Scores still remain comparatively low, however, and Miner is concerned that this foreshadows a future shortage of managerial talent. On the positive side, the gap between males and females has closed. Historically, female business students scored lower in motivation to manage than did their male counterparts. In a more recent study, researchers found that MBA students with higher motivation to manage scores tended to earn more money after graduation. But students with higher motivation to manage did not earn better grades or complete their degree program sooner than those with lower motivation to manage.[10]

---

[9] See Eugene Linden, "Frederick W. Smith of Federal Express: He Didn't Get There Overnight," *Inc.*, April 1984, p. 89.

[10] These research results are discussed in detail in John B. Miner and Norman R. Smith, "Decline and Stabilization of Managerial Motivation Over a 20-Year Period," *Journal of Applied Psychology*, June 1982, pp. 297–305; and Kathryn M. Bartol and David C. Martin, "Managerial Motivation among MBA Students: A Longitudinal Assessment," *Journal of Occupational Psychology*, March 1987, pp. 1–12.

■ **TABLE 1–4** How Strong Is Your Motivation to Manage? (*Circle one number for each factor*)

Factor	Description	Scale
1. Authority figures	A desire to meet managerial role requirements in terms of positive relationships with superiors	Weak 1—2—3—4—5—6—7 Strong
2. Competitive games	A desire to engage in competition with peers involving games or sports and thus meet managerial role requirements in this regard	Weak 1—2—3—4—5—6—7 Strong
3. Competitive situations	A desire to engage in competition with peers involving occupational or work-related activities and thus meet managerial role requirements in this regard	Weak 1—2—3—4—5—6—7 Strong
4. Assertive role	A desire to behave in an active and assertive manner involving activities that in this society are often viewed as predominantly masculine and thus to meet managerial role requirements	Weak 1—2—3—4—5—6—7 Strong
5. Imposing wishes	A desire to tell others what to do and to utilize sanctions in influencing others, thus indicating a capacity to fulfill managerial role requirements in relationships with subordinates	Weak 1—2—3—4—5—6—7 Strong
6. Standing out from group	A desire to assume a distinctive position of a unique and highly visible nature in a manner that is role-congruent for managerial jobs	Weak 1—2—3—4—5—6—7 Strong
7. Routine administrative functions	A desire to meet managerial role requirements regarding activities often associated with managerial work that are of a day-to-day administrative nature	Weak 1—2—3—4—5—6—7 Strong Total = _____

SOURCE: Adapted from John B. Miner and Norman R. Smith, "Decline and Stabilization of Managerial Motivation Over a 20-Year Period," *Journal of Applied Psychology*, June 1982, p. 298.

■ **THE FIELD OF ORGANIZATIONAL BEHAVIOR: PAST AND PRESENT**

Organizational behavior, commonly referred to as OB, is an interdisciplinary field dedicated to better understanding and managing people at work. By definition, organizational behavior is both research- and application-oriented.

Because it is a relative newcomer, the field of OB does not possess the same depth of knowledge found in other more established disciplines. Biology, for example, has evolved into such an exact science that gene splicing is now possible. Present knowledge about organizational behavior does not allow the same degree of precision in predicting and fine-tuning behavior in organizations. But knowledge about organizational behavior is rapidly accumulating. In fact, a recent study by one organizational behavior researcher found 110 distinct theories about behavior within the field of OB.[11]

Every academic discipline has a theoretical foundation that shapes its future. As an interdisciplinary field, OB draws from many different bodies of knowledge. For example, consider the diversity of professional degrees held by 41 theorists credited with developing "established" theories about OB shown in Table 1–5. Table 1–5 also shows that psychology is the predominant discipline underlying the study of organizational behavior.[12] Much of the material in

---

[11] See John B. Miner, "The Validity and Usefulness of Theories in an Emerging Organizational Science," *Academy of Management Review*, April 1984, pp. 296–306.

[12] Ibid.

■ **TABLE 1–5** Professional Degrees Held by Leading OB Theorists Indicate Diversity of Field

Type of Degree	Number of Theorists with Degree	Type of Degree	Number of Theorists with Degree
Psychology	23	Management	1
Organizational behavior	4	Social sciences	1
Sociology	4	Engineering	1
Economics	2	Law	1
Political science	2	History	1
Industrial relations	1		

SOURCE: Adapted from John B. Miner, "The Validity and Usefulness of Theories in an Emerging Organizational Science," *Academy of Management Review*, April 1984, pp. 296–306.

this book is rooted in psychology. Modern OB theories and techniques are a direct outgrowth of the field's theoretical foundation that is diverse yet biased in favor of psychology.

A historical perspective of the study of people at work helps in studying organizational behavior. According to a management history expert, this is important because:

> Historical perspective is the study of a subject in light of its earliest phases and subsequent evolution. Historical perspective differs from history in that the object of historical perspective is to sharpen one's vision of the present, not the past.[13]

In other words, we can better understand where the field of OB is today and where it appears to be headed by appreciating where it has been. A general historical perspective relating to the field of OB is displayed in Table 1–6. Four significant eras—prescientific, classical, behavioral, and modern—have paved the way for the field of OB.

■ **TABLE 1–6** Assumptions about People at Work Have Changed Dramatically through the Years

Period	Pre-1800–1880	1880–1930	1930–1960	1960–1980s
General theory of management	Prescientific	Classical	Behavioral	Modern
Nature of society	Agrarian	Industrial		Postindustrial
Locus of work	Farm/home	Factory		Office/home
Assumptions about human nature	Economic person		Social and self-actualizing person	Complex person
Role of management	Control employee behavior		Maintain employee social systems	Facilitate employee development

SOURCE: Adapted from James L. Bowditch and Anthony F. Buono, *A Primer on Organizational Behavior* (New York: John Wiley & Sons, copyright © 1985). Reprinted by permission of John Wiley & Sons, Inc.

[13] Barbara S. Lawrence, "Historical Perspective: Using the Past to Study the Present," *Academy of Management Review*, April 1984, p. 307.

The Prescientific Era

The practice of management can be traced to earliest recorded history. Abundant archaeological evidence, such as the great pyramids, stands in silent tribute to the talents of bygone managers. Illiterate workers (or slaves), miserable working conditions, primitive agrarian economies, and crude tools made the task of managers in ancient civilizations extremely difficult. Moreover, even though managers during the prescientific era did not have formal education and training in proven management methods, they accomplished amazing things.

As time passed, exploitation of natural resources and technological advances led to the Industrial Revolution. This changed the nature of society and the location of work. People left their farms and went to work in urban factories. Money economies replaced barter economies, thus expediting the payment of wages. Another outcome of the Industrial Revolution was an interest in rationalizing the managerial process. Haphazard and unsystematic management practices proved to be inadequate for large-scale factory operations. The classical management era was born out of this interest.

The Classical Era

The classical management era lasted from about 1880 to 1930, and during this time the first general theories of management began to evolve. Two major thrusts were administrative theory and scientific management. Interestingly, both theories were proposed by engineers.

Administrative Theory. Also called the universal process school of management, the administrative theory approach can be traced to Henri Fayol, a French industrialist. In his 1916 classic, *Administration Industrielle et Generale,* Fayol divided the manager's job into five functions: planning, organizing, command, coordination, and control. He then recommended 14 universal principles of management.[14] Fayol viewed workers as a potentially disruptive factor to be closely *controlled* by management. Thus, his 14 Principles emphasized division of labor, authority, discipline, and a strictly enforced chain of command.

Scientific Management. According to a time-honored definition, **scientific management** "is that kind of management which conducts a business or affairs by standards established by facts or truths gained through systematic observation, experiment, or reasoning."[15] Frederick Taylor, credited with being the father of scientific management, published *The Principles of Scientific Management* in 1911. Because Taylor conducted much of his early experimentation in the steel industry, he focused on shop floor and factory operations.

Through time and task study, standardization of tools and procedures, development of piece-rate incentive schemes, and systematic selection and training,

---

[14] For Fayol's complete work, see Henri Fayol, *General and Industrial Management,* trans. Constance Storrs (London: Isaac Pitman & Sons, 1949).

[15] George D. Babcock, *The Taylor System in Franklin Management,* 2nd ed. (New York: Engineering Magazine Company, 1917), p. 31.

Taylor dramatically improved output. Scientific management replaced haphazard rules of thumb with systematic, experimentally derived techniques. Regarding employees, Taylor's goal was to make work behavior as stable and predictable as possible so increasingly sophisticated machines and factories would achieve maximum efficiency. He relied heavily on monetary incentives because he saw workers as basically lazy beings motivated primarily by money. Although Taylor has been roundly criticized for encouraging managers to treat employees like mindless machines, many fruits of his pioneering work are still evident.[16]

The Behavioral Era

A unique combination of factors fostered the emergence of the behavioral era during the 1930s. First, following legalization of union-management collective bargaining in the United States in 1935, management began looking for new ways of handling employees. Second, behavioral scientists conducting on-the-job research started calling for more attention to the "human" factor. Managers who had lost the battle to keep unions out of their factories heeded the call for better human relations and improved working conditions. One such study, conducted at Western Electric's Hawthorne plant, was a prime stimulus for the *human relations movement*. Ironically, many of the Hawthorne findings have turned out to be more myth than fact.

The Hawthorne Legacy.   Recent interviews with three subjects in the Hawthorne studies and re-analysis of the original data with modern statistical techniques do not support initial conclusions about the positive effect of supportive supervision. Specifically, money, fear of unemployment during the Great Depression, managerial discipline, and high-quality raw materials, not supportive supervision, turned out to be responsible for high output in the relay assembly test room experiments.[17] Nonetheless, the human relations movement gathered momentum through the 1950s as academics and managers alike made stirring claims about the powerful impact individual needs, supportive supervision, and group dynamics apparently had on job performance.

New Assumptions about Human Nature.   Unfortunately, unsophisticated behavioral research methods caused the human relationists to embrace some naive and misleading conclusions. For example, human relationists believed in the axiom, "A satisfied employee is a hardworking employee." Subsequent

---

[16] For an interesting critique of Taylor's work, see Edwin A. Locke, "The Ideas of Frederick W. Taylor: An Evaluation," *Academy of Management Review,* January 1982, pp. 14–24.

[17] Evidence indicating that the original conclusions of the famous Hawthorne studies were unjustified may be found in Ronald G. Greenwood, Alfred A. Bolton, and Regina A. Greenwood, "Hawthorne a Half Century Later: Relay Assembly Participants Remember," *Journal of Management,* Fall–Winter 1983, pp. 217–31; and Richard H. Franke and James D. Kaul, "The Hawthorne Experiments: First Statistical Interpretation," *American Sociological Review,* October 1978, pp. 623–43. For a positive interpretation of the Hawthorne studies, see Jeffrey A. Sonnenfeld, "Shedding Light on the Hawthorne Studies," *Journal of Occupational Behaviour,* April 1985, pp. 111–30.

research, as discussed later in this book, shows the satisfaction-performance linkage to be more complex than originally thought.

Despite its shortcomings, the behavioral era opened the door to more progressive thinking about human nature. Rather than continuing to view employees as passive economic beings, managers began to see them as active social beings and took steps to create more humane work environments.

The Modern Era

In 1960, Douglas McGregor wrote a book titled *The Human Side of Enterprise,* which has become an important philosophical base for the modern view of people at work.[18] Drawing upon his experience as a management consultant, McGregor formulated two sharply contrasting sets of assumptions about human nature (see Table 1–7). His Theory X assumptions were pessimistic and negative and, according to McGregor's interpretation, typical of how managers traditionally perceived employees. To help managers break with this negative tradition, McGregor formulated his **Theory Y,** a modern and positive set of assumptions about people. McGregor believed managers could accomplish more through others by viewing them as self-energized, committed, responsible, and creative beings. McGregor's Theory Y challenged theorists and practicing managers to adopt a *developmental* approach to employees.

Given society's rapid change and increased complexity in recent years, McGregor's Theory Y now qualifies as an inspiring beginning rather than an adequate end. Reflecting increased complexity in the workplace, management and OB theories have become more complex and abstract. Consider, for example, the modern contingency approach to management.

A Contingency Approach. Management scholars responded to increased complexity by formulating a **contingency approach** that calls for using management techniques in a situationally appropriate manner. According to a pair of contingency theorists:

> [Contingency theories] developed and their acceptance grew largely because they responded to criticisms that the classical theories advocated ''one best way'' of organizing and managing. Contingency theories, on the other hand, proposed that the appropriate organizational structure and management style were dependent upon a set of ''contingency'' factors, usually the uncertainty and instability of the environment.[19]

The contingency approach encourages managers to view organizational behavior within a situational context. According to this modern perspective, evolving situations, not hard-and-fast rules, determine when and where various management techniques are appropriate. For example, as discussed in Chapter 13, contingency researchers have determined that there is no single best style of

---

[18] See Douglas McGregor, *The Human Side of Enterprise* (New York: McGraw-Hill, 1960).

[19] Henry L. Tosi, Jr., and John W. Slocum, Jr., ''Contingency Theory: Some Suggested Directions,'' *Journal of Management,* Spring 1984, p. 9.

■ **TABLE 1–7** McGregor's Theory X and Theory Y

Outdated (Theory X) Assumptions about People at Work	Modern (Theory Y) Assumptions about People at Work
1. Most people dislike work; they will avoid it when they can.	1. Work is a natural activity, like play or rest.
2. Most people must be coerced and threatened with punishment before they will work. People require close direction when they are working.	2. People are capable of self-direction and self-control if they are committed to objectives.
3. Most people actually prefer to be directed. They tend to avoid responsibility and exhibit little ambition. They are interested only in security.	3. People generally become committed to organizational objectives if they are rewarded for doing so.
	4. The typical employee can learn to accept and seek responsibility.
	5. The typical member of the general population has imagination, ingenuity, and creativity.

SOURCE: Adapted from Douglas McGregor, *The Human Side of Enterprise* (New York: McGraw-Hill, 1960), chap. 4.

leadership. Organizational behavior scholars embrace the contingency approach because it helps them realistically interrelate individuals, groups, and organizations.

No Simple Answers Anymore.   As an interesting example, consider the growing problem of workplace gambling (e.g., football and baseball pools). Managers complain that work remains undone when employees devote time to making and collecting bets. How would experts from earlier management eras interpret this problem? Fayol would probably say the employees were out of control because authority and the chain of command had broken down. Taylor would claim the culprits had fallen into a natural pattern of laziness because they were being paid by the hour and not by the unit of output. No doubt Taylor would allude to the economic incentive of betting. As for the human relationists, they would explain the situation in terms of the satisfaction of natural social needs and peer pressure. Here is a modern interpretation:

> Money is but one of the lures of office pools. They are social equalizers, in which junior flunkies can outwit senior executives. They are boredom antidotes, in which spread-sheets can be set aside for point-spread sheets. And, for the lucky winners, they are status-builders, in which the envious congratulations of co-workers come with a stack of crumpled bills.[20]

By examining the problem closely, an apparently simple situation turns out to be extremely complex. The path to a workable solution will be equally complex. Fortunately, the field of OB and the contingency approach to management can light the way.

In summary, each management era has enabled us to accomplish more through organized endeavor. Modern OB, which considers the contingencies among individuals, groups, the organization, and the external environment, promises

---

[20] Jeffrey Zaslow, ''Everyone in the Pool! Almost Everyone Is on This Super Friday,'' *The Wall Street Journal*, January 18, 1985, p. 1.

to help us better understand and manage people at work. Now that we have reviewed OB's historical context, we need to address how we learn about OB through a combination of theory, research, and practice.

■ LEARNING ABOUT OB FROM THEORY, RESEARCH, AND PRACTICE

As a human being, with years of interpersonal experience to draw upon, you already know a good deal about people at work. But more systematic and comprehensive understanding is possible and desirable. A working knowledge of current OB theory, research, and practice can help you develop a tightly integrated understanding of why organizational contributors think and act as they do. In order for this to happen, however, prepare yourself for some intellectual surprises from theoretical models, research results, or techniques that may run counter to your current thinking. Recognizing that surprises are what makes learning fun, let us examine the dynamic relationship between OB theory, research, and practice and the value of each.

Figure 1–2 illustrates how theory, research, and practice are related. Through-

■ **FIGURE 1–2** Learning about OB through a Combination of Theory, Research, and Practice

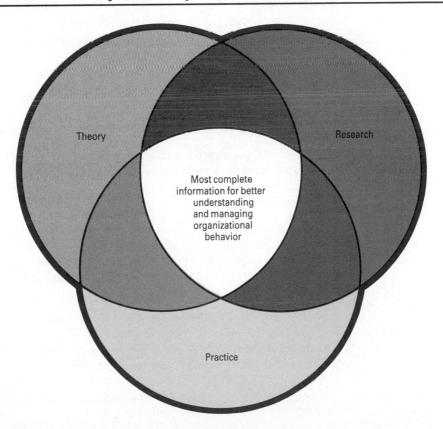

Theory

Research

Most complete
information for better
understanding
and managing
organizational
behavior

Practice

out the balance of this book, we focus primarily on the shaded portion, where all three areas overlap. Knowledge of why people behave as they do and what managers can do to improve performance is greatest within this shaded area. For each major topic, we build a foundation for understanding with generally accepted theory. This theoretical foundation is then tested and expanded by reviewing the latest relevant research findings. After interpreting the research, we discuss the nature and effectiveness of related practical applications.

Sometimes, depending on the subject matter, it is necessary to venture into the large areas outside the shaded portion of Figure 1–2. For example, an insightful theory supported by convincing research evidence might suggest an untried or different way of managing. In other instances, an innovative management technique might call for an explanatory theoretical model and exploratory research. Each area—theory, research, and practice—supports and in turn is supported by the other two. Each area makes a valuable contribution to our understanding of and ability to manage organizational behavior.

Learning from Theory

A respected behavioral scientist once said there is nothing as practical as a good theory. According to one management researcher, a **theory** is a story that explains "why."[21] A good OB theory, then, is a story that does a good job of explaining why individuals and groups behave as they do. Moreover, a good theoretical model:

1. *Defines* key terms.
2. Constructs a *conceptual framework* that explains how important factors are interrelated. (Graphic models are often used to achieve this end.)
3. Provides a *departure point* for research and practical application.

Indeed, good theories are a fundamental contributor to improved understanding and management of organizational behavior.

Learning from Research

Because of unfamiliar jargon and complicated statistical procedures, many present and future managers are put off by behavioral research. This is unfortunate because many practical lessons can be learned as OB researchers steadily push back the frontier of knowledge. Let us examine the various sources and uses of OB research evidence.

Five Sources of OB Research Insights. To enhance the instructional value of our coverage of major topics, we systematically cite "hard" evidence from five different categories. Worthwhile evidence was obtained by drawing upon the following *priority* of research methodologies:

---

[21] See Richard L. Daft, "Learning the Craft of Organizational Research," *Academy of Management Review*, October 1983, pp. 539–46.

- *Meta-analyses.* A **meta-analysis** is a statistical pooling technique that permits behavioral scientists to draw general conclusions about certain variables from many different studies.[22] They typically encompass a vast number of subjects, often reaching the thousands. Meta-analyses are instructive because they focus on general patterns of research evidence, not fragmented bits and pieces.
- *Field studies.* In OB, a **field study** probes individual or group processes in an organizational setting. Because field studies involve real-life situations, their results often have immediate and practical relevance for managers.
- *Laboratory studies.* In a **laboratory study,** variables are manipulated and measured in contrived situations. College students are commonly used as subjects. The highly controlled nature of laboratory studies enhances research precision. But generalizing the results to organizational management requires caution.[23]
- *Sample surveys.* In a **sample survey,** samples of people from specified populations respond to questionnaires. The researchers then draw conclusions about the relevant population. Generalizability of the results depends on the quality of the sampling and questioning techniques.
- *Case studies.* A **case study** is an in-depth analysis of a single individual, group, or organization. Because of their limited scope, case studies yield realistic but not very generalizable results.

Three Uses of OB Research Findings. Organizational scholars point out that managers can put relevant research findings to use in three different ways:[24]

1. *Instrumental use.* This involves directly applying research findings to practical problems. For example, a manager experiencing high stress tries a relaxation technique after reading a research report about its effectiveness.
2. *Conceptual use.* Research is put to conceptual use when managers derive general enlightenment from its findings. The impact here is less specific and more indirect than with instrumental use. For example, after reading about a study in which female managers were found to possess the same leadership abilities as their male colleagues, a manager resolves to adopt a more positive attitude about female managers.

---

[22] Complete discussion of this technique can be found in John E. Hunter, Frank L. Schmidt, and Gregg B. Jackson, *Meta-Analysis: Cumulating Research Findings across Studies* (Beverly Hills, Calif.: Sage Publications, 1982).

[23] For an interesting debate about the use of students as subjects, see Jerald Greenberg, "The College Sophomore as Guinea Pig: Setting the Record Straight," *Academy of Management Review,* January 1987, pp. 157–59; and Michael E. Gordon, L. Allen Slade, and Neal Schmitt, "Student Guinea Pigs: Porcine Predictors and Particularistic Phenomena," *Academy of Management Review,* January 1987, pp. 160–63.

[24] Based on discussion found in Janice M. Beyer and Harrison M. Trice, "The Utilization Process: A Conceptual Framework and Synthesis of Empirical Findings," *Administrative Science Quarterly,* December 1982, pp. 591–622.

3. *Symbolic use.* Symbolic use occurs when research results are relied on to verify or legitimize already held positions. Negative forms of symbolic use involve self-serving bias, prejudice, selective perception, and distortion. For example, tobacco industry spokespersons routinely deny any link between smoking and lung cancer because researchers are largely, but not 100 percent, in agreement about the negative effects of smoking. A positive example would be managers maintaining their confidence in setting performance goals after reading a research report about the favorable impact of goal setting on job performance.

By systematically reviewing and interpreting research relevant to key topics, this book provides instructive insights about OB. (The mechanics of the scientific method and OB research are discussed in detail in an appendix at the end of this chapter.)

Learning from Practice

Relative to learning more about how to effectively manage people at work, one might be tempted to ask, ''Why bother with theory and research; let's get right down to *how to do it.*'' Our answer lies in the contingency approach, discussed earlier. The effectiveness of specific theoretical models or management techniques is contingent on the situations in which they are applied. For example, one cross-cultural study of a large multinational corporation's employees working in 50 countries led the researcher to conclude that most made-in-America management theories and techniques are inappropriate in other cultures.[25] Many otherwise well-intentioned performance-improvement programs based on American cultural values have failed in other cultures because of naive assumptions about transferability (see Table 1–8).[26] Fortunately, systematic research is available that tests our ''common sense'' assumptions about what works where. Management ''cookbooks'' that provide only how-to-do-it advice with no underlying theoretical models or supporting research practically guarantee misapplication. As mentioned earlier, theory, research, and practice mutually reinforce one another.

A particularly fruitful link between research and practice comes from what OB scholars call *applied research.* The type of applied OB research we are interested in here involves the systematic study of on-the-job processes and techniques that have descriptive and goal relevance for managers. **''Descriptive relevance** refers to the extent to which a research project captures phenomena which are encountered by practitioners in applied settings.''[27] In contrast,

---

[25] For complete details, see Geert Hofstede, ''The Cultural Relativity of Organizational Practices and Theories,'' *Journal of International Business Studies,* Fall 1983, pp. 75–89.

[26] An instructive call for more managerial attention to cultural diversity can be found in Nancy J. Adler, Robert Doktor, and S. Gordon Redding, ''From the Atlantic to the Pacific Century: Cross-Cultural Management Reviewed,'' *Journal of Management,* Summer 1986, pp. 295–318.

[27] Stephen Strasser and Thomas S. Bateman, ''What We Should Study, Problems We Should Solve: Perspectives of Two Constituencies,'' *Personnel Psychology,* Spring 1984, p. 78.

■ **TABLE 1–8** Why McGregor's Theory X and Theory Y Assumptions Do Not Apply
in South East Asia

Dutch researcher Geert Hofstede's study of employees from 50 countries suggests that American management theories are not universally applicable. For example, Hofstede points out that McGregor's Theory X and Theory Y reflect America's cultural emphasis on *individualism.*

U.S. assumptions:

Work is good for people. It is God's will that people should work.

People's potentialities should be maximally utilised. It is God's will that you and I should maximally use our potentialities.

There are "organisational objectives" which exist separately from people.

People in organisations behave as unattached individuals.

These assumptions do not translate well to South East Asian cultures such as Indonesia that emphasize *collectivism.*

South East Asian assumptions:

Work is a necessity but not a goal in itself.

People should find their rightful place, in peace and harmony with their environment.

Absolute objectives exist only with God. In the world, persons in authority positions represent God, so their objectives should be followed.

People behave as members of a family and/or group. Those who do not are rejected by society.

SOURCE: Excerpted from Geert Hofstede, "The Applicability of McGregor's Theories in South East Asia," *The Journal of Management Development* 6, no. 3 (1987), pp. 9–18.

goal relevance is said to exist when researchers focus on outcomes that managers see as important (e.g., effort, performance, satisfaction). Whenever available, the results of applied OB research with descriptive and goal relevance are discussed in this text so as to test situational appropriateness.

The theory→research→practice sequence discussed in this section will help you better understand each major topic addressed later in this book. Attention now turns to a topical model that sets the stage for what lies ahead.

■ A TOPICAL MODEL FOR UNDERSTANDING AND MANAGING OB

Figure 1–3 presents a topical model intended to act as a map for what lies ahead. It shows that managers are responsible for achieving organizational effectiveness *with and through others*. Also, it reminds us that managers need to adequately understand and manage three important areas of OB to achieve organizational effectiveness. These areas are individual behavior, group processes, and organizational processes and problems. The model further empha-

■ **FIGURE 1–3** A Topical Model for What Lies Ahead

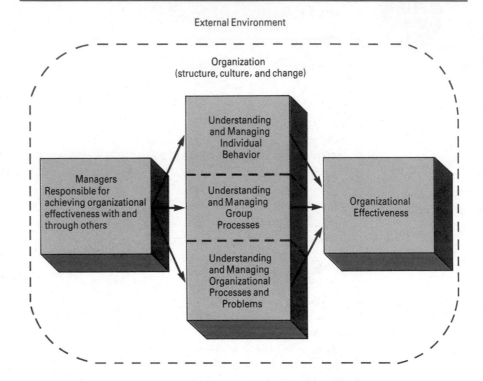

sizes that these areas do not exist in isolation. Organizational effectiveness is determined by dynamic interaction among individual, group, and organizational factors. Finally, the model illustrates that the boundary between the organization and the external environment is a permeable one. Cultural and technological changes inevitably influence the organization and its members, groups, and processes.

SUMMARY OF KEY CONCEPTS

A. This book has two key thrusts. The first underscores that people are valuable human resources needing systematic nurturing and development. A managerial thrust reminds us that the purpose of learning about organizational behavior is to accomplish organizational goals.

B. People are essential to both managerial and organizational success. One study contrasting successful managers with derailed managers found that the latter were insensitive, abrasive, and bullying. Peters and Waterman, authors of the best-seller *In Search of Excellence*, found that truly excellent companies treat their people as adults and as the primary source of productivity gains.

C. Management is defined as the process of working with and through others to achieve organizational objectives in an efficient manner. Observational studies by Mintzberg and others found that managers are not the reflective and systematic planners the traditional functional approach would have us believe. According to Mintzberg, managers play three interpersonal roles, three informational roles, and four decisional roles. Highly developed ''people'' skills are required for all these different roles.

D. Miner's motivation to manage questionnaire measures seven personal characteristics that predict managerial effectiveness. Of course, ability and opportunity round out the formula for managerial success. The steady decline in college students' motivation to manage in recent decades has stopped, and the male-female gap has closed. Still, Miner is worried that we face a shortage of managerial talent.

E. Organizational behavior (OB) is an interdisciplinary field dedicated to better understanding and managing people at work. A comparatively young field that is biased in favor of psychology, OB is both research- and application-oriented.

F. A historical perspective of OB shows how it has evolved from four eras: prescientific, classical, behavioral, and modern. Not until the behavioral era were employees viewed as active beings seeking personal growth and social recognition. In response to growing complexity, a modern contingency (or situational) approach to management is recommended. ''One best way'' is no longer adequate; situational realities need to be considered when applying OB theory and techniques.

G. Much can be learned about OB by studying the overlap of relevant theory, research, and practice. Theories, defined as stories that explain ''why,'' helpfully provide definitions, conceptual frameworks, and departure points for research and application. Five sources of OB research evidence are meta-analyses, field studies, laboratory studies, sample surveys, and case studies. OB research can be put to instrumental, conceptual, or symbolic use by managers. Applied OB research, particularly when it has descriptive and goal relevance for managers, effectively links research and practice.

H. A topical model that provides a map for what lies ahead reminds us that the manager's job is to achieve organizational effectiveness. This is accomplished only by adequately understanding and successfully managing individual behavior, group processes, and organizational processes and problems.

KEY TERMS

management	**meta-analysis**
motivation to manage	**field study**
organizational behavior	**laboratory study**
scientific management	**sample survey**
Theory Y	**case study**
contingency approach	**descriptive relevance**
theory	**goal relevance**

DISCUSSION QUESTIONS

1. Why view the typical employee as a human resource?
2. How would you respond to a fellow student who says, "I have a hard time getting along with other people, but I think I could be a good manager"?
3. Which of Mintzberg's 10 managerial roles do you think would be the most difficult to perform? Explain.
4. Which of Mintzberg's 10 managerial roles do you think is the most important? Explain.
5. Referring to Table 1–4, what is your motivation to manage? Do you believe our adaptation of Miner's scale accurately assessed your potential as a manager? Explain.
6. Why was the behavioral era essential to development of the field of OB?
7. Do you use a contingency approach in your daily affairs? Explain.
8. What "practical" theories have you formulated to achieve the things you want in life (e.g., graduating, keeping fit, getting a good job, meeting that special someone)?
9. From a manager's standpoint, which use of research is better: instrumental or conceptual? Explain your rationale.
10. What are the instructional benefits of examining OB topics through a consistent theory→research→practice format? Why not dispense with the theory and research and simply review the "three easy steps" to managing people?

BACK TO THE OPENING CASE

Now that you have read Chapter 1, you should be able to answer the following questions about the ReBecca Roloff case:

1. What is the key to Roloff's success as a manager at Pillsbury?
2. Citing specific evidence, which managerial roles has Roloff played? Which role has she played most effectively?
3. Making reasonable inferences from the facts of the case, how would you assess Roloff's motivation to manage relative to each of the seven characteristics listed in Table 1–4?
4. Is it possible that Roloff's management style would not work so well in other cultures? Explain. (Feel free to draw upon your knowledge of various cultures.)

EXERCISE 1

Objectives

1. To find out what a practicing manager thinks about the role of people in organizational success.
2. To gain a better understanding of the nature of managerial work.
3. To assess a manager's motivation to manage.

Introduction

What better way is there to test the validity of what you have just read about management and OB than to go talk to a practicing manager?

Instructions

Your task is to interview a manager. For this exercise, we will define a *manager* as anyone who supervises other people at work. You may choose a manager from any type of organization (profit or not-for-profit, large or small). Top-level executives, as well as middle managers and supervisors, are fair game. Some specific questions are provided below to help you get the most from your interview, but feel free to probe further with your own questions.

When conducting the interview, be sure to explain to the manager what you are trying to accomplish. But assure the manager that his or her name will not be mentioned in class discussion or any written assignments the instructor might require. Try to keep fairly detailed notes during the interview for later reference.

Interview Questions

1. How important are people to the success of your organization?
2. What is the most difficult part of trying to get something accomplished in your organization?
3. Basically, what does your job as a manager entail? (Relative to Mintzberg's 10 managerial roles in Table 1–3, how many different roles does this particular manager appear to play?)
4. As a manager, what do you find most rewarding?
5. During your typical workday, how do you divide your time among the following activities: desk work, telephone calls, scheduled meetings, unscheduled meetings, and tours around the facilities? (*Note:* Record your data in the blanks provided below.)

	PERCENT OF MANAGER'S TIME	AVERAGE DURATION OF EACH INSTANCE (MINUTES)
Desk work	_____	_____
Telephone calls	_____	_____
Scheduled meetings	_____	_____
Unscheduled meet- ings	_____	_____
Tours around facilities	_____	_____

6. After talking to this manager, rate his or her motivation to manage on the following scale:

   Weak = 1—2—3—4—5—6—7 = Strong

   How did you arrive at this judgment?

Questions for Consideration/Class Discussion

1. Did the manager you interviewed seem to like his or her job? How could you tell?
2. Thinking of the manager you interviewed, could you do his or her job? What, if any, skills would you need to develop first?
3. As a result of your manager interview, are you more or less attracted to a career in management? Explain.

Appendix

Research Methods in Organizational Behavior

As a future manager, you probably will be involved in developing and/or implementing programs for solving organizational behavior problems. You also may be asked to assess recommendations derived from in-house research reports or judge usefulness of management consulting proposals. These tasks might entail reading and evaluating research findings presented in scientific journal articles. Thus, it is important for managers to have a basic working knowledge of the research process. Moreover, such knowledge can help you critically evaluate research information encountered daily in newspaper, magazine, and television reports. Consider, for example, the issue of whether to wear rear-seat lap belts while riding in an automobile.

A recent study conducted by the National Transportation Safety Board (NTSB) concluded, "Instead of protecting people, rear-seat lap belts can cause serious or fatal internal injuries in the event of a head-on crash."[1] Despite previous recommendations to wear seat belts, do you now believe rear-seat lap belts are dangerous? To answer this question adequately, one needs to know more about how the NTSB's study was conducted and what has been found in related studies. Before providing you with this information, however, this

---

[1] "Buckle Up in the Rear Seat?" *University of California, Berkeley Wellness Letter,* August 1987, p. 1.

appendix presents a foundation for understanding the research process. Our purpose is not to make you a research scientist. The purpose is to make you a better consumer of research information, such as that provided by the NTSB.

■ THE RESEARCH PROCESS

Research on OB is based on the scientific method. The *scientific method* is a formal process of using systematically gathered data to test hypotheses or to explain natural phenomena. To gain a better understanding of how to evaluate this process, we discuss a model of how research is conducted, explore how researchers measure organizationally relevant variables, highlight three ways to evaluate research methods, and provide a framework for evaluating research conclusions. We also discuss how to read a research article. Finally, we return to the NTSB study and evaluate its conclusions on the basis of lessons from this appendix.

A Model of the Research Process

A flowchart of the research process is presented in Figure A–1. Organizational research is conducted to solve problems. The problem may be one of current interest to an organization, such as absenteeism or low motivation, or may be derived from published research studies. In either case, properly identifying and attempting to solve the problem necessitates a familiarity with previous research on the topic. This familiarity contributes background knowledge and insights for formulating a hypothesis to solve the problem. Students who have written formal library-research papers are well-acquainted with this type of *secondary* research.

According to a respected researcher: "A *hypothesis* is a conjectural statement of the relation between two or more variables. Hypotheses are always in declarative form, and they relate, either generally or specifically, variables to variables."[2] Regarding the problem of absenteeism, for instance, a manager might want to test the following hypothesis: "Hourly employees who are dissatisfied with their pay are absent more often than those who are satisfied." Hypothesis in hand, a researcher is prepared to design a study to test it.

There are two important, interrelated components to designing a study. The first consists of deciding how to measure independent and dependent variables. An *independent variable* is a variable that is hypothesized to affect or cause a certain state of events. For example, a recent study demonstrated that job dissatisfaction resulted in lower organizational commitment.[3] In this case, job satisfaction, the independent variable, produced lower levels of organizational

---

[2] Fred N. Kerlinger, *Foundations of Behavioral Research* (New York: Holt, Rinehart & Winston, 1973), p. 18. (Emphasis added.)

[3] For details, see Larry J. Williams and John T. Hazer, "Antecedents and Consequences of Satisfaction and Commitment in Turnover Models: A Reanalysis Using Latent Variable Structural Equation Methods," *Journal of Applied Psychology,* May 1986, pp. 219–31.

■ **FIGURE A–1**   Model of the Research Process

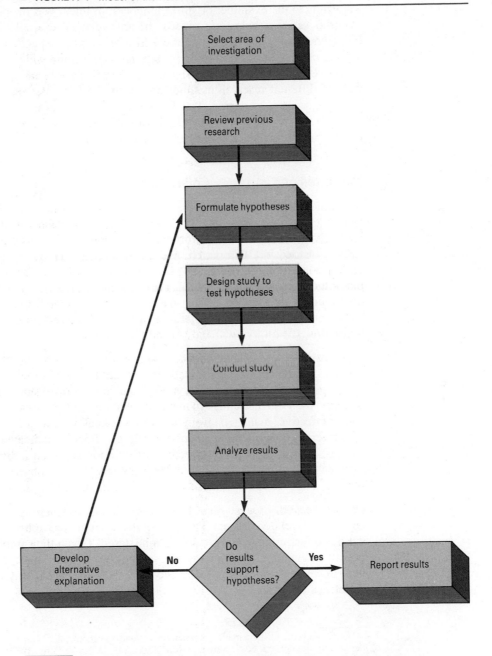

SOURCE: Virginia R. Boehm, "Research in the 'Real World': A Conceptual Model," *Personnel Psychology*, Autumn 1980, p. 496.

commitment. A *dependent variable* is the variable being explained or predicted. Returning to the example, organizational commitment was the dependent variable (the variable being explained). In an everyday example, those who eat less (independent variable) are likely to lose weight (dependent variable). The second component of designing a study is to determine which research method to use (recall the discussion in Chapter 1). Criteria for evaluating the appropriateness of different research methods are discussed in a later section.

After a study is designed and completed, data are analyzed to determine whether the hypothesis is supported. Researchers look for alternative explanations of results when a hypothesis is not supported.

Measurement and Data Collection

"In its broadest sense measurement is the assignment of numerals to objects or events according to rules."[4] Organizational researchers measure variables. Job satisfaction, turnover, performance, and perceived stress are variables typically measured in OB research. Valid measurement is one of the most critical components of any research study because research findings are open to conflicting interpretations when variables are poorly measured.[5] Poor measurement thus reduces the confidence one has in applying research findings. Four techniques are frequently used to measure variables: (1) direct observation, (2) questionnaires, (3) interviews, and (4) indirect methods.

Observation. This technique consists of recording the number of times a prespecified behavior is exhibited. For example, psychologist Judith Komaki developed and validated an observational categorization of supervisory behavior. She then used the instrument to identify behavioral differences between effective and ineffective managers from a large medical insurance firm. Managerial effectiveness was based on superior ratings. Results indicated that effective managers spent more time collecting information about an individual's performance than ineffective managers.[6] There are few "valid" observational schemes for use in OB research outside of Komaki's taxonomy.

Questionnaires. Questionnaires ask respondents for their opinions or feelings about work-related issues. They generally contain previously developed and validated instruments and are self-administered. Given their impersonal nature, poorly designed questionnaires are susceptible to rater bias. Nevertheless, a well-developed survey can be an accurate and economical way to collect large quantities of data.

---

[4] S. S. Stevens, "Mathematics, Measurement, and Psychophysics," in *Handbook of Experimental Psychology,* ed. S. S. Stevens (New York: John Wiley & Sons, 1951), p. 1.

[5] A thorough discussion of the importance of measurement is provided by Donald P. Schwab, "Construct Validity in Organizational Behavior," in *Research in Organizational Behavior,* ed. Barry M. Staw and Larry L. Cummings (Greenwich, Conn.: JAI Press, 1980), pp. 3–43.

[6] See Judith L. Komaki, "Toward Effective Supervision: An Operant Analysis and Comparison of Managers at Work," *Journal of Applied Psychology,* May 1986, pp. 270–79.

Interviews. Interviews rely on face-to-face interactions to ask respondents questions of interest. In a *structured* interview, interviewees are asked the same questions in the same order. *Unstructured* interviews do not require interviewers to use the same questions or format. Unstructured interviews are more spontaneous. Structured interviews are the better of the two because they permit consistent comparisons among people.[7] Accordingly, human resource management experts strongly recommend structured interviews during the hiring process to permit candidate-to-candidate comparisons.

Indirect Methods. These techniques obtain data without any direct contact with respondents. This approach may entail observing someone without his or her knowledge. Other examples include searching existing records, such as personnel files, for data on variables such as absenteeism, turnover, and output. This method reduces rater error and generally is used in combination with one of the previously discussed techniques.

Evaluating Research Methods

All research methods can be evaluated from three perspectives: (1) generalizability, (2) precision in control and measurement, and (3) realism of the context.[8] *Generalizability,* which also is referred to as external validity, reflects the extent to which results from one study are generalizable to other individuals, groups, or situations. *Precision in control and measurement* pertains to the level of accuracy in manipulating or measuring variables. A *realistic context* is one that naturally exists for the individuals participating in the research study. In other words, realism implies that the context is not an artificial situation contrived for purposes of conducting the study. Table A–1 presents an evaluation of the five most frequently used research methods, in terms of these three perspectives.

In summary, there is not one best research method. Choosing a method depends on the purpose of the specific study.[9] For example, if high control is necessary, as in testing for potential radiation leaks in pipes that will be used at a nuclear power plant, a laboratory experiment is appropriate (see Table A–1). In contrast, sample surveys would be useful if a company wanted to know the generalizable impact of a television commercial for light beer.

Evaluating Research Conclusions

There are several issues to consider when evaluating the quality of a research study. The first is whether results from the specific study are consistent with those from past research. If not, it is helpful to determine why discrepancies

---

[7] Advantages and disadvantages of different interviews are discussed by Richard D. Arvey and Robert H. Faley, *Fairness in Selecting Employees,* 2nd ed. (Reading, Mass.: Addison-Wesley Publishing, 1988).

[8] A complete discussion of research methods is provided by Thomas D. Cook and Donald T. Campbell, *Quasi-Experimentation: Design & Analysis Issues for Field Settings* (Chicago: Rand McNally, 1979).

[9] Ibid.

■ **TABLE A-1** Assessment of Frequently Used Research Methods

Method	Generalizability	Precision in Control and Measurement	Realistic Context
Case study	Low	Low	High
Sample survey	High	Low	Low
Field study	Moderate	Moderate	High
Laboratory experiment	Low	High	Low
Field experiment	Moderate	Moderate	Moderate

SOURCE: Adapted in part from Joseph E. McGrath, Joanne Martin, and Richard A. Kulka, *Judgment Calls in Research* (Beverly Hills, Calif.: Sage Publications, 1982).

exist. For instance, it is insightful to compare the samples, research methods, measurement of variables, statistical analyses, and general research procedures across the discrepant studies. Extreme differences suggest that future research may be needed to reconcile the inconsistent results. In the meantime, however, we need to be cautious in applying research findings from one study that are inconsistent with those from a larger number of studies.

The type of research method used is the second consideration. Does the method have generalizability (see Table A–1)? If not, check the characteristics of the sample. If the sample's characteristics are different from the characteristics of your work group, conclusions may not be relevant for your organization. Sample characteristics are very important in evaluating results from both field studies and experiments.

The level of precision in control and measurement is the third factor to consider. It is important to determine whether valid measures were used in the study. This can be done by reading the original study and examining descriptions of how variables were measured. Variables have questionable validity when they are measured with one-item scales or "ad-hoc" instruments developed by the authors. In contrast, standardized scales tend to be more valid because they typically are developed and validated in previous research studies. We have more confidence in results when they are based on analyses using standardized scales. As a general rule, validity in measurement begets confidence in applying research findings.

Finally, it is helpful to brainstorm alternative explanations for the research results. This helps to identify potential problems within research procedures.

■ READING A SCIENTIFIC JOURNAL ARTICLE

Research is published in scientific journals and professional magazines. *Journal of Applied Psychology* and *Academy of Management Journal* are examples of scientific journals reporting OB research. *Management Review* and *Personnel Administrator* are professional magazines that sometimes report research findings in general terms. Scientific journal articles report results from empirical research studies, overall reviews of research on a specific topic, and theoretical articles. To help you obtain relevant information from scientific articles, let us consider the content and structure of these three types of articles.[10]

Empirical Research Studies

Reports of these studies contain summaries of original research. They typically are comprised of four distinct sections consistent with the logical steps of the research process model shown in Figure A–1. These sections are:

- *Introduction:* This section identifies the problem being investigated and the purpose of the study. Previous research pertaining to the problem is reviewed and sometimes critiqued.
- *Method:* This section discusses the method used to conduct the study. Characteristics of the sample or subjects, procedures followed, materials used, measurement of variables, and analytic procedures typically are discussed.
- *Results:* A detailed description of the documented results is presented.
- *Discussion:* This section provides an interpretation, discussion, and implications of results.

Review Articles

These articles "are critical evaluations of material that has already been published. By organizing, integrating, and evaluating previously published material, the author of a review article considers the progress of current research toward clarifying a problem."[11] Although the structure of these articles is not as clear-cut as reports of empirical studies, the general format is:

- A statement of the problem.
- A summary or review of previous research that attempts to provide the reader with the state of current knowledge about the problem (meta-analysis frequently is used to summarize past research).
- Identification of shortcomings, limitations, and inconsistencies in past research.
- Recommendations for future research to solve the problem.

Theoretical Articles

These articles draw on past research to propose revisions to existing theoretical models or to develop new theories and models. The structure is similar to that of review articles.

---

[10] This discussion is based on material presented in the *Publication Manual of the American Psychological Association,* 3rd ed. (Washington, D.C.: American Psychological Association, 1983).

[11] Ibid., p. 21.

■ BACK TO THE NTSB STUDY

This appendix was introduced with a National Transportation Safety Board study that suggested it is not safe to wear rear-seat lap belts while riding in an automobile. Given what we have just discussed, take a few minutes now to jot down any potential explanations for why the NTSB findings conflict with past research supporting the positive benefits of rear-seat lap belts. Compare your thoughts with an evaluation presented in the *University of California, Berkeley Wellness Letter*.

Critics claim that the NTSB study paints a misleadingly scary picture by focusing on 26 unrepresentative accidents, all unusually serious and all but one frontal. The National Highway Traffic Safety Administration has strongly disputed the board's findings, citing five earlier studies of thousands of crashes showing that safety belts—including lap belts—are instrumental in preventing death and injury. And a new study of 37,000 crashes in North Carolina shows that rear-seat lap belts reduce the incidence of serious injury and death by about 40%. . . .

In the meantime, most evidence indicates that you should continue to use rear-seat lap belts. You can minimize the risk of injury by wearing them as low across the hips as possible and keeping them tight.[12]

The NTSB findings were based on a set of unrepresentative serious frontal accidents. In other words, the NTSB's sample was not reflective of the typical automobile accident. Thus, the generalizability of the NTSB results is very limited.

---

[12] "Buckle Up in the Rear Seat?" *University of California, Berkeley Wellness Letter*, August 1987, p. 1.

Chapter **2**

Dynamics of Organizational Life

LEARNING OBJECTIVES

When you finish studying the material in this chapter,
you should be able to:

- Identify five megatrends that promise to reshape organizational life.
- Discuss the term *work.*
- Identify the various reasons people work.
- Explain why the work ethic is not dead among American employees.
- Explain how job and life satisfaction interact.
- Describe at least three major characteristics of the new economy.
- Discuss three significant demographic shifts in the U.S. work force.

The Trials and Tribulations of Becoming a High-Tech Manager

With high-tech concerns springing up in bunches, the companies of tomorrow are turning to the companies of yesterday for . . . managerial talent. [Here's how two managers—Harry Caunter and William Westman—handled the transition.]

Harry Caunter Pays His High-Tech Dues

For years, Harry Caunter managed battery and electrical-products businesses for Gould Inc. In recent times, however, the suburban-Chicago company has dumped many of its older businesses and gone full bore into electronics. Mr. Caunter faced a choice: Go high tech or go elsewhere. He stayed and began his difficult ascent up the learning curve.

"I used to be able to look at financials and figure out problems and solutions," he says, somewhat wistfully. Now, he says, there is little time for such reflection: "It's all marketing and products. . . . [The market] just goes south, and you're out." He cites a device the company introduced a few years ago to test computer logic. The product was oversophisticated, and Gould's market share sank like a stone within a few months. Things didn't happen that quickly in batteries, Mr. Caunter observes.

The 49-year-old executive has felt keenly his lack of technical knowledge, he says. One of the company's four executive vice presi-dents, Mr. Caunter says he is only now settling in—after 23 months on the job.

To bone up, he has spent hours studying technical trade journals. He also confers frequently with knowledgeable colleagues, and he has hired more consultants than he used to. He is making progress, he believes. But he will still dispatch a technically proficient underling on an important call to neighboring Motorola Inc. rather than make the visit himself. He acknowledges that he lacks the knowledge to talk up the product, but he insists, "As time passes, I'll correct that."

Mr. Caunter has also had to change his management style considerably. A self-described introvert, he used to rely on what he calls a "fear-respect" relationship with subordinates. "I don't need anyone," he says. "That may be terrible to say, but it's made me a good manager." Now, however, he talks of keeping things "warm and toasty" for technical wizards with sensitive psyches and an abundance of job offers.

In the last year and a half, 16 of the top 20 people at Mr. Caunter's Santa Clara, California, design and test systems division have been lured elsewhere. "In Silicon Valley, they have no work ethic. If they get frustrated, they go get another job or sit in their hot tubs or something," Mr. Caunter says. "These are different people, this electronics bunch."

Gould gambled on Mr. Caunter because

of his troubleshooting skills and his ability to get the best out of his subordinates. So far, things seem to be working out.

William Westman Has the High-Tech Blues

Once, Mr. Westman was vice president for finance of high-flying Intel Corp., the Silicon Valley semiconductor maker. Now, chain-smoking in his office, he muses on an aborted run at high technology that left him "extremely disappointed. I looked and said, 'What the hell am I doing here?' "

Mr. Westman was an executive of Hooker Chemicals & Plastics Corp. when Intel recruited him. "I was a little awed," he recalls. "I wasn't used to powerful people coming after me. I don't have a big degree to flash around. I'm not six-foot-four and beautiful." He envisioned Intel as a flexible place where he could "make a mark and a lot of money."

Instead, the 38-year-old executive says, he found Intel to be suspicious of outsiders and resistant to change. When he proposed a cost-control project, he claims, his new bosses rejected it out of hand. And because he wore a tie instead of the standard open-necked sport shirt, he says, colleagues considered him a snob; his dress habits were even mentioned in the company newsletter.

Laurence Hootnick, the Intel senior vice president who hired him, remembers things differently. He now thinks that bringing Mr. Westman aboard was a "horrendous mis-take." Mr. Westman was "a good example of somebody who came from old-line business and really belonged there," the Intel official says. "He was a really bright guy, but he was too authoritarian. It was 'King William,' and we don't have kings here."

Mr. Westman admits that "my own stupidity and lack of flexibility" may have contributed to his problems. "I made a lot of mistakes at Intel," he says. Still, he places much of the blame on the company. "The culture was very high on my list for why I left high tech and came back to smokestack industry. The people out there went out of their way to say, 'You don't fit.' "

After less than a year with the chip maker, Mr. Westman jumped at the chance to get out. He worked briefly at Memorex Corp., then left high tech completely to become the chief financial officer of Tennessee Chemical Co., whose main product is sulfuric acid. . . . Surveying the plant from a driveway, he says. "In reality, I have made out very well, thank you."

For Discussion

What did Caunter do right that Westman did wrong?

SOURCE: Excerpted from John Bussey, "Smokestack Managers Moving to High Tech Find the Going Tough." Reprinted by permission of *The Wall Street Journal*, © Dow Jones & Company, Inc., January 10, 1985. All rights reserved.

■ Additional discussion questions linking this case with the following material appear at the end of this chapter.

Suppose some friends called and asked if you would be interested in going on a 10-day hiking and camping trip. First, you would want to know where they planned to go. A trip to the seashore would require different clothing and gear than a trip to the mountains. Primitive trails without water and facilities would require more planning than established hiking trails. Next, you would be wise to ask your friends if they had checked the weather forecast. Late spring snowstorms can prove fatal for campers in the mountains, and a few days of heavy rain can break the spirits of even the hardiest lowland hikers. In short, forehand knowledge of terrain and weather conditions are crucial to a safe and enjoyable camping trip. Intelligent preparation for any endeavor requires relevant contextual knowledge. So, too, if you are to get full benefit from the study of organizational behavior, you first need to explore its relevant context.

This chapter provides a context for the study and practice of organizational behavior. After reviewing relevant "megatrends," or major trends reshaping today's workplace, we focus on (1) the meaning of work, (2) the work ethic, (3) the relationship between job and life satisfaction, (4) significant changes in the workplace, and (5) changing work force demographics. Each section is followed by a discussion of the implications for organizational behavior. Just as it would be foolish to go on a hiking and camping trip without first studying the conditions and getting a weather report, it would be equally naive to embark upon the study of OB without first examining important changes in its real-world context.

■ MEGATRENDS: A GENERAL PICTURE OF THINGS TO COME

John Naisbitt's best-seller, *Megatrends: Ten New Directions Transforming Our Lives,* does an excellent job of synthesizing an otherwise mind-boggling array of social, political, economic, and technological changes and events into a meaningful preview of what lies ahead. Naisbitt's research method was somewhat unusual. Instead of interviewing supposed experts, Naisbitt and his *Trend Report* staff methodically searched 6,000 local newspapers every month for 12 years. As the years passed, 10 major trends (called megatrends) became evident as changes percolated up through American society (see Table 2–1). Five of Naisbitt's megatrends are particularly relevant to understanding and managing organizational behavior, and these are highlighted in this section.

Five Megatrends Reshaping Organizational Life

For each of the five megatrends, an arrow indicates what we are moving away from and what we seem to be moving toward.

1. *Industrial society* → *information society.* In today's service economy, more than 60 percent of available jobs involve creating, processing, and distributing information. Naisbitt sums up U.S. economic history in the following three words: farmer → laborer → clerk. Where yesterday's workers looked into blast furnaces, today's look into computer display terminals (and many are complaining of stressful complications).

Important among the new "information workers" are managers and administrators, whose ranks grew by 58 percent during the 1970s. The total labor force recorded a more modest 18 percent growth for the same period. In the

■ **TABLE 2–1** Naisbitt's Megatrends Paint a General Picture of What Lies Ahead

Megatrend	General Thrust
1. Industrial society ⟶ information society	Because of computers and automation, the typical employee today manages information instead of producing a tangible product. The technological displacement of workers is a growing labor-management issue.
2. Forced technology ⟶ high tech/high touch	Employees are striving for an acceptable balance between impersonal technology and the need for meaningful human interaction.
3. National economy ⟶ world economy	Regionalized "sunset" industries such as steel and autos are giving way to globalized "sunrise" industries such as biotechnology, telecommunications, and electronics.
4. Short term ⟶ long term	Strategic attention to long-term survival is replacing management's traditional preoccupation with short-term profits. Managers are beginning to view employees as a valuable resource rather than an expendable commodity.
5. Centralization ⟶ decentralization	In both government and business, the trend is toward local power and control.
6. Institutional help ⟶ self-help	Dissatisfaction and frustration with institutions have fostered a return to the traditional value of self-reliance (as evidenced by the entrepreneurial explosion).
7. Representative democracy ⟶ participative democracy	Citizens and employees are demanding and getting greater say in the key decisions affecting their lives.
8. Hierarchies ⟶ networking	Formal, vertically oriented bureaucracies are giving way to informal, horizontally oriented networks.
9. North ⟶ south	The U.S. labor force is moving south and west as the Sun Belt states benefit more from the high-tech revolution than the Frost-Belt states.
10. Either/or ⟶ multiple option	Yesterday's either/or distinctions are being tempered by wider ranging choices in lifestyle, work, and play. Gender roles are changing dramatically as more women enter the work force.

SOURCE: Reprinted by permission of Warner Books/New York from *Megatrends*. Copyright © 1982 by John Naisbitt.

information society, Naisbitt believes generalist managers will replace specialists. Generalists, he contends, can adapt, whereas specialists are soon obsolete due to the rapid turnover of information and knowledge. Managers are challenged to deal effectively with information overload.

Thanks to the computer and telecommunications revolutions, information is both a renewable and self-generating resource. But not everyone is greeting the age of computers and high technology with open arms. Workers in traditional smokestack industries, such as steel and autos, who have lost their jobs to robots and other forms of automation view computers and modern technology as a threat rather than a promise. The same goes for white-collar employees who see their jobs being simplified or "de-skilled" by office automation. Naisbitt believes computer literacy training is a must for virtually all employees.

2. *Forced technology* → *high tech/high touch.* The typical modern employee resents being forced to interact with cold, impersonal machines. Naisbitt contends that very few employees will be content to stay at home in their "electronic cottages" tapping out computerized messages to their employer's office. Organizations are an alternative to isolation. Many people need and enjoy the chance to visit and gossip with other employees during breaks, not to mention face-to-face interaction with the boss and the usual office politics. Basic human needs for interpersonal interaction and support are fostering development of humane workplace innovations. For example, Naisbitt notes the concurrent development of high-tech robots and high-*touch* quality circles (small, voluntary quality improvement groups). The human factor will become more important, not less important, as advanced technology increasingly invades the workplace.

3. *Representative democracy → participatory democracy.* At the heart of this megatrend is individuals' growing desire to have a direct say in the key political and organizational decisions that affect their lives. According to Naisbitt:

> Just as we seek a greater voice in political decisions, through initiatives and referenda, we are reformulating corporate structures to permit workers, shareholders, consumers, and community leaders a larger say in determining how corporations will be run. [A key feature of this scenario is] the trend toward greater worker participation and employee rights.[1]

Naisbitt believes today's leader/manager needs to be a *facilitator*, not simply an order giver or dictator.

4. *Hierarchies → networking.* Traditionally, government and business organizations have been oriented strongly toward vertical authority structures. The trend today is away from a vertical orientation and toward horizontal, overlapping, and multidirectional links between individuals and groups. Networks tend to develop spontaneously and are characterized by informality and equality. Competence, not arbitrary status, counts in interdisciplinary, goal-oriented networks.

5. *Either/or > multiple option.* Naisbitt says we live in a Baskin-Robbins society where all manner of things now come in 31 flavors, including jobs and lifestyles. The long-standing 40-hour, five-day workweek is being pushed aside in favor of work schedule innovations such as flexitime, permanent part-time, and compressed workweeks (e.g., four 10-hour days). Self-employment is increasing, and highly personalized work-leisure patterns are evolving. Given these multiple options, individuals now have more personal choice and responsibility for their life experiences.

Implications for OB

Naisbitt's megatrends contain many implications for those who wish to more fully understand and effectively manage people at work. Because the pace of change has quickened in the information society, overcoming resistance to change among employees is an even more important managerial task. Resistance to change and organization development strategies for implementing planned change are discussed in Chapter 18.

As the automation of factories and offices continues, employees will demand quality-of-work-life improvements to create new high-tech/high-touch balances. Along the same lines, participative management schemes will spread and flourish as employees demand and get a greater say in directing their work lives.

---

[1] John Naisbitt, *Megatrends: Ten New Directions Transforming Our Lives* (New York: Warner Books, 1982), pp. 175–76.

Techniques and innovations in these areas are treated throughout the balance of this book.

The legitimacy and usefulness of rigid, top-down hierarchical organization structures are giving way to more fluid and flexible structures. Horizontal and upward communication are increasingly replacing a historical downward

■ **TABLE 2–2**　Jobs and Organizations Are Changing to Fit Individual Needs and Lifestyles

What should be the most important objective of a company? "To make money and have fun," according to W. L. Gore & Associates. "To build something to last, to survive me . . . Not to take the money and run," according to Irwin Mintz, president of JBM Electronics Company. "To be autonomous *and* accountable," suggests Don Vlcek, president of Domino Pizza Distribution Company. "To put a lot into an enterprise or relationship, and to get a lot out of it," according to Lewis Weinberg of Fel-Pro, Incorporated.

Most forward-looking business leaders do feel that the worker-employer relationship is a vital company objective and concern. Indeed, a few of them are so sensitive to this relationship that they even choose not to refer to "workers" and "employers," per se. Don Vlcek's business card reads, "Leader of Excellence." And at W. L. Gore, the authority structure is redefined into "leaders" and "sponsors." Company owner William Gore once allegedly wrote a memo to an associate who referred to himself as a "manager," reminding him that at Gore, people *manage themselves;* they do not manage others.

The work force indeed is starting to manage itself more fully, and with this new self-responsiblity comes the increased importance of the workplace. As the Institute for Alternative Futures points out, workers are evolving into "something more than interchangeable parts in the production machine . . . not merely [people] who come to work and give 'eight-for-eight.'"

Perceptions of work and the workplace are drastically different than ever before. Twenty years ago, for instance, the professional working woman was a rare bird. And being a corporate boss, more often than not, meant holding the corner office, riding the luxury limo, patronizing the executive dining room, and boasting when the organization added more layers of employees to the company charts—for that was a signal of successful corporate growth. Hours were rigid, compensation patterns were fixed, and employees usually stayed with one company for life.

Now, women account for more than half of all professionals, and family and work considerations are increasingly at the fore; "boss" is considered by some to be an impolite term; company charts are becoming streamlined, lean, and mean; work-hour and even work-at-home options are becoming more viable; compensation patterns are changing to include the likes of merit pay; and employees—or "associates"—value personal fulfillment highly, and will change jobs, if necessary, to obtain it.

The workplace may be evolving into "a setting in which a larger variety of human needs are met and human services provided," according to the Institute for Alternative Futures. Changing perceptions and workplace considerations mean that the promotion of health, well being, and other self-enhancement opportunities will become increasingly important. Workers want more flexibility, more accountability, more of a "stake" in the corporation, and more (and different sorts of) benefits. In light of all this, companies must redefine what their workplace should offer if they want to be considered attractive places of employment in the future. And several companies right now are redefining their workplaces in innovative ways.

SOURCE: Excerpted, by permission of the publisher, from "The Future Workplace," *Management Review*, July 1986, p. 22, © 1986 American Management Association, New York. All rights reserved.

pattern. Managers are doing less telling and dictating and more *selling* and *facilitating*. Jobs and organizations are being reshaped to accommodate individual needs and lifestyles rather than vice versa (see Table 2–2). Traditionally, labor was viewed as a commodity to be bent to management's wishes. Progressive managers, as discussed in Chapter 1, now view people as the organization's most precious resource. Later discussion of motivation, rewards, group dynamics, communication, leadership, job design, and organizational cultures provides useful insights relative to productively matching individual and organizational needs.

With these megatrends in mind, let us examine the meaning of work.

■ WORK AND THE MEANING OF WORK

Are the terms *job* and *work* synonymous? Many people probably would answer yes. But William (Least Heat Moon) Trogdon, author of the bestseller *Blue Highways,* came across a man during his transcontinental travels who perceived an important difference. While passing through Kentucky, Trogdon joined an interesting couple for dinner. As often occurs, the conversation turned to what each person did for a living. The man, a metallurgical engineer, told Trogdon:

> I notice that you use *work* and *job* interchangeably. Oughten to do that. A job's what you force yourself to pay attention to for money. With work, you don't have to force yourself. There are a lot of jobs in this country, and that's good because they keep people occupied. That's why they're called "occupations."[2]

In this textbook, we define a **job** as the organizational activities or tasks one performs for monetary return. In contrast, **work** has a more encompassing meaning than a job, because it involves producing something of value for oneself or others.[3] A job may or may not deserve to be called work. A dull and unchallenging job is just that, a *job*. But a job that excites and fulfills higher-level ego needs qualifies as work.

Chrysler Corp. Chairman Lee Iacocca quickly learned the difference between a job and work upon launching his career at Ford. According to Iacocca's autobiography:

> I was nine months into the [training] program with another nine to go. But engineering no longer interested me. The day I'd arrived, they had me designing a clutch spring. It had taken me an entire day to make a detailed drawing of it, and I said to myself: "What on earth am I doing? Is this how I want to be spending the rest of my life?"
>
> I wanted to stay at Ford, but not in engineering. I was eager to be where the

---

[2] William Least Heat Moon (William Trogdon), *Blue Highways: A Journey into America* (New York: Fawcett Crest, 1982), p. 11.

[3] Based on a similar definition found in *Work in America: Report of a Special Task Force to the Secretary of Health, Education and Welfare* (Cambridge, Mass.: MIT Press, 1973), p. 3.

real action was—marketing or sales. I like working with people more than machines. . . .

[After getting permission to transfer,] I was hired for a low-level desk job in
fleet sales. . . .

Eventually, I got out from behind the telephone. I went from the desk to the
field, visiting dealers as a traveling truck and fleet representative to give them
pointers on selling. I loved every minute of it. Finally, I was out of school and
into the real world. I spent my days driving around in a brand-new car, sharing
my newly found wisdom with a couple of hundred dealers—each one hoping I
could turn him into a millionaire.[4]

For young Iacocca, drawing clutch springs was just a job, but getting out in
the field and interacting with dealers was real work.

Additional insights into the meaning and functions of work can be obtained
by interviewing the unemployed, discovering why people work, considering
the new work ethic, and examining the relationship between work and life
satisfaction.

Work: Looking In from the Outside

As the saying goes, "You never know how good something is until you've
lost it." This section examines the meaning of work from the perspective of
the unemployed. After reviewing and analyzing the unemployment experiences
of many people, one researcher identified several basic functions of work.
As depicted in Figure 2–1, work:

- Encourages setting general life goals (such as owning a new home).
- Provides economic security (paying the bills).
- Provides personal status and identity (see Table 2–3).
- Enforces goal-oriented activity (such as getting out of bed and going to
  a job instead of hiding under the covers).
- Facilitates social contact with others outside the family.
- Provides a sense of teamwork and camaraderie. (For example, at Apple
  Computer, the team that designed the successful Macintosh computer
  raised a pirate flag above its building as a competitive challenge to the
  rest of the company.)[5]
- Imposes a time structure (such as attending scheduled meetings).[6]

The list above underscores that work means different things to different
people. A research study that examined the impact of joblessness on 100
managers and professionals provides further insights into the meaning of work.
One fifth of those sampled felt as if they had lost a very significant part of

---

[4] Lee Iacocca, *Iacocca: An Autobiography* (New York: Bantam Books, 1984), pp. 30–33.

[5] See Michael Moritz, "Apple Launches a Mac Attack," *Time*, January 30, 1984, pp. 68–69.

[6] Adapted in part from Stephen Fineman, "Work Meanings, Non-Work, and the Taken-for-Granted," *Journal of Management Studies*, April 1983, pp. 143–57.

■ **FIGURE 2–1** Functions of Work Identified by Unemployed Workers

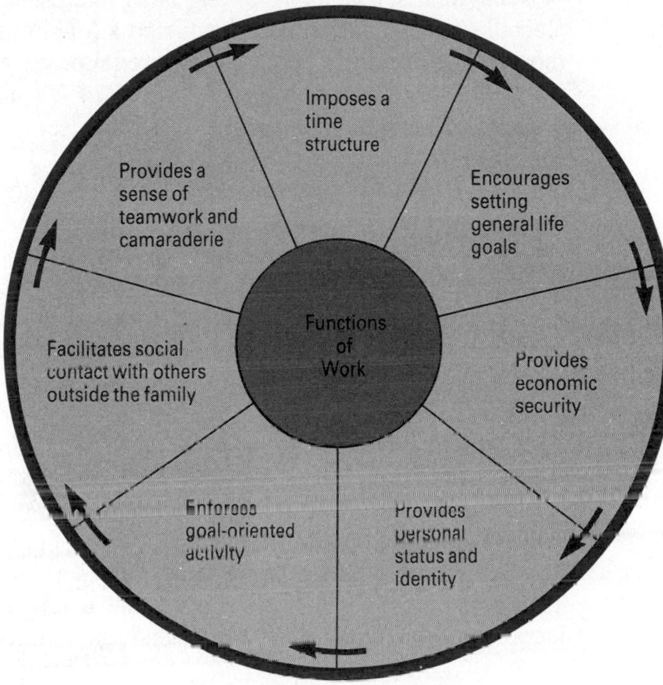

SOURCE: Adapted in part from Stephen Fineman, "Work Meanings, Non-Work, and the Taken-for-Granted," *Journal of Management Studies,* April 1983, pp. 143–57.

■ **TABLE 2–3** A Job Is a Major Determinant of One's Status and Identity

> According to a receptionist for a large midwestern organization:
>
> I changed my opinion of receptionists because now I'm one. It wasn't the dumb broad at the front desk who took telephone messages. She had to be something else because I thought I was something else. I was fine until there was a press party. We were having a fairly intelligent conversation. Then they asked me what I did. When I told them, they turned around to find other people with name tags. I wasn't worth bothering with. I wasn't being rejected because of what I said or the way I talked, but simply because of my function.
>
> SOURCE: Studs Terkel, *Working* (New York: Pantheon Books, 1974), p. 29.

their lives. They were devastated over losing their jobs. Surprisingly, one third of those interviewed were very happy about being unemployed. These professionals were happy because their former jobs made them feel alienated, stressed, and trapped.[7] A job truly is a many-sided experience.

———
[7] Ibid.

Work: More than a Stream of Income

Behavioral scientists have long been interested in *why* people work. Robert Vecchio, an OB researcher, conducted a longitudinal investigation of people's motives for working. Vecchio compared motives established in a 1955 national sample of 401 employed men with a 1974–77 national survey of 1,099 male workers. To permit comparison, a similar set of procedures was used in the follow-up study.

In the 1955 survey, respondents were asked to indicate whether they would continue working if they inherited enough money to live comfortably. Overall, 80 percent of the sample indicated they would continue working. Respondents in the follow-up study were asked: "If you were to get enough money to live as comfortably as you would like for the rest of your life, would you continue to work or would you stop working?"[8] Seventy-two percent responded they would continue working. Except for people between the ages of 45 and 54, there was a statistically significant downward trend in the number of workers who would continue working (see Figure 2–2). The largest difference occurred for people 65 and older. For this age group, 82 percent of the 1955 sample would have continued working, compared with 56 percent in the 1974–77 survey. Assuming the trend detected by Vecchio is true today, we can conclude that the commitment to work, although declining, is still relatively strong. This commitment to work suggests that a job means more than a stream of income and the work ethic is not dead, as claimed by some observers.

Implications for OB

Work, as opposed to a job, creates value and is motivational and satisfying to perform. This difference highlights a managerial need to design jobs that offer the personal fulfillment associated with work. In other words, jobs need to be structured so workers experience satisfaction and believe they are doing something of value (see Chapter 15).

Work means different things to different people. This suggests that each of us is an individual who is satisfied and motivated by different types of rewards. Chapter 3 discusses the foundation of important individual differences. Chapters 5 and 6 go one step further by applying individual differences to several models of motivation.

Most people still want to work even when they do not need the money. This suggests that people work for more than economic reasons. For example, people satisfy social and self-esteem needs through their work. Employee motivation may thus be increased by offering employees a variety of rewards that satisfy both financial and nonfinancial needs.

---

[8] Robert P. Vecchio, "The Function and Meaning of Work and the Job: Morse and Weiss (1955) Revisited," *Academy of Management Journal*, June 1980, p. 363.

■ **FIGURE 2–2** How Many Employees Would Work if They Could Afford Not to?

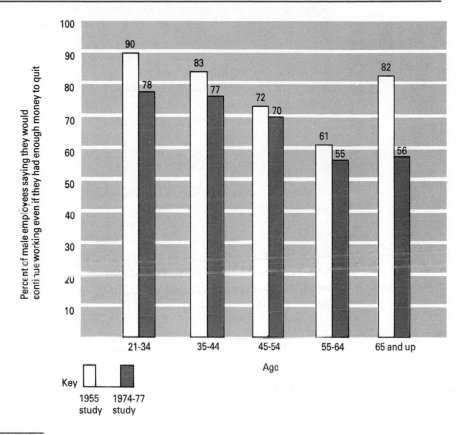

SOURCE: Based on data from Robert P. Vecchio, "The Function and Meaning of Work and the Job: Morse and Weiss (1955) Revisited," *Academy of Management Journal*, June 1980, p. 364.

■ IS THE WORK ETHIC DEAD?

The **work ethic** involves a positive attitude about work and a belief that hard work is the key to success and happiness. Researchers have found that a strong work ethic is associated with greater earnings, initiative, job satisfaction, and productivity.[9] In recent years, there has been widespread concern that the work ethic is dead or dying. This worry is based on findings from observational studies and employee attitude surveys.

For instance, according to an observational study of employee behavior over a two-year period, employees spent only 51 percent of the typical workday

[9] For example, see Paul J. Andrisani and Herbert S. Parnes, "Commitment to the Work Ethic and Success in the Labor Market: A Review of Research Findings," in *The Work Ethic— A Critical Analysis*, ed. Jack Barbash, Robert J. Lampman, Sar A. Levitan, and Gus Tyler (Madison, Wis.: Industrial Relations Research Association Series, 1983).

actually working. The remaining 49 percent was taken up by unproductive activities such as drinking coffee, chatting with co-workers, and arriving late and leaving early.[10] Employee attitude surveys have uncovered similar evidence. For example, in a national survey of 845 American employees conducted by the Public Agenda Foundation, 23 percent indicated they were not working to their full potential. In addition, 44 percent said they did not put more effort into their jobs than was required. Finally, 62 percent agreed with the belief that people do not work as hard as they used to. Other evidence, however, suggests that these findings portray an unrealistically negative picture.

Some Encouraging Evidence

Fifty-two percent of the Public Agenda Foundation sample mentioned above indicated they had a strong desire to do the very best job they could.[11] This suggests a majority of American workers possesses a strong work ethic, but for some reason this majority is not working to its potential.

Additional indicators support the existence of a vibrant work ethic. Absenteeism and turnover (quitting the job) are two indexes of commitment to the work ethic. High absenteeism and turnover rates are indicative of low commitment. As shown in Figure 2–3, absenteeism declined from 2.6 percent of the total scheduled work time in 1980 to 1.8 percent for the first nine months of 1987, a drop that also reflected aftershocks of the recession in the early 1980s. Similarly, turnover decreased from 1.4 percent of the total work force in 1980 to 1.1 percent for the first nine months of 1987. (The 0.2 percentage point jump in turnover between 1982–83 and 1984 likely resulted from the vigorous economic upturn at that time.)

Stifled Work Ethic

How then can it be claimed that workers who work halfheartedly have a strong work ethic? According to one pair of experts, management is to blame. Rather than bringing out the work ethic, management too often thwarts it by taking actions that cripple the incentive to work hard.[12] For example, paying people by the hour gives them an incentive to show up for work but not necessarily to be fully productive. Moreover, a dull, repetitive, and unchallenging job makes it more desirable to loaf than to work hard. In contrast, another management researcher believes society at large is the culprit.

---

[10] From Marc Miller, "The 'Wild Card' of Business: How to Manage the Work Ethic in the Automated Workplace," *Management Review*, September 1983, pp. 8–12.

[11] Ibid.

[12] See Daniel Yankelovich and John Immerwahr, "The Emergence of Expressivism Will Revolutionize the Contract between Workers and Employers," *Personnel Administrator*, December 1983, pp. 34–39, 114.

■ **FIGURE 2–3** Absenteeism and Turnover Rates Have Been Declining

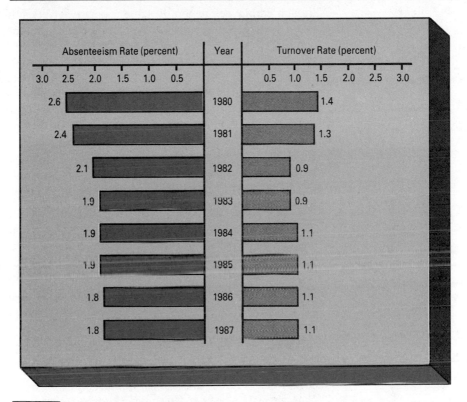

SOURCE: Based on data from *BNA's Quarterly Report on Job Absence and Turnover* (Washington: The Bureau of National Affairs, 1984); 1985–87 data from *BNA's Quarterly Report on Job Absence and Turnover* (Washington: The Bureau of National Affairs, 1987).

In our society, mechanisms for reducing the frustrations, anxieties, disappointments, and losses of personal pride and property resulting from failure are on the increase. . . . Alternative jobs exist in relative abundance, making it possible for those who fail at one job to be retrained for another, or find employment in another company. Legislation now makes it difficult to release employees for failure to perform. Psychologists have convinced managers not to use various disciplinary procedures and penalties for poor performance. Finally, unions have negotiated freedom from penalty for numerous types of nonperformance. The evidence is clear: penalties for lack of success are fast becoming extinct.[13]

In conclusion, the work ethic appears to be alive and well, but managerial and societal forces sometimes encourage employees to exert less effort.

[13] Phillip C. Grant, "Why Employee Motivation Has Declined in America," *Personnel Journal*, December 1982, p. 907.

Implications for OB

Although employees generally have a positive work ethic, boring jobs and haphazard managerial practices too often encourage them to put minimum effort into their work. This likely will lead managers to believe workers do not care about their jobs. If such is the case, managers may come to view subordinates as lazy, thus prompting the use of punishment and an authoritarian or heavy-handed leadership style. Given the importance of the work ethic, management needs to attempt to nurture it. This can be done by linking pay with performance. Consider General Motors' new compensation system, for example (see Table 2–4). Another approach is to identify what motivates, as opposed to satisfies, an individual. A two-factor theory that explains the interaction between motivation and satisfaction is presented in Chapter 5. Finally, organizational structures need to be reexamined (see Chapter 17). This reexamination will help identify whether organizational policies and practices are inhibiting the work ethic.

■ **TABLE 2–4**   General Motors Links Pay to Performance

> For decades the automaker appeared to be running a white-collar welfare system: salaried employees, regardless of individual performance or market conditions, were practically assured of high pay and lifetime employment. But this month, GM is setting up a new compensation system that it hopes will push its salaried employees to work harder—will help push those who don't out the door. . . .
>
> GM made major changes two years ago when it dropped annual cost-of-living raises for salaried employees and established a "pay-for-performance" system. . . .
>
> Also under GM's new compensation plan, managers are encouraged to give immediate, "spontaneous" rewards—such as theater tickets or trips—for a clever idea or a great report. The plan is also designed to encourage better cooperation among co-workers. Recognition awards will stem from "team" performance.
>
> SOURCE: Excerpted from Jacob M. Schlesinger, "GM's New Compensation Plan Reflects General Trend Tying Pay to Performance," *The Wall Street Journal,* January 26, 1988, p. 33.

■ THE DYNAMICS OF JOB AND LIFE SATISFACTION

Job satisfaction is an affective or emotional response toward various facets of one's job. In other words, job satisfaction involves a person's positive (or negative) feelings about his or her job. The popular press generally contends that the American work force is in the midst of a job-satisfaction crisis. But recent evidence suggests these claims probably are overstated. Internationally, the American labor force seems to be faring quite well. For example, one study contrasted the average job satisfaction of 3,600 American blue-collar workers with that of a matched sample of 3,600 Japanese workers. As shown in Table 2–5, the Americans were substantially more satisfied with their jobs. Another sample of 450 managers similarly indicated that 53 percent were

■ TABLE 2–5 U.S. and Japanese Job Satisfaction

	American Workers	Japanese Workers
Satisfaction with supervision	78%	50%
Satisfaction with co-workers	92	75
Satisfaction with work tasks	83	53
Overall job satisfaction	81	53
Life satisfaction	83	45

SOURCE: Based on data from "Surprise Gap in U.S., Japan Work Commitment," *Management Review*, October 1983, p. 65.

satisfied with their jobs. In addition, a survey of 2,000 readers of *Black Enterprise*, a periodical with a readership representative of middle-income blacks, revealed that 68 percent were satisfied with their jobs. Researchers have found that job satisfaction tends to be greater among people in higher occupational levels, among those who grew up in smaller communities (2,500 to 10,000 persons) and among individuals with higher socioeconomic status and income.[14] Work organizations are not completely responsible for the current level of job satisfaction among U.S. employees, however. As illustrated in Figure 2–4, job satisfaction also is influenced by nonwork factors.

■ FIGURE 2–4 Impact of Work and Nonwork Factors on Quality of Life

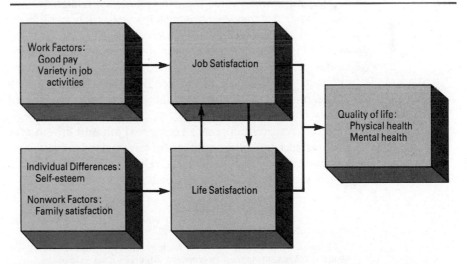

[14] See Guisseppi A. Forgionne and Vivian E. Peeters, "Race and Sex Related Differences in Job Satisfaction and Motivation among Managers," *Personnel Administrator*, February 1983, pp. 66–72; and Joel Dreyfuss, "Speaking Out about Work," *Black Enterprise*, August 1982, pp. 51–53, 55–56; for evidence of satisfaction by segments of the work force, see Oscar B. Martinson and E. A. Wilkening, "Rural-Urban Differences in Job Satisfaction: Further Evidence," *Academy of Management Journal*, March 1984, pp. 199–206; and Garnett Stokes Shaffer, "Patterns of Work and Nonwork Satisfaction," *Journal of Applied Psychology*, February 1987, pp. 115–24.

Reciprocal Relationship

Have you ever done poorly on a test you were really prepared for because you had an argument with a friend the night before? If you have, you know your personal life can influence your work and vice versa. As exemplified by Lulu Wang, senior vice president of the Equitable Capital Management Group, the same goes for job and life satisfaction.

> Wang . . . refuses to separate business from home life, because trying to do so increases stress. At the age of 12, Wang's son could read the stock pages of *The Wall Street Journal* and join in a lively discussion about a merger at the dinner table. Why not? As a pension fund portfolio manager, his mom controls over $1 billion in assets.
>
> "I've always made it a point to integrate my professional and family lives," says Wang. Keeping the two lives separate produces stress and anxiety. "Your family sees your job as something which strings you out and competes with them for your time." But if you let them share in your highs and lows, "they can't help but be supportive partners," she says.[15]

Behavioral scientists have proposed three rival hypotheses to explain the dynamic interaction between job and life satisfaction.

The first, called the *spillover effect,* hypothesizes that job satisfaction or dissatisfaction spills over into one's life and vice versa. For example, a recent study used 48 males to examine the relationship between stressful work events and wife abuse. Consistent with the spillover effect, the frequency and negativity of stressful work events were significantly related to wife abuse.[16] On the other hand, the *compensation effect* suggests job and life satisfaction are negatively related. In other words, we compensate for low job or life satisfaction by seeking satisfying activities in the other domain. Finally, the *segmentation model* proposes that job satisfaction and life satisfaction are independent—one supposedly does not influence the other. Much research has been devoted to determining the accuracy of these hypotheses.[17] None of the three is completely correct.

Recent research supports a **reciprocal job and life satisfaction relationship.** Each affects the other both positively and negatively on an ongoing basis. Research also has shown that the relationship between job and life satisfaction is stronger for people with more education and higher income levels. Ultimately,

---

[15] Sharon Nelton and Karen Berney, "Women: The Second Wave," *Nation's Business,* May 1987, pp. 20, 22.

[16] Results are presented in Julian Barling and Alan Rosenbaum, "Work Stressors and Wife Abuse," *Journal of Applied Psychology,* May 1986, pp. 346–48.

[17] See Robert Karasek, Bertil Gardell, and Jan Lindell, "Work and Non-Work Correlates of Illness and Behaviour in Male and Female Swedish White Collar Workers," *Journal of Occupational Behaviour,* July 1987, pp. 187–207; and Janet P. Near, C. Ann Smith, Robert W. Rice, and Raymond G. Hunt, "A Comparison of Work and Nonwork Predictors of Life Satisfaction," *Academy of Management Journal,* March 1984, pp. 184–89. For a review of the strength of the job and life satisfaction relationship, see Richard E. Kopelman, Jeffrey H. Greenhaus, and Thomas F. Connolly, "A Model of Work, Family, and Interrole Conflict: A Construct Validation Study," *Organizational Behavior and Human Performance,* October 1983, pp. 198–215.

■ **TABLE 2–6**   Attitude Surveys Produce Positive Results for Leaseway Transportation Corp. and Hartmarx Corp.

Truck drivers for Leaseway Transportation Corp. were asked earlier this year in an anonymous company survey how they felt about their bosses. Their response appalled the company's management.

"They said the supervisors didn't encourage ideas from them, they weren't receptive to them, they were curt to them," recalls Charles T. Deeble, the company's training and development manager. "It was, 'You're a truck driver, here are the keys, go down the road.' They were treating them like children."

Soon after, Cleveland-based Leaseway began offering management-training courses. The survey, Mr. Deeble says, "woke management up to the deficiencies, and it also bought us time with the employees because they felt, 'They (management) must really want to listen.' ". . .

Hartmarx began surveying its 25,000 employees last year, a process the company plans to repeat every three years. After the results were compiled by computer, workers met with personnel staffers in small groups, where they were encouraged to expand on their responses.

The company has already taken several steps on issues raised, Mr. Rosen [vice president of human resources] says, including the installation of a new cafeteria in a North Carolina plant and the distribution of a new orientation handbook. Complaints about poor feedback from bosses also prompted the company to revive a program to teach managers how to conduct performance appraisals.

SOURCE: Excerpted from Larry Reibstein, "A Finger on the Pulse: Companies Expand Use of Employee Surveys." Reprinted by permission of *The Wall Street Journal,* © Dow Jones & Company, Inc., October 27, 1986. All rights reserved.

---

as illustrated in Figure 2–4, the reciprocal interaction between job and life satisfaction affects the individual's overall quality of life and physical and mental health.

A person's job is a key part of a complex and dynamic package called life. For example, in 1983, when unemployment in the U.S. industrial heartland remained high despite an improving economy, *The Wall Street Journal* reported: "Nancy Fouche, the director of Barberton's [Ohio] mental-health clinic, says 40 percent of her caseload is related to joblessness—depressions, family breakdowns, violence, alcoholism."[18] (More is said about the nature and causes of job satisfaction in Chapter 5.)

Implications for OB

Since job satisfaction and life satisfaction affect the quality of our lives, managers need to keep abreast of employee attitudes and problems. Many organizations have responded to this need by creating employee relations departments. These departments concentrate on solving employee problems before they erupt into a crisis. Other organizations—like Leaseway Transportation Corp. and Hartmarx Corp.—use attitude surveys to keep their finger on the pulse of employee sentiments (see Table 2–6). A 1983 survey of 50 companies

---

[18] Geraldine Brooks, "Despite the Recovery, Some Lose Jobs Now, and It's a Hard Blow," *The Wall Street Journal,* August 5, 1983, p. 10.

listed among the Fortune 500 revealed that 43 percent conducted attitude surveys yearly while 21 percent did so every other year. Significantly, unionized firms conducting attitude surveys were less likely to have experienced a labor strike within the previous six years.[19] Finally, employee assistance programs are becoming the dominant method of helping individuals solve personal and work-related problems such as alcohol and drug abuse (see Chapter 16).

■ THE CHANGING WORKPLACE

America's economy and work force are undergoing profound changes that promise to significantly alter the practice of management. As one respected observer predicted in 1985:

> Tomorrow's work force will probably be older, more diverse in terms of gender and race, marked by intense competition for jobs and promotions, less unionized, and better educated.
> . . . social values developed during the 1960s and 1970s will create a high priority for work environment reforms, such as participative decision making, pleasant work conditions, considerate management, and such supportive facilities as day care centers.[20]

Because the work force is increasingly diverse, some managerial practices that worked well in the past are no longer appropriate. For example, unlike the obedient "organization man" of the 1950s who strived to blend in, many of today's aspiring managers and technical specialists are risk takers who are not afraid to rock the boat to make their own contribution. As exemplified in Table 2–7, progressive companies are learning how to encourage and reward rather than stifle creative risk takers.

■ **TABLE 2–7**   Hewlett-Packard Gives an Award for Contempt and Defiance

> Hewlett-Packard is highly regarded in Silicon Valley for fostering innovation. In 1982 Engineer Charles House was given a medal for "extraordinary contempt and defiance beyond the normal call of engineering duty." He had ignored an order from Founder David Packard to stop working on a type of high-quality video monitor. Despite the rebuke, House pressed ahead and succeeded in developing the monitor, which has been used to track NASA's manned moon landings and also in heart transplants. Although there were early estimates that the market for such large-screen displays would be only 30 units, more than 17,000 of them, worth about $35 million, were sold.
>
> SOURCE: John S. DeMott, "Here Come the Intrapreneurs," *Time,* February 4, 1985, p. 37.

---

[19] For complete details, see Robert J. Aiello, "Employee Attitude Surveys: Impact on Corporate Decisions," *Public Relations Journal,* March 1983, p. 21.

[20] Fred Best, "The Nature of Working in a Changing Society," *Personnel Journal,* January 1985, pp. 40–41.

To help you get a better understanding of this important context for organizational behavior, we will now explore work patterns in the current economy and discuss work in the dominant service sector.

Working in the New Economy

Technological advances have created a new economy. According to *Time,* this new economy is plagued by some troublesome inconsistencies:

> It is a two-tiered economy marked by swift change and stark contrasts. While traditional smokestack industries are reeling from foreign competition, surging high-technology companies are leading the world in innovation. Though hundreds of thousands of blue-collar assembly-line workers have lost their livelihoods, white-collar engineers have had their pick of high-paying jobs. . . . [In 1982,] 25,346 businesses went bankrupt, the most since the Great Depression, but 566,942 new companies opened their doors.[21]

While high-tech occupations will grow rapidly during the next decade, they will account for a comparatively small proportion of new job opportunities.

Low-Tech Jobs in a High-Tech Revolution. It is estimated that high technology fields will be responsible for only 6 percent of all new jobs created in the next 10 years. Occupations projected to create the most new job openings in the foreseeable future are in the relatively low-paying, low-tech service sector. Contrary to the impression created by popular media accounts of the high-tech revolution, building custodians and cashiers will be the big gainers. Next in line for vigorous job opportunity growth will be secretaries, general office clerks, and salesclerks.[22] Some lofty expectations are bound to be dashed on the rocks of this reality.

Good-Bye 40-Hour Workweek. The number of hours people spend at work has been decreasing. As presented in Figure 2–5, the private sector labor force worked an average of 40.1 hours per week in 1940. This figure dropped to an average of 34.8 hours per week for the first six months of 1987. Although liberalized policies on vacations and holidays are largely responsible for this decrease, the point emerges that the work-leisure balance is tipping in favor of more leisure. Not everyone is working less, however. Employment surveys indicate that chief executive officers, vice presidents, and middle managers work more than 40 hours a week.

> Chief executive officers spend, on average, 10 to 12 hours a day on the job, according to a survey by Canny, Bowen Inc., a search firm. The CEOs work a further 10 hours on weekends. Another survey by Robert Half International, a recruiting firm, finds that corporate vice presidents say they work 10.5 hours a week at home on nights and weekends; middle managers, they say, put in only 6.9 hours at home.[23]

---

[21] "The New Economy," *Time,* May 30, 1983, p. 62.

[22] For additional details, see Bryant Robey and Cheryl Russell, "A Portrait of the American Worker," *American Demographics,* March 1984, pp. 16–21.

[23] "Labor Letter: A Special News Report on People and Their Jobs in Offices, Fields and Factories," *The Wall Street Journal,* June 10, 1986, p. 1.

■ **FIGURE 2–5** Americans Are Working Fewer Hours

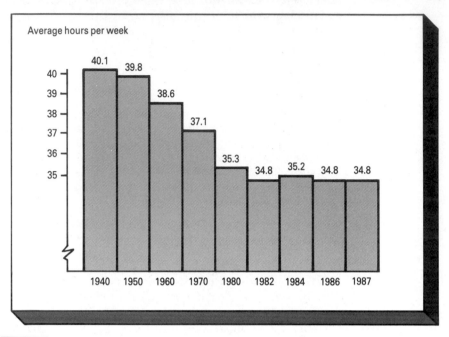

SOURCES: "Employment Conditions and Wages," *Survey of Current Business,* February 1941, p. 73; "Current Labor Statistics," *Monthly Labor Review,* June 1984, p. 75; 1986–87 data obtained from "Current Labor Statistics," *Monthly Labor Review,* August 1987, pp. 81, 85.

More Part-Timers. More and more companies are hiring people to work part-time. The total number of part-time or temporary employees had grown to 34.3 million by 1987, about 33 percent of the U.S. labor force.[24] Not only does hiring part-timers reduce an organization's labor costs (see Table 2–8), but it also accommodates the flexibility desired by a growing segment of the labor force.

Working in a Service Economy

As depicted in Figure 2–6, employment has shifted dramatically in the U.S. economy's three main sectors: agriculture, goods producing, and service producing. Sixty-four percent of the work force was employed in agriculture in 1850, as opposed to 3 percent in 1985. In contrast, employment in the service sector increased from 18 percent in 1850 to 73 percent in 1985. A leading futurist predicts that 88 percent of the U.S. work force will be employed in the service sector by the year 2000.[25]

---

[24] See Deborah C. Wise, Aaron Bernstein, and Alice Z. Cuneo, "Part-Time Workers: Rising Numbers, Rising Discord," *Business Week,* April 1, 1985, pp. 62–63; and Michael J. McCarthy, "On Their Own: In Increasing Numbers, White-Collar Workers Leave Steady Positions," *The Wall Street Journal,* October 13, 1987, pp. 1, 30.

[25] See Peter Nulty, "The Economy of the 1990s: How Managers Will Manage," *Fortune,* February 2, 1987, pp. 47–50.

■ **TABLE 2–8** Part-Time Workers Cost Less to Employ

> Part-time workers grow in number as employers cut costs.
> Western Airlines is using more part-time ticket agents and baggage handlers since it switched to a "hub-and-spoke" flight system. Maximum staffing is only needed early and late in the day. Sloans Supermarkets, New York, says part-timers account for about 40 percent of its employees. Red Apple, another New York grocer, says its largest store has 3 full-time workers and 43 part-timers: that helps avoid night-pay premiums.
> The Labor Department says that the number of temporary workers jumped by a total of more than 261,000 in 1983 and 1984, while the ranks of the self-employed also grew by 140,000. "It's a new way for employers to add to work forces without adding as much cost as regular employees," says the Conference Board.
> "It makes more sense to pay someone $3.35 an hour instead of someone who earns $9.95 an hour" as a full-timer, says a Sloan spokeswoman.
>
> SOURCE: "Labor Letter: A Special News Report on People and Their Jobs in Offices, Fields and Factories." Reprinted by permission of *The Wall Street Journal,* © Dow Jones & Company, Inc., February 12, 1985, p. 1. All rights reserved.

■ **FIGURE 2–6** Distribution of U.S. Employment by Major Sector

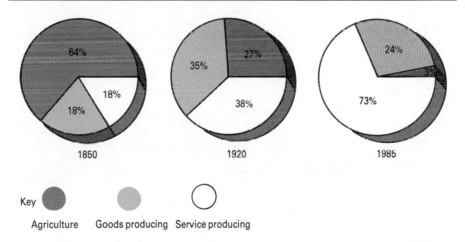

SOURCE: Historical data obtained from Michael Urquhart, "The Employment Shift to Services: Where Did It Come From?" *Monthly Labor Review,* April 1984, p. 16; 1985 data obtained from "Service Industries," *The Wall Street Journal,* August 7, 1985, p. 21.

After analyzing these employment shifts, one economist noted:

> Suggested explanations for the faster growth of services employment include changes in the demand for goods and services as a result of rising income and relative price movements, slower productivity growth in services, the increasing participation of women in the labor force since World War II, and the growing importance of the public and nonprofit sector in general.[26]

---

[26] Michael Urquhart, "The Employment Shift to Services: Where Did It Come From?" *Monthly Labor Review,* April 1984, p. 15.

■ **FIGURE 2–7**   Although on the Upswing, U.S. Service-Sector Productivity Still Lags

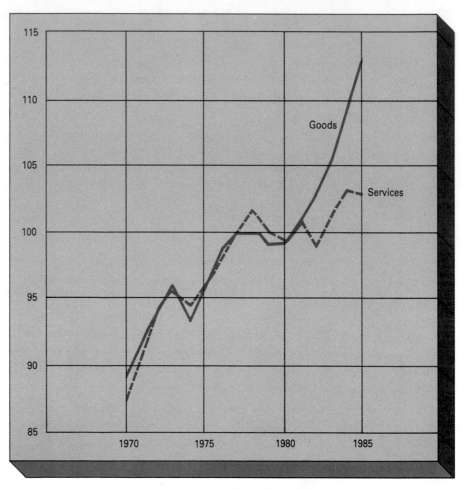

Productivity index: 1977 = 100

SOURCE: *Productivity Perspectives* (Houston: American Productivity Center, 1987), p. 3. Used with permission.

This economic scenario presents management with a significant challenge. Specifically, the service sector, the largest source of employment in the United States, has the lowest productivity.

Evidence indicates that sluggish productivity growth in the United States is directly attributable to low productivity in the service sector. During the early 1980s, service-sector productivity still lagged far behind manufacturing productivity (see Figure 2–7). Attempts to reverse this trend have not been successful. As noted in *Fortune:*

> Productivity has declined in services despite vast investments in technology, and costs have risen faster than in manufacturing. . . . [In 1985,] wages in the

labor-intensive service sector rose 4.7 percent versus 3.5 percent in manufacturing.[27]

In conclusion, a high-priority managerial task is to boost productivity of the "people-intensive" service sector.

Implications for OB

Part-timers, who now number more than ever before, have more negative attitudes toward work than full-timers. Moreover, researchers find that part-timers exhibit less organizational loyalty and have a greater tendency to quit than full-time employees.[28] These negative work outcomes are probably due to the fact that "part-timers typically get few fringe benefits—no health care, no life insurance, no pensions. Wages are lower too. On average, part-timers pull in only $4.50 an hour [in 1985], compared with $7.80 for full-time workers."[29] Consequently, management needs to identify and appeal to the needs, motives, and sources of satisfaction for this growing segment of the work force. Failing to do so may lead to further declines in overall job satisfaction and the work ethic among American workers.

Service industries have the distinction of employing the most people and having the lowest productivity. This highlights the need to identify causes of the service-sector productivity problem. Interviews, survey questionnaires, and direct observation can be used for this purpose. Virtually this entire book deals with productivity enhancement.

In response to growing service-sector employment and automation, unions are stepping up recruitment of service employees. This suggests management needs to pay better attention to the wants and desires of this segment of the work force.

■ DEMOGRAPHICS OF THE NEW WORK FORCE

Work force demographics, statistical profiles of the characteristics and composition of the adult working population, are an invaluable human resource planning aid. They enable managers to anticipate and adjust for surpluses or shortages of appropriately skilled individuals. In addition, general population demographics give managers a preview of the values and motives of future

---

[27] Thomas Moore, "What's Taking the Punch out of Profits?" *Fortune,* June 9, 1986, p. 114.

[28] Supporting evidence is found in Ellen F. Jackofsky and Lawrence H. Peters, "Part-Time versus Full-Time Employment Status Differences: A Replication and Extension," *Journal of Occupational Behaviour,* January 1987, pp. 1–9; and Douglas S. Wakefield, James P. Curry, Charles W. Mueller, and James L. Price, "Differences in the Importance of Work Outcomes between Full-Time and Part-Time Hospital Employees," *Journal of Occupational Behaviour,* January 1987, pp. 25–35.

[29] See Wise, Bernstein, and Cuneo, "Part-Time Workers: Rising Numbers, Rising Discord," p. 62.

employees. Demographic changes in the U.S. work force during the last two or three decades have immense implications for organizational behavior. Imagine the ripple effect of changes associated with a 58 percent increase in the number of workers from 1960 to 1982, largely due to the baby-boom generation's entry into the job market. Significantly, women accounted for the major share of this growth.

More Women in the Work Force

Women have been entering the labor force in increasing numbers. Since 1960, the number of working women and men has increased 109 and 36 percent, respectively. Working mothers account for a large percentage of this growth. The Labor Department reported about 60 percent of all mothers with children younger than 18 were working in 1985, and dual-worker couples increased to 23 million, or 46 percent of all married couples in 1986.[30] Women currently account for 43 percent of the U.S. labor force. They also are expected to contribute an additional two thirds of the estimated 15 million new entrants into the labor market through 1995.[31]

Female employment is concentrated in relatively lower-level, low-paying occupations. For example, women now occupy 60 percent of all service jobs and hold 8 out of every 10 clerical positions. Approximately 50 percent of all female professionals are employed as nurses or noncollege teachers. Recent figures, however, suggest a change in this pattern. Women working in executive, administrative, or managerial positions increased from 18 percent in 1970 to roughly 35 percent in 1987.[32] Moreover, 1986 found more than 1,000 women in state legislatures, 80 female mayors of cities with populations of more than 30,000, and 1,300 female judges in the state court system.[33] This demographic shift has created a unique set of dynamics between young female managers and their male and female subordinates (see Table 2-9).

Educational Mismatches

The education level of American workers has been rising. As of 1985, 17.5 percent of the labor force had a college degree. This represented a 5 percent increase from 1970. By 1985, 18 percent of all male workers had

---

[30] See "Labor Letter: A Special News Report on People and Their Jobs in Offices, Fields and Factories, *The Wall Street Journal,* February 18, 1986, p. 1; and "Labor Letter: A Special News Report on People and Their Jobs in Offices, Fields and Factories," *The Wall Street Journal,* November 4, 1986, p. 1.

[31] See Aaron Bernstein, "Business Starts Tailoring Itself to Suit Working Women," *Business Week,* October 6, 1986, pp. 50–54.

[32] Data were obtained from "Women at Work," *Business Week,* January 28, 1985, pp. 80–85; Nancy F. Rytina and Suzanne M. Bianchi, "Occupational Reclassification and Changes in Distribution by Gender," *Monthly Labor Review,* March 1984, pp. 11–17; and Anne B. Fisher, "Where Women Are Succeeding," *Fortune,* August 3, 1987, pp. 78–80, 82, 84, 86.

[33] Reported by Basia Hellwig, "How Working Women Have Changed America," *Working Woman,* November 1986, pp. 129–51.

■ **TABLE 2–9** Demographic Shifts Can Cause Conflict and Problems

After 20 years of cooking, cleaning, and kids, a middle-aged woman gets a job and finds herself working for a woman 10 or more years her junior. How does she feel?

"It's a double whammy," says 45-year-old Joanna Henderson, who helped organize a seminar at Boston's Simmons College on the subject after she was hired by a younger woman. "The stigma is more intense if your boss is both younger and a woman."

The phenomenon of older women working for younger women is the latest of a series of social upheavals unsettling corporate psyches. While older women long have accepted the inevitability of working for younger men in a largely male domain, and even older men know that aggressive younger men may surpass them, other pairings meet greater resistance. Many white workers still resent taking orders from blacks and many men chafe at working for women.

But experts say the conflict between older women and their younger-women bosses can be especially intense.

The older woman generally has entered the work force late after raising a family, or has been stuck for years in a dead-end, traditionally female job—secretary, nurse, or teacher. So she often resents younger managers, who have advantages she generally was denied—a business-school education, specialized training, and fewer barriers to the corporate fast track.

Meanwhile, the younger women managers harbor their own resentments toward their older colleagues. And because this situation was once so rare, younger women managers have few role models who have handled such conflicts.

Today more than 1.3 million women under age 35 hold managerial or administrative posts, up from only 322,000 a dozen years ago. Meanwhile, more than half the women over age 45 also work. "Your first reaction" to having a younger woman boss, says Eileen Bergquist, a 39-year-old Wheaton College career counselor, "is what the heck does this kid know?". . .

Older women workers admit that they are sometimes deferential with colleagues and maternal with superiors. "I freaked out when I started working for younger people," says a 46-year-old software specialist at Data General Corp. "You sort of want to pick up after them and wipe their noses."

But such an attitude infuriates younger women managers, raised on the feminism of the 1970s. "I don't respond to a mother, because I've got one and that was plenty," says Lori King, a Boston University career counselor, who supervises women 10 and 20 years older.

SOURCE: Excerpted from Amy Glickman, "Women Clash: Older Worker vs. Young Boss." *The Wall Street Journal,* February 19, 1985, p. 31. Reprinted by permission of *The Wall Street Journal,* © Dow Jones & Company, Inc., February 19, 1985. All rights reserved.

one to three years of college and 20 percent had four or more years. The corresponding figures for females in 1985 were 18 and 15 percent (see Figure 2–8). Unfortunately, many of these more highly educated workers may find their lofty expectations shortchanged by the new economy. According to a pair of labor economists:

From a national standpoint, a better trained work force is highly desirable. However, with respect to the college educated, the growth in the number of adult workers with degrees carries with it the possibility of an uncertain future for many young college graduates. This is because the greatest increase in the number of jobs over the decade to come is projected for such occupations as janitors, salesclerks, secretaries, and so forth. Thus, the potential exists for a growing mismatch between actual educational levels and those required for occupations with the greatest anticipated growth. In other words, many college graduates—perhaps 20 percent—will not be able to get jobs requiring a college degree, continuing the situation that has prevailed in recent years. Such mismatches could seriously affect the lives of many young workers and their families for years to come.[34]

This situation has created *under*employment.

Underemployment exists when a job requires less than a person's full potential as determined by his or her formal education, training, or skills. Unfortunately, highly educated people may experience underemployment due to a surplus of college graduates. Consider, for example, the competition for jobs given a surplus of 4 million college graduates by 1980 coupled with an expected surplus of 2 million to 3 million from 1983 to 1993.[35] Managers thus need to devise strategies for coping with underemployment and its associated

■ **FIGURE 2–8** Educational Profile of U.S. Work Force

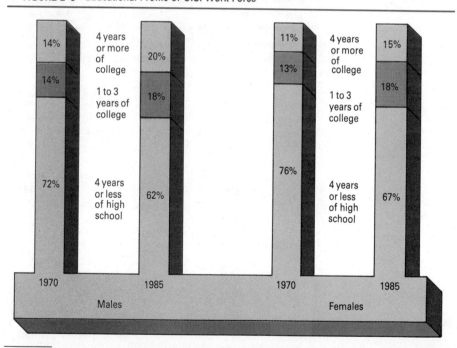

SOURCE: Based on data from "Educational Attainment of the Civilian Labor Force By Sex, Race, and Hispanic Origin, March, Selected Years, 1959–84," *Handbook of Labor Statistics, Bulletin 2217* (June, 1985), p. 164; and Thomas O. Snyder, *Digest of Education Statistics 1987* (Washington, D.C.: U.S. Government Printing Office), p. 14.

---

[34] Anne McDougall Young and Howard Hayghe, "More U.S. Workers Are College Graduates," *Monthly Labor Review,* March 1984, p. 48.

[35] See Samuel M. Enrenhalt, "What Lies Ahead for College Graduates?" *American Demographics,* September 1983, pp. 29–33.

expectations gap as the proportion of college graduates in the labor force continues to increase.

There are even more serious problems at the other end of the educational spectrum in the United States. Buried in the average increase in educational attainment statistic is a worsening public high school dropout problem.

> These days, almost 29% of each entering class doesn't make it to graduation. Says Pat Choate, a vice president at TRW's public policy office in Arlington, Virginia, and the author of a 1986 book titled *The High-Flex Society:* "The top third of America's young people is the best educated in the world, but the middle third is slipping into mediocrity, and the bottom third is at Third World standards."[36]

Increasingly, employers of young entry-level workers are finding them to be deficient in basic reading, math, and social skills. Once again we find a mismatch between educational attainment and occupational requirements. But this time, directly opposite to the problem of underemployment, many job applicants are not up to the challenge.

An Older Work Force

America's population and its work force are getting older. The median age in the United States climbed from just under 28 in 1970 to 30 at the outset of the 1980s. The median age of the work force is projected to reach 39 by the year 2000.[37] "By 2020, almost one third of the U.S. population is expected to be at least age 55."[38] Top-heavy organizations and a shortage of entry-level workers are inevitable consequences of this trend.

The U.S. Bureau of Labor Statistics estimates the number of entry-level workers will decrease 11 percent from 1984 to 1990.[39] Coupled with an increasing number of entry-level job openings, organizations will need to adjust the way they recruit and retain younger workers. Consider, for example, the different approaches used by a sample of national and local companies.

> Safeway Stores have begun using "more and more retired and senior and handicapped people," reports Milt Kegley, Safeway's vice president for human resources. . . .
>
> Burger King has just begun to offer good employees tuition grants. Wendy's pays cash bonuses to employees who refer new workers. The Roy Rogers chain has created intermediate "career" positions to encourage workers to stay. . . .
>
> During the peak sales season, Abraham & Straus transports busloads of young workers from its Brooklyn headquarters to its department stores in suburban counties.

---

[36] Louis S. Richman, "Tomorrow's Jobs: Plentiful, But . . . ," *Fortune*, April 11, 1988, p. 48.

[37] Data from Ibid., p. 56.

[38] "Aging of America," *The Wall Street Journal*, February 22, 1985, p. 31.

[39] See Martha Brannigan, "Help Wanted: A Shortage of Youths Brings Wide Changes to the Labor Market, *The Wall Street Journal*, September 2, 1986, pp. 1, 22.

Bergmann's Laundry and Dry Cleaning, which is based in a Virginia suburb of Washington but draws most of its labor force from the inner city, uses its own trucks to transport workers between their homes and their jobs. . . .

In Florida, the famed Disney World has expanded its recruiting to 60 colleges, some of them abroad, and provides formal management training to attract student workers.[40]

The next section considers the implications of a demographically changed work force.

Implications for OB

Women now account for nearly half of the U.S. labor force. A wide variety of interpersonal, group, and organizational processes have been affected. Consequently, this book contains numerous discussions of gender-related topics. For example, interpersonal dynamics between men and women have a significant impact on communication processes. While at work, males and females must strive to communicate in a professional manner free from sexual connotations. A solid grounding in OB and basic communication processes, as discussed in Chapter 12, can help.

Additionally, women will be in high demand, given future labor shortages. To attract the best workers, companies need to adopt policies and programs that meet the needs of women. Programs such as day care, night care (recent studies indicate one third of all dual-worker couples with children contain a spouse working the night shift),[41] flexible work hours and benefits, paternal leaves, and less rigid relocation policies are likely to become more common.

Mismatches between the amount of education needed to perform current jobs and the amount of education possessed by members of the work force are growing. Underemployment among college graduates threatens to erode job satisfaction and work motivation. As well-educated workers begin to look for jobs commensurate with their qualifications and expectations, absenteeism and turnover likely will increase. This problem underscores the need for job redesign (see the discussion in Chapter 15). In addition, organizations will need to consider interventions, such as realistic job previews and positive reinforcement programs, to reduce absenteeism and turnover. On-the-job remedial skills training will be necessary to help the growing number of dropouts cope with job demands.

With labor force size not expected to increase significantly during the late 1980s and 1990s, a shortage of qualified entry-level workers and late-career managers is predicted. However, as the baby-boom generation reaches retirement age after the turn of the century, the work force will be top heavy with older employees, blocking the career progress of younger workers. Because promotions satisfy an individual's need for recognition and achievement, managers

---

[40] Harry Bacas, "Where Are the Teenagers?" *Nation's Business,* August 1986, p. 21.

[41] See "Labor Letter: A Special News Report on People and Their Jobs in Offices, Fields and Factories," *The Wall Street Journal,* August 26, 1986, p. 1.

will need to find alternative ways to help employees satisfy these needs. In addition, organizations may need to devise more flexible and creative retirement plans. Polaroid Corporation's innovative retirement program is a sign of things to come:

> Polaroid Corp. in Cambridge, Mass., uses "retirement rehearsal" and phased retirement to ease the anxieties of senior workers who want to test the waters before retiring. Rehearsal retirement allows older employees a three-month, unpaid leave of absence with all fringe benefits. Phased retirement enables them to cut back to four days a week or less at reduced pay.[42]

If managers are to be more responsive to older workers, they need to be aware of how aging affects one's values and attitudes. Employee values and attitudes are discussed in the next chapter.

SUMMARY OF KEY CONCEPTS

A. After a long-term and exhaustive content analysis of newspapers from around the United States, John Naisbitt's team of researchers identified 10 major changes (megatrends) reshaping America. Five megatrends relevant to the field of OB point in the direction of an information society, high tech/high touch, participatory democracy, networking, and multiple options.

B. "Work" has a more encompassing meaning than a "job" because work produces something of value, beyond money. Surveys of unemployed people have revealed seven basic functions of work. They center around life goals, economic security, status and identity, goal-oriented activity, nonfamily social contact, teamwork and camaraderie, and time structure.

C. Some claim the work ethic—defined as a positive attitude about work and a belief that hard work is the key to success and happiness—is dead in America. However, survey evidence and rates of absenteeism and turnover indicate most employees have a strong desire to do their very best. Both management and societal forces have been blamed for stifling an otherwise strong work ethic among employees in the United States.

D. Job satisfaction involves one's positive or negative feelings about his or her job. Compared to their Japanese counterparts, American workers generally are more satisfied with their jobs. Job satisfaction tends to increase as education and income increase.

E. Research points toward a reciprocal relationship between job and life satisfaction in which each affects the other on an ongoing basis. One's physical and mental health are affected by this reciprocal relationship. Employee relations departments, attitude surveys, and employee assistance

---

[42] "Why Late Retirement Is Getting a Corporate Blessing," *Business Week*, January 16, 1984, p. 72.

programs for such problems as alcohol and drug abuse are modern organizational attempts to enhance the job and life satisfaction connection.

F. The new American economy is a two-tiered economy. A comparative few will end up with high-paying, high-tech jobs, while many will find themselves occupying lower-paying service jobs. Americans are working fewer hours per week and engaging in more part-time work. The service sector of the economy is the biggest in employment and the lowest in productivity.

G. Demographically, the U.S. work force is 43 percent female. Despite recent gains, women are still overrepresented in lower-paying, lower-level occupations. As the educational level of the labor force continues to increase, the problem of underemployment will worsen. A growing army of inadequately skilled high school dropouts poses a serious threat to the economy. As the baby-boom generation grows older, the average age of the work force will rise steadily (39 by the year 2000).

KEY TERMS

job
work
work ethic
job satisfaction

reciprocal job and life satisfaction
  relationship
work force demographics
underemployment

DISCUSSION QUESTIONS

1. Which megatrend do you think will have the greatest impact on work behavior? Explain.

2. Thinking of your last (or present) job, why would it or would it not qualify as work?

3. From your standpoint, which of the seven functions of work in Figure 2–1 is most important? Explain your reasoning.

4. Have you ever worked for an organization that stifled your work ethic? Describe the circumstances. What should have been done to correct the situation?

5. How would you describe the relationship between your satisfaction with school and your life satisfaction? Is the strength of your work ethic a controlling factor?

6. How could the encouragement of risk takers backfire on management?

7. As you look ahead to working in the new economy, what are your concerns?

8. Have you experienced any conflict in the workplace that might be attributed to the increase of women in the managerial ranks? From an OB standpoint, what could management have done to prevent this conflict?

9. Why is underemployment a serious human resource management problem? If you have ever been underemployed, what were your feelings about it?

10. How is the graying of America likely to affect organizational life?

BACK TO THE OPENING CASE

Now that you have read Chapter 2, you should be able to answer the following questions about Harry Caunter's and William Westman's experiences with high-tech organizations.

1. How would a working knowledge of Naisbitt's megatrends have helped Caunter and Westman make an easier switch to high tech?

2. Why did Caunter handle the switch to the high-tech sector better than Westman?

3. How would you respond to Caunter's remark about the electronics people in Silicon Valley (the San Jose, California, area) having no work ethic?

4. Based on what you have read about the new economy and new work force, what advice would you offer Caunter and Westman?

EXERCISE 2 ──

Objectives

1. To measure your work ethic.
2. To determine how well your work ethic score predicts your work habits.

Introduction

People differ in terms of how much they believe in the work ethic. These differences influence a variety of behavioral outcomes. What better way to gain insight into the work ethic than by measuring your own work ethic and seeing how well it predicts your everyday work habits?

Instructions

To assess your work ethic, complete the eight-item instrument developed by a respected behavioral scientist.[43] Being honest with yourself, circle your

---

[43] Adapted from Milton R. Blood, "Work Values and Job Satisfaction," *Journal of Applied Psychology,* December 1969, pp. 456–59.

responses on the rating scales following each of the eight items. There are no right or wrong answers. Add up your total score for the eight items and record it in the space provided. *The higher your total score, the stronger your work ethic.*

Following the work ethic scale is a short personal work habits questionnaire. Your responses to this questionnaire will help you determine whether your work ethic score is a good predictor of your work habits.

1. When the workday is finished, people should forget their jobs and enjoy themselves.
   Agree completely   1——2——3——4——5   Disagree completely
2. Hard work does not make an individual a better person.
   Agree completely   1——2——3——4——5   Disagree completely
3. The principal purpose of a job is to provide a person with the means for enjoying his or her free time.
   Agree completely   1——2——3——4——5   Disagree completely
4. Wasting time is not as bad as wasting money.
   Agree completely   1——2——3——4——5   Disagree completely
5. Whenever possible, a person should relax and accept life as it is, rather than always striving for unreachable goals.
   Agree completely   1——2——3——4——5   Disagree completely
6. A person's worth should not be based on how well he or she performs a job.
   Agree completely   1——2——3——4——5   Disagree completely
7. People who do things the easy way are the smart ones.
   Agree completely   1——2——3——4——5   Disagree completely
8. If all other things are equal, it is better to have a job with little responsibility than one with a lot of responsibility.
   Agree completely   1——2——3——4——5   Disagree completely
   Total = _____

Personal Work Habits Questionnaire

1. How many unexcused absences from classes did you have last semester or quarter?
   _____ absences
2. How many credit hours are you taking this semester or quarter?
   _____ hours
3. What is your overall grade point average?
   _____ GPA
4. What percentage of your school expenses are you earning through full- or part-time employment?
   _____ percent
5. In terms of percent, how much effort do you typically put forth at school and/or work?
   School = _____ %   Work = _____ %

Questions for Consideration/Class Discussion

1. How strong is your work ethic?
   Weak = 8–18   Moderate = 19–29   Strong = 30–40

2. How would you rate your work habits/results?
   Below average _____   Average _____   Above average _____
3. How well does your work ethic score predict your work habits or work results?
   Poorly _____   Moderately well _____   Very well _____

PART TWO

Understanding and Managing Individual Behavior

EXTERNAL ENVIRONMENT

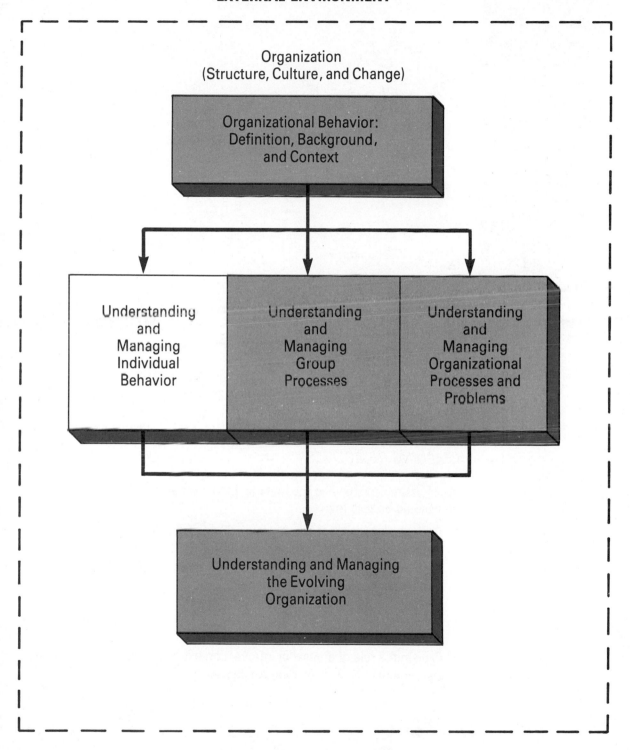

Organization
(Structure, Culture, and Change)

Organizational Behavior:
Definition, Background,
and Context

Understanding
and
Managing
Individual
Behavior

Understanding
and
Managing
Group
Processes

Understanding
and
Managing
Organizational
Processes and
Problems

Understanding and Managing
the Evolving
Organization

Chapter **3**

Individual Differences and Values

LEARNING OBJECTIVES

When you finish studying the material in this chapter,
you should be able to:

- Distinguish between instrumental and terminal values.
- Identify three types of value conflict.
- Explain how attitudes influence behavior in terms of the Fishbein and Ajzen model of behavioral intentions.
- Explain Carl Jung's cognitive styles typology.
- Discuss how an internal locus of control differs from an external locus of control.
- Explain the role of arousal in introversion-extroversion.
- Describe the dilemma of Type A behavior.

OPENING CASE 3

What Makes Ted Turner Tick?

Ted Turner, owner of the Atlanta superstation WTBS, has been called everything but dull during his business career. In addition to revolutionizing the American cable television industry with offerings such as Cable Network News (CNN), the colorful and controversial Turner owns the Atlanta Braves (a professional baseball team) and the Atlanta Hawks (a professional basketball team). Turner gained notoriety by making a daring but futile takeover bid for CBS in 1985. Despite a great deal of scrutiny by the popular press, one of the most revealing interviews with Ted Turner was conducted in the late 1970s by Chicago radio personality Studs Terkel. The following excerpts from Terkel's interview reveal the roots of Turner's personality, attitudes, values, and behavior.

I always wanted to win. I didn't win at that many things. I eventually found sailing and business. It's not the actual winning. Something's over, it's done with. It's *trying* to win. Whether it's the World Series or a boat race, getting there is half the fun. Then I think about what I'm going to do next.

I'd say I'm from the upper middle class, but I don't like to use the word "class." In certain ways, my father was real low class. He was a wild man. He used to drink a lot and got in barroom fights. He was one of those rugged individualists. He was fifteen, sixteen when the depression hit. . . .

My father had to drop out of college and go to work, but that didn't bother him. He went into business for himself, outdoor advertising. Small, but it got pretty big before he passed away.

My father was bitter about the fact that they were dirt poor. He decided, when he was about seventeen, that he was going to be a millionaire when he was thirty. He didn't accomplish it until he was fifty. When he achieved his dream, he was dead by his own hand, two years later. He told me, when I was twenty-four: "Don't ever set your goal. Don't let your dream be something you can accomplish in your lifetime. . . ."

When I lay my baseball bat in the rack for the final game, I'd like to have people look back and just gasp at what I did in my lifetime. In my time, I think maybe I can do it. When Columbus sailed, discovering the New World was the thing to do. The territories have been pretty well discovered. I'm blazing a new frontier. I'm a pioneer in this satellite technology. I'm building a fourth network. It won't be as big as CBS or ABC or NBC, but it's gonna be big.

I would like to think I'm a very humble person because of the things I haven't done. I consider my limited ability, but I'm proud of myself because I got the most out of it. I worked really hard in school, and the most I could get was ninety-five percent. I never was valedictorian. I couldn't make the football team, I couldn't make the track team. That's kinda how I got into sailing.

I've won the America's Cup. It's considered the Holy Grail of yachting. I've won the yachtsman of the year award three times. No one else has ever won it that many times. It's like the most valuable player award. . . .

I want to win the World Series. I want to set up a dynasty in baseball. I want to win the NBA championship and set up a dynasty in basketball. I'm running so fast, I'm gonna burn myself out. So I'm taking up photography. I'm gonna become a wildlife and nature photographer. Hey, that's not competitive, is it?

Money is nothing. In America, anybody can be a billionaire, if they put their mind to it. Look at Ray Kroc, started McDonald's when he was fifty. Between fifty and seventy he made, I don't know, a billion or two. Seven years ago, I was almost broke. Today,

I'm well-off. On paper. It could all go tomorrow. I've been broke before. Easy come, easy go. You never know whether a depression's coming. Money is something you can lose real easy.

Being something big to yourself, that's important. Being a star. Everybody's a star in the movie of their life.

For Discussion

Why has Ted Turner been so successful?

SOURCE: Excerpted from Studs Terkel, *American Dreams: Lost & Found* (New York: Ballantine Books, 1980), pp. 73–76. From *American Dreams: Lost and Found* by Studs Terkel. Copyright © 1980 by Studs Terkel. Reprinted by permission of Pantheon Books, a Division of Random House, Inc.

■ Additional discussion questions linking this case with the following material appear at the end of this chapter.

Present and future managers need a systematic understanding of individual differences because, as a management consultant recently observed: "With today's growing diversity in the lifestyles, values and behavior of the work force, it has become vital for all managers to develop a much deeper understanding of human behavior."[1] Managers who understand how people differ in systematic ways are likely to make better decisions in the following areas:

- Hiring.
- Assigning jobs.
- Appraising job performance.
- Assessing training needs.
- Communicating.
- Leading and motivating.
- Granting promotions and rewards.
- Building teamwork and cooperation.
- Dealing with personality clashes.

This chapter explores the following important dimensions of individual differences: (1) the nature and importance of values, (2) the relationship between

---

[1] Joseph D. Levesque, "Selecting and Managing Competent Managers," *Personnel Administrator,* March 1985, p. 67.

attitudes and behavior, (3) abilities and performance, and (4) significant personality traits. The purpose is to demonstrate that individuals can be different in some ways and remarkably alike in others, depending on one's perspective. Managers cannot achieve personal and organizational success if they do not strike a workable balance between appreciating individual differences and detecting common characteristics.

■ PERSONAL VALUES

An established cognitive approach to explaining behavior involves the study of personal values. As used here, the term *value* does not mean the worth we attach to specific goods or objects. For example, if McDonald's began offering Big Macs for $1, regular customers would see the offer as a good value. Cognitive psychologists use the term *value* in a more fundamental way. They talk of a cognitive structure (of values) that provides criteria, or standards, for choosing from among alternative behaviors. The degree to which values are acted on is influenced by changing attitudes, motives, and circumstances.

Lifelong behavior patterns are dictated by values that are fairly well set by the time the individual is in his or her early teens. For example, consider how early experiences shaped the values of the young founder of Lotus Development Corp., producer of the highly successful 1–2–3® personal computer spreadsheet program.

> In the 1960s, Mitchell D. Kapor revered the Beatles, grew his hair long, and joined protest marches against the Vietnam War. . . .
> While he now describes much of the turmoil of the 1960s as "no more than standard, adolescent growth pains," he says the period imparted a sense of social obligation that he has carried into corporate life. "Many people who came of age in the 60s share a common set of experiences and values," Kapor says. "It's possible to make money and at the same time to have a company where people are proud to work and can be happy."[2]

Although values tend to jell early in life, significant life events—such as having a child, suffering the death of a loved one, or surviving a serious accident—can reshape one's value system during adulthood.

Values Are Enduring Beliefs

According to Milton Rokeach, a leading researcher of values, a **value** is "an enduring belief that a specific mode of conduct or end-state of existence is personally or socially preferable to an opposite or converse mode of conduct or end-state of existence."[3] An individual's **value system** is defined by Rokeach as an "enduring organization of beliefs concerning preferable modes of conduct

---

[2] "A Bit of the '60s Lives on at Lotus," *Business Week,* July 2, 1984, p. 59.
[3] Milton Rokeach, *The Nature of Human Values* (New York: Free Press, 1973), p. 5.

■ **TABLE 3–1**   The Rokeach Value Survey

Instructions: Study the two lists of values presented below. Then rank the instrumental values in order of importance to you (1 = Most important, 18 = Least important). Do the same with the list of terminal values.

Instrumental Values

Rank

_____ Ambitious (hardworking, aspiring)

_____ Broadminded (open-minded)

_____ Capable (competent, effective)

_____ Cheerful (lighthearted, joyful)

_____ Clean (neat, tidy)

_____ Courageous (standing up for your beliefs)

_____ Forgiving (willing to pardon others)

_____ Helpful (working for the welfare of others)

_____ Honest (sincere, truthful)

_____ Imaginative (daring, creative)

_____ Independent (self-sufficient)

_____ Intellectual (intelligent, reflective)

_____ Logical (consistent, rational)

_____ Loving (affectionate, tender)

_____ Obedient (dutiful, respectful)

_____ Polite (courteous, well-mannered)

_____ Responsible (dependable, reliable)

_____ Self-controlled (restrained, self-disciplined)

Terminal Values

Rank

_____ A comfortable life (a prosperous life)

_____ An exciting life (a stimulating, active life)

_____ A sense of accomplishment (lasting contribution)

_____ A world at peace (free of war and conflict)

_____ A world of beauty (beauty of nature and the arts)

_____ Equality (brotherhood, equal opportunity for all)

_____ Family security (taking care of loved ones)

_____ Freedom (independence, free choice)

_____ Happiness (contentedness)

_____ Inner harmony (freedom from inner conflict)

_____ Mature love (sexual and spiritual intimacy)

_____ National security (protection from attack)

_____ Pleasure (an enjoyable, leisurely life)

_____ Salvation (saved, eternal life)

_____ Self-respect (self-esteem)

_____ Social recognition (respect, admiration)

_____ True friendship (close companionship)

_____ Wisdom (a mature understanding of life)

SOURCE: (c) 1967, 1982 by M. Rokeach. Reprinted by permission of HALGREN TESTS, NW 1145 Clifford, Pullman, WA 99163 (509) 334-5636.

or end-states of existence along a continuum of relative importance."[4] In line with Rokeach's distinction between modes of conduct and end-states of existence, he developed a value survey instrument based on what he calls instrumental and terminal values. Take the time now to complete the Rokeach value survey in Table 3–1. Rokeach contends that his value survey can be used to assess the value systems of individuals or groups. According to Rokeach and his followers, differing value systems go a long way toward explaining individual differences in behavior.

Instrumental Values.   The 18 instrumental values listed alphabetically in Rokeach's value survey involve different categories of behavior. **Instrumental values** are alternative behaviors or means by which we achieve desired ends (terminal values). Someone who ranks the instrumental value "honest" high is likely to be honest more often than someone who ranks it low. Thus, instrumental values are a fairly good, but not perfect, predictor of actual behavior. What is your most important instrumental value? In a study of 83 female and

---

[4] Ibid.

107 male college students, "loving" turned out to be the most highly rated instrumental value.[5]

Terminal Values.   Highly ranked **terminal values,** such as wisdom or salvation, are end-states or goals the individual would like to achieve during his or her lifetime. Some would say terminal values are what life is all about. History is full of examples of people who were persecuted or put to death for their passionately held terminal values. Which of the 18 terminal values in Table 3–1 did you rank the highest? In the survey of 190 college students mentioned above, "happiness" was the highest-ranked terminal value.[6]

Value Conflicts

Managers need to be aware of three types of value conflict, both in themselves and their co-workers. These are intrapersonal, interpersonal, and individual-organization value conflict.

Intrapersonal Value Conflict.   Inner conflict and resultant stress typically are experienced when highly ranked instrumental or terminal values pull the individual in different directions. For example, in the category of instrumental values, "honest" can be pushed aside by "ambitious" and "obedient" in hard-driving managers. Former President Nixon's assistant, John Dean, discussed being victimized by this particular value conflict in his biography, *Blind Ambition.* Similarly, intrapersonal conflicts between terminal values such as "pleasure" and "a sense of accomplishment" can be a problem. Otherwise serious students who have been tempted away from their homework by partying friends are well aware of this conflict of terminal values.

Yet another type of intrapersonal value conflict occurs when highly ranked instrumental and terminal values clash. For example, someone who assigns a high ranking to the instrumental value "independent" may be too aloof to achieve the terminal value "true friendship." Regarding your own value system, as measured by the Rokeach value survey, it is instructive to ask yourself if your top-ranked instrumental values will enable you to achieve your top-ranked terminal values. The value clarification exercise in Table 3–2 has been used in counseling situations to help resolve intrapersonal value conflicts.

Interpersonal Value Conflict.   This problem generally is at the core of so-called personality clashes common at work and elsewhere. According to Rokeach and a colleague:

> Interpersonal value conflicts usually exist whenever a person is encountering difficulties in interpersonal relations with, say, spouse, parent, boss, employee, or group with which one identifies.[7]

---

[5] See Anthony J. DeVito, Janet F. Carlson, and Joanne Kraus, "Values in Relation to Career Orientation, Gender, and Each Other," *Counseling and Values,* July 1984, pp. 202–6.

[6] Ibid.

[7] Milton Rokeach and John F. Regan, "The Role of Values in the Counseling Situation," *Personnel and Guidance Journal,* May 1980, p. 578.

■ **TABLE 3–2**   A Value Clarification Exercise for Resolving Intrapersonal Value Conflicts

Instructions: Probe the value implications of your own or someone else's statement of intention or belief, by answering each of the following value clarification questions.

Choosing from alternatives
1. Have you considered any alternatives to that?
2. How long did you look around before you decided?

Choosing after considering consequences
1. What is the best thing you like about that idea?
2. What would happen if everyone held your belief?

Choosing freely
1. Is that really your own choice?
2. Where do you suppose you first got that idea?

Prizing and cherishing
1. Is that something that is important to you?
2. Are you proud of how you handled that?

Publicly affirming
1. Is this something you'd like to share with others?
2. Who would you be willing to tell that to?

Acting
1. Is that something you'd be willing to try?
2. What would your next step be if you choose to pursue that direction?

Acting repeatedly
1. Is this typical of you?
2. Will you do it again?

SOURCE: Barbara Glaser and Howard Kirschenbaum, "Using Values Clarification in Counseling Settings," *Personnel and Guidance Journal,* May 1980, p. 570.

Rokeach and other value scholars believe managers must consider value differences when attempting to resolve interpersonal conflicts.

Individual-Organization Value Conflict.   As discussed later in Chapter 18, every organization has a distinct culture complete with its own prevailing value system. Not surprisingly, individual employees often find themselves at odds with their employing organization's value system. Generally, the individual's only options are to join the system, leave the system, or fight the system. One widely publicized and controversial way of fighting the organization's value system is whistle-blowing, reporting questionable practices to the media or outside agencies. Research draws a rough profile of employees who blow the whistle on their employers. In a survey of 8,587 federal employees, whistle blowers, compared with nonwhistle blowers, tended to be nonsupervisors with greater seniority and higher pay but less education.[8] The related issues of blind conformity and groupthink are probed further in Chapter 10.

Research on Male-Female Value Differences

Given women's increasing role in the workplace, managers should be aware of and sensitive to all relevant gender differences. A study of 50 female and 50 male technical school students in Israel, who ranged in age from 20 to

___
[8] For details, see Marcia Parmerlee Miceli and Janet P. Near, "The Relationships among Beliefs, Organizational Position, and Whistle-Blowing Status: A Discriminant Analysis," *Academy of Management Journal,* December 1984, pp. 687–705.

26, demonstrated that values vary systematically by gender. The researcher concluded:

> For men the following seven values were more important than for women: intellectual, ambitious, broad-minded, imaginative, mature love, a comfortable life, and inner harmony. For women the following six values were more important than for men: logical, independent, clean, polite, forgiving, and national security.[9]

These value profiles might be different in other cultures. Nonetheless, the statistically significant gender differences underscore the need for managers to carefully consider each *individual's* unique value system when making judgments and decisions about people at work.

■ ATTITUDES AND BEHAVIOR

Attitudes influence behavior at a different level than do values. While values represent global beliefs that influence behavior across all situations, attitudes relate only to behavior directed toward specific objects or situations.[10] Thus, an **attitude** is defined as "a learned predisposition to respond in a consistently favorable or unfavorable manner with respect to a given object."[11] Researchers recently found the *job* attitudes of 5,000 middle-aged male employees to be very stable over a five-year period.[12] Employees with positive attitudes toward the job tended to maintain their positive attitudes. Negative-attitude employees tended to remain negative. Even those who changed jobs or occupations tended to maintain their prior job attitudes. Thus, attitudes tend to be consistent over time *and* across related situations.

Values and attitudes generally, but not always, are in harmony. A manager who strongly values helpful behavior may have a negative attitude toward helping an unethical co-worker.

Because our cultural backgrounds and experiences vary, our attitudes and behavior vary (see Table 3–3). Attitudes are translated into behavior via behavioral intentions. Let us examine an established model of this important process.

---

[9] Y. Rim, "Importance of Values According to Personality, Intelligence and Sex," *Personality and Individual Differences* 5, no. 2 (1984), p. 246. An interesting study of the relationship between instrumental values and career choices among 11th-grade females may be found in Richard A. Young, "Vocational Choice and Values in Adolescent Women," *Sex Roles,* April 1984, pp. 485–92. Research linking personal values and ethics is discussed in Rick Wartzman, "Nature or Nurture? Study Blames Ethical Lapses on Corporate Goals," *The Wall Street Journal,* October 9, 1987, p. 27.

[10] For a discussion of the difference between values and attitudes, see Boris W. Becker and Patrick E. Connor, "Changing American Values—Debunking the Myth," *Business,* January–March 1985, pp. 56–59.

[11] Martin Fishbein and Icek Ajzen, *Belief, Attitude, Intention and Behavior: An Introduction to Theory and Research* (Reading, Mass.: Addison-Wesley Publishing, 1975), p. 6.

[12] See Barry M. Staw and Jerry Ross, "Stability in the Midst of Change: A Dispositional Approach to Job Attitudes," *Journal of Applied Psychology,* August 1985, pp. 469–80.

■ **TABLE 3–3** Contrasting Values and Attitudes between High-Level Soviet and American Female Managers

The commonly held Western perception of working women in the U.S.S.R. is that there is a high proportion of them, but the image of the weather-wrinkled 'babouska' predominates. In contrast, the confident, attractively presented American female executive currently finds particular favour in the media. But are these images true to life? What are the characteristics and styles of women in managerial roles? We interviewed and surveyed women of chief executive or comparable organizational levels in the U.S. and U.S.S.R.

In the U.S., females occupying only chief executive officer (CEO) positions were interviewed. The vast majority of the interviewees came from the service industries, in particular transportation and distribution, health care, communication, publishing and management consultancy. The top executive females interviewed in the U.S.S.R. held a wider spectrum of positions, ranging from the deputy premier of the Georgian Soviet Socialist Republic, to a government minister in charge of the social services and environment, a government minister in charge of trade unions and labour, the leader of the Komsomol (Young Communist Party) of Georgia, and top directors in the arts and health care. . . .

In terms of striving for success, U.S. and Soviet top women shared one attribute—total commitment. Like the Americans, the Soviet women were well educated and trained to university standards, often holding more than one degree. Again, like the Americans, the Soviet women made their own opportunities. . . .

What does it take to be a top female executive? The U.S. female executives emphasized their analytical abilities and skills and specialized knowledge in areas such as marketing, sales or finance, as primary reasons for successful performance in their role as CEOs. 'It's fine attention to detail and efficient administration that makes the business run well,' were the words of one executive in the retail business. . . .

The individualistic, competitive, but disciplined nature of the U.S. female executive emerged as the most commonly utilized aspect of her managerial style. Consequently, honesty (saying what you think) and a high drive to achieve personal and organizational goals were identified as high-priority attributes.

Adopting a different attitude, the Soviet executives considered themselves as generalists and team-oriented. They had long since discarded the use of particular technical skills (except for the director of the health care institute). Great emphasis was placed on 'handling people skills'—managing individuals and teams within the organization, and interacting with relevant interest groups outside the organization.

SOURCE: Excerpted from Andrew Kakabadse and Gill McWilliam, "Superpowers' Superwomen," *Management Today*, September 1987, pp. 73–74. Used with permission.

Attitudes and Behavioral Intentions

Behavioral scientists Martin Fishbein and Icek Ajzen developed a comprehensive model of behavioral intentions used widely to explain attitude-behavior relationships.[13] As depicted in Figure 3–1, an individual's intention to engage

---

[13] For a complete discussion of the model, see Fishbein and Ajzen, *Belief, Attitude, Intention and Behavior: An Introduction to Theory and Research*.

■ **FIGURE 3–1** A Model of Behavioral Intention

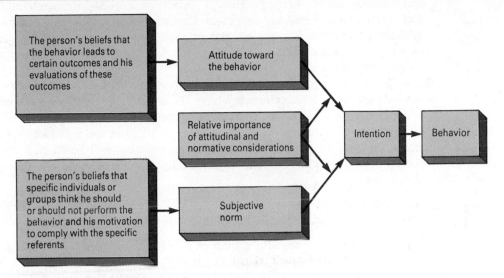

The person's beliefs that the behavior leads to certain outcomes and his evaluations of these outcomes → Attitude toward the behavior

Relative importance of attitudinal and normative considerations

The person's beliefs that specific individuals or groups think he should or should not perform the behavior and his motivation to comply with the specific referents → Subjective norm

→ Intention → Behavior

Note: Arrows indicate the direction of influence.

SOURCE: Icek Ajzen and Martin Fishbein, *Understanding Attitudes and Predicting Social Behavior,* © 1980, p. 8. Reprinted by permission of Prentice-Hall, Inc., Englewood Cliffs, New Jersey.

in a given behavior is the best predictor of that behavior. For example, the quickest and possibly most accurate way of determining whether an individual will quit his or her job is to have an objective third party ask if he or she intends to quit. A meta-analysis of 34 employee turnover studies, involving more than 83,000 employees, validated this direct approach. The researchers found stated behavioral intentions to be a better predictor of employee turnover than job satisfaction, satisfaction with the work itself, or organizational commitment.[14]

Although asking about intentions enables one to predict who will quit, it does not help explain *why* an individual would want to quit. Thus, to better understand why employees exhibit certain behaviors, such as quitting their jobs, one needs to consider their relevant attitudes. As shown in Figure 3–1, behavioral intentions are influenced both by one's attitude toward the behavior and by perceived norms about exhibiting the behavior. In turn, attitudes and subjective norms are determined by personal beliefs.

Beliefs Influence Attitudes. A person's belief system is a mental representation of his or her relevant surroundings, complete with probable cause-and-effect relationships. Beliefs are the result of direct observation and inferences from previously learned relationships. For example, we tend to infer that a laughing

---

[14] See Robert P. Steel and Nestor K. Ovalle II, "A Review and Meta-Analysis of Research on the Relationship between Behavioral Intentions and Employee Turnover," *Journal of Applied Psychology,* November 1984, pp. 673–86.

co-worker is happy. In terms of the strength of the relationship between beliefs and attitudes, beliefs do not have equal impacts on attitudes. Research indicates that attitudes are based on salient or important beliefs that may change as relevant information is received. For example, your beliefs about the quality of a particular automobile may change after hearing the car has been recalled for defective brakes.

In Figure 3–1, you can see that an individual will have positive attitudes toward performing a behavior when he or she believes the behavior is associated with positive outcomes. An individual is more likely to quit a job when he or she believes quitting will result in a better position and a reduction in job stress. In contrast, negative attitudes toward quitting will be formed when a person believes quitting leads to negative outcomes, such as the loss of money and status.

Beliefs Influence Subjective Norms.

Subjective norms refer to perceived social pressure to perform a specific behavior. As noted by Ajzen and Fishbein:

> Subjective norms are also a function of beliefs, but beliefs of a different kind, namely the person's beliefs that specific individuals or groups think he should or should not perform the behavior. These beliefs underlying a person's subjective norms are termed *normative beliefs*. Generally speaking, a person who believes that most referents [role models] with whom he is motivated to comply think he should perform the behavior will perceive social pressure to do so. Conversely, a person who believes that most referents with whom he is motivated to comply think he should not perform the behavior will have a subjective norm that puts pressure on him to avoid performing the behavior.[15]

Subjective norms can exert a powerful influence on behavior among those who are sensitive to the opinions of others.

Attitudes versus Norms: A Test of Strength.

Which has a stronger impact on intentions and behavior: attitudes or norms? The answer depends on how important the behavior is to the individual. In some situations, such as predicting intentions to buy different brands of toothpaste, research has found that social pressures were more important.[16] This finding supports the business practice of using social pressure in advertisements for consumer products. In contrast, attitudes have been found to exert greater influence than norms on intentions to donate blood.[17] Hence, it appears that attitudes have a greater influence over personally important or risky behavior, while norms have greater influence over less important behavior.

---

[15] Icek Ajzen and Martin Fishbein, *Understanding Attitudes and Predicting Social Behavior* (Englewood Cliffs, N.J.: Prentice-Hall, 1980), p. 7.

[16] See Michael J. Ryan, "Behavioral Intention Formation: The Interdependency of Attitudinal and Social Influence Variables," *Journal of Consumer Research*, December 1982, pp. 263–76.

[17] From Robert E. Burnkrant and Thomas J. Page, Jr., "An Examination of the Convergent, Discriminant, and Predictive Validity of Fishbein's Behavioral Intention Model," *Journal of Marketing Research*, November 1982, pp. 550–61.

Attitudinal Research and Application

Research has demonstrated that Fishbein and Ajzen's model accurately predicted intentions to buy consumer products, have children, and choose a career versus becoming a homemaker. Weight loss intentions and behavior, voting for political candidates, and reenlisting in the National Guard also have been predicted successfully by the model.[18] In fact, the model correctly identified 82 percent of the 225 National Guard personnel in the study who actually reenlisted.[19]

A Work-Related Example. Fishbein and Ajzen's model has been applied to voting behavior in union certification elections (see Figure 3–2). This application demonstrates how the model can be used to explain and predict work-related behavior. It also demonstrates the important role attitudes play in determining behavior. An individual's intention to vote for or against a union is dependent on both his or her attitude toward voting for a union *and* a subjective norm toward unions. People are more likely to have a favorable attitude toward voting for a union when they believe unionization will result in a more favorable economic package for them. On the other hand, people are more likely to have a negative attitude toward voting for a union when they believe the organization already provides reasonable economic wages and benefits.

Norms Play an Important Role. Normative influences also need to be considered when determining whether a person will engage in a certain behavior, such as voting for a union. For example, if an employee likes his or her supervisor, and the supervisor is strongly opposed to unions, the employee likely will yield to the supervisor's pressure to vote against the union. On the other hand, if an employee dislikes his or her supervisor, the supervisor's antiunion sentiments are likely to fall on deaf ears. The same is true for co-workers.

Finally, individual characteristics strongly affect subjective norms and voting behavior. If you grew up in a pro-union family located in a unionized community, you likely will possess a predisposition to vote for unions. In contrast, growing up with antiunion parents who live in a nonunionized community probably would produce norms against voting for unions.

To summarize, the behavioral intention model makes it clear that managers

---

[18] For an overall review of attitude formation research, see Ajzen and Fishbein, *Understanding Attitudes and Predicting Social Behavior*. Also see Shelly Chaiken and Charles Stangor, "Attitudes and Attitude Change," in *Annual Review of Psychology*, ed. Mark R. Rosenzweig and Lyman W. Porter (Palo Alto, Calif.: Annual Reviews, 1987), pp. 575–630.

[19] See Peter W. Hom and Charles L. Hulin, "A Competitive Test of the Prediction of Reenlistment by Several Models," *Journal of Applied Psychology*, February 1981, pp. 23–39. Also see Paul R. Warshaw, Roger Calantone, and Mary Joyce, "A Field Study Application of the Fishbein and Ajzen Intention Model," *The Journal of Social Psychology*, February 1986, pp. 135–36.

■ **FIGURE 3–2**   Attitudes Influence Union Certification Voting Behavior

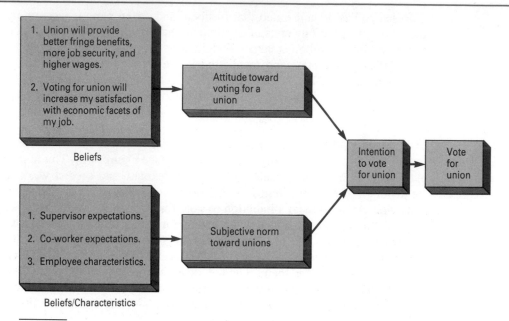

SOURCE: Adapted in part from Arthur P. Brief and Dale E. Rude, "Voting in Union Certification Elections: A Conceptual Analysis," *Academy of Management Review,* April 1981, pp. 261–67.

cannot afford to ignore attitudes, perceived norms, and intentions when attempting to get individuals to engage in productive behavior.

■ ABILITIES AND PERFORMANCE

Individual differences in abilities and accompanying skills are a central concern for managers because nothing can be accomplished without appropriately skilled personnel. An **ability** represents a broad and stable characteristic responsible for a person's maximum—as opposed to typical—performance on mental and physical tasks. A **skill,** on the other hand, is the specific capacity to physically manipulate objects. Consider this difference as you imagine yourself being the only passenger on a small commuter airplane in which the pilot has just passed out. As the plane nose-dives, your effort and abilities will not be enough to save yourself and the pilot if you do not possess flying skills. As shown in Figure 3–3, successful performance (be it landing an airplane or performing any other job) depends on the right combination of effort, ability, and skill.

Abilities can profoundly affect an organization's bottom line. Selecting em-

■ **FIGURE 3–3**   Performance Depends on the Right Combination of Effort, Ability, and Skill

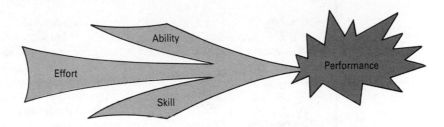

ployees who have the ability to perform assigned jobs can significantly affect the organization's labor costs. A pair of personnel selection experts noted:

> The use of cognitive ability tests for selection in hiring can produce large labor cost savings, ranging from $18 million per year for small employers such as the Philadelphia police department . . . to $16 billion per year for large employers such as the federal government.[20]

This section explores important cognitive abilities and cognitive styles related to job performance.

Intelligence and Cognitive Abilities

Although experts do not agree on a specific definition, **intelligence** represents an individual's capacity for constructive thinking and reasoning. Historically, intelligence was believed to be an innate capacity, passed genetically from one generation to the next. Research since has shown, however, that intelligence also is a function of environmental influences.[21] Stated another way: Nature + Nurture = Intelligence. The lingering question is: Which has a greater influence, nature or nurture? (See Table 3–4.)

Two Types of Abilities.   Human intelligence has been studied predominantly through the empirical approach. By examining the relationships between measures of mental abilities and behavior, researchers have statistically isolated major components of intelligence. Using this empirical procedure, pioneering psychologist Charles Spearman proposed in 1927 that all cognitive performance is determined by two types of abilities. The first can be characterized as a general mental ability needed for *all* cognitive tasks. The second is unique to the task at hand. For example, an individual's ability to complete crossword puzzles is a function of his or her broad mental abilities as well as the specific ability to perceive patterns in partially completed words.

---

[20] Frank L. Schmidt and John E. Hunter, "Employment Testing: Old Theories and New Research Findings," *American Psychologist,* October 1981, p. 1128.

[21] For a historical review of intelligence testing, see John R. Graham and Roy S. Lilly, *Psychological Testing* (Englewood Cliffs, N.J.: Prentice-Hall, 1984), chaps. 5 and 14; and Anne Anastasi, "Evolving Trait Concepts," *American Psychologist,* February 1983, pp. 175–84.

■ **TABLE 3–4** Are We the Product of Nature or Nurture?

Like many identical twins reared apart, Jim Lewis and Jim Springer found they had been leading eerily similar lives. Separated four weeks after birth in 1940, the Jim twins grew up 45 miles apart in Ohio and were reunited in 1979. Eventually they discovered that both drove the same model blue Chevrolet, chain-smoked Salems, chewed their fingernails and owned dogs named Toy. Each had spent a good deal of time vacationing at the same three-block strip of beach in Florida. More important, when tested for such personality traits as flexibility, self-control and sociability, the twins responded almost exactly alike.

The two Jims were the first of 348 pairs of twins studied at the University of Minnesota, home of the Minnesota Center for Twin and Adoption Research. Much of the investigation concerns the obvious question raised by siblings like Springer and Lewis: How much of an individual's personality is due to heredity? The center's answer: about half.

The project, summed up in a scholarly paper that has been submitted to the *Journal of Personality and Social Psychology,* is considered the most comprehensive of its kind. The Minnesota researchers report the results of six-day tests of their subjects, including 44 pairs of identical twins who were brought up apart. Well-being, alienation, aggression and the shunning of risk or danger were found to owe as much or more to nature as to nurture. Of eleven key traits or clusters of traits analyzed in the study, researchers estimated that a high of 61% of what they call "social potency" (a tendency toward leadership or dominance) is inherited, while "social closeness" (the need for intimacy, comfort and help) was lowest, at 33%.

The study finds that even a penchant for conservatism seems to have a genetic base. One of the eleven traits, traditionalism (respect for authority, rules, standards and high morals), was discovered to be 60% inherited. Among other traits listed at more than 50% were vulnerability or resistance to stress, dedication to hard work and achievement and the capacity for being caught up in imaginative experiences.

The director of the study, Thomas Bouchard, cautions that the numbers so far may not be strictly accurate. "In general," he says, "the degree of genetic influence tends to be around 50%."

SOURCE: John Leo, "Exploring the Traits of Twins," *Time,* January 12, 1987, p. 63. Copyright 1987 Time Inc. All rights reserved. Reprinted by permission from *Time.*

Seven Major Mental Abilities. Through the years, much research has been devoted to developing and expanding Spearman's ideas on the relationship between cognitive abilities and intelligence. One research psychologist listed 120 distinct mental abilities. Table 3–5 contains definitions of the seven most frequently cited mental abilities. Of the seven abilities, personnel selection researchers have found verbal ability, numerical ability, spatial ability, and inductive reasoning to be valid predictors of job performance for both minority and majority applicants.[22]

---

[22] See Schmidt and Hunter, "Employment Testing: Old Theories and New Research Findings." For evidence of the economic impact of using cognitive ability tests to select employees, see John E. Hunter and Frank L. Schmidt, "Quantifying the Effects of Psychological Interventions on Employee Job Performance and Work-Force Productivity," *American Psychologist,* April 1983, pp. 473–78.

■ **TABLE 3–5** Mental Abilities Underlying Performance

Ability	Description
1. Verbal comprehension	The ability to understand what words mean and to readily comprehend what is read
2. Word fluency	The ability to produce isolated words that fulfill specific symbolic or structural requirements (such as all words that begin with the letter *b* and have two vowels)
3. Numerical	The ability to make quick and accurate arithmetic computations such as adding and subtracting
4. Spatial	Being able to perceive spatial patterns and to visualize how geometric shapes would look if transformed in shape or position
5. Memory	Having good rote memory for paired words, symbols, lists of numbers, or other associated items
6. Perceptual speed	The ability to perceive figures, identify similarities and differences, and carry out tasks involving visual perception
7. Inductive reasoning	The ability to reason from specifics to general conclusions

SOURCE: Adapted from Marvin D. Dunnette, "Aptitudes, Abilities, and Skills," in *Handbook of Industrial and Organizational Psychology,* ed. Marvin D. Dunnette (Skokie, Ill.: Rand McNally, 1976), pp. 478–83.

Jung's Cognitive Styles Topology

Defined formally, the term **cognitive style** refers to mental processes associated with how people perceive and make judgments from information. Although the landmark work on cognitive styles was completed in the 1920s by the noted Swiss psychoanalyst Carl Jung, his ideas did not catch on in the United States until the 1970s, when a complete English translation became available.[23]

Four Different Cognitive Styles. According to Jung, two dimensions influence perception and two others affect individual judgment. Perception is based on either *sensation,* using one's physical senses to interpret situations, or *intuition,* relying on past experience. In turn, judgments are made by either *thinking* or *feeling.* Finally, Jung proposed that an individual's cognitive style is determined by the pairing of one's perception and judgment tendencies. The resulting four cognitive styles are:

- Sensation/thinking (ST).
- Intuition/thinking (NT).
- Sensation/feeling (SF).
- Intuition/feeling (NF).

Characteristics of each style are presented in Figure 3–4.[24] (The exercise at the end of this chapter will help you determine your cognitive style.)

---

[23] See John L. Bledsoe, "Your Four Communicating Styles," *Training,* March 1976, pp. 18–21.

[24] For a complete discussion of each cognitive style, see John W. Slocum, Jr., and Don Hellriegel, "A Look at How Managers' Minds Work," *Business Horizons,* July–August 1983, pp. 58–68; and William Taggart and Daniel Robey, "Minds and Managers: On the Dual Nature of Human Information Processing and Management," *Academy of Management Review,* April 1981, pp. 187–95.

■ **FIGURE 3–4**   People Have Different Cognitive Styles and Corresponding Characteristics

	Decision Style			
	ST Sensation/Thinking	**NT** Intuition/Thinking	**SF** Sensation/Feeling	**NF** Intuition/Feeling
Focus of Attention	Facts	Possibilities	Facts	Possibilities
Method of Handling Things	Impersonal analysis	Impersonal analysis	Personal warmth	Personal warmth
Tendency to Become	Practical and matter of fact	Logical and ingenious	Sympathetic and friendly	Enthusiastic and insightful
Expression of Abilities	Technical skills with facts and objects	Theoretical and technical developments	Practical help and services for people	Understanding and communicating with people
Representative Occupation	Technician	Planner — Manager	Teacher	Artist

SOURCE: William Taggart and Daniel Robey, "Minds and Managers: On the Dual Nature of Human Information Processing and Management," *Academy of Management Review,* April 1981, p. 190. Used with permission.

An individual with an ST style uses senses for perception and rational thinking for judgment. The ST-style person uses facts and impersonal analysis, and develops greater abilities in technical areas involving facts and objects. A successful engineer could be expected to exhibit this cognitive style. In contrast, a person with an NT style focuses on possibilities rather than facts and displays abilities in areas involving theoretical or technical development. This style would enhance the performance of a research scientist. Although an SF person likely is interested in gathering facts, he or she tends to treat others with personal warmth, sympathy, and friendliness. Successful counselors or teachers probably use this style. Finally, an individual with an NF style tends to exhibit artistic flair while relying heavily on personal insights rather than objective facts (see Figure 3–4).

Practical Research Findings.   If Jung's cognitive styles typology is valid, then individuals with different cognitive styles should seek different kinds of information when making a decision. A study of 50 master of business administration students found that those with different cognitive styles did in fact use qualitatively different information while working on a strategic planning problem.[25] Research also has shown that people with different cognitive styles prefer different careers. For example, people who rely on intuition prefer careers in psychology, advertising, teaching, and the arts. Findings have further shown that individuals who make judgments based on the "thinking" approach have higher work motivation and quality of work life than those who take a "feeling" approach. In addition, individuals with a sensation mode of perception have higher job satisfaction than those relying on intuition.[26]

■ KEY PERSONALITY TRAITS AND ORGANIZATIONAL BEHAVIOR

Personality traits are stable characteristics that can be used to explain and describe behavior patterns. Although using personality to explain work behavior has been limited, there is a growing interest in examining the role of personality in organizational behavior. As two researchers have noted:

> Researchers in Organizational Psychology have not had much regard for personality constructs in recent years. Personality differences, once fundamental to the study of work motivation, attitudes, and leadership are now assigned only secondary roles in most theories of organizational behavior, if they are given any role at all. . . .
>
> We disagree with those who advocate relegating personality to minor or nonexistent positions in theories of individual behavior in organizations. . . . Historically, personality research on organizational behavior has suffered from inadequate conceptual development and poor methodology and these factors have conspired to give personality a bad name. It is simply premature and unproductive to make any general normative statements about restricting the role of personality in organizational research.[27]

In the spirit of this statement, we will look more closely at three personality traits that have a significant impact on organizational behavior. They are locus of control, introversion-extroversion, and Type A (stress-prone) personality.

Perceived Causes of Behavior: Self or Environment?

Individuals vary in terms of how much personal responsibility they take for their behavior and its consequences. Julian Rotter, a personality researcher, identified a dimension of personality he labeled *locus of control* to explain

---

[25] See Bruce K. Blaylock and Loren P. Rees, "Cognitive Style and the Usefulness of Information," *Decision Sciences,* Winter 1984, pp. 74–91.

[26] Additional material on cognitive styles may be found in Ferdinand A. Gul, "The Joint and Moderating Role of Personality and Cognitive Style on Decision Making," *The Accounting Review,* April 1984, pp. 264–77; Brian H. Kleiner, "The Interrelationship of Jungian Modes of Mental Functioning wth Organizational Factors: Implications for Management Development," *Human Relations,* November 1983, pp. 997–1012; and James L. McKenney and Peter G. W. Keen, "How Managers' Minds Work," *Harvard Business Review,* May–June 1974, pp. 79–90.

[27] Howard M. Weiss and Seymour Adler, "Personality and Organizational Behavior," in *Research in Organizational Behavior,* ed. Barry M. Staw and L. L. Cummings (Greenwich, Conn.: JAI Press, 1984), p. 2.

■ **TABLE 3–6**   Kathy Kolbe: An Internal Locus of Control Enabled Her to Become a Successful Entrepreneur

Strongly encouraged by her father, Chicago Personnel Psychologist Eldon Wonderlic, [Kathy] Kolbe went to Northwestern, tried journalism, then moved with her husband and two children to Arizona. Dissatisfied with their education in Scottsdale, she decided to start a summer school of her own. "It has been written for centuries that thinking is important," she says, "but that is a lot different from saying, 'I have a method of showing how to do that.'" She wanted to teach children how to think creatively and critically, to use both the analytical left side of the brain and the more intuitive right side, to improve both verbal and nonverbal communication. In five years, her school swelled from 40 students to 200, at $60 per week each.

But by now she had encountered a new problem: the lack of special materials for gifted children. So she decided to produce her own. Several major publishers rejected her ideas, telling her that the market was too small to be profitable. In 1979 she took $500 from her savings and launched a firm called Resources for the Gifted. She wrote what she calls Think-ercises. One typical example requires pupils to make a series of logical deductions to figure out how many points were scored by various members of a basketball team. Another tries to get children to think critically about language in terms of slang. How has the computer changed the meaning of common words like memory or menu? What might become slang terms of future technology?

Though her only office was a spare bedroom and her only warehouse the closet, Kolbe wrote a catalog and sent it to 3,500 teachers and parents. Orders began to trickle in, then to flow. The first years were hard. She bought a warehouse, and it caught fire. An employee embezzled money. She divorced her husband. "I never, never feel overwhelmed," Kolbe says, a little grimly. "I enjoy a challenge."

She is now grossing about $3.5 million per year, and she is proud of never having received either government or corporate grants. Says she: "I'm a believer in the concept that if it's good, the way you'll know it is that people will pay. The bottom line is crucial because it's my report card."

these differences. He proposed that people tend to attribute the causes of their behavior primarily to either themselves or environmental factors. This personality trait produces distinctly different behavior patterns.

People who believe they control the events that affect their lives are said to possess an **internal locus of control.** For example, such a person tends to attribute positive outcomes, like getting a passing grade on an exam, to his or her own abilities. Similarly, an "internal" tends to blame negative events, like failing an exam, on personal shortcomings—not studying hard enough, perhaps. Entrepreneurs such as Kathy Kolbe, profiled in Table 3–6, succeed because their *internal* locus of control helps them overcome setbacks and disappointments. They see themselves as masters of their own fate.

■ **TABLE 3–7** Where Is Your Locus of Control?

Circle one letter for each pair of items, in accordance with your beliefs:

1. A. Many of the unhappy things in people's lives are partly due to bad luck.
    B. People's misfortunes result from the mistakes they make.

2. A. Unfortunately, an individual's worth often passes unrecognized no matter how hard he tries.
    B. In the long run, people get the respect they deserve.

3. A. Without the right breaks one cannot be an effective leader.
    B. Capable people who fail to become leaders have not taken advantage of their opportunities.

4. A. I have often found that what is going to happen will happen.
    B. Trusting to fate has never turned out as well for me as making a decision to take a definite course of action.

5. A. Most people don't realize the extent to which their lives are controlled by accidental happenings.
    B. There really is no such thing as "luck."

6. A. In the long run, the bad things that happen to us are balanced by the good ones.
    B. Most misfortunes are the result of lack of ability, ignorance, laziness, or all three.

7. A. Many times I feel I have little influence over the things that happen to me.
    B. It is impossible for me to believe that chance or luck plays an important role in my life.

Note: In determining your score, A = 0 and B = 1.

SOURCE: Excerpted from Julian B. Rotter, "Generalized Expectancies for Internal Versus External Control of Reinforcement," *Psychological Monographs,* Vol. 80 (Whole No. 609, 1966), pp. 11–12.

On the other side of this personality dimension are those who believe their performance is the product of circumstances beyond their immediate control. These individuals are said to possess an **external locus of control** and tend to attribute outcomes to environmental causes such as luck or fate. Unlike someone with an internal locus of control, an "external" would attribute a passing grade on an exam to something external (an easy test or a good day) and attribute a failing grade to an unfair test or problems at home. A shortened version of an instrument Rotter developed to measure one's locus of control is presented in Table 3–7. (Arbitrary norms for this shortened version are: 1–3 = External locus of control; 4 = Balanced internal and external locus of control; 5–7 = Internal locus of control.) Where is your locus of control: internal, external, or a combination?

Research Findings on Locus of Control. Researchers have found significant and important behavioral differences between internals and externals:

- Internals display greater work motivation.
- Internals have stronger expectations that effort leads to performance.
- Internals exhibit higher performance on tasks involving learning or problem solving, when performance leads to valued rewards.
- There is a stronger relationship between job satisfaction and performance for internals than externals.

- Internals obtain higher salaries and greater salary increases than externals.
- Externals tend to be more anxious than internals.[28]

Implications of Locus of Control Differences for Managers.   The above summary of research findings on locus of control has important implications for managing people at work. Let us examine two of them. First, since internals have a tendency to believe they control the work environment through their behavior, they will attempt to exert control over the work setting. This can be done by trying to influence work procedures, working conditions, task assignments, or relationships with peers and supervisors. As these possibilities imply, internals may resist a manager's attempts to closely supervise their work. Therefore, management may want to place internals in jobs requiring high initiative and low compliance. Externals, on the other hand, might be more amenable to highly structured jobs requiring greater compliance.

Second, locus of control has implications for reward systems. Given that internals have a greater belief that their effort leads to performance, internals likely would prefer and respond more productively to incentives such as merit pay or sales commissions.[29]

Introversion-Extroversion

Picture two friends at a large party; one is introverted and the other is extroverted. Why is it the introvert probably will retreat to a quiet corner while the extrovert might end up being the life of the party? H. J. Eysenck, an esteemed psychologist, proposed a theory of personality that answers this question.

Arousal Is the Key.   Eysenck's theory centers on the concept of arousal. Arousal refers to an individual's level of activation, alertness, or vigor. A combination of both internal (physiological) and external stimulation determines the level of arousal. Greater stimulation means greater arousal. Eysenck's theory is based on three key ideas supported by many years of research. First, introverts and extroverts inherently are different in terms of their level of arousal. On the average, introverts have a higher level of internal arousal than extroverts. Second, there is an optimal level of arousal. Finally, individuals will try to alleviate the difference between their inherent and optimal levels of arousal. By considering these ideas simultaneously, we can better understand the systematic differences in behavior exhibited by introverts and extroverts.

---

[28] For an overall review of research on locus of control, see Paul E. Spector, "Behavior in Organizations as a Function of Employee's Locus of Control," *Psychological Bulletin,* May 1982, pp. 482–97; the relationship between locus of control and performance and satisfaction is examined in Dwight R. Norris and Robert E. Niebuhr, "Attributional Influences on the Job Performance-Job Satisfaction Relationship," *Academy of Management Journal,* June 1984, pp. 424–31; salary differences between internals and externals was examined by Paul C. Nystrom, "Managers' Salaries and Their Beliefs about Reinforcement Control," *The Journal of Social Psychology,* August 1983, pp. 291–92.

[29] These recommendations are from Spector, "Behavior in Organizations as a Function of Employee's Locus of Control."

■ **TABLE 3–8** Introverts and Extroverts Exhibit Different Patterns of Behavior

Behavioral Characteristics	
Extroverts	**Introverts**
Are more highly aroused in the afternoon	Are more highly aroused in the morning
Like to work with people or things	Like to work with ideas
More expressive with words	Have a hard time expressing ideas in a clear fashion
Work best when they are stimulated by competing stimuli (noise)	Work best when they are not bothered by competing stimuli (interruptions)
Do not perform well on unstimulating tasks	Do better on tasks requiring vigilance
Tend to be talkative and outgoing	Tend to be cautious and careful

SOURCE: Adapted from D. W. J. Corcoran, "Introversion-Extroversion, Stress, and Arousal," in *Dimensions of Personality: Papers in Honour of H J Eysenck,* ed. Richard Lynn (New York: Pergamon Press, 1981).

A personality expert noted:

> Extroverts and introverts, in learning to adapt to their environments, adopt different strategies for resolving the conflict between inherent level of arousal and optimum level of arousal. The extrovert must work to raise his level of arousal to the optimum. Therefore he seeks stimulation: interaction with others, novel experiences, stimuli of greater complexity, variety and intensity. Stimuli, if repeated often, lose their arousing quality. Much of the extrovert's behavior can be seen in terms of this constant quest for stimulation. . . . Introverts, on the other hand, must work to reduce incoming stimulation: they prefer their own company, or the company of well-established companions, they follow well-worn and predictable paths, they shun excessive sensory input.[30]

Important behavioral differences between introverts and extroverts are highlighted in Table 3–8.

Implications for Management. Eysenck's theory and supporting research provide guidance for understanding and appropriately managing introverts and extroverts.[31] For example, a person's level of arousal should be considered when providing feedback about performance. Feedback, as an important source of external stimulation, would increase arousal. Because extroverts actively seek outside stimulation to compensate for their lower internal stimulation, they can be expected to respond more favorably than introverts to supervisory coaching and feedback. Likewise, extroverts feel more comfortable serving on committees and participating in problem-solving teams than do introverts. Considering the contrasting characteristics in Table 3–8, introverts and extroverts

---

[30] Anthony Gale, "EEG Studies of Extraversion-Introversion: What's the Next Step?" in *Dimensions of Personality: Papers in Honour of H J Eysenck,* ed. Richard Lynn (New York: Pergamon Press, 1981), p. 184.

[31] For a review of research on the relationship between introversion-extroversion, motivation, and performance, see Michael S. Humphreys and William Revelle, "Personality, Motivation, and Performance: A Theory of the Relationship between Individual Differences and Information Processing," *Psychological Review,* April 1984, pp. 153–84.

require different motivational approaches and job assignments. Managers cannot afford to overlook tendencies toward introversion or extroversion when hiring, placing, and motivating employees.

Type A (Stress-Prone) Personality

Personality characteristics can be hazardous to your health, according to some medical and behavioral scientists. Cardiovascular disease is the leading cause of death among adults in western industrialized countries, exceeding cancer and accidents combined. Not long ago the American Heart Association added the Type A (stress-prone) personality trait to its list of coronary risk factors. Other coronary risk factors that increase one's chances of suffering a heart attack or stroke are cigarette smoking, high blood pressure, obesity, high blood cholesterol, genetic predisposition, and physical inactivity.[32] Researchers have found that Type A individuals tend to express greater and longer-lasting anger and impatience with tasks involving urgency and competition than non-Type A's.[33] This tendency is said to multiply or worsen the impact of the other coronary risk factors (see Figure 3–5).

Type A Behavior Defined.   According to Meyer Friedman and Ray H. Rosenman, the cardiologists who isolated the Type A syndrome in the 1950s:

> **Type A behavior pattern** is an action-emotion complex that can be observed in any person who is *aggressively* involved in a *chronic, incessant* struggle to achieve more and more in less and less time, and if required to do so, against the opposing efforts of other things or persons. It is not psychosis or a complex of worries or fears or phobias or obsessions, but a socially acceptable—indeed often praised—form of conflict. Persons possessing this pattern also are quite prone to exhibit a free-floating but extraordinarily well-rationalized hostility. As might be expected, there are degrees in the intensity of this behavior pattern.[34]

Since Type A behavior is a matter of degree, it is measured on a continuum. This continuum has the stress-prone Type A behavior pattern at one end and the more relaxed Type B behavior pattern at the other. The Type B behavior pattern is defined as the relative absence of Type A characteristics.

A Methodological Debate.   Type A's, according to one body of research, experience significantly more cardiovascular disease than Type B's because Type A behavior is associated with higher blood cholesterol levels.[35] But another body of research has led some to question the link between Type A

---

[32] Coronary risk factors are reviewed in William B. Kannel, ''Status of Coronary Heart Disease Risk Factors,'' *Journal of Nutrition Education,* January–March 1978, pp. 10–14.

[33] For details, see Kenneth E. Hart and John L. Jamieson, ''Type A Behavior and Cardiovascular Recovery from a Psychosocial Stressor,'' *Journal of Human Stress,* March 1983, pp. 18–24.

[34] Meyer Friedman and Ray H. Rosenman, *Type A Behavior and Your Heart* (Greenwich, Conn.: Fawcett Publications, 1974), p. 84. (Boldface added.)

[35] For an instructive overview and model of Type A behavior, see Marilyn J. Davidson and Cary L. Cooper, ''Type A Coronary-Prone Behavior in the Work Environment,'' *Journal of Occupational Medicine,* June 1980, pp. 375–83.

■ **FIGURE 3–5** Type A Personality and Cardiovascular Disease

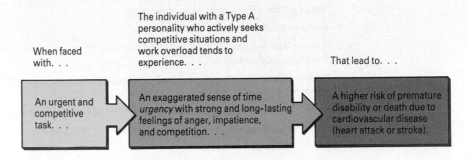

When faced with. . .

The individual with a Type A personality who actively seeks competitive situations and work overload tends to experience. . .

That lead to. . .

| An urgent and competitive task. . . | An exaggerated sense of time *urgency* with strong and long-lasting feelings of anger, impatience, and competition. . . | A higher risk of premature disability or death due to cardiovascular disease (heart attack or stroke). |

behavior and cardiovascular disease.[36] Much of the ensuing debate has centered on a methodological issue. Specifically, should Type A behavior be measured with a structured interview, as recommended by Friedman and Rosenman, or with various self-report instruments?[37] Friedman and Rosenman insist that properly measured Type A behavior is associated with an increased risk of heart attack or stroke. A recent meta-analysis of 87 studies strongly supports their belief in the structured interview approach to measuring Type A behavior.[38]

Type A Characteristics.   While labeling Type A behavior as "hurry sickness," Friedman and Rosenman have noted that individuals with a Type A personality frequently tend to exhibit most of the behaviors listed in Table 3–9. In high-pressure, achievement-oriented schools and work organizations, Type A behavior unwittingly is cultivated and even admired. For example, in early 1985, *Business Week* described William G. McGowan, founder and head of MCI Communications Corp., as follows:

> McGowan, 57, is a vigorous, driven man. He often spends weekends at the office and rarely takes vacations. . . . He is unmarried, and his singular devotion to MCI has led some to say that it has become his family.[39]

Less than two years later, McGowan suffered a nonfatal heart attack.[40] Many managers thrive on life in the corporate fast lane because of a favorable genetic background or an exceptional ability to cope with undue stress. Unfortunately,

---

[36] For an informative and interesting discussion of this contrary evidence, see Joshua Fischman, "Type A on Trial," *Psychology Today,* February 1987, pp. 42–50.

[37] The validity of the most popular Type A self-report instrument is empirically challenged in Frank Shipper, Robert Kreitner, William E. Reif, and Kathryn E. Lewis, "A Study of Four Psychometric Properties of the Jenkins Activity Survey Type A Scale with Suggested Modifications and Validation," *Educational and Psychological Measurement* 46, no. 3 (1986), pp. 551–64.

[38] See Stephanie Booth-Kewley and Howard S. Friedman, "Psychological Predictors of Heart Disease: A Quantitative Review," *Psychological Bulletin*, May 1987, pp. 343–62.

[39] John Wilke, "McGowan: The Man Who Cracked AT&T," *Business Week*, January 21, 1985, p. 69.

[40] "MCI's Chief Suffers a Heart Attack," *Business Week*, January 19, 1987, p. 40.

■ **TABLE 3–9**   Type A Characteristics

1. Hurried speech; explosive accentuation of key words.

2. Tendency to walk, move, and eat rapidly.

3. Constant impatience with the rate at which most events take place (e.g., irritation with slow-moving traffic and slow-talking and slow-to-act people).

4. Strong preference for thinking of or doing two or more things at once (e.g., reading this text and doing something else at the same time).

5. Tendency to turn conversations around to personally meaningful subjects or themes.

6. Tendency to interrupt while others are speaking to make your point or to complete their train of thought in your own words.

7. Guilt feelings during periods of relaxation or leisure time.

8. Tendency to be oblivious to surroundings during daily activities.

9. Greater concern for things worth *having* than with things worth being.

10. Tendency to schedule more and more in less and less time; a chronic sense of time urgency.

11. Feelings of competition rather than compassion when faced with another Type A person.

12. Development of nervous tics or characteristic gestures.

13. A firm belief that success is due to the ability to get things done faster than the other guy.

14. A tendency to view and evaluate personal activities and the activities of other people in terms of "numbers" (e.g., number of meetings attended, telephone calls made, visitors received).

SOURCE: Adapted from Meyer Friedman and Ray H. Rosenman, *Type A Behavior and Your Heart* (Greenwich, Conn.: Fawcett Publications, 1974), pp. 100–102.

some Type A managers, like MCI's McGowan, are likely to suffer premature death or disability from cardiovascular disease.[41]

The Dilemma of Type A Behavior.   From an organizational standpoint, Type A behavior presents management with a troublesome dilemma. One side of the dilemma is the evidence that Type A organizational contributors have a higher risk of heart attack or stroke. For example, in one study of 236 managers from 12 organizations, managers diagnosed as Type A tended to be cigarette smokers and had significantly higher blood pressure and cholesterol. The Type A's also were less interested in exercise than their Type B counterparts.[42]

On the other hand, OB research has demonstrated that Type A employees

---

[41] A recently reported study of 231 men who had survived their first heart attack for at least 24 hours found that Type A's tended to live significantly longer than Type B's. More research is needed to explain this unexpected result. It could be possible that Type A behavior works *against* the individual before a heart attack and *in favor of* those who are fortunate enough to survive their first attack. Details may be found in David R. Ragland and Richard J. Brand, "Type A Behavior and Mortality from Coronary Heart Disease," *The New England Journal of Medicine*, January 14, 1988, pp. 65–69.

[42] See John H. Howard, David A. Cunningham, and Peter A. Rechnitzer, "Health Patterns Associated with Type A Behavior: A Managerial Population," *Journal of Human Stress*, March 1976, pp. 24–31.

■ **TABLE 3-10** Saving Type A Personalities from Themselves

Type A's—those irascible, anxious, driven people who often pay for their obsessive behavior with heart attacks—can be helped. Scientists at Stanford University, Harvard University, and San Francisco's Mt. Zion Hospital & Medical Center spent close to five years studying 862 Type A personalities, all of whom had suffered at least one heart attack. They discovered that individuals who were counseled on how to change their behavior had a 46% lower rate of recurring heart attacks than those who weren't.

The therapy was surprisingly simple: Participants kept track of occurrences that made them angry, or they listened to other Type A's describe their hostile behavior on tape. According to Mt. Zion cardiologist Meyer Friedman, the counseling helped because Type A's are unusually frustrated people, and that causes the body to secrete large amounts of certain hormones such as norepinephrine. They raise blood pressure, which can eventually cause heart damage if it isn't controlled. Work out the frustration and the risk of heart disease drops.

SOURCE: Emily T. Smith, ed., "Developments to Watch," *Business Week,* November 3, 1986, p. 140. Reprinted from November 3, 1986, issue of *Business Week* by special permission, © 1986 by McGraw-Hill, Inc.

tend to be more productive than their Type B co-workers. For instance, in a study of 278 university professors, 86 percent male and 14 percent female, a positive correlation was found between Type A tendency and the quantity and quality of academic publications. This relationship applied equally to male and female professors. The researchers attributed the superior performance of the Type A's to setting higher performance goals and getting more done by working simultaneously on multiple projects.[43] Type A's are their own worst enemy because they overload themselves and seek competitive, stress-producing situations. Hence, the Type A dilemma: While superior performance driven by Type A behavior may be good from a short-run organizational standpoint, the Type A individual's long-run health is at stake. Unfortunately, the typical drive for short-term results in organizations encourages Type A's to overload themselves.

Does this dilemma signal the need for Type A's to quit their jobs and run for their lives? Not necessarily. Stress researchers, as discussed in Chapter 16, have developed coping techniques to help Type A's pace themselves more realistically and achieve better balance in their lives (see Table 3–10). Care should be taken to not overload Type A employees with work, despite their apparent eagerness to take on an ever-increasing work load. Managers need

[43] See M. Susan Taylor, Edwin A. Locke, Cynthia Lee, and Marilyn E. Gist, "Type A Behavior and Faculty Research Productivity: What Are the Mechanisms?" *Organizational Behavior and Human Performance,* December 1984, pp. 402–18.

to actively help rather than unthinkingly exploit Type A's because the premature disability or death of valued employees erodes long-run organizational effectiveness.

SUMMARY OF KEY CONCEPTS

A. Managers who understand the various psychological bases for individual differences and similarities can work with and through others more effectively. Some cognitive psychologists contend that instrumental and terminal values, defined as enduring beliefs in modes of conduct and desired end-states of existence, determine much of our behavior. Organizational members can experience intrapersonal, interpersonal, and individual-organization value conflicts.

B. Attitudes are another popular way of explaining individual differences in behavior. Whereas values are global in scope, attitudes involve predispositions to behave favorably or unfavorably toward specific objects or persons. According to Fishbein and Ajzen's model, beliefs influence attitudes and subjective norms. Depending on their relative importance, attitudes and norms together foster a behavioral intention, the best predictor of actual behavior. The Fishbein and Ajzen behavioral intention model has stood up well under research.

C. Organizations require individuals with appropriate abilities and skills. Abilities relate to one's maximum physical and mental potential, while skills involve one's capacity to actually manipulate objects. Successful performance depends on the right combination of effort, ability, and skill. Human intelligence is said to be based on seven mental abilities.

D. By combining two dimensions of perception (sensation and intuition) with two dimensions of judgment (thinking and feeling), Carl Jung identified four cognitive styles. Each style has its own distinct pattern of characteristics and abilities.

E. Personality is receiving renewed attention in OB circles as a way of explaining important individual differences. Three organizationally important personality traits are locus of control, introversion-extroversion, and Type A (stress-prone) behavior pattern. People with an *internal* locus of control, such as entrepreneurs, believe they are masters of their own fate. Those with an *external* locus of control attribute their behavior and its results to situational forces.

F. Researchers tell us that introverts avoid external stimulation such as social contacts with strangers because of their innate, optimal level of internal arousal. Extroverts, in contrast, achieve their optimum level of arousal through exposure to external stimulation.

G. Individuals exhibiting the Type A behavior pattern (an exaggerated sense of time urgency) may have a higher risk of heart attack or stroke. While the Type A person's preference for work overload can lead to high performance, the danger of stress-related disease or burnout presents management with a dilemma.

KEY TERMS

value	intelligence
value system	cognitive styles
instrumental values	personality traits
terminal values	internal locus of control
attitude	external locus of control
ability	Type A behavior pattern
skill	

DISCUSSION QUESTIONS

1. From a managerial standpoint, why is it important to understand common patterns in behavior rather than assuming each individual is unique?

2. Since becoming an adult, have you experienced any events that realigned your value system? Explain.

3. In your opinion, which of the three types of value conflict is the most troublesome for a young manager? Explain your rationale.

4. Which factor, your attitudes or your subjective norms, presently has a greater impact on your performance in school (or at work)? How do you know?

5. Regarding the seven major mental abilities listed in Table 3–5, which one do you think is your strongest and how would it help or hinder your effectiveness as a manager of people?

6. According to Jung's typology, which cognitive style do you exhibit? How can you tell? Is it an advantage or a disadvantage?

7. Which of Jung's four cognitive styles would be most appropriate for a top-level executive who has to deal with many different insiders and outsiders possessing widely varying technical and professional backgrounds?

8. How would you respond to the following statement? "Whenever possible, managers should hire people with an external locus of control."

9. Why is it crucial to consider the concept of optimal level of arousal when discussing introversion-extroversion?

10. What would be your response to the following statements by a co-worker? "Type A people are their own worst enemy. They deserve what they get."

BACK TO THE OPENING CASE

Now that you have read Chapter 3, you should be able to answer the following questions about the Ted Turner case:

1. What are Turner's top instrumental and terminal values? How can you tell? Could Turner's value system have been affected by his father's suicide? Explain.

2. What value conflicts could Turner face during the balance of his business career?

3. Which of Jung's four cognitive styles best characterizes Turner? Explain. How will this style likely help or hinder Turner's managerial role? (Refer to Figure 3–4.)

4. Would you classify Turner as an introvert or an extrovert? How can you tell?

5. How strong is Turner's Type A tendency? What is your evidence? If you were a friend of Turner's, what advice would you give him?

EXERCISE 3

Objectives

1. To identify your cognitive style, according to Carl Jung's typology.[44]
2. To consider the managerial implications of your cognitive style.

Instructions

Please respond to the 16 items below. There are no right or wrong answers. After you have completed all the items, refer to the scoring key and follow its directions.

Questionnaire

Part I. Circle the response that comes closest to how you usually feel or act.

1. Are you more careful about:
   A. People's feelings
   B. Their rights

---

[44] The questionnaire and scoring key portions of this exercise have been excerpted from John W. Slocum, Jr., and Don Hellriegel, "A Look at How Managers' Minds Work," *Business Horizons*, July–August 1983, pp. 58–68.

2. Do you usually get along better with:
   A. Imaginative people
   B. Realistic people

3. Which of these two is the higher compliment:
   A. A person has real feeling
   B. A person is consistently reasonable

4. In doing something with many other people, does it appeal more to you:
   A. To do it in the accepted way
   B. To invent a way of your own

5. Do you get more annoyed at:
   A. Fancy theories
   B. People who don't like theories

6. It is higher praise to call someone:
   A. A person of vision
   B. A person of common sense

7. Do you more often let:
   A. Your heart rule your head
   B. Your head rule your heart

8. Do you think it is worse:
   A. To show too much warmth
   B. To be unsympathetic

9. If you were a teacher, would you rather teach:
   A. Courses involving theory
   B. Fact courses

Part II. Which word in each of the following pairs appeals to you more? Circle A or B.

10. A. Compassion
    B. Foresight

11. A. Justice
    B. Mercy

12. A. Production
    B. Design

13. A. Gentle
    B. Firm

14. A. Uncritical
    B. Critical

15. A. Literal
    B. Figurative

16. A. Imaginative
    B. Matter of fact

Scoring Key

To categorize your responses to the questionnaire, count one point for each response on the following four scales and total the number of points recorded in each column. Instructions for classifying your scores are indicated below.

SENSATION	INTUITION	THINKING	FEELING
2 B _____	2 A _____	1 B _____	1 A _____
4 A _____	4 B _____	3 B _____	3 A _____
5 A _____	5 B _____	7 B _____	7 A _____
6 B _____	6 A _____	8 A _____	8 B _____
9 B _____	9 A _____	10 B _____	10 A _____
12 A _____	12 B _____	11 A _____	11 B _____
15 A _____	15 B _____	13 B _____	13 A _____
16 B _____	16 A _____	14 B _____	14 A _____
Totals = _____	_____	_____	_____

Classifying Total Scores

Write *intuitive* if your intuition score is equal to or greater than sensation score.

Write *sensation* if sensation is greater than intuition.

Write *feeling* if feeling is greater than thinking.

Write *thinking* if thinking is greater than feeling.

When thinking equals feeling, you should write feeling if a male and thinking if a female.

Questions for Consideration/Class Discussion:

1. What is your cognitive style?
   Sensation/thinking (ST) _____
   Intuition/thinking (NT) _____
   Sensation/feeling (SF) _____
   Intuition/feeling (NF) _____
2. Do you agree with this assessment? Why or why not?
3. Will your cognitive style, as determined in this exercise, help you achieve your career goal(s)?
4. Would your style be an asset or liability for a managerial position involving getting things done through others?

Chapter 4

Perception, Attributions, and Learning

LEARNING OBJECTIVES:

When you finish studying the material in this chapter,
you should be able to:

- Describe perception in terms of social information processing.
- Discuss the nature and managerial implications of the following perceptual outcomes: stereotypes and the self-fulfilling prophecy.
- Explain, according to Kelley's model, how external and internal causal attributions are formulated.
- Identify the four major causes of achievement behavior in Weiner's model of attribution.
- Contrast fundamental attribution bias and self-serving bias.
- Explain Skinner's distinction between respondent and operant behavior.
- Discuss how Bandura's social learning theory extends Skinner's operant model.

OPENING CASE 4

Asian-Americans Find Prejudice on the Corporate Ladder

They've been tagged "the model minority." They often rise to the top of their college classes and then earn recognition on the job as diligent and dependable workers. Employers scramble to offer them technical positions.

But many Asian-Americans hoping to climb the corporate ladder face an arduous ascent. Ironically, the same companies that pursue them for technical jobs often shun them when filling managerial and executive positions. Because many of their cultural values don't always mesh with those of an American corporation, they are frequently victims of lingering stereotypes that depict them as passive and self-effacing, with poor social and communications skills—traits that would rule them out as managerial material.

David Lam, for one, says he suspects he was denied a low-level management job at Hewlett-Packard Co. a few years ago because he is an Asian-American. A valued engineer at the electronics manufacturer for more than three years, he had expressed an active interest in the position. But although most promotions at the company are based on seniority, experience, and performance, the job went to a colleague, a Caucasian whom Mr. Lam had hired a year earlier. A spokesman for Hewlett-Packard refused to comment about Mr. Lam's claim.

The problem, Mr. Lam believes, is twofold. "Part of it is there's strong prejudice prevailing in the corporate world," he says.

"The other half is that Asians don't try hard enough to integrate."

Some management consultants also say that the prejudice has worsened with Japan's growing role in several industrial and high-technology sectors previously dominated by the U.S. All Asian-Americans, they say, are suffering because of the resulting anti-Japanese sentiment. . . .

Jim Tso, a lawyer and president of the Organization of Chinese Americans, in northern Virginia, sees the situation of Asian-Americans as a Catch-22. He feels that the competence and discipline they show in low-level supervisory and technical positions make American companies reluctant to promote them. "In the past," he says, "we had the coolie who slaved; today we have the high-tech coolie." A major U.S. bank sent Mr. Tso to the Far East as an officer several years ago. But the bank refused to transfer him to a post he had requested in Europe, explaining, "You're Asian, and you're better suited for Asia." He quit. . . .

Many Asian-Americans, in contending with racial stereotypes, find that of passivity to be the most frustrating. Terry Kuroda, now a vice president at Securities Industry Automation Corp., says he shocked his colleagues at Merrill Lynch, Pierce, Fenner & Smith, Inc., a few years ago when he aggressively offered to negotiate the purchase of an office computer package at a lower price. The purchasing department hesitated initially, he says, because they viewed him as simply "analytical and quiet." He persisted and eventually saved the company about $30,000 a month on computer costs.

Some Asian-Americans say, though, that negative perceptions of them as retiring individuals, however demeaning, have some basis in fact. Kung Lee Wang, who started the Organization of Chinese Americans, says that Asians' cultural heritage contributes to their modesty and often to a certain cliquishness. "Asians think that what you achieve should be recognized, but you shouldn't brag," he says. "They are also more family-oriented and less socially active with colleagues. . . ."

Despite the difficulties they encounter here, however, few Asian-Americans aspire to management positions merely to be put in charge of their company's business in the Far East. Says Terry Kuroda, "We just want to be like everyone else here, to handle business in the U.S."

For Discussion

Have you ever been unfairly stereotyped? Explain.

SOURCE: Excerpted from Winifred Yu, "Asian-Americans Charge Prejudice Slows Climb to Management Ranks." Reprinted by permission of *The Wall Street Journal*, © Dow Jones & Company, Inc. September 11, 1985. All rights reserved.

■ Additional discussion questions linking this case with the following material appear at the end of this chapter.

As human beings, we constantly strive to make sense of the world around us. The resulting knowledge influences our behavior and helps us negotiate our way through life. Think of the everyday act of driving a car. Imagine you are driving down a one-way street, with cars parked on both sides and children playing on the sidewalk. Suddenly, one of the children darts into the street in hot pursuit of a small dog. Although your response of stepping on the brake is an apparently simple one, it actually is the culmination of a complicated process involving perception, causal attributions, and performance of a learned behavioral response.

A similar process occurs when meeting someone for the first time. Your attention is drawn to the individual's physical appearance, mannerisms, actions, and reactions to what you say and do. As with driving a car, you will arrive at conclusions based on your perceptions of this social interaction. The brown-haired, green-eyed individual turns out to be friendly and fond of outdoor activities. You may further conclude that you like this person and want to get to know him or her better. This person eventually may become a behavior model from whom you learn new behaviors through imitation. These situations point out that our daily lives are governed by a complex web of perceptions, subsequent interpretations, and learned responses controlled by the environment.

This chapter clarifies three important person-environment linkages—perception, attribution, and learning processes—to help present and future managers better understand how their behavior affects and is affected by others. Because they play a central role in employees' perception, attribution, and learning processes, managers often have a surprisingly large impact on employee behavior. Consider the case of Glenn Davis:

> Glenn Davis of Houston, a chain-smoking former executive of Oceaneering International, Inc., was called into his boss's office last year for a frank talk. "The boss said, 'Glenn, you look like hell,'" Mr. Davis recalls.
>
> He had to agree. Heredity and years of job stress had left a pair of fleshy bags draped like funeral bunting under Mr. Davis's eyes. "Have you ever thought of going to a plastic surgeon?" the boss asked, and before long a surgeon was snipping the fatty deposits from Mr. Davis's eyes.
>
> . . . [Davis's] new, younger-looking face invigorated him with such a surge of entrepreneurial spirit that he started a new company, replaced his wardrobe, and splurged on a turbo-charged, jet-black sports car.[1]

A circle of perception-learning-perception is at the heart of this incident. Mr. Davis acquired new behavior patterns because of his boss's perception and his own self-perception. Let us explore these processes more closely.

After examining a basic model of perception, we will focus on: (1) perceptual outcomes, (2) how causal attributions are used to interpret behavior, and (3) four models of learning.

■ A SOCIAL INFORMATION PROCESSING MODEL OF PERCEPTION

Perception is a mental and cognitive process that enables us to interpret and understand our surroundings. Recognition of objects is one of this process's major functions. For example, both people and animals recognize familiar objects in their environments. You would recognize a picture of your best friend; dogs and cats can recognize their food dishes or a favorite toy. Reading involves recognition of visual patterns representing letters in the alphabet. People must recognize objects to meaningfully interact with their environment. But since OB's principal focus is on people, the following discussion emphasizes *social* perception rather than object perception.

The study of how people perceive one another has been labeled *social cognition* and *social information processing*. In contrast to the perception of objects:

> Social cognition is the study of how people make sense of other people and themselves. It focuses on how ordinary people think about people and how they think they think about people. . . .
>
> Research on social cognition also goes beyond naive psychology. The study of social cognition entails a fine-grained analysis of how people think about themselves and others, and it leans heavily on the theory and methods of cognitive psychology.[2]

---

[1] Dianna Solis, "Plastic Surgery Wooing Patients Hoping to Move Up Career Ladder," *The Wall Street Journal,* September 6, 1985, p. 31.

[2] Susan T. Fiske and Shelley E. Taylor, *Social Cognition* (Reading, Mass.: Addison-Wesley Publishing, 1984), pp. 1–2.

■ **TABLE 4–1** Important Differences between Person and Object Perception

- People intentionally influence the environment; they attempt to control it for their own purposes. Objects, of course, are not intentional causal agents.
- People perceive back; as you are busy forming impressions of them, they are doing the same to you. Social cognition is mutual cognition.
- A social stimulus may change upon being the target of cognition. People worry about how they come across and may adjust their appearance or behavior accordingly; coffee cups obviously do not.
- People's traits are nonobservable attributes that are vital to thinking about them. An object's nonobservable attributes are somewhat less crucial. Both a person and a cup can be fragile, but the inferred characteristic is both less important and more directly seen in the cup.
- People change over time and circumstances more than objects typically do. This can make cognitions rapidly obsolete or unreliable.
- The accuracy of one's cognitions about people is harder to check than the accuracy of one's cognitions about objects. Even psychologists have a hard time agreeing on whether a given person is extroverted, sensitive, or honest, but most ordinary people easily could test whether a given cup is heat resistant, fragile, or leaky.
- People are unavoidably complex. One cannot study cognitions about people without making numerous choices to simplify. The researcher has to simplify in object cognition, too, but it is less of a distortion. One cannot simplify a social stimulus without eliminating much of the inherent richness of the target.
- Because people are so complex, and because they have traits and intents hidden from view, and because they affect us in ways objects do not, social cognition automatically involves social explanation. It is more important for an ordinary person to explain why a person is fragile than to explain why a cup is.

SOURCE: Susan T. Fiske and Shelley E. Taylor, *Social Cognition* (Reading, Mass.: Addison-Wesley Publishing, 1984), pp. 16–17. Copyright © 1984 by Newbery Award Records, Inc., and Random House, Inc.

Although the cognitive or mental processes guiding object perception also can be used to describe aspects of social perception, fundamental differences exist (see Table 4–1). Moreover, while general theories of perception date back many years, the study of social perception is relatively new, having originated about 1976.[3]

Four-Stage Sequence and a Working Example

Social perception involves a four-stage information processing sequence (hence, the label "social information processing"). Figure 4–1 illustrates a basic social information processing model. Three of the stages in this model—selective attention/comprehension, encoding and simplification, and storage and retention—describe how specific social information is observed and stored in memory. The fourth and final stage, retrieval and response, involves turning mental representations into real-world judgments and decisions.

Keep the following everyday example in mind as we look at the four stages of social perception. Suppose you were thinking of taking a course in, say, personal finance. Three professors teach the same course, using different types of instruction and testing procedures. Through personal experience, you have

---

[3] For a review of the history of social cognition, see Janet Landman and Melvin Manis, "Social Cognition: Some Historical and Theoretical Perspectives," in *Advances in Experimental Social Psychology*, Vol. 16, ed. Leonard Berkowitz (New York: Academic Press, 1983).

■ **FIGURE 4–1** Social Perception: A Social Information Processing Model

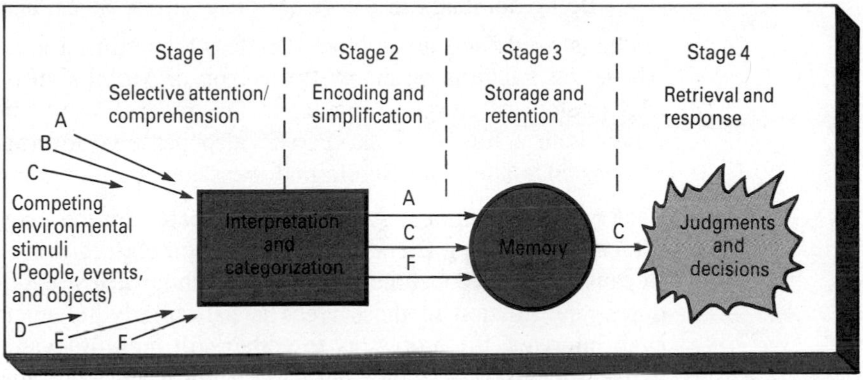

come to prefer good professors who rely on the case method of instruction and essay tests. According to social perception theory, you would likely arrive at a decision regarding which professor to take as follows.

Stage 1: Selective Attention/Comprehension

People are constantly bombarded by physical and social stimuli in the environment. Since they do not have the mental capacity to fully comprehend all this information, they selectively perceive subsets of environmental stimuli. This is where attention plays a role. **Attention** is the process of becoming consciously aware of something or someone. Attention can be focused on information either from the environment or from memory. Regarding the latter situation, if you sometimes find yourself thinking about totally unrelated events or people while reading a textbook, your memory is the focus of your attention. Research has shown that people tend to pay attention to salient stimuli.

Salient Stimuli. Something is *salient* when it stands out from its context. For example, a 250-pound man would certainly be salient in a women's aerobics class but not at a meeting of the National Football League Players' Association. Social salience is determined by several factors, including:

- Being novel (the only person in a group of that race, gender, hair color, or age).
- Being bright (wearing a yellow shirt).
- Being unusual for that person (behaving in an unexpected way, like a person with a fear of heights climbing a steep mountain).
- Being unusual for a person's social category (like a company president driving a motorcycle to work).
- Being unusual for people in general (driving 20 miles per hour in a 55 mph speed zone).

- Being extremely positive (a noted celebrity) or negative (the victim of a bad traffic accident).
- Being dominant in the visual field (sitting at the head of the table).[4]

One's needs and goals often dictate which stimuli are salient. For a driver whose gas gauge is on empty, an Exxon or Mobil sign is more salient than a McDonald's or Burger King sign. The reverse would be true for a hungry driver with a full gas tank. People also perceive information that is outside of conscious attention. Subliminal messages are an example (see Table 4–2).

Back to Our Example.   You begin your search for the "right" personal finance professor by asking friends who have taken classes from the three professors. Because you are concerned about the method of instruction and testing procedures, information in those areas is particularly salient to you. Perhaps you even interview the professors to gather still more relevant information. Meanwhile, thousands of competing stimuli fail to get your attention.

Stage 2: Encoding and Simplification

Observed information is not stored in memory in its original form. Encoding is required; raw information is interpreted or translated into mental representations. To accomplish this, perceivers assign pieces of information to **cognitive categories.** "By *category* we mean a number of objects which are considered equivalent. Categories are generally designated by names, e.g., *dog, animal.*"[5] People, events, and objects are interpreted and categorized by comparing their characteristics with *schemata* (or *schema* in singular form).

Schemata.   According to social information processing theory, a **schema** represents a person's mental picture or summary of a particular event or type of stimulus.[6] For example, your restaurant schema probably is quite similar to the description provided in Table 4–3.

Cognitive category labels are needed to make schemata meaningful. For example, read the passage in Table 4–4 *now* and determine how comprehensive it is by using the scale at the bottom of the table. Having done this, look at the label for this schema printed upside down below.[7] Read the passage again and rate it for comprehensiveness. Your comprehension improved because the cognitive category label bridged the gap between the description and the laundry schema in your memory.

Back to Our Example.   Having collected relevant information about the three personal finance professors and their approaches, your mind creates a mental picture of each by drawing upon your relevant schemata (see Figure 4–2).

---

[4] Adapted from discussion in Fiske and Taylor, *Social Cognition,* pp. 186–87.

[5] Eleanor Rosch, Carolyn B. Mervis, Wayne D. Gray, David M. Johnson, and Penny Boyes-Braem, "Basic Objects in Natural Categories," *Cognitive Psychology,* July 1976, p. 383.

[6] A thorough discussion of how scripts and schema may be used to interpret organizational behavior is presented by Dennis A. Gioia and Peter P. Poole, "Scripts in Organizational Behavior," *Academy of Management Review,* July 1984, pp. 449–59.

[7] Washing clothes.

■ **TABLE 4–2** People Are Influenced by Stimuli Outside of Conscious Attention

The number of stores using hidden messages in background music rises as retailers find other antitheft methods ineffective. "The problem is so bad that retailers can't stop it by just arresting people," says Lawrence A. Conner, director of Shoplifters Anonymous. He says the number of subliminal systems has jumped to over 300 from about 25 five years ago. Viaticus Group of Cranston, Rhode Island, which claims its taped messages can cut losses by 25 percent, says business has doubled every year for four years.

Some systems play messages such as "You are honest, don't steal." Others use anticrime symbols. An extreme example: police car sirens or jail doors closing.

SOURCE: "Business Bulletin: A Special Background Report on Trends in Industry and Finance," *The Wall Street Journal,* January 30, 1986, p. 1.

■ **TABLE 4–3** Restaurant Schema

Schema: Restaurant.
Characters: Customers, hostess, waiter, chef, cashier.

Scene 1: Entering.
 Customer goes into restaurant.
 Customer finds a place to sit.
  He may find it himself.
  He may be seated by a hostess.
   He asks the hostess for a table.
   She gives him permission to go to the table.

Scene 2: Ordering.
 Customer receives a menu.
 Customer reads it.
 Customer decides what to order.
 Waiter takes the order.
  Waiter sees the customer.
  Waiter goes to the customer.
  Customer orders what he wants.
 Chef cooks the meal.

Scene 3: Eating.
 After some time the waiter brings the meal from the chef.
 Customer eats the meal.

Scene 4: Exiting.
 Customer asks the waiter for the check.
 Waiter gives the check to the customer.
 Customer leaves a tip.
  The size of the tip depends on the goodness of the service.
 Customer pays the cashier.
 Customer leaves the restaurant.

SOURCE: From *Memory, Thought and Behavior* by Robert W. Weisberg. Copyright © 1980 by Oxford University Press, Inc. Reprinted by permission.

■ **TABLE 4–4** How Comprehensive Is This Passage?

The procedure is actually quite simple. First you arrange things into different groups. Of course, one pile may be sufficient depending on how much there is to do. If you have to go somewhere else due to lack of facilities that is the next step, otherwise you are pretty well set. It is important not to overdo things. That is, it is better to do too few things at once than too many. In the short run this may not seem important but complications can easily arise. A mistake can be expensive as well. At first the whole procedure will seem complicated. Soon, however, it will become just another facet of life. It is difficult to foresee any end to the necessity for this task in the immediate future, but then one never can tell. After the procedure is completed one arranges the materials into different groups again. Then they can be put into their appropriate places. Eventually they will be used once more and the whole cycle will then have to be repeated. However, that is part of life.

Comprehensiveness Scale

Very uncomprehensive						Very comprehensive
	1	2	3	4	5	
			Neither			

SOURCE: John D. Bransford and Marcia K. Johnson, "Contextual Prerequisites for Understanding: Some Investigations of Comprehension and Recall," *Journal of Verbal Learning and Verbal Behavior,* December 1972, p. 722. Used with permission.

Thus, by selectively attending to environmental and mental information, you have created simplified mental representations of what it would be like to take a class from each of the three professors. This enables you to render a good decision, as opposed to your life being dictated by random chance.

Stage 3: Storage and Retention

This phase involves storage of information in long-term memory. Long-term memory is like an apartment complex consisting of separate units connected to one another. Although different people live in each apartment, they sometimes interact. In addition, large apartment complexes have different wings (like A, B, and C). Long-term memory similarly consists of separate but related categories. Like the individual apartments inhabited by unique residents, the connected categories contain different types of information. Information also passes among these categories. Finally, long-term memory is made up of three compartments (or wings) containing categories of information about events, semantic materials, and people (see Figure 4–3).[8]

---

[8] The discussion of these three compartments is based on material in Robert S. Wyer, Jr., and Thomas K. Srull, "The Processing of Social Stimulus Information: A Conceptual Integration," in *Person Memory: The Cognitive Basis of Social Perception,* ed. Reid Hastie, Thomas M. Ostrom, Ebbe B. Ebbesen, Robert S. Wyer, Jr., David L. Hamilton, and Donal E. Carlston (Hillsdale, N.J.: Lawrence Erlbaum, 1980). For some practical advice on managerial memory, see Walter Kiechel III, "Unlocking the Managerial Memory," *Fortune,* December 21, 1987, pp. 183–84.

■ **FIGURE 4-2** Examples of Mental Schemata in Social Perception

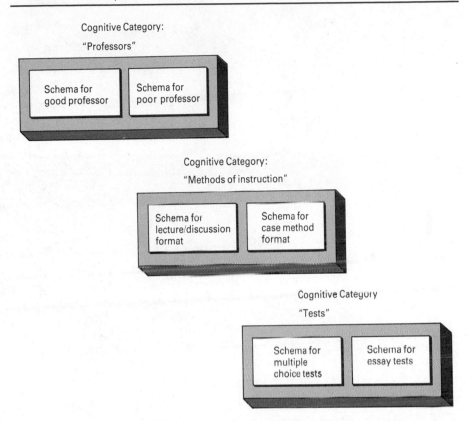

Event Memory. This compartment is composed of categories containing information about both specific and general events. Information in these categories is stored chronologically (or relative to time). Thus, for example, your memory of your last vacation would flow from beginning to end.

Semantic Memory. Semantic memory functions as a mental dictionary of concepts. Each concept contains a definition (a good leader, for example) and associated traits (outgoing), emotional states (happy), physical characteristics (tall), and behaviors (works hard). Just as there are schemata for general events, concepts in semantic memory are stored as schemata.

Person Memory. Categories within this compartment contain information about a single individual (your supervisor) or groups of people (managers).

Back to Our Example. As the time draws near for you to decide which personal finance professor to take, your schemata of them are stored in the three categories of long-term memory. These schemata are available for immediate comparison and/or retrieval.

■ **FIGURE 4–3** The Structure of Memory

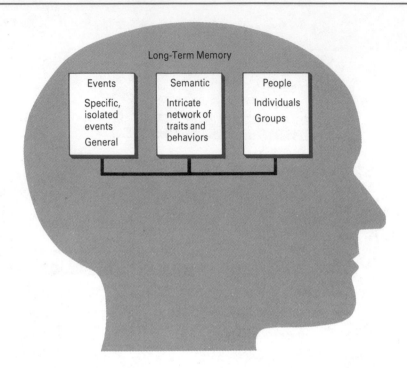

Stage 4: Retrieval and Response

Concluding our example, it is registration day and you have to choose which professor to take for personal finance. After retrieving from memory your schemata-based impressions of the three professors, you select a good one who uses the case method and gives essay tests.

Managerial Implications

Social information processing is the window through which all organizational members view, interpret, and prepare their responses to people and events. A wide variety of organizational processes thus are affected by the quality of social perception. Consider, for example, the following implications:

- *Performance appraisal:* Faulty schemata about what constitutes good-versus-poor performance can lead to inaccurate performance appraisals, thus eroding work motivation, commitment, and loyalty. One study compared the accuracy of raters who were trained to use valid performance schemata with a second group who relied on their own (untrained) schemata. Results indicated raters evaluated other people's performance more accurately when trained to use "realistic" schemata.[9]

---

[9] See Elaine D. Pulakos, "A Comparison of Rater Training Programs: Error Training and Accuracy Training," *Journal of Applied Psychology*, November 1984, pp. 581–88.

■ **TABLE 4–5**   Good Intentions Can Be Insulting in Cross-Cultural Exchanges

> The mayor of a major American city gave a miniature replica of the "Liberty Bell" (which is a symbol of independence and freedom in America) to a group of visiting Chinese artisans as a token of appreciation for their contribution to the beautification of the city. Both bells and clocks are not suitable because the words sound the same as "end" or "death" in Chinese. To compound the problem, the presentation was made on Chinese New Year's Eve and just prior to the Chinese delegation's departure for home on the following day.
>
> SOURCE: Excerpted from Rosalie L. Tung, "Corporate Executives and Their Families in China: The Need for Cross-Cultural Understanding in Business," *Columbia Journal of World Business,* Spring 1986, p. 22.

- *Selection:* Recruiters with racist or sexist schemata can undermine the accuracy and legality of hiring decisions. Those invalid schemata need to be confronted and improved through coaching and training.
- *Leadership:* Research has demonstrated that employees' evaluations of leader effectiveness are influenced strongly by their schemata of good and poor leaders.[10]
- *Communication:* Managers need to remember that social perception is a screening process that can distort communication, both coming and going. Messages are interpreted and categorized according to schemata developed through past experiences and influenced by one's age, gender, and ethnic, geographic, and cultural orientations (see Table 4–5). Effective communicators try to tailor their messages to the receiver's perceptual schemata. This requires well-developed listening and observation skills and cross-cultural sensitivity.

■ PERCEPTUAL OUTCOMES

While it is often true that beauty is in the eye of the beholder, perception does result in some predictable outcomes. Managers aware of the perception process and its outcomes enjoy a competitive edge. Grocery stores, for instance, take full advantage of perceptual tendencies to influence buying behavior.

Why, for example, are bakeries in stores so frequently placed in front near the door? "The smell literally turns on your tastebuds," says Martin Roberts, a store designer and vice president of Landor Associates. . . . "And when you smell, you tend to buy."

Grocery planners pay particular attention to specialty departments like the bakery, deli, produce, and meat counters, which bring the highest profit margins.

---

[10] For complete details, see Robert G. Lord, "An Information Processing Approach to Social Perceptions, Leadership and Behavioral Measurement in Organizations," in *Research in Organizational Behavior,* ed. L. L. Cummings and Barry M. Staw (Greenwich, Conn.: JAI Press, 1985), pp. 87–128.

Shoppers should be "romanced" through the produce department with theatrical lighting in an otherwise dark atmosphere. . . .

Good lighting throughout the store is crucial to its ambiance. . . . Soft, indirect lights are preferred because they supposedly put shoppers in a more cheerful, free-spending mood. . . . But Mr. Roberts says a new incandescent white light that brings out the reds in the color spectrum has become popular with his clients. That's because it makes produce look brighter and fresher, he says, and also because it makes the shoppers themselves look ruddier and happier.[11]

Likewise, managers can use knowledge of perceptual outcomes to help them interact more effectively with employees. For example, Table 4–6 describes five common perceptual errors. Since these perceptual errors distort evaluation

■ **TABLE 4–6** Commonly Found Perceptual Errors

Perceptual Error	Description	Example
Halo	A rater forms an overall impression about an object and then uses that impression to bias ratings about the object.	Rating a professor high on the teaching dimensions of ability to motivate students, knowledge, and communication because we like him or her.
Leniency	A personal characteristic that leads an individual to consistently evaluate other people or objects in an extremely positive fashion.	Rating a professor high on all dimensions of performance regardless of his or her actual performance. The rater who hates to say negative things about others.
Central tendency	The tendency to avoid all extreme judgments and rate people and objects as average or neutral.	Rating a professor average on all dimensions of performance regardless of his or her actual performance.
Recency effects	The tendency to remember recent information. If the recent information is negative, the person or object is evaluated negatively.	Although a professor has given good lectures for 12 of 15 weeks, he or she is evaluated negatively because lectures over the last three weeks were done poorly.
Contrast effects	The tendency to evaluate people or objects by comparing them to characteristics of recently observed people or objects.	Rating a good professor as average because you compared his or her performance to three of the best professors you have ever had in college. You are currently taking courses from the three excellent professors.

---

[11] Betsy Morris, "Romanced by the Produce: How Design Sells Groceries." Reprinted by permission of *The Wall Street Journal,* Dow Jones & Company, Inc., August 26, 1985. All rights reserved.

of job applicants and employee performance, managers need to guard against them. This section examines two important outcomes associated with person perception: stereotypes and the self-fulfilling prophecy or Pygmalion effect.

Stereotypes

Stereotypes represent grossly oversimplified beliefs or expectations about groups of people. "Stereotyping is said to occur when a perceiver makes inferences about a person because of the person's membership in some group."[12] Despite equal employment opportunity laws that discourage the use of stereotypes when making employment decisions, stereotypes persist. Since stereotypes influence how people respond to others, managers need to consciously avoid relying on them. Let us take a closer look at sex-role and age stereotypes.

Sex-Role Stereotypes. A **sex-role stereotype** is the belief that differing traits and abilities make men and women particularly well suited to different roles. This perceptual tendency was documented in a classic 1972 study. After administering a sex-role questionnaire to 383 women and 599 men, the researchers drew the following conclusion: "Our research demonstrates the contemporary existence of clearly defined sex-role stereotypes for men and women contrary to the phenomenon of 'unisex' currently touted in the media."[13] They further explained:

> Women are perceived as relatively less competent, less independent, less objective, and less logical than men; men are perceived as lacking interpersonal sensitivity, warmth, and expressiveness in comparison to women. Moreover, stereotypically masculine traits are more often perceived to be desirable than are stereotypically feminine characteristics. Most importantly, both men and women incorporate both the positive and negative traits of the appropriate stereotype into their self-concepts. Since more feminine traits are negatively valued than are masculine traits, women tend to have more negative self-concepts than do men.[14]

More recent research indicates that men and women do not systematically differ in the manner suggested by traditional stereotypes.[15] Sex-role stereotypes are indeed gross oversimplifications of reality. Women and men need to be judged as individuals, when making personnel decisions, not as members of supposedly homogeneous groups. (The same holds true for racial and ethnic minorities.)

Recent laboratory studies reveal that sex-role stereotypes do not influence

---

[12] David L. Hamilton, "A Cognitive-Attributional Analysis of Stereotyping," in *Advances in Experimental Social Psychology*, ed. L. Berkowitz (New York: Academic Press, 1979), Vol. 12, pp. 53–84.

[13] Inge K. Broverman, Susan Raymond Vogel, Donald M. Broverman, Frank E. Clarkson, and Paul S. Rosenkrantz, "Sex-Role Stereotypes: A Current Appraisal," *Journal of Social Issues* 28, no. 2 (1972), p. 75.

[14] Ibid.

[15] This research is discussed by Berna J. Skrypnek and Mark Snyder, "On the Self-Perpetuating Nature of Stereotypes about Women and Men," *Journal of Experimental Social Psychology*, May 1982, pp. 277–91.

■ **FIGURE 4–4** An Eight-Year Review of Attitudes toward Women Executives

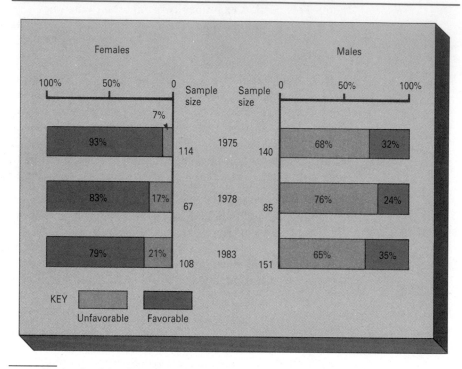

SOURCE: (Data from Peter Dubno, "Attitudes Toward Women Executives: A Longitudinal Approach," *Academy of Management Journal,* March 1985, pp. 235–39.)

the evaluation and interpretation of performance. Further, a recent meta-analysis of 19 experimental studies found no significant relationship between applicant gender and hiring recommendations. However, applicant qualifications were predictive of hiring decisions.[16] This is encouraging evidence in light of the fact that male attitudes toward female executives, although slowly improving, still remain generally unfavorable. This trend was discovered by Peter Dubno, who tracked male and female MBA students' attitudes toward female executives over eight years (see Figure 4–4). His research also found a threefold increase (7 percent to 21 percent) in *women's* unfavorable attitudes toward female executives. The reason for the narrowing of the gap between male and female attitudes toward female executives is not clear. Possibly a growing number

[16] See Angelo J. Kinicki and Rodger W. Griffeth, "The Impact of Sex-Role Stereotypes on Performance Ratings and Causal Attributions of Performance," *Journal of Vocational Behavior,* April 1985, pp. 155–70; and Lawrence H. Peters, Edward J. O'Connor, Jeff Weekley, Abdullah Pooyan, Blake Frank, and Bruce Erenkrantz, "Sex Bias and Managerial Evaluations: A Replication and Extension," *Journal of Applied Psychology,* May 1984, pp. 349–52. Results from the meta-analysis are discussed in Judy D. Olian, Donald P. Schwab, and Yitchak Haberfeld, "The Impact of Applicant Gender Compared to Qualifications on Hiring Recommendations: A Meta-Analysis of Experimental Studies," *Organizational Behavior and Human Decision Processes,* April 1988, pp. 180–95.

"I'm a vice president now, Frank, I don't make the bed anymore. Making the bed is just a stereotype, as you'd find out if you ever made vice president." (U.S. News & World Report, *December 8, 1986, p. 56. Used with permission.*)

of both females and males are now evaluating managers in terms of their accomplishments, rather than on the basis of hopeful expectations or naive stereotypes.

What are your attitudes toward female executives? To find out, complete our shortened version of the questionnaire used by Dubno and his colleagues (see Table 4–7). Compute your score by adding your nine responses. (Revised norms for comparison purposes are: total score of 9–20 = Unfavorable attitude toward female executives; 21–33 = Middle of the road; 34–45 = Favorable.) What are the organizational and career implications of your attitudes toward women executives? (See Table 4–8.)

Age Stereotypes. Long-standing age stereotypes depict older workers as less satisfied, not as involved with their work, less motivated, not as committed, and less productive then their younger co-workers. Older employees also are perceived as being more accident prone.[17] As with sex-role stereotypes, these age stereotypes are more fiction than fact.

OB researcher Susan Rhodes sought to determine whether age stereotypes were supported by data from 185 studies. She discovered that as age increases

---

[17] A thorough review of age stereotypes is presented in Benson Rosen and Thomas H. Jerdee, *Older Employees: New Roles for Valued Resources* (Homewood, Ill.: Dow Jones-Irwin, 1985).

■ **TABLE 4–7** What Are Your Attitudes toward Female Executives?

Read each question and mark your answer by circling whether you:

1 = Strongly disagree
2 = Disagree
3 = Neither disagree nor agree
4 = Agree
5 = Strongly agree

Females have the capabilities for responsible managerial positions	1 2 3 4 5
A female executive merits the same trust and respect as a male executive	1 2 3 4 5
Women in responsible managerial positions must have the capabilities for their positions and therefore men should honor their decisions	1 2 3 4 5
It's about time we had some women executives in organizations	1 2 3 4 5
Women executives are not ignorant when it comes to highly technical subjects	1 2 3 4 5
It is unfair to say women become top executives by using sexual favors	1 2 3 4 5
A man is not better suited for handling executive responsibility than a woman is	1 2 3 4 5
There are no problems with a male working for a female executive if both are dedicated, competent, and learned workers	1 2 3 4 5
Women are not taking men's positions nowadays	1 2 3 4 5
Total score = _____	

SOURCE: Based on Peter Dubno, John Costas, Hugh Cannon, Charles Wankel, and Hussein Emin, "An Empirically Keyed Scale for Measuring Managerial Attitudes toward Women Executives," *Psychology of Women Quarterly,* Summer 1979, pp. 360–61. (Copyrighted by and reprinted with the permission of Cambridge University Press.)

so do the employee's job satisfaction, job involvement, internal work motivation, and organizational commitment. Moreover, older workers were not more accident prone.[18]

Regarding job performance, a recent meta-analysis of 13 studies found that, as employees grew older, their objective performance generally *improved.* However, subjective appraisals of their performance became more negative with age. In other words, aging employees got poorer ratings from their supervisors despite doing a better job. The researchers offered this explanation:

> A possible explanation is that individual productivity . . . [is] a fairer representation of performance, whereas supervisory ratings may reflect a tendency on the part of raters to bias their appraisals, resulting in lower ratings for older workers.[19]

Older employees thus are victimized by invalid stereotypes.

A Challenge for Management. The invalidation of sex-role and age stereotypes by OB researchers represents a clear challenge to management to consciously

---

[18] For a complete review, see Susan R. Rhodes, "Age-Related Differences in Work Attitudes and Behavior: A Review and Conceptual Analysis," *Psychological Bulletin,* March 1983, pp. 328–67.

[19] David A. Waldman and Bruce J. Avolio, "A Meta-Analysis of Age Differences in Job Performance," *Journal of Applied Psychology,* February 1986, p. 36.

■ **TABLE 4–8**   Like Father Like *Daughter*

When Laura Oreffice was in high school, her father urged her to study bookkeeping and economics. He also suggested that she play sports to learn competition and "team dynamics."

By her senior year, Ms. Oreffice, under her father's tutelage, was analyzing companies' earnings reports. And when she began to plan a career, her father strongly suggested sales. "It's the fast track, and that's where he started," she says, sounding a lot like him.

Laura Oreffice's father is Paul Oreffice, chief executive of Dow Chemical Co. And like more and more of his colleagues in the business world, Mr. Oreffice is preparing his daughter for something besides marriage and motherhood. He's grooming her to be an executive.

In recent years, many executive fathers have begun to realize that their daughters will probably work—and may even have to support themselves or their families. The change is slow and sporadic. But an increasing number of fathers are realizing that women's careers can be helped or hampered by their upbringing. "Even fathers have seen that their daughters have been limited, and there's no reason they can't do what their sons have done," says Elizabeth Chittick, president of the National Women's Party, a nonprofit organization that promotes equal rights.

25 Years to Work

The daughters also have different attitudes than their counterparts of a generation ago. "Young women now know that if they marry, they'll still work 25 years of their life," says Irma Finn Brosseau, chief executive of the National Federation of Business and Professional Women's Clubs. "They also know that with a high divorce rate, they are likely to find themselves at the head of a household."

Women whose fathers have encouraged, trained, and advised them say that has given them a head start in the work world. Ms. Oreffice, now 26 years old and a bank credit analyst, says her father's help put her "one jump ahead" of many of her business-school colleagues. And he didn't treat her as if she were the son he never had. Her 24-year-old brother, Andrew, a recent business school graduate, got much the same instruction.

That's a big change from past generations, when many women were sent to college to learn to be enlightened housewives. Twenty-five years ago, says Rebecca Stafford, president of Chatham College, a women's school in Pittsburgh, many executives sent their daughters to college "so we could talk to our future husbands. . . ."

Teaching about Discrimination

Another executive father, Fred Miller, president of Nacco Mining Co. in Ohio, says he warned his daughters about sex discrimination in the "normal man's world of engineering" when they expressed interest in the field. "I told them they could do it if they set their minds to it," he says. Today, one of his daughters is a mining engineer, another is a civil engineer, and the third is studying law.

avoid such biases. Accurate and legal personnel decisions can be made by training managers to detect and avoid both invalid stereotypes and the perceptual errors listed in Table 4–6.

Self-Fulfilling Prophecy: The Pygmalion Effect

According to Greek mythology, Pygmalion was a sculptor who fell in love with a statue he carved of a beautiful woman. Through his own will, and some help from the goddess Aphrodite, Pygmalion's statue came to life. The essence of the **self-fulfilling prophecy** or Pygmalion effect is that people's expectations or beliefs determine their behavior and performance, thus serving to make their expectations come true. In other words, we strive to validate our *perceptions* of reality, no matter how faulty they may be. Thus, the self-fulfilling prophecy is an important perceptual outcome we need to better understand.

The following example illustrates how the self-fulfilling prophecy can dramatically affect an entire company:

> The folks who run Epoch Group, Inc., say that if you "create your own reality," you may be much more successful in business than you ever thought you could be.
>
> Michael D. Topf, president of the management consulting firm, . . . once challenged the head of a formal wear retail chain who said that he had had a great spring season but that now the company was "gearing down" for the summer.
>
> The firm and its employees had been operating under the mindset that spring, with its proms and weddings, was the busy season and that summer was slow, says Topf. So when summer came, they would relax. And sure enough, summer turned out to be slow.
>
> Topf got the retailer to make a declaration to his people: "We're going to have the busiest summer we've ever had." At first, there was disbelief, but the retailer, with Epoch's support, was insistent that it was going to be a busy season. So his marketing and promotion people began to come up with some strategies, pushing more formal weddings in the summer, promoting formal parties, and looking at other items, such as jewelry, that the stores could sell.
>
> And of course you know the ending to the story. The chain had the busiest summer of all its 50 years.[20]

Research and an Explanatory Model. The self-fulfilling prophecy was first demonstrated in an academic environment. After giving a bogus test of academic potential to students from grades 1 to 6, researchers informed teachers that certain students had high potential for achievement. In reality, students were randomly assigned to the "high potential" and "control" (normal potential) groups. Results showed that children designated as having "high potential" obtained significantly greater increases in both IQ scores and reading ability

---

[20] "Break the Tie that Binds," *Nation's Business,* November 1985, p. 66. Reprinted by permission from *Nation's Business,* November 1985, Copyright 1985, U.S. Chamber of Commerce.

■ **FIGURE 4–5** A Model of the Self-Fulfilling Prophecy

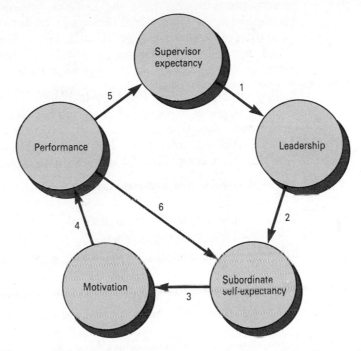

SOURCE: Dov Eden, "Self-Fulfilling Prophecy as a Management Tool: Harnessing Pygmalion," *Academy of Management Review,* January 1984, p 67. Used with permission.

than did the control students.[21] The teachers of the supposedly high-potential group got better results because their high expectations caused them to give harder assignments, more feedback, and more recognition of achievement. Students in the normal potential goup did not excel because their teachers did not expect outstanding results.

Research similarly has shown that by raising instructors' and managers' expectations for individuals performing a wide variety of tasks, higher levels of achievement/productivity can be obtained.[22] The subjects in these field studies included airmen at the United States Air Force Academy Preparatory School, disadvantaged people in job training programs, electronics assemblers, trainees in a military command course, and U.S. naval personnel.

Figure 4–5 presents a model of the self-fulfilling prophecy that helps explain these results. This model attempts to outline how supervisory expectations

---

[21] The background and results for this study are presented in Robert Rosenthal and Lenore Jacobson, *Pygmalion in the Classroom: Teacher Expectation and Pupils' Intellectual Development* (New York: Holt, Rinehart & Winston, 1968).

[22] Research on the Pygmalion effect is summarized in Dov Eden, "Self-Fulfilling Prophecy as a Management Tool: Harnessing Pygmalion," *Academy of Management Review,* January 1984, pp. 64–73.

affect employee performance. As indicated, high supervisory expectancy produces better leadership (linkage 1), which subsequently leads employees to develop higher self-expectations (linkage 2). Higher expectations motivate workers to exert more effort (linkage 3), ultimately increasing performance (linkage 4) and supervisory expectancies (linkage 5). Successful performance also improves an employee's self-expectancy for achievement (linkage 6).

Putting the Self-Fulfilling Prophecy to Work.   Largely due to the Pygmalion effect, managerial expectations powerfully influence employee behavior and performance. Consequently, managers need to harness the Pygmalion effect by building a supportive framework of positive expectations for their people. This may be accomplished by using various combinations of the following:

1. Recognize that everyone has the potential to increase his or her performance.
2. Instill confidence in your staff.
3. Set high performance goals.
4. Positively reinforce employees for a job well done.
5. Provide constructive feedback when necessary.
6. Help employees advance through the organization.
7. Introduce new employees as if they have outstanding potential.
8. Become aware of your personal prejudices and nonverbal messages that may discourage others.[23]

■ CAUSAL ATTRIBUTIONS

Attribution theory is based on the premise that people attempt to infer causes for observed behavior. Rightly or wrongly, we constantly formulate cause-and-effect explanations for our own and others' behavior. Attributional statements such as the following are common: "Joe drinks too much because he has no willpower; but I need a couple of drinks after work because I'm under a lot of pressure." Formally defined, **causal attributions** are suspected or inferred causes of behavior. Even though our causal attributions tend to be self-serving and are often invalid, it is important to understand how people formulate attributions because they profoundly affect organizational behavior. For example, a supervisor who attributes an employee's poor performance to a lack of effort might reprimand that individual. On the other hand, training might be deemed necessary if the supervisor attributes the poor performance to a lack of ability.

Generally speaking, people formulate causal attributions by considering the events preceding an observed behavior (see Figure 4–6). This section introduces

---

[23] These recommendations were adapted from Robert W. Goddard, "The Pygmalion Effect," *Personnel Journal,* June 1985, p. 10.

■ **FIGURE 4–6** A General Model of Attribution

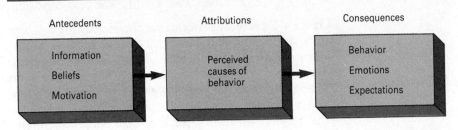

Antecedents	Attributions	Consequences
Information Beliefs Motivation	Perceived causes of behavior	Behavior Emotions Expectations

SOURCE: Adapted from Harold H. Kelley and John L. Michela, "Attribution Theory and Research," in *Annual Review of Psychology* 31, ed. Mark R. Rosenzweig and Lyman W. Porter (Palo Alto, Calif.: Annual Reviews 1980), p. 459. Reproduced, with permission, from the *Annual Review of Psychology*, Volume 31, © 1980 by Annual Reviews Inc.

and explores two different widely cited attribution models proposed by Harold Kelley and Bernard Weiner. Attributional tendencies, research, and related managerial implications also are discussed.

Kelley's Model of Attribution

Current models of attribution, such as Kelley's, are based on the pioneering work of Fritz Heider. Heider, the founder of attribution theory, proposed that behavior can be attributed either to internal factors within a person (such as ability) or to external factors within the environment (such as a difficult task). This line of thought parallels the idea of an internal versus external locus of control, as discussed in Chapter 3. Building on Heider's work, Kelley attempted to pinpoint major antecedents of internal and external attributions. Kelley hypothesized that people make causal attributions after gathering information about three dimensions of behavior: consensus, distinctiveness, and consistency.[24] These dimensions vary independently, thus forming various combinations and leading to differing attributions.

One needs a working knowledge of all three dimensions if Kelley's model is to be understood and applied.

- *Consensus* involves comparison of an individual's behavior with that of his or her peers. There is high consensus when one acts like the rest of the group and low consensus when one acts differently.
- *Distinctiveness* is determined by comparing a person's behavior on one task with his or her behavior on other tasks. High distinctiveness means the individual has performed the task in question differently than other tasks. Low distinctiveness means stable performance or quality from one task to another.
- *Consistency* is determined by judging if the individual's performance on a given task is consistent over time. High consistency means one

[24] Kelley's model is discussed in detail in Harold H. Kelley, "The Processes of Causal Attribution," *American Psychologist*, February 1973, pp. 107–28.

performs a certain task the same, time after time. Unstable performance of a given task over time would mean low consistency.

Figure 4–7 presents performance charts showing low versus high consensus, distinctiveness, and consistency. It is instructive to remember that consensus relates to other *people,* distinctiveness relates to other *tasks,* and consistency relates to *time.* The question now is: How does information about these three dimensions of behavior lead to internal or external attributions?

Kelley hypothesized that people attribute behavior to *external* causes (environmental factors) when they perceive high consensus, high distinctiveness, and low consistency. *Internal* attributions (personal factors) tend to be made when observed behavior is characterized by low consensus, low distinctiveness, and high consistency. So, for example, when all employees are performing poorly (high consensus), when the poor performance occurs on only one of several tasks (high distinctiveness), and the poor performance occurs during only one time period (low consistency), a supervisor will probably attribute an employee's poor performance to an external source such as peer pressure or an overly difficult task. In contrast, performance will be attributed to an employee's personal characteristics (an internal attribution) when only the individual in question is performing poorly (low consensus), when the inferior performance is found across several tasks (low distinctiveness), and when the low performance has persisted over time (high consistency).

Weiner's Model of Attribution

Bernard Weiner, a noted motivation theorist, developed an attribution model to explain achievement behavior and to predict subsequent changes in motivation and performance. His model proposes that ability, effort, task difficulty, and luck are the primary causes of achievement behavior (see Figure 4–8). Weiner also developed an expanded list of antecedents that includes cues such as: past performance history, task difficulty, social norms, task characteristics, patterns of performance, perceived muscular tension, sweating, and randomness of performance outcomes.[25]

Weiner's model proposes that attributions for success and failure influence how individuals perceive themselves. In turn, these self-perceptions are said to affect employee motivation. In support of this model, research shows that when individuals attribute their success to *internal* rather than external factors, they (1) have a greater desire for achievement, (2) report higher job satisfaction, (3) experience elevated self-esteem, and (4) set higher performance goals.[26]

---

[25] Weiner's complete model is presented in Bernard Weiner, *Human Motivation* (New York: Holt, Rinehart & Winston, 1980).

[26] See Dwight R. Norris and Robert E. Niebuhr, "Attributional Influences on the Job Performance-Job Satisfaction Relationship," *Academy of Management Journal,* June 1984, pp. 424–30; and Thomas I. Chacko and James C. McElroy, "The Cognitive Component in Locke's Theory of Goal Setting: Suggestive Evidence for a Causal Attribution Interpretation," *Academy of Management Journal,* March 1983, pp. 104–18.

■ **FIGURE 4–7** Performance Charts Showing Low and High Consensus, Distinctiveness, and Consistency Information

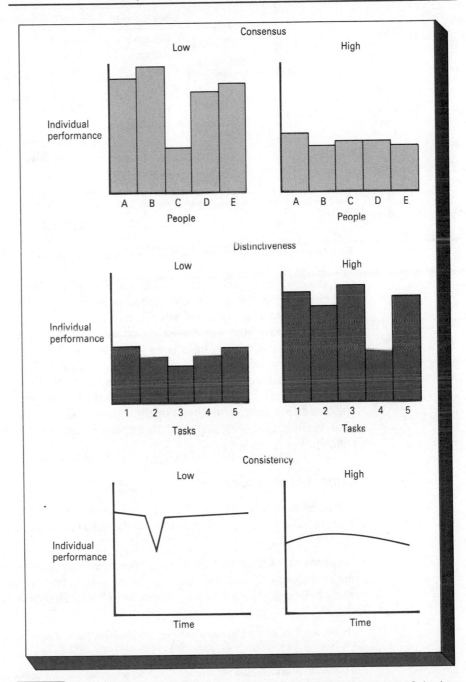

SOURCE: Karen A. Brown, "Explaining Group Poor Performance: An Attributional Analysis," *Academy of Management Review,* January 1984, p. 56. Used with permission.

■ **FIGURE 4–8**   A Modified Version of Weiner's Attribution Model

	Internal (personal)	External (environmental)
Good performance	• High ability • Hard work	• Easy job • Good luck • Help from co-workers • Good boss
Poor performance	• Low ability • Little effort	• Tough job • Bad luck • Unproductive co-workers • Unsympathetic boss

SOURCE: Adapted, by permission of the publisher, from "The 'Why' Behind Individual Work Performance," Thomas S. Bateman, Gerald R. Ferris, and Stephen Strasser, *Management Review*, October 1984, p. 71, © 1984 American Management Association, New York. All rights reserved.

But when people attribute their *failure* to a lack of ability, they tend to give up, develop lower expectations for future success, and experience decreased self-esteem. Fortunately, attributional retraining can improve both motivation and performance. Research shows that employees can be taught to attribute their failures to a lack of effort rather than to a lack of ability.[27] This attributional realignment paves the way for improved motivation and performance.

Moreover, attributions have been found to affect the way managers handle poorly performing employees. One study revealed that corrective action was taken when managers attributed poor performance to low effort. On the other hand, managers tended to transfer employees whose poor performance was attributed to a lack of ability. Finally, no immediate action was taken when poor performance was attributed to external factors beyond the individual's control.[28]

Attributional Tendencies

Researchers have uncovered two attributional tendencies that distort one's interpretation of observed behavior—*fundamental attribution bias* and *self-serving bias*.

Fundamental Attribution Bias.   The **fundamental attribution bias** reflects one's tendency to attribute another person's behavior to his or her personal characteristics, as opposed to situational factors. This bias causes perceivers

---

[27] For a review of attributional retraining, see Friedrich Forsterling, "Attributional Retraining: A Review," *Psychological Bulletin*, November 1985, pp. 495–512.

[28] See Earl C. Pence, William C. Pendleton, Greg H. Dobbins, and Joseph A. Sgro, "Effects of Causal Explanations and Sex Variables on Recommendations for Corrective Actions Following Employee Failure," *Organizational Behavior and Human Performance*, April 1982, pp. 227–40.

to ignore important environmental forces that often significantly affect behavior. For example, people typically believe criminal behavior is due to inherent dishonesty or personality flaws rather than to environmental factors such as high unemployment, broken homes, poor housing, or inadequate schools.

Self-Serving Bias. The **self-serving bias** represents one's tendency to take more personal responsibility for success than for failure. Referring again to Figure 4–8, employees tend to attribute their successes to internal factors (high ability and/or hard work) and their failures to uncontrollable external factors (tough job, bad luck, unproductive co-workers, or an unsympathetic boss). This self-serving bias is evident in how students typically analyze their performance on exams. "A" students are likely to attribute their grade to high ability or hard work. "D" students, meanwhile, tend to pin the blame on factors like an unfair test, bad luck, or unclear lectures.

For a job-related example of self-serving bias, consider the reactions of employees who worked on the Challenger space shuttle that exploded shortly after launch in 1986. According to a news report at the time:

> At a bar in Downey, Calif., angry Rockwell International Corp. employees who built the Challenger orbiter blamed other shuttle contractors for the disaster as they watched television news reports of debris being hauled out of the ocean. . . .
>
> Many shuttle workers are now blaming the fatal mistake on teams of space workers with whom they have little contact. . . . Some Rockwell employees say Cape Canaveral workers employed by archrival Lockheed could be to blame because, as one worker puts it, "they're the last ones to have anything to do with the shuttle" before launch.[29]

Because of self-serving bias, it is very difficult to pin down personal responsibility for mistakes in today's complex organizations.

Attributional Research and Managerial Implications

Attribution models and hypotheses have been extensively investigated. Some important conclusions from the vast amount of research evidence are:

- People formulate spontaneous causal attributions in two different situations: when they encounter an unexpected event (an underdog wins a football game) and when they observe the failure to achieve a goal (a politician is defeated).
- Weiner's model has been reasonably well supported.
- Fundamental attribution and self-serving biases have been consistently observed.
- A meta-analysis of 104 studies involving almost 15,000 subjects found that people who attributed negative events to their lack of ability (as

---

[29] Francine Schwadel, Matt Moffett, Roy J. Harris, Jr., and Roger Lowenstein, "Thousands Who Work on Shuttle Now Feel Guilt, Anxiety and Fear," *The Wall Street Journal*, February 6, 1986, p. 25.

opposed to bad luck) experienced greater psychological depression. The exact opposite attributions (good luck rather than high ability) tended to trigger depression in people experiencing positive events. In short, perceived bad luck can take the sting out of a negative outcome, but perceived good luck can take the joy out of a positive outcome.[30]

Attribution theory has important implications for managers. First, managers tend to disproportionately attribute behavior to *internal* causes. This can result in inaccurate evaluations of performance, leading to reduced employee motivation. No one likes to be blamed because of factors they perceive to be beyond their control. Further, since managers' responses to employee performance vary according to their attributions, attributional biases may lead to inappropriate managerial actions, including promotions, transfers, layoffs, and so forth. This can dampen motivation and performance. Attributional training sessions for managers are in order. Basic attributional processes can be explained, and managers can be taught to detect and avoid attributional biases. Finally, an employee's attributions for his or her own performance have dramatic effects on subsequent motivation, performance, and personal attitudes such as self-esteem. Managers need to keep a finger on the pulse of employee attributions if they are to make full use of the motivation concepts in the next two chapters.

■ LEARNING

What do the following situations have in common?

- The error rate for a computer programmer at a bank drops after her supervisor begins praising her for paying better attention to detail.
- After watching a training film, a sales trainee demonstrates during a role-playing exercise that he is able to overcome a customer's objections.

Although these situations vary in terms of the specific people and tasks involved, each exemplifies a different type of learning. Technically speaking, the two situations illustrate operant conditioning and vicarious learning, respectively. But before we explore these alternative types of learning, we need to formally define the term *learning*.

Learning is a psychological process through which behavior is acquired and redirected as a result of personal experience with behavior models, cues, and consequences. Noted learning theorist Robert M. Gagné observed:

The kind of change called learning exhibits itself as a change in behavior, and the inference of learning is made by comparing what behavior was possible

---

[30] For reviews of attributional research, see Bernard Weiner, " 'Spontaneous' Causal Thinking," *Psychological Bulletin,* January 1985, pp. 74–84; John H. Harvey and Gifford Weary, "Current Issues in Attribution Theory and Research," *Annual Review of Psychology* 35 (1984), pp. 427–59; and Paul D. Sweeney, Karen Anderson, and Scott Bailey, "Attributional Style in Depression: A Meta-Analytic Review," *Journal of Personality and Social Psychology,* May 1986, pp. 974–91.

before the individual was placed in a "learning situation" and what behavior can be exhibited after such treatment. The change may be, and often is, an increased capability for some type of performance.[31]

Regarding our examples above, the computer programmer's job behavior was *redirected* with conditional praise, whereas the sales trainee *acquired* a new behavior by observing and imitating a behavior model. The types of learning discussed here are more precisely termed *behavioral* learning because they focus primarily on acquisition of behavior rather than acquisition of knowledge in the form of principles, facts, or concepts (e.g., learning how to solve algebraic equations). Knowledge acquisition is better explained in terms of the perception and memory processes discussed earlier. A working knowledge of behavioral learning processes gives managers practical insights about how both good and bad work habits are first acquired and then controlled by situational factors.

To provide a background for discussion in this and later chapters, a historical perspective of learning theory, including four different models, is introduced and discussed here. The four models of learning are Watson's stimulus-response behaviorism, Thorndike's law of effect, Skinner's operant conditioning model, and Bandura's social learning. Figure 4–9 illustrates how each of these perspectives of learning has contributed to the evolution of modern learning theory.

Watson's Stimulus-Response Behaviorism

This most primitive interpretation of learning is traced to 19th century Russian physiologists such as Ivan Pavlov. Pavlov trained dogs to salivate at the sound of a bell by initially pairing a ringing bell with the presentation of food. The animals reflexively salivated at the sight and smell of the food. However, several pairings later, Pavlov's dogs salivated when the bell was rung but the food was withheld. This conditioned reflex amounted to a rudimentary form of learning, called **classical conditioning.** Through repeated exposure to bell-food pairings, Pavlov's dogs *learned* to associate the sound of the bell with eating. Interestingly, movie producers take full advantage of classical conditioning in thrillers like *Jaws* and *Jaws II*. By getting viewers to associate a thumping music score with a man-eating white shark, stomachs in the audience soon tighten merely upon hearing the music.

He Caused Psychology to Lose Its Mind. Classical conditioning was brought into the mainstream of American psychology by a researcher named John B. Watson. Before he left academe to become a successful advertising executive, Watson stood the young field of psychology on its ear during the early 1900s by rejecting the then-popular instinct theory. In its stead, he proposed a stimulus-

---

[31] Robert M. Gagné, *The Conditions of Learning* (New York: Holt, Rinehart & Winston, 1977), p. 3.

■ **FIGURE 4–9** The Evolution of Modern Behavioral Learning Theory

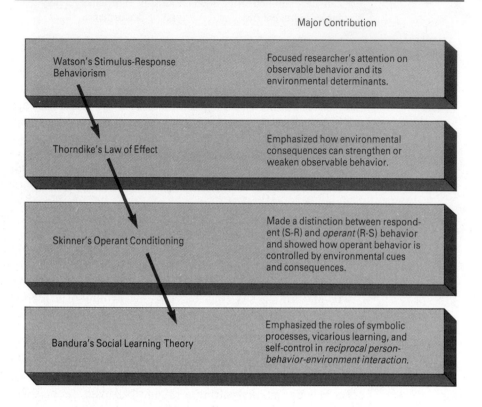

Major Contribution

Watson's Stimulus-Response Behaviorism — Focused researcher's attention on observable behavior and its environmental determinants.

Thorndike's Law of Effect — Emphasized how environmental consequences can strengthen or weaken observable behavior.

Skinner's Operant Conditioning — Made a distinction between respondent (S-R) and *operant* (R-S) behavior and showed how operant behavior is controlled by environmental cues and consequences.

Bandura's Social Learning Theory — Emphasized the roles of symbolic processes, vicarious learning, and self-control in *reciprocal person-behavior-environment interaction.*

response (S-R) approach that focused on observable behavior rather than mental processes. In 1929, Watson wrote:

> Why don't we make what we can observe the real field of psychology? Let us limit ourselves to things that can be observed, and formulate laws concerning only the observed things. Now what can we observe? Well, we can observe behavior—what the organism does or says.[32]

Thus, Watson launched a philosophy of human learning known as **behaviorism.** As a behaviorist, Watson rejected notions of mental processes and self-control when explaining human behavior. Critics chided Watson for causing American psychology to lose its mind!

Finding the Right Stimulus. Watson made the conceptual leap from reflex physiology to psychology by claiming virtually all human behavior was elicited by specific prior stimulation. In other words, he viewed all human behavior in S-R terms. According to Watson's S-R model of learning, the key to getting

---

[32] J. B. Watson and W. MacDougall, *The Battle of Behaviorism* (New York: W. W. Norton, 1929), p. 18.

someone to learn a new behavior was to find the causal stimulus for that response. From that point on, as Watson saw it, the individual would reflexively engage in the target behavior when exposed to the appropriate stimulus.

Thorndike's Law of Effect

Also during the early 1900s, Edward L. Thorndike observed in his psychology laboratory that a cat would behave randomly and wildly when placed in a small box with a secret trip lever that opened a door. However, once the cat accidentally tripped the lever and escaped, the animal would go straight to the lever when placed back in the box. Hence, Thorndike formulated his **law of effect,** which said *behavior with favorable consequences tends to be repeated, while behavior with unfavorable consequences tends to disappear.*[33] Although Thorndike adhered to Watson's notion of S-R pairings, his belief that behaviors also are controlled by their consequences caused him to subsequently be labeled a reinforcement theorist.

Skinner's Operant Conditioning Model

After an initial wave of support for Watson's S-R model, many psychologists rejected it in favor of more mentalistic and cognitive interpretations that centered on variables such as needs, drives, attitudes, and perception. However, a soon-to-be famous psychologist named B. F. Skinner adopted and refined behaviorism. Skinner agreed with Watson that *behavior* should be the primary unit of analysis. But rather than explaining all behavior in S-R terms, Skinner contended that most human behavior is controlled primarily by its *consequences.* According to Skinner, behavior is a function of its consequences, as opposed to prior causal stimulation or self-determination. Hence, Skinner endorsed and refined Thorndike's law of effect. By merging Watson's and Thorndike's ideas, Skinner qualified as a combination behaviorist and reinforcement theorist.

Respondent versus Operant Behavior. In his 1938 classic, *The Behavior of Organisms,* Skinner drew an important distinction between two types of behavior: respondent behavior and operant behavior.[34] He labeled unlearned reflexes or (S-R) connections **respondent behavior.** This category of behavior was said to describe a very small proportion of adult human behavior. Examples of respondent behavior would include crying while peeling onions and withdrawing one's hand from a hot stove. Skinner attached the label **operant behavior** to behavior that is learned when one "operates on" the environment to produce desired consequences. Some call this a response-stimulus (R-S) model. Years of controlled experiments with pigeons in "Skinner boxes" helped Skinner develop a sophisticated technology of operant conditioning. For example, he

---

[33] See Edward L. Thorndike, *Educational Psychology: The Psychology of Learning, Vol. II* (New York: Columbia University Teachers College, 1913).

[34] See B. F. Skinner, *The Behavior of Organisms* (New York: Appleton-Century-Crofts, 1938).

taught pigeons how to pace figure eights and how to bowl by reinforcing them with food whenever they more closely approximated target behaviors. Skinner's work has significant implications for OB because the vast majority of organizational behavior falls into the operant category.

Behavior Modification.   The systematic application of Skinner's operant conditioning techniques to everyday behavior is called behavior modification. On-the-job behavior modification is examined in detail in Chapter 8.

Bandura's Social Learning Theory

Albert Bandura, a Stanford psychologist, recently built on Skinner's work by initially demonstrating how people acquire new behavior by imitating role models (called vicarious learning) and later exploring the cognitive processing of cues and consequences. Like Skinner's operant model, Bandura's approach makes observable behavior the primary unit of analysis. Bandura also goes along with Skinner's contention that behavior is controlled by environmental cues and consequences. However, Bandura has extended Skinner's operant model by emphasizing that cognitive or mental processes affect how one responds to surroundings. In short, Bandura considers factors inside the individual, whereas the operant model stays outside the person. This newest addition to the evolution of behavioral learning theory is called social learning theory.

Reciprocal Determinism.   According to Bandura:

Social learning theory approaches the explanation of human behavior in terms of a continuous reciprocal interaction between cognitive, behavioral, and environmental determinants. Within the process of reciprocal determinism lies the opportunity for people to influence their destiny as well as the limits of self-direction. This conception of human functioning then neither casts people into the role of powerless objects controlled by environmental forces nor free agents who can become whatever they choose. Both people and their environments are reciprocal determinants of each other.[35]

Social Learning Defined.   Working from Bandura's comments, we define **social learning** as the process of acquiring behavior through the reciprocal interaction of the person's cognitions, behavior, and environment. The concept of reciprocal determination means we control our environment (e.g., dropping a boring class) as much as it controls us (e.g., buying a new product after seeing it advertised on television). As indicated in Figure 4–10, symbolic processes, vicarious learning, and self-control facilitate this reciprocal relationship in which each point of the triangle influences the other two points. An example of a symbolic process is relying on the mental picture of a wood pile to remember the name Woodstock.

---

[35] Albert Bandura, *Social Learning Theory* (Englewood Cliffs, N.J.: Prentice-Hall, 1977), p. vii.

■ **FIGURE 4–10** A Basic Model of Social Learning

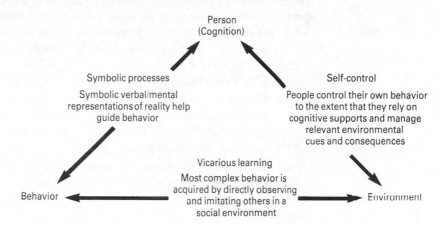

Person
(Cognition)

Symbolic processes

Symbolic verbal/mental
representations of reality help
guide behavior

Self-control

People control their own behavior
to the extent that they rely on
cognitive supports and manage
relevant environmental
cues and consequences

Vicarious learning

Most complex behavior is
acquired by directly observing
and imitating others in a
social environment

Behavior

Environment

SOURCE: Adapted, by permission of the publisher, from "A Social Learning Approach to Behavioral Management: Radical Behaviorists 'Mellowing Out,'" Robert Kreitner and Fred Luthans, *Organizational Dynamics*, Autumn 1984, p. 55, © 1984 American Management Association, New York. All rights reserved.

SUMMARY OF KEY CONCEPTS

A. Perception is a mental and cognitive process that enables us to interpret and understand our surroundings. Social perception, also known as social cognition and social information processing, is a four-stage process. The four stages are selective attention/comprehension, encoding and simplification, storage and retention, and retrieval and response. During social cognition, salient stimuli are matched with schemata, assigned to cognitive categories, and stored in long-term memory for events, semantic materials, or people.

B. Two important outcomes of person perception are stereotypes and the self-fulfilling prophecy. Managers need to be particularly aware of sex-role and age stereotypes because they can adversely affect personnel decisions. The self-fulfilling prophecy, also known as the Pygmalion effect, describes how people behave so their expectations come true. High managerial expectations foster high employee self-expectations. These in turn lead to greater effort and better performance, and yet higher expectations. Conversely, a downward spiral of expectations-performance may occur.

C. Attribution theory attempts to describe how people infer causes for observed behavior. According to Kelley's model of causal attribution, external attributions tend to be made when consensus and distinctiveness are high and consistency is low. Internal (personal responsibility) attributions tend to be made when consensus and distinctiveness are low and consistency is high.

D. Weiner's model of attribution predicts achievement behavior in terms of perceived ability, effort, task difficulty, and luck. Fundamental attribution bias involves emphasizing personal factors more than situational factors while formulating causal attributions for behavior. Self-serving bias involves personalizing the causes of one's successes and externalizing the causes of one's failures.

E. Learning is a psychological process through which behavior is acquired and redirected as a result of personal experience with behavior models, cues, and consequences. Skinner formulated his operant conditioning model by combining Watson's emphasis on observable behavior and Thorndike's emphasis on consequences.

F. According to Albert Bandura, we acquire behavior through the reciprocal interaction of the person's cognitions, behavior, and environment. This social learning involves symbolic processes, vicarious learning, and self-control.

KEY TERMS

perception   **self-serving bias**
attention   **learning**
cognitive categories   **classical conditioning**
schema   **behaviorism**
stereotypes   **law of effect**
sex-role stereotype   **respondent behavior**
self-fulfilling prophecy   **operant behavior**
causal attributions   **social learning**
fundamental attribution bias

DISCUSSION QUESTIONS

1. Why is it important for managers to have a working knowledge of perception, attribution, and behavioral learning?

2. When you are sitting in class, what stimuli are salient? What is your schema for classroom activity?

3. What evidence of self-fulfilling prophecies have you seen lately?

4. How would you formulate an attribution, according to Kelley's model, for the behavior of a classmate who starts arguing in class with your professor?

5. In what situations do you tend to attribute your successes/failures to

luck? How well does Weiner's attributional model in Figure 4–8 explain your answers? Explain.

6. Are poor people victimized by a fundamental attribution bias?
7. What evidence of the self-serving bias have you observed lately?
8. What sort of classical conditioning occurs on the job?
9. What behaviors have you learned through operant conditioning? Explain.
10. Why is social learning a potentially powerful management tool?

BACK TO THE OPENING CASE

Now that you have read Chapter 4, you should be able to answer the following questions about the Asian-American prejudice case:

1. How are Asian-American employees victimized by stereotyping? What do you think could be done to correct this problem?
2. What role does the self-fulfilling prophecy play in this case?
3. If, as Skinner claims, behavior is a function of its consequences, what are some likely behavioral outcomes of David Lam's experience at Hewlett-Packard?
4. From the standpoint of vicarious learning (acquiring behavior by imitating relevant role models), how could a shortage of Asian-American managers affect the careers of aspiring Asian-Americans?

EXERCISE 4 ———————————————————————————————

Objectives

1. To gain experience determining the causes of performance.
2. To decide on corrective action for employee performance.

Introduction

Attributions are typically made to internal and external factors. Perceivers arrive at their assessments by using various informational cues or antecedents. To determine the types of antecedents people use, we have developed a case containing various informational cues about an individual's performance. You will be asked to read the case and make attributions about the causes of performance. To assess the impact of attributions on managerial behavior, you will also be asked to recommend corrective action.

Instructions

Presented below is a case that depicts the performance of Mary Martin, a computer programmer. Please read the case and then identify the causes of her behavior by answering the questions following the case. After completing this task, decide on the appropriateness of various forms of corrective action. A list of potential recommendations has been developed. The list is divided into four categories. Read each action and evaluate its appropriateness by using the scale provided. Next, compute a total score for each of the four categories.

The Case of Mary Martin

Mary Martin, 30, received her baccalaureate degree in computer science from a reputable state school in the Midwest. She also graduated with above-average grades. Mary is currently working in the computer support/analysis department as a programmer for a nationally based firm. During the past year, Mary has missed 10 days of work. She seems unmotivated and rarely has her assignments completed on time. Mary is usually given the harder programs to work on.

Past records indicate Mary, on the average, completes programs classified as "routine" in about 45 hours. Her co-workers, on the other hand, complete "routine" programs in an average time of 32 hours. Further, Mary finishes programs considered "major problems," on the average, in about 115 hours. Her co-workers, however, finish these same "major problem" assignments, on the average, in about 100 hours. When Mary has worked in programming teams, her peer performance reviews are generally average to negative. Her male peers have noted she is not creative in attacking problems and she is difficult to work with.

The computer department recently sent a questionnaire to all users of its services to evaluate the usefulness and accuracy of data received. The results indicate many departments are not using computer output because they cannot understand the reports. It was also determined that the users of output generated from Mary's programs found the output chaotic and not useful for managerial decision making.[36]

Causes of Performance

To what extent were each of the following a cause of Mary's performance? Use the following scale:

Very little				Very much
1————	—2————	—3————	—4————	—5

a.	High ability	1 2 3 4 5
b.	Low ability	1 2 3 4 5
c.	Low effort	1 2 3 4 5
d.	Difficult job	1 2 3 4 5
e.	Unproductive co-workers	1 2 3 4 5
f.	Bad luck	1 2 3 4 5

---

[36] Adapted from Kinicki and Griffeth, "The Impact of Sex-Role Stereotypes on Performance Ratings and Causal Attributions of Performance," pp. 160–61.

Appropriateness of Corrective Action

Evaluate the following courses of action by using the scale below:

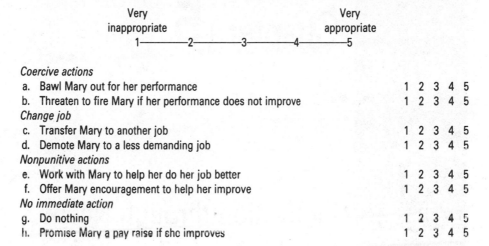

Very
inappropriate

Very
appropriate

1————2————3————4————5

Coercive actions
a. Bawl Mary out for her performance   1 2 3 4 5
b. Threaten to fire Mary if her performance does not improve   1 2 3 4 5
Change job
c. Transfer Mary to another job   1 2 3 4 5
d. Demote Mary to a less demanding job   1 2 3 4 5
Nonpunitive actions
e. Work with Mary to help her do her job better   1 2 3 4 5
f. Offer Mary encouragement to help her improve   1 2 3 4 5
No immediate action
g. Do nothing   1 2 3 4 5
h. Promise Mary a pay raise if she improves   1 2 3 4 5

Compute a score for the four categories:[37]

Coercive actions = a + b =
Change job = c + d =
Nonpunitive actions = e + f =
No immediate actions = g + h =

Questions for Consideration/Class Discussion

1. How would you evaluate Mary's performance in terms of consensus, distinc-
    tiveness, and consistency?
2. Is Mary's performance due to internal or external causes?
3. What did you identify as the top two causes of Mary's performance? Are
    your choices consistent with Weiner's classification of internal and external
    factors? Explain.
4. Which of the four types of corrective action do you think is most appropriate?
    Explain. Can you identify any negative consequences of this choice?

---

[37] Based on Pence, Pendleton, Dobbins, and Sgro, "Effects of Causal Explanations and Sex
Variables on Recommendations for Corrective Actions Following Employee Failure," pp. 227–
40.

Chapter **5**

Motivation·through Needs and Satisfaction

When you finish studying the material in this chapter,
you should be able to:

- Define the term *motivation.*
- Distinguish between content and process theories of motivation.
- Highlight the evolution of modern motivation theory.
- Contrast Maslow's and Alderfer's need theories of motivation.
- Describe the economic significance of McClelland's need for achievement theory.
- Explain the practical significance of Herzberg's distinction between motivators and hygiene factors.
- Put the job satisfaction controversy into proper perspective.

Goofy and Pluto Gripe about Disney Policies

Some of the people who play the beloved characters at Disney World . . . in Orlando, Florida—Goofy, Winnie the Pooh, Pluto and whatnot—are caught in a midlife career crisis, so to speak.

Projecting themselves in roles designed to be played by young people, who in the best of worlds would have a good time for a couple of years being, say, Mickey Mouse, and then move on to a real job, they find themselves stuck in the fantasy.

There are 125 characters in the Magic Kingdom, played by 200 people, about 40 of whom are full-time. Their hourly earnings [in 1981] range from $4.10 to $5.20 and, like everyone, they want to earn more. They work eight-hour shifts, alternating one-half hour in costume, one-half hour out, but they have been working late to rehearse for the 10th anniversary celebration of Walt Disney World, and they are getting paid at time-and-a-half rates after hours.

Recently at midnight, when rehearsals ended, Winnie the Pooh and Eeyore, the donkey from the same A. A. Milne classics; Pluto, Br'er Fox, Br'er Bear, Goofy, Mr. Walrus, and two of the Three Little Pigs sought out a secret meeting in Orlando, for the purpose of exposing their plight.

They requested anonymity because under Disney policy an unauthorized interview is grounds for dismissal. . . .

Eeyore spoke about the 35-pound donkey head.

"It's heavy," he said. "You can't see, and you can't breathe. . . . We've had a lot of back problems in the character department."

Mr. Walrus said her costume was such a burden that she has had back problems and at times her arms have gone numb.

"When I was in Winnie the Pooh, I had my nose broken because some guy shoved the honey pot right into my face. The pig's heads aren't great, either. They have metal parts right up against your head."

Pluto said, "We all wear metal taps and other metal parts, and in a thunderstorm, we feel like lightning rods."

Another pig complained of being physically abused by many guests.

"Some of them want to find out if you're a woman," she said. "But retaliation is grounds for termination." It makes her want to go take her costume off, she said, and come back and deck the offender.

Goofy said it all comes down to money and job security. He said the Kids of the Kingdom, who dance and mime songs, are paid more then $7 an hour, but did not take anywhere near the risks taken by the characters who wear cumbersome costumes and dance on floats.

To boot, he said, Disney has gone to a two-year contract with the characters, after which they audition and then their contract is renewed for another year, or they are trans-

Effective employee motivation has long been one of management's most difficult and important duties. Success in this area is even more difficult in light of the changing dynamics of organizational life, as discussed in Chapter 2. Reviewing briefly, the following realities make motivating individuals to pursue and achieve organizational objectives especially challenging today:

- The growing ranks of part-time employees tend to have more negative attitudes toward work than their full-time counterparts.
- The largest sector of the U.S. economy, the service sector, suffers from low productivity growth.
- Observational studies indicate that people typically work only 49 percent of the workday.
- Proportionately more people are seeking jobs for which they are either overqualified (hence, underemployment) or undereducated.
- Many administrative practices are crippling the incentive to work hard.

These realities add up to an immense challenge to better motivate today's employees. But experts say this motivational challenge is not being adequately met. For example, one management consultant concluded:

Employee motivation is on the decline in America, and has been for some time. Managers regularly assert that employees today just will not work like they used to. Further, my own observations suggest that more employees than in years past exert just enough effort at work to get by—no more.

In my opinion, employee motivation has been declining for a long time. This trend, however, has been camouflaged by rapid technological advance. . . . Few cared whether employees were motivated because it was believed that improvements in technology would overcome any human frailties.

But a new era is upon us. Technological growth in numerous sectors is slowing and the impact of declining motivation is becoming evident. . . .

To remain competitive in world markets, America can no longer neglect its human resources. Further decline in employee motivation cannot be tolerated.[1]

---

[1] Philip C. Grant, "Why Employee Motivation Has Declined in America," *Personnel Journal,* December 1982, p. 905.

The purpose of this chapter is to build a definitional and conceptual foundation for the topic of motivation so a rich variety of motivation theories and techniques can be introduced and discussed. Coverage of employee motivation extends to Chapter 6. In this chapter, we focus on the following: (1) need theories of motivation, (2) satisfaction theories of motivation, and (3) causes and consequences of job satisfaction. Attention turns to equity, expectancy, and goal-setting motivation theory, research, and practice in the next chapter.

■ WHAT DOES MOTIVATION INVOLVE?

The term *motivation* was derived from the Latin word *movere* meaning "to move." In the present context, **motivation** represents "those psychological processes that cause the arousal, direction, and persistence of voluntary actions that are goal directed."[2] Managers need to understand these psychological processes if they are to successfully guide employees toward accomplishing organizational objectives. After considering a general model of the motivational process, this section examines the historical roots of motivational concepts and the relationship between motivation and performance.

General Model of Motivation

A general model of the interdependent variables basic to work motivation is presented in Figure 5–1. This model provides a framework for understanding the dynamic nature of the motivation process. As shown in Figure 5–1, the basic components of motivation are: (1) needs, desires, or expectations; (2) behavior; (3) goals; and (4) feedback. The concept of homeostasis helps explain the dynamic relationship among these variables.

The Role of Homeostasis in Motivation.   Biologists use the term **homeostasis** to refer to the body's natural ability to maintain a life-sustaining balance of bodily fluids and nutrients, such as water, sodium, protein, and oxygen. One's body automatically attempts to restore equilibrium when a vital component is deficient and the system is out of balance. For example, the desire to drink liquids naturally develops when one's body becomes dehydrated. Similarly, an exhausting hour of aerobics may deplete the level of sodium in the body, producing a hunger for salt. Motivation theorists translated this biological model into psychological terms.

Referring to our definition of motivation, psychological disequilibrium arouses behavior directed toward satisfying a specific incentive or goal thought to restore equilibrium. Moreover, one will persist in trying to attain the relevant

---

[2] Terence R. Mitchell, "Motivation: New Direction for Theory, Research, and Practice," *Academy of Management Review*, January 1982, p. 81. For an interesting discussion of the central importance of motivation in OB, see Martin G. Evans, "Organizational Behavior: The Central Role of Motivation," *Journal of Management*, Summer 1986, pp. 203–22.

■ **FIGURE 5–1** A General Model of the Motivation Process

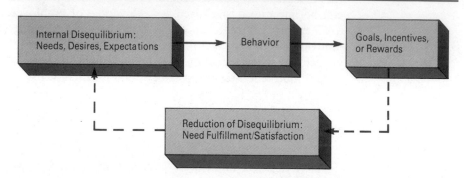

SOURCE: Adapted from Marvin D. Dunnette and Wayne K. Kirchner, *Psychology Applied to Industry* (New York: Meredith Publishing Company, 1965), p. 125.

incentive or goal until balance is restored. Therein lie the arousal, direction, and persistence aspects of our definition of motivation. As the incentive or goal is attained, internal feedback decreases both disequilibrium and motivation.

An Illustrative Example. An on-the-job example clarifies these motivational processes. Suppose a product design engineer with a need for more creative expression (disequilibrium) asks his or her manager for a more challenging project (the behavior) hoping this will lead to professional growth (the goal). Upon receiving a more challenging job assignment, the engineer enjoys greater creative expression. Because the engineer's psychological equilibrium for creative expression has been restored, his or her attention shifts away from seeking a more challenging assignment and toward other goals, perhaps a pay raise. If the design engineer was not reassigned to more challenging work, his or her disequilibrium would continue and the need for professional growth would persist.

Historical Roots of Modern Motivation Theories

Most contemporary theories of motivation are rooted partially in the principle of **hedonism,** which states that people are motivated to consciously seek pleasure and avoid pain. Hedonism dates to the Greek philosophers. As a separate and self-contained theory of human motivation, hedonism proved unsatisfactory for two reasons. First, hedonism failed to adequately reconcile the relationship between short-term and long-term consequences. For example, hedonism cannot explain why some people choose to become professional football players who willingly risk their health during bruising Sunday afternoon games. Obviously, the football players are sustaining short-term pain in order to attain longer-term rewards such as recognition and lucrative contracts. Second, due to the rich variation among people, hedonists could not neatly categorize hundreds of different activities and consequences into distinct pleasure and pain categories. Writing, for example, may be a pleasure for professional writers, but it is definitely a pain for many college students. Let us now examine the historical development of subsequent theories of motivation.

Five ways of explaining behavior—instincts, needs, rewards, cognitions, and job characteristics—underlie the evolution of modern theories of human motivation. These theories fall into one of two categories, content and process theories. **Content theories** of motivation focus on internal factors such as instincts, needs, and satisfaction that are said to energize purposeful behavior. **Process theories** of motivation, on the other hand, explain how behavior is given purpose and direction through person-environment interaction.[3] Rewards, cognitions, and job characteristics fall into this second category. Content theories of motivation tend to be static and relatively simple, whereas process theories are dynamic and more complex.

As we proceed through this review, remember the objective of each alternative motivation theory is to explain and predict purposeful or goal-directed behavior. As will become apparent, the differences between theoretical perspectives lie in the causal mechanisms used to explain behavior.

Instincts.   An instinct represents an inherited or innate predisposition to behave in a certain way. In contrast to the rational processes guiding hedonism, instinct theorists proposed that behavior was due to unconscious rather than conscious motives. Sigmund Freud, the pioneering psychoanalyst, proposed that behavior was determined largely by unconscious or instinctive motives relating primarily to sex and aggression. Instinct-based theories came under strong attack from scholars within the budding discipline of psychology during the late 1920s. Citing a list of instincts that had mushroomed to nearly 6,000, critics said instincts were too imprecise for serious scientific inquiry. The notion of instincts gave way to the concept of needs.

Needs.   According to early need theorists, psychological deprivation or disequilibrium gives behavior purpose and direction. Thus, individuals were said to be motivated by unsatisfied needs. Early need theories seemed to do a better job of explaining variations in behavior in terms of unsatisfied and satisfied needs, rather than in terms of unrelenting instincts. Henry Murray, a 1930s psychologist, was the first behavioral scientist to propose a list of needs thought to underlie goal-directed behavior (see Table 5–1). From Murray's work sprang a wide variety of need theories, some of which remain influential today. Recognized need theories of motivation are explored in the next section of this chapter.

Rewards.   Reinforcement theorists, such as Edward L. Thorndike and B. F. Skinner, proposed that behavior is controlled by its consequences, not the result of hypothetical internal states such as instincts, drives, or needs. This proposition is based on research data demonstrating that people repeat behaviors

---

[3] For an elaboration of the difference between content and process theories, see John P. Campbell, Marvin D. Dunnette, Edward E. Lawler III, and Karl E. Weick, Jr., *Managerial Behavior, Performance, and Effectiveness* (New York: McGraw-Hill, 1970).

■ **TABLE 5–1** Murray's Taxonomy of Needs

Needs	Characteristics
Abasement	Complying with and giving in to others
Achievement	Overcoming obstacles and succeeding at challenging tasks
Affiliation	Establishing meaningful social relationships, joining groups, and wanting to be loved
Aggression	Physically or psychologically injuring another person
Autonomy	Resisting the influence of others and striving for independence
Counteraction	Defending one's honor and proudly using retaliation to overcome defeat
Deference	Serving others by following direction and guidance
Defendance	Defending oneself by offering explanations, causes, and excuses
Dominance	Directing, leading, or controlling others
Exhibition	Drawing attention to oneself
Harm avoidance	Avoiding activities or situations that may be dangerous
Infavoidance	Attempting to avoid failure, shame, humiliation, or ridicule
Nurturance	Aiding or helping someone in need
Order	Being tidy, organized, and extremely precise
Play	Relaxing, joking, being entertained, or just having fun
Rejection	Ignoring or excluding others from activities
Sentience	Desiring sensuous gratifications, particularly by having objects contact the body
Sex	Desiring an erotic relationship or engaging in sexual intercourse
Succorance	Seeking help or sympathy from others
Understanding	Defining relationships and abstract ideas and concepts

SOURCE: Adapted from Henry A. Murray, *Explorations in Personality* (New York: John Wiley & Sons, 1938), pp. 77–83.

followed by favorable consequences and avoid behaviors resulting in unfavorable consequences. Few would argue with the statement that organizational rewards have a motivational impact on job behavior. However, behaviorists and cognitive theorists do disagree over the role of internal states and processes in motivation.

Cognitions.   Uncomfortable with the idea that behavior is shaped completely by environmental consequences, cognitive motivation theorists contend that behavior is a function of beliefs, expectations, values, and other mental cognitions. Behavior is therefore viewed as the result of rational and conscious choices among alternative courses of action. In Chapter 6, we discuss cognitive motivation theories involving equity, expectancies, and goal setting.

Job Characteristics.   According to this most recent addition to the evolution of motivation theory, the task itself is said to be the key to employee motivation. Specifically, a boring and monotonous job stifles motivation to perform well, whereas a challenging job enhances motivation. Three ingredients of a more challenging job are variety, autonomy, and decision authority. Two popular ways of adding variety and challenge to routine jobs are job enrichment (or job redesign) and job rotation. A prime example of an attempt to motivate

■   **FIGURE 5–2**   Motivation: A Psychological Puzzle

employees through job characteristics is General Motors' "self-managed" assembly line at its Packard Electric Division plant in Austintown, Ohio.

To avoid the tedium of working at the same station day after day, workers rotate line jobs and—most important—get to work off the line several times a month to handle material and repairs. The team members also perform many of the foreman's functions: setting the line speed, ordering material, establishing rules for handling disputes, checking quality, and doing paperwork. Each day a different worker serves as the "coordinator," the person who makes decisions.[4]

A Motivational Puzzle.   Figure 5–2 depicts the subject of motivation as a puzzle. Motivation theory presents managers with a psychological puzzle composed of alternative interpretations. Managers can learn important lessons about employee motivation from each piece of the puzzle. Within a contingency management framework, managers need to pick and choose motivational techniques best suited to the people and situation involved.

Motivation Is Only One Factor in the Performance Equation

All too often, motivation and performance are assumed to be one and the same. This faulty assumption can lead to poor managerial decisions. The following formula for performance helps put motivation into proper perspective:

---

[4] "The Revolutionary Wage Deal at GM's Packard Electric," *Business Week*, August 29, 1983, p. 56.

Performance = Level of ability × Level of skill × Motivation × Knowledge about how to complete the task × Facilitating and inhibiting conditions not under the individual's control.[5]

Thus, we see motivation is a necessary but insufficient contributor to job performance. (Multiplication signs are used to emphasize how a weakness in one factor can negate other factors.)

Drawing a distinction between performance and motivation has its advantages. According to one motivation expert:

> The implication is that there probably are some jobs for which trying to influence motivation will be irrelevant for performance. These circumstances can occur in a variety of ways. There may be situations in which ability factors or role expectation factors are simply more important than motivation. For example, the best predictor of high school grades typically is intellectual endowment, not hours spent studying. . . .
>
> Another circumstance may occur in which performance is controlled by technological factors. For example, on an assembly line, given that minimally competent and attentive people are there to do the job, performance may not vary from individual to individual. Exerting effort may be irrelevant for performance.[6]

Managers are better able to identify and correct performance problems when they recognize that poor performance is not solely due to inadequate motivation. This awareness can foster better interpersonal relations in the workplace.

■ NEED THEORIES OF MOTIVATION

As previously mentioned, theories of motivation either identify the content of what motivates individuals or describe the motivation process. The need theories discussed in this section qualify as content theories of motivation because they attempt to pinpoint factors that energize behavior. **Needs** are physiological or psychological deficiencies that arouse behavior. In contrast to the innate and fixed nature of instincts, needs can be strong or weak and are influenced by environmental factors. Thus, human needs vary over time and place.

Three popular need theories are presented: Maslow's need hierarchy theory; Alderfer's existence, relatedness, and growth (ERG) theory; and McClelland's need for achievement theory. Managers with a working knowledge of these three content theories of motivation can take appropriate steps to improve job performance.

---

[5] Adapted from John P. Campbell and Robert D. Pritchard, "Motivation Theory in Industrial and Organizational Psychology," in *Handbook of Industrial and Organizational Psychology,* ed. Marvin D. Dunnette (Skokie, Ill.: Rand McNally, 1976).

[6] Mitchell, "Motivation: New Direction for Theory, Research, and Practice," p. 83.

■ **FIGURE 5–3** Maslow's Need Hierarchy

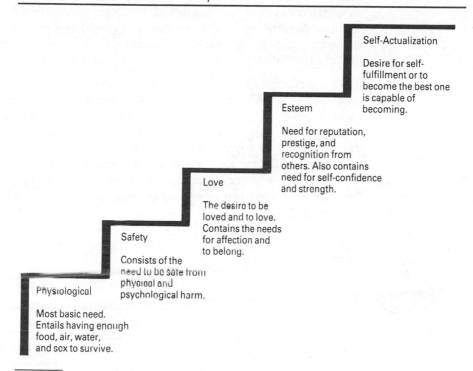

SOURCE: Adapted from descriptions provided by Abraham H. Maslow, "A Theory of Human Motivation," *Psychological Review*, July 1943, pp. 370–96.

Maslow's Need Hierarchy Theory

In 1943, psychologist Abraham Maslow published his now-famous need hierarchy theory of motivation. Although the theory was based on his clinical observation of a few neurotic individuals, it has subsequently been used to explain the entire spectrum of human behavior. Relying on Murray's taxonomy of needs as a starting point, Maslow proposed that motivation is a function of five basic needs—physiological, safety, love, esteem, and self-actualization (see Figure 5–3).

Maslow said these five need categories are arranged in a prepotent hierarchy. In other words, he believed human needs generally emerge in a predictable stair-step fashion. Accordingly, when one's physiological needs are relatively satisfied, one's safety needs emerge, and so on up the need hierarchy one step at a time. Once a need is satisfied it activates the next higher need in the hierarchy. This process continues until the need for self-actualization is activated.[7] Maslow viewed the need for self-actualization as a never-ending pursuit because one cannot achieve perfection.

---

[7] For a complete description of Maslow's theory, see Abraham H. Maslow, "A Theory of Human Motivation," *Psychological Review*, July 1943, pp. 370–96.

Cultural Translation Required.   It is important to note, from an international management perspective, that different cultures yield different need hierarchies. Because Maslow's five-level hierarchy is rooted in American culture, it does not necessarily fit significantly different cultures (see Figure 5–4). In fact, cultural translation is required for all ''made in America'' motivation theories.

A Misconception about Maslow's Theory.
We must be careful not to misinterpret Maslow's theory by characterizing the hierarchy of needs as a fixed and rigid structure. If it were, virtually all human behavior would be activated in a uniform and predictable sequence. To the contrary, Maslow stated that there are exceptions to moving up the hierarchy in a fixed stair-step fashion (see Table 5–2). Maslow also proposed that behavior is multimotivated. In other words, behavior is often motivated by some, if not all, of the needs simultaneously. It is important to remember Maslow proposed a *relative* rather than absolute hierarchy of needs.

■ **FIGURE 5–4**   Need Hierarchies Vary from Culture to Culture: An Example from the People's Republic of China

After conducting research in the People's Republic of China, Edwin C. Nevis concluded that the Chinese hierarchy of needs is arranged differently and has fewer levels than Maslow's American hierarchy. These differences owe primarily to the Chinese cultural emphasis on service and loyalty to society and the American cultural emphasis on self-determination and individualism. Nevis's Chinese hierarchy of needs is arranged as follows:

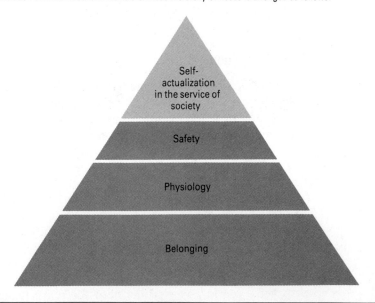

SOURCE: Reprinted with permission from NTL Institute, "Using an American Perspective in Understanding Another Culture: Toward a Hierarchy of Needs for the People's Republic of China," by Edwin C. Nevis, p. 256, *The Journal of Applied Behavioral Science,* Vol. 19, No. 3; copyright 1983.

■ **TABLE 5–2** Reversals within the Need Hierarchy

1. For some people, esteem needs are more important than love needs.
2. Self-actualization can take precedence over all other needs for people who possess a strong desire to be creative.
3. The desire to advance in life can be destroyed by chronic periods of failure. This would tend to focus people at lower-level needs.
4. Some people, like psychopathic personalities, have lost the need to love.
5. A need may become underevaluated when an individual has been satisfied with it for an extended period.
6. Even though a need may be prepotent, people do not always act on their desires. Organizational or personal constraints may inhibit an individual from satisfying an important need.
7. Ideals, high standards, or high values can lead people to give up everything in pursuit of the ideal (a martyr).

SOURCE: Derived from Abraham H. Maslow, "A Theory of Human Motivation," *Psychological Review,* July 1943, pp. 370–96.

Research Findings on Maslow's Theory. Although Maslow's theory was eagerly espoused by those seeking to understand and manage human behavior, it was not empirically tested until the mid-1960s. Since then, researchers have concluded:

- Evidence does not clearly support the existence of five distinct categories of needs.
- Categories of needs are not structured into a hierarchy of prepotency.
- There is a lack of strong evidence demonstrating that deprived needs are highly motivational.
- Need satisfaction has not consistently been found to decrease as one moves up the hierarchy of needs.[8]

Unfortunately, the bulk of these results are drawn from studies that did not test Maslow's theory appropriately. This turn of events has led one motivation scholar to conclude:

> In balance, Maslow's theory remains very popular among managers and students of organizational behavior, although there are still very few studies that can legitimately confirm (or refute) it. . . . It may be that the dynamics implied by Maslow's theory of needs are too complex to be operationalized and confirmed by scientific research. If this is the case, we may never be able to determine how valid the theory is, or—more precisely—which aspects of the theory are valid and which are not.[9]

---

[8] For an overall review of research on Maslow's need hierarchy, see Mahmoud A. Wahba and Lawrence G. Bridwell, "Maslow Reconsidered: A Review of Research on the Need Hierarchy Theory," *Organizational Behavior and Human Performance,* April 1976, pp. 212–40. More recent studies were conducted by John Rauschenberger, Neal Schmitt, and John E. Hunter, "A Test of the Need Hierarchy Concept by a Markov Model of Change in Need Strength," *Administrative Science Quarterly,* December 1980, pp. 654–70; and Ellen L. Betz, "Two Tests of Maslow's Theory of Need Fulfillment," *Journal of Vocational Behavior,* April 1984, pp. 204–20.

[9] Craig C. Pinder, *Work Motivation: Theory, Issues, and Applications* (Glenview, Ill.: Scott, Foresman, 1984), p. 52.

■ **TABLE 5–3** Maslow Recommended More Research

My work on motivations came from the clinic, from a study of neurotic people. The carry-over of this theory to the industrial situation has some support from industrial studies, but certainly I would like to see a lot more studies of this kind before feeling finally convinced that this carry-over from the study of neurosis to the study of labor in factories is legitimate.

The same thing is true of my studies of self-actualizing people—there is only this one study of mine available. There were many things wrong with the sampling, so many in fact that it must be considered to be, in the classical sense anyway, a bad or poor or inadequate experiment. I am quite willing to concede this—as a matter of fact, I am eager to concede it—because I'm a little worried about this stuff which I consider to be tentative being swallowed whole by all sorts of enthusiastic people, who really should be a little more tentative, in the way that I am.

SOURCE: Abraham H. Maslow, *Eupsychian Management* (Homewood, Ill.: Richard D. Irwin, 1965), pp. 55–56.

Interestingly, more than 20 years after his original formulation of the need hierarchy, Maslow called for more rigorous research to assess the validity of what he still considered to be a *tentative* theory (see Table 5–3).

Managerial Implications of Maslow's Theory. Although research does not clearly support this theory, it does teach managers a valuable lesson. Specifically, a satisfied need may lose its motivational potential. Therefore, managers are advised to motivate employees by devising programs or practices aimed at satisfying emerging or unmet needs. For example, in the face of technological displacement and high unemployment, employers can possibly boost motivation by giving workers a job-security pledge (see Table 5–4). Subsequently, management could attempt to satisfy esteem needs. While this can be done in a variety of ways, the use of status symbols to enhance esteem can sometimes backfire. For example, before a shift in corporate culture in 1982, Procter & Gamble (P&G) relied heavily on status symbols. Unfortunately, the following situation arose:

A Procter & Gamble Co. manager remembers moving into his new office and discovering his ceiling had half a row of tiles too many.

According to P&G tradition, branch managers' office ceilings measured 12 tiles by 12—only higher ranks got bigger offices and more tiles. His measured 12 by 12½. "People would come in and look at the ceiling and mutter things like, 'Young whippersnapper!' "[10]

As part of a more constructive approach, participative management and positive feedback programs can satisfy esteem needs. When relative satisfaction of employee esteem needs activates self-actualization needs, management can enhance motivation by redesigning jobs to provide more autonomy and responsibility.

---

[10] Jolie B. Solomon and John Bussey, "Cultural Change Pressed by Its Rivals, Procter & Gamble Co. Is Altering Its Ways," *The Wall Street Journal*, May 20, 1985, p. 1.

■ **TABLE 5-4** Increasing Physiological and Safety Need Satisfaction through Job Security Pledges

> Giving workers employment security by easing their job-loss fears makes them easier to manage. That's one conclusion of "Employment Security in Action," a study of more than 30 corporations, including IBM, Honeywell, Advanced Micro Devices, and Dana Corp., by economists Jocelyn Gutchess and researchers at the Work in America Institute, Scarsdale, New York.
>
> Job security takes many forms. Some companies have written "no layoff" policies. Others use "buffers" to protect the full-time workers by using part-timers and subcontractors and by spreading out the work. The promise of retraining eases workers' fears, too. As a result, they are more willing to adapt to new ideas.
>
> SOURCE: "A Special News Report on People and Their Jobs in Offices, Fields, and Factories," *The Wall Street Journal,* May 14, 1985, p. 1.

Alderfer's ERG Theory

Dissatisfied with Maslow's need theory, Clayton Alderfer developed an alternative theory of human needs in the late 1960s. Alderfer's theory differs from Maslow's in three major respects. First, a smaller set of core needs is used to explain behavior. From lowest to highest level they are: existence needs (E), relatedness needs (R), and growth needs (G). Hence, Alderfer's ERG theory. In addition, ERG theory does not assume needs are related to each other in a prepotent or stairstep hierarchy. Finally, frustration of higher-order needs is thought to influence the desire for lower-order needs.[11] In other words, unlike the primarily upward thrust of Maslow's hierarchy, Alderfer's theory has both upward and downward thrusts. This feature of Alderfer's ERG theory will become apparent as we examine it more closely.

The ERG Needs. **Existence needs** include all types of physiological and materialistic desires. **Relatedness needs** center around the need to have meaningful relationships with significant others. Satisfaction results from the mutual sharing of thoughts and feelings. **Growth needs** encompass the need to grow as a human being and to use one's abilities to their fullest potential.

Dynamic Relationships among the ERG Needs. Figure 5–5 depicts seven relationships among the ERG needs, as proposed by Alderfer. Each proposition has been numbered for discussion purposes. The first proposition states that a lack of satisfaction with existence needs leads to a greater desire for existence needs. For instance, when we lack money, we tend to want it. Existence needs also motivate behavior when an individual is frustrated by a lack of relatedness satisfaction (proposition 2). For example, employees may demand higher pay or better benefits when they are dissatisfied with the quality of their interpersonal relationships at work. Akin to Maslow's notion of a need

---

[11] For a complete review of ERG theory, see Clayton P. Alderfer, *Existence, Relatedness, and Growth: Human Needs in Organizational Settings* (New York: Free Press, 1972).

■ **FIGURE 5-5** Underlying Propositions of ERG Theory

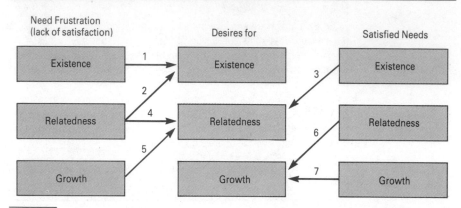

SOURCE: Adapted from Clayton P. Alderfer, "An Empirical Test of a New Theory of Human Needs," *Organizational Behavior and Human Performance,* May 1969, pp. 142–75.

hierarchy, proposition 3 suggests that people desire more relatedness activities when they are satisfied with existence needs. This helps explain why highly paid employees socialize a great deal at work. The desire for relatedness also increases when a person's relatedness (proposition 4) and growth (proposition 5) needs are not being satisfied. Finally, propositions 6 and 7 predict that satisfaction with relatedness and growth needs will increase desire for growth-related activities.

Research on ERG Theory.   On the positive side, research supports Alderfer's premise that there are three categories of needs. However, findings do not clearly support the relationships outlined in ERG's seven theoretical propositions. For example, Alderfer used participants from seven organizations to test the propositions outlined in Figure 5–5. Results confirmed propositions 1, 2, and 4. Proposition 3 was not supported. Support for propositions 5, 6, and 7 was dependent on the type of organization being surveyed. This suggests the validity of ERG theory depends on the type of organization employees work in. More recent research similarly found mixed results for ERG.[12]

Managerial Implications of ERG Theory.   Alderfer himself believes the contribution of ERG theory is indirect. The practical relevance of ERG theory appears to lie in its ability to help managers think through motivational problems. For example, ERG theory suggests employee desires are a function of both need satisfaction and frustration. Let us consider a real-life case that highlights this dynamic relationship among needs. In 1985, the going rate for truck drivers hired under the Teamsters' national contract was $13.30 an hour.[13]

---

[12] For a review of research conducted by Alderfer, see note 11. More recent research was conducted by John P. Wanous and Abram Zwany, "A Cross-Sectional Test of Need Hierarchy Theory," *Organizational Behavior and Human Performance,* February 1977, pp. 78–97.

[13] See "The Double Standard That's Setting Worker against Worker," *Business Week,* April 8, 1985, pp. 70–71.

Without overtime, this amounted to $27,664 annually. How would you interpret the Teamsters' demand for higher wages? Perhaps the truck drivers needed more money to satisfy their existence needs. However, ERG theory also proposes that the demand for yet higher wages could have been symptomatic of the drivers' frustration with relatedness. Long-distance truck drivers generally spend many hours alone. Trucking company managers who were aware of the dynamics of ERG theory might have reduced their drivers' demands for increased wages by creating a work environment that allowed greater satisfaction of relatedness needs (e.g., husband-and-wife driving teams).

McClelland's Need for Achievement Theory

Achievement theories propose that motivation varies according to the strength of one's need for achievement. Henry Murray, the psychologist who proposed the list of needs presented in Table 5–1, was the first to call attention to the **need for achievement.** He defined this need as the desire:

> to accomplish something difficult. To master, manipulate or organize physical objects, human beings, or ideas. To do this as rapidly and as independently as possible. To overcome obstacles and attain a high standard. To excel one's self. To rival and surpass others. To increase self-regard by the successful exercise of talent.[14]

Measuring Need for Achievement.   David McClelland, a behavioral scientist who has been studying achievement needs since the late 1940s, formulated a comprehensive theory of achievement motivation. His initial contribution was to refine the Thematic Apperception Test (TAT). This instrument has been used to measure the strength of an individual's achievement motive. In completing the TAT, people are asked to write stories about ambiguous pictures. (At this time, we would like you to examine Figure 5–6 and write what you think is happening regarding the people in the picture and what you think will happen to them in the future.)

The TAT stories are then analyzed to determine if they contain achievement imagery. For example, if you think Figure 5–6 shows three people talking about or working on an invention or a major accomplishment, this indicates you have a high need for achievement. (Murray's definition of the need for achievement can be used to score other achievement-oriented imagery.) On the other hand, your story may reveal your affiliation or power needs. If you think the picture depicts one individual counseling or helping others, this suggests you have a high need for affiliation. Alternatively, if you see one person trying to dominate or control the others, your need for power probably is dominant.

The TAT is a *projective* instrument because the story writer projects his or her own motives onto the figures in the picture. (Although the TAT is the dominant method used to measure the achievement motive, evidence reveals

---

[14] Henry A. Murray, *Explorations in Personality* (New York: John Wiley & Sons, 1938), p. 164.

■ **FIGURE 5-6**   A Thematic Apperception Test (TAT)

What is happening in this picture?

that it does not provide reliable evaluations of individuals' need states. Researchers thus have developed alternative techniques for measuring achievement needs.[15]) McClelland's next major accomplishment was to examine the relationship between achievement motives and economic development.

Achievement Motivation and Economic Development.   According to McClelland, achievement motivation ties directly to the economic development of entire societies. Figure 5–7 shows the theoretical framework underlying this relationship. The core of this theory involves the relationship between parental values and child-rearing practices. McClelland's theory holds that parents with

---

[15] Alternative techniques for measuring achievement needs can be found in Aharon Tziner and Dov Elizur, "Achievement Motive: A Reconceptualization and New Instrument," *Journal of Occupational Behavior,* July 1985, pp. 209–28; and Michael J. Stahl and Adrian M. Harrell, "Evolution and Validation of a Behavioral Decision Theory Measurement Approach to Achievement, Power, and Affiliation," *Journal of Applied Psychology,* December 1982, pp. 744–51.

■ **FIGURE 5–7** Need for Achievement Influences Economic Development

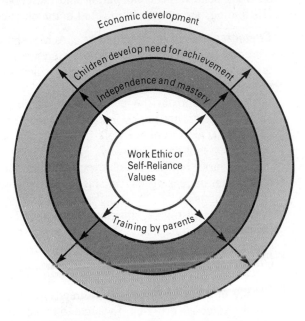

SOURCE: Adapted from David C. McClelland, *The Achieving Society* (New York: Free Press, 1961).

a strong work ethic instill independence and a need for mastery in their children. In turn, this training is thought to produce increased achievement motivation, and subsequently economic development. Thomas A. Vanderslice, who took over the reins of Apollo Computer Inc. after successful stints with industry giants General Electric and GTE Corp., exemplifies the link between achievement motivation and parental influence:

> Although his high-tech credits are superb—Vanderslice, 53, holds PhDs in both chemistry and physics—he [has] a reputation as a stern taskmaster and a temperamental executive. "He's very deliberate and results-oriented," says management consultant Walter R. Mahler. "If anyone around him is not a top-notch performer, they'll be gone soon. . . ."
>
> Some of Vanderslice's stiffness may be due to his intensely competitive upbringing. "If one of the Vanderslice boys came home with a B on his report card, their father would threaten to take them out of school," Mahler says. "They were one-upping each other all the time, and he's still doing that to his peers."[16]

To test his theory, McClelland examined the relationship between achievement motivation and economic development from the time of ancient Greece through the 1950s. Achievement motivation for past civilizations was assessed by evaluating the amount of achievement imagery contained in written docu-

---

[16] Alex Beam and Marc Frons, "How Tom Vanderslice Is Forcing Apollo Computer to Grow Up," *Business Week,* March 25, 1985, pp. 96, 98.

ments from relevant time periods. McClelland documented a positive correlation between achievement motivation and the economic rise and fall of societies. His findings are examined in detail in the classic book *The Achieving Society*.[17]

Characteristics of High Achievers.

Achievement-motivated people share three common characteristics. One is a preference for working on tasks of *moderate* difficulty. For example, when high achievers are asked to stand wherever they like while tossing rings at a peg on the floor, they tend to stand about 10 to 20 feet from the peg. This distance presents the ring tosser with a challenging but not impossible task. People with a low need for achievement, in contrast, tend to either walk up to the peg and drop the rings on or gamble on a lucky shot from far away. The high achiever's preference for moderately difficult tasks reinforces achievement behavior by reducing the frequency of failure and increasing the satisfaction associated with successfully completing challenging tasks.

Achievers also like situations in which their performance is due to their own efforts rather than to other factors, such as luck. The founder of the company that bears his name, Booth Organization Inc., demonstrates this characteristic. In explaining why he left IBM to start his own company, Barclay Booth told *The Wall Street Journal*, "I wanted to call the shots. I wanted to see my efforts contribute more directly to my own rewards. . . . Instead of making someone else rich, I wanted to make myself rich."[18] A third identifying characteristic of high achievers is that they desire more feedback on their successes and failures than do low achievers. Given these characteristics, McClelland proposes that high achievers, like Mr. Booth, are more likely to be successful entrepreneurs.

Motives and Managerial Success.

In his book *Power: The Inner Experience*, McClelland argues that individuals with high achievement motivation are not best suited for top-level executive positions. Rather, he proposes that top managers should have a high to moderate need for power coupled with a low need for affiliation.[19] Several studies support these propositions. One study compared motives for 161 scientists and engineers, 149 Air Force graduate students, and 94 executives. Results indicated the executive group possessed the highest need for power, while the other two samples were high on achievement motivation.[20] In another study, McClelland tracked the managerial success of

---

[17] See David C. McClelland, *The Achieving Society* (New York: Free Press, 1961).

[18] Ellen Graham, "The Entrepreneurial Mystique," *The Wall Street Journal*, May 20, 1985, p. 4c.

[19] See David C. McClelland, *Power: The Inner Experience* (New York: John Wiley & Sons, 1975).

[20] This study was part of the following series of research reports: Adrian M. Harrell and Michael J. Stahl, "A Behavioral Decision Theory Approach for Measuring McClelland's Trichotomy of Needs," *Journal of Applied Psychology*, April 1981, pp. 242–47; Michael J. Stahl and Adrian M. Harrell, "Evolution and Validation of a Behavioral Decision Theory Measurement Approach to Achievement, Power, and Affiliation," *Journal of Applied Psychology*, December 1982, pp. 744–51; and Michael J. Stahl, "Achievement, Power and Managerial Motivation: Selecting Managerial Talent with the Job Choice Exercise," *Personnel Psychology*, Winter 1983, pp. 775–89.

246 entry-level managers at American Telephone & Telegraph Co. over a 16-year period. Findings demonstrated that high power and low affiliation needs were associated with management success for nontechnical managers. In addition, McClelland found the need for achievement was associated with managerial success among lower-level managers.[21]

Managerial Implications.   Given that adults can be trained to increase their achievement motivations,[22] organizations should consider the benefits of providing achievement training for employees. Moreover, achievement, affiliation, and power needs can be considered during the selection process, for better placement. For example, in light of the research discussed above, recruiters might want to look for high power motivation when hiring top-level executives. On the other hand, a high need for achievement would be a good staffing prerequisite for lower- and middle-level managers. Finally, managers should create challenging task assignments or goals because challenge arouses the need for achievement.[23] Fred Carr, chairman of First Executive Corporation, endorsed this recommendation when interviewed by *The Wall Street Journal*. Mr. Carr concluded: " 'If you can motivate people to be happy, that's great. But I don't think you can do it all the time.' He believes 'continuous challenge' is how you get the most from workers.' '[24] Challenge can be created by setting difficult goals, providing a more autonomous work environment, and delegating.

■ HERZBERG'S MOTIVATOR-HYGIENE THEORY OF JOB SATISFACTION

Frederick Herzberg, a widely known behavioral scientist, developed the motivator-hygiene theory during the late 1950s.[25] Based on his studies of the relationship between job attitudes and work performance, Herzberg proposed that motivation is a direct offshoot of job satisfaction. This satisfaction → motivation linkage has supporters and detractors. Still, Herzberg's theory provides valuable insights about work motivation.

---

[21] See David C. McClelland and Richard E. Boyatzis, "Leadership Motive Pattern and Long-Term Success in Management," *Journal of Applied Psychology*, December 1982, pp. 737–43. These results were also supported by Edwin T. Cornelius III and Frank B. Lane, "The Power Motive and Managerial Success in a Professionally Oriented Service Industry Organization," *Journal of Applied Psychology*, February 1984, pp. 32–39.

[22] For a review of the foundation of achievement motivation training, see David C. McClelland, "Toward a Theory of Motive Acquisition," *American Psychologist*, May 1965, pp. 321–33. Evidence for the validity of motivation training can be found in Heinz Heckhausen and Siegbert Krug, "Motive Modification," in *Motivation and Society*, ed. Abigail J. Stewart (San Francisco: Jossey-Bass, 1982).

[23] Supporting evidence is contained in Sharon Rae Jenkins, "Need for Achievement and Women's Careers Over 14 Years: Evidence for Occupational Structure Effects," *Journal of Personality and Social Psychology*, November 1987, pp. 922–32; and Robert J. House and Jitendra V. Singh, "Organizational Behavior: Some New Directions for I/O Psychology," in *Annual Review of Psychology*, ed. Mark Rosenzweig and Lyman W. Porter (Palo Alto, Calif.: Annual Reviews, 1987).

[24] "Labor Letter: A Special News Report on People and Their Jobs in Offices, Fields and Factories," *The Wall Street Journal*, December 29, 1987, p. 1.

[25] See Frederick Herzberg, Bernard Mausner, and Barbara B. Snyderman, *The Motivation to Work* (New York: John Wiley & Sons, 1959).

Motivators versus Hygiene Factors

In his landmark study, Herzberg and his colleagues interviewed a total of 203 accountants and engineers. These interviews sought to determine the factors responsible for job satisfaction and dissatisfaction. Using a methodology called the critical incident technique, Herzberg's team asked respondents to think of an occasion in which they felt especially good about their jobs. Detailed descriptions were recorded. An opposite line of questioning was then initiated. During the second round of questioning, the respondents were asked to describe an incident in which they felt especially negative about their jobs. Detailed descriptions again were recorded. Herzberg and his colleagues then examined these critical incidents for consistencies relative to satisfaction and dissatisfaction. As an initial step, all the critical incident descriptions were classified according to 14 job-attitude factors:

- Recognition.
- Achievement.
- Possibility of growth.
- Advancement.
- Salary.
- Interpersonal relations with superiors, subordinates, or peers.
- Technical supervision.
- Responsibility.
- Company policies and administration.
- Working conditions.
- The work itself.
- Factors in personal life.
- Status.
- Job security.

Herzberg found separate and distinct clusters of factors associated with job satisfaction and dissatisfaction. Job satisfaction was more frequently associated with achievement, recognition, characteristics of the work, responsibility, and advancement. These factors were all related to outcomes associated with the *content* of the task being performed. Herzberg labeled these factors **motivators** because each was associated with strong effort and good performance. He hypothesized that motivators cause a person to move from a state of no satisfaction to satisfaction (see Figure 5–8). Therefore, Herzberg's theory predicts managers can motivate individuals by incorporating his ''motivators'' into an individual's job, a process called job enrichment.

Herzberg found job *dissatisfaction* to be associated primarily with factors in the work *context* or environment. Specifically, company policy and administration, technical supervision, salary, interpersonal relations with one's supervisor, and working conditions were most frequently mentioned by employees expressing job dissatisfaction. Herzberg labeled this second cluster of factors **hygiene factors.** He further proposed that they were not motivational. At best, according to Herzberg's interpretation, an individual will experience no

■ **FIGURE 5–8** Herzberg's Motivator-Hygiene Model

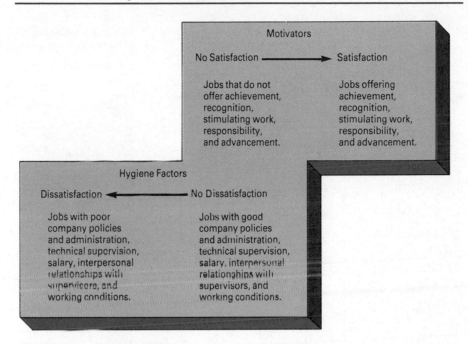

SOURCE: Adapted in part from David A. Whitsett and Erik K. Winslow, "An Analysis of Studies Critical of the Motivator-Hygiene Theory," *Personnel Psychology*, Winter 1967, pp. 391–415.

job dissatisfaction when he or she has no grievances about hygiene factors (refer to Figure 5–8).[26]

A Zero Midpoint.   The key to adequately understanding Herzberg's motivator-hygiene theory is recognizing that he does not place dissatisfaction and satisfaction on opposite ends of a single, unbroken continuum. Instead, he believes there is a zero midpoint between dissatisfaction and satisfaction. Conceivably, an organization member who has good supervision, pay, and working conditions but a tedious and unchallenging task with little chance of advancement would be at the zero midpoint. That person would have no dissatisfaction (because of good hygiene factors) and no satisfaction (because of a lack of motivators). Consequently, Herzberg warns managers that it takes more than good pay and good working conditions to motivate today's employees. It takes an "enriched job" that offers the individual opportunity for achievement and recognition, stimulation, responsibility, and advancement.

Research on the Motivator-Hygiene Theory.   Herzberg's theory generated a great deal of research and controversy. Figure 5–9 presents results obtained by Herzberg after using the critical incident technique with 1,685 workers

---

[26] Ibid.

■ **FIGURE 5–9** A Summary of Factors Affecting Job Satisfaction and Dissatisfaction

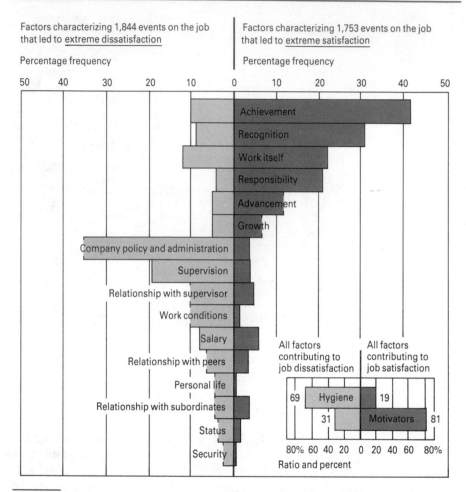

employed in 12 organizations. This study generally supported Herzberg's theory. Accordingly, motivators were associated with job satisfaction 81 percent of the time. The most frequently mentioned sources of job satisfaction were achievement, recognition, and the work itself. Hygiene factors, on the other hand, were cited as causes of job dissatisfaction 69 percent of the time. Company policy and administration was followed by supervision as the most frequently cited sources of job dissatisfaction. But these results have come under fire by other OB researchers.

The most damaging criticism is that Herzberg's neat distinction between hygiene factors and motivators may be an artifact of the critical incident technique. In other words, the critical incident technique may bias the data in such a way that Herzberg's theory becomes a self-fulfilling prophecy. Moreover, one researcher detected a self-serving bias on the part of Herzberg's subjects:

> It is still possible that obtained differences between stated sources of satisfaction and dissatisfaction stem from defensive processes within the individual respondent. Persons may be more likely to attribute the causes of satisfaction to their own achievements and accomplishments on the job. On the other hand, they may be more likely to attribute their dissatisfaction, not to personal inadequacies or deficiencies, but to factors in the work environment; i.e., obstacles presented by company policies or supervision.[27]

This criticism appears to be valid because research using the critical incident technique supports Herzberg's theory, while other studies using different methods do not.

Herzberg's research also has been criticized on the grounds there are sizable overlaps between the hygiene factors and motivators. For example, as illustrated in Figure 5–9, the work itself, a motivator, caused *dissatisfaction* in a significant number of cases. Salary, a hygiene factor, was associated with extreme *satisfaction* nearly as often as it was with dissatisfaction. In addition, the validity of Herzberg's job-attitude categorization system has been questioned.[28] Pro-Herzberg researchers respond by saying nonsupportive studies were conducted improperly.[29] A motivation scholar attempted to sort out the Herzberg controversy by concluding:

> In balance, when we combine all of the evidence with all of the allegations that the theory has been misinterpreted, and that its major concepts have not been assessed properly, one is left, more than twenty years later, not really knowing whether to take the theory seriously, let alone whether it should be put into practice in organizational settings. . . . There is support for many of the implications the theory has for enriching jobs to make them more motivating. But the two-factor aspect of the theory—the feature that makes it unique—is not really a necessary element in the use of the theory for designing jobs, per se.[30]

Implications for Managers.   As indicated in the foregoing conclusion, managers can attempt to increase work motivation by designing Herzberg's motivators into the job. This can be done by providing employees with the opportunity to experience achievement, recognition, stimulating work, responsibility, and

---

[27] Victor H. Vroom, *Work and Motivation* (New York: John Wiley & Sons, 1964), p. 129.

[28] For reviews of the criticisms of motivator-hygiene theory, see Robert J. House and Lawrence A. Wigdor, "Herzberg's Dual-Factor Theory of Job Satisfaction and Motivation: A Review of the Evidence and a Criticism," *Personnel Psychology,* Winter 1967, pp 369–89; and Nathan King, "Clarification and Evaluation of the Two-Factor Theory of Job Satisfaction," *Psychological Bulletin,* July 1970, pp. 18–31.

[29] Reviews supporting the motivator-hygiene theory may be found in David A. Whitsett and Erik K. Winslow, "An Analysis of Studies Critical of the Motivator-Hygiene Theory," *Personnel Psychology,* Winter 1967, pp. 391–415; and Ben Grigaliunas and Yoash Wiener, "Has the Research Challenge to Motivation-Hygiene Theory Been Conclusive? An Analysis of Critical Studies," *Human Relations,* December 1974, pp. 839–71.

[30] Pinder, *Work Motivation: Theory, Issues, and Applications,* p. 28.

advancement. A prime example of this sort of job enrichment is the customer satisfaction program established through joint labor-management cooperation at the General Motors Fiero plant in Pontiac, Michigan. According to a *Business Week* report at the time:

> Under the program 50 workers each follow five Fiero buyers for a year, surveying them with phone calls every three months. Workers on the assembly line, such as John Hughes, who installs trim, make the calls on their own time, usually from home, and Pontiac pays the phone bill. The information they glean is fed back to the plant—to line operators and to departments where the problems may have originated. It is also sent to service experts who educate dealers about repairs.[31]

Unfortunately, this progressive program was not enough to save the Fiero, which was discontinued in 1988 because of sagging sales. Additional job enrichment and redesign techniques are discussed in Chapter 15.

■ UNRAVELING THE CONTROVERSY SURROUNDING JOB SATISFACTION

Job satisfaction is one of the most frequently studied variables in OB. One researcher estimated there were 3,350 articles written on the subject between 1957 and 1976.[32] Hundreds more have appeared since. A good measure of this preoccupation with job satisfaction stems from Herzberg's motivator-hygiene theory. As just discussed, Herzberg's theory assumes there is a causal linkage from job satisfaction to motivation, and ultimately to job performance. This suggests that the best way to increase performance is to improve job satisfaction. Unfortunately, subsequent research has found the job satisfaction → performance relationship to be less than clear-cut. Consequently, we need to sort out the various causes and consequences of job satisfaction.

The Causes of Job Satisfaction

Job satisfaction was defined in Chapter 2 as an affective or emotional response toward various facets of one's job. This definition means job satisfaction is not a unitary concept. Rather, a person can be relatively satisfied with one aspect of his or her job and dissatisfied with one or more other aspects. For example, researchers at Cornell University developed the Job Descriptive Index (JDI) to assess one's satisfaction with the following job dimensions: work, pay, promotions, co-workers, and supervision.[33] Taking a more analytical ap-

---

[31] "A GM Plant with a Hot Line between Workers and Buyers," *Business Week,* June 11, 1984, p. 165.

[32] See Edwin A. Locke, "The Nature and Causes of Job Satisfaction," in *Handbook of Industrial and Organizational Psychology,* ed. Marvin D. Dunnette (Skokie, Ill.: Rand McNally, 1976).

[33] For a review of the development of the JDI, see Patricia C. Smith, L. M. Kendall, and Charles L. Hulin, *The Measurement of Satisfaction in Work and Retirement* (Skokie, Ill.: Rand McNally, 1969).

■ **TABLE 5–5** How Satisfied Are You with Your Present Job?

1. The way I am noticed when I do a good job	Very dissatisfied	1	2	3	4	5	Very satisfied
2. The way I get full credit for the work I do	Very dissatisfied	1	2	3	4	5	Very satisfied
3. The recognition I get for the work I do	Very dissatisfied	1	2	3	4	5	Very satisfied
4. The way they usually tell me when I do my job well	Very dissatisfied	1	2	3	4	5	Very satisfied
5. The praise I get for doing a good job	Very dissatisfied	1	2	3	4	5	Very satisfied
6. The amount of pay for the work I do	Very dissatisfied	1	2	3	4	5	Very satisfied
7. The chance to make as much money as my friends	Very dissatisfied	1	2	3	4	5	Very satisfied
8. How my pay compares with that for similar jobs in other companies	Very dissatisfied	1	2	3	4	5	Very satisfied
9. My pay and the amount of work I do	Very dissatisfied	1	2	3	4	5	Very satisfied
10. How my pay compares with that of other workers	Very dissatisfied	1	2	3	4	5	Very satisfied

Total score for satisfaction with recognition (add questions 1–5) and compensation (add questions 6–10).

SOURCE: Adapted from David J. Weiss, Rene V. Dawis, George W. England, and Lloyd H. Lofquist, *Manual for the Minnesota Satisfaction Questionnaire* (Minneapolis: Industrial Relations Center, University of Minnesota, 1967). Used with permission.

proach, researchers at the University of Minnesota concluded there are 20 different dimensions underlying job satisfaction. Selected Minnesota Satisfaction Questionnaire (MSQ) items measuring satisfaction with recognition and compensation are listed in Table 5–5. Please take a moment now to determine how satisfied you are with these two aspects of your present or most recent job. (Comparative norms for each dimension of job satisfaction are: total score of 5–10 = Low job satisfaction; 11–19 = Moderate satisfaction; 20 and above = High satisfaction.)[34] How do you feel about your job?

Four predominant models of job satisfaction specify its causes. They are need fulfillment, discrepancy, value attainment, and equity. A brief review of these models will provide insight into the complexity of this seemingly simple concept.

Need Fulfillment. These models propose that satisfaction is determined by the extent to which the characteristics of a job allow an individual to fulfill his or her needs. Although these models have intuitive appeal, they have been sharply criticized. As two management experts noted:

> The need-satisfaction model must be seriously reexamined, and does not warrant the unquestioning acceptance it has attained in organizational psychology literature. . . . The principal concepts of the model—needs and job characteristics— are both open to serious questioning and to alternative interpretations. The calculus relating needs to job satisfaction, through the mechanism of job characteristics, has not been well specified.[35]

---

[34] For norms on the MSQ, see David J. Weiss, Rene V. Dawis, George W. England, and Lloyd H. Lofquist, *Manual for the Minnesota Satisfaction Questionnaire* (Minneapolis: Industrial Relations Center, University of Minnesota, 1967).

[35] Gerald R. Salancik and Jeffrey Pfeffer, "An Examination of Need-Satisfaction Models of Job Attitudes," *Administrative Science Quarterly*, September 1977, p. 453.

Discrepancies.   These models propose that satisfaction is a result of met expectations. **Met expectations** represent the difference between what an individual expects to receive from a job, like good pay and promotional opportunities, and what he or she actually receives. When expectations are greater than what is received, a person will be dissatisfied. In contrast, this model predicts the individual will be satisfied when he or she obtains outcomes above and beyond expectations. Support for this theoretical position is rather weak.[36]

Value Attainment.   The idea underlying **value attainment** is that satisfaction results from the perception that a job allows for fulfillment of an individual's important work values.[37] In general, research consistently supports the prediction that value fulfillment is positively related to job satisfaction. However, results from one study indicate that fulfillment of important values leads to satisfaction only in certain situations.[38] Therefore, managers do not have to concentrate solely on satisfying an employee's most important values. Gains in satisfaction can be obtained by providing workers with outcomes of lesser value.

Equity.   In this model, satisfaction is a function of how "fairly" an individual is treated at work. Satisfaction results from one's perception that work outcomes, relative to inputs, compare favorably with a significant other's outcomes/inputs. Chapter 6 explores this promising model in detail.

The Consequences of Job Satisfaction

This area has significant managerial implications. As previously mentioned, thousands of studies have examined the relationship between job satisfaction and other organizational variables. Since it is impossible to examine them all, we will consider a subset of the more important variables, from the standpoint of managerial relevance (see Table 5–6).

Absenteeism.   Absenteeism is costly and managers are constantly on the lookout for ways to reduce it. One recommendation has been to increase job satisfaction. If this is a valid recommendation, there should be a strong negative relationship (or negative correlation) between satisfaction and absenteeism. In other words, as satisfaction increases, absenteeism should decrease. Two researchers recently tracked this prediction across 62,308 individuals who participated in a total of 31 studies. The results revealed a very weak negative

---

[36] See Clifford Mottaz and Glenn Potts, "An Empirical Evaluation of Models of Work Satisfaction," *Social Science Research,* June 1986, pp. 153–73.

[37] A complete description of this model is provided by E. A. Locke, "Job Satisfaction," in *Social Psychology and Organizational Behavior,* ed. Michael Gruneberg and Toby Wall (New York: John Wiley & Sons, 1984).

[38] For a test of the value fulfillment model, see John K. Butler, Jr., "Value Importance as a Moderator of the Value Fulfillment—Job Satisfaction Relationship: Group Differences," *Journal of Applied Psychology,* August 1983, pp. 420–28. For a review of earlier research, see Locke, "The Nature and Causes of Job Satisfaction."

■ **TABLE 5–6** Correlates of Job Satisfaction

Variable Related with Satisfaction	Direction of Relationship	Strength of Relationship
Absenteeism	Negative	Weak
Lateness	Negative	Weak
Turnover	Negative	Moderate
Heart disease	Negative	Moderate
Stress	Negative	Moderate
Pro-union voting	Negative	Moderate
Job performance	Positive	Weak
Life satisfaction	Positive	Moderate
Mental health	Positive	Moderate

relationship between satisfaction and absenteeism.[39] It is unlikely, therefore, that managers will realize any significant decrease in absenteeism by increasing job satisfaction.

Turnover.   Turnover is important to managers because it both disrupts organizational continuity and is very costly. For example, a 1977 study of bank tellers indicated turnover cost the bank $23,404.44 per month, or $208,853.28 per year.[40] These costs would be higher today. A meta-analysis of 28 studies demonstrated a moderate negative relationship between satisfaction and turnover.[41] (See Table 5–6.) Given the strength of this relationship, managers would be well advised to try to reduce turnover by increasing employee job satisfaction.

Job Performance.   One of the biggest controversies within organizational research revolves around the relationship between satisfaction and job performance. Some, such as Herzberg, argue that satisfaction leads to higher performance, while others contend that high performance leads to satisfaction. In an attempt to resolve this controversy, a recent meta-analysis accumulated results from 74 studies. Overall, the relationship between job satisfaction and job performance was examined for 12,192 people. It was discovered that satisfaction and performance were only slightly related.[42] This suggests managers

[39] See Rick D. Hackett and Robert M. Guion, "A Reevaluation of the Absenteeism-Job Satisfaction Relationship," *Organizational Behavior and Human Decision Processes,* June 1985, pp. 340–81.

[40] The costs of turnover were assessed by Philip H. Mirvis and Edward E. Lawler III, "Measuring the Financial Impact of Employee Attitudes," *Journal of Applied Psychology,* February 1977, pp. 1–8.

[41] Results are presented in John L. Cotton and Jeffrey M. Tuttle, "Employee Turnover: A Meta-Analysis and Review with Implications for Research," *Academy of Management Review,* January 1986, pp. 55–70.

[42] The relationship between performance and satisfaction was reviewed by Michelle T. Iaffaldano and Paul M. Muchinsky, "Job Satisfaction and Job Performance: A Meta-Analysis," *Psychological Bulletin,* March 1985, pp. 251–73.

are unlikely to enjoy substantial increases in job performance as a result of enhancing job satisfaction.

Pro-Union Voting.   Results from 11 studies revealed a significant negative correlation between job satisfaction and pro-union voting.[43] In other words, people tend to vote for unions when they are dissatisfied with their jobs. Union organizers have taken advantage of this reality for decades. This suggests organizations may want to monitor employee satisfaction if they desire to maintain a nonunionized status.

Broader Implications.   In a general sense, job satisfaction has important implications because it affects an individual's quality of work life. The term *quality of work life* refers to the overall quality of an individual's experiences at work. As suggested by research results listed in Table 5–6, job dissatisfaction is associated with increased heart disease, increased stress, and poor mental health.[44] It is hoped enlightened managers will develop an interest in reducing these negative work-related outcomes by improving job satisfaction.

SUMMARY OF KEY CONCEPTS

    A. *Motivation* is defined as those psychological processes that cause the arousal, direction, and persistence of voluntary, goal-oriented actions. The biological concept of homeostasis is used to explain how the basic motivational process works.

    B. Historically, motivation theory has evolved from hedonism to instincts, needs, rewards, cognitions, and job characteristics. *Content* theories of motivation focus on internal energizers of behavior such as instincts, needs, and satisfaction. *Process* motivation theories, which deal in terms of rewards, cognitions, and job characteristics, focus on more complex person-environment interactions.

    C. There is no single, universally accepted theory of motivation. Each alternative theory holds important managerial lessons. Managers need to pick and choose ideas from the various motivation theories as the situation dictates. When attempting to understand and manage job performance, motivation is a necessary but insufficient factor.

    D. Three well-known need theories of motivation are Maslow's need hierarchy

---

[43] For an overall review of the satisfaction–pro-union voting relationship, see Herbert G. Heneman III and Marcus H. Sandver, "Predicting the Outcome of Union Certification Elections: A Review of the Literature," *Industrial and Labor Relations Review,* July 1983, pp. 537–59. Two recent studies were conducted by Mary D. Zalesny, "Comparison of Economic and Noneconomic Factors in Predicting Faculty Vote Preference in a Union Representation Election," *Journal of Applied Psychology,* May 1985, pp. 243–56; and Thomas A. DeCotiis and Jean-Yves LeLouarn, "A Predictive Study of Voting Behavior in a Representation Election Using Union Instrumentality and Work Perceptions," *Organizational Behavior and Human Performance,* February 1981, pp. 103–18.

[44] See John M. Ivancevich and Michael T. Matteson, *Stress and Work: A Managerial Perspective* (Glenview, Ill.: Scott, Foresman, 1980). For a review of the causes of heart disease, see C. David Jenkins, "Psychologic and Social Precursors of Coronary Disease," *The New England Journal of Medicine,* February 1971, pp. 307–16.

theory, Alderfer's ERG theory, and McClelland's need for achievement theory. Maslow's notion of a prepotent or stairstep hierarchy of five levels of needs has not stood up well under research. Unlike Maslow, Alderfer's ERG theory proposes that failure to achieve a higher-level need may motivate one to seek lower-level need satisfaction. McClelland believes the need for achievement can be developed in cultures that desire a healthy economy. High achievers prefer moderate risks and situations where they can control their own destiny.

E.   Herzberg believes job satisfaction motivates better job performance. His *hygiene* factors, such as policies, supervision, and salary, erase sources of dissatisfaction. On the other hand, his *motivators,* such as achievement, responsibility, and recognition, foster job satisfaction. Although Herzberg's motivator-hygiene theory of job satisfaction has been criticized on methodological grounds, it has practical significance for job enrichment.

F.   Owing to Herzberg's work, the satisfaction-performance relationship has stirred much controversy in OB circles. Actually, job satisfaction has a complex web of causes and consequences. The correlation between job satisfaction and turnover, heart disease, stress, and pro-union voting is moderately negative. A moderately positive relationship has been found between job satisfaction and life satisfaction and mental health.

KEY TERMS

motivation	relatedness needs
homeostasis	growth needs
hedonism	need for achievement
content theories	motivators
process theories	hygiene factors
needs	met expectations
existence needs	value attainment

DISCUSSION QUESTIONS

1.   Why should the average manager be well versed in the various motivation theories?
2.   From a practical standpoint, what is a major drawback of the content theories of motivation?
3.   Despite weak research support, why is Maslow's theory still valuable?
4.   What role does frustration play in Alderfer's ERG theory?
5.   Has Alderfer improved on Maslow? Explain.
6.   Are you a high achiever? How can you tell? How will this help or hinder your path to top management?
7.   How have hygiene factors and motivators affected your job satisfaction and performance?

8.   How could your present (or past) job be enriched?

9.   Do you think job satisfaction leads directly to better job performance? Explain.

10.   What are the three most valuable lessons about employee motivation that you have learned from this chapter?

BACK TO THE OPENING CASE

Now that you have read Chapter 5, you should be able to answer the following questions about the Disney case:

1.   Using Maslow's need hierarchy theory as a point of reference, what is likely to happen to the motivation of someone who works full-time as one of the characters in Disney's Magic Kingdom for more than a couple of years?

2.   How would Herzberg interpret Goofy's complaints and comment about his job being "an incredible turn-on"?

3.   If you were a Disney manager, how would you put lessons from this chapter to work motivating the character players?

4.   What does this case seem to say about the satisfaction-performance connection?

EXERCISE 5

Objectives

1. To determine how accurately you perceive the needs of nonmanagerial employees.
2. To examine the managerial implications of inaccurately assessing employee needs.

Introduction

One thousand employees were given a list of 10 outcomes people want from their work. They were asked to rank these items from most important to least important.[45] We are going to have you estimate how you think these workers ranked the various outcomes. This will enable you to compare your perceptions with the average rankings documented by a researcher. Since the results are presented at the end of this exercise, please do not read them until indicated.

---

[45] Results from this study are reported in Kenneth A. Kovach, "What Motivates Employees? Workers and Supervisors Give Different Answers," *Business Horizons,* September–October 1987, pp. 58–65.

Instructions

Below is a list of 10 outcomes people want from their work. Read the list and then rank each item according to how you think the typical nonmanagerial employee would rank them. Rank the outcomes from 1 to 10, 1 = Most important and 10 = Least important. (Please do this now before reading the rest of these instructions.) After you have completed your ranking, calculate the discrepancy between your perceptions and the actual results. Take the absolute value of the difference between your ranking and the actual ranking for each item and then add them to get a total discrepancy score. For example, if you gave job security a ranking of 1, your discrepancy score would be 3, because the actual ranking was 4. The lower your discrepancy score, the more accurate your perception of the typical employee's needs. The actual rankings are shown below under the heading *Survey Results*.

How do you believe the typical nonmanagerial employee would rank these outcomes?

———— Full appreciation of work done
———— Job security
———— Good working conditions
———— Feeling of being in on things
———— Good wages
———— Tactful discipline
———— Personal loyalty to employees
———— Interesting work
———— Sympathetic help with personal problems
———— Promotion and growth in the organization

Questions for Consideration/Class Discussion

1. Were your perceptions accurate? Why or why not?
2. What would the discrepancy model of satisfaction suggest you should do? How about the value attainment model?
3. Would you generalize the actual survey results to all nonmanagerial employees? Why or why not?

Survey Results

Employee Ranking

  1 Interesting work
  2 Full appreciation of work done
  3 Feeling of being in on things
  4 Job security
  5 Good wages
  6 Promotion and growth in the organization
  7 Good working conditions
  8 Personal loyalty to employees
  9 Tactful discipline
10 Sympathetic help with personal problems

Chapter **6**

Motivation through Equity, Expectancy, and Goal Setting

LEARNING OBJECTIVES

When you finish studying the material in this chapter,
you should be able to:

- Discuss the role of perceived inequity in employee motivation.
- Distinguish between positive and negative inequity.
- Define Vroom's concepts of expectancy, instrumentality, and valence.
- Discuss the practical implications of Vroom's expectancy theory of motivation.
- Explain how goal setting motivates the individual.
- Identify four practical lessons from goal-setting research.
- Specify issues that should be addressed before implementing a motivational program.

OPENING CASE 6

Nordstrom's Motivational Program Keeps the Customers Happy

In the low-margin, highly competitive world of department-store sales, Seattle-based Nordstrom has turned exacting standards of customer service into a billion-dollar annual business. The rapidly expanding chain, which has 45 stores in California, Washington, Oregon, Alaska, Montana, and Utah, has drilled its staff incessantly with the venerable dogma that the customer is always right. Results: the chain's sales, 73% derived from women's retailing, passed the $1 billion mark for the first time in 1985 and reached an estimated $1.6 billion for 1986. Sales per square foot of space, a basic retail performance yard stick, is about double the average for the industry.

A major ingredient in Nordstrom's success is the quality of the salesclerks. They are paid about 20% better than those of competitors, and they are well trained and encouraged to do almost anything within reason to satisfy customers. In Seattle, a store salesclerk personally ironed a customer's newly bought shirt so that it would look fresher for an upcoming meeting. Thomas Skidmore, vice president of a Los Angeles–area real estate brokerage, tells of bringing back a squeaky pair of year-old shoes to a local Nordstrom outlet, hoping merely for repairs. Instead, he got a new pair of shoes free.

Throughout the chain, the sales help strictly follow a dictum laid down by the company's president, James Nordstrom, 46: replace anything on demand, no matter how expensive, no questions asked. Although the policy is sometimes abused by shoppers (who may, for example, order a $500 dress, wear it once to a party, and then return it), it works well for Nordstrom. Says Skidmore: "I couldn't believe how nice they were being. I bought another pair of shoes on the spot."

Nordstrom was founded in Seattle in 1901 as a retail shoe store by a Swedish prospector, John Nordstrom, who had struck it rich in the Klondike. Now a publicly traded concern, the firm is still closely controlled by members of the founder's family and propelled by their hands-on style. Says Edward Weller, a senior analyst in the San Francisco office of the Montgomery Securities investment firm: "Nordstrom's motivates people, not just by paying them well but by congratulating them and encouraging them."

For Discussion

Considering that many people roundly criticize the quality of service in the United States today, what do you think is Nordstrom's "secret of success"? Explain.

SOURCE: Excerpted from George Russell, "Where the Customer Is Still King," February 2, 1987, pp. 56–57. Copyright 1987 Time Inc. All rights reserved. Reprinted by permission from *Time*.

■ Additional discussion questions linking this case with the following material appear at the end of this chapter.

In Chapter 5, we drew a distinction between content and process theories of motivation. Content theories focus on internal factors, such as unsatisfied needs that are said to subconsciously energize or motivate behavior, and process theories explain work motivation in terms of how people perceive and consciously respond to their environment. Keeping the content theories of motivation discussed in Chapter 5 in mind, let us turn our attention to cognitive process theories of work motivation.

The process theories of motivation presented in this chapter involve three distinct thought processes or cognitions. **Cognitions** represent ''any knowledge, opinion, or belief about the environment, about oneself, or about one's behavior.''[1] As shown in Figure 6–1, cognitions involving social comparisons, expectancies, and goal setting affect behavior differently. This chapter explores equity, expectancy, and goal-setting theories of motivation anchored to these three types of cognitions. Consistent with our goal of helping you apply what you have learned about OB, we conclude the chapter by highlighting the prerequisites of successful motivational programs.

■ ADAMS' EQUITY THEORY OF MOTIVATION

Defined generally, **equity theory** is a model of motivation that explains how people strive for *fairness* and *justice* in social exchanges or give-and-take relationships. Equity theory is based on the cognitive dissonance theory, developed by social psychologist Leon Festinger in the 1950s.[2]

According to Festinger's theory, people are motivated to maintain consistency between their cognitive beliefs and their behavior. Perceived inconsistencies

■ **FIGURE 6–1** Cognitions Enable People to Interpret and Respond Rationally to Their Surroundings

Stimulus ▶	Cognition ▶	Behavior
	Social Comparisons	
Kathi, a graduating business major, is offered a good job with the federal government.	*Cognition:* "My three best friends are all taking jobs in private industry because they say that's where the real growth opportunities are."	Kathi turns down the government job and schedules interviews with some large corporations.
	Expectancies	
Mary sees a poster announcing the deadline for graduate school applications.	*Cognition:* "I believe I could get good grades and that would help me land a high-paying job."	Mary completes an application for graduate school.
	Goal Setting	
Carlos is offered a challenging administrative position in a foreign country.	*Cognition:* "A foreign assignment would certainly help me achieve my goal of being a vice president by age 35."	Carlos accepts the foreign assignment.

---

[1] Leon Festinger, *A Theory of Cognitive Dissonance* (Stanford, Calif.: Stanford University Press, 1957), p. 3.

[2] Ibid.

■ **TABLE 6–1** A Matter of Equity

> Snow days can be harder on some workers than on others.
>
> When Hewlett-Packard Co. closed a facility in Paramus, N.J., because of heavy snow, salaried workers got regular pay for the missed time. But 200 hourly employees, mostly clerical workers, were told they had to work a Saturday or lose a vacation day. . . .
>
> Honeywell, Inc. says it docks hourly workers when it closes its doors. However, it assumes salaried personnel will make up for lost time, so they get regular pay. Taking another tack, Polaroid Corp. pays everyone kept from work by severe weather. "A manager wouldn't be docked, and its the same for hourly employees," a spokesman says.
>
> SOURCE: "Labor Letter: A Special News Report on People and Their Jobs in Offices, Fields, and Factories," *The Wall Street Journal*, February 10, 1987, p. 1.

create cognitive dissonance (or psychological discomfort), which in turn motivates corrective action.[3] For example, a cigarette smoker who sees a heavy-smoking relative die of lung cancer probably would be motivated to quit smoking if he or she attributes the death to smoking. Accordingly, when victimized by unfair social exchanges, our resulting cognitive dissonance prompts us to correct the situation. As an example, consider the snowed-in hourly employee at Hewlett-Packard, Honeywell, or Polaroid (see Table 6–1). Based on your perceptions of fair and equitable treatment, which company does the best job of building commitment and satisfaction among its hourly employees? Perceived inequity is a serious threat to job satisfaction and performance.

Psychologist J. Stacy Adams pioneered application of the equity principle to the workplace. Central to understanding Adams' equity theory of motivation is an awareness of key components of the individual-organization exchange relationship. This relationship is pivotal in the formation of employees' perceptions of equity and inequity.

The Individual-Organization Exchange Relationship

Adams points out that two primary components are involved in the employee-employer exchange, *inputs* and *outcomes*. An employee's inputs, for which he or she expects a just return, include education, experience, skills, and effort. On the outcome side of the exchange, the organization provides such things as pay, fringe benefits, and recognition. These outcomes vary widely, depending on one's organization and rank. For example, top managers at Adolph Coors Co. get company cars, club memberships, and financial planning, while executives at Georgia-Pacific Corp. get corner offices and access to

---

[3] For a review of research on dissonance theory, see Joel Cooper and Russell H. Fazio, "A New Look at Dissonance Theory," in *Advances in Experimental Social Psychology*, ed. Leonard Berkowitz (New York: Academic Press, 1984), Vol. 17. A recent test of dissonance theory was conducted by S. J. Kantola, G. J. Syme, and N. A. Campbell, "Cognitive Dissonance and Energy Conservation," *Journal of Applied Psychology*, August 1984, pp. 416–21.

■ **TABLE 6–2** Factors Considered When Making Equity Comparisons

Inputs	Outcomes
Time	Pay/bonuses
Education/training	Fringe benefits
Experience	Challenging assignments
Skills	Job security
Creativity	Career advancement/promotions
Seniority	Status symbols
Loyalty to organization	Pleasant/safe working environment
Age	Opportunity for personal growth/development
Personality traits	Supportive supervision
Effort expended	Recognition
Personal appearance	Participation in important decisions

SOURCE: Based in part on J. Stacy Adams, "Toward an Understanding of Inequity," *Journal of Abnormal and Social Psychology,* November 1963, pp. 422–36.

fancy dining rooms.[4] Potential on-the-job inputs and outcomes are listed in Table 6–2.

Let us briefly examine the perception of equity inputs and outcomes.

Inputs and Outcomes Must Be Recognizable and Relevant.

Equity perceptions are formulated on the basis of *recognizable* and *relevant* inputs and outcomes. For example, corner offices would likely be recognized as a potential outcome for executives at Georgia-Pacific Corp. because they know these offices are reserved for certain employees. Whether or not a recognizable input or outcome is perceived as important depends on its relevance. If an individual expects a just return for a particular input variable, such as education, that characteristic is relevant to the exchange and will be perceived as an input. If an outcome such as a corner office has no value to an individual, he or she will not consider it relevant to the exchange.

Input-Outcome Inconsistencies.

People often disagree about the relevance of specific inputs and outcomes. An employee with 25 years of service may believe seniority should be rewarded, whereas a new employee may not. Because of such inconsistencies, people may expect to receive outcomes for inputs viewed as irrelevant by the organization. For example, high achievers generally believe superior performance should be rewarded. However, equity analysis of industry pay practices suggests these pay-for-performance advocates may be disappointed, dissatisfied, and unmotivated during various phases of their careers. According to the vice president of the Work in America Institute:

In the vast majority of cases, employees get annual increases in salary with no relation to performance. . . .

In the government sector, salary increases are based on seniority, and in most

---

[4] Reported in "Labor Letter: A Special News Report on People and Their Jobs in Offices, Fields and Factories," *The Wall Street Journal,* August 10, 1985, p. 1.

■ **FIGURE 6–2**   A Basic Model of Equity Theory

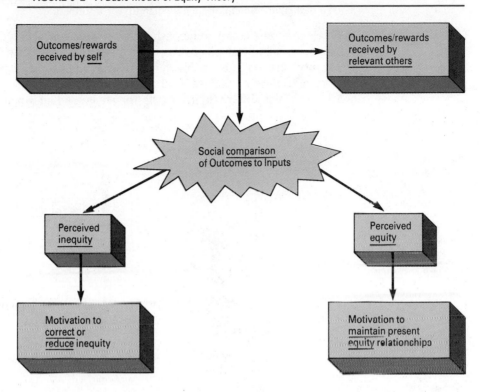

industrial and white-collar fields there is a standard annual increase. In the blue-collar sector, annual increases are based on union contracts.[5]

Fortunately, as discussed later, pay for performance is on the upswing.

Negative and Positive Inequity

On the job, feelings of inequity revolve around a person's evaluation of whether he or she receives adequate rewards to compensate for inputs. As shown in Figure 6–2, people perform these evaluations by comparing the perceived fairness of their employment exchange to that of relevant others. OB scholar Robert Vecchio identified three major categories of relevant others:

(1) *other* (including referent others inside and outside the organization, and referent others in similar or different jobs), (2) *self* (self-comparisons over time and against one's ideal ratio), and (3) *system* (based on exchanges between an individual and the organization). In addition to these categorizations, it should be noted that a group or even multiple groups can serve as referents. The selection

---

[5] "Paying for Performance: Does Salary Always Equal Productivity?" *Management World*, November 1982, p. 25.

of a specific referent is assumed to be a function of the attractiveness or relevance of a particular referent and the availability of information.[6]

Three different equity relationships are illustrated in Figure 6–3: equity, negative inequity, and positive inequity. Assume the two people in each of the equity relationships in Figure 6–3 have equivalent backgrounds (equal education, seniority, and so forth) and perform identical tasks. Only their hourly pay rates differ. Equity exists for an individual when his or her ratio

THE WALL STREET JOURNAL

"It's one of life's inequities, my boy . . . there's a *'Labor* Day,' but there's no *'Management* Day.'" (*Reprinted from* The Wall Street Journal; *permission Cartoon Features Syndicate.*)

of perceived outcomes to inputs is equal to the ratio of outcomes to inputs for a relevant co-worker (see part A in Figure 6–3). Since equity is based on comparing *ratios* of outcomes to inputs, inequity will not necessarily be perceived just because someone else receives greater rewards. If the other person's additional outcomes are due to his or her greater inputs, a sense of equity may still exist. However, if the comparison person enjoys greater outcomes for similar inputs, **negative inequity** will be perceived (see part B in Figure 6.3). On the other hand, a person will experience **positive inequity** when his or her outcome to input ratio is greater than that of a relevant co-worker (see part C in Figure 6–3).

---

[6] Robert P. Vecchio, "Models of Psychological Inequity," *Organizational Behavior and Human Performance*, October 1984, pp. 268–69. (Emphasis added.)

■ **FIGURE 6–3** Negative and Positive Inequity

A. An equitable situation

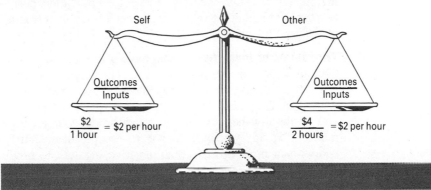

B. Negative inequity

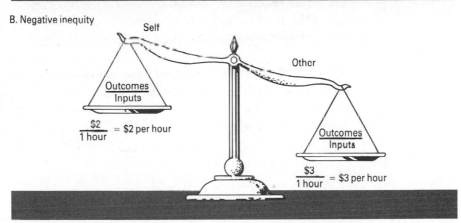

C. Positive inequity

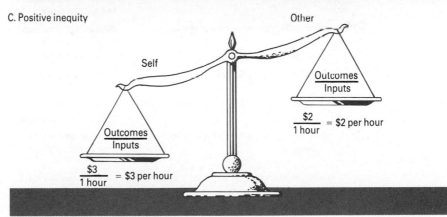

Dynamics of Perceived Inequity

Managers can derive practical benefits from Adams' equity theory by recognizing: (1) negative inequity is less tolerable than positive inequity, (2) the two types of inequity trigger different emotions, and (3) inequity can be reduced in a variety of ways.

Thresholds of Inequity. People have a lower tolerance for negative inequity than they do for positive inequity. Those who are shortchanged are more powerfully motivated to correct the situation than those who are excessively rewarded. For example, if you have ever been overworked and underpaid, you know how negative inequity can erode your job satisfaction and performance. Perhaps you quit the job to escape the negative inequity. Hence, it takes much more positive than negative inequity to produce the same degree of motivation.

Emotional Reactions to Inequity. Negative and positive inequity tend to produce different emotions. Anger often results when individuals believe they have received less than they deserve. Positive inequity tends to produce guilt.

Reducing Inequity. Table 6–3 lists eight possible ways to reduce inequity. It is important to note that equity can be restored by altering one's equity ratios behaviorally and/or cognitively. Equity theorists propose that the many possible combinations of behavioral and cognitive adjustments are influenced by the following tendencies:

1. An individual will attempt to maximize the amount of positive outcomes he or she receives.

■ **TABLE 6–3** Eight Ways to Reduce Inequity

Method	Examples
1. Person can increase his or her inputs.	Work harder; attend school or a specialized training program.
2. Person can decrease his or her inputs.	Don't work as hard; take longer breaks.
3. Person can attempt to increase his or her outcomes.	Ask for a raise; ask for a new title; seek outside intervention.
4. Person can decrease his or her outcomes.	Ask for less pay.
5. Leave the field.	Absenteeism and turnover.
6. Person can psychologically distort his or her inputs and outcomes.	Convince self that certain inputs are not important; convince self that he or she has a boring and monotonous job.
7. Person can psychologically distort the inputs or outcomes of comparison other.	Conclude that other has more experience or works harder; conclude that other has a more important title.
8. Change comparison other.	Pick a new comparison person; compare self to previous job.

SOURCE: Adapted from J. Stacy Adams, "Toward an Understanding of Inequity," *Journal of Abnormal and Social Psychology,* November 1963, pp. 422–36.

2. People resist increasing inputs when it requires substantial effort or costs.

3. People resist behavioral or cognitive changes in inputs important to their self-concept or self-esteem.

4. Rather than change cognitions about oneself, an individual is more likely to change cognitions about the comparison other's inputs and outcomes.

5. Leaving the field (quitting) is chosen only when severe inequity cannot be resolved through other methods.[7]

Equity Research Findings

The basic approach in equity research is to pay an experimental subject more (overpayment) or less (underpayment) than the standard rate for completing a task. People are paid on either an hourly or piece-rate basis. After subjects complete the task, the quantity and quality of production and attitudinal responses are measured. The following insights are based on numerous studies involving this procedure.

- Across 12 experimental conditions, *overpaid* subjects on a piece-rate system lowered the *quantity* of their performance 17 percent and increased the *quality* of their performance 26 percent. *Underpaid* subjects on a piece-rate system increased the *quantity* of their performance 34 percent while decreasing the *quality* of performance 12 percent.
- Subjects underpaid on an hourly basis tended to reduce inputs.
- Research evaluating the behavior of people overpaid on an hourly basis is inconclusive.
- People sometimes develop internal standards of equity in lieu of comparing themselves to a relevant other.
- There has been little research on the choice of method to reduce inequity.
- Perceived inequity tends to reduce satisfaction and increase interpersonal conflict.[8]

Although some of the studies responsible for these conclusions have been criticized for using poor experimental methods, recent research correcting these problems supports equity theory. Specifically, it has been found that: (1) individual tolerance for positive and negative inequity varies a great deal, (2) perceived

[7] Adapted from a discussion in Robert L. Opsahl and Marvin D. Dunnette, "The Role of Financial Compensation in Industrial Motivation," *Psychological Bulletin*, August 1966, pp. 94–118.

[8] The first conclusion is from Robert P. Vecchio, "Predicting Worker Performance in Inequitable Settings," *Academy of Management Review*, January 1982, pp. 103–10. For evidence pertaining to the remaining conclusions, see Michael R. Carrell and John E. Dittrich, "Equity Theory: The Recent Literature, Methodological Considerations, and New Directions," *Academy of Management Review*, April 1978, pp. 202–10; Paul S. Goodman and Abraham Friedman, "An Examination of Adams' Theory of Inequity," *Administrative Science Quarterly*, September 1971, pp. 271–88; and Victor D. Wall, Jr., and Linda L. Nolan, "Perceptions of Inequity, Satisfaction, and Conflict in Task-Oriented Groups," *Human Relations*, November 1986, pp. 1033–52.

■ **TABLE 6–4**   Equity Perceptions Vary from Culture to Culture

> The American manager who promised to be fair thought he was telling his Japanese staff that their hard work would be rewarded; but when some workers received higher salary increases than others, there were complaints. "You told us you'd be fair, and you lied to us," accused one salesman. "It took me a year and a half," sighed the American, "to realize that 'fair,' to my staff, meant being treated equally."
>
> SOURCE: Excerpted from Michael Berger, "Building Bridges over the Cultural Rivers," *International Management,* July–August 1987, p. 61.

pay equity correlates positively with job performance and organizational commitment, and (3) perceived inequity is a strong predictor of intention to quit.[9]

Practical Lessons from Equity Theory

Equity theory has at least three important practical implications. First, equity theory provides managers with yet another explanation of how beliefs and attitudes affect job performance (recall the discussion of attitudes and values in Chapter 3). According to this line of thinking, the best way to manage job behavior is to adequately understand underlying cognitive processes. Indeed, we are motivated powerfully to correct the situation when our ideas of fairness and justice are offended.

Second, research on equity theory emphasizes the need for managers to pay attention to employees' perceptions of what is fair and equitable. No matter how fair management thinks the organization's policies, procedures, and reward system are, each employee's *perceptions* of the equity of those factors are what count. For example, as described in Table 6–4, an American employee may interpret the word *fair* to mean equitable treatment, whereas a Japanese employee thinks it means *equal* treatment. Cross-cultural training can help managers be more sensitive to equity perceptions in multinational situations.

Equity perceptions can be monitored through informal conversations, interviews, or attitude surveys. Please take a moment now to complete the brief equity/fairness questionnaire in Table 6–5. If you perceive your work organization as unfair, you probably are dissatisfied and have contemplated quitting.

[9] See Richard C. Huseman, John D. Hatfield, and Edward W. Miles, "A New Perspective on Equity Theory: The Equity Sensitivity Construct," *Academy of Management Review,* April 1987, pp. 222–34; Richard W. Scholl, Elizabeth A. Cooper, and Jack F. McKenna, "Referent Selection in Determining Equity Perceptions: Differential Effects on Behavioral and Attitudinal Outcomes," *Personnel Psychology,* Spring 1987, pp. 11–24; and James E. Martin and Melanie M. Peterson, "Two-Tier Wage Structures: Implications for Equity Theory," *Academy of Management Journal,* June 1987, pp. 297–315.

■ **TABLE 6–5**   Measuring Perceived Organizational Equity/Fairness

Instructions: Evaluate your present (or most recent) job according to the following five dimensions.

Dimensions	Item	Score
		False True
1. Pay rules	The rules for granting pay raises in my organization are fair.	1—2—3—4—5—6—7
2. Pay administration	My supervisor rates everyone fairly when considering them for promotion.	1—2—3—4—5—6—7
3. Pay level	My employer pays me more for my work than I would receive from other organizations in this area.	1—2—3—4—5—6—7
4. Work pace	My supervisor makes everyone meet their performance standards.	1—2—3—4—5—6—7
5. Rule administration	My supervisor makes everyone come to work on time and adhere to the same rules of conduct.	1—2—3—4—5—6—7

Total score = _____

Norms

Very fair organization = 26–35

Moderately fair organization = 16–25

Unfair organization = 5–14

SOURCE: Adapted in part from John E. Dittrich and Michael R. Carroll, "Organizational Equity Perceptions, Employee Job Satisfaction, and Departmental Absence and Turnover Rates," *Organizational Behavior and Human Performance*, August 1979, pp. 29–40.

In contrast, your organizational loyalty and attachment likely are greater if you believe you are treated fairly at work.

Finally, treating employees inequitably can lead to litigation and costly court settlements. For example, consider the following events:

> Unequal punishment for workers smoking marijuana or drinking was costly to Heldor Industries Inc., Morristown, N.J. An arbitrator gave full back pay to 14 pot smokers who were fired and then reinstated after two months. Previous pot smokers had been suspended only briefly, while some drinkers weren't punished at all.[10]

Employees denied justice at work are turning increasingly to arbitration and the courts. Managers knowledgeable about equity theory can keep things from getting that far out of hand.

■ EXPECTANCY THEORY OF MOTIVATION

Expectancy theory holds that people are motivated to behave in ways that produce desired combinations of expected outcomes. Perception plays a central role in expectancy theory because it emphasizes cognitive ability to anticipate likely consequences of behavior. Embedded in expectancy theory is the principle

---

[10] "Labor Letter: A Special News Report on People and Their Jobs in Offices, Fields and Factories," *The Wall Street Journal*, July 2, 1985, p. 1.

■ FIGURE 6–4 Expectancy Theory Has Broad Application to Many Choice Situations

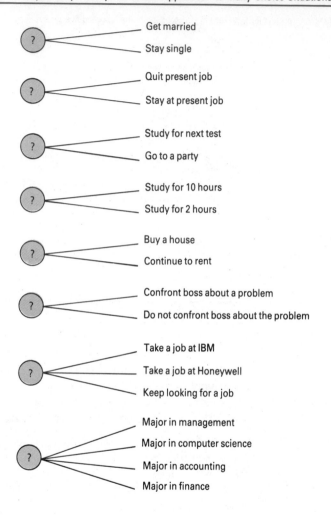

of hedonism. As mentioned in Chapter 5, hedonistic people strive to maximize their pleasure and minimize their pain. Generally, expectancy theory can be used to predict behavior in any situation in which a choice between two or more alternatives must be made (see Figure 6–4). It probes how we calculate our chances of success for various decision alternatives. Relative to organizational behavior, expectancy theory has been used primarily to predict effort and occupational/organizational choice.

This section introduces and explores a well-established expectancy theory of motivation. Understanding this cognitive process theory can help managers develop organizational policies and practices that enhance rather than inhibit employee motivation.

■ **FIGURE 6–5** A General Model of Expectancy Theory

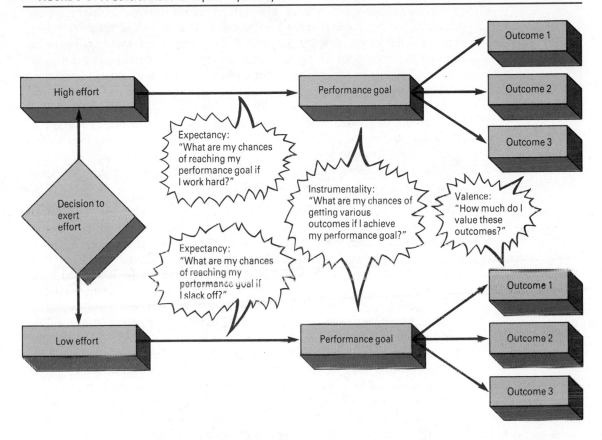

Vroom's Expectancy Theory

Victor Vroom formulated a mathematical model of expectancy theory in his 1964 book *Work and Motivation*.[11] Vroom's theory has been summarized as follows:

> The strength of a tendency to act in a certain way depends on the strength of an expectancy that the act will be followed by a given consequence (or outcome) and on the value or attractiveness of that consequence (or outcome) to the actor.[12]

A general model of Vroom's theory is presented in Figure 6–5. It outlines the variables that influence an individual's level of motivation. Motivation, according to Vroom, boils down to the decision of how much effort to exert

---

[11] For a complete discussion of Vroom's theory, see Victor H. Vroom (New York: John Wiley & Sons, 1964).

[12] Edward E. Lawler III, *Motivation in Work Organizations* (Belmont, Calif.: Wadsworth, 1973), p. 45.

in a specific task situation. This choice is based on a two-stage sequence of expectations (effort→performance and performance→outcome). First, motivation is affected by an individual's expectation that a certain level of effort will produce the intended performance goal. For example, if you do not believe increasing the amount of time you spend studying will significantly raise your grade on an exam, you probably will not study any harder than usual. Motivation also is influenced by the employee's perceived chances of getting various outcomes as a result of accomplishing his or her performance goal. Finally, individuals are motivated to the extent that they value the outcomes received.

Vroom used a mathematical equation to integrate these concepts into a predictive model of motivational force or strength. For our purposes, however, it is sufficient to define and explain the three key concepts within Vroom's model—*expectancy, instrumentality,* and *valence.*

Expectancy.

An **expectancy,** according to Vroom's terminology, represents an individual's belief that a particular degree of effort will be followed by a particular level of performance. In other words, it is an effort→performance expectation. Expectancies take the form of subjective probabilities. As you may recall from a course in statistics, probabilities range from zero to one. An expectancy of zero indicates effort has no anticipated impact on performance.

For example, suppose you do not know how to use a typewriter. No matter how much effort you exert, your perceived probability of typing 30 error-free words per minute likely would be zero. An expectancy of one suggests that performance is totally dependent on effort. If you decided to take a typing course as well as practice a couple of hours a day for a few weeks (high effort), you should be able to type 30 words per minute without any errors. In contrast, if you do not take a typing course and only practice an hour or two per week (low effort), there is a very low probability (say, a 20 percent chance) of being able to type 30 words per minute without any errors.

The following factors influence an employee's expectancy perceptions:

- Self-esteem.
- Previous success at the task.
- Help received from a supervisor and subordinates.
- Information necessary to complete the task.
- Good materials and equipment to work with.[13]

Instrumentality.

An **instrumentality** is a performance→outcome perception. As shown in Figure 6–5, it represents a person's belief that a particular outcome is contingent on accomplishing a specific level of performance. Performance is *instrumental* when it leads to something else. For example, studying is instrumental in passing exams.

Instrumentalities range from −1.0 to 1.0. An instrumentality of 1.0 indicates attainment of a particular outcome is totally dependent on task performance.

---

[13] See Craig C. Pinder, *Work Motivation* (Glenview, Ill.: Scott, Foresman, 1984), chap. 7.

For instance, consider an audio equipment salesperson being paid on commission. The amount of pay received depends solely on the number of units sold. An instrumentality of zero indicates there is no relationship between performance and outcome. For example, most companies link the number of vacation days to seniority, not job performance. Finally, an instrumentality of -1.0 reveals high performance reduces the chance of obtaining an outcome while low performance increases the chance. For example, the more time you spend studying to get an A (high performance) on an exam, the less time you will have for enjoying leisure activities. Similarly, as you lower the amount of time spent studying (low performance), you increase the amount of time that may be devoted to leisure activities.

Valence.   As Vroom used the term, **valence** refers to the positive or negative value people place on outcomes. Valence mirrors our personal preferences.[14] For example, most employees have a positive valence for receiving additional money or recognition. In contrast, job stress and being laid off would likely be negatively valent for most individuals. In Vroom's expectancy model, *outcomes* refer to different consequences that are contingent on performance, such as pay, promotions, or recognition. An outcome's valence depends on an individual's needs and can be measured for research purposes with scales ranging from a negative value to a positive value. For example, an individual's valence toward more recognition can be assessed on a scale ranging from -2 (very undesirable) to 0 (neutral) to $+2$ (very desirable).

Vroom's Expectancy Theory in Action.   Vroom's expectancy model of motivation can be used to analyze a real-life motivation program (see Table 6–6). The general expectancy model in Figure 6–5 can be our explanatory road map. Federal Express did a good job of motivating its college-age cargo handlers to switch from the low-effort portion of Figure 6–5 to the high-effort portion. According to Vroom's model, the student workers originally exerted low effort because they were paid on the basis of time, not output. It was in their best interest to work slowly and accumulate as many hours as possible. By offering to let the student workers go home early *if and when they completed their assigned duties,* Federal Express prompted high effort. This new arrangement created two positively valued outcomes: guaranteed pay plus the opportunity to leave early. The motivation to exert high effort became greater than the motivation to exert low effort.

Judging from the impressive results, the student workers had both high effort→performance expectancies and positive performance→outcome instrumentalities. Moreover, the guaranteed pay and early departure opportunity evidently had strongly positive valences for the student workers.

---

[14] For a discussion of the definition and measurement of valence, see Anthony Pecotich and Gilbert A. Churchill, Jr., "An Examination of the Anticipated-Satisfaction Importance Valence Controversy," *Organizational Behavior and Human Performance,* April 1981, pp. 213–26.

■ **TABLE 6–6**   Federal Express Tells Its Cargo Handlers: "Get Done Early and You Can Leave with Full Pay"

Here is an excerpt from a recent interview between *Inc.* magazine and Frederick W. Smith, founder and chief executive officer of Federal Express Corp., the successful overnight delivery company:

Inc.: Can you give an example of an innovation that solved people-related problems?

Smith: There's one from our cargo terminal here in Memphis. It was several years ago, when we were having a helluva problem keeping things running on time. The airplanes would come in, and everything would get backed up. We tried every kind of control mechanism that you could think of, and none of them worked. Finally, it became obvious that the underlying problem was that it was in the interest of the employees at the cargo terminal—they were college kids, mostly—to run late, because it meant that they made more money. So what we did was give them all a minimum guarantee and say, "Look, if you get through before a certain time, just go home, and you will have beat the system." Well, it was unbelievable. I mean, in the space of about 45 days, the place was way ahead of schedule. And I don't even think it was a conscious thing on their part.

SOURCE: Excerpted from "Federal Express's Fred Smith," p. 38. Reprinted with permission, *Inc.* magazine, October 1986. Copyright © 1986 by *Inc.* Publishing Company, 38 Commercial Wharf, Boston, MA 02110.

Research on Expectancy Theory and Managerial Implications

From the time Vroom's model was originally published in 1964 to about 1976, research did not support his theory. Subsequently, however, several OB researchers concluded that these discouraging results were due to various methodological difficulties and errors.[15] Having corrected those methodological problems, researchers found:

- In more than 16 studies with an average sample size of 200, expectancy theory correctly predicted occupational or organizational choice 63.4 percent of the time. This was significantly better than chance predictions.[16]
- In order to accurately predict effort, managers need to compare the individual's motivation to exert both high and low effort.[17] (For a working example, see exercise 6 at the end of this chapter.)

[15] For reviews of the problems and errors associated with this research, see Frank J. Landy and Wendy S. Becker, "Motivation Theory Reconsidered," in *Research In Organizational Behavior*, Vol. 9, ed. L. L. Cummings and Barry M. Staw (Greenwich, Conn.: JAI Press, 1987), pp. 1–38; and Terence R. Mitchell, "Expectancy Models of Job Satisfaction, Occupational Preference and Effort: A Theoretical, Methodological, and Empirical Appraisal, *Psychological Bulletin*, December 1974, pp. 1053–77.

[16] See John P. Wanous, Thomas L. Keon, and Janina C. Latack, "Expectancy Theory and Occupational/Organizational Choices: A Review and Test," *Organizational Behavior and Human Performance*, August 1983, pp. 66–86.

[17] See Charles W. Kennedy, John A. Fossum, and Bernard J. White, "An Empirical Comparison of Within-Subjects and Between-Subjects Expectancy Theory Models," *Organizational Behavior and Human Performance*, August 1983, pp. 124–43.

■ **TABLE 6–7** Managerial and Organizational Implications of Expectancy Theory

Implications for Managers	Implications for Organizations
Determine the outcomes employees value.	Reward people for desired performance and do not keep pay decisions secret.
Identify good performance so appropriate behaviors can be rewarded.	Design challenging jobs.
Make sure employees can achieve targeted performance levels.	Tie some rewards to group accomplishments to build teamwork and encourage cooperation.
Link desired outcomes to targeted levels of performance.	Reward managers for creating, monitoring, and maintaining expectancies, instrumentalities, and outcomes that lead to high effort and goal attainment.
Make sure changes in outcomes are large enough to motivate high effort.	Monitor employee motivation through interviews or anonymous questionnaires.
Monitor the reward system for inequities.	Accommodate individual differences by building flexibility into the motivation program.

- Job satisfaction, voting behavior in a union representation election (over 75 percent), reenlistment in the National Guard (about 66 percent), and decisions to retire (correct 63 percent of the time) were accurately predicted by expectancy theory.
- Contrary to Vroom's theory, job satisfaction and reenlistment decisions were more strongly related to instrumentalities than to the full model (expectancy, instrumentality, and valence interaction).[18]

Expectancy theory has important practical implications for individual managers and organizations as a whole (see Table 6–7). Managers are advised to create, monitor, and maintain expectancies, instrumentalities, and valences that lead to desired performance levels. A weak link in the effort→performance→ outcome chain could spoil an otherwise well-intentioned motivational program. In turn, organizations need policies and procedures that support and reinforce the principles of expectancy theory. Federal Express achieved a motivational boost by switching from hourly pay to a performance-contingent plan.

■ MOTIVATION THROUGH GOAL SETTING

Regardless of the nature of their specific achievements, successful people tend to have one thing in common. Their lives are goal-oriented. This is as

---

[18] These results are based on the following studies: Elaine D. Pulakos and Neal Schmitt, "A Longitudinal Study of a Valence Model Approach for the Prediction of Job Satisfaction of New Employees," *Journal of Applied Psychology*, May 1983, pp. 307–12; Thomas A. DeCotiis and Jean-Yves LeLouarn, "A Predictive Study of Voting Behavior in a Representation Election Using Union Instrumentality and Work Perceptions," *Organizational Behavior and Human Performance*, February 1981, pp. 103–18; Peter W. Hom, "Expectancy Prediction of Reenlistment in the National Guard," *Journal of Vocational Behavior*, April 1980, pp. 235–48; and Donald F. Parker and Lee Dyer, "Expectancy Theory as a Within-Person Behavioral Choice Model: An Empirical Test of Some Conceptual and Methodological Refinements," *Organizational Behavior and Human Performance*, October 1976, pp. 97–117.

■ **TABLE 6–8** A 14-Year-Old World Champion's Secret to Success

Dubbed as the top Girl Scout cookie seller of all time [14-year-old Markita], Andrews last year [1984] sold 8,006 boxes—$16,000—not bad for a little over three weeks of work. [She] . . . has sold well over 30,000 boxes of cookies in the past eight years, with sales increasing around 30 percent each year.

By comparison, in 1984, Girl Scouts sold 130,250,000 boxes of cookies, . . . that averages out to somewhat less than 100 boxes of cookies per Girl Scout.

The first step in selling, she says, is setting short- and long-term goals. Andrews tries to take 100 orders a day after school during the three-week selling period. "If I don't reach my goal of 100 on one day, I'll work harder the next day, and I'll try to think of new places to go."

. . . With only a couple of years left in Girl Scouts, she wants to reach her goal of selling 40,000 boxes of cookies.

SOURCE: Excerpted from Nancy L. Croft, "The Champion Seller of Girl Scout Cookies Can Provide Tips to Her Elders," *Nation's Business,* December 1985, p. 32.

true for politicians seeking votes as it is for rocket scientists probing outer space or Girl Scouts selling cookies (see Table 6–8). In Lewis Carroll's delightful tale of *Alice's Adventures in Wonderland,* the smiling Cheshire cat advised the bewildered Alice, "If you don't know where you're going, any road will take you there." Goal-oriented managers tend to find the right road because they know where they are going. Within the context of employee motivation, this section explores the theory, research, and practice of goal setting.

Goals: Definition and Background

Edwin Locke, a respected goal-setting scholar, and his colleagues define a **goal** as "what an individual is trying to accomplish; it is the object or aim of an action."[19] Expanding this definition, they add:

The concept is similar in meaning to the concepts of purpose and intent. . . . Other frequently used concepts that are also similar in meaning to that of goal include performance standard (a measuring rod for evaluating performance), quota (a minimum amount of work or production), work norm (a standard of acceptable behavior defined by a work group), task (a piece of work to be accomplished), objective (the ultimate aim of an action or series of actions), deadline (a time limit for completing a task), and budget (a spending goal or limit).[20]

The motivational impact of performance goals and goal-based reward plans has been recognized for a long time. At the turn of the century, Frederick Taylor attempted to scientifically establish how much work of a specified

[19] Edwin A. Locke, Karyll N. Shaw, Lise M. Saari, and Gary P. Latham, "Goal Setting and Task Performance: 1969–1980," *Psychological Bulletin,* July 1981, p. 126.

[20] Ibid.

quality an individual should be assigned each day. He proposed that bonuses be based on accomplishing those output standards. More recently, goal setting has been promoted through a widely used management technique called management by objectives (MBO). Along similar lines, merit pay plans anchored to measurable goals are growing in popularity.[21] A 1985 survey of 71 of the nation's largest health care institutions revealed that 54 percent had incentives for accomplishing goals. Just five years earlier, only 15 percent of those organizations offered such incentives.[22] Pay for performance is catching on in some unexpected places, as well. For example, the Episcopal Diocese of Newark, New Jersey, has begun to pay priests for attaining goals. "Under the merit-pay plan, priests can qualify for salary raises based on goals that could include parish growth, education and choir programs, and quality of sermons."[23]

How Does Goal Setting Work?

Despite abundant goal-setting research and practice, goal-setting theories are surprisingly scarce. An instructive model was formulated by Locke and his associates (see Figure 6–6). According to Locke's model, goal setting has four motivational mechanisms.

Goals Direct Attention. Goals that are personally meaningful tend to focus one's attention on what is relevant and important. If, for example, you have a term project due in a few days, your thoughts tend to revolve around completing that project. Similarly, the members of a home appliance sales force who are told they can win a trip to Hawaii for selling the most refrigerators will tend to steer customers toward the refrigerator department.

Goals Regulate Effort. Not only do goals make us selectively perceptive, they also motivate us to act. The instructor's deadline for turning in your term project would prompt you to complete it, as opposed to going out with friends, watching television, or studying for another course. Generally, the level of effort expended is proportionate to the difficulty of the goal.

Goals Increase Persistence. Within the context of goal setting, **persistence** represents the effort expended on a task over an extended period of time. It takes effort to run 100 meters; it takes persistence to run a 26-mile marathon. Persistent people tend to see obstacles as challenges to be overcome rather than as reasons to fail. A difficult goal that is important to the individual is a constant reminder to keep exerting effort in the appropriate direction (see Table 6–9).

---

[21] An instructive overview of merit pay may be found in Frederick S. Hills, Robert M. Madigan, K. Dow Scott, and Steven E. Markham, "Tracking the Merit of Merit Pay," *Personnel Administrator,* March 1987, pp. 50–57.

[22] See "Labor Letter: A Special News Report on People and Their Jobs in Offices, Fields and Factories," *The Wall Street Journal,* July 9, 1985, p. 1.

[23] "Labor Letter: A Special News Report on People and Their Jobs in Offices, Fields and Factories," *The Wall Street Journal,* March 5, 1985, p. 1.

■ **FIGURE 6–6**   Locke's Model of Goal Setting

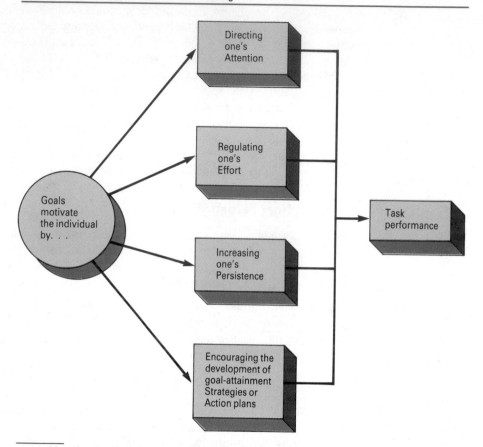

SOURCE: Adapted from discussion in Edwin A. Locke, Keryll N. Shaw, Lise M. Saari, and Gary P. Latham, "Goal Setting and Task Performance: 1969–1980," *Psychological Bulletin,* July 1981, pp. 125–52.

Goals Foster Strategies and Action Plans.   If you are here and your goal is out there somewhere, you face the problem of getting from here to there. For example, the person who has resolved to lose 20 pounds must develop a plan for getting from ''here'' (his or her present weight) to ''there'' (20 pounds lighter). Goals can help because they encourage people to develop strategies and action plans that enable them to achieve their goals.[24] By virtue of setting a weight-reduction goal, the dieter may choose a strategy of exercising more, eating less, or some combination of the two.

---

[24] Recent research evidence may be found in P. Christopher Earley and Brian C. Perry, ''Work Plan Availability and Performance: An Assessment of Task Strategy Priming on Subsequent Task Completion,'' *Organizational Behavior and Human Decision Processes,* June 1987, pp. 279–302; and P. Christopher Earley, Pauline Wojnaroski, and William Prest, ''Task Planning and Energy Expended: Exploration of How Goals Influence Performance,'' *Journal of Applied Psychology,* February 1987, pp. 107–14.

■ **TABLE 6-9** Persistence Pays Off

At the age of 15, Robert Lewis Dean borrowed $1,500 from his parents, bought a 1972 Cadillac, taught himself how to fix it up, and sold it at a profit. That venture five years ago was the beginning of an entrepreneurial career that has seen him start a business at 16, sell it for $100,000, launch another business—and then launch a series of others.

Dean is a prime representative of a new crop of entrepreneurs, business whiz kids who are exhibiting a clarity of purpose that belies their tender years. . . .

When Robert Dean sold that Cadillac he had fixed up, he decided an opportunity was staring him in the face. And he decided to seize it.

He opened Coach House Cars, Inc., an Arlington, Va., antique auto business, and kept his hands greasy as he labored to restore classic American vehicles ranging from a '42 Packard to a '57 Thunderbird. He sold the business when he was 17, after grossing $600,000 in a single year.

At 18, he abandoned plans to go to college. He opted instead to open Dynasty Limousine Corporation, . . . "I had a little bit of difficulty at first," he recalls. "People weren't sure they wanted to trust their business to a teen-ager, so I had to use some extra tactics. . . ."

Catching up with Dean is difficult. Operating under a variety of corporate umbrellas, he owns Town & Country Limousine Service of Washington, is opening a similar firm in Boston, consults for Town & Country Limousine Service of New York, and is in the process of setting up Limo-Net, an international network of individually owned and operated limousine services.

How does he feel about his $2 million revenue level? "I'm far off my goals," he complains.

SOURCE: Excerpted from Cynthia Poulos and William Hoffer, "The Business Whiz Kids." Reprinted with permission, *Nation's Business*, November 1986, U.S. Chamber of Commerce.

Insights from Goal-Setting Research

Research consistently has supported goal setting as a motivational technique. As a general backdrop for our discussion of goal-setting research, Table 6–10 presents the results of 10 research studies that examined the impact of goal setting on performance. The median increase in performance for this broad range of tasks was 16 percent. This sort of performance improvement can mean the difference between success and failure for some organizations.

Reviews of the many goal-setting studies conducted over the last couple of decades have given managers four practical insights.

Difficult Goals Lead to Higher Performance.   **Goal difficulty** reflects the amount of effort required to meet a goal. It is more difficult to sell nine cars a month than it is to sell three cars a month. An extensive review of goal-setting studies by Locke and his associates led them to conclude that performance tends to increase as goals become more difficult, but only to a point. As illustrated in Figure 6–7, the positive relationship between goal difficulty and performance breaks down when goals are perceived to be impossible. Of 57 research studies, 48 demonstrated that performance goes up when employees are given hard goals as opposed to easy or moderate goals (section A of

■ **TABLE 6-10** Results from Field Studies of Goal Setting

Task	Duration of Study	Percent Change in Performance
Servicing soft drink coolers	Unknown	+27
Keypunching	3 months	+27
Skilled technical jobs	9 months	+15
Sales	9 months	+24
Telephone service jobs	3 months	+13
Loading trucks	9 months	+26
Logging	2 months	+18
Typing	5 weeks	+11
Mass production	2 years	+16
Coding land parcels	1–2 days	+16

SOURCE: Adapted from Gary P. Latham and Edwin A. Locke, "Goal Setting—A Motivational Technique That Works," *Organizational Dynamics,* Autumn 1979, pp. 68–80.

Figure 6–7).[25] However, as the difficulty of a goal increases, performance stabilizes (section B) and eventually decreases when the goal becomes impossible (section C).

A recent meta-analysis of 70 goal-setting studies conducted between 1966 and 1984, involving 7,407 subjects, led the researchers to the following conclusion: "Clearly, difficult goals have a dramatic effect on performance outcomes."[26]

Specific, Difficult Goals Lead to Higher Performance.   **Goal specificity** pertains to the quantifiability of a goal. For example, a goal of selling nine cars a month is more specific than telling a salesperson to do his or her best. In the Locke review of goal-setting research, 99 out of 110 studies (90 percent) found that specific, hard goals led to better performance than did easy, medium, do-your-best, or no goals.[27] This result was confirmed in the 1966–1984 meta-analysis when the researchers concluded: "Overall, goal specificity/difficulty was found to be strongly related to task performance."[28] The practical value of quantified, challenging goals is clear.

Feedback Enhances the Effect of Specific, Difficult Goals.   The 1966–1984 meta-analysis of goal-setting studies led the researchers to conclude "the presence of feedback had a considerable impact on performance when used in

---

[25] Drawn from Locke, Shaw, Saari, and Latham, "Goal Setting and Task Performance: 1969–1980."

[26] Anthony J. Mento, Robert P. Steel, and Ronald J. Karren, "A Meta-Analytic Study of the Effects of Goal Setting on Task Performance: 1966–1984," *Organizational Behavior and Human Decision Processes,* February 1987, p. 69.

[27] See Locke, Shaw, Saari, and Latham, "Goal Setting and Task Performance: 1969–1980."

[28] Mento, Steel, and Karren, "A Meta-Analytic Study of the Effects of Goal Setting on Task Performance: 1966–1984," p. 72.

■ **FIGURE 6–7** Relationship between Goal Difficulty and Performance

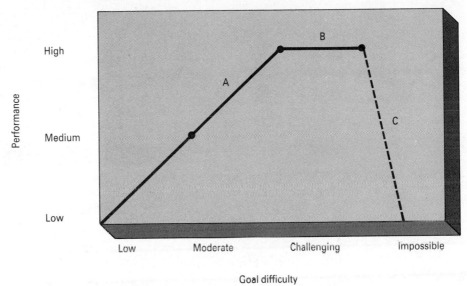

A: Performance of committed individuals with adequate ability
B: Performance of committed individuals who are working at capacity
C: Perfomance of individuals who lack commitment to high goals

SOURCE: Edwin A. Locke/Gary P. Latham, *Goal Setting: A Motivational Technique That Works!* © 1984, p. 22. Reprinted by permission of Prentice-Hall, Inc., Englewood Cliffs, New Jersey.

conjunction with difficult specific goals."[29] Feedback lets people know if they are headed toward their goals or if they are off-course and need to redirect their efforts. A recent study, for example, demonstrated the effectiveness of using both goal setting and feedback. Individuals from a college hockey team were given goals and feedback about legal body checking. The head coach hoped that this intervention would increase the amount of legal body checking, decrease penalties, and lead to more victories. Results supported these expectations. Moreover, feedback significantly improved hockey performance beyond the level solely attributed to goal setting.[30]

Participative Goals Are Superior to Assigned Goals. Again drawing upon the results of the meta-analysis of goal-setting studies conducted between 1966 and 1984, participatively set goals led to a 4 percent increase in productivity over assigned goals. However, these results were based exclusively on laboratory

[29] Ibid. p. 73.

[30] Results are presented in D. Chris Anderson, Charles R. Crowell, Mark Doman, and George S. Howard, "Performance Posting, Goal Setting, and Activity-Contingent Praise as Applied to a University Hockey Team," *Journal of Applied Psychology,* February 1988, pp. 87–95.

■ **FIGURE 6–8** Three Key Steps in Implementing a Goal-Setting Program

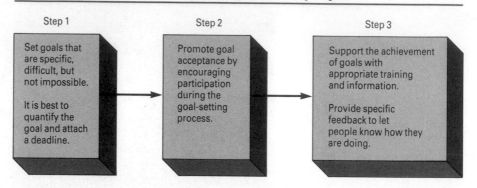

studies that controlled the level of goal difficulty.[31] Future research is needed to determine the generalizability of the positive effects of participatively set goals.

Practical Application of Goal Setting

There are three general steps to follow when implementing a goal-setting program (see Figure 6–8). Serious deficiencies in one step cannot make up for strength in the other two. The three steps need to be implemented in a systematic fashion.

Step 1: Goal Setting.   A number of sources can be used as input during this goal-setting stage.[32] Time and motion studies are one source. Goals also may be based on the average past performance of job holders. Third, the employee and his or her manager may set the goal participatively, through give-and-take negotiation. Fourth, goal setting often is constrained by external factors. For example, the production schedule of a firm with a government contract may be dictated largely by the terms of that agreement. Finally, the overall strategy of a company (e.g., become the lowest-cost producer) may affect the goals set by employees at various levels in the organization.

In accordance with available research evidence, goals should be specific and difficult, yet attainable through persistent effort. For complex tasks, however, managers should set slightly less difficult goals because difficult goals lead to lower performance than do easier goals.[33] Specificity can be achieved by stating goals in quantitative terms (e.g., units of output, dollars, or percent of desired increase or decrease). With respect to measuring performance, it

---

[31] See Mento, Steel, and Karren, "A Meta-Analytic Study of the Effects of Goal Setting on Task Performance."

[32] These recommendations are taken from Gary P. Latham and Edwin A. Locke, "Goal Setting— A Motivational Technique That Works," *Organizational Dynamics*, Autumn 1979, pp. 68–80.

[33] For results from this study, see Lewis A. Taylor III, "Decision Quality and Commitment within a Probabilistic Environment," *Organizational Behavior and Human Decision Processes*, April 1987, pp. 203–27.

■ TABLE 6–11 Goals That Ignore Quality Create Problems for the IRS

Austin, Texas—The Internal Revenue Service's sprawling 12-acre regional office here in many ways resembles a large factory.

Each day hundreds of thousands of tax returns move through the complex in assembly-line fashion. Managers hold "production meetings" to check the speed of the operation, and employees are given weekly computer printouts comparing their average hourly output with that of their peers. "Productivity" is measured and encouraged at every juncture.

This unrelenting emphasis on rapid production is an absolute necessity for the IRS. The Reagan administration's tight budget policies have forced it to service a steadily expanding population with a shrinking staff. . . .

Destroyed Letters

Late last month the IRS disclosed that a supervisor here had ordered the destruction of several thousand letters from businesses requesting adjustments or protesting errors in their tax bills. According to service-center employees, the act was a desperate attempt by the supervisor to reduce a rising backlog of complaints and maintain a high "production" rating. . . .

Union employees at the Austin center complain of tremendous pressure to increase the average number of documents they process an hour. As a result, they contend, sloppy work and errors have increased.

"Quality Work"

"When I started in the adjustment branch eight years ago, the production rate was 2.5 letters per hour," says an employee who answers correspondence from businesses claiming that their tax bills are incorrect. "We were a very efficient bunch. We put out quality work."

Since that time, however, "The production rate has doubled and tripled" as managers have worked to meet rising standards. "If you don't meet the productivity rate, the supervisors won't get their merit pay," she says.

SOURCE: Excerpted from Alan Murray, "IRS Foul Ups Likely to Continue as Returns Rise and Staff Is Cut. Reprinted by permission of *The Wall Street Journal,* © Dow Jones & Company, Inc., May 6, 1985, p. 39. All rights reserved.

is important to achieve a workable balance between quantity and quality. Failing to do so created serious problems for the U.S. Internal Revenue Service (see Table 6–11). Well-conceived goals also have a built-in time limit or deadline. Priorities need to be established in multiple-goal situations.

Finally, because of individual differences in skills and abilities, it may be necessary to establish different goals for employees performing the same job. For example, a recent study revealed that more difficult goals were set by individuals with high rather than low task abilities. Moreover, results indicated a positive goal difficulty→performance relationship for individuals with high as opposed to low self-esteem.[34] If an employee has low self-esteem or lacks the ability to perform the job, then progressively harder developmental goals may be in order. But this practice may create feelings of inequity among co-

---

[34] Results are contained in John R. Hollenbeck and Arthur P. Brief, "The Effects of Individual Differences and Goal Origin on Goal Setting and Performance," *Organizational Behavior and Human Decision Processes,* December 1987, pp. 392–414.

workers, necessitating other alternatives. For example, inability to perform at the standard may suggest a training deficiency or the need to transfer the individual to another job. In any event, managers need to keep in mind that motivation diminishes when people continually fail to meet their goals.

Step 2: Goal Acceptance.   **Goal acceptance** is the extent to which an individual is committed personally to achieving an organizational goal. This step is important because employees will not be motivated to pursue goals they view as unreasonable, unobtainable, or unfair. Goal acceptance may be increased by using one or more of the following techniques:

1. Provide instructions and an explanation for implementing the program.
2. Be supportive and do not use goals to threaten employees.
3. Encourage employees to participate in the goal-setting process.
4. Train managers in how to conduct goal-setting sessions.
5. Use selection procedures that identify applicants who have the ability to accomplish the typical goal.
6. Provide monetary incentives or other rewards for accomplishing goals.[35]

Before considering Step 3, something needs to be said about participation in the goal-setting process. As previously mentioned, participatively set goals seem to have a positive effect on performance. Goal-setting experts say participation indirectly affects performance by encouraging goal acceptance.[36] When people resist assigned goals, participation can lead to greater acceptance, which may lead to higher performance. Employees who participate in establishing performance goals tend to view those goals as "mine" rather than "theirs." On the other hand, participation is not necessary when individuals readily accept imposed or assigned goals.

Step 3: Support and Feedback.   Step 3 calls for providing employees with the necessary support elements or resources to get the job done. This includes ensuring that each employee has the necessary abilities and information to reach his or her goals. As a pair of goal-setting experts succinctly stated: "Motivation without knowledge is useless."[37] Training often is required to help employees achieve difficult goals. Moreover, employees should be provided with specific feedback (knowledge of results) on how they are doing. As discussed in detail in the next chapter, performance tends to improve when people receive feedback relative to the goals being pursued.[38]

---

[35] These recommendations are adapted from Edwin A. Locke and Gary P. Latham, *Goal Setting: A Motivational Technique That Works!* (Englewood Cliffs, N.J.: Prentice-Hall, 1984).

[36] Results are shown in P. Christopher Earley, "Influence of Information, Choice and Task Complexity upon Goal Acceptance, Performance, and Personal Goals," *Journal of Applied Psychology,* August 1985, pp. 481–91; and Miriam Erez, P. Christopher Earley, and Charles L. Hulin, "The Impact of Participation on Goal Acceptance and Performance: A Two-Step Model," *Academy of Management Journal,* March 1985, pp. 50–66.

[37] Latham and Locke, "Goal Setting—A Motivational Technique That Works," p. 79.

[38] See the results presented by Robert A. Reber and Jerry A. Wallin, "The Effects of Training, Goal Setting, and Knowledge of Results on Safe Behavior: A Component Analysis," *Academy of Management Journal,* September 1984, pp. 544–60.

■ A PRACTICAL MODEL FOR PUTTING MOTIVATIONAL THEORIES TO WORK

Successfully designing and implementing motivational programs is not easy. Managers cannot simply take one of the theories discussed in this book and apply it word for word. Dynamics within organizations interfere with the ability to apply motivation theories in "pure" form. According to management scholar Terence Mitchell:

> There are situations and settings that make it exceptionally difficult for a motivational system to work. These circumstances may involve the kinds of jobs or people present, the technology, the presence of a union, and so on. The factors that hinder the application of motivational theory have not been articulated either frequently or systematically.[39]

With Mitchell's cautionary statement in mind, this section raises issues that need to be addressed before implementing a motivational program (see Figure 6–9). Our intent here is not to discuss all relevant considerations, but rather to highlight a few important ones.

Assuming a motivational program is being considered to improve productivity, the first issue revolves around the difference between motivation and performance. As pointed out in Chapter 5, motivation and performance are not one and the same. Motivation is only one of several factors that influence performance. For example, poor performance may be more a function of either a lack of ability or technological factors. Motivation is not a good substitute for low ability or obsolete equipment. Managers, therefore, need to gauge the extent to which motivation significantly affects performance.

The method used to evaluate employee performance also needs to be considered. Without a valid performance appraisal system, it is difficult, if not impossible, to accurately distinguish between good and poor performers. Being unable to accurately measure performance also makes it difficult to evaluate the effectiveness of any motivational program, so it is beneficial for managers to assess the accuracy and validity of their appraisal systems.

If rewards are used as motivators, managers should consider the accuracy and fairness of the reward system. As discussed under expectancy theory, the promise of increased rewards will not prompt higher effort and good performance unless those rewards clearly are tied to performance. Moreover, equity theory tells us that motivation is influenced by employee perceptions about the fairness of reward allocations. Rewards also need to be integrated appropriately into the appraisal system. If performance is measured at the individual level, individual achievements need to be rewarded. On the other hand, when performance is the result of group effort, rewards should be allocated to the group.

Finally, as indicated in Figure 6–9, it is helpful to identify individual and situational factors that affect motivation. This enables managers to take a broader

---

[39] Terence R. Mitchell, "Motivation: New Directions for Theory, Research, and Practice," *Academy of Management Review,* January 1982, p. 81.

■ **FIGURE 6–9**   A Flow Diagram of Questions to Consider When Developing Motivational Programs

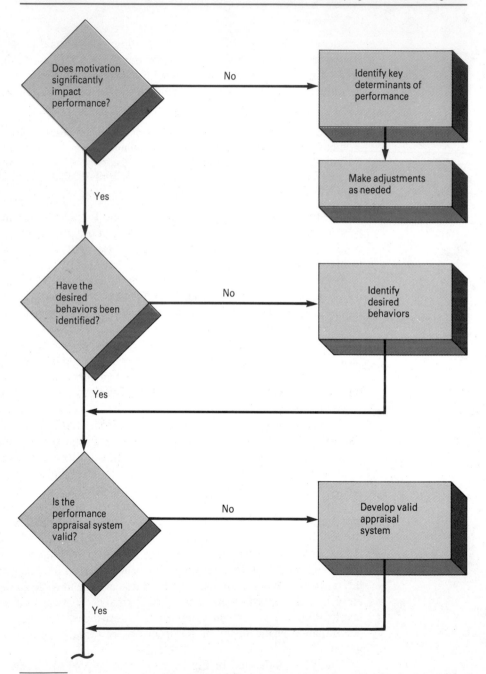

SOURCE: Adapted in part from discussion in Terence R. Mitchell, "Motivation: New Directions for Theory, Research, and Practice," *Academy of Management Review,* January 1982, pp. 80–88.

■ **FIGURE 6–9** *(concluded)*

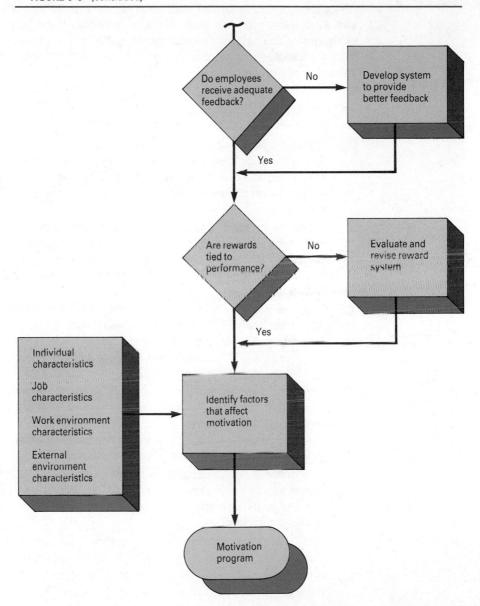

perspective when developing motivational programs. For example, motivation is not solely affected by the individual characteristics discussed in Chapters 3 and 4. A variety of job characteristics (autonomy and responsibility), work environment characteristics (peer group and supervisor), and external environmental characteristics (technological advances and economic cycles) similarly affect job performance.[40]

SUMMARY OF KEY CONCEPTS

A. Unlike the subconscious content theories of motivation presented in Chapter 5, the three process theories discussed in this chapter deal in terms of perception and conscious decision making. Equity, expectancy, and goal-setting theories involve different cognitive processes that affect one's motivation.

B. Adams' equity theory focuses on the perceived fairness of social exchanges. It is based on Festinger's cognitive dissonance theory. People perform equity evaluations by comparing their ratio of outcomes to inputs to those of relevant others. Outcomes and inputs must be recognizable and relevant if they are to play a role in equity comparisons.

C. Negative inequity occurs when someone is underrewarded. Positive inequity occurs when someone is overrewarded. People tend to have a lower tolerance for negative inequity than for positive inequity. We reduce perceived inequity through various combinations of behavioral and cognitive adjustments. Managers need to monitor employees' equity perceptions.

D. Expectancy theory assumes motivation is determined by one's perceived chances of achieving valued outcomes. Vroom's expectancy model of motivation reveals how effort→performance expectancies and performance→outcome instrumentalities influence the degree of effort expended to achieve desired (positively valent) outcomes.

E. Four motivational mechanisms of goal setting are: (1) goals direct one's attention, (2) goals regulate effort, (3) goals increase one's persistence, and (4) goals encourage development of goal-attainment strategies and action plans.

F. Goal-setting research recommends difficult, quantified, participatively set goals that are followed by specific feedback on performance.

G. Well-conceived goals include a deadline. Participation in goal setting indirectly affects performance by fostering goal acceptance.

H. When implementing a motivational program, managers should consider

---

[40] For a discussion of such characteristics, see James L. Perry and Lyman W. Porter, "Factors Affecting the Context for Motivation in Public Organizations," *Academy of Management Review*, January 1982, pp. 89–98.

the key determinants of performance, the behavior desired, and the validity of the performance appraisal system. Also requiring careful consideration are the adequacy of feedback, performance-reward linkages, and individual, task, organizational, and external factors that affect motivation.

KEY TERMS

cognitions	valence
equity theory	goal
negative inequity	persistence
positive inequity	goal difficulty
expectancy theory	goal specificity
expectancy	goal acceptance
instrumentality	

DISCUSSION QUESTIONS

1. Have you experienced positive or negative inequity at work? Describe the circumstances in terms of the inputs and outcomes of the comparison person and yourself.

2. Could a manager's attempt to treat his or her employees equally lead to perceptions of inequity? Explain.

3. What work outcomes (refer to Table 6–2) are most important to you? Do you think different age groups value different outcomes? What are the implications for managers who seek to be equitable?

4. Relative to Table 6–3, what techniques have you relied on recently to reduce either positive or negative inequity?

5. What is your definition of studying hard? What is your expectancy for earning an A on the next exam in this course? What is the basis of this expectancy?

6. If someone who reported to you at work had a low expectancy for successful performance, what could you do to increase this person's expectancy?

7. Do goals play an important role in your life? Explain.

8. How would you respond to a manager who said, "Participative goal setting is a waste of time."

9. Goal-setting research suggests that people should be given difficult goals. How does this prescription mesh with expectancy theory? Explain.

10. How could a professor use equity, expectancy, and goal-setting theory to motivate students?

BACK TO THE OPENING CASE

Now that you have read Chapter 6, you should be able to answer the following questions about the Nordstrom case:

1. What role does perceived equity probably play in this case?
2. Using the version of Vroom's expectancy theory displayed in Figure 6–5 as an explanatory device, how does the company motivate its salespeople to exert high effort?
3. What are three goals that would effectively guide Nordstrom's salespeople to render good service? (*Note:* Feel free to make reasonable assumptions about the people and situational factors involved.)

EXERCISE 6 ————————————————————————————————

Objectives

1. To better understand the mechanics of expectancy theory.
2. To conduct a personal application of expectancy theory.

Introduction

Given the choice between two or more courses of action, expectancy theory proposes that the individual will exhibit the behavior with the greatest motivational force. That force depends on one's perceived chances of achieving valued outcomes. To see if this is true, use yourself as a case in point. To do this, the three components of Vroom's expectancy theory of motivation (expectancy, instrumentality, and valence) will be measured for the behaviors of putting either a good deal of effort or moderate effort into studying for the course in which you are using this text.[41]

Instructions

This exercise has two parts, each involving three similar steps. In part A, you will be calculating your motivational force score for *high* effort. Part B will assess your motivational force score for *moderate* effort. For the purpose of this exercise, we will define high effort as "studying three or more hours a week" for this course. Moderate effort, on the other hand, is defined as "studying less than three hours a week." The performance goal for this exercise is the grade you desire (A, B, C, or D).

---

[41] This exercise is adapted from one developed by Professor Peter W. Hom, Arizona State University.

Desired grade = _____

Complete the following three steps for each part:
Step 1: Effort → performance expectancy calculation
Step 2: Performance → outcome calculation
Step 3: Motivational force calculation

Part A: High Effort Motivational Force

Step 1: Effort → performance calculation:
   What are the chances that you can earn the grade you desire in this course by studying three or more hours a week? (Be sure to consider your other commitments.) Circle a number from 1 to 5 on the following rating scale:

No Chance	25% Chance	50% Chance	75% Chance	100% Chance
1	2	3	4	5

Step 1 score = _____(record below in step 3)

Step 2: Performance ———→ outcome calculation:
   Listed below are three possible outcomes associated with completing this course. Circle your valence (V) and instrumentallty (I) ratings for each of the three outcomes, multiply those two figures, and record the resulting figure in the space at the far right. Be sure to include the sign (+ or −) of the product. (Remember that a minus times a plus is a minus and a minus times a minus is a plus.) Finally, add the three subscores to derive your step 2 score.

Valence (V): Indicate the desirability of each outcome by circling a number for each of the three items. Use the following scale:

Very undesirable = −2
Undesirable = −1
Neutral = 0
Desirable = +1
Very desirable = +2

Instrumentality (I): Indicate your chances of attaining each outcome if you earn the grade you desire in this course. Use the following scale:

Definitely will not result = −1
Probably will not result = −.5
Uncertain = 0
Probably will result = +.5
Definitely will result = +1

Possible outcomes of this course:

	Valence	×	Instrumentality

1. Help me get a good job.   −2 −1 0 +1 +2   ×   −1 −.5 0 +.5 +1   = _____
2. Hurt my social life.   −2 −1 0 +1 +2   ×   −1 −.5 0 +.5 +1   = _____
3. Give me great personal
   satisfaction.   −2 −1 0 +1 +2   ×   −1 −.5 0 +.5 +1   = _____

Total   = _____
(This is your step 2 score; record it below in step 3.)

Step 3: High motivational force calculation:

Step 1
score _____   × score _____ = _____ for *high* effort

Step 2

Motivational force

Part B: Moderate Effort Motivational Force

Step 1: Effort ⟶ performance calculation:

What are the chances that you can earn the grade you desire in this course by studying less than three hours a week? (Be sure to consider your other commitments.) Circle a number from 1 to 5 on the following rating scale:

No Chance	25% Chance	50% Chance	75% Chance	100% Chance
1	2	3	4	5

Step 1 score = _____(record below in step 3)

Step 2: Performance ⟶ outcome calculation:

Record your step 2 score from Part A in step 3 below.

Step 3: Low motivational force calculation:

Step 1   Step 2   Motivational force
score _____ × score _____ = _____ for *low* effort

Questions for Consideration/Class Discussion

1. What is your motivation to exert high and low effort?
   Motivational force for high effort = ____
   Motivational force for low effort = ____
2. According to expectancy theory, you are motivated to put forth the effort associated with the higher of the two scores. Do the results of this expectancy exercise accurately reflect your real motivation? Explain.
3. On the average, how many hours per week have you spent studying for this course? Does this exercise suggest you need to adjust your present level of effort? Explain.
4. How has this exercise helped you better understand the mechanics of Vroom's expectancy theory of motivation?

Chapter **7**

Performance Appraisal, Feedback, and Rewards

LEARNING OBJECTIVES

When you finish studying the material in this chapter,
you should be able to:

- Identify four key components of the performance appraisal process.
- Explain how the trait, behavioral, and results approaches to performance appraisal vary and discuss why a contingency approach has been suggested.
- Contrast the following three performance appraisal techniques: management by objectives (MBO), critical incidents, and behaviorally anchored rating scales (BARS).
- Define the term *feedback* and identify its two main functions.
- Identify three different sources of feedback and discuss how we perceive and cognitively evaluate feedback.
- List at least three practical lessons we have learned from feedback research.
- Contrast the following reward norms: equity and equality.
- Explain how Deci's cognitive evaluation theory runs counter to what expectancy theorists and behaviorists say about tying rewards to performance.

Big Brother Is Watching You!

Vaughn Foster has U.S. 85 all to himself as he swings his truck onto the highway for his last trip of the day. To his right, the sun is disappearing behind the Rockies; ahead, the road stretches straight and empty for miles. With one eye on the speedometer, he eases into the right lane and starts creeping ahead at 50 miles an hour.

"I've been out all week," he says. "My wife's home, my kids are home, and I'd just as soon be there with them. There's no doubt about it: If that computer wasn't there I'd be running 60 easy."

Mr. Foster is talking about a black box the size of a dictionary that sits in a compartment above his right front tire. At the end of his trip, his boss at Leprino Foods Co. in Denver will pull a cartridge out of the box and pop it into a personal computer. In seconds the computer will print out a report showing all the times the truck was speeding. "It's like a watchdog," Mr. Foster grumbles. "You just can't get as far away from that supervisor as you used to. . . ."

At Leprino Foods, executives concede that their monitoring program has distasteful features. "There's no one in their right mind who'd want to have that computer watching them," admits Jerry Sheehan, the vice president of transportation for the closely held concern.

Like other trucking managers, Mr. Sheehan used to spend much of his time urging his drivers to observe the speed limit and take it easy on their engines. Truckers who drive too fast and strain their engines get too few miles per gallon and run up undue maintenance bills.

But urging wasn't accomplishing much. Leprino hired a vehicle-tailing service to follow a sampling of trucks and gauge their speeds. The service reported that most Leprino truckers were driving about 10 miles over the speed limit. That didn't surprise Mr. Sheehan, who has a theory about employee rules. "I'm a great one for believing that people really will do what's *inspected* and not what's *expected*," he says.

Three years ago, the nonunion company started outfitting its fleet with portable computers that hook up to sensors in a truck's engine and transmission. Now all 160 Leprino trucks have them. The devices gather detailed information about a truck's trip: what times it stopped and started, how fast the engine ran, how fast the truck was going throughout the trip.

The last statistic is especially potent at Leprino, which wields both carrot and stick to encourage its drivers to stay under 60 miles an hour (the extra five miles above the [old] national speed limit allows for speedometer errors and quick surges starting down a hill). A trucker gets a bonus of three cents a mile for every trip he makes without breaking 60.

But the first time a printout shows a driver sped at 65 miles an hour or faster, he gets an official reprimand. The second time, he is suspended without pay for a week. The third time, he is fired. Mr. Sheehan says Lep-

Concluded:

rino has fired half a dozen truckers for speeding since the computers were installed.

Drivers at Leprino aren't enchanted with the system. "I started driving trucks because I'm kind of an independent sort of a guy that didn't like having the boss always looking over my shoulder," says E. K. Blaisdell, a former Leprino driver who recently became a dispatcher. "Then they managed to invent a machine that looks over my shoulder." Others gripe that they have become the butt of CB-radio jokes about states setting up extra-slow speed limits for Leprino drivers.

Mr. Sheehan, the vice president, sees another side. He says Leprino trucks now get 1.1 more miles per gallon—5.7 instead of 4.6—which is nearly a 25 percent improvement. A year after the first computers were installed, maintenance costs had dropped about one fifth and a declining accident rate had knocked $50,000 off the company's annual insurance premiums. Each $1,500 system paid for itself in about six months, Mr. Sheehan says, and in all, Leprino's $250,000 worth of computers have saved the company three times that much so far.

For Discussion

Do you think the truck-speed computers are a good managerial technique? Explain your rationale.

SOURCE: Excerpted from Michael W. Miller, "Computers Keep Eye on Workers and See If They Perform Well." Reprinted by permission of *The Wall Street Journal,* © Dow Jones & Company, Inc., June 3, 1985, pp. 1, 15. All rights reserved.

■ Additional discussion questions linking this case with the following material appear at the end of this chapter.

Productivity experts tell us that we need to work smarter, not harder. While it is true that a sound education and appropriate training are needed if one is to work smarter, the process does not end there. Today's employees need instructive performance appraisals, supportive feedback, and desired rewards if they are to translate their knowledge into improved productivity. As Figure 7–1 illustrates, constructive performance appraisals, feedback, and rewards channel effort into stable, strong job performance. As coordinated and systematic human resource management tools, performance appraisals, feedback, and rewards turn the motivation theories presented earlier into practice. On the other hand, a weak or uncoordinated appraisal/feedback/reward system can derail even well-intentioned effort. This chapter will help you integrate and apply concepts you have acquired about individual differences, learning, and motivation.

■ **FIGURE 7–1** Performance Appraisal, Feedback, and Rewards Translate Effort into Strong Performance

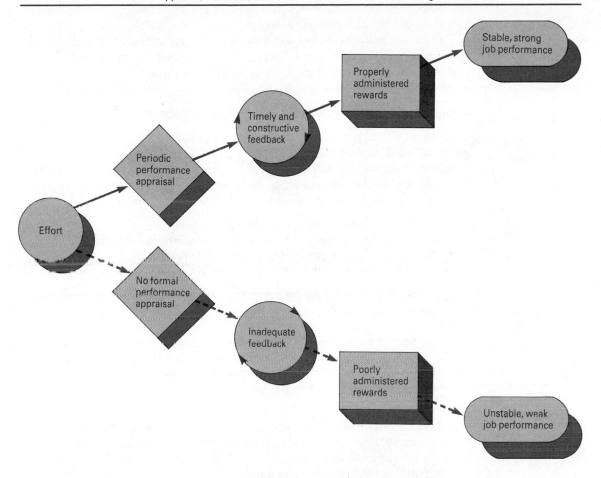

■ **PERFORMANCE APPRAISAL: DEFINITION AND COMPONENTS**

In everyday life, it is hard to escape being on the receiving end of some sort of performance appraisal. There are report cards all through school, win-loss records in organized sports, and periodic meetings with one's boss. For managers, who are in the position of both giving and receiving them, performance appraisals are an especially important consideration. As used here, **performance appraisal** involves the judgmental evaluation of a jobholder's traits, behavior, or accomplishments as a basis for making important personnel decisions. A survey of 588 companies by the American Management Association (AMA) found that management-level appraisals were used as follows: ''compensation (85.6 percent), counseling (65.1 percent), training and development (64.3 percent), promotion (45.3 percent), manpower planning (43.1 percent), retention/discharge (30.3 percent), and validation of a selection technique (17.2

percent).''[1] Economic efficiency and the principle of fairness dictate that these decisions be made on the basis of valid and reliable evidence, rather than as the result of prejudice and guesswork.

This section analyzes the key components of the performance appraisal process and summarizes recent research findings relative to those components. Specific performance rating formats are then presented, followed by practical tips.

Components of the Performance Appraisal Process

Although formal performance appraisals are practically universal in the managerial ranks (91 percent in the AMA study cited above), few express satisfaction with them. Appraisers and appraisees alike are unhappy with the process. Much of the problem stems from the complexity of the appraisal process. One writer has captured this issue with the following example:

> If you wonder why evaluating an employee's performance can be so difficult, consider a simpler appraisal: one made by the barroom fan who concludes that his team's quarterback is a bum because several of his passes have been intercepted. An objective appraisal would raise the following questions: Were the passes really that bad or did the receivers run the wrong patterns? Did the offensive line give the quarterback adequate protection? Did he call those plays himself, or were they sent in by the coach? Was the quarterback recovering from an injury?
>
> And what about the fan? Has he ever played football himself? How good is his vision? Did he have a good view of the TV set through the barroom's smoky haze? Was he talking to his friends at the bar during the game? How many beers did he down during the game?[2]

Further complicating things are Equal Employment Opportunity laws and guidelines that constrain managers' actions during the appraisal process.[3] Let us begin to sort out the complex appraisal process by examining its key components. Four key components, as shown in Figure 7–2, are the appraiser, the appraisee, the appraisal method, and the outcomes.

The Appraiser.   Managers generally express discomfort with playing the role of performance appraiser. After finding that 95 percent of the mid- to lower-level management performance appraisals at 293 U.S. companies were conducted by immediate supervisors, researchers concluded that ''most supervisors dislike 'playing God' and that many try to avoid responsibility for providing subordinates with feedback of unflattering appraisal information.''[4]

---

[1] ''Performance Appraisal: Current Practices and Techniques,'' *Personnel*, May–June 1984, p. 57.

[2] Berkeley Rice, ''Performance Review: The Job Nobody Likes,'' *Psychology Today*, September 1986, p. 32.

[3] For a review of relevant EEO laws and guidelines, see Gerald V. Barrett and Mary C. Kernan, ''Performance Appraisal and Terminations: A Review of Court Decisions Since *Brito v. Zia* with Implications for Personnel Practices,'' *Personnel Psychology*, Autumn 1987, pp. 489–503.

[4] Robert I. Lazer and Walter S. Wikstrom, *Appraising Managerial Performance: Current Practices and Future Directions*, Report 723 (New York: The Conference Board, 1977), p. 26.

■ **FIGURE 7–2**   Components of the Performance Appraisal Process

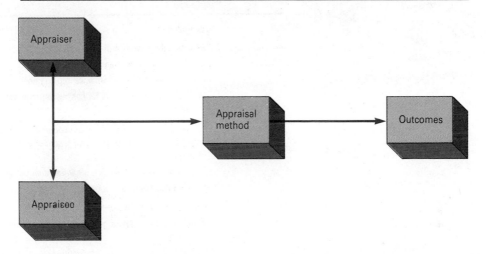

Charges of racism, sexism, and perceptual distortion also have been leveled at appraisers. Common perceptual errors include those discussed in Chapter 4 (halo, leniency, central tendency, recency, and contrast). In a survey of 267 corporations, 62 percent of the respondents reported that leniency error was their number one appraisal problem.[5] Everyday experience shows stereotyping and the self-fulfilling prophecy can contaminate the appraisal process. Moreover, because performance appraisers engage in social cognition (see Chapter 4), problems can occur in comprehending, encoding, retaining, or retrieving performance-related information.

Finally, managers typically lack the necessary performance appraisal skills. In the study just mentioned, researchers concluded, "At 52 percent of the responding companies, evaluators are simply not conducting performance interviews or filling out appraisal forms correctly."[6] Experts on the subject have specified four criteria for a willing and able performance appraiser:

> The person doing the assessment must: (1) be in a position to observe the behavior and performance of the individual of interest; (2) be knowledgeable about the dimensions or features of performance; (3) have an understanding of the scale format and the instrument itself; and (4) must be motivated to do a conscientious job of rating.[7]

Managers need to ensure that all four criteria are satisfied if performance appraisals are to be conducted properly.

---

[5] See "Performance Appraisals—Reappraised," *Management Review*, November 1983, p. 5. Eight common performance appraisal errors are discussed in Terry R. Lowe, "Eight Ways to Ruin a Performance Review," *Personnel Journal*, January 1986, pp. 60–62.

[6] "Performance Appraisals—Reappraised," p. 5.

[7] Kenneth N. Wexley and Richard Klimoski, "Performance Appraisal: An Update," in *Research in Personnel and Human Resources Management*, Vol. 2, ed. Kendrith M. Rowland and Gerald R. Ferris (Greenwich, Conn.: JAI Press, 1984), pp. 55–56.

■ **TABLE 7–1** Proactive Appraisee Roles during Performance Appraisal

Role	Description
Analyzer	Performs self-assessment of goal achievement.
	Identifies performance strengths and weaknesses.
	Makes suggestions for performance improvement.
	Takes personal responsibility for solving performance problems.
Influencer	Improves communication skills (e.g., negotiations, advocating, providing information, advising, soliciting feedback, listening).
	Questions old assumptions and organizational roadblocks.
	Strives for collaborative relationship with boss.
Planner	Develops a clear vision of why his or her job exists.
	Identifies quality-of-service goals relative to "customers" or "clients."
	Understands what his or her job contributes (or does not contribute) to the organization.
Protégé	Learns from high-performing role models without compromising personal uniqueness.
	Learns through personal initiative rather than by waiting for instructions from others.

SOURCE: Adapted from Betsy Jacobson and Beverly L. Kaye, "Career Development and Performance Appraisal: It Takes Two to Tango," *Personnel,* January 1986, pp. 26–32.

The Appraisee.   Employees play a characteristically passive listening and watching role when their own performance is being appraised. This experience can be demeaning and often threatening. According to a pair of human resource consultants:

> Whatever method is used, performance appraisals are always manager-driven. Managers are in charge of the schedule, the agenda, and the results, and managers are the ones that receive any training and/or rewards concerning performance appraisals. Subordinates generally are given no responsibility or particular preparation for their roles in the process beyond attending the appraisal meetings.[8]

Consequently, these consultants recommend four *proactive* roles (see Table 7–1) for appraisees. They suggest formal *appraisee* training so that analyzer, influencer, planner, and protégé roles are performed skillfully. This represents a marked departure from the usual practice of training appraisers only. The goal of this promising approach is to marry performance appraisal and career development through enhanced communication and greater personal commitment.

The Appraisal Method.   Three distinct approaches to appraising job performance have emerged over the years—the trait approach, the behavioral approach,

---

[8] Betsy Jacobson and Beverly L. Kaye, "Career Development and Performance Appraisal: It Takes Two to Tango," *Personnel,* January 1986, p. 27.

and the results approach. Figure 7–3 displays examples of these three approaches. Controversy surrounds the question of which of these three approaches (and a recently suggested contingency approach) is best.

- *Trait approach:* This approach involves rating an individual's personal traits or characteristics. Commonly assessed traits are initiative, decisiveness, and dependability. Although the trait approach is widely used by managers, it is generally considered by experts to be the weakest. Trait ratings are deficient because they are ambiguous relative to actual performance. For instance, rating someone low on initiative tells him or her nothing about how to improve job performance. Also, employees tend

■ **FIGURE 7–3**   Three Basic Approaches to Appraising Job Performance

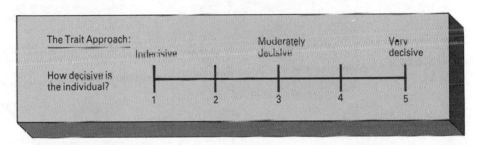

■ **FIGURE 7–4**   Six Criteria of Legally Defensible Performance Appraisal Systems

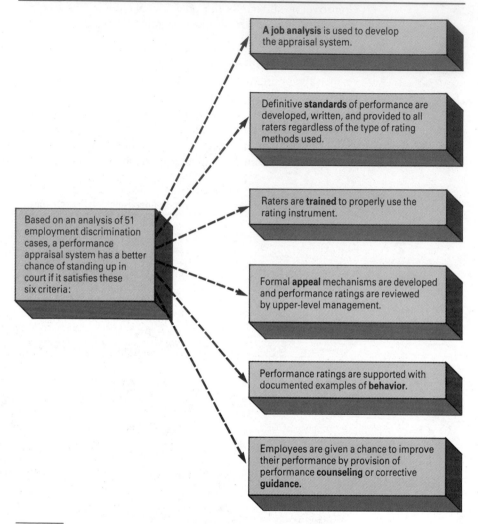

Based on an analysis of 51 employment discrimination cases, a performance appraisal system has a better chance of standing up in court if it satisfies these six criteria:

A job analysis is used to develop the appraisal system.

Definitive **standards** of performance are developed, written, and provided to all raters regardless of the type of rating methods used.

Raters are **trained** to properly use the rating instrument.

Formal **appeal** mechanisms are developed and performance ratings are reviewed by upper-level management.

Performance ratings are supported with documented examples of **behavior**.

Employees are given a chance to improve their performance by provision of performance **counseling** or corrective **guidance**.

SOURCE: Adapted from Gerald V. Barrett and Mary C. Kernan, "Performance Appraisal and Terminations: A Review of Court Decisions Since *Brito* v. *Zia* with Implications for Personnel Practices," *Personnel Psychology*, Autumn 1987, pp. 489–503.

to react defensively to feedback about their personality (who or what they are).[9]

- *Behavioral approach:* How the person actually behaves, rather than his or her personality, matters in the behavioral approach. As indicated in Figure 7–4, the legal defensibility of performance appraisals is enhanced

[9] Supporting discussion is provided by Kenneth N. Wexley, "Appraisal Interview," in *Performance Assessment,* ed. Ronald A. Berk (Baltimore, Md.: The Johns Hopkins Press Ltd., 1986).

■ **TABLE 7–2** A Contingency Approach to Performance Appraisals

Function of Appraisal	Appraisal Method	Comments
Promotion decisions	Trait	Appropriate when competing appraisees have *dissimilar* jobs
	Behavioral	Appropriate when competing appraisees have *similar* jobs
	Results	Same as above
Development decisions	Trait	Tends to cause defensiveness among low self-esteem employees
	Behavioral	Pinpoints specific performance improvement needs
	Results	Identifies deficient results, but does not tell *why*
Pay decisions	Trait	Weak performance-reward linkage
	Behavioral	Enhances performance-reward linkage
	Results	Same as above
Layoff decisions	Trait	Inappropriate, potentially discriminatory
	Behavioral	Weighted combination of behaviors, results, and seniority is recommended
	Results	Same as above

SOURCE: Adapted from Kenneth N. Wexley and Richard Klimoski, "Performance Appraisal: An Update," in *Research in Personnel and Human Resources Management,* Vol. 2, od. Kendrith M. Rowland and Gerald R. Ferris (Greenwich, Conn.: JAI Press, 1984), pp. 35–79.

when performance ratings are supported with behavioral examples of performance.

- *Results approach:* While the trait approach focuses on the "person" and the behavioral approach focuses on the "process," the results approach focuses on the "product" of one's efforts. In other words, what has the individual accomplished? Management by objectives, discussed in the next section, is the most common format for the results approach.

- *Contingency approach:* A pair of performance appraisal experts recently called the trait-behavioral-results controversy a "pseudo issue." They contend that each approach has its appropriate use, depending on the demands of the situation. Thus, they recommend a contingency approach (see Table 7–2). Notice how the poorly regarded trait approach is appropriate when a promotion decision needs to be made for candidates with dissimilar jobs. Although it has widespread applicability, the results approach is limited by its failure to specify why the appraisee's objectives have not been met. Overall, the behavioral approach emerges as the strongest. But it too is subject to situational limitations, such as when employees with dissimilar jobs are being evaluated for a promotion.

Outcomes of the Appraisal. According to a researcher from the Center for Creative Leadership, there are three indicators of a useful performance appraisal. They are:

- Timely feedback on performance.
- Input for key personnel decisions.
- Individual and organizational planning tool.[10]

Appraisal outcomes cannot be left to chance. They need to be a forethought rather than an afterthought.

Recent Performance Appraisal Research Findings

Researchers have probed many facets of the appraisal process. Recent evidence provides the following insights:

- Appraisers typically rate same-race appraisees higher. A meta-analysis of 74 studies and 17,159 individuals revealed that white superiors tended to favor white subordinates. Similarly, black superiors tended to favor black subordinates in a meta-analysis of 14 studies and 2,248 people.[11]
- No consistent pattern of gender bias is evident.
- More experienced appraisers tend to render higher-quality appraisals. Along the same line, comprehensive appraiser training and practice can reduce rater errors.
- High-performing managers tend to render higher-quality performance appraisals.
- Peer ratings and self-evaluations tend to be more lenient than those rendered by supervisors.
- Although a great deal of effort has been devoted to creating more precise rating formats, only 4 to 8 percent of the variance in appraisals is accounted for by the appraisal format.
- The appraiser's information-processing abilities significantly affect the quality of appraisals.
- Appraisers can be trained to provide more accurate performance ratings.[12]

■ ALTERNATIVE PERFORMANCE APPRAISAL TECHNIQUES

A rich variety of performance appraisal techniques and formats has evolved over the years. This is probably because any given appraisal technique rarely satisfies all affected parties. Managers are always looking for something new and better. In the AMA study of 588 companies referred to earlier, no less

---

[10] See Ann M. Morrison, "Performance Appraisal: Getting from Here to There," *Human Resource Planning* 7, no. 2 (1984), pp. 73–77.

[11] Results are presented in Kurt Kraiger and J. Kevin Ford, "A Meta-Analysis of Ratee Race Effects in Performance Ratings," *Journal of Applied Psychology*, February 1985, pp. 56–65.

[12] Research results extracted from Frank J. Landy and James L. Farr, "Performance Rating," *Psychological Bulletin*, January 1980, pp. 72–107; Wexley and Klimoski, "Performance Appraisal: An Update"; Rice, "Performance Review: The Job Nobody Likes"; and Jerry W. Hedge and Michael J. Kavangh, "Improving the Accuracy of Performance Evaluations: Comparisons of Three Methods of Performance Appraiser Training," *Journal of Applied Psychology*, February 1988, pp. 68–73.

than 10 appraisal techniques were reportedly used. As depicted in Figure 7–5, goal setting was the most extensively used technique, followed closely by written essays and critical incidents. A brief overview of each of these techniques follows.

Goal Setting/Management by Objectives

Challenging yet attainable goals, as discussed in the last chapter, can be a powerful motivational force. They also can be a handy appraisal tool when goal setting occurs within a management by objectives (MBO) framework. (The terms *goal* and *objective* are used interchangeably here.)

Peter Drucker ignited the MBO spark in his 1954 classic *The Practice of Management* by suggesting that a hierarchy of objectives would get hired managers to act more like owners. From that modest beginning, MBO has grown into a comprehensive and extensively used administrative technique. Formally defined, **management by objectives** is a comprehensive planning, evaluation, development, and control system based on quantifiable objectives

■ **FIGURE 7–5**   Reported Use of Various Performance Appraisal Techniques

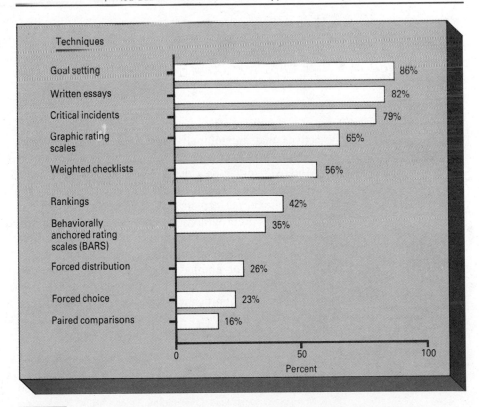

SOURCE: Data from "Performance Appraisal: Current Practices and Techniques," *Personnel,* May–June 1984, pp. 57–59.

"The fact that you've rolled up your sleeves since our last talk has been noted, Parminger. However, there's still something I'd like to discuss with you." (The New Yorker, August 11, 1986, p. 74. Drawing by W. Miller; © 1986, The New Yorker Magazine, Inc.)

that are participatively set.[13] Participation ideally fosters personal "ownership" of objectives that are mutually agreeable to both superior and subordinate. Goal setting in MBO starts at the top and trickles down through the managerial ranks. Moreover, objectives that are measurable in terms of units, dollars, or percentage of change are a good tool for holding people accountable for important aspects of their job performance. For example, the performance of managers in Xerox Corp.'s Reprographic Business Group is appraised on the basis of four sets of objectives: (1) personal and professional development, (2) task, (3) financial, and (4) human resource management.[14]

MBO is praised for emphasizing results rather than activities, generating measurable goals, and fostering participation. However, as pointed out in Table 7–2, MBO has two significant drawbacks: (1) It does not facilitate head-to-head comparisons of employees with different jobs, and (2) it does not reveal why the individual has fallen short of his or her goals.

---

[13] A good review of MBO research may be found in Jack N. Kondrasuk, "Studies in MBO Effectiveness," *Academy of Management Review*, July 1981, pp. 419–30.

[14] See Norman R. Deets and D. Timothy Tyler, "How Xerox Improved Its Performance Appraisals," *Personnel Journal*, April 1986, pp. 50–52.

■ **TABLE 7–3** A SMART Way to Keep Job Performance on Track

One of the toughest parts of designing a performance appraisal system is coming up with objective standards for measuring people's work.

If you're going to conduct formal performance appraisals (and who isn't these days?), you've got to have some reliable yardsticks. The ones you use must be fair to both employee and employer, should provoke as little argument and interpretation as possible and must be balanced across all groups of employees. Short of calling in a federal mediator, how do you design such standards?

One widely accepted way to evaluate your standards is to make sure they're smart—better make that SMART. The letters stand for Specific, Measurable, Attainable, Results-oriented and Time-related. The idea isn't new, but it's usually workable. And, according to John Reddish and George Bickley, SMART is a great way to measure the progress of employees toward just about any goal.

Reddish, a West Chester, PA, management consultant, and Bickley, president of Glenn Industries, Inc., a real estate company, define SMARTly designed performance standards as:

Specific—that is, not defined in vague, global terms, but in precise language that leaves no doubt as to what's expected. They illustrate with an analogy about a man with two cars, two sons and two gallons of antifreeze. The father tells each son to put a gallon of antifreeze in one of the cars. One son puts it in the radiator, the other stows it in the trunk. Both are right, because the message wasn't clear enough.

Measurable—in quantifiable terms that are meaningful, but that leave no doubt about when a performance goal has been achieved. For example, you wouldn't measure sales performance by number of calls made or sales courses attended; you'd look at the revenue the salesperson generated.

Attainable—in that employees should be able to reach the measurable standard at least half the time. If a standard is unrealistic, people will feel they're being set up for failure.

Results-oriented—to ensure that you're measuring output, and not the process of achieving it. Hours spent on the job, paperwork shuffled, courses logged—all become meaningless if they produce no results.

Time-related—to the extent that the results expected have a time frame. Every job standard should have a maximum time line, and only results achieved within it should count.

Standards such as these, Reddish and Bickley say, put the responsibility for performance in any job on the person doing the job, and make it difficult for marginal performers to maintain excuses such as, "You really can't measure my job."

An interesting and useful way of remembering the criteria for well-written performance appraisal goals is the SMART technique presented in Table 7–3.

Written Essays

This appraisal technique involves narrative descriptions of an individual's job performance. As one might expect, poor writing skills and an unstructured format can render this popular technique ineffective. Sharp, probing questions on the appraisal instrument are needed to keep appraisers on the right track.

Critical Incidents

Critical incidents are notable examples of good or bad performance that are written down soon after they occur. Collections of such critical incidents can provide an objective basis for a performance appraisal. The value of critical incidents is increased when managers focus on specific behavior and/or results rather than on personality traits. On the negative side, busy managers often fall behind in promptly recording critical incidents.

Graphic Rating Scales

This technique involves rating the individual's traits or performance along a graphic continuum. Graphic rating scales may be "anchored" with numbers, adjectives, or behavioral descriptions. For example, the trait "confidence" could be evaluated on the following numerically anchored scale (low = 1—2—3—4—5—6—7 = high). Although this is one of the weakest appraisal techniques when based upon traits, it can be one of the strongest when anchored to specific behaviors. Behaviorally anchored rating scales are discussed below.

Weighted Checklists

Performance appraisers are given lists of adjectives or performance descriptions and asked to check the ones that best describe the person's performance. Predetermined weights, unknown to the appraiser at the time of the review, are used to compute a final performance appraisal score.

Rankings

This technique involves the rank ordering of work group or department members on specific dimensions of performance. For instance, a book publisher's sales representatives could be ranked according to how well they service the special needs of their customers. A global ranking could then be obtained by averaging each employee's ranking across several dimensions of performance. One drawback of rankings is that they do not reveal absolute differences between appraisees. Specifically, the top-ranked sales representative might be twice as good as the second-ranked one who is only slightly better than the third-ranked one.

Behaviorally Anchored Rating Scales

Behaviorally anchored rating scales (BARS) are graphic rating scales with behavioral descriptions attached at specific points as determined by a consensus of those familiar with the job in question. For example, panels of students helped develop the BARS exhibited in Figure 7–6. The BARS technique is praised for bringing rating scales to life for the appraisers and reducing common sources of rater error (e.g., halo, leniency, and central tendency). On the

■ **FIGURE 7-6** A Behaviorally Anchored Rating Scale for College Professors

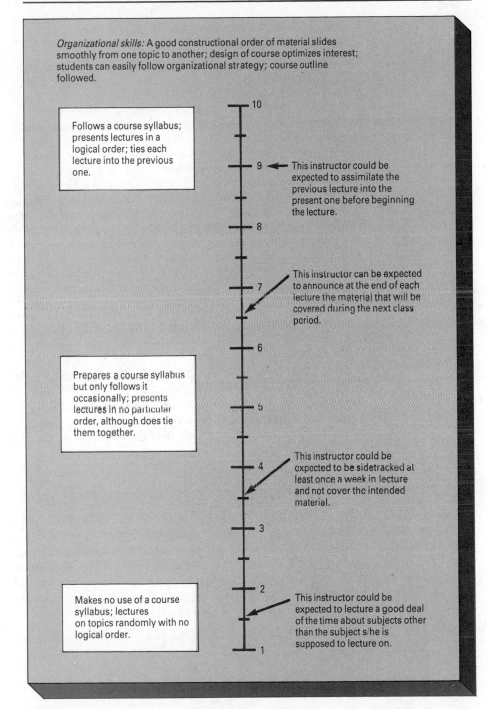

Organizational skills: A good constructional order of material slides smoothly from one topic to another; design of course optimizes interest; students can easily follow organizational strategy; course outline followed.

Follows a course syllabus; presents lectures in a logical order; ties each lecture into the previous one.

← This instructor could be expected to assimilate the previous lecture into the present one before beginning the lecture.

This instructor can be expected to announce at the end of each lecture the material that will be covered during the next class period.

Prepares a course syllabus but only follows it occasionally; presents lectures in no particular order, although does tie them together.

This instructor could be expected to be sidetracked at least once a week in lecture and not cover the intended material.

Makes no use of a course syllabus; lectures on topics randomly with no logical order.

This instructor could be expected to lecture a good deal of the time about subjects other than the subject s/he is supposed to lecture on.

SOURCE: From H. John Bernardin and Richard W. Beatty, *Performance Appraisal: Assessing Human Behavior at Work* (Boston: Kent Publishing Company, 1984), p. 84. © by Wadsworth, Inc. Reprinted by permission of PWS-KENT Publishing Company, a division of Wadsworth, Inc., and H. John Bernardin.

■ **TABLE 7–4** Forced Distributions Are a Way of Life at Exxon

Exxon doesn't rely on intuition or hit-and-miss methods to spot talent. It's incredibly methodical. Each of the company's 175,000 worldwide employees is rated once a year. The company tries to make it as objective and impersonal as possible. Each person is evaluated by several superiors rather than just by his or her immediate supervisor.

The six-page "appraisal review" form contains 21 different categories, from the quality of somebody's work to creativity and leadership. The review even includes an E.E.O. (equal employment opportunity) category, where Exxon employees are rated according to their "sensitivity to the needs of minorities, females, and other protected groups." In each category, supervisors rate employees from 1.0 for "outstanding" to 4.0 for "inadequate."

Other firms evaluate employees regularly. What makes Exxon's system unique is that everyone is then compared with his or her peers. Supervisors send the results of the appraisal reviews to a departmental committee composed of senior managers. The committee prepares a list of all employees at the same level within the department and asks the supervisors to rank them from best to worst. This is done on a bell curve; if more than 10 percent are rated as "outstanding," the departmental committee reduces a few to the next category. Based on these detailed comparisons, Exxon establishes succession plans for each job in the firm.

SOURCE: Excerpted from Robert Levering, Milton Moskowitz and Michael Katz, *The 100 Best Companies to Work For in America*, © 1984, Addison-Wesley Publishing Company, Inc., Reading, Massachusetts, pp. 108–109. Reprinted with permission.

negative side, three problems have emerged: (1) midscale anchors are difficult to specify; (2) BARS developed for one situation often are not applicable for other situations; and (3) development of BARS is costly. These problems led a pair of OB researchers to conclude: "That major objection to the BARS currently is whether the ratings that these scales produce are so error free that they justify the cost of scale development."[15]

Forced Distribution

Just as students resist the notion of a forced grade distribution with 10 percent As and 10 percent Fs, employees generally resist this technique. Critics contend it is unrealistic to assume the performance ratings in any given work group will fit a uniform bell-shaped curve. On the positive side, however, the common problem of leniency error is avoided. Exxon, the world's largest oil company, enhanced the effectiveness of the forced distribution technique by pairing it with rating scales (see Table 7–4).

Forced Choice

While noting that this technique is growing in popularity, two performance appraisal experts offered the following description:

---

[15] This critique of BARS was drawn from discussion in Landy and Farr, "Performance Rating," pp. 83–84.

A forced-choice scale is a checklist of statements that are grouped together according to certain statistical properties. The basic rationale underlying the approach is that the statements that are grouped have equal importance or social desirability. The rater is "forced" to select from each group of statements a subset of those statements that are "most descriptive" of each ratee. With this approach, raters have difficulty deliberately distorting ratings in favor of or against particular individuals because they have no idea [of how the statements are weighted].[16]

Paired Comparisons

This technique calls for head-to-head comparisons of all group members along specified performance dimensions. Rank orderings are then derived from the composite comparisons. Paired comparisons are most appropriate for small work groups because they can become cumbersome as the group grows. For example, a manager with 10 subordinates would have to make 45 paired comparisons. The formula for this determination is $[N(N - 1)]/2$. N = Number of subordinates. Thus, 10 times 9 divided by 2 equals 45. How many paired comparisons would a supervisor with 20 subordinates have to make? (See note 17 for the answer.)

Concluding Comment

Research evidence suggests that the particular appraisal technique used is not as critical to effective ratings as are basic contextual factors. Specifically, the six criteria of a legally defensible performance appraisal system need to be followed and managers need to receive hands-on training with the appraisal instrument. Once the appraisal is completed, the appraiser and appraisee need to sit down in an interruption-free setting for a performance review meeting (see Table 7–5). Managers can better handle performance review meetings if they understand the dynamics of feedback.

■ FEEDBACK

Achievement-oriented students have a hearty appetite for feedback. Following a difficult exam, for instance, students want to know two things: how they did and how their peers did. By letting students know how their work measures up to grading and competitive standards, an instructor's feedback permits the students to adjust their study habits so they can reach their goals. Likewise, managers in well-run organizations follow up goal setting with a feedback program to provide a rational basis for adjustment and improvement. For

---

[16] H. John Bernardin and Richard W. Beatty, *Performance Appraisal: Assessing Human Behavior at Work* (Boston: Kent, 1984), p. 96.

[17] For each dimension of performance, 190 paired comparisons would have to be conducted, a very time-consuming job.

■ **TABLE 7-5** Some Practical Tips on Performance Reviews

A majority of employees believe their bosses botch appraisals of their work, if they give reviews at all. Psychological Associates Inc. of St. Louis, surveying 4,000 employees at 190 companies recently, found that 70 percent believed review sessions hadn't given them a clear picture of what was expected of them on the job, or where they could advance in the company. Only half said their bosses helped them set job objectives, and only one in five said reviews were followed up during the ensuing year. . . .

Increasingly managers must do a better job of appraising employees—not only to help employees mature but to increase productivity and company loyalty. Comprehensive performance reviews also reduce the chances that a fired employee who has been warned of unsatisfactory performance will sue the company.

Employees have a right to expect a performance review at least once a year, personnel experts say. A manager should listen to an employee's self-appraisal before offering his own evaluation, then give a balanced picture of the employee's strengths and weaknesses, discuss differences and offer specific suggestions on how to improve. And he or she should work with the employee to develop goals. . . .

Personnel experts also have tips for what not to do during a review. Don't try to become a therapist to employees with marital, drinking or other personal problems, they advise managers. Instead, refer those employees to programs within the company or to outside help.

It's also best not to discuss salaries during reviews, they say. For one thing, whether or not an employee gets a raise often depends not only on his performance but on the financial condition of the company and the economy, and wages paid by competitors.

SOURCE: Excerpted from Carol Hymowitz, "Bosses: Don't Be Nasty (and Other Tips for Reviewing a Worker's Performance)." Reprinted by permission of *The Wall Street Journal,* © Dow Jones & Company, Inc., January 17, 1985, eastern edition p. 20. All rights reserved.

example, Sam Walton, founder of the fast-growing chain of Wal-Mart Stores, is a strong proponent of feedback:

> To keep his people focused on the bottom line, Walton insists that all employees have access to complete financial results. Each month, [the company] sends out monthly summaries ranking every department in every store. The overachievers are recognized and rewarded—and the laggards, while seldom fired, are sometimes demoted.[18]

This helps explain why Wal-Mart's profits have been 33 percent higher than the industry average in recent years.

As the term is used here, **feedback** is objective information about the adequacy of one's own job performance. Subjective assessments such as, "You're doing a lousy job," "You're really a jerk," or "We truly appreciate your hard work" do not qualify as objective feedback. But hard data such as units sold, days absent, dollars saved, projects completed, and quality control rejects are all candidates for objective feedback programs. Because we are dealing with objective feedback here, we are focusing on a specialized subset of the interper-

---

[18] Todd Mason, "Sam Walton of Wal-Mart: Just Your Basic Homespun Billionaire," *Business Week,* October 14, 1985, pp. 143, 146.

■ **TABLE 7-6** Six Advantages of Objective Feedback

1. *Abundant data*—The typical organization generates a great deal of objective data through MBO programs, financial and accounting procedures, and government reports that can be used in feedback programs.
2. *Small investment in time and money*—Research has shown that feedback programs that saved an average of $77,000 per year generally cost less than $1,000 to develop and implement.
3. *A natural control tool*—Straightforward presentation of objective performance data need not involve gimmicks such as lotteries or other contrived motivational techniques.
4. *Rapid results*—Immediate performance improvement is common.
5. *Suitable for most settings*—Objective feedback can be used in not-for-profit and governmental organizations that have strict limits on incentives and rewards.
6. *Complements other productivity improvement techniques*—Objective feedback is an essential part of training and management development programs and organization development (OD) interventions.

SOURCE: Adapted from Richard E. Kopelman, *Managing Productivity in Organizations: A Practical People-Oriented Perspective* (New York: McGraw-Hill, 1986), p. 174.

sonal communication process presented in Chapter 12. Six advantages of objective feedback are listed in Table 7–6.

Experts say feedback serves two functions for those who receive it, one is *instructional* and the other *motivational*. Feedback instructs when it clarifies roles or teaches new behavior. For example, an assistant accountant might be advised to handle a certain entry as a capital item rather than as an expense item. On the other hand, feedback motivates when it serves as a reward or promises a reward.[19] Having the boss tell you that a grueling project you worked on earlier has just been completed can be a rewarding piece of news. We expand upon these two functions in this section by examining feedback as a control mechanism, analyzing a conceptual model of feedback, and reviewing the practical implications of recent feedback research.

Feedback Is a Control Mechanism

The notion of feedback has an interesting history. According to one observer: "Though not a new idea, the term feedback is of relatively recent vintage, owing coinage to engineer Norbert Wiener, formulator of cybernetic theory, the hot-button topic of the 1950s."[20] Wiener limited his context to mechanical systems, but behavioral scientists eagerly embraced the concept of feedback because they sought to explain how people behave as dynamic self-adjusting systems.

---

[19] Both the definition of feedback and the functions of feedback are based on discussion in Daniel R. Ilgen, Cynthia D. Fisher, and M. Susan Taylor, "Consequences of Individual Feedback on Behavior in Organizations," *Journal of Applied Psychology*, August 1979, pp. 349–71; and Richard E. Kopelman, *Managing Productivity in Organizations: A Practical People-Oriented Perspective* (New York: McGraw-Hill, 1986), p. 175.

[20] Ron Zemke, "Feedback Technology and the Growing Appetite for Self-Knowledge," *Training*, April 1982, p. 28.

A Basic Feedback Control Model.   Figure 7–7 illustrates how feedback, in conjunction with a standard and a mechanism for comparing actual and standard, can control virtually any system. Take the familiar home thermostat, for example. If the room feels too hot, you lower the temperature setting (thus adjusting the standard). The thermostat, which constantly monitors the room temperature, turns on the cooling unit because it detects a gap between actual (feedback) and standard. When the room reaches the desired temperature, the thermostat turns off the cooling unit. Despite the imperfect analogy between mechanical and human behavioral systems, OB scholars believe feedback control is necessary and desirable in work organizations. All that is required is a set of performance standards and a mechanism for monitoring performance and providing objective feedback. Self-control is the objective of all feedback control systems, whether mechanical or behavioral.

A Hierarchy of Standards.   The basic model in Figure 7–7 can be humanized by expanding the idea of standards. Feedback control becomes less mechanical

■ **FIGURE 7–7** Feedback Control

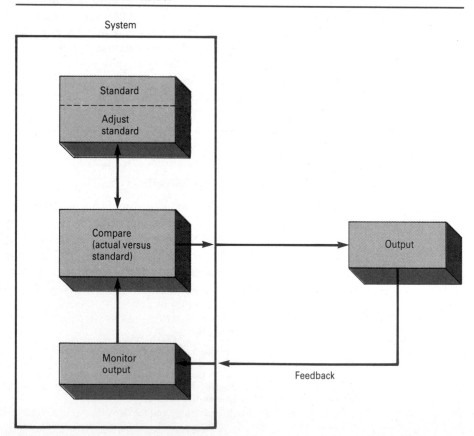

■ **FIGURE 7–8** A Model of Feedback on Job Performance

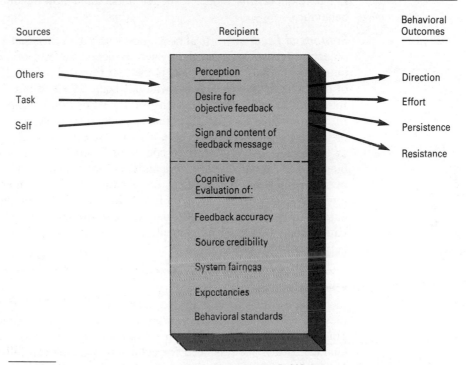

SOURCE: Based in part on discussion in M. Susan Taylor, Cynthia D. Fisher, and Daniel R. Ilgen, "Individuals' Reactions to Performance Feedback in Organizations: A Control Theory Perspective," in *Research in Personnel and Human Resources Management*, Vol. 2, ed. Kendrith M. Rowland and Gerald R. Ferris (Greenwich, Conn.: JAI Press, 1984), pp. 81–124.

when one realizes that employees conform to varying combinations of three types of standards. From general to specific, they are:

- *Principle standards* (conceptual or moral).
- *Program standards* (if-then decision rules).
- *Action standards* (specific behaviors).[21]

Humans stand apart from machines in their unique ability to conceive, formalize, and act on general moral standards.

Conceptual Model of the Feedback Process

The influence of objective feedback on job behavior is a much more complex process than one might initially suspect. To begin with, as shown in Figure 7–8, feedback comes from different sources. Moreover, perceptual and cognitive

---

[21] Adapted from discussion in M. Susan Taylor, Cynthia D. Fisher, and Daniel R. Ilgen, "Individuals' Reactions to Performance Feedback in Organizations: A Control Theory Perspective," in *Research in Personnel and Human Resources Management*, Vol. 2, ed. Kendrith M. Rowland and Gerald R. Ferris (Greenwich, Conn.: JAI Press, 1984), pp. 81–124.

hurdles must be jumped if the desired behavioral outcomes are to be achieved. Let us explore this model to better understand how feedback influences job behavior.

Sources of Feedback. It almost goes without saying that employees receive objective feedback from others such as peers, supervisors, subordinates, and outsiders. Perhaps less obvious is the fact that the task itself is a ready source of objective feedback. Anyone who has been "hooked into" pumping quarters into a video game like Pac-Man® or Pole Position can appreciate the power of task-provided feedback. Similarly, skilled tasks like computer programming or landing a jet airplane provide a steady stream of feedback about how well or poorly one is doing. A third source of feedback is oneself, but self-serving bias and other perceptual problems can contaminate this source. Those high in self-confidence tend to rely on personal feedback more than those with low self-confidence. Although circumstances vary, an employee can be bombarded by feedback from all three sources simultaneously. This is where the gatekeeping functions of perception and cognitive evaluation are needed to help sort things out.

Perception and Cognitive Evaluation of Feedback. As with other stimuli, we selectively perceive feedback. One's desire for objective feedback is an important factor here. Many people ask for objective feedback when it is the last thing they truly want. Restaurant servers who ask, "How was everything?" before presenting the bill, typically turn a deaf ear to constructive criticism. Personality characteristics, such as need for achievement, also can influence one's desire for feedback. In a laboratory study, Japanese psychology students who scored high on need for achievement responded more favorably to feedback than did their classmates who had low need for achievement. This particular relationship likely exists in Western cultures as well. Moreover, 331 employees in the marketing department of a large public utility in the United States were found to seek feedback on important issues and when faced with uncertain situations. Long-tenured employees from this sample also were less likely to seek feedback than employees with little tenure.[22] Consequently, managers need to consider each individual's readiness for objective feedback, based on relevant personality and situational variables.

The *sign* of feedback refers to whether it is positive or negative. Generally, people tend to perceive and recall positive feedback more accurately than negative feedback.[23] Feedback with a negative sign or threatening content tends to make employees defensive.

Upon receiving feedback, people cognitively evaluate factors such as its

[22] See Tamao Matsui, Akinori Okada, and Takashi Kakuyama, "Influence of Achievement Need on Goal Setting, Performance, and Feedback Effectiveness," *Journal of Applied Psychology,* October 1982, pp. 645–48; and Susan J. Ashford, "Feedback-Seeking in Individual Adaptation: A Resource Perspective," *Academy of Management Journal,* September 1986, pp. 465–87.

[23] See Brendan D. Bannister, "Performance Outcome Feedback and Attributional Feedback: Interactive Effects on Recipient Responses," *Journal of Applied Psychology,* May 1986, pp. 203–10.

accuracy, the credibility of the source, the fairness of the system (e.g., performance appraisal system), their expectancies, and the reasonableness of the standards. Any feedback that fails to clear one or more of these cognitive hurdles will be rejected or downplayed. Personal experience largely dictates how these factors are weighed. For instance, you would probably discount feedback from someone who exaggerates or from someone who performed poorly on the same task you have just successfully completed. Of course, a poor performer might be a credible source if you also have done poorly on the same task. Feedback from a source that apparently shows favoritism or relies on unreasonable behavior standards would be suspect. Also, as predicted by expectancy motivation theory, feedback must foster high effort→performance expectancies and performance→reward instrumentalities if it is to motivate desired behavior. For example, many growing children have been cheated out of the rewards of athletic competition because they were told by respected adults they were too small, too short, too slow, too clumsy, and so forth. Feedback can have a profound and lasting impact on behavior.

Behavioral Outcomes of Feedback.   In the last chapter, we discussed how goal setting gives behavior direction, increases expended effort, and fosters persistence. Because feedback is intimately related to the goal-setting process, it involves the same behavioral outcomes: direction, effort, and persistence. However, while the fourth outcome of goal setting involves formulating goal-attainment strategies, the fourth possible outcome of feedback is *resistance*. Feedback schemes that smack of manipulation or fail one or more of the perceptual and cognitive evaluation tests just discussed breed resistance. Steve Jobs, the young cofounder of Apple Computer, left the firm amid controversy in 1985 partly because his uneven and heavy-handed feedback bred resistance.

> According to several insiders, Jobs, a devout believer that new technology should supersede the old, couldn't abide the success of the venerable Apple II. Nor did he hide his feelings. He once addressed the Apple II marketing staff as members of the "dull and boring product division." As chairman and largest stockholder, with an 11.3% block, Jobs was a disproportionately powerful general manager. And he had disproportionate enthusiasm for the [Macintosh] staff. Says one of them: "He was so protective of us that whenever we complained about somebody outside the division, it was like unleashing a Doberman. Steve would get on the telephone and chew the guy out so fast your head would spin."[24]

Practical Lessons from Feedback Research

After reviewing dozens of laboratory and field studies of feedback, a trio of OB researchers cited the following practical implications for managers:

- The acceptance of feedback should not be treated as a given; it is often misperceived or rejected. This is especially true in intercultural situations, as indicated in Table 7–7.

---

[24] Bro Uttal, "Behind the Fall of Steve Jobs," *Fortune*, August 5, 1985, p. 22.

■ **TABLE 7–7** The Meaning of Feedback Cannot Be Taken for Granted in Intercultural Situations

American versus European (performance appraisal):

 In appraisal and in training, American managers look for feedback much more often. Senior managers in many European companies would not dare to propose that they should be frequently and formally appraised or retrained. It is seldom that a European executive will look to his boss or his subordinates for a genuine reflection of how well he is doing.

American versus Japanese (negotiation):

 In the . . . spirit of maintaining harmony, the Japanese tradition is to avoid a direct "no" at practically any cost. They may ask a counterquestion, promise an answer at some later date, change the subject and even occasionally leave the room. Another common response is no response at all, a dead silence. "This drives Americans up the wall," [says a cross-cultural negotiation researcher].

SOURCES: Excerpted from Paul Thorne and Bill Meyer, "The Care and Feeding of Your American Management," *International Management,* October 1987, p. 114; and John Pfeiffer, "How Not to Lose the Trade Wars by Cultural Gaffes," *Smithsonian,* January 1988, pp. 150–51.

- Managers can enhance their credibility as sources of feedback by developing their expertise and creating a climate of trust.
- Feedback from the task is effective only if it is perceived to be in response to the recipient's own actions, not as a result of technology or the actions of others.
- Negative feedback is typically misperceived or rejected.
- Although very frequent feedback may erode one's sense of personal control and initiative, feedback is too infrequent in most work organizations.
- Feedback needs to be tailored to the recipient.
- While average and below-average performers need extrinsic rewards for performance, high performers respond to feedback that enhances their feelings of competence and personal control.[25]
- More recently, a team of researchers, who experimentally manipulated attributional elements (consistency, distinctiveness, and consensus) in a classroom setting, found that students preferred specific feedback that included information about their own past performance and the performance of their peers to nonspecific feedback.[26]
- Computer-based performance feedback leads to greater improvements

---

[25] Based on discussion in Ilgen, Fisher, and Taylor, "Consequences of Individual Feedback on Behavior in Organizations," pp. 367–68.

[26] Drawn from Robert C. Liden and Terence R. Mitchell, "Reactions to Feedback: The Role of Attributions," *Academy of Management Journal,* June 1985, pp. 291–308.

■ **TABLE 7–8** A Management Consultant's Advice on Giving Feedback

1. Verbal feedback is desired even when nonverbal feedback is positive.
2. Verbal feedback must accompany nonverbal to ensure complete clarity.
3. Immediate feedback is almost always more useful than delayed feedback.
4. Negative feedback may be better than no feedback, but positive feedback produces the best results.
5. Undeserved praise does not produce positive results.
6. People need to be primed to be more receptive to later feedback.
7. Employees tend to remember longest what they hear first and last in a message.
8. If you want a subordinate to react to your feedback, you must direct it personally—in many cases, privately—to the subordinate.
9. Low amounts of feedback cause low confidence and may result in hostility.
10. Absence of feedback also communicates approval of or agreement with ideas and behaviors.

SOURCE: Adapted from Priscilla Diffie-Couch, "How to Give Feedback," *Supervisory Management,* August 1983, pp. 27–31.

in performance when it is received directly from the computer system rather than via an immediate supervisor.[27]

Managers who enact these research implications and the practical advice in Table 7–8 can be credible and effective sources of feedback.[28]

Our attention now turns to rewards, a natural follow-up to any discussion of performance appraisal and feedback.

ORGANIZATIONAL REWARD SYSTEMS

Rewards are an ever-present feature of organizational life. Some employees see their jobs as the source of a paycheck and little else. Others derive great pleasure from their jobs and association with co-workers. Even volunteers who donate their time to charitable organizations, such as the Red Cross, walk away with rewards in the form of social recognition and pride of having given unselfishly of their time. Hence, the subject of organizational rewards includes, but goes far beyond, monetary compensation. This section examines key components of organizational reward systems to provide a conceptual background for discussing the controversial practice of tying rewards to job performance.

Despite the fact that reward systems vary widely, it is possible to identify and interrelate some common components. The model in Figure 7–9 focuses on four important components: (1) types of rewards, (2) reward norms, (3) distribution criteria, and (4) desired outcomes.

---

[27] See P. Christopher Earley, "Computer-Generated Performance Feedback in the Magazine-Subscription Industry," *Organizational Behavior and Human Decision Processes*, February 1988, pp. 50–64.

[28] Practical tips for giving feedback also may be found in Robert Kreitner, "People Are Systems, Too: Filling the Feedback Vacuum," *Business Horizons*, November 1977, pp. 54–58.

■ **FIGURE 7–9** A General Model of Organizational Reward Systems

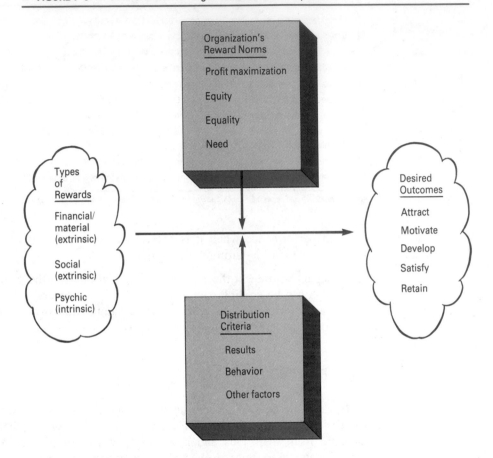

Types of Rewards

Including the usual paycheck, the variety and magnitude of organizational rewards boggles the mind (see Table 7–9). For instance, a 1984 survey found that U.S. employers spent $610 billion annually just on benefits such as disability, insurance and pensions, and paid vacations. That figure equaled 33.8 percent of the 1984 payroll.[29] In addition to the obvious pay and benefits, there are less obvious social and psychic rewards. Social rewards include praise and recognition from others both inside and outside the organization. Psychic rewards come from personal feelings of self-esteem, self-satisfaction, and accomplishment.

An alternative typology for organizational rewards is the distinction between extrinsic and intrinsic rewards. Financial, material, and social rewards qualify as **extrinsic rewards** because they come from the environment. Psychic rewards,

---

[29] Data drawn from Morton E. Grossman and Margaret Magnus, ''Benefits: Costs & Coverage,'' *Personnel Journal,* May 1986, pp. 74–79.

■ **TABLE 7-9** There Are Many Possible Rewards for Working

Consumables	Status Symbols	Monetary	Social	Opportunity
Coffee-break treats	Desk accessories	Money	Friendly greetings	Job with more responsi-
Free lunches	Personal computer	Stocks	Informal recognition	bility
Food baskets	Wall plaques	Stock options	Formal acknowledgment	Job rotation
Easter hams	Company car	Movie passes	of achievement	Early time off with pay
Christmas turkeys	Watches	Trading stamps (green	Feedback about perfor-	Extended breaks
Dinners for the family on	Trophies	stamps)	mance	Extended lunch period
the company	Commendations	Paid-up insurance	Solicitations of sugges-	Personal time off with pay
Company picnics	Rings/tie pins	policies	tions	Work on personal project
After-work wine and	Clothing	Dinner theater/sports	Solicitations of advice	on company time
cheese parties	Club privileges	tickets	Compliment on work	Use of company machin-
	Office with a window	Vacation trips	progress	ery or facilities for
	Piped-in music	Coupons redeemable at	Recognition in organiza-	personal projects
	Redecoration of work en-	local stores	tional publications	Use of company recre-
	vironment	Profit sharing	Pat on the back	ation facilities
	Company literature		Smile	Special assignments
	Private office		Verbal or nonverbal rec-	
	Popular speakers or		ognition or praise	
	lecturers			
	Book club subscriptions			

SOURCE: Adapted with permission from Fred Luthans and Robert Kreitner, *Organizational Behavior Modification and Beyond: An Operant and Social Learning Approach* (Glenview, Ill.: Scott, Foresman, 1985), p. 127.

however, are **intrinsic rewards** because they are self-granted. An employee who works to obtain extrinsic rewards, such as money or praise, is said to be extrinsically motivated. One who derives pleasure from the task itself or experiences a sense of competence or self-determination is said to be intrinsically motivated.[30]

Organizational Reward Norms

As discussed in Chapter 6 under the heading of equity theory, some OB scholars view the employer-employee linkage as an exchange relationship. Employees exchange their time and talent for rewards. Ideally, four alternative norms dictate the nature of this exchange. In pure form, each would lead to a significantly different reward distribution system. They are:

- *Profit Maximization:* The objective of each party is to maximize its net gain, regardless of how the other party fares. A profit-maximizing company would attempt to pay the least amount of wages for maximum effort. Conversely, a profit-maximizing employee would seek maximum rewards, regardless of the organization's financial well-being, and leave the organization for a better deal.
- *Equity:* According to the **reward equity norm,** rewards should be allo-

---

[30] For complete discussions, see Arthur P. Brief and Ramon J. Aldag, "The Intrinsic-Extrinsic Dichotomy: Toward Conceptual Clarity," *Academy of Management Review,* July 1977, pp. 496–500; and Edward L. Deci, *Intrinsic Motivation* (New York: Plenum Press, 1975), chap. 2.

cated proportionate to contributions. Those who contribute the most should be rewarded the most.

- *Equality:* The **reward equality norm** calls for rewarding all parties equally, regardless of their comparative contributions.
- *Need:* This norm calls for distributing rewards according to employees' needs, rather than their contributions.[31]

After defining these exchange norms, a pair of researchers concluded that these contradictory norms are typically intertwined.

> We propose that employer-employee exchanges are governed by the contradictory norms of profit maximization, equity, equality, and need. These norms can coexist; what varies is the extent to which the rules for correct application of a norm are clear and the relative emphasis different managements will give to certain norms in particular allocations.[32]

Conflict often arises over the perceived fairness of reward allocations because of disagreement about reward norms. Stockholders might prefer a profit-maximization norm, while technical specialists would like an equity norm, and unionized hourly workers would argue for a pay system based on equality. A reward norm anchored to need might prevail in a family owned and operated business. Effective reward systems are based on clear and consensual exchange norms.

Reward Distribution Criteria

According to one expert on organizational reward systems, three general criteria for the distribution of rewards are:

- *Performance: Results.* Tangible outcomes such as individual, group, or organization performance; quantity and quality of performance.
- *Performance: Actions and Behaviors.* Such as teamwork, cooperation, risk-taking, creativity.
- *Nonperformance Considerations.* Customary or contractual, where the type of job, nature of the work, equity, tenure, level in hierarchy, etc., are rewarded.[33]

Well-managed organizations integrate these reward distribution criteria with the performance appraisal system. For example, an MBO system facilitates granting rewards for results, while BARS appraisals help pinpoint rewardable behavior. Nonperformance factors such as seniority are simply taken at face value.

---

[31] Adapted from Jone L. Pearce and Robert H. Peters, ''A Contradictory Norms View of Employer-Employee Exchange,'' *Journal of Management,* Spring 1985, pp. 19–30.

[32] Ibid., p. 25.

[33] Mary Ann Von Glinow, ''Reward Strategies for Attracting, Evaluating, and Retaining Professionals,'' *Human Resource Management,* Summer 1985, p. 193.

Desired Outcomes of the Reward System

As listed in Figure 7–9, a good reward system should attract talented people and motivate and satisfy them once they have joined the organization. Further, a good reward system should foster personal growth and development and keep talented people from leaving. IBM, the most profitable company in the world, scores high on all these outcomes. For example, the computer giant's turnover was only 2.8 percent in 1985, far below the industry average. Not surprisingly, IBM employees enjoy twice-the-average benefits, including 12 paid holidays a year (versus the usual 10), assistance programs for employees with handicapped children, adoption assistance, a retirement education program, a mortgage-financing program, and a college scholarship program for employees' children.[34]

■ THE CONTINGENT REWARDS CONTROVERSY

Should rewards be tied directly to performance? Depending on one's theoretical perspective, the answer may vary from a confident yes to an adamant no. As the term is used here, a **contingent reward** is given for a specified behavior, task, or accomplishment.[35] Examples of on-the-job contingent rewards include piece-rate pay, commissions, merit pay, and conditional praise or recognition. On-the-job rewards are noncontingent when an employee receives them for merely showing up. Hourly pay and salaries are prime examples of noncontingent rewards. While we cannot hope to resolve this complex controversy here, we can provide useful insights by framing the pros and cons of the issue.

Pro: Performance-Contingent Rewards Enhance Motivation

Despite their significantly different assumptions about human behavior, expectancy theorists and behaviorists agree that contingent rewards enhance performance. Expectancy theorist Edward Lawler offered the following prescription for handling pay, the "universal" reward:

> Pay systems can play a role in increasing individuals' motivation to perform effectively, improving productivity in organizations, and off-setting the lack of involvement and commitment which is characteristic of today's work force. The key is appropriately tying pay to performance. A good case can be made that it

---

[34] Data drawn from "How IBM Employee Benefits Stack Up," *The Wall Street Journal*, April 7, 1986, p. 21.

[35] For an instructive distinction between task-noncontingent, task-contingent, and performance-contingent rewards, see Richard M. Ryan, Valerie Mims, and Richard Koestner, "Relation of Reward Contingency and Interpersonal Context to Intrinsic Motivation: A Review and Test Using Cognitive Evaluation Theory," *Journal of Personality and Social Psychology*, October 1983, pp. 736–50.

is more important now than it ever has been in the history of modern work organizations that pay be tied to performance in a motivating manner.[36]

Mixed Research Findings.   Research evidence on contingent rewards is mixed. In one study of 1,946 government and hospital employees, researchers found a positive relationship between leaders' contingent reward behavior (e.g., praising and acknowledging high performers) and subordinates' performance and satisfaction.[37] On the other hand, another group of researchers found no significant improvement in the performance of U.S. Social Security Administration managers after implementation of a merit pay system. The new merit pay system, mandated by the Civil Service Reform Act of 1978, tied 50 percent of the annual pay raise allocation to performance ratings.[38]

The Behaviorist Perspective.   Meanwhile, proponents of operant conditioning and social learning point out that behavior is strengthened, or reinforced, by favorable contingent consequences. According to this behaviorist perspective, noncontingent rewards do little more than encourage the individual to come to work. Our discussion of behavior modification in the next chapter delves into the mechanics of this behaviorist perspective.

Con: Performance-Contingent Rewards Erode Intrinsic Motivation

In the early 1970s, psychologist Edward L. Deci conducted a series of lab experiments with college students demonstrating that contingent reward schemes tend to erode intrinsic motivation. This conclusion flew in the face of the conventional wisdom that extrinsic and intrinsic rewards have an additive, or complementary, effect on motivation.

Deci's Research Design.   Deci's subjects had a choice of working on a puzzle task or reading popular magazines. Their intrinsic motivation was measured in terms of how long they worked on the puzzles, rather than being distracted by the magazines, during an eight-minute observation period. Subjects in the experimental group were paid $1 for each puzzle they solved; subjects in the control group were not paid. After observing a decrease in intrinsic motivation for the paid subjects but not for the unpaid ones, Deci concluded: "When rewards are contingent on performance they are more likely to decrease intrinsic

---

[36] Edward E. Lawler III, *Pay and Organization Development* (Reading, Mass.: Addison-Wesley Publishing, 1981), p. 224.

[37] See Philip M. Podsakoff, William D. Todor, Richard A. Grover, and Vandra L. Huber, "Situational Moderators of Leader Reward and Punishment Behaviors: Fact or Fiction?" *Organizational Behavior and Human Performance,* August 1984, pp. 21–63. A positive relationship between leader contingent reward behavior and group factors (drive, cohesiveness, and productivity) is reported in Philip M. Podsakoff and William D. Todor, "Relationships between Leader Reward and Punishment Behavior and Group Processes and Productivity," *Journal of Management,* Spring 1985, pp. 55–73.

[38] Details of this study may be found in Jone L. Pearce, William B. Stevenson, and James L. Perry, "Managerial Compensation Based on Organizational Performance: A Time Series Analysis of the Effects of Merit Pay," *Academy of Management Journal,* June 1985, pp. 261–78.

■ FIGURE 7–10 Deci's Cognitive Evaluation Theory

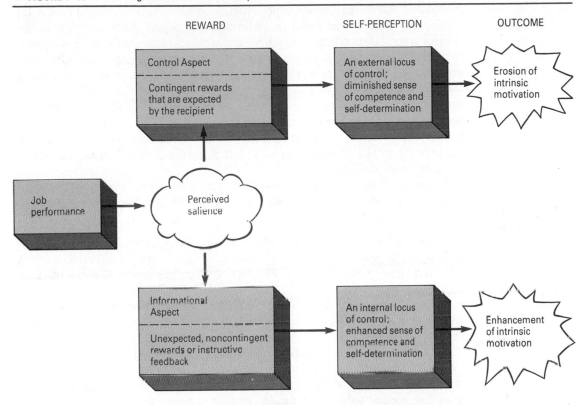

motivation. Further, when rewards are expected before the behavior begins they are more likely to decrease intrinsic motivation.''[39] Stated differently, Deci found that contingent rewards can take the fun out of a task. For example, people who love to fish probably would be less enthusiastic about fishing if they had to do it for a living.

Deci's Cognitive Evaluation Theory.   Deci formulated his **cognitive evaluation theory** to explain how contingent rewards can either enhance or erode intrinsic motivation by affecting one's feelings of competence and self-determination. The mechanisms of this theory are illustrated in Figure 7–10.

A key point in Deci's theory is his assumption that virtually all rewards and feedback have a control aspect and an informational aspect. The control aspect becomes salient (recall the discussion of salience in Chapter 4) when rewards are clearly linked to performance. A piece-rate pay system in which

---

[39] Deci, *Intrinsic Motivation*, p. 158. Methodological concerns about Deci's work are debated in Bobby J. Calder and Barry M. Staw, ''Interaction of Intrinsic and Extrinsic Motivation: Some Methodological Notes,'' *Journal of Personality and Social Psychology*, January 1975, pp. 76–80; and Edward L. Deci, Wayne F. Cascio, and Judith Krusell, ''Cognitive Evaluation Theory and Some Comments on the Calder and Staw Critique,'' *Journal of Personality and Social Psychology*, January 1975, pp. 81–85.

the employee receives a specified amount of money for each unit of work completed makes the control aspect highly salient. An unexpected bonus for a job well done would make the informational aspect more salient than the control aspect. Depending on which reward aspect is more salient to the recipient, two very different perceptual processes and outcomes swing into action. Employees who believe they are working primarily for contingent rewards, according to Deci's theory, will feel less competent and less self-determining. Hence, the fun will go out of their work. Deci's theory also contends that contingent punishment will lead to this same downward spiral. Oppositely, rewards that have a surprise effect or provide helpful information about how well the individual is doing will build competence and self-determination and bolster the enjoyment of doing the job.

When asked how managers should motivate employees, in light of his complaint about contingent rewards and punishments, Deci recommends job enrichment and participation.

More Mixed Research Findings.   After dozens of replications of Deci's studies, a clear picture about the erosion of intrinsic motivation by contingent rewards does not exist. One review of 24 Deci-type studies found that 14 of them confirmed Deci's hypothesis.[40] Interestingly, only one of the 24 studies involved actual employees, and all 14 of the confirming studies used preschool, elementary, high school, or college students as subjects. This led reviewers to conclude Deci's theory has limited value for explaining motivation in the *workplace*. Nonetheless, the issue is still unresolved; a recent field study of 48 health care technicians found that contingent rewards *did* decrease intrinsic motivation.[41] Methodological refinements and more field studies in actual work settings are needed to sort out the interaction between contingent rewards and intrinsic motivation.[42]

Practical Implications

In the foregoing debate a tough dilemma surfaces for managers whose job it is to dispense rewards and foster motivation. There are no easy answers or quick detours around the dilemma that extrinsic rewards can alternatively bolster or cripple motivation. When establishing reward systems, managers need to remember Deci's recommendations about job enrichment and participation. Additionally, factors such as the size of the reward and perceived fairness,

---

[40] See Kimberly B. Boal and L. L. Cummings, "Cognitive Evaluation Theory: An Experimental Test of Processes and Outcomes," *Organizational Behavior and Human Performance*, December 1981, pp. 289–310.

[41] Details of this study may be found in Paul C. Jordan, "Effects of an Extrinsic Reward on Intrinsic Motivation: A Field Experiment," *Academy of Management Journal*, June 1986, pp. 405–12.

[42] An overall review of research on Deci's theory is provided in Thane S. Pittman and Jack F. Heller, "Social Motivation," in *Annual Review of Psychology*, Vol. 38, ed. Mark R. Rosenzweig and Lyman W. Porter (Palo Alto, Calif.: Annual Reviews Inc., 1987). A management-oriented discussion of Deci's work can be found in Alfie Kohn, "Incentives Can Be Bad for Business," *Inc.*, January 1988, pp. 93–94.

■ **TABLE 7–10** Lincoln Electric Company: A Reward System That Works

While many U.S. companies are currently in search of new and effective ways to motivate their employees, the Lincoln Electric Company of Cleveland is still successfully running a motivation program that was put into effect when the United States was just seven years into the 20th Century.

The basis of Lincoln's effective program is pay incentives. Most of its 2,500 employees are paid on a piecework system, with an annual bonus tacked on. The bonus is a result of the employee's performance, and it can exceed their regular pay. However, an employee's mistake can lead to a deduction in his or her bonus. Because this method seems pressure-packed, one might find it hard to believe that Lincoln's turnover rate is a mere 0.3 percent a month, which indicates its employees' satisfaction with this system.

The company was founded by John C. Lincoln in 1895 to produce electric motors. (Along with the three-phase industrial motor they now produce, Lincoln has become the world's leading manufacturer of arc-welding equipment.) By 1907 his brother James joined on and began employing worker motivation programs reinforced with the idea that workers benefit when the company prospers. They made stock available for purchase at book price to employees, encouraging worker pride and participation.

Employees are solely responsible for the quality of their work. They inspect their own parts and, if a flaw exists, they remain to fix it on their own time. The company keeps track of workers by recording the names of the persons working on each piece of equipment. If a defect slips by an employee, but is spotted by one of Lincoln's quality-control people (Lincoln was recognized by *Quality Magazine*, August 1983, for outstanding product quality), or complained about by a customer, the employee involved has his bonus, pay, or merit rating reduced. Merit ratings are based on points accumulated throughout the year. Acquiring points can create tension within groups since only a specific amount of points is allocated to each department. But not all merit points come from within the group. In fact, a company spokesman says that only the first 10 points above 100 come from the group. Everything beyond that is from a pool of points set aside especially for rewarding outstanding achievements in the company.

Because of the poor industrial market [in the early 1980s], most employees average a 30-hour work week. However, due to the incentive program, the average pay in 1982 was still above $30,000. According to the spokesman, there are instances when an employee will work up to or beyond 50-hours a week, but he attributes this to Lincoln's cautious hiring plan—instead of hiring new employees in a boom economy, the company asks existing workers to take on additional hours, thus enabling Lincoln to guarantee 30-hour work weeks for employees with the company for two or more years. And Lincoln has not laid anyone off in over 30 years.

The rigorous demands on the employees can be bothersome. Besides the unfriendly competition sometimes generated from merit points, workers also face a fast-paced environment that can be both mentally and physically draining. Lincoln has no unions, no seniority system, and all promotions are done from within. If an employee desires a position outside the piecework factory environment, he must apply for a job posted on bulletin-boards throughout the company and compete for that position with other employees, both old and new.

And while some employees have gripes about the program, Lincoln's overall results speak for themselves. Last year's [1983] recession cut earnings by 42 percent and sales by 28 percent as compared with 1981 figures. However, volume and profit have increased. Over a seven-year period ending in 1981, sales escalated to a record $526.9 million, up from $232.8 million, and earnings during that period advanced to $39.7 million, also a record.

SOURCE: Reprinted, by permission of the publisher, from "Lincoln Electric's Past Enhances Its Future," *Management Review*, January 1984, pp. 40–41, © 1984 American Management Association, New York. All rights reserved.

equity, and managerial credibility need to be considered. These factors, melded in a climate of trust, help explain why some organizations such as Lincoln Electric Company get extraordinary results with contingent reward plans (see Table 7–10). Organizational reward systems that are perceived by employees to be blatantly manipulative and demeaning will breed resistance and dampen motivation.

SUMMARY OF KEY CONCEPTS

A. *Performance appraisal* involves the judgmental evaluation of a jobholder's traits, behavior, or accomplishments as a basis for making important personnel decisions (e.g., compensation, counseling, training and development, promotion, manpower planning, retention/discharge).

B. Four key components of the performance appraisal process are the appraiser, the appraisee, the appraisal method, and the outcomes. Appraisers need to be wary of perceptual errors and experts recommend a more active role for appraisees. Although the trait approach to appraisals is considered much weaker than the behavioral or results approaches, each can play a role in a contingency approach.

C. Goal setting or management by objectives (MBO) is the most widely used appraisal technique. Other techniques, listed in diminishing order of use, include written essays, critical incidents, graphic rating scales, weighted checklists, rankings, behaviorally anchored rating scales (BARS), forced distribution, forced choice, and paired comparisons.

D. *Feedback* is defined as objective information about the adequacy of one's own job performance. Feedback serves both instructional and motivational functions. The idea of feedback as a control tool for systems traces back to cybernetic theory.

E. Three sources of feedback are others, the task, or oneself. If feedback is to be believed and acted upon, it must pass several perceptual and cognitive evaluation tests. Four behavioral outcomes of feedback are direction, effort, persistence, and resistance. Positive feedback seems to work better than negative feedback.

F. Organizational reward systems are based on extrinsic (financial/material and social) and intrinsic (psychic) rewards distributed according to various reward norms and distribution criteria. A good reward system should attract, motivate, develop, satisfy, and retain talented people.

G. Contingent rewards, those tied to a specific behavior, task, or accomplishment, are recommended by expectancy theorists and behaviorists for boosting motivation and performance.

H. Deci's cognitive evaluation theory holds that the quickest way to kill intrinsic motivation is to get the individual hooked on contingent rewards. He prefers noncontingent rewards, job enrichment, and participative management for building motivation.

KEY TERMS ───

performance appraisal   **extrinsic rewards**
management by objectives (MBO)   **intrinsic rewards**
critical incidents   **reward equity norm**
behaviorally anchored rating   **reward equality norm**
   scales (BARS)   **contingent reward**
feedback   **cognitive evaluation theory**

DISCUSSION QUESTIONS ────────────────────────────────────

1. How could a weak link in the performance appraisal-feedback-rewards cycle damage the entire process?

2. Would you prefer to have your academic and/or work performance appraised in terms of traits, behavior, or results? Explain.

3. How would you respond to a manager who said, "The format of the performance appraisal instrument is everything"?

4. Why do you suppose goal setting/MBO has become the most popular appraisal technique?

5. How has feedback instructed or motivated you lately?

6. Which of the five cognitive evaluation criteria for feedback—feedback accuracy, source credibility, system fairness, expectancies, behavioral standards—do you think ranks as most important? Explain.

7. What is the most valuable lesson feedback research teaches us? Explain.

8. Which of the three organizational reward norms do you prefer? Why?

9. Why would expectancy motivation theorists recommend that rewards be closely linked to performance?

10. What is the practical significance of Deci's distinction between the control and informational aspects of rewards?

BACK TO THE OPENING CASE

Now that you have read Chapter 7, you should be able to answer the following questions about the Leprino Foods truck driver case:

1. Using the feedback model in Figure 7–8 as a guide, what is your analysis of the feedback system in this case?

2. What organizational reward norm is Leprino Foods Co. enacting? What norm would the truck drivers probably prefer? Why is conflict inevitable?

3. Will Mr. Sheehan's theory about employee rules build or weaken trust between management and the drivers? Explain.

4. What would a proponent of Deci's cognitive evaluation theory say about the feedback and reward system at Leprino Foods?

EXERCISE 7

Objectives

1. To provide actual examples of on-the-job feedback from three primary sources: organization/supervisor, co-workers, and self/task.
2. To provide a handy instrument for evaluating the comparative strength of positive feedback from these three sources.

Introduction

A pair of researchers from Georgia Tech recently developed and tested a 63-item feedback questionnaire to demonstrate the importance of both the sign and content of feedback messages.[43] Although their instrument contains both positive and negative feedback items, we have extracted 18 positive items for this self-awareness exercise.

Instructions

Thinking of your present job (or your most recent job), circle one number for each of the 18 items. Alternatively, you could ask one or more other employed individuals to complete the questionnaire. Once the questionnaire has been completed, calculate subtotal and total scores by adding the circled numbers. Then try to answer the discussion questions.

Instrument

How frequently do you experience each of the following outcomes in your present job?

Organizational/Supervisory Feedback

	RARELY	OCCASIONALLY	VERY FREQUENTLY
1. My supervisor complimenting me on something I have done.		1——2——3——4——5	
2. My supervisor increasing my responsibilities.		1——2——3——4——5	
3. The company expressing pleasure with my performance.		1——2——3——4——5	

---

[43] This exercise is adapted from material in David M. Herold and Charles K. Parsons, "Assessing the Feedback Environment in Work Organizations: Development of the Job Feedback Survey," *Journal of Applied Psychology,* May 1985, pp. 290–305.

		RARELY	OCCASIONALLY	VERY FREQUENTLY

4. The company giving me a raise.   1——2——3——4——5
5. My supervisor recommending me for a promotion
   or raise.   1——2——3——4——5
6. The company providing me with favorable data
   concerning my performance.   1——2——3——4——5

                                                        Subscore = _____

Co-Worker Feedback

7. My co-workers coming to me for advice.   1——2——3——4——5
8. My co-workers expressing approval of my work.   1——2——3——4——5
9. My co-workers liking to work with me.   1——2——3——4——5
10. My co-workers telling me that I am doing a good
    job.   1——2——3——4——5
11. My co-workers commenting favorably on some-
    thing I have done.   1——2——3——4——5
12. Receiving a compliment from my co-workers.   1——2——3   4   —5

                                                        Subscore = _____

Self/Task Feedback

13. Knowing that the way I go about my duties is supe-
    rior to most others.   1——2——3——4——5
14. Feeling I am accomplishing more than I used to.   1——2——3——4——5
15. Knowing that I can now perform or do things which
    previously were difficult for me.   1——2——3——4——5
16. Finding that I am satisfying my own standards for
    "good work."   1——2——3——4——5
17. Knowing that what I am doing "feels right."   1——2——3——4——5
18. Feeling confident of being able to handle all aspects
    of my job.   1——2——3——4——5

                                                        Subscore = _____
                                                        Total score = _____

Questions for Consideration/Class Discussion

1. Which items on this questionnaire would you rate as primarily instructional in function? Are all of the remaining items primarily motivational? Explain.
2. In terms of your own feedback profile, which of the three types is the strongest (has the highest subscore)? Which is the weakest (has the lowest subscore)? How well does your feedback profile explain your job performance and/or satisfaction?
3. How does your feedback profile measure up against those of your classmates? (Arbitrary norms, for comparative purposes, are: Deficient feedback = 18–42; Moderate feedback = 43–65; Abundant feedback = 66–90.)
4. Which of the three sources of feedback is most critical to your successful job performance and/or job satisfaction? Explain.

Chapter **8**

Behavior Modification and Self-Management

LEARNING OBJECTIVES

When you finish studying the material in this chapter,
you should be able to:

- Define the term *behavior modification* and explain the A→B→C model.
- Differentiate the following consequence management strategies: positive reinforcement, negative reinforcement, punishment, and extinction.
- Explain why the scheduling of reinforcement is so important in B. Mod.
- Define and give your own example of behavior shaping.
- Identify and briefly explain each step in the four-step B. Mod. process.
- Specify the six guidelines for managing consequences during B. Mod.
- Explain how behavioral self-management differs from B. Mod.
- Discuss the mechanics of Kanfer's model of self-regulation.
- Demonstrate your familiarity with the four major components of the social learning model of self-management.

OPENING CASE 8

How to Earn "Well Pay"

The woman in blue jeans and a logger's shirt looks up from the production line and says grimly: "I can't miss work today. It's almost the end of the month, and I'm going to earn that 'well pay' if it kills me."

At Parsons Pine Products Inc. in Ashland, Ore., "well pay" is the opposite of sick pay. It is an extra eight hours' wages that the company gives workers who are neither absent nor late for a full month. It is also one of four incentives that owner James W. Parsons has built into a "positive reinforcement plan" for workers: well pay, retro pay, safety pay, and profit-sharing pay.

Beating the Tax Man

The formula, Parsons says, enables him and his wife to beat the combination of federal and state income taxes that leaves them only 14% of any increase in earnings; it allows them to pass along much of the potential tax money to the workers. Under the Parsons system, an employee earning $10,000 a year can add as much as $3,500 to his income by helping the plant operate economically.

Parsons Pine employs some 100 workers to cut lumber into speciality items—primarily louver slats for shutters, bifold doors, and blinds, and bases for rat traps. It is reportedly the U.S.'s biggest producer of these items, with sales last year [1977] of $2.5 million.

The company began handing out "well pay" in January 1977. "We had a problem with lateness," Parsons explains. "Just be-

fore the 7 A.M. starting time, the foreman in a department would take a head count and assign three people to this machine and six over there. Then a few minutes later someone else comes in and he has to recalculate and reshuffle. Or he may be so short as to leave a machine idle."

"Well pay" brought lateness down to almost zero and cut absenteeism more than Parsons wanted it reduced, because some workers came to work even when they were sick. He dealt with this awkwardness by reminding them of "retro pay." Says Parsons: "I'd say, 'By being here while not feeling well, you may have a costly accident, and that will not only cause you pain and suffering, but it will also affect the retro plan, which could cost you a lot more than one day's 'well pay.'"

Reducing Accidents

The retro pay plan offers a bonus based on any reductions in premiums received from the state's industrial accident insurance fund. Before the retro plan went into effect in 1976, Parsons Pine had a high accident rate, 86% above the statewide base, and paid the fund accordingly. Parsons told his workers that if the plant cut its accident rate, the retroactive refund would be distributed to them. The upshot was a 1977 accident bill of $2,500 compared to a 1976 bill of $28,500. After deducting administrative expenses, the state will return $89,000 of a $100,000 premium, some $900 per employee.

The retro plan did not improve the accident

Concluded:

rate unaided, Parsons concedes. "We showed films and introduced every safety program the state has," he says. "But no matter what you do, it doesn't really make a dent until the people themselves see that they are going to lose a dollar by not being safe. When management puts on the pressure, they say, 'He's just trying to make a buck for himself,' but when fellow workers say, 'Let's work safe,' that means a lot."

The "Little Hurts"

Employees can also earn safety pay—two hours' wages—by remaining accident-free for a month. "Six hours a quarter isn't such a great incentive," says Parsons, "but it helps. When it didn't cost them anything, workers would go to the doctor for every little thing. Now they take care of the little hurts themselves."

As its most substantial incentive, the company offers a profit-sharing bonus—everything the business earns over 4% after taxes, which is Parsons' idea of a fair profit. Each supervisor rates his employees in four categories of excellence, with a worker's bonus figured as a percentage of his wages multiplied by his category. Top-ranked employees generally receive bonuses of 8% to 10%. One year they got 16½%. Two-thirds of the bonus is paid in cash and the rest goes into the retirement fund.

To illustrate how workers can contribute to profits, and profit-sharing bonuses, Parsons presents a dramatic display that has a modest fame in Ashland. Inviting the work force to lunch, he sets up a pyramid of 250 rat trap bases, each representing $10,000 in sales. Then he knocks 100 onto the floor, saying: "That's for raw materials. See why it is important not to waste?" Then he pushes over 100 more, adding: "That's for wages." And pointing to the 50 left, he says: "Out of this little pile we have to do all the other things—maintenance, repairs, supplies, taxes. With so many blocks gone, that doesn't leave much for either you or me."

A Vote for Work

The lunch guests apparently find the display persuasive. Says one nine-year veteran: "We get the most we can out of every piece of wood after seeing that. When new employees come, we work with them to cut down waste."

The message also lingered at the last Christmas luncheon, when, after distribution of checks, someone said: "Hey, how about the afternoon off?" Parsons replied: "OK, our production is on schedule and the customers won't be hurt. But you know where the cost comes from." Parsons recalls that someone asked him, "How much?" and he replied that the loss would be about $3,000.

"There was a bit of chatter and we took a vote," he says. "Only two hands were raised for the afternoon off. That was because they knew it was not just my money. It was their money, too."

For Discussion

What makes James Parsons a good manager?

SOURCE: "How to Earn 'Well Pay.'" Reprinted from June 12, 1978, issue of *Business Week* by special permission, © 1978 by McGraw-Hill, Inc. pp. 143,146.

■ Additional discussion questions linking this case with the following material appear at the end of this chapter.

Imagine you are the general manager of the public transportation authority in a large city, and one of your main duties is overseeing the city's bus system. During the past several years, you have noted with growing concern the increasing number and severity of bus accidents. In the face of mounting public and administrative pressure, it is clear that a workable accident-prevention program must be enacted. Large pay raises for the bus drivers and other expensive options are impossible because of a tight city budget. Based on what you have read about motivation, feedback, and rewards, what remedial action do you propose? (Please take a moment now to jot down some ideas.)

Since these facts have been drawn from a real-life field study, we can see what happened.[1] Management tried to curb the accident rate with some typical programs, including yearly safety awards, stiffer enforcement of a disciplinary code, complimentary coffee and doughnuts for drivers who had a day without an accident, and a comprehensive training program. Despite these remedial actions, the accident rate kept climbing. Finally, management agreed to a behavior modification experiment that directly attacked unsafe driver behavior.

One hundred of the city's 425 drivers were randomly divided into four experimental teams of 25 each. The remaining drivers served as a control group. During an 18-week period, the drivers received daily feedback on their safety performance on a chart posted in their lunchroom. An accident-free day was noted on the chart with a green dot, while a driver involved in an accident found a red dot posted next to his or her name. At two-week intervals, members of the team with the best competitive safety record received their choice of incentives averaging $5 in value (e.g., cash, free gas, free bus passes). Teams that went an entire two-week period without an accident received double incentives.

Unlike previous interventions, the behavior modification program reduced the accident rate. Compared to the control group, the experimental group recorded a 25 percent lower accident rate. During an 18-week period following termination of the incentive program, the experimental group's accident rate remained a respectable 16 percent better than the control group's. This indicated a positive, long-term effect. Moreover, the program was cost-effective. The incentives cost the organization $2,033.18, while it realized a savings of $9,416.25 in accident settlement expenses (a 1 to 4.6 cost/benefit ratio).

Why did this particular program work, while earlier attempts failed? It worked because a specific behavior (safe driving) was modified through *systematic* management of the drivers' work environment. If the posted feedback, team competition, and rewards had been implemented in traditional piecemeal fashion, they probably would have failed to reduce the accident rate. However, when combined in a coordinated and systematic fashion, these common techniques produced favorable results. This chapter introduces two systematic ways to manage job behavior: behavior modification and behavioral self-management.

---

[1] Complete details of this field study may be found in Robert S. Haynes, Randall C. Pine, and H. Gordon Fitch, "Reducing Accident Rates with Organizational Behavior Modification," *Academy of Management Journal*, June 1982, pp. 407–16.

Both areas have a common theoretical heritage, modern behaviorism. (Recall the discussion of Watson's, Thorndike's, Skinner's, and Bandura's contributions to behavioral learning theory in Chapter 4.)

■ PRINCIPLES OF BEHAVIOR MODIFICATION

Behavior modification can be defined very generally as the practical application of Skinner's operant conditioning techniques. More precisely, **behavior modification** (or B. Mod.) involves making specific behavior occur more or less often by systematically managing antecedent cues and contingent consequences.[2] On-the-job behavior modification has been alternatively labeled *organizational behavior modification* and *organizational behavior management.* To avoid unnecessary confusion, we use the generic term *behavior modification* throughout this chapter.

Although B. Mod. interventions in the workplace often involve widely used techniques such as goal setting, feedback, and rewards, B. Mod. is unique in its adherence to Skinner's operant model of learning. To review, operant theorists assume it is more productive to deal with observable behavior and its environmental determinants than with personality traits, perception, or inferred internal causes of behavior such as needs or cognitions. The purpose of this section is to introduce important concepts and terminology associated with B. Mod. Subsequent sections explore B. Mod. application and research and some issues, pro and con.

A→B→C Contingencies

To adequately understand the operant learning process, one needs a working knowledge of **behavioral contingencies,** as characterized by the A→B→C model. The initials stand for Antecedent→Behavior→Consequence. When person-environment interaction is reduced to A→B→C terms (as in Figure 8–1), a **functional analysis** has taken place.[3]

Within the context of B. Mod., *contingency* means the antecedent, behavior, and consequence in a given A→B→C relationship are connected in "if-then" fashion. If the antecedent is present, then the behavior is more likely to be displayed. If the behavior is displayed, then the consequence is experienced. Furthermore, as learned from Thorndike's law of effect, if the consequence

---

[2] Based on a similar definition in Robert Kreitner, "The Feedforward and Feedback Control of Job Performance through Organizational Behavior Management (OBM)," *Journal of Organizational Behavior Management* 3, no. 3 (1982), pp. 3–20. Three excellent resources, relative to B. Mod. in the workplace, are Lee W. Frederiksen, ed., *Handbook of Organizational Behavior Management* (New York: John Wiley & Sons, 1982); Stephen R. Rapp, Laura L. Carstensen, and Donald M. Prue, "Organizational Behavior Management 1978–1982: An Annotated Bibliography," *Journal of Organizational Behavior Management,* Summer 1983, pp. 5–50; and "Productivity Gains from a Pat on the Back," *Business Week,* January 23, 1978, pp. 56, 58, 62.

[3] Complete discussion of the A→B→C model may be found in Fred Luthans and Robert Kreitner, *Organizational Behavior Modification and Beyond: An Operant and Social Learning Approach* (Glenview, Ill.: Scott, Foresman, 1985), pp. 46–49.

■ **FIGURE 8–1** Productive Job Behavior Requires Supportive Antecedents and Consequences

Antecedent ⟶	Behavior ⟶	Consequence	Behavioral Outcome
Manager: "I suppose you haven't finished the payroll report yet."	*Payroll clerk:* "No way! I'm behind schedule because the supervisors didn't submit their payroll cards on time."	*Manager:* "I'm sure everyone will enjoy getting their paychecks late again!"	The payroll clerk continues to make excuses while missing important deadlines because of the manager's negative antecedents and sarcastic consequences.
Manager: "How are you coming along on this week's payroll report?"	*Payroll clerk:* "I'm a little behind schedule. But if I work during my lunch hour, I'll have it in on time."	*Manager:* "I appreciate the extra effort! How would you like to spend tomorrow working on that bonus-pay project you suggested last week?"	The payroll clerk continues to meet important deadlines because of the manager's nonthreatening antecedents and rewarding consequences.

is pleasing, the behavior will be strengthened (meaning it will occur more often). According to a pair of writers, one a clinical psychologist and the other a manager:

> Some contingencies occur automatically; others we set up by linking our behavior with the behavior of others in an attempt to design an environment that will best serve our purposes. Setting up a contingency involves designating behaviors and assigning consequences to follow. We design contingencies for children fairly simply ("If you finish your homework, I'll let you watch television"), but influencing the behavior of people in the work force is more difficult.
>
> As a result, managers often fail to use contingencies to their full advantage.[4]

Let us look more closely at antecedents, behavior, and consequences to fully understand A→B→C contingencies.

The Role of Antecedents. Unlike the S in the reflexive stimulus-response (S-R) model, antecedents *cue* rather than cause behavior. For example, in classic S-R fashion, a blistering hot piece of pizza *causes* you to quickly withdraw it from your mouth. In contrast, a yellow traffic light *cues* rather than causes you to step on the brake. Because many motorists step on the gas when green traffic signals change to yellow, traffic signals have probable rather than absolute control over driving behavior. Antecedents get the power to cue certain behaviors from associated consequences. For instance, if you have just received a ticket for running a red light, you will probably step on the brake when encountering the next few yellow traffic signals.

Focusing on Behavior. True to Watsonian and Skinnerian behaviorism, B. Mod. proponents emphasize the practical value of focusing on behavior. According to one on-the-job B. Mod. advocate:

> Managers who deliberately set out to change employee behavior and admit this are much farther ahead of their colleagues who motivate employees to "change

---

[4]Douglas H. Ruben and Marilyn J. Ruben, "Behavioral Principles on the Job: Control or Manipulation?" *Personnel*, May 1985, p. 61.

■ **TABLE 8–1** Passing Shots in the Operant-Cognitive Debate

The Operant Side (Skinner)	The Cognitive Side (Locke)
"The objection to inner states is not that they do not exist, but that they are not relevant in a functional analysis. We cannot account for the behavior of any system while staying wholly inside it; eventually we must turn to forces operating upon the organism from without."	"I am unalterably opposed to behaviorism . . . because it flies in the face of the most elementary and self-evident facts about human beings: that they possess consciousness and that their minds are their guides to action, or more fundamentally: their means of survival. I am not against the judicious use of contingent rewards and punishments; it is the behaviorist philosophy that I oppose."

SOURCES: B. F. Skinner, *Science and Human Behavior* (New York: Free Press, 1953), p. 35; and Edwin A. Locke, "Myths in 'The Myths of the Myths about Behavior Mod in Organizations,'" *Academy of Management Review,* January 1979, p. 135.

their attitudes'' or ''affect their personalities.'' . . . Managers who use behavioral technology to get their staff to do the job are merely doing with foresight and in a carefully planned fashion what they formerly did haphazardly—changing employee *behavior*.[5]

This exclusive focus on behavior, without regard for personality traits or cognitive processes, is referred to as radical behaviorism. As one might suspect, this extreme perspective has stirred debate and controversy (for an example, see Table 8–1).

Contingent Consequences

Contingent consequences, according to Skinner's operant theory, control behavior in four ways: positive reinforcement, negative reinforcement, punishment, and extinction.[6] These contingent consequences are managed systematically in B. Mod. programs. To avoid the all-too-common mislabeling of these consequences, let us review some formal definitions.

Positive Reinforcement Strengthens Behavior. **Positive reinforcement** is the process of strengthening a behavior by contingently presenting something pleasing (see Table 8–2). (Remember that a behavior is strengthened when it increases in frequency and weakened when it decreases in frequency.) A young design engineer who works overtime because of praise and recognition from the boss is responding to positive reinforcement. Similarly, people tend to return to restaurants where they are positively reinforced with good food and friendly service.

Negative Reinforcement Also Strengthens Behavior. **Negative reinforcement** is the process of strengthening a behavior by contingently withdrawing something displeasing. For example, an army sergeant who stops yelling when a recruit jumps out of bed has negatively reinforced that particular behavior. Similarly, the behavior of clamping our hands over our ears when watching a jumbo jet take off is negatively reinforced by relief from the noise. Negative reinforcement is often confused with punishment. But the two strategies have opposite effects

---

[5] Thomas K. Connellan, *How to Improve Human Performance: Behaviorism in Business and Industry* (New York: Harper & Row, 1978), p. 32.

[6] See Luthans and Kreitner, *Organizational Behavior Modification and Beyond,* pp. 49–56.

■ **TABLE 8–2** Creating a Positively Reinforcing Workplace in a Swiss Department Store Chain

Make your salespeople feel good, and they will make your customers feel good.

That's the advice of Francis Loeb, managing director of Loeb AG, a department store chain in Berne, Switzerland. . . .

Among the methods his company uses to make employees feel valuable:

- An annual "theater day" is held for all employees, who dress in costume for a riverboat ride.

   Says Loeb in his charming Swiss-German accent: "I have the possibility to go down on my knees before a salesperson and sing him an opera song. How else could I do this but in costume?"

   Pictures of Loeb serenading an employee become a popular souvenir of the event.
- Representative sales clerks are invited to air problems at meetings of the chain's general managers. Not only do the employees benefit from letting off steam, but "we learn a lot," Loeb says.
- An annual celebration dinner is held to recognize employees who have contributed to a suggestion box in the previous 12 months.
- Each member of the sales staff is invited to name his or her best customer each year. That individual is sent a cake in the salesperson's name—but at the company's expense.
- Employees are given a day off on their birthdays—plus a piece of birthday cake from the company restaurant.
- Retired salespeople are asked to join a quality circle, where active workers can gain the benefit of the retirees' experience.
- Loeb is often at hand to open the door and bid goodnight to workers who have been on duty during some of the less desirable work periods—Saturdays and nights.

Whatever the specific techniques of making employees feel valued, they must reflect genuine concern for the employees. As Loeb sums up, "It must come from the heart."

SOURCE: Excerpted from Sharon Nelton, "Psychological Hugs for Employees." Reprinted with permission, *Nation's Business,* March 1986, Copyright 1986, U.S. Chamber of Commerce. p. 63.

on behavior. Negative reinforcement, as the word *reinforcement* indicates, strengthens a behavior because it provides relief from an unpleasant situation.

Punishment Weakens Behavior. **Punishment** is the process of weakening behavior through either the contingent presentation of something displeasing or the contingent withdrawal of something positive. A manager assigning a tardy employee to a dirty job exemplifies the first type of punishment. Docking a tardy employee's pay is an example of the second type of punishment, called ''response cost'' punishment. Legal fines involve response cost punishment. Salesclerks who must make up any cash register shortages out of their own pockets are being managed through response cost punishment.

Extinction Also Weakens Behavior. **Extinction** is the weakening of a behavior by ignoring it or making sure it is not reinforced. Getting rid of an old boyfriend or girlfriend by refusing to answer their phone calls is an extinction strategy.

"This one's for keeping a neat and tidy cubicle at all times, and this one's for not tying up lines with personal calls, and this one's for not horsing around at the water cooler." (*Management Review,* January 1982, p. 12. Drawing by H. Martin; © 1975 The New Yorker Magazine, Inc.)

A good analogy for extinction is to imagine what would happen to your houseplants if you stopped watering them. Like a plant without water, a behavior without occasional reinforcement eventually dies. Although very different processes, both punishment and extinction have the same weakening effect on behavior.

How to Properly Categorize Contingent Consequences.

In B. Mod., consequences are defined in terms of their demonstrated impact on behavior (see Figure 8–2), not subjectively or by their intended impact. For example, notice how one expert in the field distinguishes between reinforcement and rewards:

> Reinforcement is distinguished from reward in that a reward is something that is perceived to be desirable and is delivered to an individual after performance. An increase in pay, a promotion, and a comment on good work performance may all be rewards. But rewards are not necessarily reinforcers. Reinforcers are defined by the increase in the rate of behavior.[7]

---

[7] Lawrence M. Miller, *Behavior Management: The New Science of Managing People at Work* (New York: John Wiley & Sons, 1978), p. 106.

■ **FIGURE 8–2** Contingent Consequences in Behavior Modification

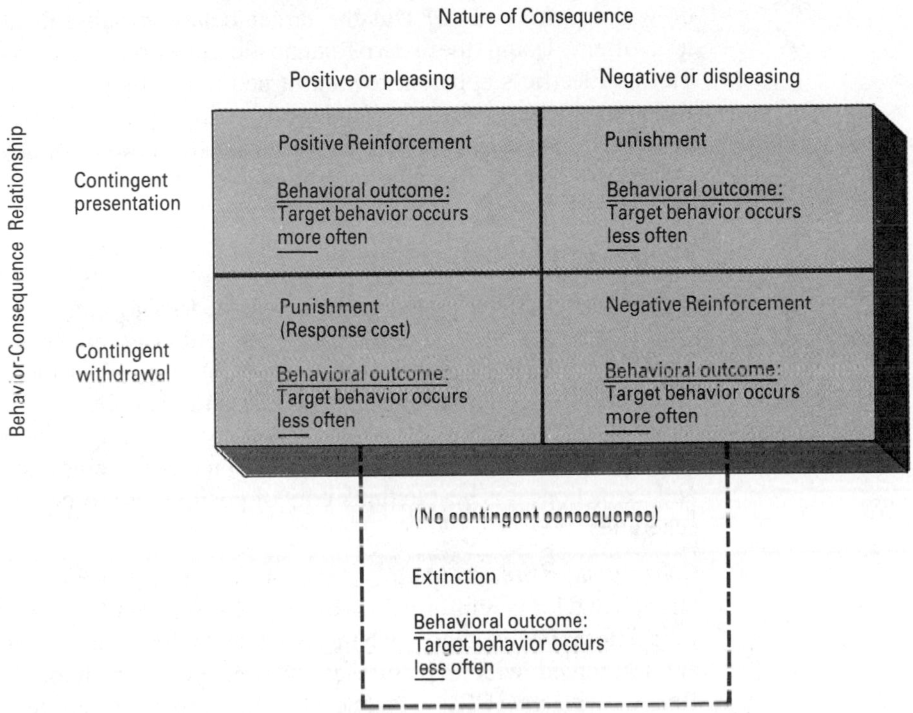

Nature of Consequence

A promotion is both a reward and a positive reinforcer if the individual's performance subsequently improves. On the other hand, apparent rewards may turn out to be the opposite. For example, consider Tampa Electric Co.'s successful "positive discipline" program, which gives misbehaving employees *a paid day off* (see Table 8–3).

■ **TABLE 8–3** "You've Been Misbehaving, Take a Day Off with Pay!"

Tampa Electric Company's "positive discipline" program:

It works like this: Employees who come in late, do a sloppy job, or mistreat a colleague first get an oral "reminder" rather than a "reprimand." Next comes a written reminder, then the paid day off—called a "decision-making leave day."

. . . After a pensive day on the beach, naughty employees must agree in writing— or orally, at some union shops—that they will be on their best behavior for the next year. The paid day off is a one-shot chance at reform. If the employee doesn't shape up, it's curtains. The process is documented, so employees often have little legal recourse.

SOURCE: Laurie Baum, "Punishing Workers with a Day Off," *Business Week,* June 16, 1986, p. 80.

Contingent consequences are always categorized "after the fact" by answering the following two questions: (1) Was something contingently presented or withdrawn? and (2) Did the target behavior subsequently occur more or less often? Using these two diagnostic questions, can you figure out why Tampa Electric's apparent reward turned out to be punishment for employees? Referring to the upper-right-hand quadrant in Figure 8–2, something was contingently presented and the target behavior (tardiness, sloppy work, etc.) was weakened. Hence, it was a punishment contingency.

Schedules of Reinforcement

As just illustrated, contingent consequences are an important determinant of future behavior. The *timing* of behavioral consequences can be even more important. Based on years of tedious laboratory experiments with pigeons in highly controlled environments, Skinner and his colleagues discovered distinct patterns of responding for various schedules of reinforcement.[8] Although some of their conclusions can be generalized to negative reinforcement, punishment, and extinction, it is best to think only of positive reinforcement when discussing schedules.

Continuous Reinforcement. As indicated in Table 8–4, every instance of a target behavior is reinforced when a **continuous reinforcement** (CRF) schedule is in effect. For instance, when your television set is operating properly, you are reinforced with a picture every time you turn it on (a CRF schedule). But, as with any CRF schedule of reinforcement, the behavior of turning on the television will undergo rapid extinction if the set breaks.

Intermittent Reinforcement. Unlike CRF schedules, **intermittent reinforcement** involves reinforcement of some but not all instances of a target behavior. Four subcategories of intermittent schedules, described in Table 8–4, are fixed and variable ratio schedules and fixed and variable interval schedules. Reinforcement in *ratio* schedules is contingent on the number of responses emitted. *Interval* reinforcement is tied to the passage of time. Some common examples of the four types of intermittent reinforcement are:

- *Fixed ratio* (piece-rate pay; bonuses tied to the sale of a fixed number of units).
- *Variable ratio* (slot machines that pay off after a variable number of lever pulls; lotteries that pay off after the purchase of a variable number of tickets).
- *Fixed interval* (hourly pay; annual salary paid on a regular basis).
- *Variable interval* (random supervisory praise and pats on the back for employees who have been doing a good job).

---

[8] See C. B. Ferster and B. F. Skinner, *Schedules of Reinforcement* (New York: Appleton-Century-Crofts, 1957).

■ **TABLE 8–4** Schedules of Reinforcement

Schedule	Description	Probable Effects on Responding
Continuous (CRF)	Reinforcer follows every response.	Steady high rate of performance as long as reinforcement continues to follow every response.
		High frequency of reinforcement may lead to early satiation.
		Behavior weakens rapidly (undergoes extinction) when reinforcers are withheld.
		Appropriate for newly emitted, unstable, or low-frequency responses.
Intermittent	Reinforcer does not follow every response.	Capable of producing high frequencies of responding.
		Low frequency of reinforcement precludes early satiation.
		Appropriate for stable or high-frequency responses.
Fixed ratio (FR)	A fixed number of responses must be emitted before reinforcement occurs	A fixed ratio of 1:1 (reinforcement occurs after every response) is the same as a continuous schedule.
		Tends to produce a high rate of response which is vigorous and steady.
Variable ratio (VR)	A varying or random number of responses must be emitted before reinforcement occurs.	Capable of producing a high rate of response which is vigorous, steady, and resistant to extinction.
Fixed interval (FI)	The first response after a specific period of time has elapsed is reinforced.	Produces an uneven response pattern varying from a very slow, unenergetic response immediately following reinforcement to a very fast, vigorous response immediately preceding reinforcement.
Variable interval (VI)	The first response after varying or random periods of time have elapsed is reinforced.	Tends to produce a high rate of response which is vigorous, steady, and resistant to extinction.

SOURCE: Fred Luthans and Robert Kreitner, *Organizational Behavior Modification and Beyond: An Operant and Social Learning Approach* (Glenview, Ill.: Scott, Foresman, 1985), p. 58. Used with permission.

Scheduling Is Critical. The schedule of reinforcement can more powerfully influence behavior than the magnitude of reinforcement. Although this proposition grew out of experiments with pigeons, subsequent on-the-job research confirmed it. Consider, for example, a field study of 12 unionized beaver trappers employed by a lumber company to keep the large rodents from eating newly planted tree seedlings.[9]

The beaver trappers were randomly divided into two groups that alternated weekly between two different bonus plans. Under the first schedule, each trapper earned his regular $7 per hour wage plus $1 for each beaver caught. Technically, this bonus was paid on a continuous reinforcement (CRF) schedule. The second bonus plan involved the regular $7 per hour wage plus a one-in-four chance (as determined by rolling the dice) of receiving $4 for each beaver trapped. This second bonus plan qualified as a variable ratio (VR-4) schedule. In the long run, both incentive schemes averaged out to a $1-per-beaver bonus. Surprisingly, however, when the trappers were under the VR-4 schedule, they were 58 percent more productive than under the CRF schedule, despite the fact that the net amount of pay averaged out the same for the two groups during the 12-week trapping season.

Organizations Rely on the Weakest Schedule. Generally, variable ratio and variable interval schedules of reinforcement produce the strongest behavior that is most resistant to extinction. As gamblers will attest, variable schedules hold the promise of reinforcement after the next target response. Time-based pay schemes such as hourly pay and salaries that have become predominant in today's service economy are the weakest schedule of reinforcement (fixed interval). In a recent postretirement article, B. F. Skinner questioned this state of affairs (see Table 8–5).

Behavior Shaping

Have you ever wondered how trainers at Sea World and other aquarium parks manage to get bottle-nosed dolphins to do flips, killer whales to carry people on their backs, and seals to juggle balls? The results are seemingly magical. Actually, a mundane learning process called shaping is responsible for the animals' antics.

Two-ton killer whales, for example, have a big appetite and they find buckets of fish very reinforcing. So if the trainer wants to ride a killer whale, he or she reinforces very basic behaviors that will eventually lead to the whale being ridden. The killer whale is contingently reinforced with a few fish for coming near the trainer, then for being touched, then for putting its nose in a harness, then for being straddled, and eventually for swimming with the trainer on its back. In effect, the trainer systematically raises the behavioral requirement for reinforcement. Thus, **shaping** is defined as the process of reinforcing closer and closer approximations to a target behavior.

---

[9] See Lise M. Saari and Gary P. Latham, ''Employee Reactions to Continuous and Variable Ratio Reinforcement Schedules Involving a Monetary Incentive,'' *Journal of Applied Psychology,* August 1982, pp. 506–8.

■ **TABLE 8–5** B. F. Skinner Doesn't Like the Way Employees Are Paid Today

The reinforcing effect of money is especially weak when it is paid on contract. The contingencies are aversive. Workers do not work "in order to be paid," if that means that the money they will receive at the end of the week affects their behavior during the week. They work to avoid being discharged and losing the money they would otherwise receive. Most of the time they do simply what they are told to do or have agreed to do. Having assembled part of a television set on a production line, the worker is not then more strongly inclined to assemble another. The contract must remain in force. Workers rarely put in a free day at the factory just because they have been paid when they have done so at other times.

Money is reinforcing when it is piece-rate pay or is paid on commission (technically speaking, when behavior is reinforced on a fixed-ratio schedule), or when it is paid on the variable-ratio schedule of all gambling systems; however, other schedules are far commoner, and wages do not, strictly speaking, reinforce at all.

SOURCE: B. F. Skinner, "What Is Wrong with Daily Life in the Western World?" *American Psychologist,* May 1986, p. 569.

Shaping works very well with people, too. This led one B. Mod. proponent to conclude: "Shaping is one of the least understood, least used, but most powerful tools in behavioral technology as applied to the job situation. Its power in terms of changing job behavior is way out of proportion to its simplicity."[10] Praise, recognition, and instructive and credible feedback cost managers little more than moments of their time. Yet, when used in conjunction with a behavior-shaping program, these consequences can efficiently foster significant improvements in job performance. The key to successful behavior shaping lies in reducing a complex target behavior to easily learned steps and then faithfully (and patiently) reinforcing any improvement. Table 8–6 lists practical tips on shaping.

■ A MODEL FOR MODIFYING JOB BEHAVIOR

Someone once observed that children and pets are the world's best behavior modifiers. In fact, one of your authors responds obediently to his cats, while the other jumps to satisfy contingencies arranged by his dogs! Despite their ignorance of operant theory, children and pets are good behavior modifiers because they (1) know precisely what behavior they want to elicit, (2) provide clear antecedents, and (3) wield situationally appropriate and powerful contingent consequences. Let us learn from these "masters" of behavior modification and examine a four-step B. Mod. process for managing on-the-job behavior[11] (see Figure 8–3).

---

[10] Connellan, *How to Improve Human Performance,* pp. 133–34.

[11] An alternative five-step model—Pinpoint, Record, Involve, Coach, Evaluate—may be found in Kenneth Blanchard and Robert Lorber, *Putting the One Minute Manager to Work* (New York: Berkley Books, 1984), p. 58.

■ **TABLE 8–6** Ten Practical Tips for Shaping Job Behavior

1. *Accommodate the process of behavioral change.* Behaviors change in gradual stages, not in broad, sweeping motions.
2. *Define new behavior patterns specifically.* State what you wish to accomplish in explicit terms and in small amounts that can be easily grasped.
3. *Give individuals feedback on their performance.* A once-a-year performance appraisal is not sufficient.
4. *Reinforce behavior as quickly as possible.*
5. *Use powerful reinforcements.* In order to be effective, rewards must be important to the employee—not to the manager.
6. *Use a continuous reinforcement schedule.* New behaviors should be reinforced *every time* they occur. This reinforcement should continue until these behaviors become habitual.
7. *Use a variable reinforcement schedule for maintenance.* Even after behavior has become habitual, it still needs to be rewarded, though not necessarily every time it occurs.
8. *Reward teamwork—not competition.* Group goals and group rewards are one way to encourage cooperation in situations in which jobs and performance are interdependent.
9. *Make all rewards contingent on performance.*
10. *Never take good performance for granted.* Even superior performance, if left unrewarded, will eventually deteriorate.

SOURCE: Adapted from A. T. Hollingsworth and Denise Tanquay Hoyer, "How Supervisors Can Shape Behavior," *Personnel Journal,* May 1985, pp. 86, 88.

Step 1: Identify Target Behavior

Managers who strictly follow the operant principle of focusing on observable behavior rather than on inferred internal states, have two alternatives in Step 1. They can pinpoint a *desirable* behavior that occurs too *seldom* (e.g., contributing creative ideas at staff meetings), or they can focus on an *undesirable* behavior that occurs too *often* (e.g., making disruptive comments at staff meetings). Organizational behavior modification proponents prefer the first alternative because it requires managers to see things in a positive, growth-oriented manner instead of in a negative, punitive manner. As a case in point, researchers have documented the benefits of "well pay" versus the costs of traditional sick pay.[12] In short, every undesirable behavior has a desirable opposite. Just a few of many possible examples are: being absent/being on time, having an accident/working safely, remaining aloof/participating actively, procrastinating/completing assignments on time, competing destructively/being a team player.

Pointers for Identifying Behaviors.   According to the former editor of the *Journal of Organizational Behavior Management,* a journal devoted to the study of B. Mod. in the workplace, too many B. Mod. programs focus on process (rule following) rather than on accomplishments. Thus, he offers the following three pointers for identifying target behaviors:

1. The primary focus should be on accomplishments or outcomes. These accomplishments should have *significant* organizational impact. . . .
2. The targeting of process behaviors (rule adherence, etc.) should only occur when that behavior can be functionally related to a significant organizational accomplishment. . . .

---

[12] For example, see Barron H. Harvey, Judy A. Schultze, and Jerome F. Rogers, "Rewarding Employees for Not Using Sick Leave," *Personnel Administrator,* May 1983, pp. 55–59.

■ **FIGURE 8–3** Modifying On-the-Job Behavior

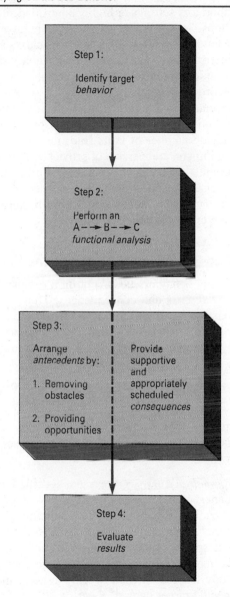

> Step 1:
>
> Identify target
> *behavior*

> Step 2:
>
> Perform an
> A — → B — → C
> *functional analysis*

> Step 3:
>
> Arrange   Provide
> *antecedents* by: supportive
>   and
> 1. Removing   appropriately
>   obstacles   scheduled
>   *consequences*
> 2. Providing
>   opportunities

> Step 4:
>
> Evaluate
> *results*

    3. There should be broad participation in the development of behavioral targets. . . .[13]

These pointers are intended to prevent managers from falling victim to charges of blatant and pointless manipulation.

---

[13] Lee W. Frederiksen, ''The Selection of Targets for Organizational Interventions,'' *Journal of Organizational Behavior Management,* no. 4 (1981–1982), p. 4.

A Word of Caution about Shifting the Focus from Behavior to Results.   In laboratory settings or highly controlled situations such as classrooms or machine shops, it is possible to directly observe and record the frequency of specific behaviors. Asking a question in class, arriving late at work, and handing in an error-free report are all observable behavioral events. However, in today's complex organizations, it is not always possible (or desirable) to observe and record work behaviors firsthand. For example, top-level managers and technical specialists often spend time alone in closed offices. When work behavior cannot be monitored firsthand, the next best alternative is to track results. Examples include number of units sold, number of customer complaints, degree of goal attainment, and percent of project completed. Managers who build contingencies around results need to keep in mind that those contingencies will be less precise than ones anchored to observable behavioral events. For instance, the wrong person could be reinforced because organizational politicians sometimes take credit for others' results.

Step 2: Functionally Analyze the Situation

Any behaviors occurring on a regular basis necessarily have their own supportive cues and consequences. Thus, it is important for managers to identify existing A→B→C contingencies before trying to rearrange things. For example, it is important to know that a recently uncooperative employee is being pressured by co-workers to vote yes in an upcoming union certification election.

Step 3: Arrange Antecedents and Provide Consequences

In this step, analysis gives way to action. An instructive way to discuss step 3 is to explore separately antecedent management and consequence management. In practice, antecedent and consequence management are closely intertwined.

Managing Antecedents.   As specified in step 3 of Figure 8–3, antecedent management involves two basic strategies: (1) removing obstacles and/or (2) providing opportunities. Some practical suggestions are listed in Table 8–7. Based on the discussion of goal setting in Chapter 6, challenging objectives that specify what and when something is to be accomplished are probably the most potent antecedent management tool. For instance, supervisors in one study handed in their weekly reports more promptly when they were given specific target dates.[14]

By rearranging apparently insignificant antecedents, significant results can be achieved. Importantly, these must be *contingent* antecedents, as identified through an A→B→C functional analysis. For example, a telephone company was losing an estimated $250,000 annually because its telephone installers

---

[14] See James Conrin, ''A Comparison of Two Types of Antecedent Control over Supervisory Behavior,'' *Journal of Organizational Behavior Management,* Fall–Winter 1982, pp. 37–47.

■ **TABLE 8–7** Paving the Way for Good Job Performance with Helpful Antecedents

Remove Obstacles	Provide Opportunities
Eliminate unrealistic plans, schedules, and deadlines	Formulate difficult but attainable goals
Identify and remedy skill deficiencies through training	Provide clear instructions
Eliminate confusing or contradictory rules	Give friendly reminders, constructive suggestions, and helpful tips
Avoid conflicting orders and priorities	Ask nonthreatening questions about progress
Remove distracting co-workers	Display posters with helpful advice
	Rely on easy-to-use forms
	Build enthusiasm and commitment through participation and challenging work assignments
	Promote personal growth and development through training

were not reporting the installation of ''ceiling drops.'' A ceiling drop involves installing extra wiring to compensate for a lowered ceiling. Despite comprehensive training on how to install and report ceiling drops, a large percentage of ceiling drops remained unreported and thus unbilled by the company. The following turn of events then took place.

> A specialist in training design was called in to find out why the training had failed. She noted a curious thing. The form that the installers were required to fill out was extremely complicated and the part dealing with ceiling drops was even more complicated. . . .
>
> One small change was made by adding a box where the installer could merely check ''ceiling drop installed.'' Now the installer no longer had to fill out an extensive explanation of what took place in the house. Within one week after the change in the form, the number of ceiling drops reported and charged back to the customers had increased dramatically, far above what it was immediately after the training sessions.[15]

Summarizing, from a B. Mod. perspective the telephone installers did not have an attitude or motivation problem. Nor did they have a knowledge deficiency requiring more training. They simply did not report ceiling drops because it was too complicated to do so. The streamlined reporting form presented the installers with an opportunity to behave properly, whereas the old form was an obstacle to good performance. In A→B→C terms, the streamlined reporting form became an antecedent that efficiently cued the desired behavior.

Managing Consequences.   Step 3 in Figure 8–3 calls for providing supportive and appropriately scheduled consequences. Six guidelines for successfully managing consequences during B. Mod. are:

1. *Reinforce improvement, not just final results.* Proper shaping cannot occur if the behavioral requirement for reinforcement is too demanding. Behavior undergoes extinction when it is not shaped in achievable step-by-step increments.

---

[15] Connellan, *How to Improve Human Performance*, p. 27.

■ **TABLE 8–8** Japanese Employers Emphasize Natural Rewards

> If there is a single element of the Japanese approach to labor relations that has not received substantial attention in this country, despite its potential for success, it is the Japanese desire to find ways to make work easier for employees. It is an understatement to say that the work ethic is alive and well in Japan, but Japanese manufacturing plants are by no means sweatshops. On the contrary, major Japanese employers believe it is essential not to overburden their workers, not only because of a moral commitment to the people who work for them, but also because they have found that overburdening results in inefficiency, product defects, and safety problems.
>
> SOURCE: Excerpted from Stanley J. Brown, "The Japanese Approach to Labor Relations: Can It Work in America?" *Personnel*, April 1987, p. 26.

2. *Fit the consequences to the behavior.* A pair of B. Mod. scholars interpreted this guideline as follows:

> Overrewarding a worker may make him feel guilty and certainly reinforces his current performance level. If the performance level is lower than that of others who get the same reward, he has no reason to increase his output. When a worker is underrewarded, he becomes angry with the system. His behavior is being extinguished and the company may be forcing the good employee (underrewarded) to seek employment elsewhere while encouraging the poor employee (overrewarded) to stay on.[16]

Note how this recommendation is consistent with the discussion of equity theory in Chapter 6.

3. *Emphasize natural rewards over contrived rewards.* **Natural rewards** are potentially reinforcing consequences derived from day-to-day social and administrative interactions (see Table 8–8). Typical natural rewards include supervisory praise, assignment to favored tasks, early time off with pay, flexible work schedules, and extended breaks. Contrived rewards include money and other tangible rewards. Regarding this distinction, it has been pointed out that:

> Natural social rewards are potentially the most powerful and universally applicable reinforcers. In contrast to contrived rewards, they do not generally lead to satiation (people seldom get tired of compliments, attention, or recognition) and can be administered on a very contingent basis.[17]

4. *Provide individuals with objective feedback whenever possible.* As we discussed in the last chapter, objective feedback can have a positive impact on future behavior. This is particularly true when people have the opportunity

---

[16] W. Clay Hamner and Ellen P. Hamner, "Behavior Modification on the Bottom Line," *Organizational Dynamics,* Spring 1976, p. 8.

[17] Luthans and Kreitner, *Organizational Behavior Modification and Beyond,* p. 128.

■ **TABLE 8–9** Emery Air Freight's Successful Behavior Modification Program

---

According to the manager primarily responsible for developing the B. Mod. program that reportedly saved Emery Air Freight over $3 million, this is what took place:

The firm used large containers to forward small packages in order to cut handling and delivery times to airlines, and since usage of these containers had been promulgated by management, it and dock workers assumed that the containers were being used 90 percent of the time when possible. But an on-the-job analysis found the figure closer to 45 percent. Since most of the workers knew how and when to use the containers, it was reasoned that an educational program would have little impact.

Management concluded that the answer was to tell the workers how much they were falling short of the 90 percent utilization rate and how profits would be increased if the containers were used at an optimum level.

To start, management developed a checklist on which the dock worker would indicate each time he or she used a container. At the end of each shift, the worker totaled his or her own results to see whether the 90 percent goal had been reached. Supervisors and regional managers were encouraged to provide positive reinforcement by praising any improvement in employee performance. If a worker's improvement was minimal, he or she was not criticized. Instead, he or she was lauded for keeping an honest record of container usage.

The results were impressive. In 80 percent of the offices where the technique was tried, the use of containers rose from 45 percent to 95 percent. The increase was matched throughout the company and meant a saving of nearly $650,000 a year.

SOURCE: Reprinted, by permission of the publisher, "Modifying Employee Behavior: Making Rewards Pay Off," Edward J. Feeney, *Supervisory Management,* December 1985, p. 26, © (1985 American Management Association, New York. All rights reserved.

to keep track of their own performance, as was the case at Emery Air Freight[18] (see Table 8–9). The three-way marriage of goal setting, objective feedback, and positive reinforcement for improvement can be fruitful indeed. For example, the hockey player study cited in Chapter 6 demonstrated that a B. Mod. intervention of goal setting, feedback, and praise increased the team's winning percentage by almost 100 percent for two consecutive years.[19]

5. *Emphasize positive reinforcement; de-emphasize punishment.* Proponents of B. Mod. in the workplace, as mentioned earlier, recommend building up good behavior with positive reinforcement instead of tearing down bad behavior with punishment. For instance, the authors of the best-seller, *The One Minute Manager,* told their readers to "catch them doing something right!"[20] In other

---

[18] For details, see "At Emery Air Freight: Positive Reinforcement Boosts Performance," *Organizational Dynamics,* Winter 1973, pp. 41–50.

[19] See D. Chris Anderson, Charles R. Crowell, Mark Doman, and George S. Howard, "Performance Posting, Goal Setting, and Activity-Contingent Praise as Applied to a University Hockey Team," *Journal of Applied Psychology,* February 1988, pp. 87–95.

[20] Kenneth Blanchard and Spencer Johnson, *The One Minute Manager* (New York: Berkley Books, 1982), p. 39. Interestingly, managers were given this identical bit of advice, "Catch them doing something right!" five years earlier by Robert Kreitner, "People Are Systems, Too: Filling the Feedback Vacuum," *Business Horizons,* November 1977, pp. 54–58.

words, managers who focus on what's right with job performance unavoidably end up emphasizing positive reinforcement.

Regarding the use of punishment, operant reseachers found it tends to suppress undesirable behavior only temporarily while prompting emotional side effects. For example, a computer programmer who is reprimanded publicly for failing to "debug" an important program may get even with the boss by skillfully sabotaging another program. Moreover, those punished come to fear and dislike the person administering the punishment.[21] Thus, it is unlikely that punitive managers can build the climate of trust so necessary for success in modern organizations. For example, the "giant retailer W. T. Grant, which went bankrupt in 1975, made it a practice to cut the tie of any sales manager who did not meet his quota."[22]

6. *Schedule reinforcement appropriately.* Once again, immature behavior requires the nurture of continuous reinforcement. Established or habitual behavior, in contrast, can be maintained with fixed or variable schedules of intermittent reinforcement.

Step 4: Evaluate Results

A B. Mod. intervention is effective if (1) a desirable target behavior occurs more often or (2) an undesirable target behavior occurs less often. Since *more* or *less* are relative terms, managers need a measurement tool that provides an objective basis for comparing preintervention with postintervention data. This is where baseline data and behavior charting can make a valuable contribution.

Baseline data are preintervention behavioral data collected without the target person's knowledge. This "before" measure later provides a basis for assessing an intervention's effectiveness. For example, in Table 8–10, notice the role of baseline data in Little Rock, Arkansas, Union National Bank's successful B. Mod. program.

A **behavior chart** is a B. Mod. program evaluation tool that includes both preintervention baseline data and postintervention data. The vertical axis of a behavior chart can be expressed in terms of behavior frequency, percent, or results attained. A time dimension is typically found on the horizontal axis of a behavior chart. When a goal is included, as shown in Figure 8–4, a behavior chart quickly tells the individual where his or her performance has been, is, and should be. As the successful bus driver safety program discussed at the opening of this chapter illustrates, posted feedback can be a very effective management tool. Moreover, a behavior chart provides an ongoing evaluation of a B. Mod. program.

---

[21] For a review of this research, see Luthans and Kreitner, *Organizational Behavior Modification and Beyond,* pp. 139–44. An alternative view of the benefits of punishment is discussed by Richard D. Arvey and John M. Ivancevich, "Punishment in Organizations: A Review, Propositions, and Research Suggestions," *Academy of Management Review,* January 1980, pp. 123–32.

[22] Susan Narod, "Off-Beat Company Customs," *Dun's Business Month,* November 1984, p. 66.

■ **TABLE 8–10** A Company That Banks on B. Mod.

We first started paying incentives in the proof department. The employees of a bank's proof department encode machine readable numbers on the bottom of checks so they can then be processed by a computer. Accuracy is essential, as is a short processing time. Checks not encoded cannot be credited to the bank's account and, therefore, represent lost interest.

Before the program began, data were collected for five weeks showing the number of checks each operator processed each hour. . . . This period, called a "baseline," is important because it allows us to measure performance before implementing a program. In that way we know exactly how much improvement the program produced. During the baseline period, average production was 1,065 items/hour. This was in line with the industry norm of 900–1,100 items/hour. When a weekly graph was posted and high performers praised, production increased to 2,100 items/hour. Later, the supervisor stopped posting the graph and performance dropped again. This unfortunate occurrence had the happy result of showing clearly that it was the feedback which increased performance.

At that time, UNB's management decided to change the program slightly. In addition to reinstating the graph, they paid proof operators a bonus based on their daily output. This bonus was figured each day but paid at normal payroll times.

In three months, production had increased to 2,800 items/hour, which was the maximum rate for which incentive money was paid. Production above this point did not produce any more incentive pay. When the maximum was raised to 3,000 items/hour, production again increased quickly. There is currently no maximum, and performance averages 3,500 items/hour, more than three times baseline levels. Interestingly, the manufacturers of the proof machine specify that its maximum rate is 3,500 items/hour. We have seen individual production of 4,460 items/hour.

The proof department program has been in effect for six years, and proof operators currently earn incentive equal to 50 to 70 percent of their base salary. From a personnel standpoint, the proof department was once the biggest problem area of the bank. The incentive program turned it into one of our smoothest operations. Prior to the incentive program, the turnover was 110 percent; now it is 0 percent. Absenteeism went from 4.24 percent to 2.23 percent; employees were reduced from 11 full-time, three part-time, to three full-time, six part-time; over-time went from 475 hours a year to 13 hours, and savings from float or processing checks faster is about $100,000 a year.

SOURCE: Excerpted from Wayne Dierks and Kathleen McNally, "Incentives You Can Bank On," pp. 61–62. Reprinted from the March 1987 issue of *Personnel Administrator*, copyright, 1987, The American Society for Personnel Administration, 606 North Washington street, Alexandria, Virginia 22314.

■ B. MOD. IN THE WORKPLACE: RESEARCH AND PRACTICAL IMPLICATIONS

As recently as the mid-1970s, when B. F. Skinner was being hailed as the most influential living psychologist, operant theory and B. Mod. were virtually ignored in mainstream OB texts. Since that time, however, job-oriented B. Mod. theory and research have mushroomed. Let us selectively examine key research findings from this growing body of knowledge with an eye toward gleaning practical lessons for more effective management.

■ **FIGURE 8–4** Behavior Charts Help Evaluate B. Mod. Programs and Provide Feedback

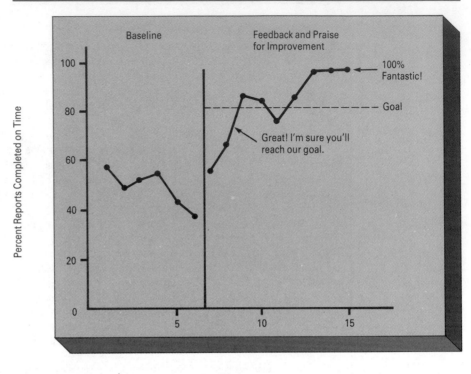

Recent Research Evidence

After reviewing 41 on-the-job B. Mod. studies, a team of researchers concluded:

- Because of mixed research results, laboratory conclusions about schedules of reinforcement do not necessarily apply to organizational behavior. More research is needed in this area.
- While B. Mod. programs have had a generally positive impact on product quantity, absenteeism, employee safety, and employee theft, the impact on product *quality* has not been adequately researched.[23] More sophisticated B. Mod. programs are needed to tackle complex organizational problems such as poor quality products.

[23] See Kirk O'Hara, C. Merle Johnson, and Terry A. Beehr, "Organizational Behavior Management in the Private Sector: A Review of Empirical Research and Recommendations for Further Investigation," *Academy of Management Review*, October 1985, pp. 848–64.

Another researcher examined supervisory behavior from an operant perspective and found:

- Management by exception (focusing on what is wrong with performance) was the major reason supervisors did not use positive reinforcement as often as they could have.[24]
- Contrary to what one might expect, effective managers did not use positive reinforcement more often than did their less effective peers. However, comparatively speaking, effective managers spent nearly 50 percent more time monitoring performance firsthand (e.g., sampling work by watching and listening to employees). Less effective managers tended to rely on secondary sources and self-reports. These findings led the researcher to conclude:

> What these results may signify is the importance of *contingent* consequences. Performance monitoring, particularly work sampling, may enable managers to obtain fair and accurate information. Thus, effective managers may not necessarily provide more consequences than those who are marginally effective. Rather, they may be more likely to provide contingent consequences.[25]

Some Practical Implications

Some believe B. Mod. does not belong in the workplace.[26] They see it as blatantly manipulative and demeaning. But even the severest critics admit it works. Although, they rightly point out that on-the-job applications of B. Mod. have focused on superficial rule-following behavior such as getting to work on time. Indeed, B. Mod. is still in early transition from highly controlled and simple laboratory and clinical settings to loosely controlled and complex organizational settings. Despite the need for more B. Mod. research and application in complex organizations, some practical lessons already have been learned.

First, it is very difficult and maybe impossible to change organizational behavior without systematically managing antecedents and contingent consequences. Second, even the best-intentioned reward system will fail if it does not include clear behavior-consequence contingencies. Third, behavior shaping is a valuable developmental technique. Fourth, goal setting, objective feedback, and positive reinforcement for improvement, when combined in systematic A→B→C fashion, are a powerful management tool. Finally, because formal program evaluation is fundamental to B. Mod., those who use it on the job can be held accountable.

---

[24] Complete discussion may be found in Judi Komaki, "Why We Don't Reinforce: The Issues," *Journal of Organizational Behavior Management*, Fall–Winter 1982, pp. 97–100.

[25] Judith L. Komaki, "Toward Effective Supervision: An Operant Analysis and Comparison of Managers at Work," *Journal of Applied Psychology*, May 1986, p. 277.

[26] For example, see Fred L. Fry, "Operant Conditioning in Organizational Settings: Of Mice or Men?" *Personnel*, July–August 1974, pp. 17–24; and Edwin A. Locke, "The Myths of Behavior Mod in Organizations," *Academy of Management Review* 2 (1977), pp. 543–53.

■ BEHAVIORAL SELF-MANAGEMENT

Judging from the number of diet books that appear on the best-seller lists each year, self-control seems to be in rather short supply. Historically, when someone sought to wage the war of self-control, he or she was told to exercise willpower, be self-disciplined, resist temptation, or seek divine guidance. Although well-intentioned, this advice gives the individual very little to go on relative to actually changing behavior. Fortunately, social learning theorists formulated step-by-step self-management models that have helped individuals conquer serious behavioral problems. Typical among those problems are alcohol and drug abuse, overeating, cigarette smoking, phobias, and antisocial behavior. True to its interdisciplinary nature, the field of OB has recently translated self-management theory and techniques from the clinic to the workplace. In this section, we define behavioral self-management and build its managerial context. We also discuss the notion of self-regulation, introduce a social learning model of self-management, and explore the practical implications of relevant research.

Behavioral Self-Management and the Practice of Management

Formally defined, **behavioral self-management** (BSM) is the process of modifying one's own behavior by systematically managing cues, cognitive processes, and contingent consequences. The term *behavioral* signifies that BSM focuses primarily on modifying behavior, rather than on changing values, attitudes, or personalities. At first glance, BSM appears to be little more than self-imposed B. Mod. But BSM differs from B. Mod. in that cognitive processes are considered in BSM, while ignored in B. Mod. This adjustment reflects the influence of Bandura's extension of operant theory into social learning theory, as discussed in Chapter 4.

In 1979, OB scholars Fred Luthans and Tim Davis developed the managerial context for BSM as follows:

> Research and writing in the management field have given a great deal of attention to managing societies, organizations, groups, and individuals. Strangely, almost no one has paid any attention to managing oneself more effectively. . . . Self-management seems to be a basic prerequisite for effective management of other people, groups, organizations, and societies.[27]

Moreover, some have wrapped BSM in ethical terms: "Proponents of self-control contend that it is more ethically defensible than externally imposed behavior control techniques when used for job enrichment, behavior modification, management by objectives, or organization development."[28] Still others have placed self-management within a managerial context by discussing it as

---

[27] Fred Luthans and Tim R. V. Davis, "Behavioral Self-Management—The Missing Link in Managerial Effectiveness," *Organizational Dynamics,* Summer 1979, p. 43.

[28] Luthans and Kreitner, *Organizational Behavior Modification and Beyond,* p. 158.

■ **FIGURE 8–5** Kanfer's Model of Self-Regulation

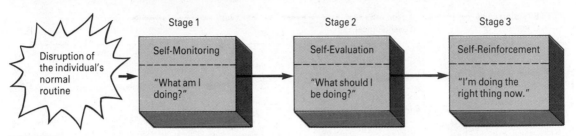

SOURCE: Adapted from discussion in Frederick H. Kanfer, "Self-Management Methods," in *Helping People Change: A Textbook of Methods,* 2nd ed., ed. Frederick H. Kanfer and Arnold P. Goldstein (New York: Pergamon Press, 1980), p. 340.

a substitute for hierarchical leadership.[29] BSM is an important first step toward effectively managing others.

The Mechanics of Self-Regulation

Given that people are capable of self-control, what are the mechanics of this psychological process? One answer to this question is Frederick Kanfer's deceptively simple three-stage model of self-regulation (see Figure 8–5). According to Kanfer, as creatures of habit people tend to go about their daily lives without giving much conscious thought to alternative ways of behaving. But when unforeseen events disrupt habitual ways, people shift into a self-examining mode Kanfer calls self-regulation.

For instance, we may leave for school or work feeling good about our appearance when all of a sudden a close friend points out that our clothes are "really out of date." If we are sensitive to peer pressure, this disruptive event triggers thoughts about how we are dressing and how we should dress differently (Stages 1 and 2 in Kanfer's model). Self-evaluation in Stage 2 involves comparing actual behavior with some standard or criterion. We acquire behavior standards through socialization, peer pressure, relevant role models, and other behavior-shaping influences such as advertising. Finally, after we have adjusted our behavior and the disruptive influences cease, we reinforce ourselves with good thoughts for behaving appropriately (Stage 3).

The representation of Kanfer's model in Figure 8–5 has been rationalized for instructional purposes. Self-regulation actually is a more subtle and subconscious process. Kanfer explains:

It is quite likely that the total sequence of criterion setting, self-observation, evaluation, reinforcement, and planning of new actions proceeds rather quickly,

---

[29] See, for example, Charles C. Manz and Henry P. Sims, Jr., "Self-Management as a Substitute for Leadership: A Social Learning Theory Perspective," *Academy of Management Review,* July 1980, pp. 361–67; Charles C. Manz, *The Art of Self-Leadership* (Englewood Cliffs, N.J.: Prentice-Hall, 1983); and Charles C. Manz, "Self-Leadership: Toward an Expanded Theory of Self-Influence Processes in Organizations," *Academy of Management Review,* July 1986, pp. 585–600.

■ **FIGURE 8–6**   A Social Learning Model of Self-Management

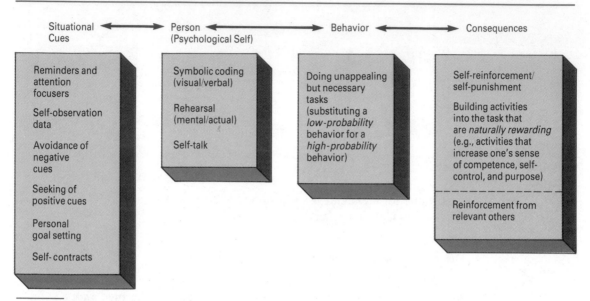

SOURCE: Adapted in part from material found in Charles C. Manz, *The Art of Self-Leadership* (Englewood Cliffs, N.J.: Prentice-Hall, 1983), chap. 3; and Fred Luthans and Robert Kreitner, *Organizational Behavior Modification and Beyond: An Operant and Social Learning Approach* (Glenview, Ill.: Scott, Foresman, 1985), p. 163.

often without much thought by the person. Nevertheless, . . . [the three-stage model] can help us to organize some of the essential features of the process by which an individual manages his own behavior.[30]

Using Kanfer's model of self-regulation as a conceptual springboard, let us examine a how-to-do-it model of self-management.

Social Learning Model of Self-Management

As discussed in Chapter 4, social learning theorists hold that behavior results from the *reciprocal* interaction among three elements. Those three elements are (1) the person's cognitive processes, (2) environmental cues and consequences, and (3) the behavior itself. According to Albert Bandura, the pioneering social learning theorist:

[A] distinguishing feature of social learning theory is the prominent role it assigns to self-regulatory capacities. By arranging environmental inducements, generating cognitive supports, and producing consequences for their own actions, people are able to exercise some measure of control over their own behavior.[31]

---

[30] Frederick H. Kanfer, ''Self-Management Methods,'' *Helping People Change: A Textbook of Methods,* 2nd ed., ed. Frederick H. Kanfer and Arnold P. Goldstein (New York: Pergamon Press, 1980), p. 339.

[31] Albert Bandura, *Social Learning Theory* (Englewood Cliffs, N.J.: Prentice-Hall, 1977), p. 13.

In other words, to the extent that you can control your environment and your cognitive representations of your environment, you are the master of your own behavior. The practical BSM model displayed in Figure 8–6 is derived from social learning theory; hence, the two-headed arrows indicating reciprocal interaction. Each of the four major components of this BSM model requires a closer look. Since this is a *behavioral* model, let us begin our examination with the behavior component.

Behavioral Dilemmas.   Any form of self-control is difficult because it involves engaging in behaviors that are unappealing in the short run but beneficial or necessary in the long run. All too often, people engage in behaviors that are appealing in the short run but damaging to health, career, and friendships in the long run. For example, an overweight junk-food connoisseur would find it unappealing to pass up a hot fudge sundae. Yet his or her health and happiness may eventually depend on doing just that, and doing it over and over. Table 8–11 lists several unappealing but necessary managerial tasks. Notice how the challenge of self-management pivots around the substitution of a low-probability behavior for its high-probability counterpart. For instance, a manager who does not delegate (low probability behavior) tends to perform all tasks him or herself (high-probability behavior). Managers need BSM to tackle the behavioral dilemmas in Table 8–11 that keep them from reaching their full potential.

■ TABLE 8–11   Doing Unappealing but Necessary Managerial Tasks: A Challenge for Better Self-Management

Substituting Low-Probability Behavior	for	High-Probability Behavior
Sticking to schedules and deadlines		Procrastinating
Preparing for and accepting changes in the workplace		Prejudicially resisting changes in the workplace
Catching people doing things *right*		Managing strictly by exception
Doing paperwork		Putting off paperwork
Delegating		Doing everything oneself
Positively reinforcing performance improvement		Taking performance improvement for granted and ignoring it
Giving corrective feedback during performance review meetings		Conducting "good news only" performance review meetings
Planning and scheduling activities		Doing everything at the last moment
Addressing ethical questions and dilemmas		Avoiding ethical issues
Anticipating and preventing problems		Reacting to existing problems ("fire fighting")
Getting ahead through competence and hard work		Getting ahead through political maneuvering
Confronting personality conflicts		Running away from personality conflicts
Conveying bad news to one's superiors		Falsely telling one's superiors that "everything's fine"
Assertively pursuing one's desires		Passively giving in to others
Listening		Communicating without listening

As a procedural note, behavior charts can be used in BSM to evaluate progress toward one's goals, but baseline data ideally should be collected by someone else to ensure objectivity.

Managing Situational Cues. When people try to give up a nagging habit like smoking, the cards are stacked against them. Many people (friends who smoke) and situations (after dinner, when under stress at work, or when relaxing) serve as subtle yet powerful cues telling the individual to light up. If the behavior is to be changed, the cues need to be rearranged so as to trigger the alternative behavior. Six techniques for managing situational cues are listed in the left-hand column of Figure 8–6.

Reminders and attention focusers do just that. For example, many students and managers cue themselves about deadlines and appointments with yellow Post-it™ notes stuck all over their work areas, refrigerators, and dashboards. Self-observation data, when compared against a goal or standard, can be a potent cue for improvement. Those who keep a weight chart near their bathroom scale will attest to the value of this tactic (see Table 8–12). Successful self-management calls for avoiding negative cues while seeking positive cues. Managers in Northwestern Mutual Life Insurance Company's new-business department appreciate the value of avoiding negative cues: "On Wednesdays, the department shuts off all incoming calls, allowing workers to speed processing of new policies. On those days, the unit averages 23 percent more policies than on other days."[32]

Goals, as repeatedly mentioned in this text, are the touchstone of good management. So it is with challenging yet attainable personal goals and effective self-management. Goals simultaneously provide a target and a measuring stick of progress.[33] Finally, a self-contract is an "if-then" agreement with oneself. For example, if you can define all the key terms at the end of this chapter, then treat yourself to something special.

Arranging Cognitive Supports. This component makes BSM distinctly different from conventional behavior modification. Referring to the *person* portion of the self-management model in Figure 8–6, three cognitive supports for behavior change are symbolic coding, rehearsal, and self-talk. These amount to psychological, as opposed to environmental, cues. Yet they prompt appropriate behavior in the same manner. Each requires brief explanation.

- *Symbolic coding:* From a social learning theory perspective, the human brain stores information in visual and verbal codes. For example, a sales manager could use the visual picture of a man chopping down a huge tree to remember Woodman, the name of a promising new client. In contrast, people commonly rely on acronyms to recall names, rules for

---

[32] "Labor Letter," *The Wall Street Journal,* October 15, 1985, p. 1.

[33] Helpful instructions on formulating career goals may be found in Dorothy Heide and Elliot N. Kushell, "I Can Improve My Management Skills by: _____ ," *Personnel Journal,* June 1984, pp. 52–54.

■ **TABLE 8-12** A Best-Selling Novelist Shares His Self-Management Secret

Here is how Irving Wallace, author of such best-sellers as *The Prize* (later a movie starring Paul Newman) and *The Man*, got himself to sit down and complete his manuscripts on time:

I kept a work chart when I wrote my first book—which remains unpublished—at the age of 19. I maintained work charts while writing my first four published books. These charts showed the date I started each chapter, the date I finished it, and the number of pages written in that period. With my fifth book, I started keeping a more detailed chart, which also showed how many pages I had written by the end of every working day. . . . I am not sure why I started keeping such records. I suspect that it was because, as a free-lance writer, entirely on my own, without employer or deadline, I wanted to create disciplines for myself, ones that were guilt-making when ignored. A chart on the wall served as such a discipline, its figures scolding me or encouraging me.

SOURCE: Irving Wallace, *The Writing of One Novel* (Richmond Hill, Ontario: Simon & Schuster of Canada, 1971), as found in Irving Wallace, "Self-Control Techniques of Famous Novelists," *Journal of Applied Behavior Analysis*, Fall 1977, p. 516.

behavior, and other information. An acronym (or verbal code) that is often heard in managerial circles is the KISS principle, standing for "Keep It Simple, Stupid."

■ *Rehearsal:* While it is true that practice often makes perfect, mental rehearsal of challenging tasks also can increase one's chances of success. Dwight Stones, for example, a former world record holder in the high jump, would not begin his approach until he mentally rehearsed each footstep, his takeoff, and ascent over the bar. Job-finding seminars are very popular on college campuses today because they typically involve mental and actual rehearsal of tough job interviews. This sort of manufactured experience can build the confidence necessary for real-world success.

■ *Self-talk:* According to an expert on the subject, **"self-talk** is the set of evaluating thoughts that you give yourself about facts and events that happen to you."[34] Personal experience tells us that self-talk tends to be a self-fulfilling prophecy (recall the discussion in Chapter 4). Negative self-talk tends to pave the way for failure, whereas positive self-talk often facilitates success. Replacing negative self-talk ("I'll never get a raise") with positive self-talk ("I deserve a raise and I'm going to get it") is fundamental to better self-management.

Self-Reinforcement. The satisfaction of self-contracts and other personal achievements calls for self-reinforcement. According to Bandura, three criteria must be satisfied before self-reinforcement can occur:

---

[34] Charles Zastrow, *Talk to Yourself: Using the Power of Self-Talk* (Englewood Cliffs, N.J.: Prentice-Hall, 1979), p. 60.

1. The individual must have *control over desired reinforcers.*
2. Reinforcers must be *self-administered on a conditional basis.* Failure to meet the performance requirement must lead to self-denial.
3. *Performance standards must be adopted* to establish the quantity and quality of target behavior required for self-reinforcement.[35]

In view of the following realities, self-reinforcement strategies need to be resourceful and creative:

> Self-granted rewards can lead to self-improvement. But as failed dieters and smokers can attest, there are short-run as well as long-run influences on self-reinforcement. For the overeater, the immediate gratification of eating has more influence than the promise of a new wardrobe. The same sort of dilemma plagues procrastinators. Consequently, one needs to weave a powerful web of cues, cognitive supports, and internal and external consequences to win the tug-of-war with status-quo payoffs. Primarily because it is so easy to avoid, self-punishment tends to be ineffectual. As with managing the behavior of others, positive instead of negative consequences are recommended for effective self-management.[36]

In addition, it helps to solicit positive reinforcement for self-improvement from supportive friends and relatives.

Research and Managerial Implications

There is ample evidence that behavioral self-management works. For example, in one controlled study of 20 college students, 17 were able to successfully modify their own behavior problems involving smoking, lack of assertiveness, poor study habits, overeating, sloppy housekeeping, lack of exercise, and moodiness.[37] But because BSM has only recently been transplanted from clinical and classroom applications to the workplace, on-the-job research evidence is sparse. One pair of researchers reported successful BSM interventions with managerial problems including overdependence on the boss, ignoring paperwork, leaving the office without notifying anyone, and failing to fill out expense reports.[38] Also, absenteeism of unionized state government employees was significantly reduced with BSM training.[39] These preliminary studies need to

---

[35] Drawn from discussion in Albert Bandura, "Self-Reinforcement: Theoretical and Methodological Considerations," *Behaviorism,* Fall 1976, pp. 135–55.

[36] Robert Kreitner and Fred Luthans, "A Social Learning Approach to Behavioral Management: Radical Behaviorists 'Mellowing Out,' " *Organizational Dynamics,* Autumn 1984, p. 63.

[37] See Richard F. Rakos and Mark V. Grodek, "An Empirical Evaluation of a Behavioral Self-Management Course in a College Setting," *Teaching of Psychology,* October 1984, pp. 157–62.

[38] Luthans and Davis, "Behavioral Self-Management—The Missing Link in Managerial Effectiveness," pp. 52–59.

[39] Results are presented in Colette A. Frayne and Gary P. Latham, "Application of Social Learning Theory to Employee Self-Management of Attendance," *Journal of Applied Psychology,* August 1987, pp. 387–92.

be supplemented by research of how, why, and under what conditions BSM does or does not work. In the meantime, present and future managers can fine-tune their own behavior by taking lessons from proven self-management techniques.

SUMMARY OF KEY CONCEPTS ─────────────────────────────

A.   *Behavior modification* (B. Mod.) is defined as the process of making specific behavior occur more or less often by systematically managing (1) antecedent cues and (2) contingent consequences.

B.   B. Mod. involves managing person-environment interactions that can be functionally analyzed into antecedent→behavior→consequence (A→B→C) relationships. Antecedents cue rather than cause subsequent behavior. Contingent consequences, in turn, either strengthen or weaken that behavior.

C.   Positive and negative reinforcement are consequence management strategies that strengthen behavior, whereas punishment and extinction weaken behavior. These strategies need to be defined objectively, in terms of their actual impact on behavior frequency, not subjectively on the basis of intended impact.

D.   Every instance of a behavior is reinforced with a continuous reinforcement (CRF) schedule. Under intermittent reinforcement schedules—fixed and variable ratio or fixed and variable interval—some, rather than all, instances of a target behavior are reinforced. Variable schedules produce the most extinction-resistant behavior. Behavior shaping occurs when closer approximations of a target behavior are contingently reinforced.

E.   On-the-job behavior can be modified with the following four-step model: (1) Identify target behavior, (2) functionally analyze the situation, (3) arrange antecedents and provide consequences, and (4) evaluate results. Improvement should be reinforced equitably and with natural rewards whenever possible. New behavior requires continuous reinforcement. Intermittent reinforcement can maintain established behavior. Behavior charts, with baseline data for before-and-after comparison, are a practical way of evaluating the effectiveness of a B. Mod. program.

F.   *Behavioral self-management* (BSM) is the process of modifying one's own behavior by systematically managing cues, cognitive processes, and contingent consequences. Because BSM is based on social learning theory, rather than pure operant theory (radical behaviorism), it deals with cognitive processes such as visual and verbal symbolic coding, mental rehearsal, and self-talk.

G.   According to Kanfer's model, the three stages of self-regulation triggered by a disruption in normal routine are self-monitoring, self-evaluation, and self-reinforcement.

H.   A social learning model of self-management holds that one's behavior results from the reciprocal interaction among four components: (1) situational cues, (2) the person's psychological self, (3) the behavior itself, and (4) consequences. Self-management represents a dilemma because it involves replacing high-probability (appealing but unnecessary) behavior with low-probability (unappealing but necessary) behavior.

KEY TERMS

behavior modification   intermittent reinforcement
behavioral contingencies   shaping
functional analysis   natural rewards
positive reinforcement   baseline data
negative reinforcement   behavior chart
punishment   behavioral self-management
extinction   self-talk
continuous reinforcement

DISCUSSION QUESTIONS

1. What would an A→B→C functional analysis of your departing your residence *on time* for school or work look like? How about a functional analysis of your leaving late?

2. Why is the term *contingency* central to understanding the basics of B. Mod.?

3. What real-life examples of positive reinforcement, negative reinforcement, both forms of punishment, and extinction can you draw from your recent experience? Were these strategies appropriately or inappropriately used?

4. From a schedules of reinforcement perspective, why do people find gambling so addictive?

5. What sort of behavior shaping have you engaged in lately? Explain your success or failure.

6. Regarding the six guidelines for successfully managing consequences, which do you think ranks as the most important? Explain your rationale.

7. Why is valid baseline data essential in a B. Mod. program?

8. What sort of luck have you had with self-management recently? Which of the self-management techniques discussed in this chapter would help you do better?

9. Do you agree with the assumption that managers need to do a good job with self-management before they can effectively manage others? Explain.

10. What importance would you attach to self-talk in self-management? Explain.

BACK TO THE OPENING CASE

Now that you have read Chapter 8, you should be able to answer the following questions about the Parsons Pine Products case:

1. How would you rate James W. Parsons, the owner, as a behavior modifier? Explain in technical B. Mod. terms.
2. What sort of antecedent management has taken place in this case?
3. In A→B→C terms, which of Parsons' plans—well pay, retro pay, safety pay, and profit-sharing pay—probably has the most powerful influence on the target behavior?
4. Could any of Parsons' elaborate reinforcement schemes backfire? Explain potential problems and offer suggestions.

EXERCISE 8

Objectives

1. To better understand the principles of behavior modification through firsthand experience.
2. To improve your own or someone else's behavior by putting to use what you have learned in this chapter.

Introduction

Because the areas of B. Mod. and BSM are application oriented, they need to be put to practical use if they are to be fully appreciated. In a general sense, everyone is a behavior modifier. Unfortunately, those without a working knowledge of behavioral principles tend to manage their own and others' behavior rather haphazardly. They tend to unwittingly reinforce undesirable behavior, put desirable behavior on extinction, and rely too heavily on punishment and negative reinforcement. This exercise is designed to help you become a more systematic manager of behavior.

Instructions

Selecting the target behavior of your choice, put the four-step behavior modification model in Figure 8–3 into practice. The target may be your own behavior (e.g., studying more, smoking fewer cigarettes, eating less or eating more nutritionally, or one of the managerial BSM problems in Table 8–11) or someone else's (e.g., improving a roommate's housekeeping behavior). Be sure to construct a behavior chart (as in Figure 8–4) with the frequency of the target behavior on the vertical axis and time on the horizontal axis. It is best to focus on a behavior that occurs daily so a three- or four-day baseline period can be followed by a one- to two-week intervention period. Make sure you follow as many of the six consequence management guidelines as possible.

You will find it useful to perform an A→B→C functional analysis of the target behavior to identify its supporting (or hindering) cues and consequences. Then you will be in a position to set a reasonable goal and design an intervention strategy involving antecedent and consequence management. When planning a self-management intervention, give careful thought to how you can use cognitive supports. Make sure you use appropriate schedules of reinforcement.

Questions for Consideration/Class Discussion

1. Did you target a specific behavior (e.g., eating) or an outcome (e.g., pounds lost)? What was the advantage or disadvantage of tracking that particular target?
2. How did your B. Mod. or BSM program turn out? What did you do wrong? What did you do right?
3. How has this exercise increased your working knowledge of B. Mod. and/or BSM?

PART THREE

Understanding and Managing Group Processes

EXTERNAL ENVIRONMENT

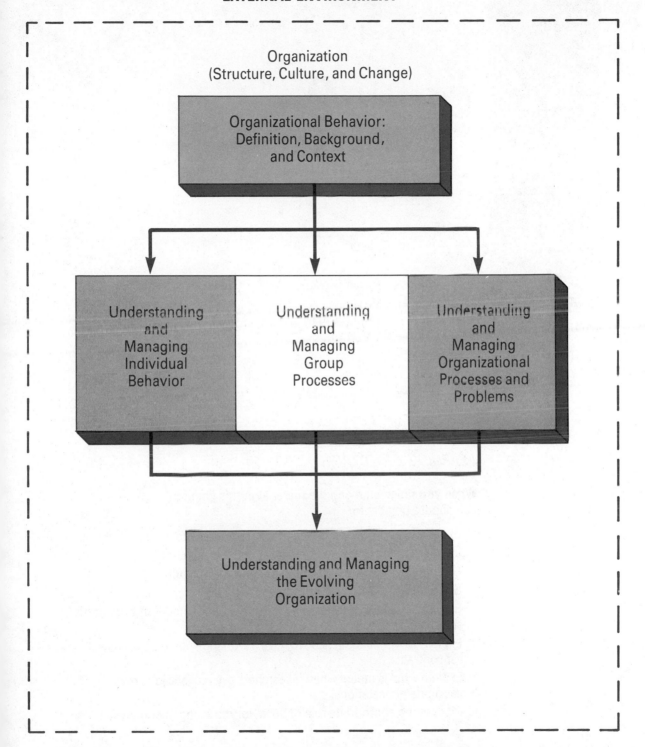

Organization
(Structure, Culture, and Change)

Organizational Behavior:
Definition, Background,
and Context

Understanding
and
Managing
Individual
Behavior

Understanding
and
Managing
Group
Processes

Understanding
and
Managing
Organizational
Processes and
Problems

Understanding and Managing
the Evolving
Organization

Chapter **9**

Organizational Socialization

LEARNING OBJECTIVES

When you finish studying the material in this chapter,
you should be able to:

- Explain what has been learned from social facilitation research.
- Identify and describe the five social network functions.
- Distinguish between role conflict and role ambiguity.
- Specify four reasons why norms are enforced in organizations.
- Briefly describe the three phases in Feldman's model of organizational socialization.
- Explain why managers need to have a working knowledge of psychological contracts.
- Explain what is meant when researchers say realistic job previews (RJPs) vaccinate expectations.
- Discuss the appropriate role of behavior modeling in employee training.

OPENING CASE 9

Doing Things the IBM Way

If you work for IBM, you're working for the company that makes more profit after taxes than any other company in the world. You're also working for the company that's the acknowledged leader of the industry of the future. That IBMers wear these "titles" with a minimum of arrogance reflects an extraordinary culture that goes back to the company's founder.

Thomas J. Watson created an environment where employees could take pride in their work and thereby identify their interests with IBM's. . . .

Needless to say, IBM has never been unionized. And no one can recall IBMers walking off their jobs in protest. Why should they when the company virtually guarantees lifetime employment. . . . Watson laid down his "no layoff" policy in the darkest days of the Depression. [Critics point out, however, that IBM has stretched the definition of its no-layoff policy in recent years. For example, during a 1986–87 cost-cutting program, the firm trimmed more than 5,000 people from its U.S. work force by offering early-retirement incentives. Many others were given the option of accepting transfers to less desirable jobs and/or locations or resigning.]

Perhaps his most signal achievement was to foster at IBM a culture in which people felt good about what they were doing. It was tantamount to empowering workers. . . . Watson ran IBM from 1914 to 1956, when the reins were taken by his son, Thomas J. Watson, Jr., who retired as chief executive officer in 1971. The younger Watson, who still serves on the IBM board of directors, once said: "Our early emphasis on human relations was not motivated by altruism but by the simple belief that if we respected our people and helped them respect themselves the company would make the most profit."

IBM, more than any other big company, has institutionalized its beliefs the way a church does. They are expounded in numerous IBM internal publications to ensure that employees know what's expected of them. And they are reflected in codes of behavior, still in force even though the Watsons are no longer around. There are rules for everything. The Watsons insisted that salespersons wear dark business suits and white shirts; that's no longer a strict regulation but most IBM salesmen continue to dress that way. The Watsons wouldn't permit drinking, on or off the job; today, an IBMer can drink off the job but anyone who drinks at lunch is expected to take the rest of the day off. . . .

Everyone at IBM is graded, at least once a year. You get a Performance Plan for the year, which sets goals. You're reviewed at the end of the year to see whether you met those goals. People who sell IBM equipment have quotas—and they are ruthlessly held to them. If a customer returns an IBM machine that he bought, IBM forces the salesperson who sold the equipment to return the commission.

The result is a company filled with ardent believers. (If you're not ardent, you may not be comfortable.) Susan Chace, a perceptive reporter for *The Wall Street Journal*, profiled IBM in 1982, concluding that the IBM culture "is so pervasive that, as one nine-year (for-

Concluded:

mer) employee put it, 'leaving the company is like emigrating.' '' She also quoted George McQuilken, who left IBM to found his own company, Spartacus Computers, as saying, ''The hardest part about being gone was the first few times I tried to make a decision on my own about anything, like what hotel to stay in, or who I wanted to hire.''

Indeed, IBM is a world unto itself. One of the 10 largest industrial corporations in America, with a work force [now 216,000] exceeded by only three other firms (GM, Ford, and GE), IBM has employees in almost every city of any size and in lots of smaller ones. The company has long had a reputation for transferring its people around. A long-standing joke among employees is that their company's initials really stand for ''I've Been Moved.''. . . The company currently relocates 3 percent of its employees a year, down from 5 percent 10 years ago. And there is now a rule (still another IBM rule) which specifies that employees will not be transferred more than once in two years or more than three times in 10 years. Still, with 3 percent transferred every year, 6,000 IBMers in the United States pack their bags annually.

IBM maintains a company-wide open-door policy. And managers are expected to treat employees fairly. ''The easiest way to get fired around here is for a supervisor to be capricious or unfair in dealing with subordinates,'' Edward Krieg, director of management development, told us during our visit to the corporate headquarters in Armonk, New York, a suburb of New York City. If you're not satisfied with your treatment, you have the right, as an IBMer, to appeal all the way up to the head of the company, including a personal interview with the chairman if that is ''appropriate.''

Those who don't abide by IBM's rules, including its 32-page code of business ethics,

don't last long. ''If anybody does anything that's the least bit shady, the heavens descend on them from their supervisors on down,'' Krieg explained. ''People see we have a basic set of beliefs and we adhere to them.''

IBM expects its people to spend their careers with the company. According to Krieg, IBM is looking for ''people with a very positive self-image, who are willing to have their talents tested. People who can enjoy collegiality of interests with others. People who are stimulated by their peers.'' He claimed that though the company is ''competitive, it is not dog-eat-dog.''

Like any good church, IBM has powerful training programs. . . . It invests $500 million a year on employee education and training. . . .

Secrecy is one of IBM's hallmarks. It spends great amounts of money making sure its research is kept from potential competitors, and it vigorously sues any ex-IBMer it suspects of having betrayed one of its processes. Partly because of this obsession, many have remarked that there's something terribly ingroupish about IBMers. It appears to be the rule rather than the exception that IBMers socialize with each other rather than with outsiders. Because of these tendencies, some have compared joining IBM with joining a religious order or going into the military. (One longtime IBM watcher told *Time*, ''If you understand the Marines, you can understand IBM.'') You must be willing to give up some of your individual identity to survive.

For Discussion

Would you like to work for IBM? Explain.

SOURCE: Excerpted from Robert Levering, Milton Moskowitz, and Michael Katz, *The 100 Best Companies to Work For in America*, © 1984. Addison-Wesley Publishing Company, Inc., Reading, Massachusetts, pps. 156–59. Reprinted with permission.

■ Additional discussion questions linking this case with the following material appear at the end of this chapter.

If you were a waitress in a restaurant and you wanted to maximize your tips while serving male-female couples, which of the following approaches would you use?

a. Touch the male lightly and briefly on the shoulder while asking if everything was all right.

b. Do not touch either person while asking if everything was all right.

c. Touch the female lightly and briefly on the shoulder while asking if everything was all right.

Think briefly about why you have selected that answer before reading further.

According to the results of a recent social psychology field study in a Greensboro, North Carolina, restaurant, the last approach would be your most profitable alternative. This approach produced an average tip of 15 percent, whereas the first and second tactics yielded average tips of 13 percent and 11 percent, respectively.[1] Of course, different results could be expected in cultures where public physical contact is discouraged. The outcome for a male waiter might be different, too. Nonetheless, this little multiple-choice quiz illustrates the curious twists behavior can take when individuals interact. Because the management of organizational behavior is above all else a social endeavor, managers need a working knowledge of *interpersonal* behavior.

In Part Two, we drew heavily upon the field of psychology to better understand why individuals behave as they do. Now that the focus has switched to social behavior, we will be drawing useful insights from the fields of social psychology, sociology, and cultural anthropology. Like psychology, these socially oriented fields have their own distinct models and terminology. Thus, this chapter will provide a foundation of terms and concepts for the discussion of group processes in Part Three.

This chapter discusses social facilitation and social networks, explains roles and norms, presents a model of organizational socialization, and explores modern socialization techniques. With an eye toward increasing your chances of professional success, this chapter takes a career perspective. It sorts out the social influences you can expect to encounter upon joining a work organization. (Additional career perspectives are in the Appendix following this chapter.) As humorously chronicled in Table 9–1, organizational newcomers have lots of unanswered questions. Organizational socialization processes provide answers to those questions.

■ SOCIAL FACILITATION

In task situations, does the mere presence of others help or hinder one's performance? This question, centering on what social scientists call **social facilitation,** has intrigued researchers for nearly a century. Not surprisingly,

---

[1] See Renee Stephen and Richard L. Zweigenhaft, "The Effect on Tipping of a Waitress Touching Male and Female Customers," *The Journal of Social Psychology,* February 1986, pp. 141–42.

■ **TABLE 9-1** Reality Shock for a British Organizational Newcomer

In the late 1970s, I joined the British division of a large multinational company as a personnel manager, a job I held for about a year and a half. This division comprises a medium size manufacturing concern situated in the north of England and since all names and positions have been changed to protect identities, it will be referred to as Wenslow Manufacturing Company.

Any feelings of excitement or even awe that one has when first joining a multinational—the sense of being part of a worldwide family, or even a worldwide "machine"—soon disappear as one realizes that there is no sign of romance. The connecting rods of the machine are absent also. People do not dream about their counterparts in Tahiti or South America, or even in Birmingham. They go about their jobs in much the same way as does everyone else in every other organization.

Perhaps then the first feature of entry concerns the bringing down to earth of the new member. The absolute mundanity of everyday transactions is strongly reinforced by the apathetic stances individuals take towards other divisions, which are treated as irrelevant, distracting, and boring. In a way that is reassuring to a newcomer—"I shall be able to cope after all." But what does coping entail? How does a new member learn what standards are applied to coping? When does coping become not coping? And when does it become identified as super coping—leading to promotion? How are such boundaries communicated, and indeed established?

SOURCE: David Golding, "Inside Story: On Becoming a Manager," *Organization Studies* 7, no. 2 (1986), p. 194. Used with permission.

findings and recommendations have varied through the years. In the early 1900s, Frederick Taylor claimed that workers would loaf or engage in what he called "systematic soldiering" if allowed to mingle during work hours.[2] During the bank wiring room portion of the famous Hawthorne studies, researchers did observe workers conspiring to restrict output.[3] On the other hand, an early 1950s experiment showed that self-selected teams of construction workers had lower production costs, lower turnover, and greater satisfaction than workers in assigned teams.[4]

Research Insights

Thanks to a meta-analysis of 241 studies encompassing almost 24,000 subjects, decades of conflicting findings on social facilitation can be boiled down to the following conclusions:

---

[2] Details may be found in Frederick W. Taylor, *The Principles of Scientific Management* (New York: Harper & Row, 1911).

[3] See F. J. Roethlisberger and William J. Dickson, *Management and the Worker* (Cambridge, Mass.: Harvard University Press, 1939); and Henry A. Landsberger, *Hawthorne Revisited* (Ithaca, N.Y.: Cornell University, 1958).

[4] For details of this study, see Raymond H. Van Zelst, "Sociometrically Selected Work Teams Increase Production," *Personnel Psychology*, Autumn 1952, pp. 175–85.

- The mere presence of others has a relatively small (3 percent or less) impact on the performance of individuals.
- Physiological arousal occurs in the presence of others only when the task being performed is complex.
- Performance of simple tasks tends to be speeded up and made more accurate by the presence of others.
- Performance of complex tasks tends to be slowed and made less accurate by the presence of others.[5]

Implications for Studying and Managing Organizational Behavior

It is important to realize that one's job performance can be affected in a small yet meaningful way by the mere presence of others. For example, training for simple tasks can be done in groups, whereas training for complex tasks needs to include private practice sessions. But managers need to know more about what happens when employees interact in real-life fashion. Fortunately, social scientists have in recent years probed far beyond the impact of the mere presence of others. They have uncovered many instructive insights about the social networks people form, the roles they play, the norms they follow, and how they are transformed from outsiders to contributing insiders. Hence, social behavior includes but does not stop at the social facilitation effect.

■ SOCIAL NETWORKS

Everyday experience in organizations demonstrates that people are creatures of habit. Joe and Jean always share office gossip during lunch, while Maria and Mike exchange only market information during monthly sales meetings. Social network analysis measures the frequency and nature of such interactions. Although this sociological technique, in one form or another, has been around for years, it was not proposed as an OB tool until 1979. According to the scholars responsible for extending the social network perspective to the field of OB:

> In network analysis, an organization is conceived of as clusters of people joined by a variety of links which transmit goods and services, information, influence, and affect [feelings]. These clusters of people are both formal (prescribed), such as departments or work groups, and informal (emergent), such as coalitions and cliques.[6]

Thus, **social network analysis** is defined as the process of graphically mapping and categorizing social transactions to identify meaningful patterns.

The social network perspective is presented here as an instructive analytical

[5] Research conclusions drawn from Charles F. Bond, Jr., and Linda J. Titus, ''Social Facilitation: A Meta-Analysis of 241 Studies,'' *Psychological Bulletin,* September 1983, pp. 265–92.

[6] Noel Tichy and Charles Fombrun, ''Network Analysis in Organizational Settings,'' *Human Relations,* November 1979, pp. 925–26.

■ **FIGURE 9-1** Social Network Transactions

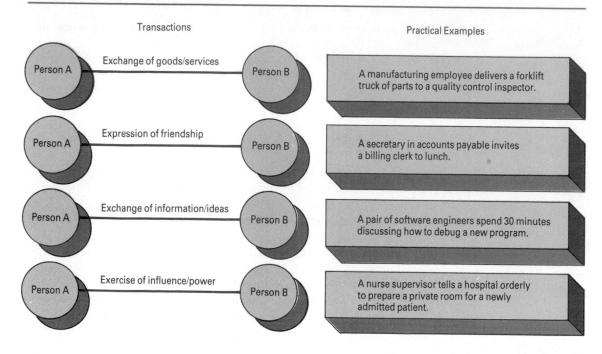

tool, which will help you better understand social processes such as socialization, group formation, power, communication, and organizational cultures. Social network analysis is instructive for managers because it:

- Is a generic tool that can be used to better understand both interpersonal and interorganizational interaction.
- Realistically characterizes organizations as complex, changing, and dynamic rather than simple and static.
- Treats formal and informal interactions as equally important. (Informal interactions too often are underemphasized or ignored.)
- Sorts out the complex web of multiple relationships among organizational members.
- Shows the relative importance of network members (including but not limited to their formal authority and status).
- Identifies the different functions performed by network members.

The following sections explore the social network perspective by considering four types of network transactions, five functions of network members, network clusters, recent research, and managerial implications.

Social Network Transactions

Four types of social network transactions are illustrated in Figure 9–1. These transactions generally are intertwined. For example, a computer programmer who, while delivering a data analysis, asks the head of another department about her sick child has engaged in two simultaneous transactions: (1) exchange of information/ideas and (2) expression of friendship. The four social transaction categories encompass virtually all interpersonal dealings.

Social Network Functions

Depending on the number and nature of their social transactions with others, individuals fulfill different network functions. They may function as stars, liaisons, bridges, gatekeepers, or isolates. Each social network function is defined as follows:

- *Star*—an individual with the most linkages in the network.
- *Liaison*—an individual who links two or more clusters without belonging to a cluster.
- *Bridge*—an individual who serves as a linking pin by belonging to two or more clusters.
- *Gatekeeper*—an individual who links his or her network to outside domains such as suppliers, clients, government agencies, and so on.
- *Isolate*—an individual who is no longer connected to the network.[7]

Figure 9–2 portrays an idealized social network to illustrate each of these five functions. Note that individuals 1 and 4 are both stars because each has five network linkages or connections. But 4 is labeled a gatekeeper because of his or her outside connection.

Prescribed and Emergent Clusters

Two types of clusters also appear in Figure 9–2. *Prescribed clusters* are task teams or formal committees carrying out assigned jobs. The *emergent cluster* is an informal, unofficial grouping of network members. The star (1) obviously is the central figure in this emergent cluster. This cluster is a *coalition* if it is a temporary alliance with a specific purpose. For example, a group of factory employees who band together to complain to management about toxic fumes in the work area is a coalition. If this emergent cluster is based on lasting friendships, then it is a **clique.**[8]

Recent Social Network Research

Organizational research of social networks is sparse because of its relatively recent introduction to the field of OB. A pioneering 1984 study conducted at a newspaper publishing company found that central (nonsupervisory) members of the various networks were promoted to supervisory positions more often than noncentral members. Central network members were those who had the

---

[7] These definitions are adapted from discussion in Noel M. Tichy, Michael L. Tushman, and Charles Fombrun, "Social Network Analysis for Organizations," *Academy of Management Review,* October 1979, pp. 507–19.

[8] Adapted from material in Tichy and Fombrun, "Network Analysis in Organizational Settings," p. 929.

■ **FIGURE 9-2** Social Network Functions

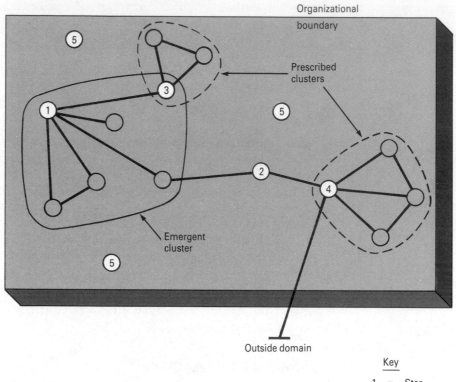

Key

1	=	Star
2	=	Liaison
3	=	Bridge
4	=	Gatekeeper
5	=	Isolate

greatest control over their co-workers' access to resources and information. This outcome prompted the researcher to conclude that, regarding promotions, it pays to be in the "right place" in organizational networks.[9]

A more recent study examined the relationship between social networks and turnover for employees in three fast-food restaurants. Findings indicated that turnover was clustered by social networks. That is, employees who perceived themselves as belonging to certain networks either stayed together or quit together.[10]

---

[9] For details, see Daniel J. Brass, "Being in the Right Place: A Structural Analysis of Individual Influence in an Organization," *Administrative Science Quarterly*, December 1984, pp. 518–39.

[10] See David Krackhardt and Lyman W. Porter, "The Snowball Effect: Turnover Embedded in Communication Networks," *Journal of Applied Psychology*, February 1986, pp. 50–55.

The Practical Value of a Social Network Perspective

Managers who view their work units and organizations as social networks have a handy early detection system for interpersonal problems and opportunities. Keeping track of those who fulfill key network functions, for example, is a good idea. A star of an emergent cluster might be a good candidate for a managerial position. Liaisons are in a good position to be objective observers and communication monitors because they link clusters without belonging to them. Those who serve as bridges may be able to help management resolve intergroup conflicts because of their familiarity with the parties involved.

Gatekeepers, meanwhile, can keep an organization properly tuned to its environment. PepsiCo's emphasis on the gatekeeper function prompted the head of the firm to tell *Business Week:* "You hear a lot of conversations around Pepsi about what's going on with the consumer, what's going on at the supermarket, what the competition is doing."[11] Thus, it is no accident that PepsiCo is widely admired for its ability to read and quickly respond to shifting markets.

Finally, employees who become isolated from the organization's social network may be experiencing serious problems. For example, people concerned about the growth of drug abuse on the job have pointed out:

> Many managers are in an excellent position to hide drug habits because they can close their office doors and delegate work to others. Company officers also travel frequently, making it easier to use narcotics on the sly.[12]

Of course, being an "isolate" does not necessarily make one a drug addict. Because some people do their best work when left alone, managers need to interpret social networks very carefully.

■ ORGANIZATIONAL ROLES AND NORMS

Employees need to behave with a fairly high degree of predictability if organizations are to accomplish their objectives. Imagine what it would be like if a teller at your local bank stopped in the middle of your transaction and said it was time to go shopping! Formal policies, rules, and regulations foster predictable job behavior. But other, more subtle forces are at work as well. In this section, the subtle yet powerful social forces behavioral scientists call roles and norms are examined.

Roles

Nearly four centuries have passed since William Shakespeare had his character Jaques speak the following memorable lines in Act II of *As You Like It:*

---

[11] Amy Dunkin, "Pepsi's Marketing Magic: Why Nobody Does It Better," *Business Week,* February 10, 1986, p. 53.

[12] Janice Castro, "Battling the Enemy Within," *Time,* March 17, 1986, p. 54.

■ **FIGURE 9–3**   A Role Episode

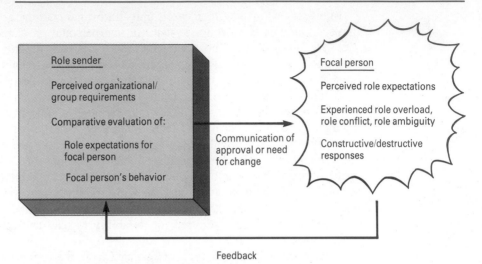

Feedback

SOURCE: Adapted in part from Robert L. Kahn, Donald M. Wolfe, Robert P. Quinn, and J. Diedrick Snoek, *Organizational Stress: Studies in Role Conflict and Ambiguity,* 1981 edition (Malabar, Fla.: Robert E. Krieger Publishing Co., 1964), p. 26.

"All the world's a stage, And all the men and women merely players; They have their exits and their entrances; And one man in his time plays many parts. . . ." This intriguing notion of all people as actors in a universal play was not lost on 20th-century sociologists who developed a complex theory of human interaction based on roles. According to an OB scholar, "**roles** are sets of behaviors that persons expect of occupants of a position."[13] By referring to the cognitive element of *expectations,* role theory sets itself apart from social network analysis, which deals primarily with observable behavior. This section explores role theory by analyzing a role episode and defining the terms *role overload, role conflict,* and *role ambiguity.*

Role Episodes.   A role episode, as illustrated in Figure 9–3, consists of a snapshot of the ongoing interaction between two people. In any given role episode, there is a role sender and a focal person who is expected to act out the role. Within a broader context, one may be simultaneously a role sender and a focal person. For the sake of social analysis, however, it is instructive to deal with separate role episodes.

Role episodes begin with the role sender's perception of the relevant organization's or group's behavioral requirements. Those requirements serve as a standard for formulating expectations for the focal person's behavior. The role sender then cognitively evaluates the focal person's actual behavior against those expectations. Appropriate verbal and nonverbal messages are then sent

[13] George Graen, "Role-Making Processes within Complex Organizations," in *Handbook of Industrial and Organizational Psychology,* ed. Marvin D. Dunnette (Chicago: Rand McNally, 1976), p. 1201.

■ **TABLE 9–2** Communicating Role Expectations via the Carrot-and-Stick Approach at Westinghouse

The carrot is a plan that, since 1984, has rewarded 134 managers with options to buy 764,000 shares of stock for boosting the company's financial performance.

The stick is quarterly meetings that are used to rank managers by how much their operations contribute to earnings per share. The soft-spoken . . . [chairman of the board] doesn't scold. He just charts in green the results of the sectors that have met their goals and charts the laggards in red. Peer pressure does the rest. Shame "is a powerful tool," says one executive.

SOURCE: Excerpted from Gregory L. Miles, "Doug Danforth's Plan to Put Westinghouse in the 'Winner's Circle,'" *Business Week,* July 28, 1986, p. 75.

to the focal person to pressure him or her into behaving as expected (see Table 9–2). A team of pioneering role theorists observed:

> Each role sender behaves toward the focal person in ways determined by his own expectations and his own anticipations of the focal person's responses. Under certain circumstances the role sender, responding to his own immediate experience, expresses his expectations overtly; he attempts to influence the focal person in the direction of greater conformity with his expectations. It is not uncommon for a role sender to be relatively unaware that his behavior is really an influence attempt. Even mild communications about actual and expected role performance usually carry an evaluative connotation.[14]

On the receiving end of the role episode, the focal person accurately or inaccurately perceives the communicated role expectations. Various combinations of role overload, role conflict, and role ambiguity are then experienced. (These three outcomes are defined and discussed in the following sections.) The focal person then responds constructively by engaging in problem solving, for example, or destructively because of undue tension, stress, and strain. Stress is discussed in detail in Chapter 16.

Role Overload. According to organizational psychologist Edgar Schein, **role overload** occurs when "the sum total of what role senders expect of the focal person far exceeds what he or she is able to do."[15] Students who attempt to handle a full course load and maintain a decent social life while working 30 or more hours a week know full well the consequences of role overload. As the individual tries to do more and more in less and less time, stress mounts and personal effectiveness slips.

[14] Robert L. Kahn, Donald M. Wolfe, Robert P. Quinn, and J. Diedrick Snoek, *Organizational Stress: Studies in Role Conflict and Ambiguity,* 1981 edition (Malabar, Fla.: Robert E. Krieger Publishing Co., 1964), p. 27. A thorough discussion of role making is presented by George B. Graen and Terri A. Scandura, "Toward a Psychology of Dyadic Organizing," in *Research in Organizational Behavior,* ed. L. L. Cummings and Barry M. Staw (Greenwich, Conn.: JAI Press, 1987), pp. 175–208.

[15] Edgar H. Schein, *Organizational Psychology,* 3rd ed. (Englewood Cliffs, N.J.: Prentice-Hall, 1980), p. 198.

Role Conflict.   Have you ever felt like you were being torn apart by the conflicting demands of those around you? If so, you were a victim of role conflict. **Role conflict** is experienced when "different members of the role set expect different things of the focal person."[16] Managers often face conflicting demands between work and family, for example. The renowned loyalty Japanese employees have to their companies sometimes leads to role conflict of tragic proportions.

> A manager at a leading Japanese company was asked by his boss to resign and move to a small subsidiary. He was willing to comply, but his wife told him not to accept the demotion because she feared it would hurt their daughter's chances of concluding an arranged marriage. Torn between the conflicting demands of his boss and his wife, the manager hanged himself.[17]

Progressive organizations offer employee counseling and stress management courses to head off this sort of tragic outcome.

Role conflict also may be experienced when internalized values, ethics, or personal standards collide with others' expectations. For instance, an otherwise ethical production supervisor may be told by a superior to "fudge a little" on the quality control reports so an important deadline will be met. The resulting role conflict forces the supervisor to choose between being loyal but unethical or ethical but disloyal. Tough ethical choices such as this mean personal turmoil, interpersonal conflict, and even resignation. Consequently, experts say business schools should do a better job of weaving ethics training into their course requirements.[18]

Role Ambiguity.   Those who experience role conflict may have trouble complying with role demands, but they at least know what is expected of them. Such is not the case with **role ambiguity,** which occurs when "members of the role set fail to communicate to the focal person expectations they have or information needed to perform the role, either because they do not have the information or because they deliberately withhold it."[19] In short, people experience role ambiguity when they do not know what is expected of them. Organizational newcomers often complain about unclear job descriptions and vague promotion criteria. According to role theory, prolonged role ambiguity can foster job dissatisfaction, erode self-confidence, and hamper job performance.

Take a moment now to complete the self-assessment exercise in Table 9–3. See if you can distinguish between sources of role conflict and sources of role ambiguity, as they affect your working life.

---

[16] Ibid.

[17] Leslie Helm and Charles Gaffney, "The High Price Japanese Pay for Success," *Business Week,* April 7, 1986, p. 52.

[18] See, for example, David Clark Scott, "As Inside Trades Boil, Business Deans Ponder Ethics Role," *The Christian Science Monitor,* June 27, 1986, pp. 16–17.

[19] Schein, *Organizational Psychology,* p. 198.

■ **TABLE 9–3** Measuring Role Conflict and Role Ambiguity

Instructions:

Step 1: While thinking of your present (or last) job, circle one response for each of the following statements. Please consider each statement carefully because some are worded positively and some negatively.

Step 2: In the space in the far right column, label each statement with either a "C" for role conflict or an "A" for role ambiguity. (See note 20 for a correct categorization.)

Step 3: Calculate separate totals for role conflict and role ambiguity and compare them with these arbitrary norms: 5–14 = low; 15–25 = moderate; 25–35 = high.

		Very False	**Very True**	
1.	I feel certain about how much authority I have.	7—6—5—4—3—2—1		_____
2.	I have to do things that should be done differently.	1—2—3—4—5—6—7		_____
3.	I know that I have divided my time properly.	7—6—5—4—3—2—1		_____
4.	I know what my responsibilities are.	7—6—5—4—3—2—1		_____
5.	I have to buck a rule or policy in order to carry out an assignment.	1—2—3—4—5—6 7		_____
6.	I feel certain how I will be evaluated for a raise or promotion.	7—6—5—4—3—2—1		_____
7.	I work with two or more groups who operate quite differently.	1—2—3—4—5—6—7		_____
8.	I know exactly what is expected of me.	7—6—5—4—3 2—1		_____
9.	I do things that are apt to be accepted by one person and not accepted by others.	1—2—3—4—5—6—7		_____
10.	I work on unnecessary things.	1—2—3—4—5—6—7		_____

Role conflict score   = _____
Role ambiguity score = _____

SOURCE: Adapted from John R. Rizzo, Robert J. House, and Sidney I. Lirtzman, "Role Conflict and Ambiguity in Complex Organizations," *Administrative Science Quarterly*, June 1970, p. 156.

Norms

Norms are more encompassing than roles. While roles involve behavioral expectations for specific positions, norms help organizational members determine right from wrong and good from bad. According to one respected team of management consultants: "A **norm** is an attitude, opinion, feeling, or action— shared by two or more people—that guides their behavior."[21] Although norms are typically unwritten and seldom discussed openly, they have a powerful influence on group and organizational behavior.[22] Referring again to PepsiCo Inc., a norm has evolved that equates corporate competitiveness with physical fitness. According to observers:

> Leanness and nimbleness are qualities that pervade the company. When Pepsi's brash young managers take a few minutes away from the office, they often head straight for the company's physical fitness center or for a jog around the museum-quality sculptures outside of PepsiCo's Purchase New York headquarters.[23]

---

[20] 1 = A; 2 = C; 3 = A; 4 = A; 5 = C; 6 = A; 7 = C; 8 = A; 9 = C; 10 = C.

[21] Robert R. Blake and Jane Srygley Mouton, "Don't Let Group Norms Stifle Creativity," *Personnel*, August 1985, p. 28.

[22] Based on discussion found in Daniel C. Feldman, "The Development and Enforcement of Group Norms," *Academy of Management Review*, January 1984, pp. 47–53.

[23] Dunkin, "Pepsi's Marketing Magic," p. 52.

At PepsiCo and elsewhere, group members positively reinforce those who adhere to current norms with friendship and acceptance. On the other hand, nonconformists experience criticism and even **ostracism,** or rejection by group members. Anyone who has experienced the "silent treatment" from a group of friends knows what a potent social weapon ostracism can be. Norms can be put into proper perspective by understanding how they develop and why they are enforced.

How Norms Are Developed.   Experts say norms evolve in an informal manner as the group or organization determines what it takes to be effective. Generally speaking, norms develop in various combinations of the following four ways:

1.   *Explicit statements by supervisors or co-workers.* . . . For instance, a group leader might explicitly set norms about not drinking at lunch. . . .

2.   *Critical events in the group's history.* At times there is a critical event in the group's history that established an important precedent. [For example, a key recruit may have decided to work elsewhere because a group member said too many negative things about the organization. Hence, a norm against such "sour grapes" behavior might evolve.]

3.   *Primacy.* The first behavior pattern that emerges in a group often sets group expectations. If the first group meeting is marked by very formal interaction between supervisors and subordinates, then the group often expects future meetings to be conducted in the same way. . . .

4.   *Carryover behaviors from past situations.* . . . Such carryover of individual behaviors from past situations can increase the predictability of group members' behaviors in new settings and facilitate task accomplishment. For instance, students and professors carry fairly constant sets of expectations from class to class.[24]

Why Norms Are Enforced.   Norms tend to be enforced by group members when they:

-   Help the group or organization survive.
-   Clarify or simplify behavioral expectations.
-   Help individuals avoid embarrassing situations.
-   Clarify the group's or organization's central values and/or unique identity.[25]

Working examples of each of these four situations are presented in Table 9–4.

Relevant Research Insights and Managerial Implications

Within the topical domain of roles and norms, OB researchers have directed their attention almost exclusively toward the correlates of role conflict and

---

[24] Feldman, "The Development and Enforcement of Group Norms," pp. 50–52.
[25] Ibid.

■ **TABLE 9-4** Four Reasons Why Norms Are Enforced

Norm	Reason for Enforcement	Example
"Make our department look good in top management's eyes."	Group/organization survival	After vigorously defending the vital role played by the Human Resources Management Department at a divisional meeting, a staff specialist is complimented by her boss.
"Success comes to those who work hard and don't make waves."	Clarification of behavioral expectations	A senior manager takes a young associate aside and cautions him to be a bit more patient with co-workers who see things differently.
"Be a team player, not a star."	Avoidance of embarrassment	A project team member is ridiculed by her peers for dominating the discussion during a progress report to top management.
"Customer service is our top priority."	Clarification of central values/unique identity	Two sales representatives are given a surprise Friday afternoon party for having received prestigious best-in-the-industry customer service awards from an industry association.

SOURCE: Four reasons adapted from Daniel C. Feldman, "The Development and Enforcement of Group Norms," *Academy of Management Review,* January 1984, pp. 47–53.

role ambiguity. Hence, we will focus on research insights in those narrower yet important areas. The following insights were uncovered in a meta-analysis of 96 role conflict and role ambiguity studies in work settings:

- As feedback from both others and the task itself increased, role ambiguity decreased.
- As direction from the leader increased, role conflict and role ambiguity decreased.
- As the quantity of written rules and procedures increased, role ambiguity decreased.
- Contrary to conventional wisdom, role conflict and role ambiguity did not increase as one moved up the organizational hierarchy.
- As participation in decision making increased, role conflict and role ambiguity decreased.
- Individuals with an external locus of control tended to report higher role conflict and role ambiguity.
- There is too little evidence available to confidently support the widespread belief that high role conflict and ambiguity have physiological stress-related consequences (e.g., elevated heart rate and blood pressure).
- As role conflict and role ambiguity increased, job satisfaction and organizational commitment decreased, and intentions to quit increased.
- Job performance tended to decrease only slightly as role conflict and role ambiguity increased.[26]

The foregoing research findings hold few surprises for managers. Generally, relative to satisfaction, commitment, and performance, it pays to reduce both role conflict and role ambiguity. Within a contingency management approach,

---

[26] Research insights drawn from Susan E. Jackson and Randall S. Schuler, "A Meta-Analysis and Conceptual Critique of Research on Role Ambiguity and Role Conflict in Work Settings," *Organizational Behavior and Human Decision Processes,* August 1985, pp. 16–78. Also see Paul E. Spector, "Perceived Control by Employees: A Meta-Analysis of Studies Concerning Autonomy and Participation at Work," *Human Relations,* November 1986, pp. 1005–16.

feedback, formal rules and procedures, directive leadership, setting specific hard goals, and participation can make positive contributions. Although the connection between role conflict/ambiguity and stress is uncertain, managers may want to be safe by taking remedial steps. Managers can use all of the socialization techniques discussed in the last section of this chapter to reduce role conflict and role ambiguity.

■ THE ORGANIZATIONAL SOCIALIZATION PROCESS

Joining the military, going to college, pledging a sorority or fraternity, taking a full-time job, and getting transferred have more in common than initially meets the eye. In each case, the individual experiences the shaping process called organizational socialization. As shown in Figure 9–4, this process involves many sources of influence, some of which are beyond management's direct control. One authority on the subject refers to **organizational socialization** as "people processing" and defines it as "the manner in which the experiences of people learning the ropes of a new organizational position, status, or role are structured for them by others within the organization."[27] In short, organizational socialization turns outsiders into fully functioning insiders. This is an anxiety-producing time because newcomers—called recruits, new hires, rookies, pledges, trainees, or apprentices—must adapt or fall by the wayside. This section introduces a three-phase model of organizational socialization and examines relevant research.

Present and future managers need to have a working knowledge of organizational socialization for at least three reasons. First, such understanding can enhance one's chances of successfully clearing the career hurdles into and through the organized world of work. Second, human resource management specialists report there is a turnover epidemic among recent college graduates. According to observers: "Turnover among managers out of college less than five years has quintupled since 1960. Today the average corporation can count on losing 50 percent of its college graduates within five years."[28] Organizations can counter this costly trend by skillfully managing the socialization process. Third, more effective socialization programs can enhance an organization's continuity and chances of survival in an increasingly competitive world.

A Three-Phase Model of Organizational Socialization

One's first year in a complex organization can be confusing. There is a constant swirl of new faces, strange jargon, conflicting expectations, and appar-

---

[27] John Van Maanen, "People Processing: Strategies of Organizational Socialization," *Organizational Dynamics,* Summer 1978, p. 19. An instructive discussion of the roles of attributions and social learning in organizational socialization may be found in Gareth R. Jones, "Psychological Orientation and the Process of Organizational Socialization: An Interactionist Perspective," *Academy of Management Review,* July 1983, pp. 464–74.

[28] Roy Rowan, "Rekindling Corporate Loyalty," *Fortune,* February 9, 1981, p. 54.

■ **FIGURE 9–4**   Newcomers Receive Information from a Variety of Sources during the Socialization Process

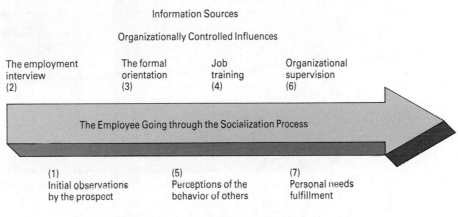

Information Sources

Organizationally Controlled Influences

| The employment interview (2) | The formal orientation (3) | Job training (4) | Organizational supervision (6) |

The Employee Going through the Socialization Process

| (1) Initial observations by the prospect | (5) Perceptions of the behavior of others | (7) Personal needs fulfillment |

Factors Influenced but not Controlled by the Organization

ently unrelated events. Some organizations treat new members in a rather haphazard, sink-or-swim manner. More typically, though, the socialization process is characterized by a sequence of identifiable steps.[29]

Organizational behavior researcher Daniel Feldman has proposed a three-phase model of organizational socialization that promotes deeper understanding of this important process. As illustrated in Figure 9–5, the three phases are: (1) anticipatory socialization, (2) encounter, and (3) change and acquisition. Each phase has its associated perceptual and social processes. Feldman's model also specifies behavioral and affective outcomes that can be used to judge how well the individual has been socialized. The entire three-phase sequence may take from a few weeks to a year to complete, depending on individual differences and the complexity of the situation.

Phase 1: Anticipatory Socialization.   Organizational socialization begins *before* the individual actually joins the organization. Anticipatory socialization information comes from many sources. U.S. Marine recruiting ads, for example, prepare future recruits for a rough-and-tumble experience. Widely circulated stories about IBM being the "white shirt" company probably deter those who would prefer working in jeans from applying. And a manager at Steelcase, a Michigan-based maker of office systems, told the editor of *Management*

---

[29] For an instructive capsule summary of five different organizational socialization models, see John P. Wanous, Arnon E. Reichers, and S. D. Malik, "Organizational Socialization and Group Development: Toward an Integrative Perspective," *Academy of Management Review*, October 1984, pp. 670–83, table 1. Also see Daniel C. Feldman, *Managing Careers in Organizations* (Glenview, Ill.: Scott, Foresman, 1988), chap. 5.

Outsider

Phases

Perceptual and
Social Processes

1. *Anticipatory Socialization*

"Learning that occurs prior
to joining the organization."

Anticipating realities about
the organization and the new job.

Anticipating organization's
needs for one's skills and
abilities.

Anticipating organization's
sensitivity to one's needs
and values.

2. *Encounter*

"Values, skills, and attitudes
start to shift as new recruit
discovers what the organization
is truly like."

Managing lifestyle-versus-
work conflicts.

Managing intergroup
role conflicts.

Seeking role definition
and clarity.

Becoming familiar with task
and group dynamics.

3. *Change and acquisition*

"Recruit masters skills and
roles and adjusts to work
group's values and norms."

Competing role demands are
resolved.

Critical tasks are mastered.

Group norms and values are
internalized.

Behavioral Outcomes

Socialized
Insider

Affective Outcomes

Performs role assignments

Remains with organization

Spontaneously innovates and
cooperates

Generally satisfied

Internally motivated to
work

High job involvement

SOURCE: Adapted from material in Daniel C. Feldman, "The Multiple Socialization of Organization Members," *Academy of Management Review*, April 1981, pp. 309–18.

Review: "We have many second- and third-generation employees, who are loyal workers before they even join the company."[30]

All of this information—whether formal or informal, accurate or inaccurate—helps the individual anticipate organizational realities. Unrealistic expectations about the nature of the work, pay, and promotions are often formulated during phase 1. Fortunately, management can curb unrealistic expectations by relying on the psychological contracting and realistic job preview techniques discussed later in this chapter.

Phase 2: Encounter.   This second phase begins when the employment contract has been signed. It is a time for surprise and making sense as the newcomer enters unfamiliar territory.[31] Behavioral scientists warn that **reality shock** can occur during the encounter phase.

> Becoming a member of an organization will upset the everyday order of even the most well-informed newcomer. Matters concerning such aspects as friendships, time, purpose, demeanor, competence, and the expectations the person holds of the immediate and distant future are suddenly made problematic. The newcomer's most pressing task is to build a set of guidelines and interpretations to explain and make meaningful the myriad of activities observed as going on in the organization.[32]

During the encounter phase, the individual is challenged to resolve any conflicts between the job and outside interests. If the hours prove too long, for example, family duties may require the individual to quit and find a more suitable work schedule. Also, as indicated in Figure 9–5, role conflict stemming from competing demands of different groups needs to be confronted and resolved.

Phase 3: Change and Acquisition.   Mastery of important tasks and resolution of role conflict signals the beginning of this final phase of the socialization process. Those who do not make the transition to phase 3 leave voluntarily or involuntarily or become network isolates.

Organizational Socialization Research

Credible research results in this area have begun to appear only recently in the OB literature. One study, relying on self-report data from 102 MBA students (73 men and 29 women), examined the effects of various socialization tactics. The researcher concluded: "The more institutionalized the form of socialization was, the greater were expressed job satisfaction and commitment, and the

---

[30] Anthony J. Rutigliano, "Steelcase: Nice Guys Finish First," *Management Review,* November 1985, p. 46.

[31] See Meryl Reis Louis, "Surprise and Sense Making: What Newcomers Experience in Entering Unfamiliar Organizational Settings," *Administrative Science Quarterly,* June 1980, pp. 226–51.

[32] Van Maanen, "People Processing: Strategies of Organizational Socialization," p. 21.

■ **TABLE 9–5** Helpfulness of Various Organizational Socialization Activities for Male and Female College Graduates

Socialization Activity	Helpfulness Ranking	
	Males	Females
Daily interactions with peers while working	1	1
Buddy relationship with a more senior co-worker	2	2
Your first supervisor	3	3
Formal on-site orientation sessions	4	9
Other new recruits (employees)	5	5
Mentor and/or sponsor relationship	6	4
Business trips with others from work	7	10
Off-site residential training programs	8	7
Secretary or other support staff	9	8
Social/recreational activities with people from work	10	6

SOURCE: Data from Barry Z. Posner and Gary N. Powell, "Female and Male Socialization Experiences: An Initial Investigation," *Journal of Occupational Psychology*, March 1985, pp. 81–85.

lower was intention to quit."[33] Socialization is considered to be institutionalized when newcomers receive formally structured orientation, guidance, and training. This study suggests managers should avoid a haphazard, sink-or-swim approach to organizational socialization. Socialization needs to be managed systematically so newcomers get a clear idea of what is expected of them.

Another study probed male-versus-female differences in socialization experiences for recent graduates of two U.S. business schools. A sample of 134 males and 83 females, on the job for only 8 to 10 months, reported the availability and helpfulness of 10 socialization activities (see Table 9–5). Statistical analysis led the researchers to the following conclusion:

> Overall the *availability,* or access, to different socialization opportunities did not seem to differ much between the sexes, but the perceived *helpfulness* of the activities available varied. In general, the men perceived their socialization experiences as more helpful than did the women.[34]

Moreover, as evident in Table 9–5, the male and female subsamples in this study disagreed about the *relative* helpfulness of the various socialization activities. While the males ranked "formal on-site orientation sessions" fourth, their female counterparts found this activity to be of little use, ranking it ninth. On the other hand, the females found "social/recreational activities with people from work" to be relatively more helpful. There also were gender-based differences regarding the perceived helpfulness of mentors/sponsors and business trips. The former being more helpful for females; the latter more

---

[33] Gareth R. Jones, "Socialization Tactics, Self-Efficacy, and Newcomers' Adjustments to Organizations," *Academy of Management Journal*, June 1986, p. 272.

[34] Barry Z. Posner and Gary N. Powell, "Female and Male Socialization Experiences: An Initial Investigation," *Journal of Occupational Psychology*, March 1985, p. 84.

helpful for males. This study suggests that while some women now may have equal access to organizational socialization activities, they still find themselves deriving fewer benefits than their male counterparts.

Finally, support for stage models is mixed. Although different stages of socialization do occur, they are not identical in order, length, or content for all people or jobs.[35] Keeping the concepts discussed so far in this chapter in mind, let us examine some practical organizational socialization techniques.

■ SOCIALIZATION TECHNIQUES

Organizational newcomers learn the ropes by receiving information from a variety of sources. Important among these sources of sense-making input are psychological contracts, realistic job previews, and behavior modeling.

Psychological Contracts

Although not readily apparent, new employees have two overlapping contracts with their employers. First, and most widely recognized, is the employment contract. This typically is a legal document specifying such things as compensation, hours, and conditions of employment. In addition, there is a *psychological* contract that encompasses and goes beyond the employment contract. According to a personnel research psychologist, ''The **psychological contract** is the sum total of all written and unwritten, spoken and unspoken, expectations of the employer and employee.''[36] Employees have implicit expectations about pay raises, promotions, and job security. Meanwhile, employers have their own expectations about the individual's loyalty, willingness to learn, and creativity.[37] Problems arise when these unwritten and unspoken expectations turn out to be unrealistic.

Unmet Expectations. Individuals begin to formulate their side of the psychological contract before they join the organization. Subsequent to the signing of an employment contract, the psychological contract evolves and shifts as employee and employer modify their expectations for each other. Problems can and do arise when either party in the psychological contract feels cheated. Anyone who has not gotten an expected promotion can attest to the dampening effect unmet expectations can have on job satisfaction and performance. Likewise, managers feel cheated when their expectations for an employee's

---

[35] A summary of socialization research is provided by Cynthia D. Fisher, "Organizational Socialization: An Integrative Review," in *Research in Personnel and Human Resources Management,* ed. Kendrith M. Rowland and Gerald R. Ferris (Greenwich, Conn.: JAI Press, 1986), pp. 101–45.

[36] Herbert George Baker, "The Unwritten Contract: Job Perceptions," *Personnel Journal,* July 1985, p. 37. (Emphasis added.)

[37] An expanded list of employer-employee expectations may be found in John Paul Kotter, "The Psychological Contract: Managing the Joining-Up Process," *California Management Review,* Spring 1973, pp. 91–99.

■ **TABLE 9–6** How the U.S. Navy Is Doing a Better Job of Handling Psychological Contracts

The Navy's enlistment program has been improved in the following ways:

1. A general increase in the amount of information delivered by the recruiter or classifier regarding Navy lifestyle, recruit training, and so on.

2. More comprehensive, factual and detailed presentation of Navy career opportunities, rating and assignment possibility in a consistent and unbiased fashion.

3. More extensive exploration of applicant job values, educational aspirations, desired working conditions, aptitudes, interests, motivations, and career goals before enlistment.

4. Improvement of the fit between Navy requirements and policies and individual aptitudes and interests.

SOURCE: Excerpted from Herbert George Baker, "The Unwritten Contract: Job Perceptions," *Personnel Journal,* July 1985, p. 40.

performance go unmet. Conflict between students and teachers over course requirements and grades generally can be traced to psychological contracts and mistaken assumptions about mutual expectations.

Surfacing the Psychological Contract. Employers and employees alike are urged to openly discuss the terms of their psychological contracts. The idea is to improve individual-organization fit by bringing unrealistic expectations into line with reality. This psychological contracting can be done before, during, and/or after actual hiring. Personnel specialists claim free discussion of mutual expectations will enhance satisfaction and performance while reducing turnover. As a practical example, the U.S. Navy is attempting to improve enlistment rates, job performance, morale, and reenlistment rates by having its recruiters discuss psychological contracts more openly and skillfully (see Table 9–6).

Although specific hard evidence on psychological contracts is lacking, the void is filled partially by research insights about a related technique, called realistic job previews.

Realistic Job Previews

During the recruiting process, newcomers typically are told about the good things they can expect from the organization. For example, they may hear about the paid holidays, the recreational facilities, and the new family dental insurance plan. Unfortunately, these good-news-only job previews tell the individual very little about what he or she will be doing each day. Too often the result is the same. The person's unrealistically high expectations come crashing down after a few weeks on the job and he or she quits. Take the case of Lynda McDermott, for example.

> To Lynda McDermott, the job offer sounded ideal. So she left her position at an accounting firm and became executive vice president of a fledgling management consulting company in New York, a job that her new boss said would allow her to play a major role in landing new business. . . .

Eleven months later she quit. Her boss, she says, had immediately relegated her to administrative duties, a far cry from the role she had expected. . . .

As Ms. McDermott sees it, she was a victim of a job bait-and-switch. Promised the world as an applicant, the new employee eventually realizes that the job is something quite different, leading to disgruntlement, stalled careers and costly turnover.[38]

Turnover can be expensive. One study determined it cost a bank $2,800 to replace each teller who quit after a 23-week training period. During one year, it cost the bank $1,680,000 to replace 600 of its 1,400 tellers. Higher turnover costs can be expected for higher-level, higher-paying jobs. For example, 1982 replacement costs for a sales manager and an officer from the U.S. Naval Academy were estimated at $399,600 and $86,000, respectively.[39]

One recommended solution is the **realistic job preview** (RJP) that involves giving recruits a realistic idea of what lies ahead by presenting both positive and negative aspects of the job. RJPs may be verbal, in booklet form, audiovisual, or hands-on as in the case of Nissan Motor Manufacturing Corp. (see Table 9–7). RJPs are a structured approach to psychological contracting because two-way discussion is replaced by a one-way presentation of facts. Importantly, RJPs are given *before* the individual signs an employment contract, whereas psychological contracting can occur at any time.

The Psychology of RJPs.   John Wanous and other proponents of RJPs hypothesized two major outcomes (see Figure 9–6). First, a frank presentation of the job's positive and negative aspects may convince recruits with unrealistic expectations to seek employment elsewhere. Thus, the possibility of avoiding some early turnover. Second, recruits whose unrealistically high expectations are lowered by an RJP may decide to join the organization. According to RJP theory, this second situation should lead to improved satisfaction and performance and decreased turnover. As shown in Figure 9–6, the key psychological component of RJPs is the lowering of unrealistically high expectations. RJP scholars refer to this process as the "vaccination of expectations." By reviewing recent research, we can determine how well the RJP technique delivers on its promises.

Recent RJP Research.   Because of differing samples, a variety of RJP media, and inconsistent statistical methods, RJP research yields mixed and often contradictory results. Two reviews of RJP research, including a meta-analysis, provide the following insights:

- RJPs tended to reduce turnover by an average of 6 percent.
- The effectiveness of RJPs tended to increase as the complexity of the job increased.

---

[38] Larry Reibstein, "Crushed Hopes: When a New Job Proves to Be Something Different," *The Wall Street Journal*, June 10, 1987, p. 21.

[39] Cost data for bank tellers from Roger A. Dean and John P. Wanous, "Effects of Realistic Job Previews on Hiring Bank Tellers," *Journal of Applied Psychology*, February 1984, pp. 61–68. Managerial cost data is presented in Wayne F. Cascio, *Costing Human Resources: The Financial Impact of Behavior in Organizations* (Boston: Kent Publishing Company, 1982).

■ **TABLE 9–7**   Hands-On RJPs at Nissan Motor

Smyrna, Tenn.—Bookkeeper Phyllis Baines has two minutes to grab 55 nuts, bolts and washers, assemble them in groups of five and attach them in order of size to a metal rack. But she fumbles nervously with several pieces and finishes the task seconds after her allotted time.

"I've got to get a little better at this, don't I?" she frets as she pulls the last of the fasteners out of a grimy plastic tray. Her tester, Harold Hicks, encourages her: "You're close. For the first night, you're probably doing a little better than normal."

It may appear that Mrs. Baines—not her real name—is going through first-night jitters at an adult-school class in home repair. But the 31-year-old department store employee will be devoting 70 hours worth of her nights and weekends over the next few months doing similar exercises, in an effort to land a job at the Nissan Motor Manufacturing Corp. plant here.

Mrs. Baines and about 270 other job seekers are participating in Nissan's "pre-employment" program. In exchange for a shot at highly paid assembly-line and other hourly jobs, and Nissan's promise not to inform their employers, the moonlighters are working up to 360 hours—without pay—being tested and instructed in employment fundamentals by the Japanese auto maker. . . .

"We hope the process makes it plain to people what the job is," says Thomas P. Groom, Nissan's manager of employment. "It's an indoctrination process" as well as a screening tool. . . .

Not all participants are fully satisfied with the program. A candidate who works as a machine adjuster at an envelope factory says that the lack of a job guarantee by Nissan "worries you, because you get your hopes up." And some candidates bemoan the lack of pay for their time.

But many participants feel that the training and experience they receive outweigh any additional obstacles to getting hired. For one thing they get a shot at some of the best paid jobs in the state, and if they don't get hired, they can take the skills they have learned elsewhere. Adds Judy McFarland, a press operator who went through the program in 1983: "It gave me a chance to see what Nissan expected of me without their having to make a commitment to me or to them."

SOURCE: Excerpted from Dale D. Buss, "Job Tryouts without Pay Get More Testing in U.S. Auto Plants." Reprinted by permission of *The Wall Street Journal,* © Dow Jones & Company, Inc., January 10, 1985, p. 31. All rights reserved.

- RJPs were about half as effective as job enrichment programs at reducing turnover.[40] (Recall the discussion of job enrichment in Chapter 5.)

A more recent meta-analysis of 21 RJP experiments that included 9,166 subjects, led to the following conclusions:

- Audiovisual RJPs tended to have a positive impact on job performance, whereas written RJPs (in booklet form) had a slight negative impact.

---

[40] See Richard R. Reilly, Barbara Brown, Milton R. Blood, and Carol Z. Malatesta, "The Effects of Realistic Previews: A Study and Discussion of the Literature," *Personnel Psychology,* Winter 1981, pp. 823–34; and Glenn M. McEvoy and Wayne F. Cascio, "Strategies for Reducing Employee Turnover: A Meta-Analysis," *Journal of Applied Psychology,* May 1985, pp. 324–53.

■ **FIGURE 9-6** The Desired Psychological Outcomes of Realistic Job Previews

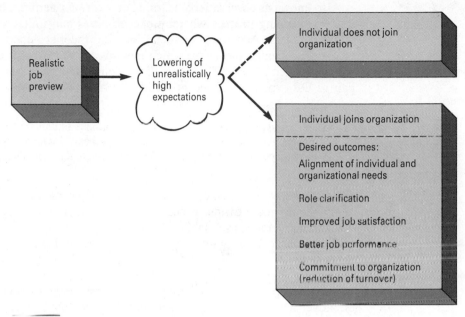

SOURCE: Adapted from John P. Wanous, "Realistic Job Previews: Can a Procedure to Reduce Turnover Also Influence the Relationship between Abilities and Performance?" *Personnel Psychology*, Summer 1978, p. 251.

- RJPs tended to lower initial expectations about the job.
- RJPs tended to increase the dropout rate among job candidates.
- Those who experienced an RJP tended to report greater initial commitment to the organization.
- RJP recipients tended to have slightly higher job satisfaction.
- RJP recipients tended to stay on the job longer (thus indicating a lower rate of early turnover).[41]

Managers and RJPs. Realistic job previews may not have as dramatic an impact on organizational outcomes as proponents have suggested, but they do seem to produce favorable results. Their most significant contribution is the vaccination of expectations. RJPs consistently bring unrealistic expectations into line with reality. Given the available evidence, the time and expense of producing audiovisual RJPs seems to be justified only for complex, higher-paying jobs. Booklet RJPs are recommended for routine jobs that pay comparatively less. Relative to reducing turnover, it appears advisable to use RJPs in combination with job enrichment programs that strive to make the work itself more internally motivating.

[41] See Steven L. Premack and John P. Wanous, "A Meta-Analysis of Realistic Job Preview Experiments," *Journal of Applied Psychology*, November 1985, pp. 706–19. An instructive critique of RJP research can be found in James A. Breaugh, "Realistic Job Previews: A Critical Appraisal and Future Research Directions," *Academy of Management Review*, October 1983, pp. 612–19. Other supportive evidence may be found in Benjamin L. Dilla, "Descriptive versus Prescriptive Information in a Realistic Job Preview," *Journal of Vocational Behavior*, February 1987, pp. 33–48.

Behavior Modeling

Also known as observational learning or vicarious learning, **behavior modeling** is a learning process whereby one observes and imitates the behavior of relevant others. According to social learning theorist Albert Bandura, ''One of the fundamental means by which new modes of behavior are acquired and existing patterns are modified entails modeling and vicarious processes.''[42] A pair of OB experts more recently added:

> The fundamental characteristic of modeling is that learning takes place, *not* through actual experience, but through observation or imitation of another individual's experience. Modeling is a ''vicarious process,'' which implies sharing in the experience of another person through imagination or sympathetic participation.[43]

Sports fans who wildly celebrate when their favorite team wins the championship are engaging in a vicarious process. Organizational newcomers, who are especially hungry for sense-making information regarding what to do, whom to trust, and so forth, acquire a great deal of adaptive behavior through behavior modeling.

From an organizational perspective, people learn both productive and counterproductive behavior by watching and imitating others. For example, a new employee in a furniture factory might observe that old-timers can turn out work faster by removing the safety guards from their power saws. Of course, the supervisor should discourage this behavior because it could lead to a painful and costly accident.

Let us examine two ways in which behavior models can influence the behavior of organizational newcomers.

Learning through Imitation. For better or for worse, people tend to act like those with whom they closely identify. For instance, many parents have cringed at the sight of their children firing imaginary guns at each other after watching a violent movie or television program. Similarly, it is no mere coincidence that middle-level managers tend to dress, act, talk, and think like their executive-level bosses. In fact, a researcher who studied 141 pairs of middle managers and first-level supervisors found that the supervisors who perceived their bosses to be successful and competent tended to imitate their bosses' leadership style.[44]

---

[42] Albert Bandura, *Principles of Behavior Modification* (New York: Holt, Rinehart & Winston, 1969), p. 118. For an instructive update on alternative observational learning theories, see Gina Green and J. Grayson Osborne, ''Does Vicarious Instigation Provide Support for Observational Learning Theories? A Critical Review,'' *Psychological Bulletin*, January 1985, pp. 3–17. Also see Dennis A. Gioia and Charles C. Manz, ''Linking Cognition and Behavior: A Script Processing Interpretation of Vicarious Learning,'' *Academy of Management Review*, July 1985, pp. 527–39.

[43] Henry P. Sims and Charles C. Manz, ''Modeling Influences on Employee Behavior,'' *Personnel Journal*, January 1982, p. 58.

[44] See Howard M. Weiss, ''Subordinate Imitation of Supervisor Behavior: The Role of Modeling in Organizational Socialization,'' *Organizational Behavior and Human Performance*, June 1977, pp. 89–105.

■ **TABLE 9–8**   Behavior Modeling Plays a Role in General Electric's Bonus System

> GE is . . . banking on the maxim that money talks. The company has always paid its managers well, and business heads now sprinkle bonuses around, rewarding those whose work exemplifies the new GE. At appliances last year [1986], a quarter of 4,200 management-level employees pocketed awards averaging $1,400. There are no elaborate ceremonies; often, checks are handed out right on the shop floor. "We like to recognize people in front of their peers. It lets them puff up their chests a little bit," says Michael P. Sullivan, a service manager at medical systems who got a check for $2,000.
>
> SOURCE: Excerpted from Russell Mitchell, "Jack Welch: How Good a Manager?" *Business Week,* December 14, 1987, p. 103.

Learning from Others' Consequences.   We not only observe and imitate relevant others' behavior, we also tend to be influenced by the consequences of their behavior. Research and practical experience reveal that behavior that is rewarded tends to be imitated, while behavior that is punished tends not to be imitated. Television advertisers exploit this tendency to the fullest by showing movie stars and sports heroes having a great time while using certain products. The power of vicarious rewards has significant implications for socialization and managerial leadership:

> Leaders should recognize that rewards given to one employee as a consequence for achievement-oriented behavior can have an impact on other employees because a model is established. Performance-contingent rewards such as compliments, favored job assignments, and material rewards can act as an incentive to employees who observe the reward, in addition to those who receive the reward. Modeling is indeed a means of diffusing knowledge about reward contingencies among employees.[45]

A prime example is General Electric's bonus system (see Table 9–8).

But what about the impact of watching someone else get punished? In a recent study of 60 college students, it was found that those who "observed a co-worker receiving a cut in pay for low productivity produced significantly more than either the control group or the groups that observed a co-worker receiving a threat of a pay cut."[46] Moreover, this effect endured beyond the first week and there was no negative impact on job satisfaction. So it seems vicarious punishment does work.

With these two dimensions of behavior modeling in mind, we are in a better position to understand the underlying process itself.

Bandura's Observational Learning Model.   According to Bandura, successful behavior modeling depends on the four subprocesses illustrated in Figure 9–7.

---

[45] Henry P. Sims and Charles C. Manz, "Social Learning Theory: The Role of Modeling in the Exercise of Leadership," *Journal of Organizational Behavior Management,* 1981–1982, p. 61.

[46] Details of this study may be found in Mel E. Schnake, "Vicarious Punishment in a Work Setting," *Journal of Applied Psychology,* May 1986, pp. 343–45.

■ FIGURE 9–7 Bandura's Observational Learning Model

Note the similarities between this model and the model of perception discussed in Chapter 4. Before someone else's behavior can be imitated, it must be attended to and retained. Then it must be attempted (or reproduced) and achieve adequate motivational support if it is to endure. As with operant conditioning, this naturally occurring process can be passively left to chance or actively managed. Relative to organizational socialization, training programs make extensive use of behavior models today via films and videotaped role playing.

Modeling: Practical Research Insights.   The primary research thrust in this area has centered on the use of behavior models in industrial training programs. A supervisory training program developed during the 1970s by Melvin Sorcher, an industrial psychologist at General Electric, is the most widely used approach. Called ''Applied Learning,'' Sorcher's training program is based on the following four steps:

1. *Modeling,* in which small groups of supervisor-trainees watch filmed supervisor and employee models interact in effective ways in a problem situation.

2. *Role-playing,* in which the trainees take part in extensive practice and rehearsal of the specific behaviors demonstrated by the models. As their role-play behaviors become more and more similar to the models,

3. *Social reinforcement* (praise, reward, constructive feedback) is provided by both the trainers and other trainees. These three procedures are implemented in such a way that

4. *Transfer of training* from classroom to job setting is encouraged.[47]

On-the-job research demonstrates the practical value of Sorcher's modeling program. In one carefully controlled experiment, 20 supervisors were encouraged to imitate filmed behavior models successfully handling common interpersonal problems. Among those problems were giving orientations and recognition, improving poor work habits, and overcoming resistance to change. One year after the training, the trainees' job performance was rated as significantly better than that for a matched control group of 20 supervisors. Additional

---

[47] Arnold P. Goldstein and Melvin Sorcher, *Changing Supervisor Behavior* (New York: Pergamon Press, 1974), p. ix.

■ **TABLE 9–9** Using Behavior Models Effectively in Employee Training Programs

Observational Learning Subprocess	Practical Tips

Attention	1. Behavior models tend to attract more attention when:
	  a. They have high status and/or credibility in the trainees' eyes.
	  b. The complexity of the modeled behavior is appropriate to the trainees' capabilities.
	  c. The modeled behavior is repeated two or more times.
	  d. The modeled behavior is presented in an appealing, detailed, and vivid manner.

Retention	2. Modeled behavior tends to be retained when trainees rehearse and practice it both mentally and behaviorally.
Reproduction/motivation	3. Modeled behavior tends to be imitated when trainees are appropriately reinforced or rewarded for doing so.

SOURCE: Adapted from Henry P. Sims, Jr., and Charles C. Manz, "Modeling Influences on Employee Behavior," *Personnel Journal,* January 1982, p. 62.

supportive evidence was then obtained when the control group's performance improved after it went through the same modeling-based training program.[48]

Thanks to this sort of practical research, experts on the subject have offered some instructive modeling tips for managers (see Table 9–9). One important lesson from these tips is that a "Do as I say, not as I do" philosophy of management is inappropriate today. Given what we now know about the role of behavior modeling in organizational socialization, managers need to be positive role models committed to a "Do as I do" approach.

SUMMARY OF KEY CONCEPTS

A. Because social facilitation research demonstrates that the mere presence of others has relatively little impact on behavior, attention needs to be directed to the "how" and "what" of social interaction.

B. Social network analysis examines organizations in terms of formal (prescribed) and informal (emergent) clusters of individuals that link to transmit goods and services, information, influence, and feelings. Various individuals perform the following social network functions: star, liaison, bridge, gatekeeper, and isolate.

---

[48] See Gary P. Latham and Lise M. Saari, "Application of Social-Learning Theory to Training Supervisors through Behavioral Modeling," *Journal of Applied Psychology,* June 1979, pp. 239–46. Additional insightful research may be found in Steven J. Mayer and James S. Russell, "Behavior Modeling Training in Organizations: Concerns and Conclusions," *Journal of Management,* Spring 1987, pp. 21–40.

C. Organizational *roles* are sets of behaviors persons expect of occupants of a position. One may experience role overload (too much to do in too little time), role conflict (conflicting role expectations), or role ambiguity (unclear role expectations).

D. While roles are specific to the person's position, norms are shared attitudes that differentiate appropriate from inappropriate behavior in a variety of situations. Norms evolve informally and are enforced because they help the group or organization survive, clarify behavioral expectations, help people avoid embarrassing situations, and clarify the group's or organization's central values.

E. Organizational outsiders are shaped into fully functioning insiders through organizational socialization. The three phases of Feldman's organizational socialization model are anticipatory socialization, encounter, and change and acquisition. Researchers have found higher job satisfaction and commitment and lower intention to quit in organizations with formalized socialization processes (e.g., orientation and training).

F. Psychological contracts encompass the mutual expectations employees and employers have for each other. The contracts may be written or unwritten, spoken or unspoken. Both parties are urged to openly discuss their perceptions of the psychological contract.

G. Proponents of realistic job previews (RJPs) recommend that managers give recruits an honest appraisal about the positive and negative aspects of the job (vaccination of expectations) so as to curb unrealistic expectations and reduce costly turnover. RJP research documented a small reduction in turnover.

H. Behavior modeling is a learning process involving imitating others' behavior. The four subprocesses in Bandura's observational learning model are attention, retention, reproduction, and motivation. Researchers documented the effectiveness of employee training programs that involve the imitation of behavior models. Like it or not, managers are influential behavior models who cannot succeed with a "Do as I say, not as I do" philosophy of management.

KEY TERMS ————————————————————————————

social facilitation	norm
social network analysis	ostracism
clique	organizational socialization
roles	reality shock
role overload	psychological contract
role conflict	realistic job preview
role ambiguity	behavior modeling

DISCUSSION QUESTIONS

1.   Does the mere presence of others help or hinder your performance? Explain your answer.
2.   In social networks, why do gatekeepers play an important role?
3.   Considering your present lifestyle, how many different roles are you playing? What sorts of role conflict and role ambiguity are you experiencing?
4.   What norms do college students usually enforce in class?
5.   Why is socialization essential to organizational success?
6.   What sort of anticipatory socialization did you undergo at your present school or job?
7.   What are the terms of the various psychological contracts you have with people in positions of authority (e.g., bosses, teachers, and so on)?
8.   How would you respond to a manager who asked you if realistic job previews are worthwhile?
9.   Can you think of any behaviors you have acquired recently through behavior modeling? Explain.
10.   Why do you suppose Sorcher's applied learning has proved to be such an effective supervisory training tool?

BACK TO THE OPENING CASE

Now that you have read Chapter 9, you should be able to answer the following questions about the IBM case:

1.   Relative to the enforcement of norms at IBM, what are the company's central values?
2.   Does IBM have a highly institutionalized socialization process? Support your conclusion with specific evidence.
3.   What would you tell a recruit if you had to give him or her a realistic job preview for a position at IBM?

EXERCISE 9

Objectives

1. To promote deeper understanding of organizational socialization processes.
2. To provide you with a useful tool for analyzing and comparing organizations.

Introduction

Employees are socialized in many different ways in today's organizations. Some organizations, such as IBM, have made an exact science out of organizational socialization. Others leave things to chance in hopes that collective goals will somehow be achieved. The questionnaire[49] in this exercise is designed to help you gauge how widespread and systematic the socialization process is in a particular organization.

Instructions

If you are presently employed and have a good working knowledge of your organization, you can complete this questionnaire yourself. If not, identify a manager or professional (e.g., corporate lawyer, engineer, nurse) and have that individual complete the questionnaire for his or her organization.

Respond to the items below as they apply to the handling of professional employees (including managers). Upon completion, compute the total score by adding up your responses. For comparison, scores for a number of strong, intermediate, and weak culture firms are provided.

Instrument

	Not true of this company				Very true of this company
1. Recruiters receive at least one week of intensive training.	1	2	3	4	5
2. Recruitment forms identify several key traits deemed crucial to the firm's success, traits are defined in concrete terms and interviewer records specific evidence of each trait.	1	2	3	4	5
3. Recruits are subjected to at least four in-depth interviews.	1	2	3	4	5
4. Company actively facilitates de-selection during the recruiting process by revealing minuses as well as pluses.	1	2	3	4	5
5. New hires work long hours, are exposed to intensive training of considerable difficulty, and/or perform relatively menial tasks in the first months.	1	2	3	4	5
6. The intensity of entry-level experience builds cohesiveness among peers in each entering class.	1	2	3	4	5
7. All professional employees in a particular discipline begin in entry-level positions regardless of experience or advanced degrees.	1	2	3	4	5
8. Reward systems and promotion criteria require mastery of a core discipline as a precondition of advancement.	1	2	3	4	5
9. The career path for professional employees is relatively consistent over the first 6 to 10 years with the company.	1	2	3	4	5

---

[49] This exercise has been adapted from Richard Pascale, ''The Paradox of 'Corporate Culture:' Reconciling Ourselves to Socialization,'' pp. 26–41. © 1985 by the Regents of the University of California. Reprinted/Condensed from the *California Management Review*, Vol. XXVII, No. 2. By permission of The Regents.

Instrument (concluded)

		Not true of this company				Very true of this company
10.	Reward systems, performance incentives, promotion criteria and other primary measures of success reflect a high degree of congruence.	1	2	3	4	5
11.	Virtually all professional employees can identify and articulate the firm's shared values (i.e., the purpose or mission that ties the firm to society, the customer, or its employees).	1	2	3	4	5
12.	There are very few instances when actions of management appear to violate the firm's espoused values.	1	2	3	4	5
13.	Employees frequently make personal sacrifices for the firm out of commitment to the firm's shared values.	1	2	3	4	5
14.	When confronted with trade-offs between systems measuring short-term results and doing what's best for the company in the long term, the firm usually decides in favor of the long term.	1	2	3	4	5
15.	This organization fosters mentor-protégé relationships.	1	2	3	4	5
16.	There is considerable similarity among high potential candidates in each particular discipline.	1	2	3	4	5

Total score = _____

For comparative purposes:

Strongly socialized firms

Weakly socialized firms

Scores:

65–80	IBM, P&G, Morgan Guaranty
55–64	ATT, Morgan Stanley, Delta Airlines
45–54	United Airlines, Coca Cola
35–44	General Foods, PepsiCo
25–34	United Technologies, ITT
Below 25	Atari

Questions for Consideration/Class Discussion

1. How strongly socialized is the organization in question? What implications does this degree of socialization have for satisfaction, commitment, and turnover?
2. In examining the 16 items in the above questionnaire, what evidence of realistic job previews and behavior modeling can you find? Explain.
3. What does this questionnaire say about how organizational norms are established and enforced? Frame your answer in terms of specific items in the questionnaire.
4. Using this questionnaire as a gauge, would you rather work for a strongly, moderately, or weakly socialized organization?

Appendix

Career Management

Some people are spectators who prefer to passively watch life go by, while others are active participants. The same is true of career management. Individuals can leave their fates in the hands of others or can influence their careers by taking charge. Skillful career management is important because people are happier and more satisfied when their personal and work lives are compatible. Moreover, failing to manage one's career may lead to professional plateauing, poor work attitudes, stress, and ultimately a lower quality of life.[1] This appendix is based on the premise that you can enhance your personal and professional success by proactively managing your career. It also helps present and future managers to address employees' career needs and aspirations. We first present a model of career management. This is followed by a discussion of career stages and tips for successfully making the transition from student to professional.

---

[1] See Suzanne K. Stout, John W. Slocum, Jr., and William L. Cron, "Dynamics of the Career Plateauing Process," *Journal of Vocational Behavior,* February 1988, pp. 74–91; Daniel C. Feldman and Barton A. Weitz, "Career Plateaus Reconsidered," *Journal of Management,* March 1988, pp. 69–80; and Janina C. Latack, "Career Transitions within Organizations: An Exploratory Study of Work, Nonwork, and Coping Strategies," *Organizational Behavior and Human Performance,* December 1984, pp. 296–322.

■ CAREER MANAGEMENT MODEL

People today change careers on the average of four to six times during their working lifetime.[2] A *career* is "the pattern of work-related experiences that span the course of a person's life."[3] Work-related experiences include "objective events or situations such as a series of job positions, job duties or activities, and work-related decisions, and subjective interpretations of work-related events (past, present, or future) such as work aspirations, expectations, values, needs, and feelings about particular work experiences."[4] In turn, **career** *management* is a problem-solving/decision-making process aimed at optimizing the match between an individual's needs and values and his or her work-related experiences. Figure 9A–1 presents a model of career management.

Career management is an ongoing process of gathering information, being aware of self and environment, setting career goals and action plans, obtaining feedback, and assessing career progress and satisfaction (see Figure 9A–1). Although this process may appear to be unrealistically rational, research indicates students can be taught to follow its guidelines. For example, researchers in a recent study successfully trained highly impulsive, dependent, or fatalistic college students to use a more rational approach to career decision making.[5] There are two key phases within the eight-step process in Figure 9A–1: Career planning and career appraisal.

Career Planning

This phase consists of steps A through D in Figure 9A–1. *Career exploration* entails gathering career-related information about oneself and the environment. Self-exploration focuses on identifying one's values, needs, aspirations, abilities, and skills. Environmental exploration, on the other hand, is occupationally focused. That is, individuals seek information about specific job requirements, job duties, and job opportunities. Although awareness of self and environment (step B) is the primary benefit of career exploration, extensive career exploration was found to generate more job interviews, job offers, and higher organizational commitment.[6]

Awareness is the extent to which one has an accurate perception of her or his personal qualities and environmental characteristics. High awareness enables individuals to set realistic career goals (step C) and career strategies (step

---

[2] See Jack Falvey, "Career Navigation: Learn to Plot Your Own Destiny Rather Than Let It Drift," *Training and Development Journal,* February 1988, pp. 32–36.

[3] Jeffrey H. Greenhaus, *Career Management* (Hinsdale, Ill.: The Dryden Press, 1987), p. 6.

[4] Ibid., pp. 6–7.

[5] Details are provided in John D. Krumboltz, Richard T. Kinnier, Stephanie S. Rude, Dale S. Scherba, and Daniel A. Hamel, "Teaching a Rational Approach to Career Decision Making: Who Benefits Most?" *Journal of Vocational Behavior,* August 1986, pp. 1–6.

[6] See Brian D. Steffy and Jack W. Jones, "The Impact of Family and Career Planning Variables on the Organizational, Career, and Community Commitment of Professional Women," *Journal of Vocational Behavior,* April 1988, pp. 196–212; and Stephen A. Stumpf, Elizabeth J. Austin, and Karen Hartman, "The Impact of Career Exploration and Interview Readiness on Interview Performance and Outcomes," *Journal of Vocational Behavior,* April 1984, pp. 221–35.

■ **FIGURE 9A–1** A Model of Career Management

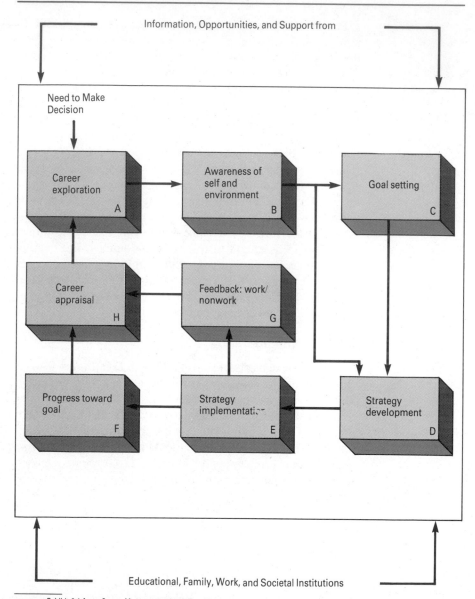

Information, Opportunities, and Support from

Need to Make Decision

Career exploration — A

Awareness of self and environment — B

Goal setting — C

Career appraisal — H

Feedback: work/ nonwork — G

Progress toward goal — F

Strategy implementation — E

Strategy development — D

Educational, Family, Work, and Societal Institutions

SOURCE: Exhibit 2.1 from *Career Management,* by Jeffrey H. Greenhaus, copyright © 1987 by the Dryden Press, a division of Holt, Rinehart and Winston, Inc., reprinted by permission of the publisher.

D). This is what happened to Barrie Christman as she advanced from a management trainee in 1974 to chief executive of Mellon Bank in Maryland ($220 million in assets).

Christman got where she is by demonstrating unusual drive and initiative. After joining Mellon with a degree in math and economics, she found that her

■ **TABLE 9A–1** Common Career Strategies

Strategy	Description
Competence in current job	Trying to perform effectively in one's current job.
Extended work involvement	Devoting more time and effort to one's job.
Skill development	Enhancing one's work-related skills and abilities through training or work experience.
Opportunity development	Promoting one's interests and aspirations to others and identifying job opportunities consistent with these interests and aspirations.
Development of mentor relationships	Trying to establish a key relationship with someone who will provide needed work-related information, career guidance, and professional support.
Image building	Promoting one's self image by communicating the appearance of potential, acceptability, and success.
Organizational politics	Obtaining career outcomes by using political behaviors to influence others.

SOURCE: Adapted from Jeffrey H. Greenhaus, *Career Management* (Hinsdale, Ill.: The Dryden Press, 1987), p. 27.

peers had MBAs. Soon she was hitting the books at night at the University of Pittsburgh's Graduate School of Business, earning an MBA in three years. "I don't like operating at a disadvantage," she says.[7]

As demonstrated by Christman's experience, *career goals* are motivational because they help individuals direct their effort and attention to specific career-related outcomes such as a promotion. Moreover, career goals foster development of career strategies (recall the discussion of goal strategies in Chapter 6). *Career strategies* are action plans that provide the direction or guidance for accomplishing career goals. A study of 414 government employees indicated males and females generally used the same career strategies and managers more actively relied on career strategies than nonmanagers.[8] Table 9A–1 presents seven commonly used career strategies.

Career Appraisal

Career appraisal consists of obtaining and using career-related feedback from both work and nonwork sources (steps E through H in Figure 9A–1). Common work sources include performance appraisals, supervisors or managers, co-workers, and people working within the organizational function of personnel/human resource management. Family members, friends, and professional acquaintances are good nonwork sources of career feedback.

---

[7] Matt Rothman, "Breathing New Life into a Failed S&L," *Business Week,* November 10, 1986, p. 93.

[8] Details are found in Sam Gould and Larry E. Penley, "Career Strategies and Salary Progression: A Study of Their Relationships in a Municipal Bureaucracy," *Organizational Behavior and Human Performance,* October 1984, pp. 244–65.

Feedback is a critical component of career management because it enables one to evaluate and monitor progress toward career goals. For instance, working long hours may lead to praise from a boss and criticism from a spouse. Interpreting career feedback, however, is dependent on one's original career goals. Returning to the example, working long hours may be consistent with a career goal of promotion, but inconsistent with a personal lifestyle goal of a happy family. Thus, depending on the career goal, feedback may reinforce or require modification of the goal.

Ultimately, career appraisal becomes a valuable piece of information used during career exploration (see Figure 9A–1). It represents a feedback loop that perpetuates the process of career management. Progressive companies such as Coca-Cola have recognized this fact by formally linking the performance appraisal process with a career development system that includes annual career development reviews.[9]

■ CAREER STAGES AND ANCHORS

Careers, like life in general, involve change. Needs, career aspirations, and job skills change over time. Nevertheless, researchers demonstrated that people encountered common work experiences at similar points in their careers. These commonalities are called *career stages* and are independent of occupation or organization. In this section we examine the four stages of a professionally oriented career. This discussion helps you to manage your own professional career and provides managers with a framework for facilitating the career development of others.

Furthermore, careers are affected by one's career anchor. Edgar Schein, a well-known career researcher, defined a *career anchor* as "the self-image that a person develops around his or her career, which both guides and constrains career decisions."[10] It is important to understand different types of career anchors because they strongly influence career-related choices such as integrating work, family, and personal priorities. Career anchors are discussed along with career stages in this section.

Professional Career Stages

Professional careers evolve over four successive stages: apprentice, colleague, mentor, and sponsor. The length of each stage varies by individual and occupation, but is not necessarily related to age. Each stage involves different tasks, different primary relationships, and different psychological issues needing to

---

[9] A description of this program is provided in Lynn Slavenski, "Career Development: A Systems Approach," *Training and Development Journal*, February 1987, pp. 56–60.

[10] Edgar H. Schein, "Individuals and Careers," in *Handbook of Organizational Behavior*, ed. Jay W. Lorsch (Englewood Cliffs, N.J.: Prentice-Hall, 1987), p. 155.

■ **TABLE 9A–2**   Four Stages of Professional Careers

	Stage I	Stage II	Stage III	Stage IV
Central activity	Helping Learning Following directions	Independent contributor	Training Interfacing	Shaping the direction of the organization
Primary relationship	Apprentice	Colleague	Mentor	Sponsor
Major psychological issues	Dependence	Independence	Assuming responsibility for others	Exercising power

be resolved.[11] The following discussion of career stages focuses on these differences (see Table 9A–2).

Stage I: Apprentice.   New professionals generally lack experience and thus work under close supervision. Central activities during this stage involve helping others, learning which elements of work are important and/or of greatest priority, and following directions. Such activities tend to be routine. The primary relationship entails being subordinate to someone else and necessitates a willingness to accept supervision and direction. This type of relationship creates dependence, the key psychological issue to be resolved.

Stage II: Colleague.   Independence is the key theme underlying this stage. It is acquired by demonstrating a high level of technical competence. Once competence is established, by developing a speciality in one content area, for example, peer relationships become more important. Consequently, supervisors are less frequently relied on for guidance as one develops his or her own resources to solve organizational problems. Coping with the responsibilities associated with independence is the critical psychological issue to be resolved during stage II. To successfully cope, an individual must develop her or his own performance standards. Organizational norms, peers, and professional associations are commonly used in this pursuit.

Stage III: Mentor.   Key activities involve training, guiding, influencing, or directing others. Individuals begin to work in more than one area and strive for greater breadth of technical competence. These activities create a drastic shift in the primary relationship. Individuals now must take care of others while also assuming responsibility for their work. Self-confidence, good interpersonal skills, and learning to derive satisfaction from the success of others are necessary for successfully surviving the career transition during this third stage.

---

[11] Thorough discussions of career stage models can be found in Douglas T. Hall, *Careers in Organizations* (Pacific Palisades, Calif.: Goodyear, 1976); and Daniel C. Feldman, *Managing Careers in Organizations* (Glenview, Ill.: Scott, Foresman, 1988).

Stage IV: Sponsor.   Shaping and influencing an organization's business strategy or direction is the key activity during the final career stage. This activity requires an individual to assume the roles of manager, idea innovator, and entrepreneur. One must learn to use one's power to be an effective sponsor.

Research and Practical Implications.   A study of 550 professionals—155 scientists, 268 engineers, 52 accountants, and 75 professors—yielded the following evidence.

- High performers did not tend to skip stages.
- Although high performers were found at all four stages, people were less likely to be valued as they grew older if they did not advance beyond the early stages.
- People moved back and forth between stages. (For example, a mentor might become an apprentice by taking on a new special project outside of his or her area of competence.)
- Individuals outside of those in formal management positions advanced to stages III and IV.[12]

The four-stage model provides a useful device for managers when discussing performance and career issues with employees. Linking back to Figure 9A–1, career stages can be used as career goals. In turn, managers can use performance feedback to help employees develop career strategies aimed at moving to successive career stages.[13]

Career Anchors

A career anchor was previously defined as that part of the self-concept relating to one's career image. Through experience, a well-developed career anchor provides answers to the following questions.

1. What are my talents, skills, areas of competence? What are my strengths and what are my weaknesses?
2. What are my main motives, drives, goals in life? What am I after?
3. What are my values, the main criteria by which I judge what I am doing? Am I in the right kind of organization or job? How good do I feel about what I am doing?[14]

As suggested by these questions, career anchors reflect an individual's important career-related values and needs. Returning to the model of career management in Figure 9A–1, identifying one's career anchor is an important component

---

[12] Results are presented in Gene W. Dalton, Paul H. Thompson, and Raymond L. Price, "The Four Stages of Professional Careers: A New Look at Performance by Professionals," *Organizational Dynamics,* Summer 1977, pp. 19–42.

[13] An organizational application is provided by Paul H. Thompson, Robin Zenger Baker, and Norman Smallwood, "Improving Professional Development by Applying the Four-Stage Career Model," *Organizational Dynamics,* Autumn 1986, pp. 49–62.

[14] Edgar H. Schein, "Individuals and Careers," p. 157.

■ **TABLE 9A–3** Characteristics of Career Anchors

Career Anchor	Preferred Type of Work	Preferred Pay and Benefits	Preferred Type of Promotion System	Preferred Type of Recognition
Security/stability	Stable and predictable, more concerned about context than content of work	Steady increments based on length of service; likes insurance and retirement programs	Seniority-based	Loyalty and steady performance
Autonomy/independence	Contract or project work within areas of expertise; low supervision and clearly defined goals	Merit pay for performance; portable benefits and cafeteria style choice of benefits	Merit-based that leads to more autonomy	Portable (medals, prizes, awards, testimonials, etc.)
Technical/functional competence	Challenging work that is intrinsically interesting; low supervision and clearly defined goals; administrative or managerial work is not desirable	Skill-based defined by work experience and education; external equity is important; portable benefits and cafeteria style choice of benefits	Professional promotional ladder that parallels the typical managerial ladder	Opportunities for self-development in speciality; peer recognition more important than awards from members of management
Managerial	High levels of responsibility; challenging, varied, and integrative in nature; prefers leadership opportunities	Internal equity is important; short-run bonuses and good retirement programs	Merit-based	Promotions and monetary recognition
Entrepreneurial	High need to create; easily bored and requires a constant new challenge	Ownership is key; wants wealth as a way of showing personal success	Total flexibility; wants to do whatever one wants at any point in time	Building a fortune; high personal visibility and public recognition
Sense of service	Work that enables one to satisfy critical values—helping people; prefers autonomy	Fair pay and portable benefits; money not a critical concern	Merit-based	Support from professional peers and superiors
Pure challenge	Any work that enables one to compete with others; seeks tougher and tougher challenges	Pay that rewards winning	Merit-based	Praise for winning
Lifestyle	Any work that enables one to balance personal and professional life; flexibility is essential	Options that permit one to integrate personal, family, and professional concerns	Flexible	Respect for personal and family considerations

SOURCE: Based in part on Edgar H. Schein, "Individuals and Careers," in *Handbook of Organizational Behavior*, ed. Jay W. Lorsch (Englewood Cliffs, N.J.: Prentice-Hall, 1987), pp. 155–71.

of self-exploration (step A) strongly affecting one's level of self-awareness (step B).

In an extensive study of career anchors, Edgar Schein identified eight distinct types. His results further revealed that people with various career anchors preferred different types of work, different types of pay and promotion systems, and different types of recognition (see Table 9A–3). Moreover, results supported the prediction that satisfaction with one's career was related to the match between a career anchor and the specific type of job being performed.[15] Thus, for example, if you have an autonomy career anchor, you will be dissatisfied with jobs in which you are closely supervised or receive pay raises based on seniority or cost of living. It thus is important for you to gain awareness of your career anchor in order to optimize the match between personal values and needs and the characteristics of a particular job. Keep in mind, however, your career anchor is largely determined by work-related experience and thus is subject to modification.

■ MAKING THE TRANSITION FROM STUDENT TO PROFESSIONAL

Career researchers have uncovered problem areas interfering with the successful transition from student to professional apprentice.[16] Table 9A–4 identifies the five most frequent transitional problems and provides recommendations for overcoming them. For example, new college graduates often are impatient with being closely supervised and performing routine tasks. You need to find ways to adjust to this problem because it is inherent to the apprentice stage of career development (see Table 9A–2). Possible solutions are: (1) acquiring technical competence, (2) learning as much as possible about the organization, and (3) demonstrating independence in solving organizational problems.

Longer feedback loops are another career transition problem. As students, you receive frequent feedback in the form of test scores and grades on assignments. This feedback can be very intensive. In contrast, organizational feedback loops are much longer. Managers typically provide formal performance feedback during annual performance appraisal review sessions. Annual feedback is inadequate for changing behavior, particularly for less experienced employees. Your challenge is to obtain the necessary feedback to help you meet your performance goals without becoming a nuisance to your boss.

How do you successfully survive the transition from student to professional? Be prepared for painful adjustments, shattered expectations, and most importantly, take charge of your career. By combining self-awareness, planning, career goals and strategies, and self-monitored feedback, you stand a much greater chance of success. We both wish you good fortune and the best of luck in your future careers!

---

[15] Ibid., pp. 155–71.

[16] See Paul H. Thompson and Gene W. Dalton, "Balancing Your Expectations," *Business Week Careers*, February–March 1987, pp. 32–35; and Jack Falvey, "Career Navigation," pp. 32–36.

■ **TABLE 9A–4** Career Transitions from Student to Professional

Transitional Problem	Solution
1. Loss of hard-earned status	Be prepared to start as an "organizational" freshman who must prove oneself.
2. Impatience with close supervision and performance of routine tasks	Acquire technical competence; learn as much as possible about the organization; and demonstrate independence in solving organizational problems.
3. Changing from a competitive academic environment to a cooperative/collaborative environment	Learn to work with others—this requires good social and interpersonal skills; and demonstrate the willingness to be a team player.
4. Identifying what constitutes competent performance	Clarify expectations with one's supervisor; demonstrate technical accuracy in completing job assignments; try to adopt the boss's broader managerial perspective; and demonstrate disciplined performance by completing tasks on time and by not avoiding difficult assignments.
5. Being resourceful and innovative	Learn when to ask for assistance and when not to. Do not be afraid to do more than is "formally" required of the position.
6. Longer feedback loops	Seek feedback at appropriate times—this necessitates learning how much feedback to ask for without becoming a nuisance.

SOURCE: Based in part on discussion in Paul H. Thompson and Gene W. Dalton, "Balancing Your Expectations," *Business Week Careers,* February–March 1987, pp. 32–35.

Chapter **10**

Group Dynamics

LEARNING OBJECTIVES

When you finish studying the material in this chapter,
you should be able to:

- Identify the four criteria of a group, from a sociological perspective.
- Describe the six stages of group development.
- Distinguish between task and maintenance functions in groups.
- Summarize the practical lessons learned from research on group size and group member ability.
- Explain the mechanics of Zand's model of trust.
- Define two different types of cohesiveness.
- Describe groupthink and identify at least four of its symptoms.
- Explain what managers can do to reduce social loafing.

OPENING CASE 10

The Wilderness Lab (Janet W. Long)

I found myself on a bus . . . winding into the Rockies west of Denver toward the base camp used by the Corporate Development Program of the Colorado Outward Bound School. There were 18 other refugees from the white-collar world, all headed for five days of management development in the woods. Outward Bound offers "Reaching Your Management Potential" in conjunction with the University of Denver Center for Management Development. . . .

Our bus carried a diverse group into the mountains. We represented organizations from Washington State to Washington, D.C. . . . from one-person consulting firms to multinational corporations. The participants included wise, understated, seasoned managers as well as bright young travelers on the corporate ladder whose rough edges were softened by the positive energy in their eyes. There were managers whose natural interests in people and leadership ability had taken them up the ranks, and highly skilled technicians, used to being independent contributors, who had recently found themselves in the uncomfortable position of needing to manage others. Ages ranged from 24 to 44, and disciplines included law, engineering, architecture, marketing and education, among others. Some participants were veterans of many training programs; others were fairly new to the realm of management development.

Most of us wanted to be there. Some had learned of the program themselves and lobbied to go. Others had been sent by their organizations to learn to work more effectively in groups—either because they were normally reticent in groups, or because they tended to dominate and compete. The outdoor medium had been selected by some because it is a more comfortable setting than the traditional classroom. Others had chosen it because it is a substantial step *beyond* the familiar corporate comfort zone and as such is a ripe environment for testing the ways we plan, solve problems, and work with others.

Most of us were a little scared. Our fears ranged from making fools of ourselves to falling off a cliff. It was hard to determine which of those fears was more serious. . . .

At the top of the hill we found a "trust ladder" nailed to one of the many pines surrounding us. There appeared to be a little more risk here than looking silly. Eric [the course director] explained that we would need to rely on one another under many circumstances in the coming week, and that the object of this exercise was to climb the ladder and fall off backwards into the arms of the group. He showed us how to line up and join hands to catch our falling teammate, and he headed for the ladder before we could ponder the matter too thoroughly. I was afraid that I wouldn't be able to hold him . . . and, of course, I couldn't have alone. One by one we climbed the ladder and thumped down into the waiting arms.

This was the first activity that we analyzed. We talked about risk taking, trusting one's support system, communicating needs and checking to be sure that the support system is ready before relying on it . . . and a little about what's involved in supporting someone effectively.

Our most physical group challenge was a 13-foot wall the entire group had to scale. It was sheer and smooth, with a platform behind it on which one could stand at about waist level with the top of the wall. This platform could be occupied by two people (once we got them up and over) to help haul up the rest of the group. A ladder was provided on the back for climbing down to earth. Thirteen feet had never seemed so imposing. We were given a few safety restrictions, and the stopwatch began ticking. Group planning and problem solving were again germane, with special attention to the first and last people over the wall.

We decided that we needed to boost some strong people up first to help pull the rest up, and keep some powerful boosters on the ground. The middle group would be relatively straightforward, with help from above and below. The final climb appeared to require two key players: someone strong enough to act as a "human rope," facing the wall and hanging with his shoulders looped over the top; and someone light and strong enough to scramble up the wall, using the human rope until he could get a hand from the pullers.

The roles clear, we began to assess our resources. I was proud of the group as we offered up both our strengths *and* limitations. We had walked past THE WALL several times over the previous two days, and it was the culmination of our group challenges. We were hungry to do it well, and the chance to play a key role was tantalizing. But the group interdependence in this exercise took on a more serious note. Despite good safety precautions (such as helmets and "spotters" whose job it would be to break anyone's fall) we really did have one another's safety in our hands. It would not do to play the hero

here and be unable to come through. Some of our most athletic team members owned up to prohibitive injuries that would keep them in the middle of the progression. Others stepped forward to fill the void, each assessing his or her own capabilities with a balance of commitment and responsibility. Soon we all knew our roles, and the adrenaline began to flow.

The scene that followed was an organized frenzy of push, pull, scramble, encourage, and keep those hands in the air in case someone fell. No one spent a moment uninvolved in the process. We all ached for our last two teammates as they completed the grueling climb. It was a tired and happy group that sat in a circle beneath the wall to talk not only about planning and problem solving but also the dynamics of sensible group risk taking, and the strength of being part of a multi-talented, interdependent and mutually supportive team.

As I leaned back against the wall and watched all this with an analytical trainer's eye, I became aware of the powerful lesson I was experiencing at gut level. [White-water canoeing had] . . . left me with a shoulder that chronically dislocates, which not only put me in the center of the progression up the wall, but made me feel like a liability to the group. As I stepped up for my boost, I told the pullers what to expect. "All right, Wayne, you can pull for all you're worth. But Mike, I can't extend this right arm very high, and if I call your name, let go in a hurry." I could feel the spotters move in around me, but I was up and over in a moment with no trouble.

During the debriefing I asked what effect my limitation had on the group, especially Wayne and Mike. "None at all," said Wayne. "None," echoed Mike, "because you told us what your needs were. I could lean down the wall further and put myself into a more vulnerable position with more leverage be-

Concluded:

cause I knew you wouldn't be pulling very hard with that arm.'' I've never been good at making my needs known, but in this situation I felt a responsibility to the group. I thought back to the office and wondered how many projects I had avoided or contributed less than I could have because I didn't give someone the chance to fill in my weak spots.

For Discussion

Why might the wilderness lab be a better learning environment than the classroom?

SOURCE: Excerpted from Janet W. Long, ''The Wilderness Lab,'' *Training and Development Journal*, May 1984, pp. 58–69. Used with permission.

■ Additional discussion questions linking this case with the following material appear at the end of this chapter.

Groups are an inescapable aspect of modern life. College students are often teamed with their peers for class projects. Parents serve on community advisory boards at their local high school. Managers find themselves on product planning committees and productivity task forces. Productive organizations simply cannot function without groups. But, as personal experience shows, group effort can bring out both the best and the worst in people. A marketing department meeting, where several people excitedly brainstorm and refine a creative new advertising campaign, can yield results beyond the capabilities of individual contributors. Oppositely, committees have become the brunt of jokes (e.g., a committee is a place where they take minutes and waste hours; a camel is a horse designed by a committee) because they all too often are plagued by lack of direction and conflict. Modern managers need a solid understanding of groups and group processes so as to avoid their pitfalls and tap their vast potential.

For example, the fate of General Motors Corp.'s multibillion dollar Saturn project will be determined to a great extent by the company's revolutionary use of groups. The Saturn project's objective is to manufacture automobiles in the United States that will be cost-competitive with the Japanese.

> The basic groups in Saturn plants will be work units of 6 to 15 UAW [United Auto Workers Union] members who will elect a ''counselor'' from their own ranks. The team will decide who does which job. It will also maintain equipment, order supplies, and set the relief and vacation schedules of its members. Each group will have a personal computer for keeping tabs on business data, ranging from production schedules to freight pickups and deliveries.[1]

---

[1] Maralyn Edid, ''How Power Will Be Balanced on Saturn's Shop Floor,'' *Business Week*, August 5, 1985, p. 65.

■ **FIGURE 10–1**   Four Criteria of a Sociological Group

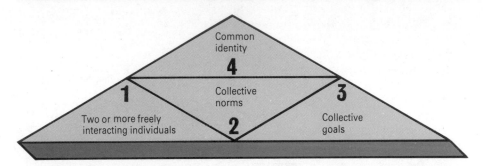

This approach, technically called job redesign (see Chapter 15), will require unprecedented degrees of cooperation and mutual trust between management and labor. But General Motors obviously believes in the power and potential of teamwork because the Saturn project's success hinges on *group* performance.

Although other definitions of groups exist, we draw from the field of sociology and define a **group** as two or more freely interacting individuals who share collective norms and goals and have a common identity.[2] Figure 10–1 illustrates how the four criteria in this definition combine to form a conceptual whole. Organizational psychologist Edgar Schein shed additional light on this concept by drawing instructive distinctions between a group, a crowd, and an organization:

> The size of a group is thus limited by the possibilities of mutual interaction and mutual awareness. Mere aggregates of people do not fit this definition because they do not interact and do not perceive themselves to be a group even if they are aware of each other as, for instance, a crowd on a street corner watching some event. A total department, a union, or a whole organization would not be a group in spite of thinking of themselves as "we," because they generally do not all interact and are not all aware of each other. However, work teams, committees, subparts of departments, cliques, and various other informal associations among organizational members would fit this definition of a group.[3]

Take a moment now to list the various groups of which you are a member. Does each of your "groups" satisfy the four criteria in Figure 10–1?

The purpose of this chapter is to improve your chances of working effectively with others. This is accomplished by analyzing group types and functions and exploring the group development process. Important aspects of group structure are examined, followed by a discussion of teamwork. The chapter concludes with steps managers can take to counteract three major threats to group effectiveness.

---

[2] This definition is based in part on one found in David Horton Smith, "A Parsimonious Definition of 'Group:' Toward Conceptual Clarity and Scientific Utility," *Sociological Inquiry*, Spring 1967, pp. 141–67.

[3] Edgar H. Schein, *Organizational Psychology*, 3rd ed. (Englewood Cliffs, N.J.: Prentice-Hall, 1980), p. 145.

■ GROUP TYPES, FUNCTIONS, AND DEVELOPMENT

Research-oriented disciplines each have classification systems that serve as a departure point for deeper understanding. Group dynamics is no exception. Three insightful ways of classifying groups are by *type*, the *functions* they perform, and their developmental *stages*.

Formal and Informal Groups

Individuals join groups, or are assigned to groups, to accomplish various purposes. If the group is formed by a manager to help the organization accomplish its goals, then it qualifies as a **formal group.** Formal groups typically wear such labels as work group, team, committee, quality circle, or task force. An **informal group** exists when the members' overriding purpose of getting together is friendship. Although formal and informal groups often overlap, such as a team of corporate auditors heading for the tennis courts after work, some employees are not friends with their co-workers. The desirability of overlapping formal and informal groups is problematic. Some managers firmly believe personal friendship fosters productive teamwork on the job while others view workplace "bull sessions" as a serious threat to productivity. Both situations are common, and it is the manager's job to strike a workable balance, based on the maturity and goals of the people involved.

Functions of Formal Groups

Researchers point out that formal groups fulfill two basic functions: *organizational* and *individual*.[4] The various functions are listed in Table 10–1. Complex combinations of these functions can be found in formal groups at any given time.

For example, consider what Mazda's new American employees experienced when they spent a month working in Japan before the opening of the firm's Flat Rock, Michigan, plant in 1987.

> After a month of training in Mazda's factory methods, whipping their new Japanese buddies at softball and sampling local watering holes, the Americans were fired up. . . . [A maintenance manager] even faintly praised the Japanese practice of holding group calisthenics at the start of each working day: "I didn't think I'd like doing exercises every morning, but I kind of like it."[5]

While Mazda pursued the organizational functions it wanted—interdependent teamwork, creativity, coordination, problem solving, and training—the American workers benefited from the individual functions of formal groups. Among those benefits were affiliation with new friends, enhanced self-esteem, exposure to the Japanese social reality, and reduction of anxieties about working for a

---

[4] Ibid., pp. 149–53.
[5] Janice Castro, "Mazda U.," *Time*, October 20, 1986, p. 65.

■ **TABLE 10–1** Formal Groups Fulfill Organizational and Individual Functions

Organizational Functions	Individual Functions
1. Accomplish *complex, interdependent tasks* that are beyond the capabilities of individuals.	1. Satisfy the individual's *need for affiliation*.
2. Generate *new or creative ideas* and *solutions*.	2. Develop, enhance, and confirm the individual's *self-esteem* and sense of *identity*.
3. *Coordinate* interdepartmental *efforts*.	3. Give individuals an opportunity to *test* and *share* their perceptions of *social reality*.
4. Provide a *problem-solving mechanism* for *complex problems* requiring varied information and assessments.	4. *Reduce* the individual's *anxieties* and feelings of *insecurity* and *powerlessness*.
5. *Implement* complex *decisions*.	5. Provide a *problem-solving mechanism* for *personal* and *interpersonal problems*.
6. *Socialize* and *train* newcomers.	

SOURCE: Adapted from Edgar H. Schein, *Organizational Psychology*, 3rd ed. (Englewood Cliffs, N.J.: Prentice-Hall, 1980), pp. 149–51.

foreign-owned company. In short, Mazda created an admirable blend of organizational and individual group functions by training its newly hired American employees in Japan.

Stages of the Group Development Process

Chapter 9 detailed how the organizational socialization process can be reduced to a sequence of identifiable phases. So it is with the group development process. This implies groups go through a predictable maturation process, such as one would find in any life-cycle situation (e.g., humans, organizations, products). However, while there is general agreement among theorists that the group development process occurs in identifiable stages, they disagree about the exact number, sequence, length, and nature of those stages.[6] An instructive model of group development is depicted in Figure 10–2. Notice how *uncertainty over authority and power* is an overriding obstacle during the first three phases. During the last three phases, *uncertainty over interpersonal relations* becomes the major obstacle.

Let us briefly examine each of the six stages.[7] You can make this process come to life by relating the various stages to your own experiences with work groups, committees, athletic teams, social or religious groups, or class project teams. Some group happenings that surprised you when they occurred may now make sense or strike you as inevitable when seen as part of a developmental process.

Stage 1: Orientation.   During this "ice-breaking" stage, group members tend to be uncertain and anxious about such things as their roles, who is in charge, and the group's goals. Mutual trust is low and there is a good deal of holding

---

[6] For an instructive overview of five different theories of group development, see John P. Wanous, Arnon E. Reichers, and S. D. Malik, "Organizational Socialization and Group Development: Toward an Integrative Perspective," *Academy of Management Review*, October 1984, pp. 670–83.

[7] Adapted from discussion in Linda N. Jewell and H. Joseph Reitz, *Group Effectiveness in Organizations* (Glenview, Ill.: Scott, Foresman, 1981), pp. 15–20.

■ **FIGURE 10–2** Six Stages of Group Development

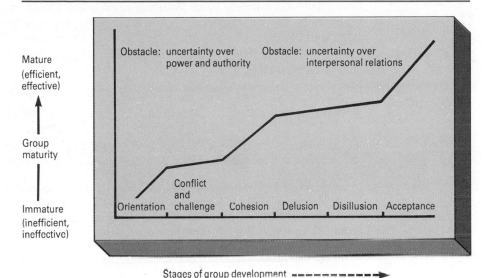

Stages of group development ----------►

back to see who takes charge and how. If the formal leader (e.g., a supervisor) does not assert his or her authority, an emergent leader will eventually step in to fulfill the group's need for leadership and direction. Leaders typically mistake this honeymoon period as a mandate for permanent control. But later problems may force a leadership change.

Stage 2: Conflict and Challenge. This is a time of testing. Individuals test the leader's policies and assumptions as they try to determine how they fit into the power structure. Subgroups take shape, and subtle forms of rebellion, such as procrastination, occur. Many groups stall in stage 2 because power politics erupts into open rebellion.

Stage 3: Cohesion. Groups that make it through stage 2 generally do so because a respected member, other than the leader, challenges the group to resolve its power struggles so something can be accomplished. Questions about authority and power are resolved rather quickly through unemotional, matter-of-fact group discussion. A renewed feeling of team spirit is experienced because members believe they have found their proper roles.

Stage 4: Delusion. Having resolved major disputes over power and authority, the group's members feel a sense of relief over having been "through the worst of it." Unfortunately, pressures build up as the quest for harmony and goodwill causes individuals to stifle their complaints. Participation is very active during this stage.

Stage 5: Disillusion. The unrealistic sense of harmony in stage 4 begins to fray around the edges as some members point out that the group is not fulfilling its potential. Conflict between subgroups may arise over whether or not individuals should reveal their relative strengths and weaknesses. A drop in group cohesiveness is evidenced by increased absenteeism, withheld commitment, and critical remarks.

Stage 6: Acceptance. The hurdle between stages 4 and 5 is much like that between stages 2 and 3. Consequently, it once again falls on an influential member of the group, typically not the leader, to challenge his or her peers to do some reality testing. This exercise promotes greater understanding about the members' expectations for each other and for the group as a whole.

> As a result of overcoming this final obstacle, the group structure can become flexible and adjust to fit the requirements of the situation without causing problems for the members. Influence can shift depending on who has the particular expertise or skills required for the group task or activity. Subgroups can work on special problems or subproblems without posing threats to the authority or cohesiveness of the rest of the group.[8]

These characteristics combine to signal that the group has matured. The B. F. Goodrich Co.'s team-oriented participative management program is a good example. The success of that program depends on mature groups that have survived the ups and downs of the group development process (see Table 10–2).

Group Development: Research and Practical Implications

Despite a vast array of group development theories, high-quality research evidence is scarce. One of the most fruitful studies to date was carried out by a pair of Dutch social psychologists. They hypothesized that interpersonal feedback would vary systematically during the group development process. "The unit of feedback measured was a verbal message directed from one participant to another in which some aspect of behavior was addressed."[9] After collecting and categorizing 1,600 instances of feedback from four different eight-person groups, they concluded:

- Interpersonal feedback increases as the group develops through successive stages.
- As the group develops, positive feedback increases and negative feedback decreases.
- Interpersonal feedback becomes more specific as the group develops.
- The credibility of peer feedback increases as the group develops.[10]

---

[8] Ibid., p. 19.

[9] Don Davies and Bart C. Kuypers, "Group Development and Interpersonal Feedback," *Group & Organization Studies,* June 1985, p. 194.

[10] Drawn from Ibid., pp. 184–208.

■ TABLE 10–2 The Systematic Development of Group Maturity Keeps B. F. Goodrich's Participative Management Program on Track

The BF Goodrich Tire Group is using work teams in its controller's organization to involve employees in problem solving and departmental planning. [These voluntary eight- to twelve-member teams meet weekly.] The purpose of this form of participative management—called the Employee Involvement Network (EIN)—is to encourage employees to use their skills and ideas in order to improve productivity. Specific objectives of EIN are:

To enlist employees' and their managers' support in identifying and solving problems by more effective two-way communication within a group or department.

To develop a sense of corporate "ownership" among employees, and create the necessary environment to improve group or department performance.

To recognize the group or department's achievements in order to encourage and stimulate employee participation. . . .

During the early stages of the work team, the group tends to center on improving the work environment. In some cases, team members test management's commitment to the employee involvement network. Management's willingness to listen and implement new ideas is very important to continued group development. Not receiving clear and full explanations, or having ideas, requests or suggestions rejected outright without good reason can be harmful to a team's development. How well the work team performs also depends upon the degree of employee involvement at the meetings and if team members use the proper problem solving techniques. Team members also should critique their own meetings.

A fully functioning work team is characterized by stable participation and steady leadership. Generally, the meetings are productive and there is ongoing problem solving. It could take up to a year for a work group to develop into a cohesive and productive team. The team at this stage focuses on improving the department's work, reviewing productivity gains, controlling costs, or making other improvements.

. . . a monitoring of the Billing Department's operations reveals the contribution EIN has made to the controller's organization. In the first year we have been able to increase the number of billing documents processed each work day by 21 percent, and the number of billing documents processed per employee-hour by 15 percent. We have been able to reduce the cost for each hour employed by 9.4 percent, the cost of each bill produced by 11 percent, and total department expense by 2.2 percent. The average number of days absent per employee went down by 40 percent.

SOURCE: Excerpted from material in Gene L. Smith, "Improving Productivity in the Controller's Organization," *Management Accounting,* January 1986, pp. 49–51. Used with permission.

These findings hold important lessons for managers. The content and delivery of interpersonal feedback among work group or committee members can be used as a gauge of whether the group is developing properly. For example, the onset of stages 2 (conflict and challenge) and 5 (disillusion) will be signaled by a noticeable increase in *negative* feedback. Effort can then be directed at generating specific, positive feedback among the members so the group's development will not stall. The feedback model discussed in Chapter 7 is helpful in this regard.

Along a somewhat different line, experts in the area of leadership contend that different leadership styles are needed as work groups develop.

> In general, it has been documented that leadership behavior that is active, aggressive, directive, structured, and task-oriented seems to have favorable results early in the group's history. However, when those behaviors are maintained throughout the life of the group, they seem to have a negative impact on cohesiveness and quality of work. Conversely, leadership behavior that is supportive, democratic, decentralized, and participative seems to be related to poorer functioning in the early group development stages. However, when these behaviors are maintained throughout the life of the group, more productivity, satisfaction, and creativity result.[11]

The practical punch line here is that managers are advised to shift from a directive and structured leadership style to a participative and supportive style as the group develops. (Leadership is discussed in detail in Chapter 13.)

■ GROUP STRUCTURE AND COMPOSITION

Individuals may be created equally, but groups are not. Work groups of varying size are made up of individuals with varying ability and motivation. Moreover, those individuals perform different roles, on either an assigned or voluntary basis. No wonder some work groups are more productive than others. No wonder some committees are tightly knit while others wallow in conflict. In this section, we examine four important dimensions of group structure and composition: (1) functional roles of group members, (2) group size, (3) gender composition, and (4) group member ability. Each of these dimensions alternatively can enhance or hinder group effectiveness, depending on how it is managed.

Functional Roles Performed by Group Members

In Chapter 9, we introduced and discussed the sociological concept of *roles*. Here we extend that concept by considering two categories of functional roles that individuals fulfill while working in groups.[12] Specifically, task and maintenance roles (see Table 10–3) need to be performed if a given work group is to get anything accomplished.

Task versus Maintenance Roles.   **Task roles** enable the work group to define, clarify, and pursue a common purpose. Meanwhile, **maintenance roles** foster supportive and constructive interpersonal relationships. In short, task roles keep the group *on track* while maintenance roles keep the group *together*. A fraternity or sorority member is performing a task function when he or she

---

[11] Donald K. Carew, Eunice Parisi-Carew, and Kenneth H. Blanchard, "Group Development and Situational Leadership: A Model for Managing Groups," *Training and Development Journal,* June 1986, pp. 48–49.

[12] See Kenneth D. Benne and Paul Sheats, "Functional Roles of Group Members," *Journal of Social Issues,* Spring 1948, pp. 41–49.

■ **TABLE 10–3**   Functional Roles Performed by Group Members

Task Roles	Description
Initiator:	Suggests new goals or ideas.
Information seeker/giver:	Clarifies key issues.
Opinion seeker/giver:	Clarifies pertinent values.
Elaborator:	Promotes greater understanding through examples or exploration of implications.
Coordinator:	Pulls together ideas and suggestions.
Orienter:	Keeps group headed toward its stated goal(s).
Evaluator:	Tests group's accomplishments with various criteria such as logic and practicality.
Energizer:	Prods group to move along or to accomplish more.
Procedural technician:	Performs routine duties (e.g., handing out materials or rearranging seats).
Recorder:	Performs a "group memory" function by documenting discussion and outcomes.

Maintenance Roles	Description
Encourager:	Fosters group solidarity by accepting and praising various points of view.
Harmonizer:	Mediates conflict through reconciliation or humor.
Compromiser:	Helps resolve conflict by meeting others "half way."
Gatekeeper:	Encourages all group members to participate.
Standard setter:	Evaluates the quality of group processes.
Commentator:	Records and comments on group processes/dynamics.
Follower:	Serves as a passive audience.

SOURCE: Adapted from discussion in Kenneth D. Benne and Paul Sheats, "Functional Roles of Group Members," *Journal of Social Issues,* Spring 1948; pp. 41–49.

stands at a business meeting and says: "What is the real issue here? We don't seem to be getting anywhere." Another individual who says, "Let's hear from those who oppose this plan," is performing a maintenance function. Importantly, each of the various task and maintenance roles may be played in varying combinations and sequences by either the group's leader or any of its members.

Checklist for Managers.   The task and maintenance roles listed in Table 10–3 can serve as a handy checklist for managers and group leaders who wish to ensure proper group development. Roles that are not always performed when needed, such as those of coordinator, evaluator, and gatekeeper, can be performed in a timely manner by the formal leader or assigned to other members.

International managers need to be sensitive to cultural differences regarding the relative importance of task and maintenance roles. In Japan, for example, cultural tradition calls for more emphasis on maintenance roles (see Table 10–4).

Group Size

How many group members is too many? The answer to this deceptively simple question has intrigued managers and academics for years. Folk wisdom says "two heads are better than one" but that "too many cooks spoil the

■ **TABLE 10-4**   What It Takes to Be a Good Group Member in Japan

In every kind of group, one quality is desired above all—interpersonal harmony. Much of members' behavior is directed toward creating a pleasant state in their unit. They are gracious, courteous, and gentle; they smile often, bow low and long to friends and to strangers they respect, avoid acts of rivalry, offer help to those in need, show agreement by repeatedly saying "yes" while a companion is speaking, and are shy with superiors. In informal gatherings participants eschew behaviors that might ruffle the composure of those assembled. They do not match wits, engage in sparkling repartee, or display hostile jocularity.

Courtesy requires that members not be conspicuous or disputatious in a meeting or class-room. If two or more members discover that their views differ—a fact that is tactfully taken to be unfortunate—they adjourn to find more information and to work toward a stance that all can accept. They do not press their personal opinions through strong arguments, neat logic, or rewards and threats. And they do not hesitate to shift their beliefs if doing so will preserve smooth interpersonal relations. (To lose is to win.)

A meeting is a joint effort to find a mutually agreeable solution; it is not a debate. Promotions within a company, moreover, are based in large part on an employee's capacity to work well with others.

SOURCE: Alvin Zander, "The Value of Belonging to a Group in Japan," *Small Group Behavior*, Vol. 14 (February 1983), pp. 7–8. Copyright © 1983 by Sage Publications, Inc. Reprinted by permission of Sage Publications, Inc.

broth.'' So where should a manager draw the line when staffing a committee? At 3? At 5 or 6? At 10 or more? Researchers have taken two different approaches to pinpointing optimum group size: mathematical modeling and laboratory simulations. Let us briefly review recent findings from these two approaches.

The Mathematical Modeling Approach.   This approach involves building a mathematical model around certain desired outcomes of group action such as decision quality. Due to differing assumptions and statistical techniques, the results of this research are inconclusive. Statistical estimates of optimum group size have ranged from 3 to 13.[13]

The Laboratory Simulation Approach.   This stream of research is based on the assumption that group behavior needs to be observed firsthand in controlled laboratory settings. A laboratory study by respected Australian researcher Philip Yetton and his colleague, Preston Bottger, provides useful insights about group size and performance.[14]

Five hundred fifty-five subjects (330 managers and 225 graduate management students, of whom 20 percent were female) were assigned to task teams ranging

---

[13] For example, see Bernard Grofman, Scott L. Feld, and Guillermo Owen, "Group Size and the Performance of a Composite Group Majority: Statistical Truths and Empirical Results," *Organizational Behavior and Human Performance*, June 1984, pp. 350–59.

[14] See Philip Yetton and Preston Bottger, "The Relationships among Group Size, Member Ability, Social Decision Schemes, and Performance," *Organizational Behavior and Human Performance*, October 1983, pp. 145–59.

in size from 2 to 6. The teams worked on the National Aeronautics and Space Administration moon survival exercise. (This exercise involves the rank ordering of 15 pieces of equipment that would enable a spaceship crew on the moon to survive a 200-mile trip between a crash-landing site and home base.)[15] After analyzing the relationships between group size and group performance, Yetton and Bottger concluded:

> It would be difficult, at least with respect to decision quality, to justify groups larger than five members. . . . Of course, to meet needs other than high decision quality, organizations may employ groups significantly larger than four or five.[16]

Managerial Implications.   Within a contingency management framework, there is no hard-and-fast rule about group size. It depends on the manager's objective for the group. If a high-quality decision is the main objective, then a three- to five-member group would be appropriate. However, if the objective is to generate creative ideas, encourage participation, socialize new members, or communicate policies, then groups much larger than five could be justified.

Odd-numbered groups with three, five, seven, and so on members are recommended if the issue is to be settled by a majority vote. Voting deadlocks (e.g., 2–2, 3–3) too often hamper effectiveness of even-numbered groups. A majority decision rule is not necessarily a good idea. A recent study found that better group outcomes were obtained by negotiation groups that used a unanimous as opposed to majority decision rule. Individuals' self-interests were more effectively integrated when groups used a unanimous decision criterion.[17]

Effects of Men and Women Working Together in Groups

As pointed out in Chapter 2, the female portion of the U.S. labor force has grown significantly in recent years. This demographic shift brought an increase in the number of organizational committees and teams composed of both men and women. Some profound effects on group dynamics might be expected. Let us see what researchers have found in the way of group gender composition effects and what managers can do about them.

Gender Composition Research.   Researchers have pondered two basic questions about men, women, and groups. First, do female task groups perform differently than male task groups? Second, are there unique group dynamics in mixed male-female groups? Laboratory studies, using college students as subjects, provided the following tentative insights:

---

[15] This copyrighted exercise may be found in Jay Hall, "Decisions, Decisions, Decisions," *Psychology Today,* November 1971, pp. 51–54, 86, 88.

[16] Yetton and Bottger, "The Relationships among Group Size, Member Ability, Social Decision Schemes, and Performance," p. 158.

[17] Details of this study are presented in Leigh L. Thompson, Elizabeth A. Mannix, and Max H. Bazerman, "Group Negotiation: Effects of Decision Rule, Agenda, and Aspiration," *Journal of Personality and Social Psychology,* January 1988, pp. 86–95.

- "Men in groups were found to generate more solutions to brainstorming tasks than were women in groups, and women in groups appeared to generate better quality solutions to discussion problems than did men."[18]
- In two-person task groups, both male and female subjects worked harder when their "more capable partner was of the opposite sex."[19]
- In six-person groups composed of three males and three females, males were more effective advocates of risky decisions than were females.[20]

Because these results come from laboratory studies, they do not necessarily carry over to complex work organizations. Additional insights are needed from field research involving actual employees. One such survey of 387 male U.S. government employees sought to determine how they were affected by the growing number of female co-workers. The researchers concluded, "Under many circumstances, including intergender interaction in work groups, frequent contact leads to cooperative and supportive social relations."[21]

Constructive Managerial Action.   Male and female employees can and often do work well together in groups, as discovered in the foregoing field study. However, as suggested by the laboratory studies reviewed, managers can expect to encounter unique group dynamics stemming from male-female interaction. Hard rules for dealing with male-female group dynamics are not yet at hand, pending more organizational studies. Meanwhile, steps can be taken to make the best of suspected gender composition effects.

For example, a trainee's performance might be enhanced by pairing him or her with a capable person of the opposite sex. Additionally, female managers can become more effective advocates of both change and risky decisions if women's support groups—both inside and outside the organization—are actively encouraged. Progressive employers know they can attract and retain talented women by creating a more supportive work environment. "Du Pont Co., for example, holds monthly workshops to make managers aware of gender-related attitudes."[22]

Individual Ability and Group Effectiveness

Imagine that you are a department manager charged with making an important staffing decision amid the following circumstances. You need to form eight

---

[18] Wendy Wood, Darlene Polek, and Cheryl Aiken, "Sex Differences in Group Task Performance," *Journal of Personality and Social Psychology,* January 1985, p. 70.

[19] Norbert L. Kerr and Robert J. MacCoun, "Sex Composition of Groups and Member Motivation II: Effects of Relative Task Ability," *Basic and Applied Social Psychology,* December 1984, p. 268.

[20] See James DiBerardinis, Kathy Ramage, and Steve Levitt, "Risky Shift and Gender of the Advocate: Information Theory versus Normative Theory," *Group & Organization Studies,* June 1984, pp. 189–200.

[21] Scott J. South, Charles M. Bonjean, William T. Markham, and Judy Corder, "Female Labor Force Participation and the Organizational Experiences of Male Workers," *The Sociological Quarterly,* Summer 1983, p. 378.

[22] Irene Pave, "A Woman's Place Is at GE, Federal Express, P&G . . . ," *Business Week,* June 23, 1986, p. 78.

3-person task teams from a pool of 24 employees. Based on each of the employee's prior work records and their scores on ability tests, you know that 12 have high ability and 12 have low ability. The crux of your problem is how to assign the 12 high-ability employees. Should you spread your talent around by making sure there are both high- and low-ability employees on each team? Then again, you may want to concentrate your talent by forming four high-ability teams and four low-ability teams. Or should you attempt to find a compromise between these two extremes? What is your decision? Why? A recent field experiment provided an instructive and interesting answer.

The Israeli Tank-Crew Study.   Aharon Tziner and Dov Eden, respected researchers from Tel Aviv University, systematically manipulated the composition of 208 three-man tank crews. All possible combinations of high- and low-ability personnel were studied (high-high-high; high-high-low; high-low-low; and low-low-low). Ability was a composite measure of (1) overall intelligence, (2) amount of formal education, (3) proficiency in Hebrew, and (4) interview ratings. Successful operation of the tanks required the three-man crews to perform with a high degree of synchronized interdependence. Tank-crew effectiveness was determined by commanding officers during military maneuvers for the Israel Defense Forces.

As expected, the high-high-high ability tank crews performed the best and the low-low-low the worst. But the researchers discovered an important *interaction effect*:

> Each member's ability influenced crew performance effectiveness differently depending on the ability levels of the other two members. A high-ability member appears to achieve more in combination with other uniformly high-ability members than in combination with low-ability members.[23]

The tank crews composed of three high-ability personnel far outperformed all other ability combinations. The interaction effect also worked in a negative direction because the low-low-low ability crews performed far below expected levels. Moreover, as illustrated in Figure 10–3, significantly greater performance gains were achieved by creating high-high-high ability crews than by upgrading low-low-low ability crews with one or two high-ability members.

This returns us to the staffing problem at the beginning of this section. Tziner and Eden recommended the following solution:

> Our experimental results suggest that the most productive solution would be to allocate six highs and all 12 lows to six teams of high-low-low ability and to assign the six remaining highs to two teams of high-high-high ability. This avoids the disproportionately low productivity of the low-low-low ability combination, while leaving some of the highs for high-high-high ability teams where they are most productive. . . . Our results show that talent is used more effectively when concentrated than when spread around.[24]

---

[23] Aharon Tziner and Dov Eden, "Effects of Crew Composition on Crew Performance: Does the Whole Equal the Sum of Its Parts?" *Journal of Applied Psychology*, February 1985, p. 91.

[24] Ibid.

■ **FIGURE 10–3** Ability of Israeli Tank-Crew Members and Improvement in Effectiveness

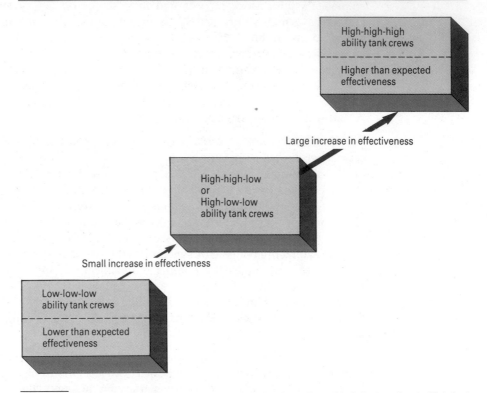

SOURCE: Based on discussion in Aharon Tziner and Dov Eden, "Effects of Crew Composition on Crew Performance: Does the Whole Equal the Sum of Its Parts?" *Journal of Applied Psychology*, February 1985, pp. 85–93.

A Managerial Interpretation.   While the real-life aspect of the tank-crew study makes its results fairly generalizable, a qualification is in order. Specifically, modern complex organizations demand a more flexible contingency approach. Figure 10–4 shows two basic contingencies. If management seeks to *improve* the performance of *all* groups or train novices, high-ability personnel can be spread around. This option would be appropriate in a high-volume production operation. But if the desired outcome is to *maximize* performance of the *best* group(s), then high-ability personnel should be concentrated. This second option would be advisable in research and development departments, for example, where technological breakthroughs need to be achieved. Extraordinary achievements require clusters of extraordinary talent.

■ **EFFECTIVE TEAMWORK THROUGH COOPERATION, TRUST, AND COHESIVENESS**

As competitive pressures intensify, organizational success increasingly will depend on teamwork rather than individual stars. Compaq Computer Corp., the fastest-growing company in American business history, has become the

■ **FIGURE 10-4** A Contingency Model for Staffing Work Groups

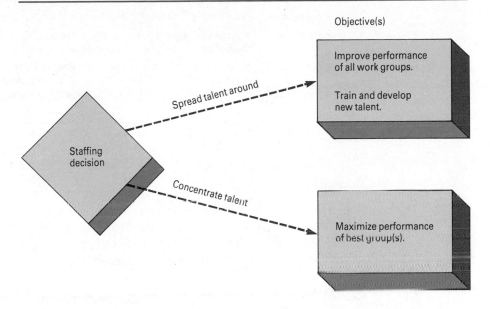

Objective(s)

Improve performance of all work groups.

Train and develop new talent.

Spread talent around

Staffing decision

Concentrate talent

Maximize performance of best group(s).

world's second-largest maker of personal computers through effective teamwork. According to *Inc.* magazine:

> "I'm not a superstar with all the vision, just a guy who moderates the consensus among a pretty bright bunch of people," explains president Rod Canion in his austere office amidst the pine forests of suburban Houston. "Our way has been to work as a team to find out the market needs and execute our product. If people say, 'Ho hum' and that we need more pizzazz, I think they miss the point."
>
> Canion's point is that entrepreneurial success is far less dependent these days on the brilliant insights and force of personality of hard-charging chief executive officers. A growing number of companies are organizing themselves around a "smart team" of experienced, savvy managers who substitute collegiality for hierarchy and keep their focus on a single goal: building a company that's going to last.[25]

If this sort of testimonial to teamwork has a familiar ring, it is because World Series baseball and Super Bowl football champions are often heard saying virtually the same thing. Unfortunately, from an analytical OB perspective, the concept of teamwork can be elusive. (Using the three criteria listed in Table 10-5 as a frame of reference, take a moment now to ponder the secrets of success of the most effective team of which you have been a member. Why did it succeed while others failed?) Whether in the athletic arena or the world of organizational behavior, three components of teamwork that turn up repeatedly are cooperation, trust, and cohesiveness. Let us carefully examine the contributions each can make to effective teamwork.

---

[25] Joel Kotkin, "The 'Smart Team' at Compaq Computer," *Inc.*, February 1986, p. 48.

■ **TABLE 10–5** Three Criteria of an Effective Team

Team effectiveness can be assessed in terms of the following three criteria:

1. Group effectiveness   "The productive output of the work group should meet or exceed the performance stan-
                           dards of the people who receive and/or review the output."

2. Group development   "The social processes used in carrying out the work should maintain or enhance the
                           capability of members to work together on subsequent team tasks."

3. Personal satisfaction "The group experience should, on balance, satisfy rather than frustrate the personal
                           needs of group members."

SOURCE: Excerpted from J. Richard Hackman, "The Design of Work Teams," in *Handbook of Organizational Behavior,* ed. Jay W. Lorsch (Englewood Cliffs, N.J.: Prentice-Hall, 1987), p. 323.

Cooperation

Individuals are said to be cooperating when their efforts are systematically *integrated* to achieve a collective objective. The greater the integration, the greater the degree of cooperation. In task groups and organizations made up of interdependent task groups, integration can be achieved in two ways: collaboration and coordination (see Figure 10–5).[26]

Collaboration versus Coordination. **Collaboration** occurs when group members share joint responsibility for certain outcomes. For instance, team members in a tug-of-war contest must collaborate if they are to succeed. Similarly, the members of a hospital's cost-containment committee must collaborate if they are to develop good recommendations. **Coordination,** on the other hand, involves arranging subtasks sequentially. Assembly lines, for example, require a high degree of coordination because task A must be completed before task B, which must be completed before task C. Because collaboration requires a mature group characterized by effective communication, mutual trust, and cohesiveness, it is administratively more difficult to achieve than coordination. Managers who desire to build teamwork in today's complex organizations need to work on both dimensions of cooperation.

Cooperation versus Competition. A widely held assumption among American managers is that "competition brings out the best in people." From an economic standpoint, business survival depends on staying ahead of the competition. But from an interpersonal standpoint, critics contend competition has been overemphasized, primarily at the expense of cooperation. According to Alfie Kohn, a strong advocate of greater emphasis on cooperation in our classrooms, offices, and factories:

> My review of the evidence has convinced me that there are two . . . important reasons for competition's failure. First, success often depends on sharing resources efficiently, and this is nearly impossible when people have to work against one another. Cooperation takes advantage of all the skills represented in a group as well as the mysterious process by which that group becomes more than the

---

[26] This distinction is drawn from Gordon O'Brien, "The Measurement of Cooperation," *Organizational Behavior and Human Performance,* November 1968, pp. 427–39.

■ **FIGURE 10–5** Two Dimensions of Cooperation

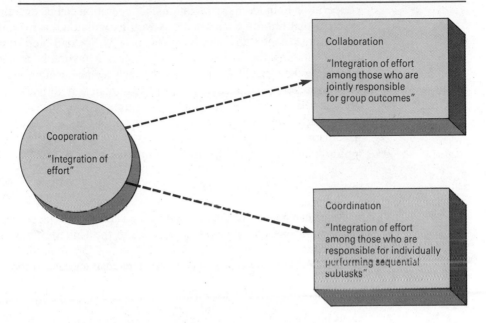

sum of its parts. By contrast, competition makes people suspicious and hostile toward one another and actively discourages this process. . . .

Second, competition generally does not promote excellence because trying to do well and trying to beat others simply are two different things. Consider a child in class, waving his arm wildly to attract the teacher's attention, crying, "Oooh! Oooh! Pick me!" When he is finally recognized, he seems befuddled. "Um, what was the question again?" he finally asks. His mind is focused on beating his classmates, not on the subject matter.[27]

Research Support for Cooperation. After conducting a meta-analysis of 122 studies encompassing a wide variety of subjects and settings, one team of researchers concluded:

1. Cooperation is superior to competition in promoting achievement and productivity. . . .
2. Cooperation is superior to individualistic efforts in promoting achievement and productivity. . . .
3. Cooperation without intergroup competition promotes higher achievement and productivity than cooperation with intergroup competition.[28]

[27] Alfie Kohn, "How to Succeed without Even Vying," *Psychology Today*, September 1986, pp. 27–28.

[28] David W. Johnson, Geoffrey Maruyama, Roger Johnson, Deborah Nelson, and Linda Skon, "Effects of Cooperative, Competitive, and Individualistic Goal Structures on Achievement: A Meta-Analysis," *Psychological Bulletin*, January 1981, pp. 56–57. An alternative interpretation of the foregoing study that emphasizes the influence of situational factors can be found in John L. Cotton and Michael S. Cook, "Meta-Analysis and the Effects of Various Reward Systems: Some Different Conclusions from Johnson et al.," *Psychological Bulletin*, July 1982, pp. 176–83.

Given the size and diversity of the research base, these findings strongly endorse cooperation in modern organizations. Cooperation can be encouraged by reward systems that reinforce teamwork as well as individual achievement.

A more recent study involving 84 male U.S. Air Force trainees uncovered an encouraging link between cooperation and favorable race relations. After observing the subjects interact in three-man teams during a management game, the researchers concluded: [Helpful] "teammates, both black and white, attract greater respect and liking than do teammates who have not helped. This is particularly true when the helping occurs voluntarily."[29] These findings suggest that managers can enhance equal employment opportunity programs by encouraging *voluntary* helping behavior in interracial work groups.

Trust

American managers have been intrigued and somewhat embarrassed in recent years as Japanese companies have come to the United States and dramatically reversed the fortunes of one losing operation after another. According to a special report in *Business Week,* the Japanese success story hinges on *trust*:

> A key element of the Japanese transplants' success is their adroit handling of American workers. The Japanese approach to production, emphasizing flexible teams, just-in-time deliveries, and attention to quality, demands extremely high employee loyalty, which is a sharp departure from the traditional adversary relationship in most U.S. factories. Workers given responsibility for running the production line will care about and catch mistakes, but only if they trust management. The trust must be mutual, too, because the just-in-time delivery system, which depends on a steady stream of components, is easy to sabotage.[30]

Clearly, given the evidence in Table 10–6, U.S. managers need to do a much better job of building labor-management trust. Trust is important off the job, too. Many friendships, budding romances, and marriages have been ruined by betrayed trust. We now turn our attention to exploring the concept of trust and discussing a research-based model of trust that has important managerial implications.

A Cognitive Leap.   **Trust** is defined as reciprocal faith in others' intentions and behavior. Scholars explain the reciprocal (give-and-take) aspect of trust as follows:

> When we see others acting in ways that imply that they trust us, we become more disposed to reciprocate by trusting in them more. Conversely, we come to distrust those whose actions appear to violate our trust or to distrust us.[31]

---

[29] Stuart W. Cook and Michael Pelfrey, "Reactions to Being Helped in Cooperating Interracial Groups: A Context Effect," *Journal of Personality and Social Psychology,* November 1985, p. 1243.

[30] Aaron Bernstein, "The Difference Japanese Management Makes," *Business Week,* July 14, 1986, p. 48.

[31] J. David Lewis and Andrew Weigert, "Trust as a Social Reality," *Social Forces,* June 1985, p. 971.

■ **TABLE 10–6** Trust Seems to Be in Short Supply in the U.S. Workplace

Most workers don't trust their bosses, a study finds.

Fully 78 percent of American workers are suspicious of management, developing an "us-against-them" syndrome that interferes with their performance, contend Boston University's Donald Kanter and Philip Mirvis. These workers, the psychologists say, "spurn innovation and create unrest. Their first loyalty is to themselves, not the firm."

Employees with the most cynical view of management are under 25, less educated and members of minority groups, the study finds. But, curiously, most say they are satisfied with their jobs and with opportunities for pay, benefits and promotion. Most also, while balking at supervision, tend to cooperate with their fellow workers on the job.

SOURCE: Excerpted from "Labor Letter: A Special News Report on People and Their Jobs in Offices, Fields, and Factories," *The Wall Street Journal*, February 10, 1987, p. 1.

In short, we tend to give what we get: trust begets trust; distrust begets distrust.

Trust involves "a cognitive 'leap' beyond the expectations that reason and experience alone would warrant"[32] (see Figure 10–6). For example, suppose a member of a newly formed class project team works hard based on the assumption that her teammates also are working hard. That assumption, on which her trust is based, is a cognitive leap that goes beyond her actual experience with her teammates. When you trust someone, you have *faith* in their good intentions. The act of trusting someone, however, carries with it the inherent risk of betrayal. Progressive managers believe that the benefits of interpersonal trust far outweigh any risks of betrayed trust.

■ **FIGURE 10–6** Interpersonal Trust Involves a Cognitive Leap

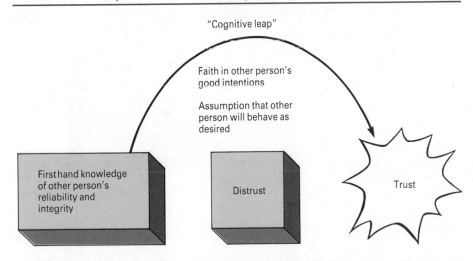

[32] Ibid., p. 970.

Zand's Model of Trust.   Dale Zand's model explains how trust evolves in problem-solving groups such as committees and task groups. It shows the interaction among three variables: information, influence, and control. As illustrated in Figure 10–7, formal and informal leaders can initiate trusting relationships by becoming more vulnerable through admitting one's limitations, claiming responsibility for one's mistakes, sharing important information, and encourag-

■ **FIGURE 10–7** Zand's Model of Trust

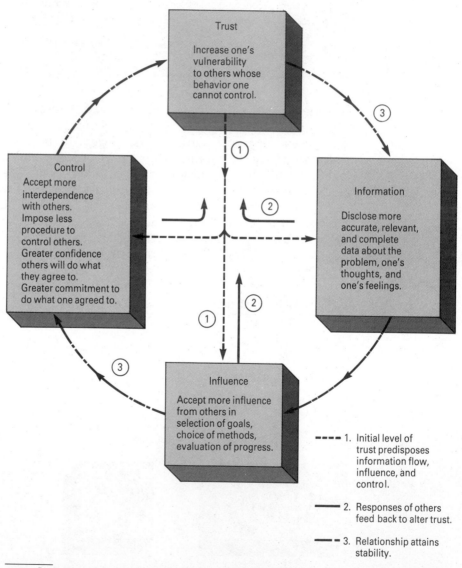

Trust

Increase one's vulnerability to others whose behavior one cannot control.

Control

Accept more interdependence with others. Impose less procedure to control others. Greater confidence others will do what they agree to. Greater commitment to do what one agreed to.

Information

Disclose more accurate, relevant, and complete data about the problem, one's thoughts, and one's feelings.

Influence

Accept more influence from others in selection of goals, choice of methods, evaluation of progress.

---- 1. Initial level of trust predisposes information flow, influence, and control.

——— 2. Responses of others feed back to alter trust.

– – – 3. Relationship attains stability.

SOURCE: Reprinted from "Trust and Managerial Problem Solving" by Dale E. Zand, published in *Administrative Science Quarterly* (June 1972) by permission of *Administrative Science Quarterly*. © 1972 by Cornell University.

ing meaningful participation and self-control. In response to this trusting posture, group members tend to share useful task-oriented information and be more open to influence by others. These factors, when combined with an emphasis on *self-control* rather than procedural control, tend to strengthen the cycle of trust. Oppositely, distrust prevails if leaders try to be invulnerable, relevant information is not shared, influence is resisted, and rules and regulations stifle self-control.

Zand tested his model of trust with 64 middle managers working in eight-person managerial problem-solving teams. Half of the teams were told to expect high trust, while the other half were told to expect low trust. As hypothesized, the high-trust groups significantly outperformed the low-trust groups. Thus, Zand concluded:

> The results indicate that it is useful to conceptualize trust as behavior that conveys appropriate information, permits mutuality of influence, encourages self-control, and avoids abuse of the vulnerability of others.[33]

Zand has given managers a behaviorally specific definition of trust.

From a practical standpoint, actions speak louder than words when it comes to trust. According to well-known management scholar George Odiorne: "The people we trust are the people whose behavior is predictable."[34] Zand's model tells managers exactly which behavior needs to be predictable if trust and teamwork are to prevail.

Cohesiveness

Cohesiveness is a process whereby "a sense of 'we-ness' emerges to transcend individual differences and motives."[35] Members of a cohesive group stick together. They are reluctant to leave the group. Cohesive group members stick together for one or both of the following reasons: (1) because they enjoy each others' company, or (2) because they need each other to accomplish a common goal. Accordingly, two types of group cohesiveness identified by sociologists are socio-emotional cohesiveness and instrumental cohesiveness.[36]

Socio-Emotional and Instrumental Cohesiveness.   **Socio-emotional cohesiveness** is a sense of togetherness that develops when individuals derive emotional satisfaction from group participation. Most general discussions of group cohesiveness are limited to this type. However, from the standpoint of getting

[33] Dale E. Zand, "Trust and Managerial Problem Solving," *Administrative Science Quarterly,* June 1972, p. 238.

[34] George S. Odiorne, "The Managerial Bait-and-Switch Game," *Personnel,* March 1986, p. 32. Also see Louis B. Barnes, "Managing the Paradox of Organizational Trust," *Harvard Business Review,* March–April 1981, pp. 107–16.

[35] William Foster Owen, "Metaphor Analysis of Cohesiveness in Small Discussion Groups," *Small Group Behavior,* August 1985, p. 416.

[36] This distinction is based on discussion in Aharon Tziner, "Differential Effects of Group Cohesiveness Types: A Clarifying Overview," *Social Behavior and Personality* 10, no. 2 (1982), pp. 227–39.

things accomplished in task groups, we cannot afford to ignore instrumental cohesiveness. **Instrumental cohesiveness** is a sense of togetherness that develops when group members are mutually dependent on one another because they believe they could not achieve the group's goal by acting separately. A feeling of we-ness is *instrumental* in achieving the common goal. Both types of cohesiveness are essential to productive teamwork.

Lessons from Group Cohesiveness Research.

After reviewing the relevant research literature, a Texas A&M University scholar concluded:

- Highly cohesive groups have greater member satisfaction than groups with low cohesiveness.
- High-cohesion groups are more effective than low-cohesion groups.
- Members of highly cohesive groups communicate more frequently and more positively than members of low-cohesion groups.[37]

In a second study of 125 groups with interaction problems, trained observers found lack of cohesiveness to be the number one problem. Leadership was the next greatest problem.[38]

The relationship between cohesiveness and performance remains ambiguous. Studies have found a mixture of positive, negative, and neutral relationships. This unexpected trend is partially due to researchers using inconsistent measures of cohesiveness.[39]

Putting Cohesiveness to Work.

Because cohesiveness has proved to be an important component of effective teamwork, managers need to take constructive steps to foster both types (see Table 10–7). A good example is Westinghouse's highly automated military radar electronics plant in College Station, Texas. Compared to their counterparts at a traditional factory in Baltimore, each of the Texas plant's 500 employees produces eight times more, at half the per-unit cost.

> The key, says Westinghouse, is not the robots but the people. Employees work in teams of 8 to 12. Members devise their own solutions to problems. Teams measure daily how each person's performance compares with that of other members and how the team's performance compares with the plant's. Joseph L. Johnson, 28, a robotics technician, says that is a big change from a previous hourly factory job where he cared only about "picking up my paycheck." Here, peer pressure "makes sure you get the job done."[40]

---

[37] See Owen, "Metaphor Analysis of Cohesiveness in Small Discussion Groups."

[38] Details may be found in Sanford B. Weinberg, Susan H. Rovinski, Laurie Weiman, and Michael Beitman, "Common Group Problems: A Field Study," *Small Group Behavior,* February 1981, pp. 81–92.

[39] For a summary of cohesiveness research, see Paul S. Goodman, Elizabeth Ravlin, and Marshall Schminke, "Understanding Groups in Organizations," in *Research in Organizational Behavior,* ed. L. L. Cummings and Barry M. Staw (Greenwich, Conn.: JAI Press, 1987), pp. 121–74.

[40] Gregory L. Miles, "The Plant of Tomorrow Is in Texas Today," *Business Week,* July 28, 1986, p. 76.

■ **TABLE 10–7** Steps Managers Can Take to Enhance the Two Types of Group Cohesiveness

Socio-Emotional Cohesiveness

Keep the group relatively small.

Strive for a favorable public image to increase the status and prestige of belonging.

Encourage interaction and cooperation.

Emphasize members' common characteristics and interests.

Point out environmental threats (e.g., competitors' achievements) to rally the group.

Instrumental Cohesiveness

Regularly update and clarify the group's goal(s).

Give every group member a vital "piece of the action."

Channel each group member's special talents toward the common goal(s).

Recognize and equitably reinforce every member's contributions.

Frequently remind group members they need each other to get the job done.

Self-selected work teams (in which people pick their own teammates) and off the job social events can stimulate socio-emotional cohesiveness. The fostering of socio-emotional cohesiveness needs to be balanced with instrumental cohesiveness. The latter can be encouraged by making sure everyone in the group recognizes and appreciates each member's vital contribution to the group goal. While balancing the two types of cohesiveness, managers need to remember that "groupthink" theory and research, discussed later, cautions against too much cohesiveness.

■ THREATS TO GROUP EFFECTIVENESS

An instructive counterpoint to the discussion of teamwork is a review of three problems that can erode and possibly destroy group effectiveness. Those problems are the Asch effect, groupthink, and social loafing. Because the first two problems relate to blind conformity, some brief background work is in order.

Very little would be accomplished in task groups and organizations without conformity to norms, role expectations, policies, and rules and regulations. After all, deadlines, commitments, and product/service quality standards have to be established and adhered to if the organization is to survive. But, as pointed out by management consultants Robert Blake and Jane Srygley Mouton, conformity is a two-edged sword:

> Social forces powerful enough to influence members to conform may influence them to perform at a very high level of quality and productivity. All too often, however, the pressure to conform stifles creativity, influencing members to cling to attitudes that may be out of touch with organizational needs and even out of kilter with the times.[41]

---

[41] Robert R. Blake and Jane Srygley Mouton, "Don't Let Group Norms Stifle Creativity," *Personnel*, August 1985, p. 29.

■ **FIGURE 10–8**   The Asch Experiment

A test of perception: Which of the lines on the comparison
card (on the right) is the same length as the standard line on the left?

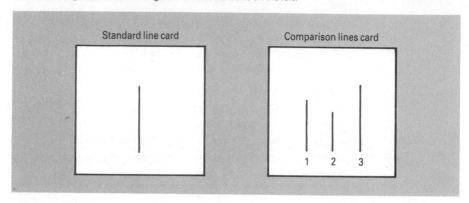

Moreover, excessive or blind conformity can stifle critical thinking, the last line of defense against unethical conduct. Almost daily accounts in the popular media of insider trading scandals, illegal dumping of hazardous wastes, and other unethical practices make it imperative that future managers understand the mechanics of blind conformity.

The Asch Effect

More than 30 years ago, social psychologist Solomon Asch conducted a series of laboratory experiments that revealed a negative side of group dynamics.[42] Under the guise of a "perception test," Asch had groups of seven to nine volunteer college students look at 12 pairs of cards such as the ones in Figure 10–8. The object was to identify the line that was the same length as the standard line. Each individual was told to announce his or her choice to the group. Since the differences among the comparison lines were obvious, there should have been unanimous agreement during each of the 12 rounds. But such was not the case.

A Minority of One.   All but one member of each group were Asch's confederates who agreed to systematically select the wrong line during seven of the rounds (the other five rounds were control rounds for comparison purposes). The remaining individual was the naive subject who was being tricked. Group pressure was created by having the naive subject in each group be among the last to announce his or her choice. Thirty-one subjects were tested. Asch's research question was: "How often would the naive subjects conform to a majority opinion that was obviously wrong?"

Only 20 percent of Asch's subjects remained entirely independent; 80 percent yielded to the pressures of group opinion at least once! Fifty-eight percent

---

[42] For additional information, see Solomon E. Asch, *Social Psychology* (Englewood Cliffs, N.J.: Prentice-Hall, 1952), chap. 16.

knuckled under to the "immoral majority" at least twice. Hence, the **Asch effect,** the distortion of individual judgment by a unanimous but incorrect opposition, was documented. (Do you ever turn your back on your better judgment by giving in to group pressure?)

A Managerial Perspective.   Asch's experiment has been widely replicated with mixed results. Both high and low degrees of blind conformity have been observed with various situations and subjects. Recent replications in Japan and Kuwait have demonstrated that the Asch effect is not unique to the United States.[43] But the point is not precisely how great the Asch effect is in a given situation or culture, but rather, managers committed to ethical conduct need to be concerned that the Asch effect exists. Even isolated instances of blind, unthinking conformity seriously threaten the effectiveness and integrity of work groups and committees. Functional conflict and assertiveness, as discussed in the following two chapters, can help employees respond appropriately when they find themselves being a minority of one.

Groupthink

Why did President Lyndon B. Johnson and his group of highly intelligent White House advisers make some very *unintelligent* decisions that escalated the Vietnam War? Those fateful decisions were made despite obvious warning signals, including stronger than expected resistance from the North Vietnamese and withering support at home and abroad. Systematic analysis of the decision-making processes underlying the war in Vietnam and other U.S. foreign policy fiascoes prompted Yale University's Irving Janis to coin the term *groupthink.* Modern managers can all too easily become victims of groupthink, just like President Johnson's staff, if they passively ignore the danger.

Definition and Symptoms of Groupthink.   Janis defines **groupthink** as "a mode of thinking that people engage in when they are deeply involved in a cohesive in-group, when members' strivings for unanimity override their motivation to realistically appraise alternative courses of action."[44] He adds, "Groupthink refers to a deterioration of mental efficiency, reality testing, and moral judgment that results from in-group pressures."[45] Unlike Asch's subjects, who were strangers to each other, members of groups victimized by groupthink are friendly, tightly knit, and cohesive.

The symptoms of groupthink listed in Figure 10–9 thrive in the sort of climate outlined in the following critique of corporate directors in the United States:

---

[43] See Timothy P. Williams and Shunya Sogon, "Group Composition and Conforming Behavior in Japanese Students," *Japanese Psychological Research* 26, no. 4 (1984), pp. 231–34; and Taha Amir, "The Asch Conformity Effect: A Study in Kuwait," *Social Behavior and Personality* 12, no. 2 (1984), pp. 187–90.

[44] Irving L. Janis, *Groupthink,* 2nd ed. (Boston: Houghton Mifflin, 1982), p. 9.

[45] Ibid.

■ **FIGURE 10–9**   Symptoms of Groupthink Lead to Defective Decision Making

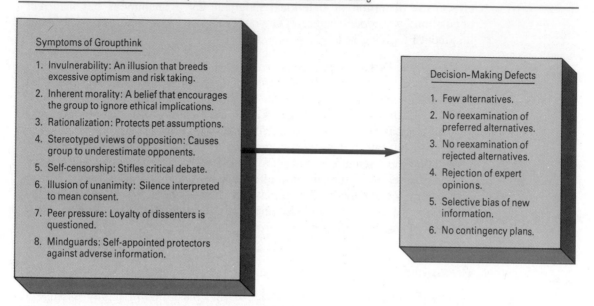

Symptoms of Groupthink

1. Invulnerability: An illusion that breeds excessive optimism and risk taking.
2. Inherent morality: A belief that encourages the group to ignore ethical implications.
3. Rationalization: Protects pet assumptions.
4. Stereotyped views of opposition: Causes group to underestimate opponents.
5. Self-censorship: Stifles critical debate.
6. Illusion of unanimity: Silence interpreted to mean consent.
7. Peer pressure: Loyalty of dissenters is questioned.
8. Mindguards: Self-appointed protectors against adverse information.

Decision-Making Defects

1. Few alternatives.
2. No reexamination of preferred alternatives.
3. No reexamination of rejected alternatives.
4. Rejection of expert opinions.
5. Selective bias of new information.
6. No contingency plans.

SOURCES: Symptoms adapted from Irving L. Janis, *Groupthink,* 2nd ed. (Boston: Houghton Mifflin, 1982), pp. 174–75. Defects excerpted from Gregory Moorhead, "Groupthink: Hypothesis in Need of Testing," *Group & Organization Studies,* December 1982, p. 434.

> Many directors simply don't rock the boat. "No one likes to be the skunk at the garden party," says [management consultant] Victor H. Palmieri. . . . "One does not make friends and influence people in the boardroom or elsewhere by raising hard questions that create embarrassment or discomfort for management."[46]

In short, policy- and decision-making groups can become so cohesive that strong-willed executives are able to gain unanimous support for poor decisions.

Groupthink Research and Prevention.   Laboratory studies using college students as subjects validate portions of Janis's groupthink concept. Specifically, it has been found that:

- Groups with a moderate amount of cohesiveness produce better decisions than low- or high-cohesive groups.
- Highly cohesive groups victimized by groupthink make the poorest decisions, despite high confidence in those decisions.[47]

Janis believes prevention is better than cure when dealing with groupthink. He recommends the following preventive measures:

---

[46] Laurie Baum, "The Job Nobody Wants," *Business Week,* September 8, 1986, p. 60.

[47] Details of this study may be found in Michael R. Callaway and James K. Esser, "Groupthink: Effects of Cohesiveness and Problem-Solving Procedures on Group Decision Making," *Social Behavior and Personality* 12, no. 2 (1984), pp. 157–64. Also see Carrie R. Leana, "A Partial Test of Janis's Groupthink Model: Effects of Group Cohesiveness and Leader Behavior on Defective Decision Making," *Journal of Management,* Spring 1985, pp. 5–17.

1. Each member of the group should be assigned the role of critical evaluator. This role involves actively voicing objections and doubts.

2. Top-level executives should not use policy committees to rubber-stamp decisions that have already been made.

3. Different groups with different leaders should explore the same policy questions.

4. Subgroup debates and outside experts should be used to introduce fresh perspectives.

5. Someone should be given the role of devil's advocate when discussing major alternatives. This person tries to uncover every conceivable negative factor.

6. Once a consensus has been reached, everyone should be encouraged to rethink their position to check for flaws.[48]

These anti-groupthink measures can help cohesive groups produce sound recommendations and decisions.

Social Loafing

Is group performance less than, equal to, or greater than the sum of its parts? Can three people, for example, working together accomplish less than, the same as, or more than they would working separately? An interesting study conducted more than a half century ago by a French agricultural engineer named Ringelmann found the answer to be "less than."[49] In a rope-pulling exercise, Ringelmann reportedly found that three people pulling together could achieve only two and a half times the average individual rate. Eight pullers achieved less than four times the individual rate. This tendency for individual effort to decline as group size increases has come to be called **social loafing.** Let us briefly analyze this threat to group effectiveness with an eye toward avoiding it.

Social Loafing Theory and Research. Among the theoretical explanations for the social loafing effect are: (1) equity of effort ("Everyone else is goofing off, so why shouldn't I?"), (2) loss of personal accountability ("I'm lost in the crowd, so who cares?"), (3) motivational loss due to the sharing of rewards ("Why should I work harder than the others when everyone gets the same reward?"), and (4) coordination loss as more people perform the task ("We're getting in each other's way").

Recent laboratory studies refined these theories by identifying situational factors that moderated the social loafing effect. Social loafing occurred when:

---

[48] Adapted from discussion in Janis, *Groupthink,* chap. 11.

[49] Based on discussion in Bibb Latane, Kipling Williams, and Stephen Harkins, "Many Hands Make Light the Work: The Causes and Consequences of Social Loafing," *Journal of Personality and Social Psychology,* June 1979, pp. 822–32; and David A. Kravitz and Barbara Martin, "Ringelmann Rediscovered: The Original Article," *Journal of Personality and Social Psychology,* May 1986, pp. 936–41.

- The task was perceived to be unimportant or simple.[50]
- Group members thought their individual output was not identifiable.[51]
- Group members expected their co-workers to loaf.[52]

Practical Implications.   These findings demonstrate the social loafing effect is not an inevitable part of group effort. Management can curb this threat to group effectiveness by making sure the task is challenging and perceived as important. Additionally, it is a good idea to hold group members personally accountable for identifiable portions of the group's task. (Recall the discussions of goal setting and management by objectives in Chapters 6 and 7.) Finally, positive expectations that everyone in the group will be working hard need to be fostered via trust and supportive leadership.

SUMMARY OF KEY CONCEPTS

A.   Sociologically, a *group* is defined as two or more freely interacting individuals who share collective norms and goals and have a common identity. There are formal (task-oriented) groups and informal (friendship-oriented) groups. Formal groups fulfill both organizational and individual functions.

B.   Groups mature through six stages of development: orientation, conflict and challenge, cohesion, delusion, disillusion, and acceptance. Interpersonal feedback increases and becomes more positive, specific, and credible as the group matures. Members of formal groups need to perform both task and maintenance roles if anything is to be accomplished.

C.   Laboratory simulation studies suggest decision-making groups should be limited to five or fewer members. Larger groups are appropriate when creativity, participation, or socialization are the main objectives. If majority votes are to be taken, odd-numbered groups are recommended, to avoid deadlocks. Judging from available research, there are no hard-and-fast rules for male-female representation in work groups. Results of the Israeli tank-crew study prompted researchers to conclude that it is better to concentrate high-ability personnel in separate groups. Within a contingency management perspective, however, there are situations in which it is advisable to spread high-ability people around.

D.   Three key components of teamwork are cooperation, trust, and cohesiveness. Cooperative integration of effort can be achieved via collaboration

---

[50] See Stephen J. Zaccaro, "Social Loafing: The Role of Task Attractiveness," *Personality and Social Psychology Bulletin,* March 1984, pp. 99–106; and Jeffrey M. Jackson and Kipling D. Williams, "Social Loafing on Difficult Tasks: Working Collectively Can Improve Performance," *Journal of Personality and Social Psychology,* October 1985, pp. 937–42.

[51] For complete details, see Kipling Williams, Stephen Harkins, and Bibb Latane, "Identifiability as a Deterrent to Social Loafing: Two Cheering Experiments," *Journal of Personality and Social Psychology,* February 1981, pp. 303–11.

[52] See Jeffrey M. Jackson and Stephen G. Harkins, "Equity in Effort: An Explanation of the Social Loafing Effect," *Journal of Personality and Social Psychology,* November 1985, pp. 1199–1206.

or coordination. Research demonstrates the value of cooperation versus competition.

E. *Trust*, defined as reciprocal faith in others' intentions and behavior, requires a cognitive leap. Zand's research-based model of trust pivots on the interaction of information, influence, and self-control.

F. Cohesive groups have a shared sense of togetherness or a "we" feeling. Socio-emotional cohesiveness involves emotional satisfaction. Instrumental cohesiveness involves goal-directed togetherness. Despite methodological inconsistencies, research is generally supportive of cohesiveness.

G. Three threats to group effectiveness are the Asch effect, groupthink, and social loafing. The first two involve blind conformity. The Asch effect occurs when a minority of one goes along with an incorrect majority. Groupthink plagues cohesive in-groups that shortchange moral judgment while putting too much emphasis on unanimity. Critical evaluators, outside expertise, and devil's advocates are among the preventive measures recommended by Irving Janis, who coined the term *groupthink*.

H. Social loafing involves the tendency for individual effort to decrease as group size increases. This problem can be contained if the task is challenging and important, individuals are held accountable for results, and group members expect everyone to work hard.

KEY TERMS

group	trust
formal group	cohesiveness
informal group	socio-emotional cohesiveness
task roles	instrumental cohesiveness
maintenance roles	Asch effect
collaboration	groupthink
coordination	social loafing

DISCUSSION QUESTIONS

1. Which of the following would qualify as a sociological group? A crowd watching a baseball game? One of the baseball teams? Explain.

2. What is your opinion about employees being friends with their co-workers (overlapping formal and informal groups)?

3. What is your personal experience with groups that failed to achieve the sixth stage of group development? At which stage did they stall?

4. Which roles do you prefer to play in work groups, task or maintenance? How could you do a better job in this regard?

5. When forming class project teams, would it be a good idea for the

instructor to concentrate the high-ability students or spread them around evenly among all the teams? Explain your rationale.

6.   Why would collaboration generally be harder to achieve than coordination?

7.   In your personal friendships, how do you come to trust someone? How fragile is that trust? Explain.

8.   Why should a group leader strive for both socio-emotional and instrumental cohesiveness?

9.   Have you ever been a victim of either the Asch effect or groupthink? Explain the circumstances.

10.   Have you observed any social loafing recently? What were the circumstances and what could be done to correct the problem?

BACK TO THE OPENING CASE

Now that you have read Chapter 10, you should be able to answer the following questions about Janet Long's Wilderness Lab experience:

1.   Did Janet Long's group satisfy the criteria of a sociological group?
2.   Using Zand's model as a conceptual framework, how did the group build trust? Explain.
3.   Why was social loafing probably not a problem during the wall-climbing exercise?

EXERCISE 10

Objectives

1. To give you firsthand experience with work group dynamics through a role-playing exercise.[53]
2. To develop your ability to evaluate group effectiveness.

Introduction

The Johnny Rocco Case

Johnny has a grim personal background. He is the third child in a family of seven. He has not seen his father for several years and his recollection is that his father used to come home drunk and beat up every member of the family; everyone ran when his father came staggering home.

---

[53] The case and instructions portions of this exercise excerpted from *Developing Management Skills* by David A. Whetten and Kim S. Cameron. Copyright © 1984 by Scott, Foresman and Company. Reprinted by permission.

His mother, according to Johnny, wasn't much better. She was irritable and unhappy and she always predicted that Johnny would come to no good end. Yet she worked when her health allowed her to do so in order to keep the family in food and clothing. She always decried the fact that she was not able to be the kind of mother she would like to be.

Johnny quit school in the seventh grade. He had great difficulty conforming to the school routine—he misbehaved often, was truant frequently, and fought with schoolmates. On several occasions he was picked up by the police and, along with members of his group, questioned during several investigations into cases of both petty and grand larceny. The police regarded him as "probably a bad one."

The juvenile officer of the court saw in Johnny some good qualities that no one else seemed to sense. Mr. O'Brien took it on himself to act as a "big brother" to Johnny. He had several long conversations with Johnny, during which he managed to penetrate to some degree Johnny's defensive shell. He represented to Johnny the first semblance of personal interest in his life. Through Mr. O'Brien's efforts, Johnny returned to school and obtained a high school diploma. Afterwards, Mr. O'Brien helped him obtain a job.

Now 20, Johnny is a stockroom clerk in one of the laboratories where you are employed. On the whole Johnny's performance has been acceptable, but there have been glaring exceptions. One involved a clear act of insubordination on a fairly unimportant matter. In another, Johnny was accused, on circumstantial grounds, of destroying some expensive equipment. Though the investigation is still open, it now appears the destruction was accidental.

Johnny's supervisor wants to keep him on for at least a trial period, but he wants "outside" advice as to the best way of helping Johnny grow into greater responsibility. Of course, much depends on how Johnny behaves in the next few months. Naturally, his supervisor must follow personnel policies that are accepted in the company as a whole. It is important to note that Johnny is not an attractive young man. He is rather weak and sickly, and he shows unmistakable signs of long years of social deprivation.

A committee is formed to decide the fate of Johnny Rocco. The chairperson of the meeting is Johnny's supervisor and should begin by assigning roles to the group members. These roles (shop steward [representing the union], head of production, Johnny's co-worker, director of personnel, and social worker who helped Johnny in the past) represent points of view the chairperson believes should be included in this meeting. (Johnny is not to be included.) Two observers should also be assigned. Thus, each group will have eight members.

Instructions

After roles have been assigned, each role player should complete the personal preference part of the work sheet, ranking from 1 to 11 the alternatives according to their appropriateness from the vantage point of his or her role.

Once the individual preferences have been determined, the chairperson should call the meeting to order. The following rules govern the meeting: (1) the group must reach a consensus ranking of the alternatives; (2) the group cannot use a statistical aggregation, or majority vote, decision-making process; (3) members should stay "in character" throughout the discussion. Treat this as a committee meeting consisting of members with different backgrounds, orientations, and interests who share a problem.

After the group has completed the assignment, the observers should conduct a discussion of the group process using the Group Effectiveness Questions as a guide. Group members should not look at these questions until after the group task has been completed.

Worksheet

PERSONAL PREFERENCE	GROUP DECISION	
_____	_____	Warn Johnny that at the next sign of trouble he will be fired.
_____	_____	Do nothing, as it is unclear if Johnny did anything wrong.
_____	_____	Create strict controls (do's and don'ts) for Johnny with immediate strong punishment for any misbehavior.
_____	_____	Give Johnny a great deal of warmth and personal attention and affection (overlooking his present behavior) so he can learn to depend on others.
_____	_____	Fire him. It's not worth the time and effort spent for such a low-level position.
_____	_____	Talk over the problem with Johnny in an understanding way so he can learn to ask others for help in solving his problems.
_____	_____	Give Johnny a well-structured schedule of daily activities with immediate and unpleasant consequences for not adhering to the schedule.
_____	_____	Do nothing now, but watch him carefully and provide immediate punishment for any future behavior.
_____	_____	Treat Johnny the same as everyone else, but provide an orderly routine so he can learn to stand on his own two feet.
_____	_____	Call Johnny in and logically discuss the problem with him and ask what you can do to help him.
_____	_____	Do nothing now, but watch him so you can reward him the next time he does something good.

Group Effectiveness Questions

A. Referring to Table 10–3, what task roles were performed? By whom?

B. What maintenance roles were performed? By whom?

C. Were any important task or maintenance roles ignored? Which?

D. Was a climate of trust established? Did the resulting trust or lack of trust affect the group's performance?

E. Was there any evidence of the Asch effect, groupthink, or social loafing? Explain.

Questions for Consideration/Class Discussion

1. Did your committee do a good job? Explain.
2. What, if anything, should have been done differently?
3. How much similarity in rankings is there among the different groups in your class? What group dynamics apparently were responsible for any variations in rankings?

Chapter **11**

Power, Mentoring, Politics, and Conflict

LEARNING OBJECTIVES

When you finish studying the material in this chapter, you should be able to:

- Distinguish between socialized and personalized power.
- Identify and briefly describe French and Raven's five bases of power.
- Describe the two basic functions of mentoring.
- Explain why informal mentoring may be superior to formal mentoring programs.
- Define organizational politics and explain what triggers it.
- Explain the role of coalitions in organizational politics.
- List at least six antecedents of conflict.
- Describe five conflict-handling styles and explain why a contingency approach to managing conflict is in order.

Kroger's Turnaround Ace Gets the Ax!

Demanding, decisive—and in a hurry. Those traits powered William Kagler's rapid advance at Kroger Co., from the job of spokesman to president and the chairman's heir apparent.

But the hard-driving ambition that marked his rise ultimately triggered his demise. Late last year, Mr. Kagler was abruptly fired by chairman Lyle Everingham—and it was style more than substance that caused his ouster.

"My behavior, over time," Mr. Kagler says slowly, was "an experience he didn't want to endure any longer. . . ."

Whatever the cause, a bad fit between boss and heir apparent often spells turmoil in the office and can lead to the crown prince being suddenly dethroned. Mr. Kagler's career at Kroger, the $17 billion Cincinnati-based supermarket company, illustrates some classic elements of such a rise and fall.

Mr. Kagler, now 54 years old, was always openly driven—labeled aggressive and confident by his admirers, heavy-handed and arrogant by his critics. His urgency, he says, stemmed in part from the death of his father at age 53, before he had time to enjoy retirement, and also from a "health scare" his wife went through more recently. Mr. Kagler says he renewed a vow to reach the chief executive's office—and make his mark there—and exit with time to spare.

On the ascent, Mr. Kagler's eager insistence paid off. He won a reputation in the supermarket industry for his negotiating style with unions, which yielded big concessions.

He traveled widely, returning with inspirations he pushed the stores to adopt, such as supermarket sushi bars and stands selling hand-dipped ice cream. Once an adviser to a U.S. Senate candidate, Mr. Kagler was very visible at Kroger, appearing up to his last day at the firm in videotaped speeches he circulated to employees.

In contrast, Kroger's chairman, Mr. Everingham, is a quiet, more private man, whose modest manner reflects in part his beginnings as a Kroger produce clerk. Opting deliberately for an aggressive successor, he chose Mr. Kagler in early 1983.

Some stock analysts and industry executives saw Mr. Kagler's firebrand manner as serving a purpose for the company and the milder Mr. Everingham in planning and carrying out a recent restructuring. His ouster came after most of the staff cuts and store closings were completed. . . .

"I've never been able to walk past anything I believed to be wrong without saying something," Mr. Kagler says. "Some people might say, 'Yeah, but you think too much is wrong.' Maybe I could have been more diplomatic. But, no, I wouldn't have done anything differently."

Impatient with the Boss

As president, Mr. Kagler rarely hesitated. He was impatient with himself and everyone else—including Mr. Everingham. For instance, he thought Mr. Everingham was too slow in disposing of Kroger's faltering

SupeRx drugstore division. And he let everyone know it—despite the fact that he had no responsibility for the division.

Mr. Kagler would burst out of his office, commenting sarcastically to secretaries about colleagues he considered slow-moving—including Mr. Everingham. At first, what he did was "strategic—to prod Everingham," says one official familiar with the situation. "Later, it was (from) sheer frustration."

Mr. Kagler says he did push hard, but adds that "there was no argument (inside Kroger) that decisions had to be made." His approach to analyzing and diagnosing the company's problems, he says, helped Kroger halt a six-quarter earnings slide, turn around its television advertising strategy, and make other innovations.

During the six months preceding his firing, Mr. Kagler recalls colleagues saying, "Whoa, slow down, you're going to run out of gas." Instead, he began approaching board members privately, prodding them about a timetable for his rise to chief executive. When word reached Mr. Everingham, the chairman quickly did his own canvass of directors and got their approval to fire his president. . . .

For Discussion

What was the real reason behind the firing of Kagler?

SOURCE: Excerpted from Jolie Solomon, "Heirs Apparent to Chief Executives Often Trip over Prospect of Power." Reprinted by permission of *The Wall Street Journal,* Dow Jones & Company, Inc., March 24, 1987. All rights reserved.

■ Additional discussion questions linking this case with the following material appear at the end of this chapter.

How do you get others to carry out your wishes? Do you simply tell them what to do? Or do you prefer a less direct approach such as promising to return the favor? Whatever approach you use, the heart of the issue is *social influence*. A large measure of social interaction involves attempts to influence others, including parents, bosses, co-workers, spouses, teachers, and children. Managers who understand subtle yet powerful social influence tactics enjoy a competitive advantage relative to achieving their organizational and career goals. As a backdrop for this chapter and the following chapters on communication and leadership, we will examine recent research evidence on the tactics organizational members typically use to get their own way at work.

Researcher David Kipnis and his colleagues asked 165 administrative employees who were attending evening graduate school to describe how they managed to get either their bosses, co-workers, or subordinates to do what they wanted them to do.[1] From the resulting 370 influence tactics, the researchers compiled a 58-item questionnaire. After a second sample of 754 employed graduate students completed the questionnaire, relative to how they generally influenced

---

[1] See David Kipnis, Stuart M. Schmidt, and Ian Wilkinson, "Intraorganizational Influence Tactics: Explorations in Getting One's Way," *Journal of Applied Psychology,* August 1980, pp. 440–52.

■ **TABLE 11–1** Eight Generic Influence Tactics: How Employees Get Their Own Way

	Tactic	Description
Tactics used to influence *superiors*, *peers*, and *subordinates*	Assertiveness	Simply ordering or demanding compliance. Setting deadlines, bawling someone out, or checking up on them.
	Sanctions	Promising or preventing salary increases. Threatening to fire someone or give them a poor performance evaluation.
	Ingratiation	Making someone feel important, acting humbly, or being friendly to someone before asking them for something.
	Rationality	Backing up a request with a detailed plan, supporting information, logic, or written documentation.
Tactics used to influence only *superiors*	Exchange of benefits	Promising to return a favor. Reminding someone of a past favor. Offering to make a personal sacrifice.
	Blocking	Seeking compliance by threatening to contact an outside agency, engaging in a work slowdown, or ceasing work.
	Upward appeal	Seeking formal or informal support from higher-ups when making a request.
Tactic used to influence only *subordinates*	Coalitions	Backing up a request with the support of peers or subordinates. Making a request at a meeting called for that purpose.

SOURCE: Adapted from discussion in David Kipnis, Stuart M. Schmidt, and Ian Wilkinson, "Intraorganizational Influence Tactics: Explorations in Getting One's Way," *Journal of Applied Psychology*, August 1980, pp. 440–52.

their co-workers, the Kipnis team factor analyzed the results into eight organizational influence tactics (see Table 11–1). Four of the tactics—assertiveness, sanctions, ingratiation, and rationality—reportedly were used to influence co-workers at all levels. Exchange of benefits, blocking, and upward appeal were used to influence only the subjects' superiors. The eighth influence tactic, coalitions, was directed at subordinates only. (A broader interpretation of coalitions is discussed later relative to organizational politics.) The various approaches can be considered generic influence tactics because they characterize social behavior in virtually all organizations. Notably, there was no gender effect. In other words, no significant difference was found between the influence tactics used either by or with men and women. A study of 125 male and 59 female middle-level managers in Israel similarly demonstrated that men and women used the same influence tactics.[2]

Regarding *upward* influence, employees in a recent study varied their influence tactics to suit the leadership style of their boss. Blocking, upward appeal, and ingratiation tended to be used most often to influence authoritarian managers.

---

[2] See Dafna N. Izraeli, "Sex Effects in the Evaluation of Influence Tactics," *Journal of Occupational Behaviour*, January 1987, pp. 79–86.

Rationality was used to influence participative managers.[3] These results suggest a contingency approach to interpersonal influence.

By demonstrating the complexity and variety of social influence, the foregoing research findings whet our appetite to learn more about how today's managers can and do get things done with and through others. The purpose of this chapter, consequently, is to enhance your understanding of three organizational influence processes: power, politics, and conflict resolution. Mentoring is discussed as an important and interesting empowerment strategy.

■ SOCIAL POWER

The term *power* evokes mixed and often passionate reactions. Citing recent instances of government corruption and corporate misconduct, many observers view power as a sinister force. To these critics, Lord Acton's time-honored statement that "power corrupts and absolute power corrupts absolutely" is as true as ever. However, OB specialists remind us that, like it or not, power is a fact of life in modern organizations. According to one management scholar:

> Power must be used because managers must influence those they depend on. Power also is crucial in the development of managers' self-confidence and willingness to support subordinates. From this perspective, power should be accepted as a natural part of any organization. Managers should recognize and develop their own power to coordinate and support the work of subordinates; it is powerlessness, not power, that undermines organizational effectiveness.[4]

Thus, power is a necessary and generally positive force in organizations. As the term is used here, **social power** is defined as "the ability to marshal the human, informational, and material resources to get something done."[5]

Dimensions of Power

While power may be an elusive concept to the casual observer, social scientists view power as having reasonably clear dimensions. Three dimensions of power that deserve our attention are: (1) the distinction between power and authority, (2) socialized versus personalized power, and (3) the five bases of power.

Power and Authority.   In our definition of power, emphasis must be placed on the word *ability* because it sets power apart from the concept of authority. **Authority** is the "right" or the "obligation" to seek compliance; power is the "demonstrated ability" to achieve compliance. As illustrated in Figure

---

[3] Details of this study are provided in Mahfooz A. Ansari and Alka Kapoor, "Organizational Context and Upward Influence Tactics," *Organizational Behavior and Human Decision Processes,* August 1987, pp. 39–49.

[4] Dean Tjosvold, "The Dynamics of Positive Power," *Training and Development Journal,* June 1984, p. 72.

[5] Morgan W. McCall, Jr., *Power, Influence, and Authority: The Hazards of Carrying a Sword,* Technical Report No. 10 (Greensboro, N.C.: Center for Creative Leadership, 1978), p. 5.

■ **FIGURE 11–1** Power and Authority Are Not Necessarily the Same Thing

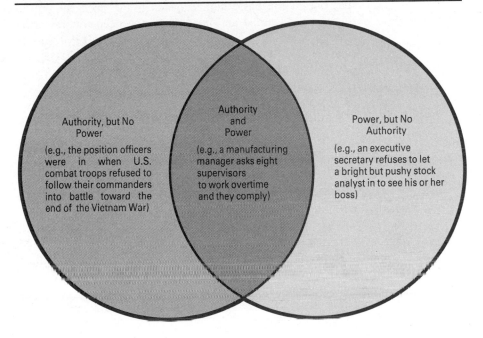

Authority, but No Power

(e.g., the position officers were in when U.S. combat troops refused to follow their commanders into battle toward the end of the Vietnam War)

Authority and Power

(e.g., a manufacturing manager asks eight supervisors to work overtime and they comply)

Power, but No Authority

(e.g., an executive secretary refuses to let a bright but pushy stock analyst in to see his or her boss)

11–1, three classic situations can arise because power and authority often do not overlap. Effective managers are able to back up their authority with power (the middle portion of Figure 11–1).

This distinction between power and authority may appear to be a simple one, but those who fail to appreciate the difference can unwittingly commit career suicide. For instance, nonmanagerial employees who have no official authority may wield a great deal of power because of who or what they know. Staff assistants, who have no real authority in the formal chain of command, often are very powerful. For example:

> At Intel Corp., Jean C. Jones, executive secretary to Chairman Gordon E. Moore, is curator of Intel's high-tech museum. But most of her influence—as well as the power most executive assistants wield—derives from many of those old-fashioned secretarial duties. Each week, she decides how much of the 30-in. stack of mail her boss will see and how many of the 125 telephone calls will gain his ear. Jones deflects 80% of those calls, weeding out the insurance salesmen and the stockbrokers. By scheduling Moore's calendar, she helps determine who gets to see the boss in person.[6]

Part of the organizational socialization process discussed in Chapter 9 involves teaching newcomers where the real power lies.

---

[6] Laurie Baum and John A. Byrne, "Executive Secretary: A New Rung on the Corporate Ladder," *Business Week*, April 21, 1986, p. 74.

Two Types of Power.   Behavioral scientists such as David McClelland contend that one of the basic human needs is the need for power (n Pwr). Because this need is learned and not innate, the need for power has been extensively studied. The Thematic Apperception Test (TAT), discussed in Chapter 5 as a tool for measuring need for achievement (n Ach), also is used to measure need for power. Historically, need for power was scored when subjects interpreted TAT pictures in terms of one person attempting to influence, convince, persuade, or control another. More recently, however, researchers have drawn a distinction between **socialized power** and **personalized power.**

> There are two subscales or "faces" in n Pwr. One face is termed "socialized" (s Pwr) and is scored in the Thematic Apperception Test (TAT) as "plans, self-doubts, mixed outcomes and concerns for others, . . ." while the second face is "personalized" power (p Pwr), in which expressions of power for the sake of personal aggrandizement become paramount.[7]

This distinction between socialized and personalized power helps explain why power has a negative connotation for many people. Managers and others who pursue personalized power for their own selfish ends give power a bad name. But managers like Dorothy Terrell, one of the most successful black female managers in America, exercise power effectively and responsibly (see Table 11–2). She does so by emphasizing socialized power and de-emphasizing personalized power.

Five Bases of Power.   A popular classification scheme for social power traces back 30 years to the work of John French and Bertram Raven. They proposed

■ **TABLE 11–2**   Dorothy Terrell: A Fast-Rising Manager Who Knows How to Handle Power

> As Dorothy Terrell approached the front door of the Digital Equipment Corporation plant in Boston three years ago, she was assailed by doubt. It was a hot July day, and she was about to start her first week as plant manager of a facility that manufactures keyboards for digital computers.
>
> Terrell admits she was very nervous. Her new responsibilities would include managing 375 workers on a three-shift operation and controlling a budget of $35 million. She made elaborate plans for how she would conduct her first week on the job. But first and foremost there was a meeting with all of her staff and plant employees, which had been planned for her without her knowledge, and she wasn't quite sure what she wanted to say. As she made her way to the plant cafeteria, where the workers were assembled, waiting for Terrell, she mustered the confidence to walk in and simply smile.
>
> "I said 'Good afternoon. My name is Dorothy Terrell and I'm the new plant manager here in Boston.'"
>
> Suddenly everyone in the cafeteria began clapping loudly and cheering their new boss.
>
> "It was unbelievable! That was the beginning of a love affair. I felt accepted by the plant. That really helped me."

[7] Leonard H. Chusmir, "Personalized vs. Socialized Power Needs among Working Women and Men," *Human Relations,* February 1986, p. 149.

■ **TABLE 11–2** *(concluded)*

Dorothy Terrell's love affair with the Boston plant began in July 1984 and has continued to grow. Her excellent performance at the Digital Equipment Corporation plant had put her in line to climb the corporate ladder quickly at the minicomputer company with annual sales exceeding $7 billion.

Terrell signed on with Digital almost eleven years ago to manage employee relations and be director of training at its Westminster, Mass., office. Terrell's advancement was swift. She moved from her employee relations job to plant personnel manager and on to group manager of personnel before being selected as the manager of Digital's Boston plant, where her annual salary is close to six figures. Her position makes Terrell, at 41, one of the most powerful women in corporate America.

"I have profit-loss responsibility for this plant. We produce a quality keyboard at competitive cost. But I have to decide what it will take to produce that keyboard in terms of money, people, space and materials. That's a major responsibility that could easily impact on the corporation's revenues."

The staff who must report to her includes the plant comptroller, personnel manager, operations manager, engineering and technology manager and the information systems and new products manager.

"How powerful am I? I'm very powerful. But power is a word that took me a little time to get comfortable with. I always thought of power as being negative, something other people had and used to oppress others. I've since understood that's not necessarily the case. You can be powerful and share what makes you powerful. I can make things happen and *that* for me is power," she says.

Dorothy Terrell uses that power on the plant floor, where she encourages her employees to manufacture the best product they can.

"I like people. I value them to the extent that I'll push them to do things that stretch them. I really believe in having employees use their brains as well as their hands," says Terrell, who regularly puts in 12-hour days at the plant.

Terrell also asks staff members and plant employees for their input. She favors a style of management that encourages participation and says she has no problem admitting she doesn't know everything.

"It's important for me to hear what people have to say. It's not important, however, for me to agree with what people have to say," explains Terrell, who describes herself as a tough but fair manager. . . .

She admits that although she wields a great deal of power in her job, there are also lots of pressures, the kind of pressures that could easily derail the career of a weak manager. "What we build here has got to be of a certain quality. Something could happen with a keyboard we sell that might endanger somebody. *That's* pressure. There are people in this plant who look to me to make sure their jobs are around. You're not just feeding them, you're feeding families and a community. *That's* a lot of pressure."

. . . While Digital has been good to Terrell, she has also made her mark on the company by becoming an important role model in the community and being a popular spokesperson, especially in the black community. "I feel a responsibility to help others. I didn't get where I am by myself," she says.

SOURCE: Excerpted from Lloyd Gite, "Dorothy Terrell," *Black Enterprise,* April 1987, pp. 46–48. Copyright The Earl G. Graves Publishing Co., Inc., 130 Fifth Avenue, New York, NY 10011. All rights reserved.

that power arises from five different bases: reward power, coercive power, legitimate power, expert power, and referent power.[8] Each involves a different approach to influencing others.

- *Reward power:* A manager has **reward power** to the extent that he or she obtains compliance by promising or granting rewards. On-the-job behavior modification, for example, relies heavily on reward power.
- *Coercive power:* Threats of punishment and actual punishment give an individual **coercive power.** A sales manager who threatens to fire any salesperson who uses a company car for family vacations is relying on coercive power.
- *Legitimate power:* This base of power is anchored to one's formal position or authority. Thus, individuals who obtain compliance primarily because of their formal authority to make decisions have **legitimate power** (see Table 11–3). Legitimate power may express itself in either a positive or negative manner in managing people. Positive legitimate power focuses constructively on job performance. Negative legitimate power tends to be threatening and demeaning to those being influenced. Its main purpose is to build the power holder's ego.
- *Expert power:* Valued knowledge or information gives an individual **expert power** over those who need such knowledge or information. The power of supervisors is enhanced because they know about work schedules and assignments before their subordinates do.
- *Referent power:* Also called charisma, **referent power** comes into play when one's personality becomes the reason for compliance. Role models have referent power over those who identify closely with them.

To further your understanding of these five bases of power and to assess your self-perceived power, please take a moment to complete the questionnaire in Table 11–4. Think of your present job or your most recent job when responding to the various items. Arbitrary norms for each of the five bases of power are: 3–6 = Weak power base; 7–11 = Moderate power base; 12–15 = Strong power base. How is your power profile?

Recent Research Insights about Social Power

In one study, a sample of 94 male and 84 female nonmanagerial and professional employees in Denver, Colorado, completed TAT tests. The researchers found that the male and female employees had similar needs for power (n Pwr) and personalized power (p Pwr). But the females had a significantly higher need for socialized power (s Pwr) than did their male counterparts.[9]

---

[8] See John R. P. French and Bertram Raven, "The Bases of Social Power," in *Studies in Social Power,* ed. Dorwin Cartwright (Ann Arbor: University of Michigan Press, 1959), pp. 150–67.

[9] Details may be found in Chusmir, "Personalized vs. Socialized Power Needs among Working Women and Men," pp. 149–59. For a review of research on individual differences in the need for power, see Robert J. House, "Power and Personality in Complex Organizations," in *Research in Organizational Behavior,* ed. Barry M. Staw and L. L. Cummings (Greenwich, Conn.: JAI Press, 1988), pp. 305–57.

■ **TABLE 11-3**   The "Power of the Pencil" in International Business

Masan, South Korea—Back home in New Jersey, Joseph Antonini wouldn't rate more than a glance and a smile of greeting while on a factory tour. So Mr. Antonini is clearly embarrassed by what is happening here.

As he rides up to the Hanil Synthetic Fiber Industrial Co. plant, security guards straighten and bark a word that sounds like "choof." Workers spring to open Mr. Antonini's door, and dozens of applauding Hanil office workers crowd around, hailing the startled visitor. Mr. Antonini and his associate, Ronald L. Buch, are handed large floral displays.

"Can you beat that?" asks Mr. Antonini, the president of K mart Apparel Corp.

Gulping Potent Liquor

Lots of people are trying. A few days earlier, Mr. Antonini survived a 21-course banquet in his honor at a Chinese clothing factory. Then there was the *mao-tai* party, an affair of fortitude at which toasts were continually exchanged in gulped servings of the potent Chinese liquor. "I tasted that for days," Mr. Antonini says.

This is an Asian buying trip. It sounds like great fun, but it is serious business for the 30 or so buyers of K mart Apparel, the clothing arm of the U.S. discount chain. The buyers, often with their bosses in tow, scour a dozen Asian nations for . . . fall merchandise worth hundreds of millions of dollars. They look for bargains, but they also use the trip to make contacts for new sources of supply and to learn what the competition is doing.

It is a demanding, ritualized process of negotiating to the third decimal point by day, cementing deals, and then renewing good will at night in an atmosphere of luxury, power, and privilege.

All for "The Pencil"

"It can go to your head," notes Mr. Antonini, a 20-year K mart veteran who remembers living in one-room apartments as a young store manager. Now he and his buyers fly first-class, stay only in luxury hotels, and drive around Hong Kong in Mercedes-Benz limousines. In Hong Kong a merchandise source treats Mr. Antonini to a $400 bottle of wine at dinner. And in Japan, a source serves him rich meals of Kobe beef at $200 a plate.

Indeed, those with "the pencil"—the buyers' term for the authority to order merchandise—are treated royally. "But once you lose the pencil, it's over," says the wife of one K mart executive. "You've got to understand it's for the pencil, not you."

SOURCE: Excerpted from Steve Weiner, "K mart Apparel Buyers Hopscotch the Orient to Find Quality Goods." Reprinted by permission of *The Wall Street Journal,* Dow Jones & Company, Inc., March 19, 1985. All rights reserved.

This bodes well for today's work organizations where women are playing an ever greater administrative role.

A 1985 reanalysis of 18 field studies that measured French and Raven's five bases of power uncovered "severe methodological shortcomings."[10] After correcting for these problems, the researchers identified the following relation-

---

[10] Philip M. Podsakoff and Chester A. Schriesheim, "Field Studies of French and Raven's Bases of Power: Critique, Reanalysis, and Suggestions for Future Research," *Psychological Bulletin,* May 1985, p. 388.

■ **TABLE 11–4**   What Is Your Self-Perceived Power?

Instructions: Score your various bases of power for your present (or former) job, using the following scale:

1 = Strongly disagree   4 = Agree
2 = Disagree   5 = Strongly agree
3 = Slightly agree

Reward power score = _____
1. I can reward persons at lower levels. _____
2. My review actions affect the rewards gained at lower levels. _____
3. Based on my decisions, lower level personnel may receive a bonus. _____

Coercive power score = _____
1. I can punish employees at lower levels. _____
2. My work is a check on lower-level employees. _____
3. My diligence reduces error. _____

Legitimate power score = _____
1. My position gives me a great deal of authority. _____
2. The decisions made at my level are of critical importance. _____
3. Employees look to me for guidance. _____

Expert power score = _____
1. I am an expert in this job. _____
2. My ability gives me an advantage in this job. _____
3. Given some time, I could improve the methods used on this job. _____

Referent power score = _____
1. I attempt to set a good example for other employees. _____
2. My personality allows me to work well in this job. _____
3. My fellow employees look to me as their informal leader. _____

SOURCE: Adapted and excerpted in part from Duncan L. Dieterly and Benjamin Schneider, "The Effect of Organizational Environment on Perceived Power and Climate: A Laboratory Study," *Organizational Behavior and Human Performance,* June 1974, pp. 316–37.

ships between power bases and work outcomes such as job performance, job satisfaction, and turnover:

- Expert and referent power had a generally positive impact.
- Reward and legitimate power had a slightly positive impact.
- Coercive power had a slightly negative impact.

Do situational factors affect the use of power? According to a laboratory study involving 90 Canadian business students, the answer is yes. Superiors used their power most constructively when working *cooperatively* with their subordinates. In contrast, superiors in both competitive and individual achievement situations did not use their power to enhance their subordinates' performance.[11]

The Effective and Responsible Management of Power

Responsible managers strive for socialized power while avoiding personalized power. This, in addition to being aware of the relative strengths of their bases

[11] See Dean Tjosvold, "Power and Social Context in Superior-Subordinate Interaction," *Organizational Behavior and Human Decision Processes,* June 1985, pp. 281–93.

■ **FIGURE 11–2**   Bases of Power and Behavior Change

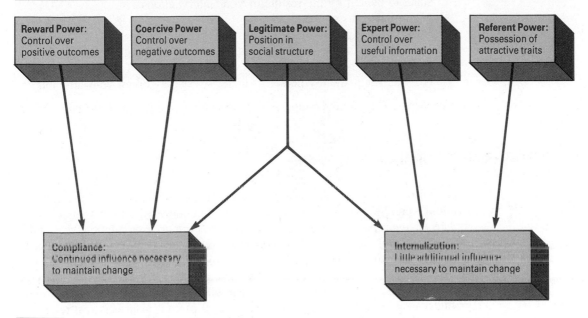

SOURCE: From *Group Effectiveness in Organizations* by Linda N. Jewell and Joseph Reitz. Copyright © 1981 by Scott, Foresman and Company. Reprinted by permission.

of power, can help managers use their power effectively. It is important to recognize, however, that the various power bases tend to produce two very different modes of behavior change. As illustrated in Figure 11–2, reward, coercive, and negative legitimate power tend to produce *compliance*. On the other hand, positive legitimate, expert, and referent power tend to foster *internalization*. Internalization is superior to compliance because it is driven by internal or intrinsic motivation. Employees who merely comply require frequent "jolts" of power from the boss to keep them headed in a productive direction. Those who internalize the task at hand tend to become self-starters who do not require close supervision.

According to the research cited above, expert and referent power have the greatest potential for improving job performance and satisfaction and reducing turnover. Formal education, training, and self-development can build a manager's expert power. At the same time, one's referent power base can be strengthened by adhering to the following practical guidelines offered by a trio of management consultants:

- Build your relationship on shared interests, motivations, and goals.
- Respect different interests, goals, and values, and do not attack or disdain another person's style.
- Use reward power and positive reinforcement.
- Invite reciprocal influence to show that you respect and want the perceptions, opinions, and information others have to offer.

- Give your expertise and share information, especially when you don't stand to benefit by the results of your interventions.
- Minimize status concerns.
- Become an expert communicator.
- Get to know the informal political structure of the organization.
- Get to know how people react to stress and crisis. Trying to negotiate requests when another person is under stress may doom your attempts.[12]

These steps will foster the cooperative teamwork associated with the supportive use of power.

■ EMPOWERMENT THROUGH MENTORING

Any discussion of social power in modern organizations would be incomplete without a parallel examination of mentoring. Countless aspiring managers have bolstered their power bases through personal one-to-one relationships with powerful senior managers. A five-year study of 3,600 Honeywell managers recently documented the importance of personal relationships in management development. The research question was simply: "How do managers learn to manage?" The Honeywell managers learned 50 percent of what they knew about managing from direct job experience, 30 percent from personal relationships, and 20 percent from formal training.[13] Mentoring was an integral part of the learning attributed to personal relationships.

Mentoring: Definition, Functions, and Phases

Definitions of the terms *mentoring* and *mentor* are many and varied. For present purposes, **mentoring** is defined as the process of forming and maintaining an intensive and lasting developmental relationship between a senior person (the mentor) and a junior person (the protégé, if male; or protégée, if female). The modern word *mentor* derives from Mentor, the name of a wise and trusted counselor in Greek mythology. Terms typically used in connection with mentoring are *teacher, coach, godfather,* and *sponsor.* Although mentoring often occurs naturally, it sometimes is actively managed as part of career development or management succession programs. Consider the mentoring programs at Johnson & Johnson, Pacific Bell, and Bell Laboratories, for example.

A Johnson & Johnson Co. unit, Ortho Pharmaceutical Corp., assigns mentors to the college graduates it hires. . . . At Pacific Bell, a unit of Pacific Telesis Group, the firm's 75 summer management interns, hired after their junior year in college, get mentors; the mentors later help decide whether the interns will

---

[12] Robert C. Benfari, Harry E. Wilkinson, and Charles D. Orth, "The Effective Use of Power," *Business Horizons,* May–June 1986, p. 15. Contingency recommendations for using the different sources of power also are provided by I. Thomas Sheppard, "The 'Pow' in Power," *The Executive Female,* Special Issue #1, 1986, pp. 29–31.

[13] Additional details may be found in Ron Zemke, "The Honeywell Studies: How Managers Learn to Manage," *Training,* August 1985, pp. 46–51.

■ **FIGURE 11–3**   The Career and Psychosocial Functions of Mentoring

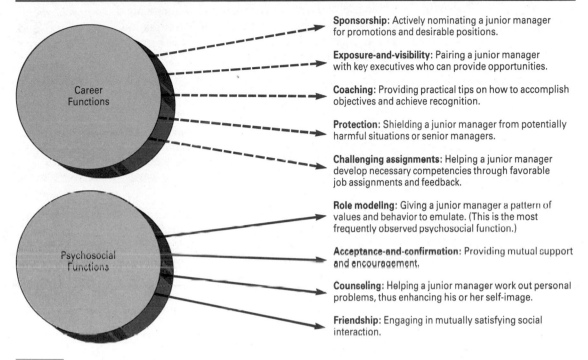

Sponsorship: Actively nominating a junior manager for promotions and desirable positions.

Exposure-and-visibility: Pairing a junior manager with key executives who can provide opportunities.

Coaching: Providing practical tips on how to accomplish objectives and achieve recognition.

Protection: Shielding a junior manager from potentially harmful situations or senior managers.

Challenging assignments: Helping a junior manager develop necessary competencies through favorable job assignments and feedback.

Role modeling: Giving a junior manager a pattern of values and behavior to emulate. (This is the most frequently observed psychosocial function.)

Acceptance-and-confirmation: Providing mutual support and encouragement.

Counseling: Helping a junior manager work out personal problems, thus enhancing his or her self-image.

Friendship: Engaging in mutually satisfying social interaction.

SOURCE: Adapted from discussion in Kathy E. Kram, *Mentoring at Work: Developmental Relationships in Organizational Life* (Glenview, Ill., Scott, Foresman, 1985), pp. 22–39.

be offered permanent jobs. The system is credited with drawing better-quality new hires.

AT&T Bell Laboratories gives new employees "technical mentors" to help them learn their jobs, and assigns advisors to women and minority hires.[14]

Mentoring specialists emphasize that "mentor programs offer things other career development programs don't—primarily individual attention."[15]

Functions of Mentoring.   Kathy Kram, a Boston University researcher, conducted in-depth interviews with both members of 18 pairs of senior and junior managers. Each pair exhibited a significant developmental relationship. All the subjects worked for a large public utility in the northeastern United States. While there were seven female protégées, only one of the mentors was female.[16] As a by-product of this study, Kram identified two general functions—career and psychosocial—of the mentoring process (see Figure 11–3). Five *career*

---

[14] "Labor Letter: A Special News Report on People and Their Jobs in Offices, Fields and Factories," *The Wall Street Journal*, February 23, 1988, p. 1.

[15] Beverly J. Bernstein and Beverly L. Kaye, "Teacher, Tutor, Colleague, Coach," *Personnel Journal*, November 1986, p. 44.

[16] See Kathy E. Kram, "Phases of the Mentor Relationship," *Academy of Management Journal*, December 1983, pp. 608–25.

functions that enhanced career development were sponsorship, exposure-and-visibility, coaching, protection, and challenging assignments. Four *psychosocial functions* were role modeling, acceptance-and-confirmation, counseling, and friendship. The psychosocial functions clarified the participants' identity and enhanced their feelings of competence.

Both members of the mentoring relationship can benefit from these career and psychosocial functions. Mentoring is not strictly a top-down proposition, as many mistakenly believe. According to Kram:

> By providing a range of career and psychosocial functions, the senior colleague gains recognition and respect from peers and superiors for developing young talent, receives support from the junior colleague who seeks counsel, and experiences satisfaction by helping a less experienced adult navigate effectively in the world of work.[17]

Phases of Mentoring.   In addition to identifying the functions of mentoring, Kram's research revealed four phases of the mentoring process: (1) initiation, (2) cultivation, (3) separation, and (4) redefinition. As indicated in Table 11–5, the phases involve *variable* rather than fixed time periods. Telltale turning points signal the evolution from one phase to the next. For example, when a junior manager begins to resist guidance and strives to work more autonomously, the separation phase begins. The mentoring relationships in Kram's sample lasted an average of five years.[18]

Research Evidence on Mentoring

Three recently reported research projects supplement Kram's study of mentoring. In the first study, 520 high-level managers (95 percent male) from Columbia University's executive development programs completed questionnaires about either their mentors or their protégés. Among the significant findings:

- "On average, respondents became protégés at 30 when their mentors were 43 (for an age difference of 13 years). In about half the cases (53 percent), mentors were immediate supervisors."[19]
- Seventy-two percent of the surveyed managers reported that their mentors substantially helped their career development.
- Eighty-three percent of the respondents preferred informal over formal mentor programs.

The second study probed the dynamics of cross-gender mentoring. Because of the underrepresentation of women in executive-level positions, the most common cross-gender mentor relationship is a male mentor and a female protégée. Relationships of this type have long been considered problematic because of the potential for romantic involvement. Results of this second study of 32

---

[17] Kathy E. Kram, *Mentoring at Work: Developmental Relationships in Organizational Life* (Glenview, Ill.: Scott, Foresman, 1985), p. 47.

[18] For additional discussion, see Kram, "Phases of the Mentor Relationship."

[19] Murray H. Reich, "Executive Views from Both Sides of Mentoring," *Personnel*, March 1985, p. 42.

■ **TABLE 11–5** Phases of the Mentor Relationship

Phase	Definition	Turning Points*
Initiation	A period of six months to a year during which time the relationship gets started and begins to have importance for both managers.	Fantasies become concrete expectations. Expectations are met; senior manager provides coaching, challenging work, visibility; junior manager provides technical assistance, respect, and desire to be coached. There are opportunities for interaction around work tasks.
Cultivation	A period of two to five years during which time the range of career and psychosocial functions provided expand to a maximum.	Both individuals continue to benefit from the relationship. Opportunities for meaningful and more frequent interaction increase. Emotional bond deepens and intimacy increases.
Separation	A period of six months to two years after a significant change in the structural role relationship and/or in the emotional experience of the relationship.	Junior manager no longer wants guidance but rather the opportunity to work more autonomously. Senior manager faces midlife crisis and is less available to provide mentoring functions. Job rotation or promotion limits opportunities for continued interaction; career and psychosocial functions can no longer be provided. Blocked opportunity creates resentment and hostility that disrupts positive interaction.
Redefinition	An indefinite period after the separation phase, during which time the relationship is ended or takes on significantly different characteristics, making it a more peerlike friendship.	Stresses of separation diminish, and new relationships are formed. The mentor relationship is no longer needed in its previous form. Resentment and anger diminish; gratitude and appreciation increase. Peer status is achieved.

* Examples of the most frequently observed psychological and organizational factors that cause movement into the current relationship phase.
SOURCE: Kathy E. Kram, "Phases of the Mentor Relationship," *Academy of Management Journal*, December 1983, p. 622. Used with permission.

mentor-protégée pairings (14 male-female; 18 female-female) suggest that male-female mentor relationships are more beneficial than harmful. According to the researcher:

> It would appear that the most productive mentoring functions occur *after* the initial attraction of identification has mellowed. From a practical perspective, it may be that we should stop advising young women to avoid or maintain their distance with male mentors despite the acknowledged possibility that sexual entanglements can emerge. If, as was found in this sample, male mentors are at least as likely (if not more so) to provide psychosocial functions for female protégées, young women may find cross-sex mentoring uniquely valuable.[20]

[20] Donald D. Bowen, "The Role of Identification in Mentoring Female Protegees," *Group & Organization Studies*, March–June 1986, p. 72. Also see James G. Clawson and Kathy E. Kram, "Managing Cross-Gender Mentoring," *Business Horizons*, May–June 1984, pp. 22–32; and Selwyn Feinstein, "Women and Minority Workers in Business Find a Mentor Can Be a Rare Commodity," *The Wall Street Journal*, November 11, 1987, p. 37.

■ **TABLE 11–6**   Practical Insights about Mentoring from the Honeywell Study

One of the surprises of phase two of the Honeywell studies was the finding that there is a big difference between "having a mentor" and "being mentored." That, at least, is the conclusion reached by Dennis J. Adsit, a key member of the "skunkworks" team that conducted the project.

According to Adsit, the study found that mentors per se—specific individuals who influenced the careers of certain managers—were not that common in the organization. Yet paradoxically, managers insisted that their relationships with others were significant factors.

"When we examined [in interviews] the reasons why managers consider different kinds of relationships developmental," Adsit says, "what emerged were descriptions associated with the literature on mentors. They said things like 'acted as a sounding board,' 'served as a good role model,' 'gave me feedback and coaching about my performance,' 'discussed career issues with me' and 'provided a broader perspective.' These are all behaviors generally attributed to mentors."

But the sounding boards and role models these managers were talking about included all sorts of people—peers, consultants and even subordinates—not just their immediate supervisors or upper-level managers.

Adsit found, in fact, that the only reliable factor in the discussions that distinguished a mentor relationship from other valuable relationships was terminology: "When a person used the term 'mentor,' it almost always implied someone at a higher level in the organization."

What this suggests to Adsit is that companies ought to shift their thinking in the mentoring area away from a focus on "people who . . ." and toward one on "behaviors that . . ." As he puts it, "Instead of asking, 'Are mentors important for development?' let's begin asking, 'How important are mentoring behaviors to a manager's development?' "

This shift from mentor as person to mentoring as behavior is important for three reasons, he argues. First, there is a terrible muddle in the professional literature over what a mentor is. "We wrestled with this amorphous concept when we designed our survey. We were unsuccessful at defining it in a way broad enough to cover the various aspects of mentoring [discussed in the literature], yet focused enough to make the survey answers interpretable."

Second, he points out, many organizations are "improving their job-rotation systems," meaning that managers are changing assignments more often. "Increasing movement between functions makes establishing traditional mentoring relationships more difficult and limits their effectiveness. It's important to understand how other relationships can provide the support, guidance and feedback that [traditional] mentors provide."

Finally, there is the blunt fact that many successful managers make no mention of ever having had a mentor. "And yet it seems doubtful," says Adsit, "that these managers could have become successful without having experienced mentoring *behaviors*." The Honeywell data supports that conclusion, he says, and thus suggests that behaviors are the critical factor. In fact, Adsit proposes, multiple sources of "mentoring" may be more valuable "due to the varied perspectives multiple sources may provide."

Having a mentor is in vogue today, but if the Honeywell studies are correct, "being mentored" is more helpful to a manager's career.

SOURCE: Ron Zemke, "Cooling Mentormania," p. 49. Reprinted with permission from the Aug. 1985 issue of *Training*, The Magazine of Human Resources Development. Copyright 1985, Lakewood Publications Inc., Minneapolis, MN (612) 333–0471. All rights reserved.

In the third and final study, a survey of 59 female lawyers from Oregon who had been mentored led to the following conclusions: "(1) Mentoring does appear to be important to career success and satisfaction. . . . (2) The recently proposed idea that group mentoring relationships are superior to traditional mentorship may be erroneous."[21]

Getting the Most Out of Mentoring

Mentoring can be an informal, spontaneous process or a formally structured one. As an example of the latter approach, Kaiser Aluminum & Chemical Corp. assigns junior managers to carefully screened mentors.[22] Regardless of the approach taken, it is important to realize that mentoring has been zealously oversold in recent years. Some managers do not want to be a mentor or a protégé. If managers are forced into such roles by a formal mentoring program, resistance and resentment could damage relationships and careers.

A workable alternative involves establishing a career development program that fosters the performance of mentoring functions and behaviors without forcing artificial relationships. This organizational climate encourages emergence of informal and trusting relationships that are essential to successful mentoring. The Honeywell study, mentioned earlier, supports this informal approach (see Table 11–6).

■ ORGANIZATIONAL POLITICS

Most students of OB find the study of organizational politics intriguing. Perhaps this topic owes its appeal to the antics of Hollywood characters like "Dallas's" J. R. Ewing who get their way by stepping on anyone and everyone. As we will see, however, organizational politics includes but is not limited to dirty dealing. Organizational politics is an ever-present and often positive force in modern work organizations. Roberta Bhasin, a district manager for Mountain Bell Telephone Company, put organizational politics into perspective by observing:

> Most of us would like to believe that organizations are rationally structured, based on reasonable divisions of labor, a clear hierarchical communication flow, and well-defined lines of authority aimed at meeting universally understood goals and objectives.
>
> But organizations are made up of *people* with personal agendas designed to win power and influence. The agenda—the game—is called corporate politics.

---

[21] Sandra Riley and David Wrench, "Mentoring among Women Lawyers," *Journal of Applied Social Psychology* 15, no. 4 (1985), p. 385.

[22] Kaiser's formal mentoring program is discussed in Jack W. Farrell, "A Unique Approach to Management Development," *Traffic Management*, January 1985, pp. 44–46. Additional practical advice may be found in John Lawrie, "How to Establish a Mentoring Program," *Training and Development Journal*, March 1987, pp. 25–27; and Daniel C. Feldman, *Managing Careers in Organizations* (Glenview, Ill.: Scott, Foresman, 1988), chap. 7.

It is played by avoiding the rational structure, manipulating the communications hierarchy, and ignoring established lines of authority. The rules are never written down and seldom discussed.

For some, corporate politics are second nature. They instinctively know the unspoken rules of the game. Others must learn. Managers who don't understand the politics of their organizations are at a disadvantage, not only in winning raises and promotions, but even in getting things *done*.[23]

We explore this important and interesting area by: (1) defining the term *organizational politics*, (2) identifying three levels of political action, (3) discussing eight specific political tactics, and (4) examining relevant research and practical implications.

Definition and Domain of Organizational Politics

"Organizational politics involves intentional acts of influence to enhance or protect the self-interest of individuals or groups."[24] An emphasis on *self-interest* distinguishes this form of social influence. Managers are endlessly challenged to achieve a workable balance between employees' self-interests and organizational interests. As demonstrated by the first example in Table 11–7, the pursuit of self-interest may serve the organization's interests. Political behavior becomes a negative force when self-interests erode or defeat organizational interests.

Uncertainty Triggers Political Behavior.   Political maneuvering is triggered primarily by *uncertainty*. Five common sources of uncertainty within organizations are:

1. Unclear objectives.
2. Vague performance measures.
3. Ill-defined decision processes.
4. Strong individual or group competition.[25]
5. Any type of change.

Regarding this last source of uncertainty, organization development specialist Anthony Raia noted "Whatever we attempt to change, the political subsystem becomes active. Vested interests are almost always at stake and the distribution of power is challenged."[26]

Thus, we would expect a field sales representative, striving to achieve an assigned quota, to be less political than a management trainee working on a

[23] Roberta Bhasin, "On Playing Corporate Politics," *Pulp & Paper*, October 1985, p. 175.

[24] Robert W. Allen, Dan L. Madison, Lyman W. Porter, Patricia A. Renwick, and Bronston T. Mayes, "Organizational Politics: Tactics and Characteristics of Its Actors," *California Management Review*, Fall 1979, p. 77.

[25] First four based on discussion in Don R. Beeman and Thomas W. Sharkey, "The Use and Abuse of Corporate Politics," *Business Horizons*, March–April 1987, pp. 26–30.

[26] Anthony Raia, "Power, Politics, and the Human Resource Professional," *Human Resource Planning* 8, no. 4 (1985), p. 203.

■ **TABLE 11–7**   Positive and Negative Faces of Organizational Politics

A Positive Face

One of the best ways to move up is by doing something patently political—proposing a new job only you can fill. . . .

For example: An engineering firm had always had trouble with basic administration because a large number of secretaries and word-processing people were needed, but the turnover was high. One engineer, Duncan R., tired of his straight engineering job, developed a scheme that allowed coverage of both the telephones and the word-processing equipment with 20% fewer people. This involved a pool approach and incorporated some part-timers and home-based workers at peak times. He wrote a job description for the person who would manage the new system, including the purchase of microcomputers and a new job title, director of staff service. . . .

It worked, as did his new organizational scheme. His boss's only comment was, "Why didn't you propose this job sooner?"

A Negative Face

"Some people have a compulsion to be considered in the same light as upper-level executives—and that can have dire consequences," says [a management consultant]. . . .

Such an obsession ruined one middle manager who found out on the sly that top executives would be monitoring a seminar he was attending. While other attendees were dressed casually—as suggested—he showed up in a three-piece suit, equipped with pointer, pocket calculator, and Cross pen. Until the top executives departed, that is. During the first break he quickly changed into slacks and sweater. The display created animosity and he was subsequently undermined by his own staff.

SOURCES: Excerpted from Marilyn Moats Kennedy, "Corporate Politics 101," *Canadian Business*, August 1985, pp. 62–63; and Charles R. Day, Jr., "The Politics Game," *Industry Week*, March 31, 1986, p. 80.

variety of projects. While some management trainees stake their career success on hard work, competence, and a bit of luck, many do not. These people attempt to gain a competitive edge through some combination of the political tactics discussed below. Meanwhile, the salesperson's performance is measured in actual sales, not in terms of being friends with the boss or taking credit for others' work. Thus, the management trainee would tend to be more political than the field salesperson because of greater uncertainty about management's expectations.

Three Levels of Political Action.   Although much political maneuvering occurs at the individual level, it also can involve group or collective action. Figure 11–4 illustrates three different levels of political action: the individual level, the coalition level, and the network level.[27] Each level has its distinguishing characteristics. At the individual level, personal self-interests are pursued by the individual. The political aspects of coalitions and networks are not so obvious, however.

[27] This three-level distinction comes from Anthony T. Cobb, "Political Diagnosis: Applications in Organizational Development," *Academy of Management Review*, July 1986, pp. 482–96.

■ **FIGURE 11–4** Levels of Political Action in Organizations

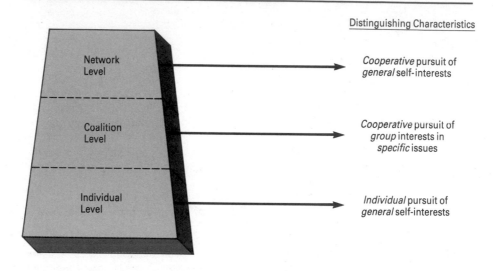

Distinguishing Characteristics

Network Level → *Cooperative* pursuit of *general* self-interests

Coalition Level → *Cooperative* pursuit of *group* interests in *specific* issues

Individual Level → *Individual* pursuit of *general* self-interests

People with a common interest can become a political coalition by fitting the following definition. In an organizational context, a **coalition** is an informal group bound together by the *active* pursuit of a *single* issue. Coalitions may or may not coincide with formal group membership. When the target issue is resolved (a sexually harrassing supervisor is fired, for example), the coalition disbands. Experts note that political coalitions have "fuzzy boundaries," meaning they are fluid in membership, flexible in structure, and temporary in duration.[28]

Coalitions are a potent political force in organizations. Consider the situation Charles J. Bradshaw faced in a finance committee meeting at Transworld Corp. in 1986. Bradshaw, president of the company, opposed the chairman's plan to acquire a $93 million nursing home company.

> [The senior vice president for finance] kicked off the meeting with a battery of facts and figures in support of the deal. "Within two or three minutes, I knew I had lost," Bradshaw concedes. "No one was talking directly to me, but all statements addressed my opposition. I could tell there was a general agreement around the board table."
>
> . . . Then the vote was taken. Five hands went up. Only Bradshaw voted "no."[29]

After the meeting, Bradshaw resigned his $530,000-a-year position, without as much as a handshake or good-bye from the chairman. In Bradshaw's case,

---

[28] An excellent historical and theoretical perspective of coalitions can be found in William B. Stevenson, Jone L. Pearce, and Lyman W. Porter, "The Concept of 'Coalition' in Organization Theory and Research," *Academy of Management Review,* April 1985, pp. 256–68.

[29] Laurie Baum, "The Day Charlie Bradshaw Kissed Off Transworld," *Business Week,* September 29, 1986, p. 68.

the finance committee was a formal group that momentarily became a political coalition aimed at sealing his fate at Transworld.

A third level of political action involves networks. Unlike coalitions, which pivot on specific issues, networks are loose associations of individuals seeking social support for their general self-interests. Politically, networks are people-oriented, while coalitions are issue-oriented. Networks have broader and longer-term agendas than do coalitions. For instance, a company's Hispanic employees might build a network to enhance the members' career opportunities.

Political Tactics

Anyone who has worked in an organization has firsthand knowledge of blatant politicking. Blaming someone else for your mistake is an obvious political ploy. But other political tactics are more subtle. Researchers have identified a range of political behavior.

One landmark study, involving in-depth interviews with 87 managers from 30 electronics companies in Southern California, identified eight political tactics. Top , middle , and lower-level managers were represented about equally in the sample. According to the researchers: "Respondents were asked to describe organizational political tactics and personal characteristics of effective political actors based upon their accumulated experience in *all* organizations in which they had worked."[30] Listed in descending order of occurrence, the eight political tactics that emerged were:

1. Attacking or blaming others.
2. Using information as a political tool.
3. Creating a favorable image.
4. Developing a base of support.
5. Praising others (ingratiation).
6. Forming power coalitions with strong allies.
7. Associating with influential people.
8. Creating obligations (reciprocity).

Table 11–8 describes these political tactics and indicates how often each reportedly was used by the interviewed managers.

The researchers distinguished between reactive and proactive political tactics. Some of the tactics, such as scapegoating, were *reactive* because the intent was to *defend* one's self-interest. Other tactics, such as developing a base of support, were *proactive* because they sought to *promote* the individual's self-interest.

Find out how political you are with the questionnaire in Table 11–9. After responding to all 10 items, determine your political tendencies by using the scoring system recommended by the author of this quiz:

[30] Allen, Madison, Porter, Renwick, and Mayes, "Organizational Politics: Tactics and Characteristics of Its Actors," p. 77.

■ **TABLE 11–8**   Eight Common Political Tactics in Organizations

Political Tactic	Percent of Managers Mentioning Tactic	Brief Description of Tactic
1. Attacking or blaming others	54%	Used to avoid or minimize association with failure. Reactive when scapegoating is involved. Proactive when goal is to reduce competition for limited resources.
2. Using information as a political tool	54	Involves the purposeful withholding or distortion of information. Obscuring an unfavorable situation by overwhelming superiors with information.
3. Creating a favorable image	53	Dressing/grooming for success. Adhering to organizational norms and drawing attention to one's successes and influence. Taking credit for others' accomplishments.
4. Developing a base of support	37	Getting prior support for a decision. Building others' commitment to a decision through participation.
5. Praising others (ingratiation)	25	Making influential people feel good ("apple polishing").
6. Forming power coalitions with strong allies	25	Teaming up with powerful people who can get results.
7. Associating with influential people	24	Building a support network both inside and outside the organization.
8. Creating obligations (reciprocity)	13	Creating social debts ("I did you a favor, so you owe me a favor").

SOURCE: Adapted from Robert W. Allen, Dan L. Madison, Lyman W. Porter, Patricia A. Renwick, and Bronston T. Mayes, "Organizational Politics: Tactics and Characteristics of Its Actors," *California Management Review*, Fall 1979, pp. 77–83.

A confirmed organizational politician will answer "true" to all 10 questions. Organizational politicians with fundamental ethical standards will answer "false" to Questions 5 and 6, which deal with deliberate lies and uncharitable behavior. Individuals who regard manipulation, incomplete disclosure, and self-serving behavior as unacceptable will answer "false" to all or almost all of the questions.[31]

Research Evidence on Organizational Politics

Research evidence in this area is rather sparse, partly because managers often are reluctant to frankly discuss their self-serving behavior. A subsequent research report on the sample of Southern California electronics industry managers discussed earlier provided the following insights:

- Sixty percent of the managers reported organizational politics was a frequent occurrence.
- The larger the organization, the greater the perceived political activity.
- Ambiguous roles and goals and increased conflict were associated with increased political activity.

---

[31] Joseph F. Byrnes, "Connecting Organizational Politics and Conflict Resolution," *Personnel Administrator*, June 1986, pp. 49–50.

■ **TABLE 11–9** How Political Are You? A Self-Quiz

The Political Behavior Inventory

To determine your political appreciation and tendencies, please answer the following questions. Select the answer that best represents your behavior or belief, even if that particular behavior or belief is not present all the time.

1. You should make others feel important through an open appreciation of their ideas and work.	___ True ___ False	6. Sometimes it is necessary to make promises that you know you will not or cannot keep. ___ True ___ False
2. Because people tend to judge you when they first meet you, always try to make a good first impression.	___ True ___ False	7. It is important to get along with everybody, even with those who are generally recognized as windbags, abrasive, or constant complainers. ___ True ___ False
3. Try to let others do most of the talking, be sympathetic to their problems, and resist telling people that they are totally wrong.	___ True ___ False	8. It is vital to do favors for others so that you can call in these IOUs at times when they will do you the most good. ___ True ___ False
4. Praise the good traits of the people you meet and always give people an opportunity to save face if they are wrong or make a mistake.	___ True ___ False	9. Be willing to compromise, particularly on issues that are minor to you, but important to others. ___ True ___ False
5. Spreading false rumors, planting misleading information, and backstabbing are necessary, if somewhat unpleasant, methods to deal with your enemies.	___ True ___ False	10. On controversial issues, it is important to delay or avoid your involvement if possible. ___ True ___ False

SOURCE: Joseph F. Byrnes, "Connecting Organizational Politics and Conflict Resolution," *Personnel Administrator*, June 1986, p. 49. Used with author's permission.

- Most of the managers (90 percent) believed middle- and upper-level managers were more political than lower-level managers.
- People in staff (advisory) positions were considered to be more political than people in line (decision-making) positions.
- Marketing staffs and members of corporate boards of directors were rated as the most political, while production, accounting, and finance personnel were viewed as the least political.
- Two situations most frequently mentioned in association with political activity were reorganization changes and personnel changes.
- Politics and power formed a self-perpetuating cycle.

According to the researchers: "The successful practice of organizational politics is perceived to lead to a higher level of power, and once a high level of power is attained, there is more opportunity to engage in political behavior.[32]

A more recent study analyzed 330 brief reports written by 90 middle managers from a variety of industries. Those reports dealt with how the managers had "taken a position on a decision" or "resisted a decision." The researchers

---

[32] See Dan L. Madison, Robert W. Allen, Lyman W. Porter, Patricia A. Renwick, and Bronston T. Mayes, "Organizational Politics: An Exploration of Managers' Perceptions," *Human Relations*, February 1980, pp. 79–100.

concluded that middle managers, often acting in coalitions, are a formidable barrier to implementing strategic plans they consider contrary to their self-interests.[33]

Managing Organizational Politics

Organizational politics can be managed to a certain extent but never eliminated. With this realization in mind, the practical steps in Table 11–10 are recommended. Notice the importance of reducing uncertainty through standardized performance evaluations and clear performance-reward linkages.[34] Measurable objectives are management's first line of defense against negative expressions of organizational politics. To resolve the conflict between middle managers' self-interests and strategy implementation, top managers need to build commitment to strategic plans through the participative management process discussed in Chapter 15.

■ **TABLE 11–10** Some Practical Advice on Managing Organizational Politics

To Reduce System Uncertainty:

Make clear what are the bases and processes for evaluation.

Differentiate rewards among high and low performers.

Make sure the rewards are as immediately and directly related to performance as possible.

To Reduce Competition:

Try to minimize resource competition among managers.

Replace resource competition with externally oriented goals and objectives.

To Break Existing Political Fiefdoms:

Where highly cohesive political empires exist, break them apart by removing or splitting the most dysfunctional subgroups.

If you are an executive, be keenly sensitive to managers whose mode of operation is the personalization of political patronage. First, approach these persons with a directive to "stop the political maneuvering." If it continues, remove them from the positions and preferably the company.

To Prevent Future Fiefdoms:

Make one of the most important criteria for promotion an apolitical attitude that puts organizational ends ahead of personal power ends.

SOURCE: Don R. Beeman and Thomas W. Sharkey, "The Use and Abuse of Corporate Politics," *Business Horizons,* March–April 1987, p. 30.

[33] For additional details, see William D. Guth and Ian C. Macmillan, "Strategy Implementation versus Middle Management Self-Interest," *Strategic Management Journal,* July–August 1986, pp. 313–27.

[34] The management of organizational politics also is discussed in Stephen L. Payne and Bernard F. Pettingill, "Coping with Organizational Politics," *Supervisory Management,* April 1986, pp. 28–31.

An individual's degree of politicalness is a matter of personal values, ethics, and temperament. People who are either strictly nonpolitical or highly political generally pay a price for their behavior. The former may experience slow promotions and feel left out, while the latter run the risk of being called self-serving and losing their credibility. People at both ends of the political spectrum may be considered poor team players. A moderate amount of prudent political behavior generally is considered a survival tool in complex organizations.

■ CONFLICT

Mention the term *conflict* and most people envision fights, riots, or war. But these extreme situations represent only the most overt and combative expressions of conflict. During the typical workday, managers encounter more subtle and nonviolent types of opposition such as arguments, criticism, and disagreement. Conflict, like power and organizational politics, is an inevitable and sometimes positive force in modern work organizations. For example, a sincere dissenting opinion by a member of an executive planning committee might prevent the group from falling victim to groupthink. OB scholar Stephen Robbins defines **conflict** as "all kinds of opposition or antagonistic interaction. It is based on scarcity of power, resources or social position, and differing value systems."[35] Research reveals that managers spend about 21 percent of their time dealing with conflict,[36] so they need to be well grounded in conflict theory, research, and practice.

Conflict occurs at three levels within organizations: interpersonal, intragroup, and intergroup. This section addresses these three levels of conflict by (1) distinguishing between functional and dysfunctional conflict, (2) identifying antecedents of conflict, (3) examining alternative styles of handling conflict, (4) reviewing recent research evidence, and (5) discussing a contingency approach to managing conflict.

A Conflict Continuum

Ideas about managing conflict have undergone an interesting evolution during this century. Initially, scientific management experts like Frederick W. Taylor believed all conflict ultimately threatened management's authority and thus had to be avoided or quickly resolved. Later, human relationists recognized the inevitability of conflict and advised managers to learn to live with it. Emphasis remained on resolving conflict whenever possible, however. Beginning in the 1970s, OB scholars realized conflict had both positive and negative outcomes, depending on its nature and intensity. This perspective introduced

---

[35] Stephen P. Robbins, *Managing Organizational Conflict: A Nontraditional Approach* (Englewood Cliffs, N.J.: Prentice-Hall, 1974), p. 23.

[36] See Kenneth W. Thomas and Warren H. Schmidt, "A Survey of Managerial Interests with Respect to Conflict," *Academy of Management Journal*, June 1976, pp. 315–18.

■ **FIGURE 11–5** The Relationship between Conflict Intensity and Outcomes

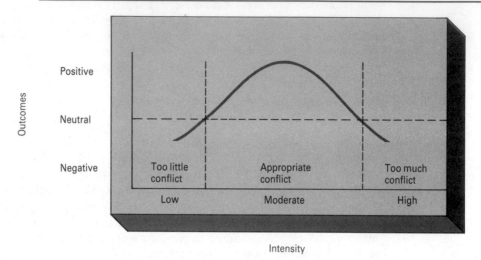

SOURCE: L. David Brown, *Managing Conflict at Organizational Interfaces,* © 1986, Addison-Wesley Publishing Co., Inc., Reading, Massachusetts. Figure 1.1 on page 8. Reprinted with permission.

the revolutionary idea that organizations could suffer from *too little* conflict. Figure 11–5 illustrates the relationship between conflict intensity and outcomes.

Work groups, departments, or organizations that experience too little conflict tend to be plagued by apathy, lack of creativity, indecision, and missed deadlines. Excessive conflict, on the other hand, can erode organizational performance because of political infighting, dissatisfaction, lack of teamwork, and turnover. Appropriate types and levels of conflict energize people in constructive directions.

Functional versus Dysfunctional Conflict

The distinction between **functional conflict** and **dysfunctional conflict** pivots on whether or not the organization's interests are served. According to Robbins:

> Some [types of conflict] support the goals of the organization and improve performance; these are functional, constructive forms of conflict. They benefit or support the main purposes of the organization. Additionally, there are those types of conflict that hinder organizational performance; these are dysfunctional or destructive forms. They are undesirable and the manager should seek their eradication.[37]

Functional conflict is commonly referred to in management circles as constructive conflict, or constructive confrontation.[38] Executives such as General Electric

---

[37] Stephen P. Robbins, " 'Conflict Management' and 'Conflict Resolution' Are Not Synonymous Terms," *California Management Review,* Winter 1978, p. 70.

[38] See Andrew S. Grove, "How to Make Confrontation Work for You," *Fortune,* July 23, 1984, pp. 73–75; and M. Michael Markowich and JoAnna Farber, "Managing Your Achilles' Heel," *Personnel Administrator,* June 1987, pp. 137–49.

■ **TABLE 11–11** Functional and Dysfunctional Conflict in Action

---

Functional Conflict

Jack Welch, chairman, General Electric.

Welch takes pleasure in giving and receiving a challenge—whether grilling a subordinate on the technical details of a project or presenting his views to the public. He once engaged a senior vice-president in a prolonged, emotional shouting match, embarrassing a roomful of managers. Then Welch thanked the subordinate for standing up to him. Welch calls this "constructive conflict."

Dysfunctional Conflict

Fred Ackman, chairman, Superior Oil.

Familiarity bred contempt. Employees say Ackman proved thoroughly autocratic, refusing even to discuss staff suggestions. He tended to treat disagreement as disloyalty. Many were put off by Ackman's abusive temper, which together with his stature (5 feet 8½ inches) and red hair earned him the nickname "Little Red Fred." Says a former subordinate, "He couldn't stand it when somebody disagreed with him, even in private. He'd eat you up alive, calling you a dumb S.O.B. or asking if you had your head up your ass. It happened all the time."

SOURCES: Excerpted from Marilyn A. Harris, "Can Jack Welch Reinvent GE?" *Business Week,* June 30, 1986; and Steven Flax, "The Toughest Bosses in America," *Fortune,* August 6, 1984, p. 21.

Company's chairman, Jack Welch, rely on constructive conflict to keep managers open to change and headed in a productive direction (see Table 11–11). In contrast, managers like Fred Ackman, chairman of Superior Oil Corp., foster dysfunctional conflict by dealing with personalities rather than issues. Not surprisingly, of 13 top executives at Superior Oil, 9 left within one year of Ackman's joining the company.

Antecedents of Conflict

Certain situations produce more conflict than others. By knowing the antecedents of conflict, managers are better able to anticipate conflict and take steps to resolve it if it becomes dysfunctional. Among the situations that tend to produce conflict are:

- Incompatible personalities or value systems.
- Overlapping or unclear job boundaries.
- Competition for limited resources.
- Inadequate communication.
- Interdependent tasks (for example, one person cannot complete his or her assignment until others have completed their work).
- Organizational complexity (conflict tends to increase as the number of hierarchical layers and specialized tasks increase).
- Unreasonable or unclear policies, standards, or rules.

- Unreasonable deadlines or extreme time pressure.
- Collective decision making (the greater the number of people participating in a decision, the greater the potential for conflict).
- Decision making by consensus (100 percent agreement often is impossible to achieve without much arguing).
- Unmet expectations (employees who have unrealistic expectations about job assignments, pay, or promotions are more prone to conflict).
- Unresolved or suppressed conflicts.[39]

Proactive managers carefully read these early warnings and take appropriate action. For example, group conflict can be reduced by making decisions on the basis of a majority vote rather than seeking a consensus.

Alternative Styles of Handling Conflict

People tend to handle conflict in patterned ways referred to as *styles*. Several conflict styles have been categorized over the years. According to conflict specialist Afzalur Rahim's recent model, five different conflict handling styles can be plotted on a 2 × 2 grid. High to low concern for *self* is found on the horizontal axis of the grid while high to low concern for *others* forms the vertical axis (see Figure 11–6). Various combinations of these variables produce the five different conflict handling styles: integrating, obliging, dominating, avoiding, and compromising. There is no single best style; each has strengths and limitations and is subject to situational constraints.

Integrating (Problem Solving).   In this style, interested parties confront the issue and cooperatively identify the problem, generate and weigh alternative solutions, and select a solution. Integrating is appropriate for complex issues plagued by misunderstanding. However, it is inappropriate for resolving conflicts rooted in opposing value systems. Its primary strength is its longer-lasting impact because it deals with the underlying problem rather than merely with symptoms. The primary weakness of this style is that it's very time-consuming.

Obliging (Smoothing).   "An obliging person neglects his or her own concern to satisfy the concern of the other party."[40] This style, often called smoothing, involves playing down differences while emphasizing commonalities. Obliging may be an appropriate conflict-handling strategy when it is possible to eventually get something in return. But it is inappropriate for complex or worsening problems. Its primary strength is that it encourages cooperation. Its main weakness is that it's a temporary fix that fails to confront the underlying problem.

Dominating (Forcing).   High concern for self and low concern for others encourages "I win, you lose" tactics. The other party's needs are largely ignored. This style is often called forcing because it relies on formal authority to force

---

[39] Adapted in part from discussion in Alan C. Filley, *Interpersonal Conflict Resolution* (Glenview, Ill.: Scott, Foresman, 1975), pp. 9–12.

[40] M. Afzalur Rahim, "A Strategy for Managing Conflict in Complex Organizations," *Human Relations,* January 1985, p. 84.

■ **FIGURE 11–6**   Five Conflict-Handling Styles

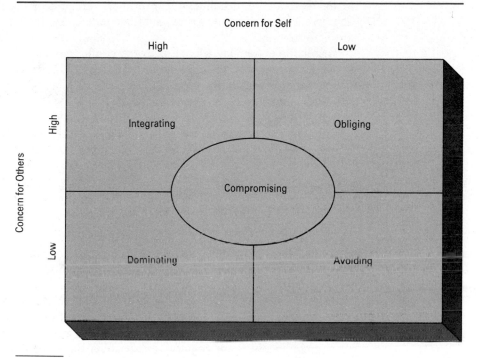

SOURCE: M. Afzalur Rahim, "A Strategy for Managing Conflict in Complex Organizations," *Human Relations,* January 1985, p. 84. Used with permission.

compliance. Dominating is appropriate when an unpopular solution must be implemented, the issue is minor, or a deadline is near. It is inappropriate in an open and participative climate. Speed is its primary strength. The primary weakness of this domineering style is that it often breeds resentment.

Avoiding.   This tactic may involve either passive withdrawal from the problem or active suppression of the issue. Avoidance is appropriate for trivial issues or when the costs of confrontation outweigh the benefits of resolving the conflict. It is inappropriate for difficult and worsening problems. The main strength of this style is that it's a natural reaction to a difficult situation. The primary weakness is that the tactic provides a temporary fix that sidesteps the underlying problem.

Compromising.   This is a give-and-take approach involving moderate concern for both self and others. "Each party is required to give up something of value. Includes external or third party interventions, negotiation, and voting."[41] Compromise is appropriate when parties have opposite goals or possess equal power (such as labor-management contract negotiations). But compromise is

[41] Robbins, " 'Conflict Management' and 'Conflict Resolution' Are Not Synonymous Terms," p. 73.

inappropriate when overuse would lead to inconclusive action (e.g., failure to meet production deadlines). The primary strength of this tactic is that the democratic process has no losers, but it's a temporary fix that can stifle creative problem solving.

To reinforce your knowledge of these conflict styles and learn more about yourself, please complete the self-quiz in Table 11–12. The instrument from which this quiz was drawn was validated through a factor analysis of responses from 1,219 managers from across the United States.[42] Are the results what you expected or are they a surprise?

With the antecedents of conflict and the five conflict-handling styles in mind, let us probe the relevant research for instructive insights.

Conflict Research Evidence

Laboratory studies, relying on college students as subjects, uncovered the following insights about organizational conflict:

- People with a high need for affiliation tended to rely on a smoothing (obliging) style while avoiding a forcing (dominating) style.[43] Thus, personality traits affect how people handle conflict.
- Confrontation (an integrating style) was associated with high task effectiveness, while smoothing was associated with low task effectiveness.[44]
- Disagreement expressed in an arrogant and demeaning manner produced significantly more negative effects than the same sort of disagreement expressed in a reasonable manner.[45] In other words, *how* you disagree with someone is very important in conflict situations.
- Threats and punishment by one party in a disagreement tended to produce intensifying threats and punishment from the other party.[46] In short, aggression breeds aggression.
- As conflict increased, group satisfaction decreased. An integrative style of handling conflict led to higher group satisfaction than did an avoidance style.[47]

A field study involving 8,938 nonsupervisory employees working for a large utility company revealed:

[42] The complete instrument may be found in M. Afzalur Rahim, "A Measure of Styles of Handling Interpersonal Conflict," *Academy of Management Journal,* June 1983, pp. 368–76.

[43] See Robert E. Jones and Bonita H. Melcher, "Personality and the Preference for Modes of Conflict Resolution," *Human Relations,* August 1982, pp. 649–58.

[44] Details may be found in Robert E. Jones and Charles S. White, "Relationships among Personality, Conflict Resolution Styles, and Task Effectiveness," *Group & Organization Studies,* June 1985, pp. 152–67.

[45] See Robert A. Baron, "Reducing Organizational Conflict: An Incompatible Response Approach," *Journal of Applied Psychology,* May 1984, pp. 272–79.

[46] See George A. Youngs, Jr., "Patterns of Threat and Punishment Reciprocity in a Conflict Setting," *Journal of Personality and Social Psychology,* September 1986, pp. 541–46.

[47] For more details, see Victor D. Wall, Jr., and Linda L. Nolan, "Small Group Conflict: A Look at Equity, Satisfaction, and Styles of Conflict Management," *Small Group Behavior,* May 1987, pp. 188–211.

■ TABLE 11–12 What Is Your Primary Conflict Handling Style?

Instructions: For each of the 15 items, indicate how often you rely on that tactic by circling the appropriate number. After you have responded to all 15 items, complete the scoring key below.

Conflict Handling Tactics	Rarely				Always
1. I argue my case with my co-workers to show the merits of my position.	1—2—3—4—5
2. I negotiate with my co-workers so that a compromise can be reached.	1—2—3—4—5
3. I try to satisfy the expectations of my co-workers.	1—2—3—4—5
4. I try to investigate an issue with my co-workers to find a solution acceptable to us.	1—2—3—4—5
5. I am firm in pursuing my side of the issue.	1—2—3—4—5
6. I attempt to avoid being "put on the spot" and try to keep my conflict with my co-workers to myself.	1—2—3—4—5
7. I hold on to my solution to a problem.	1—2—3—4—5
8. I use "give and take" so that a compromise can be made.	1—2—3—4—5
9. I exchange accurate information with my co-workers to solve a problem together.	1—2—3—4—5
10. I avoid open discussion of my differences with my co-workers.	1—2—3—4—5
11. I accommodate the wishes of my co-workers.	1—2—3—4—5
12. I try to bring all our concerns out in the open so that the issues can be resolved in the best possible way.	1—2—3 4 5
13. I propose a middle ground for breaking deadlocks.	1—2—3—4—5
14. I go along with the suggestions of my co-workers.	1—2—3—4—5
15. I try to keep my disagreements with my co-workers to myself in order to avoid hard feelings.	1—2—3—4—5

Scoring Key:

Integrating		**Obliging**		**Dominating**	
Item	Score	Item	Score	Item	Score
4.	_____	3.	_____	1.	_____
9.	_____	11.	_____	5.	_____
12.	_____	14.	_____	7.	_____
Total = _____		Total = _____		Total = _____	

Avoiding		**Compromising**	
Item	Score	Item	Score
6.	_____	2.	_____
10.	_____	8.	_____
15.	_____	13.	_____
Total = _____		Total = _____	

Your primary conflict handling style is: _____
  (The category with the highest total.)

Your backup conflict handling style is: _____
  (The category with the second highest total.)

SOURCE: Adapted and excerpted in part from M. Afzalur Rahim, "A Measure of Styles of Handling Interpersonal Conflict," *Academy of Management Journal,* June 1983, pp. 368–76.

- Both intradepartmental and interdepartmental conflict decreased as goal difficulty and goal clarity increased. Thus, as was the case with politics, challenging and clear goals can defuse conflict.
- Higher levels of conflict tended to erode job satisfaction and internal work motivation.[48]

Conflict Management: A Contingency Approach

Three realities dictate how organizational conflict should be managed. First, conflict is inevitable because it is triggered by a wide variety of antecedents. Second, too little conflict may be as counterproductive as too much. Third, there is no single best way of resolving conflict. Consequently, conflict specialists recommend a contingency approach to managing conflict. Antecedents of conflict and actual conflict need to be monitored. If signs of too little conflict such as apathy or lack of creativity appear, then conflict needs to be stimulated. This can be done by nurturing appropriate antecedents of conflict. On the other hand, when conflict becomes dysfunctional, the appropriate conflict-handling style needs to be enacted. Realistic training involving role playing can prepare managers to try alternative conflict styles.

Managers can keep from getting too deeply embroiled in conflict by applying three lessons from recent research: (1) establish challenging and clear goals, (2) disagree in a constructive and reasonable manner, and (3) refuse to get caught in the aggression-breeds-aggression spiral (see Table 11–13).

■ **TABLE 11–13** A Skillful Conflict Manager

Suzan Couch has been both a target and an arbiter of jealousy on the job. As vice president of marketing services at Warner Amex Cable Communications in New York, she sensed overt jealousy from a male executive apparently resentful of her success. He criticized her performance to colleagues as "not serious," she says, and spread snide remarks about her personal life. She retaliated, not with fire, but with friendliness. "Every time I saw him, I gave him another compliment," she says. "I was so sweet that he finally gave up" his campaign.

In her role as manager, she faced a potentially explosive rivalry between two subordinates, both "very talented, high-powered women," who were vying for the same promotion. She worried that the loser, in her bitterness, would undermine projects and poison office camaraderie. "With a lot of deadlines to meet, I couldn't afford that," says Ms. Couch, who now heads her own marketing firm, CB Communication Inc. in New York.

Her approach, after tapping her choice, was to make sure the other employee accepted the situation graciously but still felt part of the winner's circle. Ms. Couch held out the hope of a future promotion and also arranged for the two rivals to share a "no hard feelings" champagne lunch. "They're still friends," she notes.

SOURCE: Excerpted from Carol Hymowitz and Timothy D. Schellhardt, "Thy Neighbor's Job: As Insecurities Grow, Office Jealousy Flourishes." Reprinted by permission of *The Wall Street Journal*, Dow Jones & Company, Inc., July 17, 1986. All rights reserved.

---

[48] See Mel E. Schnake and Daniel S. Cochran, "Effect of Two Goal-Setting Dimensions on Perceived Intraorganizational Conflict," *Group & Organization Studies*, June 1985, pp. 168–83.

SUMMARY OF KEY CONCEPTS

A. Research by Kipnis and others identified eight generic influence tactics people use in work organizations: assertiveness, sanctions, ingratiation, rationality, exchange of benefits, blocking, upward appeal, and coalitions. No characteristic male or female tactics were found.

B. Social power is the *ability* to get things done, whereas authority is the *right* to seek compliance. Socialized power embraces a concern for the welfare of others. Personalized power is rooted in self-interest. French and Raven's five bases of power are reward power, coercive power, legitimate power, expert power, and referent power.

C. Mentoring is a common empowerment strategy whereby junior managers form intensive and lasting developmental relationships with senior managers. Mentors fulfill both career and psychosocial functions. Four phases of the mentoring process are initiation, cultivation, separation, and redefinition. Managers reportedly prefer informal mentoring over formal programs.

D. Organizational politics is defined as intentional acts of influence to enhance or protect the self-interests of individuals or groups. Uncertainty triggers most politicking in organizations. Political action occurs at individual, coalition, and network levels. Coalitions are informal, temporary, and single-issue alliances.

E. Researchers find political maneuvering associated with larger organizations, ambiguous roles and goals, conflict, upper levels of management, and staff personnel. Organizational politics can be managed but never eliminated.

F. Conflict is defined as all kinds of opposition or antagonistic interaction. It is inevitable and not necessarily destructive. Too little conflict, as evidenced by apathy or lack of creativity, can be as great a problem as too much conflict. Functional conflict enhances organizational interests while dysfunctional conflict is counterproductive.

G. There are many antecedents of conflict—including incompatible personalities, competition for limited resources, and unrealized expectations—that need to be monitored. Five alternative conflict-handling styles are integrating (problem solving), obliging (smoothing), dominating (forcing), avoiding, and compromising.

H. Conflict research demonstrates a link between personality and conflict style and that aggression breeds aggression. Challenging and measurable goals are an effective tool for containing both political behavior and conflict.

KEY TERMS

social power	**personalized power**
authority	**reward power**
socialized power	**coercive power**

legitimate power   **coalition**
expert power   **conflict**
referent power   **functional conflict**
mentoring   **dysfunctional conflict**
organizational politics

DISCUSSION QUESTIONS

1. Of the eight generic influence tactics, which do you use the most when dealing with friends, parents, your boss, or your professors? Would other tactics be more effective?

2. Before reading this chapter, did the term *power* have a negative connotation for you? Do you view it differently now? Explain.

3. What base(s) of power do you rely on in your daily affairs? (Use Table 11–4 to assess your power bases at work.) Do you handle power effectively and responsibly?

4. Have you ever had a mentor? Explain how things turned out.

5. Why would a junior manager not want to be assigned a mentor?

6. Why do you think organizational politics is triggered primarily by uncertainty?

7. What personal experience have you had with coalitions? Explain any positive or negative outcomes.

8. How political are you prepared to be at work? (Use the self-quiz in Table 11–9 as an assessment tool.) What are the career implications of your behavior?

9. What examples of functional and dysfunctional conflict have you encountered?

10. According to Table 11–12, what is your primary conflict-handling style? Would this help or hinder your effectiveness as a manager?

BACK TO THE OPENING CASE

Now that you have read Chapter 11, you should be able to answer the following questions about the Kroger case:

1. Judging from the available evidence, what was Mr. Kagler's primary base(s) of power? Did he wield power effectively and responsibly?

2. What evidence of organizational politics can you find in this case? Did coalitions enter the picture in any way? Explain.

3. Is it possible that Mr. Kagler's dominant conflict-handling style worked both for and against him? Explain.

EXERCISE 11 ——

Objectives

1. To further your knowledge of interpersonal conflict and conflict-handling styles.
2. To give you a firsthand opportunity to try the various styles of handling conflict.

Introduction

This is a role-playing exercise intended to develop your ability to handle conflict. There is no single best way to resolve the conflict in this exercise. One style might work for one person, while another gets the job done for someone else.

Instructions

Read the following short case, "Can Larry Fit In?" Pair up with someone else and decide which of you will play the role of Larry and which will play the manager. Pick up the action from where the case leaves off. Try to be realistic and true to the characters established in the case. The manager is primarily responsible for resolving this conflict situation. Whoever plays Larry should resist any unreasonable requests or demands and cooperate with any personally workable solution. *Note:* To conserve class time, try to resolve this situation in less than 15 minutes.

Case: "Can Larry Fit In?"[49]

You are the manager of an auditing team for a major accounting firm. You are sitting in your office reading some complicated new reporting procedures that have just arrived from the home office. Your concentration is suddenly interrupted by a loud knock on your door. Without waiting for an invitation to enter, Larry, one of your auditors, bursts into your office. He is obviously very upset, and it is not difficult for you to surmise why he is in such a nasty mood. You have just posted the audit assignments for the next month, and you scheduled Larry for a job you knew he wouldn't like. Larry is one of your senior auditors, and the company norm is that they get the better assignments. This particular job will require him to spend two weeks away from home, in a remote town, working with a company whose records are notorious for being a mess.

Unfortunately, you have had to assign several of these less desirable audits to Larry recently because you are short of personnel. But that's not the only reason. You have received several complaints from the junior staff members recently about Larry's treating them in an obnoxious manner. They feel he is always looking for an opportunity to boss them around, as if he were their supervisor instead of a member of the audit team. As a result, your whole operation works smoothly when you can send Larry out of town on a solo project for several days. It keeps him from coming into your office telling you how to do your job, and the morale of the rest of the auditing staff is significantly higher.

———————
[49] This case is quoted from *Developing Management Skills* by David A. Whetten and Kim S. Cameron. Copyright © 1984 by Scott, Foresman and Company. Reprinted by permission.

Larry slams the door and proceeds to express his anger over this assignment. He says you are deliberately trying to undermine his status in the group by giving him all the dirty assignments. He accuses you of being insensitive to his feelings and says that if things don't change, he is going to register a formal complaint with your boss.

Questions for Consideration/Class Discussion

1. What antecedents of conflict appear to be present in this situation? What can be done about them?
2. Having heard how others handled this conflict, did one particular style seem to work better than the others?
3. Did power and politics enter into your deliberations? Explain.

Chapter **12**

Organizational Communication Processes

LEARNING OBJECTIVES

When you finish studying the material in this chapter,
you should be able to:

- Explain why organizational communication is important.
- Describe the perceptual process model of communication.
- Explain the contingency approach to media selection.
- Discuss patterns of hierarchical communication.
- Demonstrate your familiarity with four antecedents of communication distortion.
- Describe the grapevine and its identifiable patterns.
- Contrast four different communications abilities/traits that affect communication competence.
- Discuss the primary sources of both nonverbal communication and listener comprehension.

OPENING CASE 12

Allstate's Award-Winning Communication Program

Donald Craib, Jr., the [recently retired] chief executive officer of Allstate Insurance Company, which is part of the Sears financial network, received an award for excellence in communication leadership in 1986 from the International Association of Business Communicators. The award was granted to Craib because of his leadership in developing and implementing Allstate's corporate communication program. Craib described the program as follows:

Growth in nearly any industry, during the post–World War II period, was often a matter of simply keeping up with demand. For the past 10 years, however, things have been different. Explosive growth in the economy was no longer there. Using Allstate as a case study, if we were to continue to grow in the future, we were going to have to respond positively to a more competitive marketplace, increase our market share through market segmentation and find niches that would enable us to concentrate on our strengths.

In short, we would have to place a greater emphasis on productivity and efficiencies within the company if we were to maintain our competitive position while providing our customers with superior and cost-effective service. To achieve this, certain processing centers would have to be consolidated with others to take advantage of automation.

In planning changes in our corporate structure, we recognize that it would have to become leaner, more responsive and more market-oriented. . . .

Communication Is Key to Successful Strategy

We had done our strategic planning. But we realized that it is our people—our human resources—who must make the plan work.

We turned now to our corporate communication plan. We began then placing more emphasis than ever on communication within Allstate, not as a gesture, but as a management tool in support of our growth objectives.

When I refer to corporate communication, I'm not referring to company newsletters, videotape programs or ''rap'' sessions among employees—although they are important. I'm referring to a company-wide communication strategy. It is a strategy that involves management at every level and in every operating department. It's a strategy with a goal to create a communicative culture that has a positive impact on growth and bottom-line results.

The reason for such an approach is simple. If our strategic-planning efforts are going to be successful, our 43,000 employees have to know what they need to do and why it is important.

Our first step in 1982 was to create a Communications Board. It continues to function. Membership includes myself, the president, senior vice presidents and top executives of our business units and, of course, our communication professionals. Basically, the board makes sure that our communication efforts lock step with our overall corporate strategy.

In addition, the corporate relations department established key contacts within each of our business units—executives who work with the communicators to ensure the accuracy of information in our employee publications and videotape presentations.

In the process, we revised and refined our communication media. Our research led us to introduce new publications targeted to key internal audiences. We scrapped others that were no longer useful. A new management magazine was created to communicate to this key group the goals of the organization.

For the first time, we produced an employee annual report for distribution at department kickoff meetings, thus assuring a unified message on the year's objectives.

We increased the frequency of our all-employee newspaper to accommodate the added information relating to corporate changes.

We restructured our employee videotape program, switching from a news-show format to in-depth portrayals of issues critical to employees and the company. The tapes were designed to be used as discussion-starters in staff meetings.

All of these communication vehicles were put to the test in late 1983 with the long-awaited announcement of the most sweeping reorganization in Allstate's history.

Face a Situation Head-On

In moving responsibility down the chain of command and giving more authority to managers in the field, the reorganization which we termed New Perspective would produce profound changes for thousands of people in the company—new responsibilities, new objectives, new ways of looking at traditional functions. Our strategy was to face the situation head-on. We pinpointed speed, honesty and management visibility as the key elements in the success of the effort.

With regard to speed, we never gave the rumor mill time to gear up. We made the reorganization announcement at our annual corporate conference, attended by company officers, and we videotaped the message. Within a week, videotape and the company newspaper reported the changes to all employees countrywide.

We were honest. We didn't gloss over the difficult parts. Consolidation of some field offices would lead inevitably to a loss of jobs in some cities while new jobs would be added in others. Changes were announced up to a year in advance to give affected employees all possible notice. Some employees were offered other positions with Allstate. In some cases, this necessitated relocation. Other employees were placed with other Sears companies, or assisted in finding jobs with other employers. Our *Allstate Now* newspaper, in covering the consolidation of two New York operations, featured employees who chose to stay with the company as well as those who didn't. Articles explained relocation benefits along with outplacement services for those who left Allstate. . . .

While our formal media play vital roles, we are always mindful that our managers and supervisors are the most effective communicators of all.

Studies continue to show that employees believe the people they work with much more readily than they believe any other source.

So a good communication strategy must make certain that managers themselves understand a company's basic message and objectives. To foster the kind of participative environment that makes a communication strategy succeed, Allstate's corporate training department conducts programs to improve managers' communicative skills.

A comprehensive communication strategy also recognizes that communication is a two-way street. The objective is to create a dialogue within the company, not constantly deliver pronouncements from on high. We encourage employee participation and put it to work for the company.

Every managerial function and activity involves some form of direct or indirect communication. Whether planning and organizing, or directing and leading, managers find themselves communicating with and through others. Managerial decisions and organizational policies are ineffective unless they are *understood* by those responsible for enacting them. Effective communication is a cornerstone of managerial and organizational success. In fact, the authors of the best-selling book *The 100 Best Companies to Work for in America* emphasized communication when listing the 12 characteristics of the "ideal company."

> Each company is unique, but there were certain themes we heard over and over again, and the urge to draw a kind of composite picture of the ideal company is irresistible. Beyond good pay and strong benefits, such a company would. . . . Encourage open communication, informing its people of new developments and encouraging them to offer suggestions and complaints.[1]

Empirical research studies lend additional support to this observation.

A study involving 327 hospital nurses revealed that employee satisfaction with organizational communication was positively and significantly correlated with both job satisfaction and performance. In a second study, overall organizational performance was directly related to the quality of managerial communication.[2] The importance of these findings is underscored by the fact that managers reportedly spend between 70 and 87 percent of their time communicating.[3]

A recent study expanded this insight by using self-report questionnaires

---

[1] Robert Levering, Milton Moskowitz, and Michael Katz, *The 100 Best Companies to Work for in America* (Reading, Mass.: Addison-Wesley Publishing, 1984), p. ix.

[2] Results from the nursing study are discussed in N. David Pincus, "Communication Satisfaction, Job Satisfaction, and Job Performance," *Human Communication Research,* Spring 1986, pp. 395–419. For details on the second study, see Robert A. Snyder and James H. Morris, "Organizational Communication and Performance," *Journal of Applied Psychology,* August 1984, pp. 461–65.

[3] Supporting evidence can be found in Henry Mintzberg, *The Nature of Managerial Work* (Englewood Cliffs, N.J.: Prentice-Hall, 1980); and William L. Gardner and Mark J. Martinko, "Impression Management: An Observational Study Linking Audience Characteristics with Verbal Self-Presentations," *Academy of Management Journal,* March 1988, pp. 42–65.

■ **FIGURE 12-1** Managerial Communication Behavior

Managers use the following media . . .

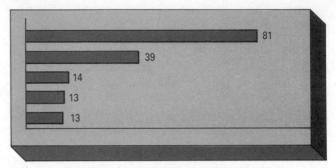

Face-to-face
Scheduled meetings
Unscheduled meetings
Telephone
Writing memos

81
39
14
13
13

Percentage of communication behaviors per week*

. . . To communicate with the following people

Total Communication Distribution†

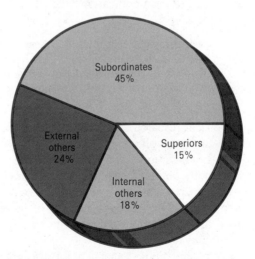

Subordinates
45%

External
others
24%

Internal
others
18%

Superiors
15%

---

*Total does not equal 100 percent because of overlapping categories.
†Equals more than 100 percent due to rounding.
SOURCE: Based on data presented in Fred Luthans and Janet K. Larsen, "How Managers Really Communicate," *Human Relations,* February 1986, pp. 167–68.

and direct observation to assess the communication behavior of 120 managers. The sample included a cross section of managers from all levels in five diverse organizations. Among the sampled organizations were a financial institution, a state department of revenue, a manufacturing plant, a campus police department, and the professional staff in ROTC units. An average of 81 percent of the managers' weekly communication behaviors involved face-to-face interactions (see Figure 12–1). They spent the least amount of time on the telephone (13 percent) and writing memos (13 percent). The various communication media were used to communicate predominantly with subordinates and individuals working outside the organization. As expected, top-level managers spent proportionately more time communicating with external others. The sample of 120 managers devoted the least amount of time and effort, 15 percent, to communicating with their superiors.[4]

Even though managers spend the majority of their time communicating, they are not necessarily effective communicators. Robert Levinson, a banking industry executive, summed up the state of managerial communication by describing the typical manager as follows: "He talks too much, expresses himself poorly, and has an uncanny ability for evading the point."[5] Levinson further concluded that most managers cannot "write a coherent letter, make a compelling presentation, dictate a concise memo, or put together a speech that doesn't have half his audience looking at their watches."[6] While some might call this appraisal too harsh, it highlights the need for better managerial communication.

This chapter will help you better understand how managers can both improve their communication skills and design more effective communication programs. We discuss (1) basic dimensions of the communication process, focusing on a perceptual process model and a contingency approach to selecting media; (2) communication patterns; (3) communication competence; and (4) nonverbal communication and active listening.

■ BASIC DIMENSIONS OF THE COMMUNICATION PROCESS

Communication is defined as "the exchange of information between a sender and a receiver, and the inference (perception) of meaning between the individuals involved."[7] Analysis of this exchange reveals that communication consists of consecutively linked elements (see Figure 12–2). Managers who understand this process can analyze their own communication patterns as well as design communication programs that fit organizational needs. This section reviews a perceptual process model of communication and discusses a contingency approach to choosing communication media.

A Perceptual Process Model of Communication

The communication process historically has been described in terms of a *conduit* model. This traditional model depicts communication as a pipeline in

---

[4] Complete details of the study can be found in Fred Luthans and Janet K. Larsen, "How Managers Really Communicate," *Human Relations,* February 1986, pp. 161–78.

[5] Robert E. Levinson, "How's That Again?: Execs: The World's Worst Communicators," *Management World,* July–August 1986, p. 40.

[6] Ibid.

[7] James L. Bowditch and Anthony F. Buono, *A Primer on Organizational Behavior* (New York: John Wiley & Sons, 1985), p. 81.

■ **FIGURE 12–2** A Perceptual Model of Communication

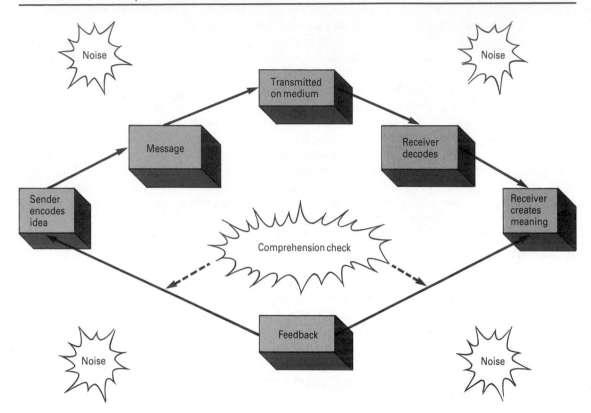

which information and meaning are transferred from person to person. Recently, however, communication scholars have criticized the conduit model for being based on unrealistic assumptions. For example, the conduit model assumes communication transfers *intended meanings* from person to person.[8] If this assumption was true, miscommunication would not exist and there would be no need to worry about being misunderstood. We could simply say or write what we want and assume the listener or reader accurately understands our intended meaning.

As we all know, communicating is not that simple or clear-cut. Communication is fraught with miscommunication. In recognition of this, researchers have begun to examine communication as a form of social information processing (recall the discussion in Chapter 4) in which receivers interpret messages by cognitively processing information. This view led to development of a **perceptual model of communication** that depicts communication as a process in

[8] For a review of these criticisms, see Stephen R. Axley, ''Managerial and Organizational Communication in Terms of the Conduit Metaphor,'' *Academy of Management Review*, July 1984, pp. 428–37.

which receivers create meaning in their own minds.[9] Let us briefly examine the elements of this perceptual process model.

Encoding. Communication begins when a sender encodes an idea or thought. Encoding translates mental thoughts into a code or language that can be understood by others. Managers typically rely on words, numbers, gestures, nonverbal cues like facial expressions, or pictures for encoding. Moreover, different methods of encoding can be used to portray similar ideas. The following short exercise highlights this point.

On a piece of paper, draw a picture of the area currently surrounding you. Now, write a verbal description of the same area. Does the pictorial encoding portray the same basic message as the verbal description? Which mode was harder to use and which more effective? Interestingly, a growing number of management consultants recommend using visual communication, such as drawings, to analyze and improve group interaction and problem solving and to reduce stress.[10]

The Message. The output of encoding is a message. There are two important points to keep in mind about messages. First, they contain more than meets the eye. Messages may contain hidden agendas as well as trigger affective or emotional reactions. Consider the following situation. You are seated in a restaurant and the server is passing near your table. You comment to the server, "I'm ready to order now." What is the meaning of this message? Consider your answer in light of the facts presented in note 11.[11] Given this situation, what underlying meanings might your apparently simple message convey? The second point to consider about messages is that they need to match the medium used to transmit them. For example, a routine memo is a poor way to announce an emotional issue like a large layoff.

Selecting a Medium. Managers can communicate through a variety of media. Potential media include face-to-face conversations, telephone calls, written memos or letters, photographs or drawings, meetings, bulletin boards, computer output, and charts or graphs. Choosing the appropriate media depends on many factors, including the nature of the message, its intended purpose, the type of audience, proximity to the audience, time horizon for disseminating the message, and personal preferences (see Table 12–1).

All media have advantages and disadvantages. Face-to-face conversations, for instance, are useful for communicating about sensitive or important issues and those requiring feedback and intensive interaction. Telephones are convenient, fast, and private, but lack nonverbal information. Although writing memos or letters is time-consuming, it is a good medium when it is difficult

---

[9] Ibid.

[10] Descriptions are provided by Robert E. Ault, "Draw on New Lines of Communication," *Personnel Journal,* September 1986, pp. 72–77.

[11] You have been waiting a long time. Because you are very hungry and the server has not been near your table, you are getting annoyed. This example was taken from Cynthia Gallois and Victor J. Callan, "Decoding Emotional Messages: Influence of Ethnicity, Sex, Message Type, and Channel," *Journal of Applied Psychology,* October 1986, pp. 755–62.

■ **TABLE 12–1** Executives Have Different Preferences for Communicating by Telephone

Reuben Mark, chief executive of Colgate-Palmolive Co., spends a third of his day on the phone and considers it valuable. But Daniel Silverman III, president of Chemfix Technologies Inc., prefers personal meetings, to "see the answer as well as hear it." . . .

Jeffrey Payson, chairman of General Homes Corp., tries to save time by having his secretary screen incoming calls. Maurice Segall, chief executive of Zayre Corp., generally doesn't take any calls. However, Millard Pryor, chairman of Lydall Inc., handles his own calls; "my secretary has more important things to do."

J. Terrence Murray, Fleet Financial Group's chairman, takes only essential calls.

SOURCE: "Labor Letter: A Special News Report on People and Their Jobs in Offices, Fields and Factories," *The Wall Street Journal*, September 30, 1986, p. 1.

to meet with the other person, when formality and a written record are important, and when face-to-face interaction is not necessary to enhance understanding. More is said later in this chapter about choosing media.

Decoding.   Decoding is the receiver's version of encoding. Decoding consists of translating verbal, oral, or visual aspects of a message into a form that can be interpreted. Receivers rely on social information processing to determine the meaning of a message during decoding. With respect to gender differences in encoding and decoding, a recent study revealed that females were both better encoders and decoders of emotional messages.[12]

Creating Meaning.   In contrast to the conduit model's assumption that meaning is directly transferred from sender to receiver, the perceptual model is based on the belief that a receiver creates the meaning of a message in his or her mind. A receiver's interpretation of a message often will differ from that intended by the sender. In turn, receivers act according to their own interpretations, not the communicator's. A communication expert concluded the following after considering this element of the communication process.

Miscommunication and unintentional communication are to be expected, for they are the norm. Organizational communicators who take these ideas seriously would realize just how difficult successful communication truly is. Presumably, they would be conscious of the constant effort needed to communicate in ways most closely approximating their intentions. . . . Communication is fraught with unintentionality and, thereby, great difficulty for communicators.[13]

Managers are encouraged to rely on *redundancy* of communication to reduce this unintentionality. This can be done by transmitting the message over multiple media. For example, a production manager might follow up a phone conversation about a critical schedule change with a memo.

---

[12] For details, see Gallois and Callan, "Decoding Emotional Messages."

[13] Axley, "Managerial and Organizational Communication in Terms of the Conduit Metaphor," p. 432.

Feedback.   Feedback is used as a *comprehension check*. It gives senders an idea of how accurately their message is understood. The double-headed arrow feedback loop in Figure 12–2 indicates that receivers become senders when they provide feedback to original communicators, who in turn become receivers.

Noise.   **Noise** represents anything that interferes with the transmission and understanding of a message. It affects all linkages of the communication process. Noise includes factors such as a speech impairment, poor telephone connections, illegible handwriting, inaccurate statistics in a memo or report, poor hearing and eyesight, and physical distance between sender and receiver. Managers can improve communication accuracy by reducing noise. Consider, for example, the approach used by Northrop Corp. to improve communication and productivity by reducing the physical barriers between engineers and production workers.

> At the company's new building in Hawthorne, Calif., where it makes the Tigershark fighter plane, engineers work right on the line so problems can be ironed out swiftly. "You can make changes on the plane together rather than sending memos," says Welko E. Gasich, senior vice-president for advanced projects. The result: The second Tigershark was made in 30% fewer work hours than the first. And the third plane "had zero defects on the fuselage, which is unheard of," Gasich says.[14]

Choosing Media: A Contingency Perspective

Managers need to determine which media to use for both obtaining and disseminating information. If an inappropriate medium is used, managerial decisions may be based on inaccurate information, and/or important messages may not reach the intended audience (see Table 12–2). Media selection therefore is a key component of communication effectiveness. This section explores a contingency model designed to help managers select communication media in a systematic and effective manner. Media selection in this model is based on the interaction between information richness and complexity of the problem/situation at hand.

Information Richness.   Respected organizational theorists Richard Daft and Robert Lengel define **information richness** in the following manner:

> Richness is defined as the potential information-carrying capacity of data. If the communication of an item of data, such as a wink, provides substantial new understanding, it would be considered rich. If the datum provides little understanding, it would be low in richness.[15]

As this definition implies, alternative media possess levels of information richness that vary from high to low.

---

[14] "The Revival of Productivity: The U.S. Is Poised for a Strong, Sustained Surge in Worker Efficiency," *Business Week,* February 13, 1984, p. 100.

[15] Richard L. Daft and Robert H. Lengel, "Information Richness: A New Approach to Managerial Behavior and Organization Design," in *Research in Organizational Behavior,* ed. Barry M. Staw and Larry L. Cummings (Greenwich, Conn.: JAI Press, 1984), p. 196.

■ **TABLE 12–2** The Chinese Language Limits the Choice of a Medium

A major problem in the transmission and storage of information is the Chinese language which consists of 30,000–40,000 separate ideograms. The traditional Chinese typewriter is a complex and cumbersome machine, while electronic video display/printers and duplicators have not yet arrived.

Written information in day to day management is scarce, and consists of handwritten notes for which no copy exists. Perforce, decisions are by consensus discussion, with perhaps a shorthand summary on file, but that is all. Information may simply be forgotten or misunderstood. Credit for a good idea or censure for a disastrous decision may be hard to pin down. This, it might be argued, applies equally to the Japanese enterprise although with their thorough sharing of information and seeking of consensus, they probably do not incur the same problems as the Chinese.

A key tool in information dissemination in the factory is a blackboard and chalk. Normally to add new information it is necessary to wipe out the old and unless that information is readily retrievable, it may be lost.

Electronic reproduction of Chinese characters combined with word processors and computers in the next few years are likely to transform Chinese management in quite unforeseeable ways.

SOURCE: J. M. Livingstone, "Chinese Management in Flux," *Euro-Asia Business Review,* April 1987, p. 19. Copyright © 1987. Reprinted by permission of John Wiley & Sons, Ltd.

Information richness is determined by four factors: (1) feedback (ranging from immediate to very slow), (2) channel (ranging from a combined visual and audio to limited visual), (3) type of communication (personal versus impersonal), and (4) language source (body, natural, or numeric). In Figure 12–3, the information richness of five different media is categorized in terms of these four factors.

Face-to-face is the richest form of communication. It provides immediate feedback, which serves as a comprehension check. Moreover, it allows for the observation of multiple language cues, like body language and tone of voice, over more than one channel. Although high in richness, the telephone is not as informative as the face-to-face medium. Formal numeric media such as quantitative computer printouts or video displays possess the lowest richness. Feedback is very slow, the channel involves only limited visual information, and the numeric information is impersonal.

Complexity of the Managerial Problem/Situation. Managers face problems and situations that range from low to high in complexity. Low-complexity situations are routine, predictable, and managed by using objective or standard procedures. Calculating an employee's paycheck is an example of low complexity. Highly complex situations, like a corporate reorganization, are ambiguous, unpredictable, hard to analyze, and often emotionally laden. Managers spend considerably more time analyzing these situations because they rely on more

■ **FIGURE 12–3** Characteristics of Information Richness for Different Media

Information Richness	Medium	Feedback	Channel	Type of Communication	Language Source
High	FACE-TO-FACE	Immediate	Visual, audio	Personal	Body, natural
↑	TELEPHONE	Fast	Audio	Personal	Natural
	PERSONAL WRITTEN	Slow	Limited visual	Personal	Natural
	FORMAL WRITTEN	Very slow	Limited visual	Impersonal	Natural
Low	FORMAL NUMERIC	Very slow	Limited visual	Impersonal	Numeric

SOURCE: Adapted from Richard L. Daft and Robert H. Lengel, "Information Richness: A New Approach to Managerial Behavior and Organization Design," in *Research in Organizational Behavior,* ed. Barry M. Staw and Larry L. Cummings (Greenwich, Conn.: JAI Press, 1984), p. 197.

sources of information during their deliberations. There are no set solutions to complex problems or situations.

Contingency Recommendations.   The contingency model for selecting media is graphically depicted in Figure 12–4. As shown, there are three zones of

■ **FIGURE 12–4** A Contingency Model for Selecting Communication Media

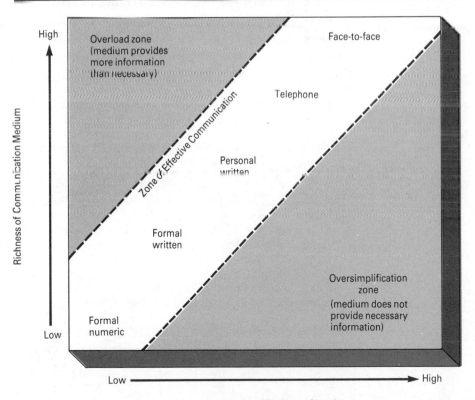

SOURCE: Adapted from Richard L. Daft and Robert H. Lengel, "Information Richness: A New Approach to Managerial Behavior and Organization Design," in *Research in Organizational Behavior,* ed. Barry M. Staw and Larry L. Cummings (Greenwich, Conn.: JAI Press, 1984), p. 199. Used with permission.

communication effectiveness. Effective communication occurs when the richness of the medium is matched appropriately with the complexity of the problem or situation. Media low in richness—formal numeric or formal written—are better suited for simple problems, while media high in richness—telephone or face-to-face—are appropriate for complex problems or situations. For example, an effective strategy would be for district sales managers to communicate monthly sales reports to each salesperson via formal numeric sales charts.

Conversely, ineffective communication occurs when the richness of the medium is either too high or too low for the complexity of the problem or situation. Extending the above example, a district sales manager would fall into the *overload zone* if he or she communicated monthly sales reports through richer media. Conducting face-to-face meetings or telephoning each salesperson would provide excessive information and take more time than necessary to communicate monthly sales data. The oversimplification zone represents another ineffective choice of communication medium. In this situation, media with inadequate richness are used to communicate complicated problems. An example would be announcing a major reorganization via a formal memo. Effective communicators, like those discussed in Table 12–3, use rich media to prepare employees for reorganizations.

Research Evidence. The relationship between media richness and problem/situation complexity has not been researched extensively because the underlying theory is relatively new. Available evidence indicates that managers used richer sources when confronted with ambiguous and complicated events.[16] This would be appropriate, according to the contingency model just discussed.

■ **TABLE 12–3** Effective Organizations Use Rich Media to Communicate about Corporate Reorganizations

---

Chevron Corp. put out more than 60 newsletters called "bluetops" to keep employees up to date on events in the year after its agreement to acquire Gulf Corp. Also used were 20-minute videos, recorded phone updates, severance and benefits seminars, and "town hall" meetings with Chevron chief George Keller. Struggling energy firms such as Transco Energy, Tenneco Inc. and United Energy hold big meetings to inform about layoffs and dispel rumors.

Eastman Kodak Co. sent videotape presentations by its top officers to all employees worldwide the day it reorganized its photographic division. When Atlantic Richfield Co.'s restructuring was announced, employees promptly got letters describing early retirement and termination plans.

But most companies handle such changes badly, viewing them as too risky to discuss openly, says Towers, Perrin, Forster & Crosby, New York consultant.

SOURCE: "Labor Letter: A Special News Report on People and Their Jobs in Offices, Fields and Factories," *The Wall Street Journal,* May 20, 1986, p. 1.

---

[16] For a summary of this research, see Daft and Lengel, "Information Richness: A New Approach to Managerial Behavior and Organization Design," pp. 191–233.

■ COMMUNICATION PATTERNS

Examining organizational communication patterns is a good way to identify factors contributing to effective and ineffective management. For example, research reveals that effective managers, in contrast to ineffective ones, tend to be: (1) more communication-oriented and willing to speak up, (2) more receptive to employees, (3) more willing to ask or persuade as opposed to tell, and (4) more open to explaining the "why" of things.[17] With these progressive practices in mind, this section promotes a working knowledge of three important communication patterns: hierarchical communication, communication distortion, and the grapevine.

Hierarchical Communication

Hierarchical communication is defined as "those exchanges of information and influence between organizational members, at least one of whom has formal (as defined by official organizational sources) authority to direct and evaluate the activities of other organizational members."[18] This category of communication involves the information exchanges depicted in Figure 12–5. Managers provide five types of information through downward communication: job instructions, job rationale, organizational procedures and practices, feedback about performance, and indoctrination of goals. Employees, in turn, communicate information upward about themselves, co-workers and their problems, organizational practices and policies, and what needs to be done and how to do it. Timely and valid hierarchical communication can promote individual and organizational success. Consider Wal-Mart, for example, a company whose success traces in part to the communication network linking its more than 900 stores.

> Mr. Walton [Wal-Mart's founder] has structured the company so that news from a store quickly percolates up to executives at headquarters, as well as spreading among the other outlets. Every Monday, Wal-Mart's regional managers fly from their base in Bentonville [Arkansas] to their respective territories for a week of exhaustive store tours. Back at headquarters on Friday, they meet with one another and report to Wal-Mart's top executives. After a second meeting on Saturday, these managers call their districts. Thus, "any gem in one store gets into all the stores," explains Mr. Ellis of Goldman Sachs.
>
> In this way, too, problems that might take another chain months to identify surface quickly. At one meeting, a regional manager reported that a K mart Corp. store in his territory was "beating us on prices." The situation was the same in another market, and Wal-Mart executives immediately ordered all stores to check their prices against K mart's.[19]

---

[17] Charles Redding, *Communication within the Organization: An Interpretive Review of Theory and Research* (New York: Industrial Communication Council, 1972).

[18] Fredric M. Jablin, "Superior-Subordinate Communication: The State of the Art," *Psychological Bulletin,* November 1979, p. 1202.

[19] Hank Gilman and Karen Blumenthal, "Two Wal-Mart Officials Vie for Top Post: David Glass Appears to Hold Leading Edge," *The Wall Street Journal,* July 23, 1986, p. 6.

■ **FIGURE 12–5** Hierarchical Communication

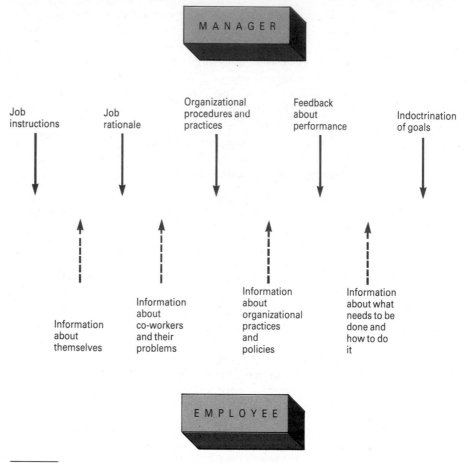

SOURCE: Adapted from Daniel Katz and Robert L. Kahn, *The Social Psychology of Organizations,* 2nd ed. (New York: John Wiley & Sons, 1978).

Unfortunately, hierarchical communication systems are not always this effective or accurate. Information distortion is common.

Communication Distortion

Communication distortion modifies the content of a message, reducing the accuracy of communication between managers and employees. Communication experts point out the organizational problems caused by distortion.

Distortion is an important problem in organizations because modifications to messages cause misdirectives to be transmitted, nondirectives to be issued, incorrect information to be passed on, and a variety of other problems related to both the quantity and quality of information.[20]

Awareness of the antecedents or causes of communication distortion can help managers avoid or limit these problems.

Antecedents of Distortion.   Studies have identified four situational antecedents of distortion in upward communication (see Figure 12–6). Distortion tends to increase when supervisors have high upward influence and/or power. Employees also tend to modify or distort information when they aspire to move upward and when they do not trust their supervisors.[21] Because managers generally do not want to reduce their upward influence or curb their subordinates' desire for upward mobility, they can reduce distortion in several ways. First, managers can de-emphasize power differences between themselves and their subordinates. Second, they can enhance trust through a meaningful performance review process that rewards actual performance. Third, managers can encourage staff feedback by conducting smaller, more informal meetings. Fourth, they can establish performance goals that encourage employees to focus on problems

THE WALL STREET JOURNAL

"It's not really all that important that we understand each other . . . just that *you* understand *me."* Reprinted from *The Wall Street Journal;* permission Cartoon Features Syndicate.

---

[20] Janet Fulk and Sirish Mani, "Distortion of Communication in Hierarchical Relationships," in *Communication Yearbook 9,* ed. Margaret L. McLaughlin (Beverly Hills, Calif.: Sage Publications, 1986), p. 483.

[21] For a review of this research, see Fulk and Mani, "Distortion of Communication in Hierarchical Relationships," pp. 483–510.

■ **FIGURE 12-6** Sources of Distortion in Upward Communication

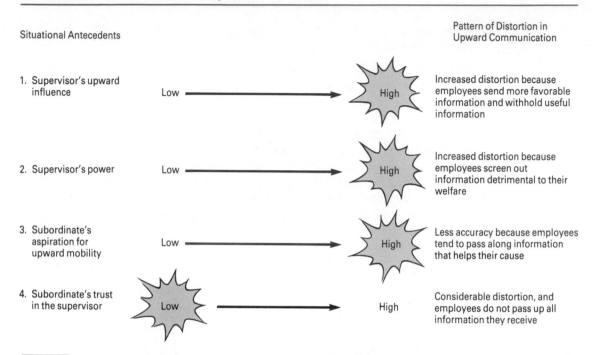

Situational Antecedents

Pattern of Distortion in
Upward Communication

1. Supervisor's upward influence   Low ⟶ High   Increased distortion because employees send more favorable information and withhold useful information

2. Supervisor's power   Low ⟶ High   Increased distortion because employees screen out information detrimental to their welfare

3. Subordinate's aspiration for upward mobility   Low ⟶ High   Less accuracy because employees tend to pass along information that helps their cause

4. Subordinate's trust in the supervisor   Low ⟶ High   Considerable distortion, and employees do not pass up all information they receive

SOURCE: Adapted in part from Janet Fulk and Sirish Mani, "Distortion of Communication in Hierarchical Relationships," in *Communication Yearbook 9*, ed. Margaret L. McLaughlin (Beverly Hills, Calif.: Sage Publications 1986).

rather than personalities. Finally, distortion can be limited by encouraging dialogue between those with opposing viewpoints.[22]

What Is Your Potential for Communication Distortion? To assess the communication pattern between you and your immediate supervisor, please take a moment to complete the survey in Table 12–4. Think of your present (or last) job when responding to the various items. Do your responses to the first three questions suggest low or high potential for distortion? (Arbitrary norms for each of the first three questions are: 1–2 = low, 3 = moderate, and 4–5 = high.) How does this assessment mesh with your responses to the last three questions, which measure three outcomes of distortion?

The Grapevine

The term *grapevine* originated from the Civil War practice of stringing battlefield telegraph lines between trees. Today, the term **grapevine** represents the unofficial communication system of the informal organization. Information traveling along the grapevine supplements official or formal channels of commu-

---

[22] Based on discussion found in William Hennefrund, "Fear of Feedback," *Association Management*, March 1986, pp. 80–83.

■ **TABLE 12–4** A Self-Assessment of Antecedents and Outcomes of Distortion in Upward Communication

Instructions: Circle your response to each question by using the following scale:

1 = Strongly disagree
2 = Disagree
3 = Neither
4 = Agree
5 = Strongly agree

Supervisor's upward influence:

In general, my immediate supervisor can have a big impact on my career in this organization.   1   2   3   4   5

Aspiration for upward mobility:

It is very important for me to progress upward in this organization.   1   2   3   4   5

Supervisory trust:

I feel free to discuss the problems and difficulties of my job with my immediate supervisor without jeopardizing my position or having it "held against" me later.   1   2   3   4   5

Withholding information:

I provide my immediate supervisor with a small amount of the total information I receive at work.   1   2   3   4   5

Selective disclosure:

When transmitting information to my immediate supervisor, I often emphasize those aspects that make me look good.   1   2   3   4   5

Satisfaction with communication:

In general, I am satisfied with the pattern of communication between my supervisor and me.   1   2   3   4   5

SOURCE: Adapted and excerpted in part from Karlene H. Roberts and Charles A. O'Reilly III, "Measuring Organizational Communication," *Journal of Applied Psychology,* June 1974, p. 323.

nication. Although the grapevine can be a source of inaccurate rumors, it functions positively as an early warning signal for organizational changes, a medium for creating organizational culture, a mechanism for fostering group cohesiveness, and a way of informally bouncing ideas off others.[23] Evidence indicates that the grapevine is alive and well in today's workplaces.

A survey conducted by the Hay Group, a large management consulting organization, revealed that employees used the grapevine as their most frequent source of information, followed by supervisors, company publications, memos, bulletin boards, and management meetings, respectively.[24] Contrary to general opinion, the grapevine is not necessarily counterproductive. Plugging into the grapevine can help employees, managers, and organizations alike achieve desired results. Consider the following examples:

> Tim Scerba, a communications specialist at Teachers Insurance, heard through the grapevine that a colleague was quietly pursuing a project originally entrusted

[23] Organizational benefits of the grapevine are discussed in Walter Kiechel III, "In Praise of Office Gossip," *Fortune,* August 19, 1985, pp. 253, 254, 256.

[24] Results are presented in "Who Told You That?" *The Wall Street Journal,* May 23, 1985, p. 37.

to him—in effect, an invasion of turf. Fueled with new ambition, Scerba worked harder and faster—and eventually won all the credit. . . .

Ted Klein, president of a public relations firm bearing his name, learned at a casual business lunch that a Fortune 500 company might be interested in retaining his services. In calling the firm to check out the rumor, he landed the account.[25]

To enhance your understanding of the grapevine, we will explore grapevine patterns and research and managerial recommendations for monitoring this often misunderstood system of communication.

Grapevine Patterns. Communication along the grapevine follows predictable patterns (see Figure 12–7). The most frequent pattern is not a single strand or gossip chain, but the cluster pattern.[26] In this case, person A passes along a piece of information to three people, one of whom—person F—tells two others, and then one of those two—person B—tells one other. As you can see in Figure 12–7, only certain individuals repeat what they hear when the cluster pattern is operating. People who consistently pass along grapevine information to others are called **liaison individuals.**

About 10 percent of the employees on an average grapevine will be highly active participants. They serve as liaisons with the rest of the staff members who receive information but spread it to only a few other people. Usually these liaisons are friendly, outgoing people who are in positions that allow them to cross departmental lines. For example, secretaries tend to be liaisons because they can communicate with the top executive, the janitor, and everyone in between without raising eyebrows.[27]

Effective managers monitor the pulse of work groups by regularly communicating with known liaisons.

Research and Practical Implications. Although research activity on this topic has slowed in recent years, past research about the grapevine provided the following insights:

- It is faster than formal channels.
- It is estimated to be 75 percent accurate.
- It is selective and discriminating in terms of the information transmitted.
- It tends to be jointly active or inactive with the formal system.
- People tend to rely on the grapevine when they are insecure, threatened, or faced with organizational changes.

[25] Robert Brody, "I Heard It through the Grapevine," *Executive Female,* September–October 1986, p. 22.

[26] See Keith Davis, "Management Communication and the Grapevine, *Harvard Business Review,* September–October 1953, pp. 43–49.

[27] Hugh B. Vickery III, "Tapping into the Employee Grapevine," *Association Management,* January 1984, pp. 59–60.

■ **FIGURE 12–7**   Grapevine Patterns

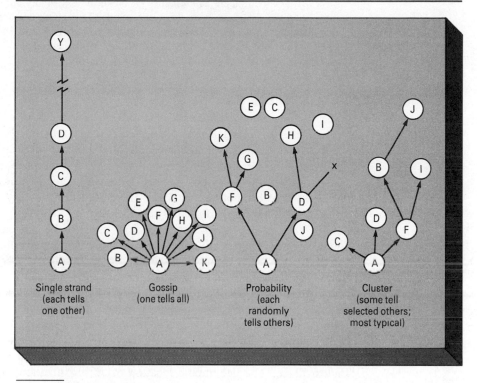

Single strand
(each tells
one other)

Gossip
(one tells all)

Probability
(each
randomly
tells others)

Cluster
(some tell
selected others;
most typical)

SOURCE: Keith Davis and John W. Newstrom, *Human Behavior at Work: Organizational Behavior,* 7th ed. (New York: McGraw-Hill, 1985), p. 317. Used with permission.

- Employees acquire almost 50 percent of their on-the-job information through the grapevine.[28]

The key managerial recommendation is to *monitor* and *influence* the grapevine rather than attempt to control it. Effective managers accomplish this by openly sharing relevant information with employees. For example, managers can increase the amount of communication by both keeping in touch with liaison individuals and making sure information travels to people "isolated" from the formal communication system. Providing advance notice of departmental or organizational changes, carefully listening to employees, and selectively sending information along the grapevine are other ways to influence and monitor the grapevine. Keith Davis, who has studied the grapevine for over 30 years, offers this final piece of advice:

---

[28] Earlier research is discussed by Davis, "Management Communication and the Grapevine"; and Roy Rowan, "Where Did *That* Rumor Come From?" *Fortune,* August 13, 1979, pp. 130–31, 134, 137. More recent research is discussed in "Pruning the Company Grapevine," *Supervision,* September 1986, p. 11; and Robert Half, "Managing Your Career: 'How Can I Stop the Gossip?' " *Management Accounting,* September 1987, p. 27.

No administrator in his right mind would try to abolish the management grapevine. It is as permanent as humanity is. Nevertheless, many administrators have abolished the grapevine from their own minds. They think and act without giving adequate weight to it or, worse, try to ignore it. This is a mistake. The grapevine is a factor to be reckoned with in the affairs of management. The administrator should analyze it and should consciously try to influence it.[29]

■ COMMUNICATION COMPETENCE

People vary a great deal in how effectively they communicate. Communication competence powerfully affects an individual's career progress. In fact, a four-year study of 90 employees from an eastern U.S. insurance company revealed that communication abilities were a strong predictor of upward mobility and the number of promotions received. Communication ability was a composite measure of an individual's ability to differentiate between liked and disliked co-workers, to self-monitor interpersonal cues, to be persuasive, and to take another person's perspective. People with more developed communication abilities tended to reach higher levels in the organization and were promoted more frequently than individuals with less developed abilities.[30]

Although there is no universally accepted definition of **communication competence,** it is a performance-based index of an individual's knowledge of "when and how to use language in the social context."[31] Communication competence is determined by three components: communication abilities and traits, situational factors, and the individuals involved in an interaction (see Figure 12–8). The geographic location of an organization, for example, is an important situational factor. As a case in point, contrast communication styles used by Seinosuke Kashima, a Japanese trading-company official, while working in both New York and Japan (see Table 12–5).

Individuals involved in an interaction also affect communication competence. For example, people are likely to withhold information and react emotionally or defensively when interacting with someone they dislike or do not trust. You can improve your communication competence through four communication abilities/traits under your control: assertiveness, aggressiveness, nonassertiveness, and interaction involvement.

Assertiveness, Aggressiveness, and Nonassertiveness

The saying "you can attract more bees with honey than with vinegar" captures the difference between using an assertive communication style and an aggressive style. Research studies indicate that assertiveness is more effective

---

[29] Davis, "Management Communication and the Grapevine," p. 49.

[30] See Beverly Davenport Sypher and Theodore E. Zorn, Jr., "Communication-Related Abilities and Upward Mobility: A Longitudinal Investigation," *Human Communication Research,* Spring 1986, pp. 420–31.

[31] Donald J. Cegala, "Interaction Involvement: A Cognitive Dimension of Communicative Competence," *Communication Education,* April 1981, p. 110.

■ **FIGURE 12–8**   Communication Competence Affects Upward Mobility

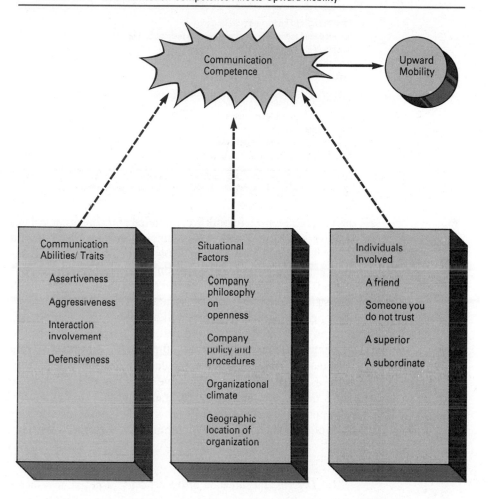

■ **TABLE 12–5**   Differing Communication Styles in the United States and Japan

> In New York Mr. Kashima did a lot of business on the telephone. In Japan, he must personally visit people in order to conduct any important business—"so they can see my eyes.". . .
> Below the surface, he says, things get even more complicated. "Suppose I want to propose something new," he says. "In Japan, the first thing I should do is take a colleague from the office to a nightclub and talk around the theme—without mentioning my idea directly. Only after my office colleagues and I understand each other would I go to my superior and propose the idea. But when I first returned from the U.S., I tended to go straight ahead with my ideas. It caused problems. Now I do it the normal [Japanese] way."
>
> SOURCE: E. S. Browning, "Unhappy Returns: After Living Abroad, Japanese Find It Hard to Adjust Back Home," *The Wall Street Journal*, May 6, 1986, p. 1.

■ **TABLE 12–6**   Assertive Bill of Rights

I have the right to be treated with respect.
I have the right to have and express my own feelings and opinions.
I have the right to be listened to and taken seriously.
I have the right to set my own priorities.
I have the right to say no without feeling guilty.
I have the right to ask for what I want.
I have the right to get what I want.
I have the right to get what I pay for.
I have the right to make mistakes.
I have the right to assert myself even though I may inconvenience others.
I have the right to choose not to assert myself.

SOURCE: Reprinted, by permission of the publisher, from *Mastering Assertiveness Skills: Positive Power and Influence at Work,* by Elaina Zuker, p. 17, © 1983 Elaina Zuker. Published by AMACOM, a division of American Management Association, New York. All rights reserved.

than aggressiveness in both work-related and consumer contexts.[32] An **assertive style** is expressive and self-enhancing and is based on the "ethical notion that it is not right or good to violate our own or others' basic human rights, such as the right to self-expression or the right to be treated with dignity and respect."[33] In contrast, an **aggressive style** is expressive and self-enhancing and strives to take unfair advantage of others. Aggressiveness violates the other person's basic "assertive bill of rights" (see Table 12–6). A **nonassertive style** is characterized by timid and self-denying behavior. Nonassertiveness is ineffective because it gives the other person an unfair advantage.

Managers may improve their communication competence by trying to be more assertive and less aggressive or nonassertive. This can be achieved by using the appropriate nonverbal and verbal behaviors listed in Table 12–7. Remember that nonverbal and verbal behaviors should complement and reinforce each other. James Waters, a communication expert, further recommends that assertiveness can be enhanced by using various combinations of the following assertiveness elements.

1.   *Describe* the situation or the behavior of people to which you are reacting.

2.   *Express* your feelings and/or *explain* what impact the other's behavior has on you.

3.   *Empathize* with the other person's position in the situation.

4.   *Specify* what changes you would like to see in the situation or in another's behavior and offer to *negotiate* those changes with the other person.

5.   *Indicate,* in a nonthreatening way, the possible consequences that will follow if change does not occur.[34]

---

[32] Results from a work-related study are presented in Dominic A. Infante and William I. Gorden, "Superiors' Argumentativeness and Verbal Aggressiveness as Predictors of Subordinates' Satisfaction," *Human Communication Research,* Fall 1985, pp. 117–25. A consumer study was conducted by Marsha L. Richins, "An Analysis of Consumer Interaction Styles in the Marketplace," *Journal of Consumer Research,* June 1983, pp. 73–82.

[33] James A. Waters, "Managerial Assertiveness," *Business Horizons,* September–October 1982, p. 25.

[34] Ibid., p. 27.

■ **TABLE 12–7** Communication Styles

Communication Style	Description	Nonverbal Behavior Pattern	Verbal Behavior Pattern
Assertive	Pushing hard without attacking; permits others to influence outcome; expressive and self-enhancing without intruding on others	Good eye contact Comfortable but firm posture Strong, steady, and audible voice Facial expressions matched to message Appropriately serious tone Selective interruptions to ensure understanding	Direct and unambiguous language No attributions or evaluations of other's behavior Use of "I" statements and cooperative "we" statements
Aggressive	Taking advantage of others; expressive and self-enhancing at other's expense	Glaring eye contact Moving or leaning too close Threatening gestures (pointed finger; clenched fist) Loud voice Frequent interruptions	Swear words and abusive language Attributions and evaluations of other's behavior Sexist or racist terms Explicit or implicit threats or putdowns
Nonassertive	Encouraging others to take advantage of us; inhibited; self-denying	Little eye contact Downward glances Slumped posture Constantly shifting weight Wringing hands Weak or whiny voice	Qualifiers ("maybe"; "kind of") Fillers ("uh," "you know," "well") Negaters ("It's not really that important"; "I'm not sure")

SOURCE: Adapted in part from James A. Waters, "Managerial Assertiveness," *Business Horizons,* September–October 1982, pp. 24–29.

Waters offers managers the following situational advice when using the various assertiveness elements: (1) *empathize* and *negotiate* with superiors or others on whom you are dependent, (2) *specify* with friends and peers, and (3) *describe* to strangers.

Interaction Involvement

Can you recall a situation in which you were talking with someone who appeared disinterested or preoccupied? How did you feel about this interaction? Contrast these feelings with those based on an interaction with someone who was highly involved in your conversation. As suggested by these examples, **interaction involvement** represents the extent to which an individual participates in or is consciously involved in an ongoing conversation. Individuals who are psychologically and communicatively removed are said to be low in interaction involvement. Such individuals appear withdrawn, preoccupied, or distanced from the interaction. On the other hand, highly involved individuals try to integrate thoughts, feelings, and both nonverbal and verbal behaviors when responding to others. These behaviors make them more sensitive and perceptive during a conversation.

Interaction involvement is influenced by both situational factors and an individual's general orientation to communicating.[35] For example, all of us experience periods of low involvement due to situational factors like embarrassment, preoccupation, boredom, bad mood, low energy, confusion, and contemplation.[36] These factors are a natural component of the communication process. We will now consider measuring interaction involvement.

Measuring General Orientation to Interaction Involvement.   An individual's general orientation to interaction involvement is composed of three interrelated factors called responsiveness, perceptiveness, and attentiveness. These factors are defined by a communication expert as follows:

> *Responsiveness* is an index of an individual's certainty about how to respond in social situations. *Perceptiveness* is an individual's general sensitivity to: (1) what meanings ought to be applied to others' behavior, and (2) what meanings others have applied to one's own behavior. *Attentiveness* is the extent to which one tends to heed cues in the immediate social environment, especially one's . . . [conversation partner].[37]

Take a moment now to assess your general orientation to interaction involvement by completing the survey in Table 12–8. Arbitrary norms for the dimensions of *responsiveness* and *attentiveness* are: 3–6 = high, 7–10 = moderate, and 11–15 = low. Norms for *perceptiveness* are: 3–7 = low, 8–11 = moderate, and 12–15 = high. What are your strongest and weakest aspects of interaction involvement?

Research Findings and Recommendations for Improving Interaction Involvement.   In contrast to people with low interaction involvement, highly involved individuals are more effective at directing the flow of a conversation, speak more frequently during an ongoing social interaction, and exhibit less distracting nonverbal body movements while speaking. Highly involved individuals also possess higher self-esteem and satisfaction with communication than low involved people.[38] Overall, research findings support the notion that interaction

---

[35] For a discussion about the components of interaction involvement, see Donald J. Cegala, Grant T. Savage, Claire C. Brunner, and Anne B. Conrad, "An Elaboration of the Meaning of Interaction Involvement: Toward the Development of a Theoretical Concept," *Communication Monographs,* December 1982, pp. 229–48.

[36] Based on discussion found in Erving Goffman, *Interaction Ritual: Essays in Face-to-Face Behavior* (Chicago: Aldine, 1967).

[37] Donald J. Cegala, "Affective and Cognitive Manifestations of Interaction Involvement during Unstructured and Competitive Interactions," *Communication Monographs,* December 1984, p. 321.

[38] Results are found in Cegala, Savage, Brunner, and Conrad, "An Elaboration of the Meaning of Interaction Involvement: Toward the Development of a Theoretical Concept," pp. 229–48; Cegala, "Affective and Cognitive Manifestations of Interaction Involvement during Unstructured and Competitive Interactions," pp. 320–38; and Cegala, "Interaction Involvement: A Cognitive Dimension of Communicative Competence."

■ **TABLE 12–8**   The Interaction Involvement Scale

Instructions: Circle your response to each item by using the following scale:
1 = Strongly disagree
2 = Disagree
3 = Neither
4 = Agree
5 = Strongly agree

Responsiveness:

1. Often in conversations, I'm not sure what my role is; that is, I'm not sure how I'm
   expected to relate to others.   1   2   3   4   5
2. Often in conversations I'm not sure what the other is really saying.   1   2   3   4   5
3. Often I feel sort of "unplugged" from the social situation of which I am part; that is,
   I'm uncertain of my role, others' motives, and what's happening.   1   2   3   4   5

Perceptiveness:

1. I am keenly aware of how others perceive me during my conversations.   1   2   3   4   5
2. During conversations I am sensitive to others' subtle or hidden meanings.   1   2   3   4   5
3. I am very observant during my conversations with others.   1   2   3   4   5

Attentiveness:

1. My mind wanders during conversations and I often miss parts of what is going on.   1   2   3   4   5
2. Often I will pretend to be listening to someone when in fact I'm thinking about something
   else.   1   2   3   4   5
3. Often I am preoccupied in my conversations and do not pay complete attention to
   others.   1   2   3   4   5

SOURCE: Excerpted from Donald J. Cegala, "Affective and Cognitive Manifestations of Interaction Involvement during Unstructured and Competitive Interactions," *Communication Monographs,* December 1984, p. 322.

involvement is an important component of communication competence. Because communication competence affects an individual's career progress and the overall quality of communication in an organization, it is worthwhile to consider methods of improving interaction involvement.

Assessment, awareness, and behavior modification are key aspects of enhancing one's interaction involvement. Your interaction involvement can be improved by consciously increasing your responsiveness, perceptiveness, and attentiveness during conversations. The self-assessment questionnaire in Table 12–8 can be used periodically to monitor your progress. If you notice that situational factors—like fatigue or preoccupation—are lowering your involvement level, try to tactfully remove yourself from the situation. No involvement may be better than low involvement, which engenders bad feelings from others more highly involved in the conversation.

■ NONVERBAL COMMUNICATION AND ACTIVE LISTENING

Nonverbal communication and active listening also affect communication effectiveness and competence. Relevant dynamics of the nonverbal and listening components of organizational communication are explored in this section.

Sources of Nonverbal Communication

Nonverbal communication is "Any message, sent or received independent of the written or spoken word, . . . [It] includes such factors as use of time and space, distance between persons when conversing, use of color, dress, walking behavior, standing, positioning, seating arrangement, office locations and furnishings."[39] Due to the prevalence of nonverbal communication and its significant impact on organizational behavior (including, but not limited to, perceptions of others, hiring decisions, work attitudes, and turnover),[40] it is important that managers become consciously aware of the sources of nonverbal communication.

Physical Features and Environmental Characteristics.   An individual's physical features and the environment in which a conversation occurs are important sources of nonverbal communication. Body type—overweight, muscular, or underweight—skin color, clothes, and physical handicaps affect what we infer about what people actually say and write. Researchers have documented that positive impressions in the United States are ascribed to those who are thin, white-skinned, and not physically handicapped.[41] Facial attractiveness, which is related to these nonverbal cues, has been found to predict scholastic success in a military academy.[42] These tendencies can be criticized as unfair, racist, or sexist, but they still play a key role in communication. Moreover, a report from a conference attended by 400 fashion trendsetters, sociologists, and psychologists concluded that clothes convey consistent and predictable impressions.[43] Bright colors draw attention, while suit jackets and blazers create positive impressions in business settings. As indicated in Table 12–9, aspiring female and male managers need to know the fine points of dressing for success.

---

[39] Walter D. St. John, "You Are What You Communicate," *Personnel Journal,* October 1985, p. 40.

[40] An interesting study of the impact of nonverbal and verbal communication on perceptions of competence was conducted by Nicole A. Steckler and Robert Rosenthal, "Sex Differences in Nonverbal and Verbal Communication with Bosses, Peers, and Subordinates," *Journal of Applied Psychology,* February 1985, pp. 157–63. The impact of nonverbal cues on selection decisions was examined by Charles K. Parsons and Robert C. Liden, "Interviewer Perceptions of Applicant Qualifications: A Multivariate Field Study of Demographic Characteristics and Nonverbal Cues," *Journal of Applied Psychology,* November 1984, pp. 557–68. Employee reactions to environmental nonverbal cues were studied by Greg R. Oldham and Yitzhak Fried, "Employee Reactions to Workspace Characteristics," *Journal of Applied Psychology,* February 1987, pp. 75–80.

[41] For a summary of this research, see Karlene H. Roberts, "Communicating in Organizations," in *Modules in Management,* ed. James E. Rosenzweig and Fremont E. Kast (Chicago: Science Research Associates, 1984).

[42] Results can be found in LeAnne Dickey-Bryant, Gary J. Lautenschlager, and Jorge L. Mendoza, "Facial Attractiveness and Its Relation to Occupational Success," *Journal of Applied Psychology,* February 1986, pp. 16–19. A research review of the relationship between physical appearance variables and performance ratings is provided by Kenneth P. DeMeuse, "A Review of the Effects of Non-Verbal Cues on the Performance Appraisal Process," *Journal of Occupational Psychology,* September 1987, pp. 207–26.

[43] See Beverly Gary Kempton, "The Language of Clothes," *Working Woman,* September 1984, pp. 157, 159.

■ **TABLE 12–9** Dressing for Success

A decade ago, "The Woman's Dress for Success Book" propelled female executives into somber suits and blouses with big floppy bows at the neck. Then, a few years ago, a barrage of media stories reported that women had achieved enough success to look more feminine. It was fine to loosen up and wear dresses. . . .

Maybe so. But interviews with dozens of executives, both male and female, found that most would be shocked to see mini-skirts on female executives. Indeed, the consensus seems to be that, despite the relaxation of dress codes, it still isn't acceptable to look too feminine— or too sexy or too cute—in corporate America.

Those interviewed say most female executives dress in a professional manner. But they can also recall vividly at least one inappropriate outfit that influenced their judgment of a woman's capability. . . .

Not surprisingly, the issue strikes some feminists as absurd. "It's a big waste of time to stand in front of your closet and worry about whether someone will think badly of you because of a lacy collar," says Letty Cottin Pogrebin, a founding editor of Ms. "It's a terrible duality. It has nothing to do with our performance."

Still, in actual practice the results of such readings can be dire. John T. Molloy, who wrote a "Dress for Success" book for men as well as the one for women, says that as part of a study he asked the managers of about 10,000 female office workers to describe the women's style of dress. Then he tracked the women's career progress over three years.

He found that the female executives whose attire was described as "extremely feminine" were typically paid less and promoted less frequently. The highest-paid women, on the other hand, were those whose dress was described as professional, dull, conservative, non-sexy or non-frilly. Women whose clothes were termed conservative or traditional were twice as likely to receive promotions as those whose dress was labeled frilly or frivolous, or occasionally frilly or occasionally sexy.

"If you wear very fluffy or sexy clothing or a miniskirt," Mr. Molloy asserts, "you are cutting short not only your skirt but your career."

Men also pay for sartorial mistakes. Though the uniform nature of men's suits provides fewer opportunities for dramatic gaffes, and men rarely have to worry about sexist responses, they are often judged harshly for looking too sloppy, too casual, too quirky or too flashy. As with women, such infractions lead some executives to question their judgment and business acumen.

While the executives interviewed agree that it's certainly possible to look both feminine and professional, just what it means to look "too feminine" is open to debate. When the executives were asked to cite specific outfits they find inappropriate, their opinions varied by industry. But both men and women mentioned outfits that were too flowery, too tight, too short, too low-cut, too "cutesy" or too loud. They also complained about spike heels, hats, and excessive makeup and jewelry. . . .

The executives queried agree that the biggest clothing mistakes seem to show up on job applicants and other visitors from outside an office. A female candidate for a job involving labor negotiation at a large Los Angeles savings-and-loan association arrived in a blue and pink flowery dress with "little flouncy sleeves" and a "little lace collar" says Patricia Benninger, a vice president of human resources there.

The dress "turned off all the credibility she could have built up during the interview," says Ms. Benninger. "My feelings were, She doesn't know the job." The outfit, she adds, said that the woman was "someone who could be easily persuaded," and that "this person couldn't stand up to toughness."

SOURCE: Excerpted from Kathleen A. Hughes, "Businesswomen's Broader Latitude in Dress Codes Goes Just So Far." Reprinted by permission of *The Wall Street Journal*, Dow Jones & Company, Inc., September 1, 1987. All rights reserved.

Environmental factors such as room temperature and darkness, furniture arrangements, and the number of people in an area also send nonverbal messages.[44]

Body Movements and Gestures.   Body movements, such as leaning forward or backward, and gestures, such as pointing, provide additional nonverbal information. Open body positions such as leaning backward, communicate *immediacy,* a term used to represent openness, warmth, closeness, and availability for communication. *Defensiveness* is communicated by gestures such as folding arms, crossing hands, and crossing one's legs.[45] Judith Hall, a communication researcher, conducted a meta-analysis of gender differences in body movements and gestures. Results revealed that women nodded their heads and moved their hands more than men. Leaning forward, large body shifts, and foot and leg movements were exhibited more frequently by men than women.[46] Although it is both easy and fun to interpret body movements and gestures, it is important to remember, "There isn't a reliable dictionary of gestures, and the meaning of gestures depends on the context, the actor, the culture, and other factors."[47]

Touch.   Touching is another powerful nonverbal cue. In many cultures, touch can signal compassion, warmth, attraction, and friendliness. People tend to touch those they like. In addition, touch may be used to establish and maintain perceptions of power. Individuals employed in jobs perceived as low in status, such as a mailroom clerk, tend to get touched more frequently. A meta-analysis of gender differences in touching indicated that women do more touching during conversations than men. Keep in mind, however, that men and women interpret touching differently. While women differentiate between touching for the purpose of conveying warmth/friendship and sexual attraction, men may not.[48] Sexual harassment claims can be reduced by keeping this perceptual difference in mind.

Facial Expressions.   Facial expressions convey a wealth of information. Smiling, for instance, typically represents warmth, happiness, or friendship, whereas frowning conveys dissatisfaction or anger. Although puckered lips are used for kissing, during conversations they might convey confusion or contemplation.

---

[44] For an instructive summary of this research, see Tim R. V. Davis, "The Influence of the Physical Environment in Offices," *Academy of Management Review,* April 1984, pp. 271–83.

[45] Supporting research is presented in Peter A. Anderson, "Nonverbal Immediacy in Interpersonal Communication," in *Multichannel Integrations of Nonverbal Behavior,* ed. Aron W. Siegman and Stanley Feldstein (Hillsdale, N.J.: Lawrence Erlbaum, 1985), pp. 1–36.

[46] Related research is summarized by Judith A. Hall, "Male and Female Nonverbal Behavior," in *Multichannel Integrations of Nonverbal Behavior,* ed. Aron W. Siegman and Stanley Feldstein (Hillsdale, N.J.: Lawrence Erlbaum, 1985), pp. 195–226.

[47] Roberts, "Communicating in Organizations," p. 15.

[48] Touching research is reviewed by Brenda Major, "Gender Patterns in Touching Behavior," in *Gender and Nonverbal Behavior,* ed. Nancy M. Henley (New York: Springer-Verlag, 1981). Meta-analytic results can be found in Hall, "Male and Female Nonverbal Behavior."

Research evidence reveals that women smile more frequently than men.[49] Because smiling sometimes is viewed as nonassertive and low-power behavior, smiling too much might lead others to form negative impressions about oneself. This does not mean one should never smile at work. Rather, facial expression should suit the occasion. A communication consultant offers the following advice on facial expressions.

> Smiling is inappropriate just about any time you want to persuade or influence, to make a claim to power. A simple rule of thumb: When you want to be taken seriously, wear an expression to match.[50]

A recent study reinforced the communicative power of facial expressions. Results indicated that network television newscasters Tom Brokaw, Dan Rather, and Peter Jennings exhibited different patterns of facial expressions when referring to candidates in the 1984 U.S. presidential election. Peter Jennings displayed more positive expressions when referring to Ronald Reagan than when talking about Walter Mondale. Brokaw and Rather displayed no such facial expression bias. A follow-up study indicated that voting behavior mirrored the newscasters' facial expressions. Reagan received significantly more votes from viewers who regularly watched Peter Jennings. There was no significant difference in voting behavior among Brokaw's or Rather's regular viewers.[51] Managers need to be wary of this subtle but potent source of bias in their own facial expressions.

Eye Contact. Eye contact is a strong nonverbal cue that serves four functions in communication. First, eye contact regulates the flow of communication by signaling the beginning and end of conversation. There is a tendency to look away from others when beginning to speak and to look at them when done. Second, gazing (as opposed to glaring) facilitates and monitors feedback because it reflects interest and attention. Third, eye contact conveys emotion. People tend to avoid eye contact when discussing bad news or providing negative feedback. Fourth, gazing relates to the type of relationship between communicators. People tend to gaze longer when conversing with others they like and/or with whom they have intense relationships.[52]

Interpersonal Distance Zones. Renowned anthropologist Edward Hall studied the impact of social and personal space on human communication and behavior. He identified four distance zones that regulate interpersonal interactions. These zones differ across cultures. The zones and accompanying distance for Americans are:

---

[49] This finding was reported in Jacqueline Shannon, ''Don't Smile When You Say That,'' *Executive Female,* March–April 1987, pp. 33, 43.

[50] Ibid.

[51] Results are discussed in Brian Mullen, David Futrell, Debbie Stairs, Dianne M. Tice, Roy F. Baumeister, Kathryn E. Dawson, Catherine A. Riordan, Christine E. Radloff, George R. Goethals, John G. Kennedy, and Paul Rosenfeld, ''Newscasters' Facial Expressions and Voting Behavior of Viewers: Can a Smile Elect a President?'' *Journal of Personality and Social Psychology,* August 1986, pp. 291–95.

[52] See the related discussion presented in Roberts, ''Communicating in Organizations.''

- *Intimate distance,* the zone for lovemaking, wrestling, comforting, and protecting, is physical contact to 18 inches.
- *Personal distance* is 1.5 to 4 feet and is used for interpersonal interactions with friends or acquaintances.
- *Social distance,* the zone used for business and casual social interactions, spans 4 to 12 feet.
- *Public distance* is used for impersonal and formal interactions and covers 12 to 25 feet.[53]

The important point to remember is that people strive to maintain a distance zone consistent with their cultural expectations and the nature of the interaction. Violating interpersonal distance zones creates discomfort, which can reduce communication effectiveness.

Practical Tips.   A communication expert offers the following advice to improve nonverbal communication skills.

Positive nonverbal actions that help to communicate include:

- Maintaining eye contact.
- Occasionally nodding the head in agreement.
- Smiling and showing animation.
- Leaning toward the speaker.
- Speaking at a moderate rate, in a quiet, assuring tone. . . .

Here are some actions . . . to avoid:

- Looking away or turning away from the speaker.
- Closing your eyes.
- Using an unpleasant voice tone.
- Speaking too quickly or too slowly.
- Yawning excessively.[54]

Practice these tips by turning the sound off while watching television, and trying to interpret emotions and interactions, and by watching yourself talk in a mirror. Honest feedback from your friends about your nonverbal communication style also may help.

Active Listening

Some communication experts contend that listening is the fundamental communication skill for today's managers.[55] Estimates suggest that managers typically spend about 9 percent of a working day reading, 16 percent writing, 30

---

[53] Based on Edward T. Hall, *The Hidden Dimension* (Garden City, N.Y.: Doubleday, 1966).

[54] St. John, "You Are What You Communicate," p. 43.

[55] See Walter Kiechel III, "Learn How to Listen," *Fortune,* August 17, 1987, pp. 107–8.

■ **FIGURE 12–9** Listener Comprehension Model

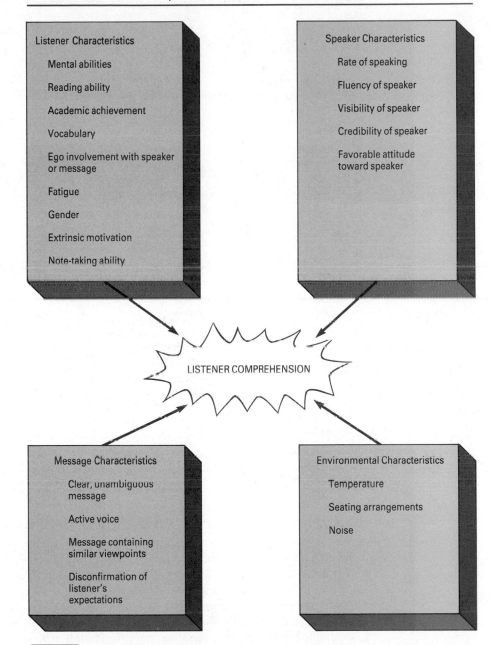

Listener Characteristics

   Mental abilities

   Reading ability

   Academic achievement

   Vocabulary

   Ego involvement with speaker
   or message

   Fatigue

   Gender

   Extrinsic motivation

   Note-taking ability

Speaker Characteristics

   Rate of speaking

   Fluency of speaker

   Visibility of speaker

   Credibility of speaker

   Favorable attitude
   toward speaker

LISTENER COMPREHENSION

Message Characteristics

   Clear, unambiguous
   message

   Active voice

   Message containing
   similar viewpoints

   Disconfirmation of
   listener's
   expectations

Environmental Characteristics

   Temperature

   Seating arrangements

   Noise

SOURCE: Adapted from discussion in Kittie W. Watson and Larry L. Barker, "Listening Behavior: Definition and Measurement," in *Communication Yearbook 8,* ed. Robert N. Bostrom (Beverly Hills, Calif.: Sage Publications, 1984), pp. 178–97.

■ **TABLE 12–10**

Keys to Effective Listening	The Bad Listener	The Good Listener
1. Find areas of interest.	Tunes out dry subjects	Opportunitizes; asks "What's in it for me?"
2. Judge content, not delivery.	Tunes out if delivery is poor	Judges content, skips over delivery errors
3. Hold your fire.	Tends to enter into arguments	Doesn't judge until comprehension is complete
4. Listen for ideas.	Listens for facts	Listens for central themes
5. Be flexible.	Takes intensive notes using only one system	Takes fewer notes. Uses four or five different systems, depending on speaker
6. Work at listening.	Shows no energy output; Attention is faked	Works hard, exhibits active body state
7. Resist distractions.	Is distracted easily	Fights or avoids distractions, tolerates bad habits, knows how to concentrate
8. Exercise your mind.	Resists difficult expository material; seeks light, recreational material	Uses heavier material as exercise for the mind
9. Keep your mind open.	Reacts to emotional words	Interprets color words; does not get hung up on them
10. Capitalize on the fact that *thought* is faster than speech.	Tends to daydream with slow speakers	Challenges, anticipates, mentally summarizes, weighs the evidence, listens between the lines to tone of voice

SOURCE: Lyman K. Steil, "How Well Do You Listen?" *Executive Female,* Special Issue No. 2 (1986), p. 37. Reprinted with permission from *Executive Female,* the bimonthly publication of the National Association for Female Executives.

percent talking, and 45 percent listening.[56] Moreover, because listening appears to be effortless—we have the cognitive ability to process information three to four times faster than people speak—it is often neglected or taken for granted. Listening involves much more than hearing a message. Hearing is merely the physical component of listening.

Listening is the process of *actively* decoding and interpreting verbal messages. Listening requires cognitive attention and information processing; hearing does

---

[56] Estimates are provided in both Donald W. Caudill and Regina M. Donaldson, "Effective Listening Tips for Managers," *Administrative Management,* September 1986, pp. 22–23; and Eugene Raudsepp, "What Do We Listen For?" *Executive Female,* Special Issue No. 1 (1986), pp. 15–18.

not. With these distinctions in mind, we will examine a model of listener comprehension and some practical advice for becoming a more effective listener.

Listener Comprehension Model.   Listener comprehension represents the extent to which an individual can recall factual information and draw accurate conclusions and inferences from a verbal message. It is a function of listener, speaker, message, and environmental characteristics (see Figure 12–9). Communication researchers Kittie Watson and Larry Barker conducted a global review of listening behavior research and arrived at the following conclusions. Listening comprehension is positively related to high mental and reading abilities, academic achievements, a large vocabulary, being ego-involved with the speaker, having energy, being female, extrinsic motivation to pay attention, and being able to take good notes. Speakers who talk too fast or too slow, possess disturbing accents or speech patterns, are not visible to the audience, lack credibility, or are disliked have a negative impact on listening comprehension. In contrast, clear messages stated in the active voice increase listening comprehension. The same is true of messages containing viewpoints similar to the listener's or those that disconfirm expectations. Finally, comfortable environmental characteristics and compact seating arrangements enhance listening comprehension.[57]

Becoming a More Effective Listener.   Table 12–10 presents 10 keys to effective listening. You can improve your listening skills by avoiding the 10 habits of bad listeners while cultivating good listening habits. Importantly, it takes awareness, effort, and practice to improve one's listening comprehension. Is anyone listening?

SUMMARY OF KEY CONCEPTS

A.   Managers spend the majority of their workday communicating with others. The effectiveness of this communication is significantly related to an individual's job satisfaction and performance as well as to overall organizational performance. Face-to-face communication is the most frequently used medium. Managers communicate more frequently with subordinates than with superiors, internal others, and external others.

B.   Communication is a process of consecutively linked elements. Historically, this process was described in terms of a conduit model. Criticisms of this model led to development of a perceptual process model of communication that depicts receivers as information processors who create the meaning of messages in their own mind. Because receivers' interpretations of messages often differ from that intended by senders, miscommunication is a common occurrence.

---

[57] For a summary of supporting research, see Kittie W. Watson and Larry L. Barker, ''Listening Behavior: Definition and Measurement,'' in *Communication Yearbook 8,* ed. Robert N. Bostrom (Beverly Hills, Calif.: Sage Publications, 1984).

C. Selecting media is a key component of communication effectiveness. Media selection is based on the interaction between the information richness of a medium and the complexity of the problem/situation at hand. Information richness ranges from low to high and is a function of four factors: speed of feedback, characteristics of the channel, type of communication, and language source. Problems/situations range from simple to complex. Effective communication occurs when the richness of the medium matches the complexity of the problem/situation. From a contingency perspective, richer media need to be used as problems/situations become more complex.

D. Hierarchical communication patterns describe exchanges of information between managers and employees they supervise. Managers provide five types of downward communication: job instructions, job rationale, organizational procedures and practices, feedback about performance, and indoctrination of goals. Employees communicate information upward about themselves, co-workers and their problems, organizational practices and policies, and what needs to be done and how to do it.

E. Communication distortion is a common problem that consists of modifying the content of a message. Employees distort upward communication when their supervisor has high upward influence and/or power. Distortion also increases when employees aspire to move upward and when they do not trust their supervisor.

F. The grapevine is the unofficial communication system of the informal organization. Communication along the grapevine follows four predictable patterns: single strand, gossip, probability, and cluster. The cluster pattern is the most common.

G. Communication competence reflects the extent to which an individual is an effective communicator. It is determined by an individual's communication abilities/traits, situational factors, and the individuals involved in an interaction. An assertive communication style is more effective than both an aggressive and nonassertive style. Effective communicators tend to exhibit high interaction involvement.

H. There are several identifiable sources of nonverbal communication that affect communication effectiveness. Physical features, body movements and gestures, touch, facial expressions, eye contact, and interpersonal distance zones are important nonverbal cues. Listening is the process of actively decoding and interpreting verbal messages. Listener characteristics, speaker characteristics, message characteristics, and environmental characteristics influence listener comprehension.

KEY TERMS

communication
perceptual model of communi-
    cation

noise
information richness
hierarchical communication

communication distortion   **aggressive style**
grapevine   **nonassertive style**
liaison individual   **interaction involvement**
communication competence   **nonverbal communication**
assertive style   **listening**

DISCUSSION QUESTIONS

1. Do you think miscommunication is the norm or exception in the typical workplace? Explain.
2. Describe a situation when you had trouble decoding a message. What caused the problem?
3. What are some sources of noise that interfere with communication during a class lecture, an encounter with a professor in his or her office, and a movie?
4. Which of the three zones of communication in Figure 12–4 (overload, effective, oversimplification) do you think is most common in today's large organizations? Explain your rationale.
5. Have you ever distorted upward communication? What was your reason? Was it related to one of the four antecedents of communication distortion? Explain.
6. What is your personal experience with the grapevine? Do you see it as a positive or negative factor in the workplace? Explain.
7. Would you describe your prevailing communication style as assertive, aggressive, or nonassertive? How can you tell? Would your style help or hinder you as a manager?
8. Are you good at reading nonverbal communication? Give some examples.
9. What are your experiences with intercultural differences in interpersonal distance zones?
10. What steps do you need to take to become a better listener? Explain.

BACK TO THE OPENING CASE

Now that you have read Chapter 12, you should be able to answer the following questions about the Allstate case:

1. What was the complexity of the problem/situation faced by Allstate? Were the company's communication media appropriate for this level of complexity? Explain.
2. Would you classify Allstate's corporate communication style as assertive, aggressive, or nonassertive? Discuss your rationale.
3. What was Allstate's apparent attitude toward the grapevine? Do you agree with this attitude? Explain.
4. How did Allstate try to reduce distortion of downward communication?

EXERCISE 12

Objectives

1. To demonstrate the relative effectiveness of communicating assertively, aggressively, and nonassertively.
2. To give you hands-on experience with different styles of communication.

Introduction

Research shows that assertive communication is more effective than either an aggressive or nonassertive style. This *role-playing exercise* is designed to increase your ability to communicate assertively. Your task is to use different communication styles while attempting to resolve the work-related problems of a poor performer.

Instructions

Read the "Poor Performer" and "Store Manager" roles shown below. Pair up with someone and decide who will initially play the poor performer role and who will play the managerial role. When playing the managerial role, you should first attempt to resolve the problem by using an *aggressive* communication style. Attempt to achieve your objective by using the nonverbal and verbal behavior patterns associated with the aggressive style shown in Table 12–7. Take about four to six minutes to act out the instructions. The person playing the manager should then try to resolve the problem with a *nonassertive* style and finally with an *assertive* style. Once again, rely on the relevant nonverbal and verbal behavior patterns presented in Table 12–7 and take four to six minutes to act out each scenario. After completing these three role plays, switch roles: Manager becomes poor performer and poor performer becomes manager. Try to be realistic and true to the characters established in the role specifications.

Role: Poor Performer

You sell shoes full-time for a national chain of shoe stores. During the last month you have been absent three times without giving your manager a reason. The quality of your work has been slipping. You have a lot of creative excuses when your boss tries to talk to you about your performance.

When playing this role, feel free to invent a personal problem that you may eventually want to share with your manager. However, make the manager dig for information about this problem. Otherwise, respond to your manager's comments as you normally would.

Role: Store Manager

You manage a store for a national chain of shoe stores. In the privacy of your office, you are talking to one of your salespeople who has had three unexcused absences from work during the last month. The quality of his or her work has been slipping. Customers have complained that this person is rude, and co-workers have told you this individual isn't carrying his or her fair share of the work. You are fairly sure this person has some sort of personal problem. You want to identify that problem and get him or her back on the right track.

Questions for Consideration/Class Discussion

1. What drawbacks of the aggressive and nonassertive styles did you observe?
2. What were the advantages of the assertive style?
3. What were the most difficult aspects of trying to use an assertive style?
4. How important was nonverbal communication during the various role plays? Explain with examples.

PART FOUR

Understanding and Managing Organizational Processes and Problems

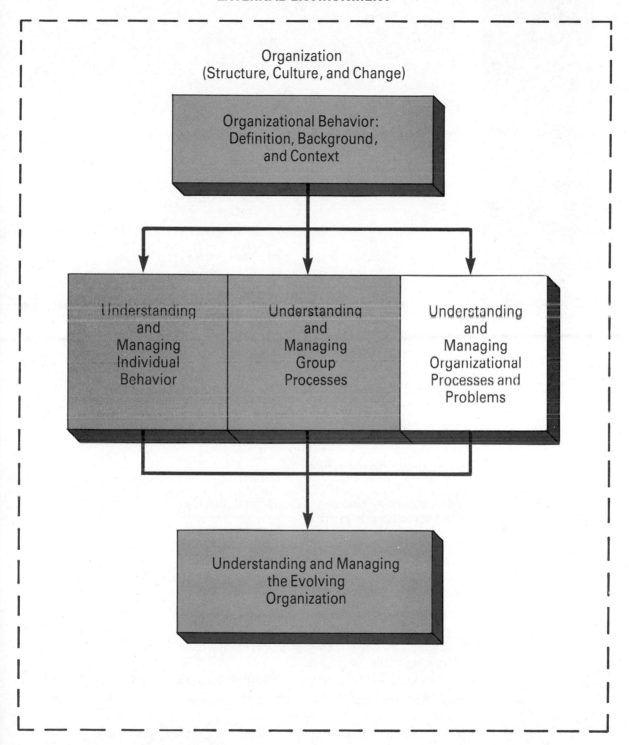

Chapter **13**

Leadership

LEARNING OBJECTIVES

When you finish studying the material in this chapter,
you should be able to:

- Define the term *leadership* and describe the evolution of modern leadership theory.
- Discuss the idea of one best style of leadership, using Blake and Mouton's Managerial Grid as a point of reference.
- Explain, according to Fiedler's contingency model, how leadership style interacts with situational control.
- Contrast House's path-goal theory with Vroom and Yetton's decision-making model of leadership.
- Discuss the role-making (VDL) and attributional models of leadership.
- Explain the practical implications of the three categories of substitutes for leadership.
- Discuss Zaleznik's distinction between leaders and managers.

Leading Domino's Pizza to Success

Bob Popiolek remembers how Tom Monaghan used to drag himself home from his pizza shop about 3 A.M., carrying the night's receipts in a brown paper bag. He would finally get around to counting the cash the next afternoon at the kitchen table in his trailer home.

"Funny, but it seemed like a burden to him, like the fun was in the work, not the money," says Popiolek, who lived in the same Ypsilanti, Mich., trailer park and swapped friendly wagers with Monaghan about who would build the tallest building, make the most money, win the most fame.

They have not seen each other in almost 20 years, but Popiolek is willing to concede that Thomas S. Monaghan, 48, founder of Domino's Pizza, the world's largest privately held restaurant chain, won each bet.

From near-bankruptcy in 1970, the chain fought its way back to solvency—and more. Revenues were $98 million in 1980. The slogan at Domino's in the past year was "One-point-five in 85." That is $1.5 billion in sales and franchise royalties, more than double the 1984 figure. [Domino's met its 1985 goal.]

In 1984 Monaghan had an estimated worth of $200 million; in 1985 he was worth $50 million more. Domino's is expanding at the rate of 21 stores each week. The days of cash in brown paper bags are over. . . .

Friends and competitors of Tom Monaghan agree his success is attributable to a few key traits:

- He is undeterred by failure. In 1970, after trying to expand too fast and go public, he was $1.5 million in debt. Refusing to file for bankruptcy, he instead fired everyone except his wife and his bookkeeper. He paid off the Internal Revenue Service and about 1,500 creditors, writing checks stamped with a personally designed logo of a man wearing only a rain barrel.

- He has kept his concept simple. For most of its 25 years, Domino's menu has included only pizza (two or three sizes, 11 toppings) and cola. No sit-down, only takeout and delivery, guaranteed in 30 minutes or less. Ninety percent of deliveries meet the guarantee, and drivers who make the most deliveries on time win trips to the Indy 500.

- Monaghan rewards his own. His top executives drive $38,000 BMWs or other expensive cars of their choice. The company owns a million-dollar, 64-foot yacht called the *Tigress II,* on which particularly successful store managers spend weekend cruises. In 1984, 68 store managers who increased their sales 50 percent won $3,800 trips for two to Hawaii. On Monaghan's wrist is a $12,000 Patek Philippe gold watch, Swiss-made, which he will give to any store manager whose weekly sales top the company record (the current record, $62,087, is held by a store in Myrtle Beach, S.C.). He has given away half a dozen. . . .

- And he tries to be good. Last spring he

Concluded:

hired a corporate chaplain, a Catholic priest who says mass each morning in a conference room off the Domino's headquarters cafeteria. Monaghan attends daily. When he is on the road, he goes to a local church. . . .

Domino's has franchised two thirds of its more than 2,800 outlets—it is the fastest-growing franchise in the nation, although it is still smaller than rival Pizza Hut, which has more than 4,000 units and had 1984 sales of $1.9 billion. Of Domino's franchisees, 98 percent are former employees. Stores have opened in Japan, Australia, West Germany and Britain, as well as Canada.

The growth comes because people want to share in Monaghan's success. "He wants you to succeed so much that you want him to succeed, too. He believes there's enough room for everyone in the high-priced seats," says Becky Belknap, who, with her husband, Gene, went to work for Monaghan in the mid-60s. Now they own seven Domino's stores in Ann Arbor.

Aside from tangible incentives, Monaghan believes in teamwork and will try anything to promote it. Two years ago, he bought a sailboat and took his executives on Michigan's annual Port Huron-to-Mackinac race. "He read somewhere that the best way to get men to cooperate and work together was in war," recalls Bill Martin, an Ann Arbor developer who helped Monaghan find the boat, "and the next best was as a crew in a major sailboat race."

Nothing is done the usual way at Domino's. "A lot of companies would say we do things wrong, because instead of Tom telling people it isn't going to work, he lets them try it, then *they* find out," says Monaghan aide Helen McNulty. "Tom always says, 'If you're not making mistakes, you're not working.' "

He keeps in his office files a folder labeled "Dream File," into which he slips clippings about things he would like to own, places he would like to see, people he would like to meet.

"I have a big appetite for so many things," he says.

Domino's Expands (An Update)*

By February 1988, Domino's had grown to 4,280 outlets. Sales climbed more than 35 percent during 1987, exceeding $1.9 billion. Monaghan even expanded to Central America by opening a pizza store in the mountains of Honduras. Part of the profits from that outlet, at Monaghan's insistence, are being used to fund a Catholic mission in the Honduran town of San Pedro Sula. Monaghan is quick to tell people that he considers the entire world to be a potential market for Domino's pizzas.

For Discussion

Is Tom Monaghan a good role model for aspiring managers? Explain.

* An update on Domino's is presented in Wendy Zellner, "Tom Monaghan: The Fun-Loving Prince of Pizza," *Business Week*, February 8, 1988, pp. 90–93.

SOURCE: Excerpted from Susan Ager, "An Appetite for More Than Pizza," pp. 81–83. Reprinted by permission from *Nation's Business,* February 1986. Copyright 1986, U.S. Chamber of Commerce.

■ Additional discussion questions linking this case with the following material appear at the end of this chapter.

Someone once observed that a leader is a person who finds out which way the parade is going, jumps in front of it, and yells "Follow me!" The plain fact is that this approach to leadership has little chance of working in today's rapidly changing world. Admired leaders, such as civil rights activist Martin Luther King, Jr., Britain's Margaret Thatcher, and Chrysler's Lee Iacocca, led people in bold new directions. They envisioned how things could be improved, rallied followers, and refused to accept failure. In short, successful leaders are those individuals who can step into a difficult situation and make a noticeable difference. But how much of a difference can leaders make in modern organizations?

OB researchers have discovered that leaders can make a *significant* difference. In one study, for example, the performance of 50 United Methodist ministers was studied over a 20-year period. After dividing the sample into effective and ineffective leaders, the researchers compared objective measures of performance for the two groups. Effective and ineffective leadership was determined by the ministers' positive or negative impact on attendance at worship services, membership in the congregation, property value, and monetary giving. Results indicated that churches with superior ministers experienced significantly greater charitable income, membership, and property value than the remaining churches.[1] Another study tracked the relationship between net profit and leadership in 167 companies from 13 industries. It also covered a time span of 20 years. Higher net profits were earned by companies with effective leaders.[2] Leadership does make a difference in today's organizations, and that difference is worth studying because it can become a competitive advantage.

After formally defining the term *leadership*, this chapter focuses on the following areas: (1) the evolution of leadership theory, (2) alternative contingency theories of leadership, (3) emerging interpretations of leadership, and (4) the distinction between leading and managing.

■ WHAT DOES LEADERSHIP INVOLVE?

Because the topic of leadership has fascinated people for centuries, definitions abound. A common thread among these definitions is social influence. As the term is used in this chapter, **leadership** is defined as "a social influence process in which the leader seeks the voluntary participation of subordinates in an effort to reach organizational objectives."[3]

Tom Peters and Nancy Austin, authors of the best seller *A Passion for Excellence*, describe leadership in broader terms:

---

[1] Results are presented in Jonathan E. Smith, Kenneth P. Carson, and Ralph A. Alexander, "Leadership: It Can Make a Difference," *Academy of Management Journal*, December 1984, pp. 765–76.

[2] See Stanley Lieberson and James F. O'Connor, "Leadership and Organizational Performance: A Study of Large Corporations," *American Sociological Review*, April 1972, pp. 117–30.

[3] Chester A. Schriesheim, James M. Tolliver, and Orlando C. Behling, "Leadership Theory: Some Implications for Managers," *MSU Business Topics*, Summer 1978, p. 35.

Leadership means vision, cheerleading, enthusiasm, love, trust, verve, passion, obsession, consistency, the use of symbols, paying attention as illustrated by the content of one's calendar, out-and-out drama (and the management thereof), creating heroes at all levels, coaching, effectively wandering around, and numerous other things. Leadership must be present at all levels of the organization. It depends on a million little things done with obsession, consistency and care, but all of those million little things add up to nothing if the trust, vision and basic belief are not there.[4]

Leadership clearly entails more than wielding power and exercising authority. The label *leadership* embraces many different managerial concepts already discussed, including values, perception, motivation, reinforcement, socialization, power, politics, and communication. Furthermore, as indicated in Table 13–1, successful leadership is exhibited in different ways.

■ THE EVOLUTION OF MODERN LEADERSHIP THEORY

To comprehend current leadership theory, we need to understand how it has evolved. This section offers a brief historical perspective of leadership theory. Three theoretical approaches are discussed: trait theory, behavioral styles theory, and situational theory. Each explains leadership from a different point of view (see Figure 13–1). All three schools of thought can teach present and future managers valuable lessons about leading.

Trait Theory

At the turn of the 20th century, the prevailing belief was that leaders were born, not made. Selected people were thought to possess inborn traits that made them successful leaders. A **leader trait** is a physical or personality characteristic that can be used to differentiate leaders from followers.

Before World War II, hundreds of studies were conducted to pinpoint the traits of successful leaders. Dozens of leadership traits were identified. During the postwar period, however, enthusiasm was replaced by widespread criticism. Studies conducted by Ralph Stogdill in 1948 and by Richard Mann in 1959, which sought to summarize the impact of traits on leadership, caused the trait approach to fall into disfavor.

Stogdill's and Mann's Findings.   Based on his review, Stogdill concluded that five traits tended to differentiate leaders from average followers. They were (1) intelligence, (2) dominance, (3) self-confidence, (4) level of energy and

[4] Tom Peters and Nancy Austin, *A Passion for Excellence* (New York: Random House, 1985), pp. 5–6.

■ **TABLE 13–1** Contrasting Leadership Styles at Liz Claiborne Inc.

Her dream was to design clothes for professional women, get her name on the label, and build a small, successful business. Instead Elisabeth Claiborne Ortenberg built an empire. In 1986 Liz Claiborne Inc. moved onto the Fortune 500 list of the largest industrial companies in the U.S. An 11-year-old enterprise, it is one of the youngest companies ever to make the cut.

Claiborne, 57, has turned a $255,000 investment into a consistently profitable apparel company with estimated 1986 revenues of $800 million. . . .

Claiborne was one of the first designers to steer executive women away from navy-blue-suit-and-bow-tie uniforms. Her comfortable, colorful clothes are fashionable but not faddish, and they fit. . . .

President Liz Claiborne and Co-chairman Arthur Ortenberg, her husband of 29 years, work their magic in ten-hour days at the company's headquarters: sleek, modern all-white offices (Liz loves white) in a prewar building a block from Manhattan's tawdry Times Square. Claiborne spends her time overseeing 14 designers, picking fabrics and colors, and "editing" their work. She regrets that she no longer has time to design herself. With customers and retailers she is extremely approachable; with others she is often aloof and impatient. She does not like talking to audiences or reporters. Wall Street analysts wish they could chat with her about the business, but she generally refuses.

Ortenberg, who shares the chairman's office with marketing expert and college roommate Jerome Chazen, heads operations. "I call Ortenberg the Wizard of Oz," says Ken Wyse, the company's former marketing director. "He's the man behind the door—intellectual and godlike, Socratic and dogmatic. He makes pronouncements." While Claiborne is shy, Ortenberg is outgoing. She is serious; he jokes a lot. She looks at details; he sees the big picture. She says she manages by doing; he says he manages by teaching.

The personalities and management styles contrast clearly in a "concept" meeting for Lizwear, the company's most casual line. Ortenberg, not officially part of the meeting, pops into Claiborne's office frequently as she and several designers and managers toss around ideas and swatches of fabric for next fall's collection. Her remarks are short: If she likes something, it is "fabulous" or "terrific." Ortenberg is more challenging: "Think about this . . . Now remember that . . ."

Claiborne and Ortenberg say their most important mission now is preparing successors. Ortenberg is developing a group of managers to run the company with the same team approach that has characterized it since the beginning. Claiborne is not looking for a single Liz Claiborne to replace her but is grooming several designers.

activity, and (5) task-relevant knowledge.[5] However, these five traits did not correlate strongly with leader emergence. That is, people with these traits often remained followers.

Mann's review was similarly disappointing for the trait theorists. Among the seven categories of personality traits he examined, Mann found intelligence

[5] For complete details, see Ralph M. Stogdill, "Personal Factors Associated with Leadership: A Survey of the Literature," *Journal of Psychology* 25 (1948), pp. 35–71; and Ralph M. Stogdill, *Handbook of Leadership* (New York: Free Press, 1974).

■ **FIGURE 13–1**   The Evolution of Leadership Theory

A. Trait Theory

B. Behavioral Styles Theory

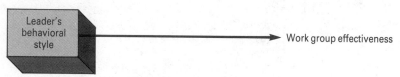

C. Situational Theory

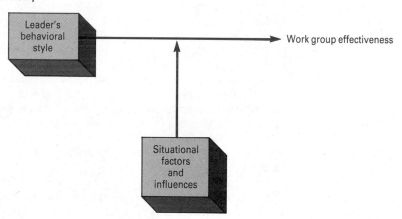

was the best predictor of leadership. However, Mann warned that all observed positive relationships between traits and leadership were weak (correlations averaged about 0.15).[6]

Together, Stogdill's and Mann's findings dealt a near deathblow to the trait approach. But now, decades later, leadership traits are once again receiving serious research attention.

Contemporary Trait Research.   Two OB researchers concluded in 1983 that past trait data may have been incorrectly analyzed. By applying modern statistical techniques to an old database, they demonstrated that the majority of a leader's

---

[6] See Richard D. Mann, ''A Review of the Relationships between Personality and Performance in Small Groups,'' *Psychological Bulletin*, July 1959, pp. 241–70.

behavior could be attributed to stable underlying traits.[7] Unfortunately, their methodology did not single out specific traits.

A 1986 meta-analysis by Robert Lord and his associates remedied this shortcoming with the following insights. First, the Lord study criticized leadership researchers for misinterpreting Stogdill and Mann's findings. Specifically, correlations between traits and *perceived leadership ability* were misinterpreted as linkages between traits and leader *effectiveness*. Second, a reanalysis of Mann's data and subsequent studies revealed that individuals tend to be perceived as leaders when they possess one or more of the following traits: intelligence, dominance, and masculinity. Thus, Lord and his colleagues concluded, "Personality traits are associated with leadership perceptions to a higher degree and more consistently than the popular literature indicates."[8] It should be noted that the masculinity finding reflects a cultural gender bias, not sexist research. Of course, equal employment opportunity laws in the United States and elsewhere prohibit the basing of employment decisions on gender.

A recent study by Warren Bennis, a well-known management consultant, pumped additional life into the trait approach to leadership. Bennis focused on leader effectiveness rather than perceived ability. He interviewed 90 successful leaders in an attempt to identify their common traits. Sixty were corporate executives in Fortune 500 firms; 30 were from the public sector. The sample included six black males and six females. Bennis identified the following four leadership traits:

1. *Management of attention.* Leaders possessing this trait can attract the attention of others through a combination of vision and strong commitment to its accomplishment (see Table 13–2).

2. *Management of meaning.* This trait involves use of exceptional communication skills to make the leader's ideas and vision tangible to others.

3. *Management of trust.* Through a clear and constant focus and consistent behavior, a leader with this trait generates trust.

4. *Management of self.* This trait is evident when leaders know their limitations but reject the notion of failure.[9]

Trait Theory in Perspective.   We can no longer afford to ignore the implications of leadership traits. Traits play a central role in how we perceive leaders. Recalling the Chapter 4 discussion of social perception, it is important to determine the traits embodied in people's schemata (or mental pictures) for leaders. If those traits are inappropriate (i.e., foster discriminatory selection and invalid performance appraisals), they need to be corrected through training and development.

---

[7] See David A. Kenny and Stephen J. Zaccaro, "An Estimate of Variance Due to Traits in Leadership," *Journal of Applied Psychology,* November 1983, pp. 678–85.

[8] Robert G. Lord, Christy L. De Vader, and George M. Alliger, "A Meta-Analysis of the Relation between Personality Traits and Leadership Perceptions: An Application of Validity Generalization Procedures, *Journal of Applied Psychology,* August 1986, p. 407.

[9] A complete discussion is provided in Warren Bennis, "The 4 Competencies of Leadership," *Training and Development Journal,* August 1984, pp. 15–19.

■ **TABLE 13–2**   The Leadership Traits of a 31-Year-Old Billionaire

It took William H. Gates III only 12 years to build the little company he helped start into the number two seller of personal computer software. By mid-1987, Gates's 45 percent share of Microsoft's stock was worth an estimated $1 billion. According to *Business Week:*

> At 31, the co-founder of Microsoft is typical in many ways of the young entrepreneurs who created the personal-computer industry in the 1970s. Competitors call him a technical genius. Gates still talks zealously about his "vision" of bringing computing power to "the masses.". . .
>
> Whether by good planning or fast footwork, the intense bachelor who likes to drive his Jaguar a little too fast has become that rarest of entrepreneurs: one with the right blend of youthful energy, technical acumen, intellectual breadth, and business savvy to adjust as his company matures.

SOURCE: Excerpted from Richard Brandt, "The Billion-Dollar Whiz Kid," *Business Week,* April 13, 1987, p. 69.

Behavioral Styles Theory

This phase of leadership research began during World War II as part of the effort to develop better military leaders. It was an outgrowth of two events: the seeming inability of trait theory to explain leadership effectiveness and the human relations movement, an outgrowth of the Hawthorne Studies. The thrust of early behavioral leadership theory was to focus on leader behavior, instead of on personality traits. As shown in part B of Figure 13–1, it was believed that leader behavior directly affected work group effectiveness. This led researchers to identify patterns of behavior (called leadership styles) that enabled leaders to effectively influence others.

The Hawthorne Studies, discussed in Chapter 1, supposedly demonstrated that supportive supervision had a positive impact on performance. We now know this was not necessarily true. In any event, this conclusion paved the way for the belief that there is *one best style of leadership.* This view was initially reinforced by Kurt Lewin's widely cited 1939 laboratory study indicating that followers preferred leaders with a democratic style, as opposed to those with either an authoritarian or *laissez-faire* (hands-off) style.[10] Table 13–3 summarizes these three classic styles of leadership.

Because Lewin and his associates used young children as subjects, critics eventually pointed out the limited generalizability of the results. Consequently, teams of researchers from two universities directed their efforts to identifying the behaviors that differentiated effective and ineffective leaders.

The Ohio State Studies.   Researchers at Ohio State University began by generating a list of behaviors exhibited by leaders. At one point, the list contained

---

[10] Details are provided in Kurt Lewin, Ronald Lippitt, and Ralph K. White, "Patterns of Aggressive Behavior in Experimentally Created 'Social Climates,' " *Journal of Social Psychology,* May 1939, pp. 271–99.

■ **TABLE 13–3**   The Three Classic Styles of Leader Behavior

	Authoritarian	Democratic	Laissez-faire
Nature	Leader retains all authority and responsibility	Leader delegates a great deal of authority while retaining ultimate responsibility	Leader denies responsibility and abdicates authority to group
	Leader assigns people to clearly defined tasks	Work is divided and assigned on the basis of participatory decision making	Group members are told to work things out themselves and do the best they can
	Primarily a downward flow of communication	Active two-way flow of upward and downward communication	Primarily horizontal communication among peers
Primary strength	Stresses prompt, orderly, and predictable performance	Enhances personal commitment through participation	Permits self-starters to do things as they see fit without leader interference
Primary weakness	Approach tends to stifle individual initiative	Democratic process is time-consuming	Group may drift aimlessly in the absence of direction from leader

SOURCE: Robert Kreitner, *Management,* 3rd ed. (Boston: Houghton Mifflin, 1986), p. 463.

1,800 statements that described nine categories of leader behavior. Using a statistical technique called *factor analysis,* the Ohio State researchers concluded there were only two independent dimensions of leader behavior: consideration and initiating structure. **Consideration** involves leader behavior associated with creating mutual respect or trust and focuses on a concern for group members' needs and desires. **Initiating structure** is leader behavior that organizes and defines what group members should be doing to maximize output.[11] These two dimensions of leader behavior were oriented at right angles to form four behavioral styles of leadership (see Figure 13–2).

It initially was hypothesized that a high structure, high consideration style would be the one best style of leadership. Through the years, this hypothesis has been tested many times. Researchers typically have used the Leader Behavior Description Questionnaire (LBDQ) to measure leader behavior and then have matched it with different aspects of group performance such as output and satisfaction. Results have been mixed.

Although some studies found that a high structure, high consideration style correlated positively with high performance and satisfaction, other studies found negative outcomes associated with the "high-high" style. A review by one respected team of leadership researchers found consideration to be negatively related to leader effectiveness. Additionally, they found high structure to be associated with high grievance rates and turnover as well as lower job satisfaction.[12] Results such as these have led many to conclude that there is not one best style of leadership. Rather, it is argued, effectiveness of a given leadership style depends on situational factors.

---

[11] This research is described in detail in Stogdill, *Handbook of Leadership,* chap. 11.

[12] For a review, see Steven Kerr, Chester A. Schriesheim, Charles J. Murphy, and Ralph M. Stogdill, "Toward a Contingency Theory of Leadership Based upon the Consideration and Initiating Structure Literature," *Organizational Behavior and Human Performance,* August 1974, pp. 62–82.

■ **FIGURE 13–2**   Four Leadership Styles Derived from the Ohio State Studies

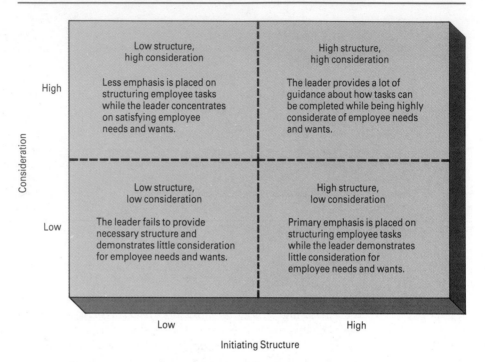

University of Michigan Studies.   As in the Ohio State studies, this research sought to identify behavioral differences between effective and ineffective leaders. Researchers identified two different styles of leadership. One was called employee-centered, while the other was referred to as job-centered. These behavioral styles parallel the consideration and initiating structure styles identified by the Ohio State group. In summarizing the results from these studies, one management expert concluded that effective leaders: (1) tend to have supportive or employee-centered relationships with employees, (2) use group rather than individual methods of supervision, and (3) set high performance goals.[13] These conclusions led Rensis Likert, one of the participating researchers, to develop a management system called System 4. This approach recommends using supportive supervision and participative decision making.[14]

Blake and Mouton's Managerial Grid.   Perhaps the most widely known behavioral styles model of leadership is the Managerial Grid. Behavioral scientists Robert Blake and Jane Srygley Mouton developed and trademarked the grid. They use it to demonstrate that there is one best style of leadership. Somewhat

---

[13] See Victor H. Vroom, "Leadership," in *Handbook of Industrial and Organizational Psychology*, ed. Marvin D. Dunnette (Chicago: Rand McNally, 1976).

[14] System 4 management is discussed in Rensis Likert, *The Human Organization* (New York: McGraw-Hill, 1967).

■ **FIGURE 13–3** Blake and Mouton's Managerial Grid®

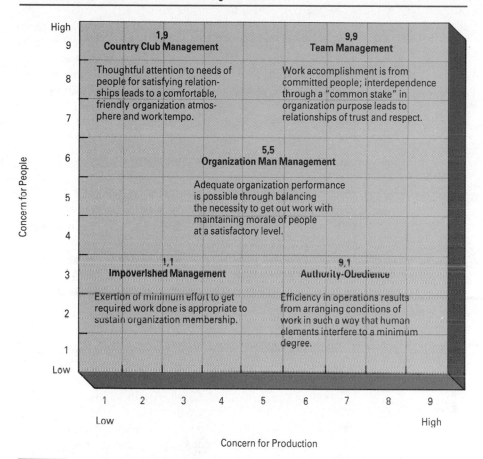

SOURCE: Robert R. Blake and Jane Srygley Mouton, *The Managerial Grid III: The Key to Leadership Excellence* (Houston: Gulf Publishing Company), Copyright © 1985, p. 12. Reproduced by permission.

akin to the Ohio State model, Blake and Mouton's **Managerial Grid** is a matrix formed by the intersection of two dimensions of leader behavior (see Figure 13–3). On the horizontal axis is "concern for production." "Concern for people" is represented on the vertical axis.

Blake and Mouton point out that "the variables of the Managerial Grid are *attitudinal* and *conceptual*, with *behavior* descriptions derived from and connected with the thinking that lies behind action."[15] In other words, concern for production and concern for people involve attitudes and patterns of thinking, as well as specific behaviors. By scaling each axis of the grid from 1 to 9, Blake and Mouton were able to plot five leadership styles. Because it emphasizes

---

[15] Robert R. Blake and Jane Srygley Mouton, "A Comparative Analysis of Situationalism and 9,9 Management by Principle," *Organizational Dynamics*, Spring 1982, p. 23.

teamwork and interdependence, the 9,9 style is considered by Blake and Mouton to be the best, regardless of the situation.

In support of the 9,9 style, Blake and Mouton cite the results of a study in which 100 experienced managers were asked to select the best way of handling 12 managerial situations. Between 72 and 90 percent of the managers selected the 9,9 style for each of the 12 situations.[16] Moreover, Blake and Mouton report, "The 9,9 orientation . . . leads to productivity, satisfaction, creativity, and health."[17] Critics point out that Blake and Mouton's research may be self-serving. At issue is the grid's extensive use as a training and consulting tool for diagnosing and correcting organizational problems.

Behavioral Styles Theory in Perspective.   By emphasizing leader *behavior*, something that is learned, the behavioral styles approach makes it clear that leaders are made, not born. This is the opposite of the trait theorists' traditional assumption. Given what we know about behavior shaping and model-based training, leader *behaviors* can be systematically improved and developed. For example, a recent study demonstrated that managers can be taught to use positive reward behavior, reprimand behavior, and goal-setting behavior.[18] On the negative side, situational theorists complain that the one-best-style approach ignores powerful situational determinants of leader effectiveness.

Situational Theory

Situational theory grew out of an attempt to explain the inconsistent findings regarding traits and styles. As shown in part C of Figure 13–1, **situational leadership theory** proposes that the effectiveness of a particular style of leader behavior depends on the situation. As situations change, different styles become appropriate. This challenges the idea of one best style of leadership. The behavior of successful leaders like Kenneth Olsen, president and chief executive officer of Digital Equipment Corp., suggests that the situational approach deserves careful study.

> Mr. Olsen's personality and his management style are a bundle of contradictions. He is an autocrat who has never named a second in command, who often terrifies subordinates by interrupting presentations, who dictates product designs. Yet he is a democrat who discusses design flaws with repair people on the assembly line, one who created a special engineers' committee that can approve research turned down by executives, and one who pushes employees to disagree. . . .
>
> And he is an egalitarian who is called "Ken" even by secretaries and has banned reserved parking spaces, executive company cars and executive dining rooms.[19]

---

[16] Ibid., pp. 28–29. Also see Robert R. Blake and Jane S. Mouton, "Management by Grid Principles or Situationalism: Which?" *Group & Organization Studies,* December 1981, pp. 439–55.

[17] Ibid., p. 21.

[18] For details, see Charles C. Manz and Henry P. Sims, Jr., "Beyond Imitation: Complex Behavioral and Affective Linkages Resulting from Exposure to Leadership Training Models," *Journal of Applied Psychology,* November 1986, pp. 571–78.

[19] William M. Bulkeley, "Digital Equipment, Still Led by Founder, Regains Momentum," *The Wall Street Journal,* April 3, 1986, pp. 1,18.

■ **TABLE 13–4** In International Management There Is No One Best Style of Leadership

Business travelers carrying their *One Minute Manager,* by Kenneth Blanchard and Spencer Johnson, get a cold splash of a different reality when they plunge into business in Abu Dhabi or Bombay. . . . A one-minute praising could even bring work to a stop in Japan, where singling out an individual causes humiliation, and the authors' recommended pat on the arm will only compound the error. Never touch in Japan. . . .

Some of the concepts in the best-selling *In Search of Excellence,* by Tom Peters and Robert Waterman, travel well; others need to be discarded in the international situation. MBWA (management by walking around), for example, can permanently tarnish a boss' image in France, where proper decorum is a mark of authority and important for maintaining respect. Participative management is viewed as incompetence in Latin America and the Arab world, where bosses make decisions and good subordinates follow orders.

SOURCE: Excerpted from Lennie Copeland, "Savoir Faire over There," *Nation's Business,* September 1986, p. 48.

Let us closely examine some alternative situational theories of leadership that reject the notion of one best leadership style (see Table 13–4).

■ FIEDLER'S CONTINGENCY MODEL

Fred Fiedler, an OB scholar who has been studying leadership since the early 1950s, developed a contingency model of leadership. It is the oldest, most widely known, and most extensively researched situational model of leadership. Fiedler's basic premise is that leader effectiveness is *contingent* upon an appropriate match between the leader's style and the degree to which he or she controls the situation. Before we examine this matching process, we need to discuss Fiedler's ideas about leadership style and situational control. After linking these variables, we conclude this section with a discussion of relevant research and a framework for applying Fiedler's model.[20]

The Leader's Style: Task-Oriented or Relationship-Oriented

Fiedler developed the least preferred co-worker (LPC) scale to identify leadership styles. (As an instructive exercise, please complete the LPC scale in Table 13–5 before continuing.) He contends that the LPC scale measures whether a leader has a **task-oriented style** or a **relationship-oriented style.** Although

---

[20] For more on this theory, see Fred E. Fiedler, "A Contingency Model of Leadership Effectiveness," in *Advances in Experimental Social Psychology,* Vol. 1, ed. Leonard Berkowitz (New York: Academic Press, 1964); Fred E. Fiedler, *A Theory of Leadership Effectiveness* (New York: McGraw-Hill, 1967).

■ TABLE 13–5 Least Preferred Co-Worker (LPC) Scale

Throughout your life you have worked in many groups with a wide variety of different people—on your job, in social clubs, in church organizations, in volunteer groups, on athletic teams, and in many others. You probably found working with most of your co-workers quite easy, but working with others may have been very difficult or all but impossible.

Now, think of all the people with whom you have ever worked. Next, think of the one person in your life with whom you could work least well. This individual may or may not be the person you also disliked most. It must be the one person with whom you had the most difficulty getting a job done, the one single individual with whom you would least want to work—a boss, a subordinate, or a peer. This person is called your "least preferred co-worker" (LPC).

On the scale below, describe this person by placing an "X" in the appropriate space.

										Scoring
Pleasant	8	7	6	5	4	3	2	1	Unpleasant	_____
Friendly	8	7	6	5	4	3	2	1	Unfriendly	_____
Rejecting	1	2	3	4	5	6	7	8	Accepting	_____
Tense	1	2	3	4	5	6	7	8	Relaxed	_____
Distant	1	2	3	4	5	6	7	8	Close	_____
Cold	1	2	3	4	5	6	7	8	Warm	_____
Supportive	8	7	6	5	4	3	2	1	Hostile	_____
Boring	1	2	3	4	5	6	7	8	Interesting	_____
Quarrelsome	1	2	3	4	5	6	7	8	Harmonious	_____
Gloomy	1	2	3	4	5	6	7	8	Cheerful	_____
Open	8	7	6	5	4	3	2	1	Guarded	_____
Backbiting	1	2	3	4	5	6	7	8	Loyal	_____
Untrustworthy	1	2	3	4	5	6	7	8	Trustworthy	_____
Considerate	8	7	6	5	4	3	2	1	Inconsiderate	_____
Nasty	1	2	3	4	5	6	7	8	Nice	_____
Agreeable	8	7	6	5	4	3	2	1	Disagreeable	_____
Insincere	1	2	3	4	5	6	7	8	Sincere	_____
Kind	8	7	6	5	4	3	2	1	Unkind	_____
									Total	_____

SOURCE: Fred E. Fiedler and Martin M. Chemers, *Improving Leadership Effectiveness* (New York: John Wiley & Sons, 1984), pp. 17–19. Used with permission.

there has been much disagreement over the definition of these styles, they have been characterized as follows:

> Low-LPC persons, those describing their least preferred co-worker in quite negative terms, are thought to be primarily concerned with task success, i.e., they are "task-oriented." On the other hand, persons describing their least pre-

ferred co-worker in relatively positive terms (high-LPC persons) are thought to be "relationship-oriented," i.e., primarily concerned with attaining and maintaining successful interpersonal relationships.[21]

Leadership styles, according to Fiedler, are relatively stable from one situation to the next because they reflect the individual's basic motivation.

Returning to the LPC scale in Table 13–5, simply add the values associated with each of your 18 responses to calculate your LPC score. If your score is 73 or above, you are classified as a high-LPC person with a relationship-oriented style. A score below 64 identifies you as a low-LPC person, indicating that you have a task-oriented style. According to Fiedler's model, one style is not better than the other. Each is appropriate and necessary in certain situations. If your total score is between 65 and 72, you are classified as a middle-LPC person. Middle-LPC leaders exhibit characteristics of both the high- and low-LPC styles.

Situational Control

Situational control refers to the amount of control and influence the leader has in his or her immediate work environment. Situational control ranges from high to low. High control implies that the leader's decisions will produce predictable results because the leader has the ability to influence work outcomes. Low control implies that the leader's decisions may not influence work outcomes because the leader has very little influence. There are three dimensions of situational control: leader-member relations, task structure, and position power. These dimensions vary independently, forming eight combinations of situational control (see Figure 13–4).

The three dimensions of situational control are defined as follows:

- **Leader-member relations** reflects the extent to which the leader has the support, loyalty, and trust of the work group. This dimension is the most important component of situational control. Good leader-member relations suggest that the leader can depend on the group, thus ensuring that the work group will try to meet the leader's goals and objectives.
- **Task structure** is concerned with the amount of structure contained within tasks performed by the work group. For example, a managerial job contains less structure than that of a bank teller. Since structured tasks have guidelines for how the job should be completed, the leader has more control and influence over employees performing such tasks. This dimension is the second most important component of situational control.
- **Position power** refers to the degree to which the leader has formal

---

[21] Robert W. Rice and F. James Seaman, "Internal Analyses of the Least Preferred Co-Worker (LPC) Scale," *Educational and Psychological Measurement* 41 (1981), p. 110.

■ **FIGURE 13–4** Representation of Fiedler's Contingency Model

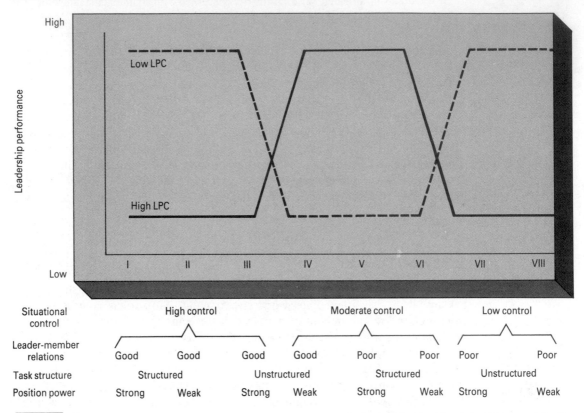

SOURCE: Adapted from Fred E. Fiedler, "Situational Control and a Dynamic Theory of Leadership," in *Managerial Control and Organizational Democracy,* ed. Bert King, Siegfried Streufert, and Fred E. Fiedler (New York: John Wiley & Sons, 1978), p. 114. Used with permission.

power to reward, punish, or otherwise obtain compliance from employees.[22]

Linking Leadership Style and Situational Control

Fiedler's complete contingency model is presented in Figure 13–4. The horizontal axis breaks out the eight control situations. Each situation represents a unique combination of leader-member relations, task structure, and position power. The vertical axis indicates the level of leader effectiveness. Plotted on the resulting quadrant are lines indicating those situations in which low-LPC (dotted line) and high-LPC (solid line) leaders are predicted to be effective.

---

[22] Additional information on the description and calculation of situational control is contained in Fred E. Fiedler, "The Contingency Model and the Dynamics of the Leadership Process," in *Advances in Experimental Social Psychology,* Vol. 11, ed. Leonard Berkowitz (New York: Academic Press, 1978).

For those situations in which the leader has high control (situations I, II, and III), task-oriented (low-LPC) leaders are hypothesized to be more effective than relationship-oriented (high-LPC) leaders. Under conditions of moderate control (situations IV, V, and VI), the interpersonal orientation of high-LPC leaders is predicted to be more effective. Finally, the task orientation of low-LPC leaders is hypothesized to be more effective under conditions of low control (situations VII and VIII). *In short, Fiedler contends that task-oriented leaders are more effective in extreme situations of either high or low control, but relationship-oriented leaders tend to be more effective in middle-of-the-road situations of moderate control.*

Research and Managerial Implications

The validity of the LPC scale is the major controversy surrounding Fiedler's contingency model. Some researchers claim the LPC scale is not reliable or valid. Others interpret the same validational evidence as support for the LPC's reliability and validity. Although the "true" validity of the LPC scale remains an unresolved issue, general consensus is that "the LPC scale may not be the best method for identifying task-oriented and relationship oriented persons."[23] Thus, some researchers are trying to refine the LPC measure.

The overall validity of Fiedler's contingency model was tested through a meta analysis of 35 studies containing 137 leader style-performance relations. According to the researchers' findings: (1) the contingency theory was correctly induced from studies on which it was based; (2) for laboratory studies testing the model, the theory was supported for all leadership situations except situation II; (3) for field studies testing the model, three of the eight situations (IV, V, and VII) produced completely supportive results, while partial support was obtained for situations I, II, III, VI, and VIII.[24] This last finding suggests that Fiedler's model may need theoretical refinement. Such refinement might entail a reconceptualization of the meaning of a least preferred co-worker.

A second study summarized research about the relationship between leadership style and follower job satisfaction. As suggested by the contingency model, followers generally had higher job satisfaction when the leader was correctly matched with the appropriate situation.[25] Finally, an "in match" group of

---

[23] Robert W. Rice, "Construct Validity of the Least Preferred Co-Worker Score," *Psychological Bulletin,* November 1978, p. 1231. Arguments about the validity of the LPC are contained in Chester A. Schriesheim, Brendan D. Bannister, and William H. Money, "Psychometric Properties of the LPC Scale: An Extension of Rice's Review," *Academy of Management Review,* April 1979, pp. 287–90; and Robert W. Rice, "Reliability and Validity of the LPC Scale: A Reply," *Academy of Management Review,* April 1979, pp. 291–94.

[24] See Lawrence H. Peters, Darrell D. Hartke, and John T. Pohlmann, "Fiedler's Contingency Theory of Leadership: An Application of the Meta-Analyses Procedures of Schmidt and Hunter," *Psychological Bulletin,* March 1985, pp. 274–85.

[25] Results are summarized in Robert W. Rice, "Leader LPC and Follower Satisfaction: A Review," *Organizational Behavior and Human Performance,* August 1981, pp. 1–25.

administrators displayed less job stress, fewer health problems, and lower absenteeism than did a comparable "out of match" group.[26]

In conclusion, except for the validity of the LPC scale, Fiedler's contingency model has considerable support. This implies that organizational effectiveness can be enhanced by appropriately matching leaders with situations. Fiedler believes it is a waste of time to try to change one's leadership style. Instead, leaders with an inappropriate style need to change their degree of situational control or be moved to a situation in which they can be effective. The following section discusses how this might be done.

Leader Match Training

Fiedler has developed a training program based on the contingency model. This program assumes that individuals are either unwilling or unable to change their leadership style. Fiedler and Chemers have observed:

> It is very difficult to change personality or long-established behaviors. We know only too well how little success has been reported in trying to remake husbands, wives, or children, and how difficult it is to break a habit like smoking. The way we interact with our subordinates and superiors is learned from childhood on and is no more easily changed. However, we do know that people behave differently in different situations, and that it is frequently very easy to change critical aspects of our leadership situations.[27]

Accordingly, the training program teaches managers to manage the situational control within their leadership environment.

Training begins by having managers assess their leadership style with the LPC. Then, diagnostic instruments are used to measure leader-member relations, task structure, and position power. After calculating the degree of situational control, managers determine whether their leadership style matches their leadership situation. Finally, managers are trained to change their leadership situations by modifying one or more of the components of situational control (see Table 13–6). For example, a high-LPC leader would not be totally effective in a high-control situation (refer to Figure 13–4). To improve performance, this leader should modify the situation so it involves moderate control. This might be done by making the task less structured—seeking new problems to solve, for example—or lowering position power through delegation. In an evaluation of this program, 13 studies found significant increases in leadership effectiveness following managerial training.[28]

---

[26] See Martin M. Chemers, Robert B. Hays, Frederick Rhodewalt, and Jay Wysocki, "A Person-Environment Analysis of Job Stress: A Contingency Model Explanation," *Journal of Personality and Social Psychology,* September 1985, pp. 628–35.

[27] Fred E. Fiedler and Martin M. Chemers, *Improving Leadership Effectiveness* (New York: John Wiley & Sons, 1984), p. 5.

[28] For documentation, see Fred E. Fiedler and Linda Mahar, "The Effectiveness of Contingency Model Training: A Review of the Validation of Leader Match," *Personnel Psychology,* Spring 1979, pp. 45–62; Fred E. Fiedler, Cecil H. Bell, Martin M. Chemers, and Dennis Patrick, "Increasing Mine Productivity and Safety through Management Training and Organization Devel-

■ **TABLE 13–6** Techniques to Modify Situational Control

Modifying leader-member relations
Spend more or less time with your subordinates.
Organize activities that take place outside of work (e.g., picnic, bowling, etc.).
Request trusted employees that you know to work for you.
Obtain positive outcomes for your employees (e.g., special bonus, time off, etc.).
Share information with your employees.

Modifying task structure
Break the job down into smaller subtasks.
Request additional training.
Develop procedures, guidelines, or diagrams related to completing tasks.
Seek advice from others.
Seek problems to solve.
Volunteer for new tasks or assignments.
Become more of a decision maker.

Modifying position power
Exercise the powers that are inherent in your position.
Become an expert on the tasks performed by your employees.
Control the type and amount of information that your employees receive.
Delegate authority.
Incorporate the work group into planning and decision-making activities.
Do not withhold information from employees.
Avoid any trappings of demonstrating power and rank.

SOURCE: Adapted from Fred E. Fiedler and Martin M. Chemers, *Improving Leadership Effectiveness* (New York: John Wiley & Sons, 1984), pp. 179–84. Used with permission.

■ PATH-GOAL AND DECISION-MAKING MODELS OF LEADERSHIP

This section examines two more situational models of leadership: House's path-goal model and Vroom and Yetton's decision-making model. A working knowledge of these models makes managers aware of additional situational determinants of leader effectiveness.

Path-Goal Theory

Path-goal theory is based on the expectancy theory of motivation discussed in Chapter 6. Expectancy theory proposes that motivation to exert effort increases as one's effort → performance → outcome expectations improve. Path-goal theory focuses on how leaders influence followers' expectations.

Robert House originated the path-goal theory of leadership. He proposed a model that describes how expectancy perceptions are influenced by the contingent relationships between four leadership styles and various employee attitudes

---

opment: A Comparative Study," *Basic and Applied Social Psychology*, March 1984, pp. 1–18. For an alternative interpretation of the success of leader match training, see Arthur G. Jago and James W. Ragan, "The Trouble with Leader Match Is That It Doesn't Match Fiedler's Contingency Model," *Journal of Applied Psychology*, November 1986, pp. 555–59.

■ **FIGURE 13-5** A General Representation of House's Path-Goal Theory

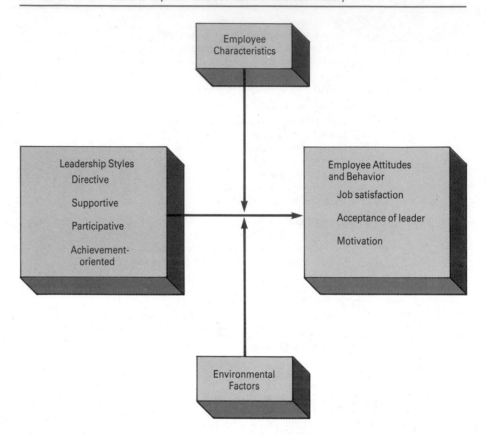

and behaviors (see Figure 13–5).[29] According to the path-goal model, leader behavior is acceptable when employees view it as a source of satisfaction or as paving the way to future satisfaction. In addition, leader behavior is motivational to the extent it (1) reduces roadblocks that interfere with goal accomplishment, (2) provides the guidance and support needed by employees, and (3) ties meaningful rewards to goal accomplishment. Because the model deals with pathways to goals and rewards, it is called the path-goal theory of leadership. House sees the leader's main job as helping employees stay on the right paths to challenging goals and valued rewards.

Leadership Styles.   House believes leaders can exhibit more than one leadership style. This contrasts with Fiedler, who proposes that leaders have one dominant style. The four leadership styles identified by House are:

- *Directive leadership.* Providing guidance to employees about what should be done and how to do it, scheduling work, and maintaining standards of performance.

---

[29] For more detail on this theory, see Robert J. House, "A Path Goal Theory of Leader Effectiveness," *Administrative Science Quarterly*, September 1971, pp. 321–38.

- *Supportive leadership*. Showing concern for the well-being and needs of employees, being friendly and approachable, and treating workers as equals.
- *Participative leadership*. Consulting with employees and seriously considering their ideas when making decisions.
- *Achievement-oriented leadership*. Encouraging employees to perform at their highest level by setting challenging goals, emphasizing excellence, and demonstrating confidence in employee abilities.[30]

Research evidence supports the idea that leaders exhibit more than one leadership style.[31] Descriptions of business leaders reinforce these findings. For example, William Ziff, who built Ziff-Davis Publishing Co. into one of the largest and most profitable special-interest magazine publishers in the United States, used more than one style of leadership.

> Ziff was the epitome of the hands-on manager. He read every issue of every magazine and would often become involved in minute details, such as headlines and newsstand displays. He set up tight operational systems, such as central departments to handle circulation, promotion, and research [directive style]. But he left most lines of authority unclear, which tended to diffuse all power but his own. He avoided rule by outright fiat and often acceded to others' views [participative style]. . . .
>
> But within his circle of close friends and colleagues, he acted like "one of the guys" [supportive style].[32]

Contingency Factors.   **Contingency factors** are situational variables that cause one style of leadership to be more effective than another. In the present context, these variables affect expectancy or path-goal perceptions. This model has two groups of contingency variables (see Figure 13–5). They are employee characteristics and environmental factors. Two important employee characteristics identified by House are locus of control (recall the discussion in Chapter 3) and task ability. He also identified three environmental factors: (1) the employee's task, (2) the authority system, and (3) the work group. All these factors have the potential for hindering or motivating employees. Table 13–7 contains a list of contingency relationships involving these factors.

Research Findings.   This theory is criticized for not clearly specifying the variables it includes or the predictions it makes. This has made it difficult to fully test path-goal theory. As a result, research has generally tested only two hypotheses drawn from the theory. The only prediction verified so far is that supportive leader behavior promotes job satisfaction when individuals are performing structured tasks.[33] A more recent field study involving 466

---

[30] Adapted from Robert J. House and Terence R. Mitchell, "Path-Goal Theory of Leadership," *Journal of Contemporary Business,* Autumn 1974, p. 83.

[31] See House, "A Path Goal Theory of Leader Effectiveness."

[32] Chris Welles, "What's Next for the Unpredictable Bill Ziff?" *Business Week,* April 14, 1986, p. 103.

[33] For a detailed discussion of relevant research, see Chester A. Schriesheim and Angelo S. DeNisi, "Task Dimensions as Moderators of the Effects of Instrumental Leadership: A Two-Sample Replicated Test of Path-Goal Leadership Theory," *Journal of Applied Psychology,* October 1981, pp. 589–97.

■ **TABLE 13–7** Contingency Relationships Suggested by Path-Goal Theory

Leadership Style	Situation in Which Most Effective
Directive	Positively affects the satisfaction of individuals with an external locus of control or low task ability.
	Negatively affects the satisfaction of individuals with high task ability.
	Positively affects the satisfaction and motivation of individuals working on ambiguous tasks.
	Negatively affects the satisfaction and motivation of individuals working in clear tasks.
Supportive	Positively affects the satisfaction of individuals working in stressful, frustrating, or dissatisfying tasks.
Participative	Positively affects the satisfaction of individuals with an internal locus of control.
	Positively affects the satisfaction and motivation of individuals who are ego-involved in an ambiguous task.
Achievement-oriented	Positively affects the motivation of individuals performing ambiguous nonrepetitive tasks.

SOURCE: Adapted from Robert J. House and Terence R. Mitchell, "Path-Goal Theory of Leadership," *Journal of Contemporary Business,* Autumn 1974, pp. 81–97.

employees from several countries who were working in Saudi Arabia found that the path-goal theory applies to different cultures. However, only the satisfaction portions of the model were supported. The motivation/performance portions were not.[34]

Managerial Implications. One important implication is that leaders possess and use more than one style of leadership. Managers should not be hesitant to try new behaviors when the situation calls for them. Second, the degree of task structure is a relevant contingency variable. Managers should consider using supportive supervision when the task is structured. Supportive supervision is satisfying in this context because employees already know what they should be doing.

Vroom and Yetton's Decision-Making Model

Victor Vroom and Philip Yetton prefer a decision-making perspective of leadership. They believe decision making is the essence of leadership. Theirs is a *prescriptive model* in that it specifies the decision-making styles that are effective in different situations. The Vroom and Yetton model is shown in Figure 13–6.[35]

Vroom and Yetton's model is represented as a decision tree. The manager's task is to move from left to right along the various branches of the diagram. In doing so, one encounters 14 problem situations. A specific set of possible solutions is prescribed for each situation. Before we apply the model, however,

---

[34] Complete details may be found in Abduhl-Rahim A. Al-Gattan, "Test of the Path-Goal Theory of Leadership in the Multinational Domain," *Group & Organization Studies,* December 1985, pp. 429–45.

[35] For more on this theory, see Victor H. Vroom and Philip W. Yetton, *Leadership and Decision-Making* (Pittsburgh, Pa.: University of Pittsburgh Press, 1973).

■ **FIGURE 13–6** Vroom and Yetton Decision-Making Model

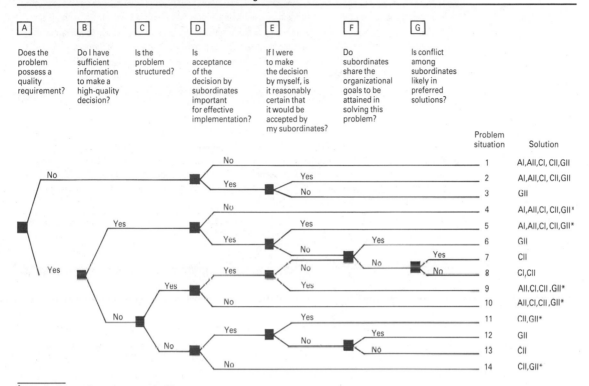

A	B	C	D	E	F	G
Does the problem possess a quality requirement?	Do I have sufficient information to make a high-quality decision?	Is the problem structured?	Is acceptance of the decision by subordinates important for effective implementation?	If I were to make the decision by myself, is it reasonably certain that it would be accepted by my subordinates?	Do subordinates share the organizational goals to be attained in solving this problem?	Is conflict among subordinates likely in preferred solutions?

Problem situation	Solution
1	AI,AII,CI, CII,GII
2	AI,AII,CI, CII,GII
3	GII
4	AI,AII,CI, CII,GII ×
5	AI,AII,CI, CII,GII*
6	GII
7	CII
8	CI,CII
9	AII,CI,CII ,GII*
10	AII,CI,CII ,GII*
11	CII,GII*
12	GII
13	CII
14	CII,GII*

*Within feasible set when answer to question F is yes.

it is necessary to consider the different decision styles managers ultimately choose from and an approach for diagnosing the leadership situation.

Five Decision-Making Styles.   Vroom and Yetton identified five distinct decision-making styles. In Table 13–8, each style is represented by a letter. The letter indicates the basic thrust of the style. For example, A stands for *autocratic*, C for *consultive*, and G for *group*. There are several important issues to consider as one moves from an AI style to a GII style. They are:

- The problem or decision is discussed with more people.
- Group involvement moves from merely providing data to recommending solutions.
- Group "ownership" and commitment to the solution increases.
- As group commitment increases, so does the time needed to arrive at a decision.[36]

[36] See Norman B. Wright, "Leadership Styles: Which Are Best When?" *Business Quarterly*, Winter 1984, pp. 20–23.

■ **TABLE 13-8**   Management Decision Styles (Vroom and Yetton Model)

AI	You solve the problem or make the decision yourself, using information available to you at that time.
AII	You obtain the necessary information from your subordinate(s), then decide on the solution to the problem yourself. You may or may not tell your subordinates what the problem is in getting the information from them. The role played by your subordinates in making the decision is clearly one of providing the necessary information to you rather than generating or evaluating solutions.
CI	You share the problem with relevant subordinates individually, getting their ideas and suggestions without bringing them together as a group. Then you make the decision that may or may not reflect your subordinates' influence.
CII	You share the problem with your subordinates as a group, collectively obtaining their ideas and suggestions. Then you make the decision that may or may not reflect your subordinates' influence.
GII	You share a problem with your subordinates as a group. Together you generate and evaluate alternatives and attempt to reach agreement (consensus) on a solution. Your role is much like that of chairman. You do not try to influence the group to adopt "your" solution and you are willing to accept and implement any solution that has the support of the entire group.

SOURCE: Reprinted, by permission of the publisher, from "A New Look at Managerial Decision Making," Victor H. Vroom, *Organizational Dynamics,* Spring 1973, p. 67, © 1973 American Management Association, New York. All rights reserved.

Style choice is dependent on the problem situation. Drawing upon decision-making research, Vroom and Yetton identified seven problem attributes that are used to diagnose or analyze the situation.

Matching the Situation to Leadership Style.   Vroom and Yetton developed seven questions that managers can use to diagnose a situation. They are labeled from A to G and are listed at the top of Figure 13–6. These questions are based on seven rules developed to protect the quality and acceptance of a decision.[37] Yes-no answers to these questions determine the problem type, which in turn identifies a set of leadership styles that are potentially effective. When more than one decision-making style is acceptable for a problem, the manager is free to choose whichever style he or she prefers. However, Vroom and Yetton advise the leader to consider the following two constraints when making this final choice of decision-making style. One involves the need to minimize the number of hours associated with making the decision. If this is the case, the manager should use the most autocratic style possible. If the manager wants to emphasize employee development, a more participative style should be chosen.

Applying the Vroom and Yetton Model.   To use the model in Figure 13–6 for a given situation, start at the left side and move toward the right by asking yourself the question (A through G) associated with each decision point (represented by a box in the figure) encountered. When you reach the end of a path, a problem situation is identified. You may choose any leadership style within the solution set.

---

[37] An expanded discussion of the problem attributes and the diagnostic questions is provided in Victor H. Vroom, "A New Look at Managerial Decision Making," *Organizational Dynamics,* Spring 1973, pp. 66–80.

Let us track a simple example through Figure 13–6. Suppose you have to determine the work schedule for a group of part-time workers who report to you. Does this decision have a quality requirement (question A)? Not really. This takes us along the path with a decision node at question D. Assuming that acceptance is important, and your employees will accept your decision (question E), we end up at problem situation 2. As shown in Figure 13–6, any of the five leadership styles would be effective in this case.

Research Insights.   Only a handful of studies have tested this model. In Vroom and Yetton's original test of their model, 136 managers were asked to describe a problem and the method used to solve it. Results indicated that in 97 of 136 problems, the manager's leadership style fell in the feasible set. Unfortunately, there was no way of knowing whether these decisions were effective. Subsequent research has demonstrated:

- Decisions were more effective when they were solved with decision processes recommended by the model.[38]
- Females followed prescriptions from the model more than did males.
- There was a preference for participative management even when an autocratic style was prescribed.[39]
- When managers possessed conflict management skills, higher group performance was obtained when group discussions were held to resolve subordinates' conflict over preferred solutions.[40]

In conclusion, although there is some support for the model, additional research is needed to adequately assess its validity.

Managerial Implications.   Consistent with path-goal theory, Vroom and Yetton's model emphasizes that there is not one style of leadership effective for all situations. It urges managers to use different styles of decision making/leadership to suit situational demands. Also, the model can help managers determine when, and to what extent, they should involve employees in decision making. By simply being aware of the seven diagnostic questions, managers can enhance their ability to structure ambiguous problems. This should ultimately enhance the quality of managerial decisions.

---

[38] Results are found in R. H. George Field, "A Test of the Vroom-Yetton Normative Model of Leadership," *Journal of Applied Psychology,* October 1982, pp. 523–32; Victor H. Vroom and Arthur G. Jago, "On the Validity of the Vroom-Yetton Model," *Journal of Applied Psychology,* April 1978, pp. 151–62.

[39] The second and third findings drawn from Arthur G. Jago and Victor H. Vroom, "Sex Differences in the Incidence and Evaluation of Participative Leader Behavior," *Journal of Applied Psychology,* December 1982, pp. 776–83; Madeline E. Heilman, Harvey A. Hornstein, Jack H. Cage, and Judith K. Herschlag, "Reactions to Prescribed Leader Behavior as a Function of Role Perspective: The Case of the Vroom-Yetton Model," *Journal of Applied Psychology,* February 1984, pp. 50–59.

[40] See Andrew Crouch and Philip Yetton, "Manager Behavior, Leadership Style, and Subordinate Performance: An Empirical Extension of the Vroom-Yetton Conflict Rule," *Organizational Behavior and Human Decision Processes,* June 1987, pp. 384–96.

■ EMERGING EXPLANATIONS OF LEADERSHIP

Now that we have discussed some well-established models of leadership, we will explore three comparatively new perspectives. The first examines leadership from a role-making standpoint. The second focuses on substitutes for leadership, and the third explains leadership from an attributional point of view. Although all three perspectives are situational, they are different from the situational models just discussed. Thus, these theories offer managers some mind-expanding insights about leader effectiveness.

Graen's Role-Making (VDL) Model of Leadership

George Graen, an industrial psychologist, believes popular theories of leadership are based on an incorrect assumption. Theories such as Blake and Mouton's Managerial Grid and Fiedler's contingency model assume that leader behavior is characterized by a stable or average leadership style. In other words, these models assume a leader treats all subordinates in about the same way. This traditional approach to leadership is shown in the left side of Figure 13–7. In this case, the leader (designated by the circled L) is thought to exhibit a similar pattern of behavior toward all employees (E_1 to E_5). In contrast, Graen contends that leaders develop unique one-to-one relationships with each of the people reporting to them. Behavioral scientists call this sort of relationship a *vertical dyad*. Hence, Graen's approach is labeled the **vertical dyad linkage (VDL) model** of leadership. The forming of vertical dyads is said to be a naturally occurring process resulting from the leader's attempt to delegate and assign work roles. As a result of this process, Graen predicts that one of two distinct types of leader-member exchange relationships will evolve.[41]

One type of leader-member exchange is called the **ingroup exchange.** In this relationship, leaders and followers develop a partnership characterized by reciprocal influence, mutual trust, respect and liking, and a sense of common fates. Figure 13–7 shows that E_1 and E_5 are members of the leader's ingroup. In the second type of exchange, referred to as an **outgroup exchange,** leaders are characterized as overseers who fail to create a sense of mutual trust, respect, or common fate.[42] E_2, E_3, and E_4 are members of the outgroup on the right side of Figure 13–7.

Research Findings.   If Graen's model is correct, there should be a significant relationship between the type of leader-member exchange and job-related outcomes. To date, research supports this prediction. For example, one study

---

[41] See Fred Dansereau, Jr., George Graen, and William Haga, "A Vertical Dyad Linkage Approach to Leadership within Formal Organizations," *Organizational Behavior and Human Performance*, February 1975, pp. 46–78; and Richard M. Dienesch and Robert C. Liden, "Leader-Member Exchange Model of Leadership: A Critique and Further Development," *Academy of Management Review*, July 1986, pp. 618–34.

[42] These descriptions were taken from Dennis Duchon, Stephen G. Green, and Thomas D. Taber, "Vertical Dyad Linkage: A Longitudinal Assessment of Antecedents, Measures, and Consequences," *Journal of Applied Psychology*, February 1986, pp. 56–60.

■ **FIGURE 13–7** A Role-Making (VDL) Model of Leadership

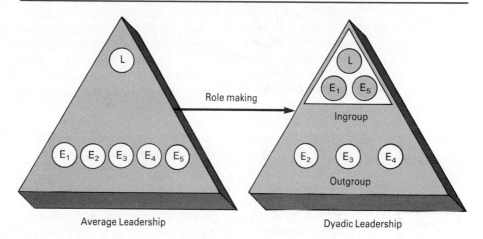

Average Leadership   Dyadic Leadership

L = Leader

E = Employee

SOURCE: Adapted from Fred Dansereau, Jr., George Graen, and William J. Haga, "A Vertical Dyad Linkage Approach to Leadership within Formal Organizations," *Organizational Behavior and Human Performance,* February 1975, p. 72.

found that ingroup members had higher performance and job satisfaction than employees in the outgroup.[43] The type of leader-member exchange also has been found to predict turnover among nurses and computer analysts, as well as career outcomes like promotability, salary level, and receipt of bonuses over a seven-year period.[44]

Managerial Implications. Graen's VDL model underscores the importance of training managers to improve leader-member relations. Ideally, this should enhance the job satisfaction and performance of employees and also reduce turnover. A large U.S. government installation in the Midwest recently conducted such a training program. Results indicated a 19 percent increase on an objective measure of productivity. This improvement resulted in an estimated annual cost savings of more than $5 million.[45] VDL researcher Robert Vecchio's

[43] Results are found in Robert P. Vecchio and Bruce C. Godbel, "The Vertical Dyad Linkage Model of Leadership: Problems and Prospects," *Organizational Behavior and Human Performance,* August 1984, pp. 5–20.

[44] Turnover studies were conducted by George B. Graen, Robert C. Liden, and William Hoel, "Role of Leadership in the Employee Withdrawal Process," *Journal of Applied Psychology,* December 1982, pp. 868–72; Gerald R. Ferris, "Role of Leadership in the Employee Withdrawal Process: A Constructive Replication," *Journal of Applied Psychology,* November 1985, pp. 777–81. The career progress study was conducted by Mitsuru Wakabayashi and George B. Graen, "The Japanese Career Progress Study: A 7-Year Follow-Up," *Journal of Applied Psychology,* November 1984, pp. 603–14.

[45] See Terri A. Scandura and George B. Graen, "Moderating Effects of Initial Leader-Member Exchange Status on the Effects of a Leadership Intervention," *Journal of Applied Psychology,* August 1984, pp. 428–36.

■ **TABLE 13–9**   In or Out: What to Do about It

In truth, the best time to manage the in or out phenomenon is very early in a person's employment. If you are a new employee or if you are developing a relationship with a newly assigned boss, it is a good idea to offer your loyalty and provide expressions of cooperativeness.

If your status as an out-member is already well established, it may be difficult or impossible to break the status quo. Short of confronting the supervisor and asking for a new start, an out-group employee's only options are to:

Accept the current situation;

Try to become an in-group member by being cooperative and loyal (this is an unattractive option for many out-groupers because they may have to swallow their pride); or

Quit.

Out-group members typically—but resentfully—come to accept the status quo.

Supervisors should be mindful that in-groups and out-groups exist within their work units, and they should control potential conflict between the two divisions. Supervisors should consciously try to expand their in-groups. This means not giving up on people who may gradually be coming to see themselves as marginal members of the work unit. Supervisors who create a greater sense of in-ness among their subordinates can expect to have more effective work units.

SOURCE: Excerpted from Robert Vecchio, "Are You *In* or *Out* with Your Boss?" *Business Horizons,* November–December 1986, p. 78.

tips for both followers and leaders in Table 13–9 are a good supplement to formal training programs.

Substitutes for Leadership

Virtually all leadership theories assume that some sort of formal leadership is necessary, whatever the circumstances. But this basic assumption has been questioned in recent years. Specifically, some OB scholars propose that there are **substitutes for leadership** that tend to negate the leader's ability to influence employee satisfaction and performance.[46] In other words, a leader's influence tactics are likely to have very little or no impact in certain situations. For example, leader behavior that initiates structure would tend to be resisted by independent-minded employees with high ability and vast experience. Consequently, such employees would be guided more by their own initiative than by managerial directives.

Table 13–10 lists various substitutes for leadership. Characteristics of the subordinate, the task, and the organization can act as substitutes for traditional hierarchical leadership. Further, different characteristics are predicted to negate

---

[46] For an expanded discussion of this approach, see Steven Kerr and John M. Jermier, "Substitutes for Leadership: Their Meaning and Measurement," *Organizational Behavior and Human Performance*, December 1978, pp. 375–403.

■ **TABLE 13–10** Substitutes for Leadership

Characteristic	Relationship-Oriented or Considerate Leader Behavior Is Unnecessary	Task-Oriented or Initiating Structure Leader Behavior Is Unnecessary
Of the subordinate		
1. Ability, experience, training, knowledge		X
2. Need for independence	X	X
3. "Professional" orientation	X	X
4. Indifference toward organizational rewards	X	X
Of the task		
5. Unambiguous and routine		X
6. Methodologically invariant		X
7. Provides its own feedback concerning accomplishment		X
8. Intrinsically satisfying	X	
Of the organization		
9. Formalization (explicit plans, goals, and areas of responsibility)		X
10. Inflexibility (rigid, unbending rules and procedures)		X
11. Highly specified and active advisory and staff functions		X
12. Closely knit, cohesive work groups	X	X
13. Organizational rewards not within the leader's control	X	X
14. Spatial distance between superior and subordinates	X	X

SOURCE: Adapted from Steven Kerr and John M. Jermier, "Substitutes for Leadership: Their Meaning and Measurement," *Organizational Behavior and Human Performance,* December 1978, pp. 375–403.

different types of leader behavior. For example, tasks that provide feedback concerning accomplishment, like taking a test, tend to negate task-oriented but not relationship-oriented leader behavior (see Table 13–10). Although the list in Table 13–10 is not all-inclusive, it shows that there are more substitutes for task-oriented leadership than for relationship-oriented leadership. Thus, managers could concentrate on providing adequate amounts of relationship-oriented leadership while letting situational factors substitute for task-oriented leader behavior.

An Attributional Model

This final model takes an information processing approach to leadership. It is based on the idea that leaders form cause-effect attributions from information about employee behavior. In turn, these attributions affect the way leaders respond to an employee's performance.

■ **FIGURE 13–8** An Attributional Model of Leadership

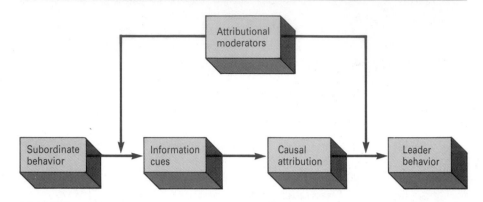

SOURCE: Adapted from Terence R. Mitchell, Stephen G. Green, and Robert E. Wood, "An Attributional Model of Leadership and the Poor Performing Subordinate," in *Research in Organizational Behavior*, ed. Larry L. Cummings and Barry M. Staw (Greenwich, Conn.: JAI Press, 1981), p. 211. Used with permission.

Figure 13–8 presents an attributional model of leadership. The process is set in motion by the occurrence of some type of employee behavior (for instance, absenteeism, outstanding performance, or poor performance). The next step consists of the leader's interpretation or attribution of the behavior. Chapter 4 noted that this step involves collecting information from three primary cues. These cues are related to the consensus, distinctiveness, and consistency of observed behavior. After processing these cues, the leader determines whether the behavior was due to external (task difficulty, boss, co-workers) or internal (ability or effort) factors. For example, the leader may conclude that an employee is performing poorly because of a lack of effort. Based on this internal attribution, the leader chooses a corrective action. The leader may offer increased incentives or take punitive action to encourage greater effort.

The above process is influenced by **attributional moderators** (see Figure 13–8). These variables produce distorted attributions and are likely to alter the consistency of a leader's behavior. For example, the fundamental attribution bias results in a leader's tendency to focus on internal as opposed to external causes of performance. Personal characteristics of the employee also act as moderators. Researchers report that leaders tend to attribute a female's success to external causes and failure to internal causes. The opposite pattern was found for males.[47]

Summary of Attributional Leadership Research.   Results from several different research studies are summarized below.

- Subordinates tend to see their poor performance as externally caused, while supervisors see it as internally caused.

[47] For a discussion of additional moderators, see Mark J. Martinko and William L. Gardner, "The Leader/Member Attribution Process," *Academy of Management Review*, April 1987, pp. 235–49.

- When supervisors have internal attributions for the poor performance of subordinates, they are more likely to be punitive and channel their response directly at the subordinate than when they have external attributions.
- A poor work history, as determined by consistency, consensus, and distinctiveness information, is likely to result in internal attributions and a personal punitive response, by the supervisor, to a poor performer.
- When the outcome of the performance failure is serious, the supervisor is more likely to have internal attributions and utilize personal punitive responses than when the outcome is not serious.
- When a subordinate apologizes or denies responsibility (gives an explanation), the supervisor is less likely to be severe or personally punitive than when there is no apology.
- Given the same performance, a supervisor will make more extreme evaluations based on an effort attribution than an ability attribution.[48]

Managerial Implications. Managers/leaders need to be aware that their behavior is influenced by their *perceptions* about the causes of an employee's performance. In addition, it is good to remember that attributional moderators may distort these perceptions. For example, managers and employees generally attribute the latter's poor performance to different causes. Employees, thus, are likely to misinterpret and become dissatisfied with a leader's corrective actions. Steps need to be taken to reduce these conflicting perceptions. As reviewed in Chapter 4, attributional training can help contain this problem.

■ LEADING VERSUS MANAGING

Throughout this chapter we have used the terms *leader* and *manager* synonymously. Some management experts and practitioners think that leading and managing involve separate and distinct behaviors and activities. For example, Abraham Zaleznik, a professor at Harvard Business School, described the difference as follows:

> Leaders . . . are often dramatic and unpredictable in style. They tend to create an atmosphere of change, ferment, even chaos. They "are often obsessed by their ideas, which appear visionary and consequently excite, stimulate and drive other people to work hard and create reality out of fantasy.". . .
> Managers . . . are typically hard-working, analytical, tolerant and fair-minded. They have a strong sense of belonging to the organization and take great pride in perpetuating and improving upon the status quo. But managerial executives focus "predominantly on process, whereas leaders focus on substance."[49]

---

[48] See Terence R. Mitchell, Stephen G. Green, and Robert E. Wood, "An Attributional Model of Leadership and the Poor Performing Subordinate," in *Research in Organizational Behavior,* ed. Larry L. Cummings and Barry M. Staw (Greenwich, Conn.: JAI Press, 1981), p. 228.

[49] Bernard Wysocki, Jr., "The Chief's Personality Can Have a Big Impact—For Better or Worse," *The Wall Street Journal,* September 11, 1984, p. 1.

Zaleznik probably would have titled this chapter "managership." While we do not believe that Zaleznik's distinction negates the many lessons in this chapter about influencing others, we do like the way it tests long-standing assumptions about leadership.

Fundamental Differences

After extensive research, Zaleznik has found that leaders and managers vary in their orientations toward their (1) goals, (2) conceptions about work, (3) interpersonal styles, and (4) self-perceptions.[50]

Goals.   Managers tend to adopt passive attitudes toward goals. They use goals out of necessity, as opposed to using them as a vehicle for creating change. In contrast, leaders are proactive instead of reactive about goals. Leaders try to shape the content of goals, thereby changing people's attitudes. They accomplish this through their enthusiasm, expectations, vision, and motivation.

Conceptions about Work.   Using a variety of skills, such as negotiating and bargaining, managers focus on establishing strategies to make decisions. In this process, they attempt to narrow the options used to solve problems. Solutions tend to be conservative. Leaders, on the other hand, attempt to develop new and possibly controversial solutions to problems. Leaders do not avoid risky challenges or problems, especially when there is opportunity for significant rewards.

Interpersonal Relations.   Managers like working with others. Their interactions generally revolve around the individual's role within the decision-making process. Conversations are more factual and goal-directed. Leaders use a different style. They often complain about others getting in the way. Leaders tend to be emotional and intuitive and readily evoke strong feelings, like love or hate.

Self-Perceptions.   Managers are likely to view themselves as members of particular organizations or social institutions. Perpetuating these organizations increases a manager's self-esteem. In contrast, a leader's self-esteem is not likely to depend on membership in an organization.

Does the Difference Matter?

The distinction between leaders and managers is more than a semantic issue. First, it is important from a hiring standpoint. Leaders quickly become frustrated with the mundane aspects of managing. This frustration may lead to job dissatisfaction and ultimately to turnover. Conversely, managers may lack the daring and vision needed to rally people around a cause. Moreover, these differences affect work group structures. Work group performance can be increased by

[50] The following discussion is based on Abraham Zaleznik, "Managers and Leaders: Are They Different?" *Harvard Business Review,* May–June 1977, pp. 67–78.

■ **TABLE 13–11**   Mixing Things Up at Banc One

Banc One Corp. in Columbus, Ohio, has grown into the largest banking organization in Ohio with a conscious strategy of thrusting "zealot"-style executives together with "implementer" and "control" executives. Working closely, these groups engage in "gentle confrontation," says R. Patrick Handley, the chief financial officer and a self-described "control" executive.

Around Banc One, it is widely understood that "zealots" such as John F. Fisher, senior vice president, are like elephants clearing new paths in consumer banking. Then come the implementers, who follow through on important details, while the "controllers" watch closely and may try to close an operation if things go radically wrong.

SOURCE: Excerpted from Bernard Wysocki, Jr., "The Chief's Personality Can Have a Big Impact—For Better or Worse," *The Wall Street Journal*, September 11, 1984, p. 1.

staffing a productive mix of leaders and managers. Banc One Corporation, for example, obtained positive results with this technique (see Table 13–11).

Finally, there are training implications. As demonstrated by research on modeling and leader match training, managerial training works. Many proven management training and development techniques are available. Unfortunately, according to Zaleznik, this is not true for leadership. Zaleznik believes the only way to nurture leadership talent is through intensive one-to-one mentor relationships. (Recall the discussion of mentoring in Chapter 11.)

We agree with Zaleznik about the importance of mentors. But we also believe a workable combination of leadership training and mentoring is necessary to ensure a much-needed supply of leadership talent.

SUMMARY OF KEY CONCEPTS

A. *Leadership* is defined as a social influence process in which the leader tries to obtain the voluntary participation of employees in an effort to reach organizational objectives. Leadership entails more than having authority and power.

B. Historically, leadership theory has evolved from traits, to behavioral styles, to situations. Although the trait approach has been roundly criticized, current research has shown that traits play an important role in perceived leader ability. Blake and Mouton's Managerial Grid emphasizes that there is one best style of leadership (9,9). Situational theories propose that effective leadership is contingent on the situation.

C. Fiedler believes leader effectiveness depends on an appropriate match between leadership style, measured with the LPC scale, and situational control. Low-LPC leaders are task-oriented and high-LPC leaders are relationship-oriented. Situational control is composed of leader-member relations, task structure, and position power. Low-LPC leaders are effective under situations of both high and low control. High-LPC leaders are more effective when they have moderate situational control. Leader match training has produced increased leader effectiveness.

D. According to path-goal theory, leaders alternately can exhibit directive, supportive, participative, or achievement-oriented styles of leadership. The effectiveness of these styles depends on various employee characteristics and environmental factors. Path-goal theory has received limited support from research.

E. Vroom and Yetton's decision-making model of leadership identifies 14 problem situations faced by leaders. Through the use of a decision tree, the model identifies appropriate leadership styles for each of the problem situations. The styles range from autocratic to highly participative.

F. There are three emerging explanations of leadership. The *role-making* approach assumes leaders develop unique vertical dyad linkages (VDL) with each employee. These leader-member exchanges qualify as either ingroup or outgroup relationships. The second explanation assumes there are *substitutes for leadership* that tend to negate the leader's ability to influence employee behavior. The *attributional* perspective proposes that leaders form causal attributions about employee behavior. In turn, these attributions affect a leader's behavior toward his or her employees.

G. Zaleznik claims leaders and managers are different because they vary in their orientations toward their goals, conceptions about work, interpersonal styles, and self-perceptions. He believes leadership can be learned only from mentors.

KEY TERMS

leadership

leader trait

consideration

initiating structure

Managerial Grid

situational leadership theory

task-oriented style

relationship-oriented style

leader-member relations

task structure

position power

contingency factors

vertical dyad linkage (VDL) model

ingroup exchange

outgroup exchange

substitutes for leadership

attributional moderators

DISCUSSION QUESTIONS

1. Are you interested in leading others? Why or why not? If yes, can you identify the source of this desire?

2. Has your college education helped you develop any of the traits characteristic of leaders? Which of Bennis's four leadership traits do you possess?

3. Do you agree with Blake and Mouton that there is one best style of leadership?

4. Does it make more sense to change a person's leadership style or the situation? How would Fred Fiedler and Robert House answer this question?

5. Based on your experience, how have managers helped clarify your path-goal perceptions?

6. Have you ever been a member of an ingroup or outgroup? For either situation, describe the pattern of interaction between you and your supervisor.

7. Have you ever experienced a situation in which a manager attributed your behavior to the wrong cause? Describe the situation and your reaction to the inappropriate attribution.

8. Do organizations develop leaders or managers? Explain your rationale.

9. Have you ever worked with or for a leader, as Zaleznik defines the term? Describe this person.

10. In your view, which leadership theory has the greatest practical application? Why?

BACK TO THE OPENING CASE

Now that you have read Chapter 13, you should be able to answer the following questions about the Tom Monaghan case:

1. Citing examples, which of Bennis's four leader traits were exhibited by Monaghan?

2. Where would you plot Monaghan's style of leadership on the Managerial Grid?

3. How did Monaghan attempt to clarify path-goal relationships?

4. Would you attribute Monaghan's success to internal or external causes? Explain.

5. Using Zaleznik's distinction, is Monaghan more of a leader or a manager? What are the implications for Domino's Pizza?

EXERCISE 13

Objectives

1. To promote understanding of the Vroom and Yetton decision-making model.
2. To develop and assess your ability to use the model.

Introduction

Vroom and Yetton proposed a decision-making model of leadership. In order to enhance your understanding of this model, we would like you to use it to analyze a brief case. You will be asked to read the case and use the information to determine an appropriate leadership style. This will enable you to compare your solution with a solution recommended by Vroom. Since Vroom's analysis is presented at the end of this exercise, please do not read it until indicated.

Instructions

Presented below is a case depicting a situation faced by the manufacturing manager of an electronics plant.[51] Read the case and then use Vroom and Yetton's model (refer to Table 13–8 and Figure 13–6) to arrive at a solution. At this point, it might be helpful to reread the material that explains how to apply the model. Keep in mind that you move toward a solution by asking yourself the questions (A through G) associated with each relevant decision point. After completing your analysis, we would like you to compare your solution with the one offered by Vroom.

Leadership Case

You are a manufacturing manager in a large electronics plant. The company's management has recently installed new machines and put in a new simplified work system, but to the surprise of everyone, yourself included, the expected increase in productivity was not realized. In fact, production has begun to drop, quality has fallen off, and the number of employee separations has risen.

You do not believe that there is anything wrong with the machines. You have had reports from other companies that are using them and they confirm this opinion. You have also had representatives from the firm that built the machines go over them and they report that they are operating at peak efficiency.

You suspect that some parts of the new work system may be responsible for the change, but this view is not widely shared among your immediate subordinates who are four first-line supervisors, each in charge of a section, and your supply manager. The drop in production has been variously attributed to poor training of the operators, lack of an adequate system of financial incentives, and poor morale. Clearly, this is an issue about which there is considerable depth of feeling within individuals and potential disagreement among your subordinates.

This morning you received a phone call from your division manager. He had just received your production figures for the last six months and was calling to express his concern. He indicated that the problem was yours to solve in any way that you think best, but that he would like to know within a week what steps you plan to take.

You share your division manager's concern with the falling productivity and know that your [people] are also concerned. The problem is to decide what steps to take to rectify the situation.

---

[51] Reprinted, by permission of the publisher, from "A New Look at Managerial Decision Making," Victor H. Vroom, *Organizational Dynamics*, Spring 1973, p. 72, © 1973 American Management Association, New York. All rights reserved.

Questions for Consideration/Class Discussion

1. What leadership style from Table 13–8 do you recommend?
2. Did you arrive at the same problem type and solution as Vroom? If not, what do you think caused the difference?
3. Based on this experience, what problems would a manager encounter in trying to apply this model?

Vroom's Analysis and Solution

Question:

   A (Quality?) = Yes
   B (Sufficient information?) = No
   C (Structured?) = No
   D (Acceptance important?) = Yes
   E (Prior probability of acceptance?) = No
   F (Subordinates share organizational goals?) = Yes
   G (Conflict?) – Yes

Problem type = 12
Leader style – GII

Chapter **14**

Decision Making and Creativity

LEARNING OBJECTIVES

When you finish studying the material in this chapter,
you should be able to:

- Define the terms *decision making, problem solving,* and *creativity.*
- Distinguish between programmed and nonprogrammed decisions.
- Discuss the four steps in the classical model of problem solving.
- Explain the garbage can model of decision making.
- Describe the five types of decision-making processes identified in case studies of decision making.
- Discuss the contingency relationships that influence the three primary strategies used to select solutions.
- Discuss the pros and cons of involving groups in the decision-making process.
- Specify at least five characteristics of creative people.

OPENING CASE 14

Decision Making at the Top

*F*ortune magazine interviewed seven chief executive officers to determine the decision-making process they used to solve a critical problem. Here are some highlights of the different approaches used by Kenneth Oshman, former head of Rolm Corp., and American Can Company's chief, William Woodside.

Co-founder Kenneth Oshman, 44, of Rolm Corp.—a classic Silicon Valley success, acquired . . . [in 1984] by IBM for $1.9 billion—believes a chief executive's job is to peer intently three to five years into the future, looking for problems. In 1971 the first flicker of an adverse change in Rolm's environment galvanized him into furious activity. Rolm was then a fast-growing $1.5-million-a-year maker of heavy-duty computers, 60% of which were sold to the military—"not a totally rational customer," Oshman recalls. That year, as he began to worry that the market for his specialized product would soon be saturated at around $15 million in annual sales, the Navy announced plans to use only one standard computer design, with specifications identical to a machine made by Sperry Univac. Oshman scrambled to find a second, related product line.

Well, remarked two employees, there's always the computerized telephone business, though that's now grinding up our former employer, Arcata Communications Inc., which distributes such gear. Oshman decided to investigate. Surely, he thought, the Federal Communications Commission's 1968 decision to let non-Bell equipment be hooked up

to the phone company's network must create a major opportunity. Six months of research produced a disappointing conclusion: to gain a worthwhile share of the potentially giant market, you'd have to stride in as a full-blown manufacturing, sales, and service behemoth, a task far beyond Rolm's capacity.

"But we didn't have a strong enough gut feeling that anything else was right for us," says Oshman. "So we decided to see how we could turn this into a business." After more months of sounding out skeptical telephone experts, he called in reinforcements by hiring a technical expert and a marketing veteran, making Rolm's top management feel even more committed to the decision.

Oshman believed Rolm could develop digital switching equipment AT&T and a handful of competitors were supplying to businesses. What big companies really wanted, Rolm's talks with potential customers found, was a phone system that would route calls over the cheapest available lines, monitor phone use to control costs, and make it easy to let employees keep the same phone number when they changed offices—tasks made to order for a computer-controlled system. The same system could solve Rolm's service problem by having a built-in diagnostic capability that would pinpoint malfunctions on its own.

"As the Boston Consulting Group would tell you, . . . the last thing you ever do is go into a new market with a completely new product." That's true—if you don't want to take the risk of building a giant new business. In this case the product worked, customers

Concluded:

bought it, and in nine years Rolm grew at an annual compound rate of 57% to the $660 million in annual sales it reached just before IBM acquired it.

And the premise that set this whole beautifully logical process in motion turned out to be completely wrong. The military-specification computer market did not stop at $15 million a year but grew to an estimated $200 million, of which Rolm today has around half. And the Navy began to loosen its single computer standard in 1976. Says Oshman: "I'd rather be lucky than right."

Sometimes a chief executive's gutsy decision is clearly more a response than a preemptive strike. American Can Co.'s chief, William Woodside, thought he was well in control of a changing world when suddenly that world changed with a vengeance. Company officers had for a decade seen the can business slowly leaking away into new containers. They had steadily been diverting cash from the can business to buy more promising businesses. In the late seventies, however, high interest rates, inflation, and overcapacity in the company's can and paper operations stopped this process dead. Says Woodside, 63, "We could see ourselves going downhill. We had to free up a lot of cash at one time so that we could then begin to invest in growing businesses."

Woodside told subordinates that the company would have to decide to do something big. But how big is big? What options were thinkable? "You gradually start with the easy stuff and then work up to the things that are unthinkable," Woodside says. "You sort of ratchet yourself along by having a picture of the future that gradually changes as you learn more facts and add more pieces to it."

Early on he looked at the plan of the paper division—which constituted a quarter of the company—to sell one mill and to enter into a joint venture with another. But dramatic as this streamlining seemed to the division, he found that it would make virtually no difference to the corporation—the paper business would still need $1 billion of investment over five years just to keep its share of a hotly competitive market. So he told the division to go back and consider every possible scenario, including selling the business.

By this time Woodside had established a "strategic work group" of half a dozen officers to help him study the alternatives, which the group discussed every week or two with everyone in top management. As is typical of the information-sifting phase of megadecision-making, this procedure had two purposes. First, it really did help Woodside make up his mind, step by step, that only the sale of a big chunk of the company would do; that the can business probably wasn't easily salable; that the paper unit, though the better business, was thus the only candidate.

And as Woodside's senior vice president for strategic planning, Robert Abramson, 42, says, "The process itself was part of the selling of the decision." Observes Woodside: "You must allow all senior managers to get a fair hearing, so you'll end up making a decision that not everybody will agree to, but all will carry out." Those who disagreed, often for fear of losing power, got a chance to see that Woodside was unshakeably determined to make big changes and that they'd serve their careers better by helping to shape the future rather than opposing it. Woodside listened patiently at the big meetings to suggestions and challenges: in his own mind he was way ahead of the group on the decision to sell the paper unit—which he finally did in 1982—and half a step ahead on deciding what kind of acquisition he wanted.

For Discussion

How do these accounts vary from the way you thought high-level decisions are made?

SOURCE: Excerpted from Myron Magnet, "How Top Managers Make a Company's Toughest Decision," *Fortune*, March 18, 1985, pp. 52–57. Used with permission.

■ Additional discussion questions linking this case with the following material appear at the end of this chapter.

Decision making is one of the primary responsibilities of being a manager. There are two principal reasons the quality of a manager's decisions are important. First, the quality of a manager's decisions directly affects his or her career opportunities, rewards, and job satisfaction. As a dramatic example, consider what happened to three executives at Film Recovery Systems Inc. when they made decisions that resulted in the death of an employee:

> Prosecutors all over the U.S. are bringing corporate officials into the dock. The trend was accelerated by the murder conviction last summer of three executives of Film Recovery Systems Inc. in Elk Grove Village, Ill. The executives were each sentenced to 25 years in jail for causing the death of an employee who inhaled cyanide fumes at work. They are appealing.[1]

Second, managerial decisions contribute to the success or failure of the organization. Take PepsiCo's crucial decision to market the first soft drink containing 100 percent NutraSweet, an artificial sweetener:

> [The company] risked millions when it rushed its diet cola by being first out with a 100% NutraSweet formula in November, 1984. Pepsi couldn't test the product before the rollout because that would have tipped off Coke. Instead, it went ahead on the basis of a gut feeling that the time was right. Since then, Diet Pepsi's volume has soared by 25%, and sales are around $1.2 billion.[2]

Decision making is "the process through which a course of action is chosen."[3] The fundamental cognitive process consists of identifying and choosing alternative solutions that lead to a desired state of affairs. The process begins with a problem and ends when a solution has been chosen. To gain an understanding of how managers may improve their decisions, this chapter focuses on: (1) the types of decisions managers make, (2) the classical model of decision making, (3) contemporary approaches to decision making, (4) the dynamics of decision making, and (5) creativity.

■ TYPES OF MANAGERIAL DECISIONS

Decision theorists have identified two types of managerial decisions: programmed and nonprogrammed.[4] It is important to distinguish between these two types because different techniques are used to solve each one (see Figure 14–1).

---

[1] Jonathan Tasini, "The Clamor to Make Punishment Fit the Corporate Crime," *Business Week,* February 10, 1986, p. 73.

[2] Amy Dunkin, "Pepsi's Marketing Magic: Why Nobody Does It Better," *Business Week,* February 10, 1986, pp. 52–53.

[3] George P. Huber, *Managerial Decision Making* (Glenview, Ill.: Scott, Foresman, 1980), p. 9.

[4] A thorough discussion is provided by Herbert A. Simon, *The New Science of Management Decision* (Englewood Cliffs, N.J.: Prentice-Hall, 1977), pp. 39–81.

■ **FIGURE 14–1**   Techniques for Solving Two Types of Decisions

	Decision-Making Techniques	
Types of Decisions	**Traditional**	**Modern**

Programmed
Routine, repetitive decisions
Organization develops specific processes for handling them
	1. Habit
	2. Clerical routine:
	   Standard operating procedures
	3. Organization structure:
	   Common expectations
	   A system of subgoals
	   Well-defined informational channels
		1. Operations research
		   Mathematical analysis
		   Models
		   Computer simulation
		2. Electronic data processing

Nonprogrammed One-shot, ill-structured, novel, policy decisions Handled by general problem-solving processes	1. Judgment, intuition, and creativity 2. Rules of thumb 3. Selection and training of executives	Heuristic problem-solving techniques applied to: a. Training human decision makers b. Constructing heuristic computer programs

SOURCE: Herbert A. Simon, *The New Science of Management Decision,* © 1977, p. 48. Reprinted by permission of Prentice-Hall, Inc., Englewood Cliffs, New Jersey.

Programmed Decisions

Programmed decisions tend to be repetitive and routine. Through time and experience, organizations develop specific procedures for handling these decisions. Getting dressed in the morning or driving to school involve personal programmed decisions. Through habit, you are likely to act on a similar chain of decisions each day. Work-related examples are determining how much vacation time to give an employee, deciding when to send customers a bill, and ordering office supplies. Habit and standard operating procedures are the most frequently used techniques for making these decisions. Today, computers handle many programmed decisions.

Nonprogrammed Decisions

Nonprogrammed decisions are novel and unstructured. Hence, there are no cut-and-dried procedures for handling the problem. These decisions also tend to have important consequences. The opening case illustrates two examples of nonprogrammed decisions. Both Oshman and Woodside faced novel situations that threatened the survival of their firms. U.S. automakers make numerous high-risk nonprogrammed decisions as they attempt to compete more effectively with the Japanese. Many of these nonprogrammed decisions involve automating outdated plants (see Table 14–1).

To solve nonprogrammed decisions, managers tend to rely on judgment, intuition, and creativity. More and more, however, heuristic computer programs (also known as artificial intelligence and expert systems) are being used in these situations. **Heuristics** provide general decision rules, if-then statements, that help managers make decisions. For example, researchers at the University

■ **TABLE 14-1**   General Motors Makes Nonprogrammed Decisions at Its Hamtramck Plant

GM management boasted that the facility, which produces GM's luxury cars, would elevate the company to absolute leadership in manufacturing technologies. But not everything at Hamtramck is working well. A fleet of robotic vehicles built to carry materials through the factory sat idle for months while GM workers tried to figure out the software needed to make them go. Problems with programming the robots in the plant's paint shop, which one consultant describes as being "on the wild, ragged edge of technology," forced GM to truck some cars to an older plant for painting. An expensive vision-inspection system was erected in the wrong spot on the assembly line to catch defective parts in time; it has now been relocated.

SOURCE: Russell Mitchell, "Detroit Stumbles on Its Way to the Future," *Business Week,* June 16, 1986, pp. 103–4.

of Pittsburgh are developing an expert system that helps doctors diagnose approximately 700 illnesses.[5]

■ DECISION MAKING: THE CLASSICAL PROBLEM-SOLVING PERSPECTIVE

Problem solving is "the conscious process of reducing the difference between an actual situation and the desired situation."[6] Problem solving involves making decisions. Decision making is a subset of those activities associated with problem solving. While people tend to use intuitive procedures to solve informal problems, the classical model of problem solving proposes that managers use a rational, four-step sequence: (1) identifying the problem, (2) generating alternative solutions, (3) evaluating and selecting a solution, and (4) implementing and evaluating the solution (see Figure 14–2). Despite criticism for being unrealistic, the classical model is instructive because it analytically breaks down the problem-solving process and serves as a conceptual anchor for newer perspectives. After studying each of these four steps, we will explore recent research findings related to the rational model.

Identifying the Problem

A **problem** exists when the actual situation and the desired situation differ. For example, a problem exists when you have to pay rent at the end of the month and don't have enough money. Your problem is not that you have to pay rent. Your problem is obtaining the needed funds. Similarly, the problem for a sales manager who has orders for 100 personal computers, but only 80 units in stock, is 20 units (the gap between actual and desired). One expert proposed that managers use one of three methods to identify problems: historical

[5] See Bob Davis, "More Firms Try to Put Skills of Key Staffers in Computer Programs," *The Wall Street Journal*, June 10, 1985, pp. 1, 12; and Andrew Kupfer, "Now, Live Experts on a Floppy Disk," *Fortune*, October 12, 1987, pp. 69–82.

[6] Huber, *Managerial Decision Making*, p. 12.

■ **FIGURE 14–2**   A Model of Decision Making and Problem Solving

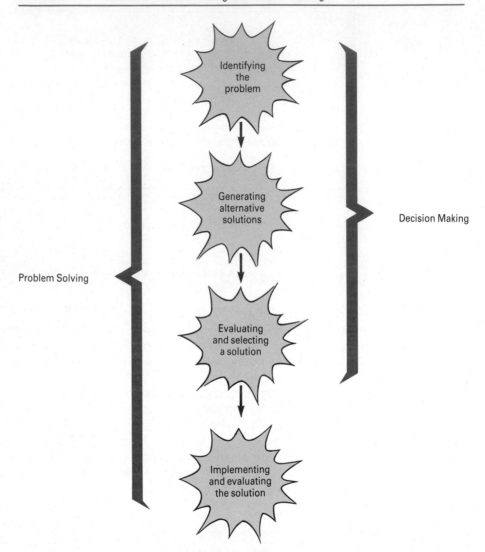

SOURCE: Adapted from George P. Huber, *Managerial Decision Making* (Glenview, Ill.: Scott, Foresman, 1980), p. 8.

cues, planning, and other people's perceptions.[7] This breakdown is useful from an OB perspective because it emphasizes cognitive processes rather than quantitative management science techniques.

Historical Cues.   This perspective assumes the recent past is the best estimate of the future. Thus, managers rely on past experience to identify discrepancies (problems) from expected trends. For example, a sales manager may conclude

---

[7] See William F. Pounds, "The Process of Problem Finding," *Industrial Management Review,* Fall 1969, pp. 1–19.

■ **TABLE 14–2** Factors That Bias the Identification of Problems

Factor	Characteristics
Informational bias	People have a reluctance to communicate information that will be negative for the recipient.
Uncertainty absorption	As people transfer information from one to another, it loses its uncertainty. Information is viewed as being more precise than it really is.
Selective perception	People seek and avoid certain types of information. In an effort to reduce stress and tension, people ignore ambiguous or uncertain aspects of the environment.
Stereotyping	People make decisions on the basis of prominent characteristics. People may not seek enough information because they believe they have an accurate perception of the situation.
Level of motivation	Motivation influences the setting of standards, which is the key determinant of identifying a difference between an actual and desired state.
Stress	Stress reduces an individual's ability to cope with informational demands.
Cognitive complexity	People vary in their ability to handle complex as well as large amounts of information.

SOURCE: Based in part on Ronald N. Taylor, *Behavioral Decision Making* (Glenview, Ill.: Scott, Foresman, 1984), pp. 16–23.

that a problem exists because first-quarter sales are less than they were a year ago. This method is prone to error because it is highly subjective.

Planning. A planning approach is more systematic and can lead to more accurate results. This method consists of using projections to estimate what is expected to occur in the future. A time period of one or more years is generally used. Companies are increasingly using the scenario technique as a planning tool. A 1982 survey of Fortune 500 firms found that 53 percent used scenarios for organizational planning.[8] The **scenario technique** is a speculative, conjectural forecasting tool used to identify future states, given a certain set of environmental conditions. For example, an organization might estimate future sales by using a scenario that assumes unemployment will be 10 percent. Multiple scenarios identify a range of future states by considering a variety of environmental conditions. In this case, a sales scenario might be based on projecting a 10 percent unemployment rate and an 8 percent inflation rate. An alternative scenario might use a 15 percent unemployment rate and a 10 percent inflation rate. By using scenarios, managers can discipline their intuition.

Other People's Perceptions. A final approach to identifying problems is to rely on the perceptions of others. Professors may realize they have unrealistic grading standards when the entire class complains about the grade distribution. In other words, students' perceptions indicate that a problem exists. Similarly, automobile manufacturers sometimes are forced to recall cars because of consumer complaints about product safety or quality. Research on decision making reveals several factors that bias or distort the identification of problems through each of these methods (see Table 14–2).

---

[8] The use of scenarios is discussed in Robert E. Linneman and Harold E. Klein, "Using Scenarios in Strategic Decision Making," *Business Horizons*, January–February 1985, pp. 64–74; and Steven P. Schnaars, "How to Develop and Use Scenarios," *Long Range Planning*, February 1987, pp. 105–14.

Generating Solutions

After identifying a problem, the next logical step is generating alternative solutions. For programmed decisions, alternatives are readily available through decision rules. This is not the case for nonprogrammed decisions. For nonprogrammed decisions, this step is the creative part of problem solving. Managers can use a number of techniques to stimulate creativity. For instance, this is how Ward Hagan, the previous chief executive at Warner-Lambert, attempted to increase managerial ability to generate solutions:

> Hagan sent his top 500 managers through a program to train them to be more critical and probing, and he took care to show by promotions that he valued such behavior. The result is that his troops were able to show him how to get from here to there, so much so that stock analysts are now high on Warner-Lambert.[9]

Techniques to increase creative thinking are discussed in the last section of this chapter.

Selecting a Solution

Optimally, decision makers want to choose the alternative with the greatest value. Decision theorists refer to this as maximizing the expected utility of an outcome. This is no easy task. First, assigning values to alternatives is complicated and prone to error. Not only are values subjective, but they also vary according to the preferences of the decision maker. Further, evaluating alternatives assumes they can be judged according to some standard or criteria. This further assumes: (1) valid criteria exist, (2) each alternative can be compared against these criteria, and (3) the decision maker actually uses the criteria. As you know from making your own decisions, people frequently violate these assumptions. Russell Ackoff, a managerial problem-solving scholar, proposed three approaches to making choices: optimizing, satisficing, and idealizing.[10]

Optimize. **Optimizing** involves solving problems by producing the best possible solution. When managers optimize, they make decisions in a completely rational fashion. This assumes that managers:

- Have knowledge of all possible alternatives.
- Have complete knowledge about the consequences that follow each alternative.
- Have a well-organized and stable set of preferences for these consequences.

---

[9] Myron Magnet, "How Top Managers Make a Company's Toughest Decision," *Fortune*, March 18, 1985, p. 55.

[10] These approaches are discussed in detail in Russell L. Ackoff, "The Art and Science of Mess Management," *Interfaces*, February 1981, pp. 20–26.

- Have the computational ability to compare consequences and to determine which one is preferred.[11]

As noted by Herbert Simon, a decision theorist who in 1978 earned the Nobel Prize for his work on decision making, ''the assumptions of perfect rationality are contrary to fact. It is not a question of approximation; they do not even remotely describe the processes that human beings use for making decisions in complex situations.''[12] Since decision makers do not follow these rational procedures, Simon proposed instead that decision makers *satisfice* when they make decisions.

Satisfice. People satisfice because they do not have the time, information, or ability to handle the complexity associated with following a rational process. This is not necessarily undesirable. **Satisficing** consists of choosing a solution that meets some minimum qualifications, one that is ''good enough.'' According to Ackoff, satisficing *resolves* problems by producing solutions that are satisfactory, as opposed to optimal. Borrowing another student's notes may satisfice for missing a class, although attending class is the best way to obtain complete information.

Idealize. **Idealizing** consists of changing a situation so the problem no longer exists. Quitting your job because you don't like your boss is an example. As opposed to solving or resolving the problem through optimizing or satisficing, this approach *dissolves* problems. By leaving the company, the problem is dissolved because you no longer have to interact with your boss. This approach is not used as frequently as satisficing.

Implementing and Evaluating the Solution

Once a solution is chosen, it needs to be implemented. Before implementing a solution, though, managers need to do their homework. For example, three ineffective managerial tendencies have been observed frequently during the initial stages of implementation (see Table 14–3). Skillful managers try to avoid these tendencies.

After the solution is implemented, the evaluation phase assesses its effectiveness. If the solution is effective, it should reduce the difference between the actual and desired states that created the problem. If the gap is not closed, the implementation was not successful and one of the following is true. Either the problem was incorrectly identified, or the solution was inappropriate. Assuming the implementation was unsuccessful, management can return to the first step, problem identification. If the problem was correctly identified, management should consider implementing one of the previously identified, but untried, solutions. This process can continue until all feasible solutions have been tried or the problem has changed.

---

[11] For a review of these assumptions, see Herbert A. Simon, ''A Behavioral Model of Rational Choice,'' *The Quarterly Journal of Economics,* February 1955, pp. 99–118.

[12] Herbert A. Simon, ''Rational Decision Making in Business Organizations,'' *The American Economic Review,* September 1979, p. 510.

■ **TABLE 14–3** Three Managerial Tendencies Reduce the Effectiveness of Implementation

Managerial Tendency	Recommended Solution
The tendency not to ensure that people understand what needs to be done.	Involve the implementors in the choice-making step. When this is not possible, a strong and explicit attempt should be made to identify any misunderstanding, perhaps by having the implementor explain what he or she thinks needs to be done and why.
The tendency not to ensure the acceptance or motivation for what needs to be done.	Once again, involve the implementors in the choice-making step. Attempts should also be made to demonstrate the payoffs for effective implementation and to show how completion of various tasks will lead to successful implementation.
The tendency not to provide appropriate resources for what needs to be done.	Many implementations are less effective than they could be because adequate resources, such as time, staff, or information, were not provided. In particular, the allocations of such resources across departments and tasks are assumed to be appropriate because they were appropriate for implementing the previous plan. These assumptions should be checked.

SOURCE: Modified from George P. Huber, *Managerial Decision Making* (Glenview, Ill.: Scott, Foresman, 1980), p. 19.

Recent Research Findings

Researchers have examined many aspects of decision making. Recent findings support the following conclusions:

- Decision makers do not follow the series of steps outlined in the classical model.[13]
- Decision makers are not able to select the most cost-effective mix of informational inputs to use in making decisions.
- Decision makers tend to obtain only moderate amounts of information. Thus, too little information is used when the decision stakes are high.
- Decision makers are more effective when they use a causal analysis to identify problems.[14]
- Information overload reduces the quality of a decision.
- Decision makers tend to satisfice.
- Decision makers can be trained to reduce the extent to which they use irrelevant information and to increase the accuracy of their judgments.[15]

---

[13] For a review of research evidence, see Charles R. Schwenk, ''The Use of Participant Recollection in the Modeling of Organizational Decision Processes,'' *Academy of Management Review*, July 1985, pp. 496–503.

[14] See studies by Terry Connolly and Brian K. Thorn, ''Predecisional Information Acquisition: Effects of Task Variables on Suboptimal Search Strategies,'' *Organizational Behavior and Human Decision Processes*, June 1987, pp. 397–416; and David M. Schweiger, Carl R. Anderson, and Edwin A. Locke, ''Complex Decision Making: A Longitudinal Study of Process and Performance,'' *Organizational Behavior and Human Decision Processes*, October 1985, pp. 245–72.

[15] The above three conclusions can be found in Shelby H. McIntyre and Adrian B. Ryans, ''Task Effects on Decision Quality in Traveling Salesperson Problems,'' *Organizational Behavior and Human Performance*, December 1983, pp. 344–69; and Thomas W. Dougherty, Ronald J. Ebert, and John C. Callender, ''Policy Capturing in the Employment Interview,'' *Journal of Applied Psychology*, February 1986, pp. 9–15.

Findings such as these prompted researchers to look for new models of organizational decision making.

■ DECISION MAKING: CONTEMPORARY PERSPECTIVES

Contemporary approaches grew from the classical model's inability to explain how decisions are actually made. Contemporary models differ from the classical approach in three fundamental ways. First, they do not assume the decision-making process is necessarily rational. Decision-making processes are viewed as ranging from rational to irrational. Second, they do not assume decision makers follow a sequential series of steps when making decisions. Finally, contemporary models do not assume all decisions are purposeful. In other words, decisions are made not only to solve problems, but they also are made for political reasons, by default or oversight, or by accident.

This section examines two recently proposed descriptions of organizational decision making. The first provides a theoretical description, and the second reviews 78 case studies that identified five additional types of decision-making processes.

The Garbage Can Model

This complex model attempts to describe the overall pattern of organizational decision making in organized anarchies. **Organized anarchies** represent any organization or decision situation that possesses three general characteristics: problematic preferences, unclear technology, and fluid participation.[16] These characteristics are described as follows:

1. *Problematic preferences:* Problems, alternatives, preferences, and solutions are ambiguous. Thus, decision makers are faced with inconsistent and ill-defined pieces of information.

2. *Unclear technology:* Decisions are not made on an absolute basis. Rather, a trial-and-error procedure is used. This makes it difficult to identify cause-and-effect relationships, resulting in a decision maker's inability to identify the causes and solutions of organizational problems.

3. *Fluid participation:* This characteristic reflects the amount of time and effort, or participation, managers put into making any single decision. Because of the variety of tasks performed by managers, they have limited time to devote to any one activity. This causes a manager's participation level to vary or change depending on the demands faced. For example, managers are willing to put more effort into solving a problem when they have fewer demands on their time.

These characteristics together create uncertainty for decision makers, which causes the decision-making process to become disorganized or chaotic. The

---

[16] The model is discussed in detail in Michael D. Cohen, James G. March, and Johan P. Olsen, ''A Garbage Can Model of Organizational Choice,'' *Administrative Science Quarterly*, March 1972, pp. 1–25.

■ **FIGURE 14–3** Relationship between Organizational Uncertainty and Organized Anarchies

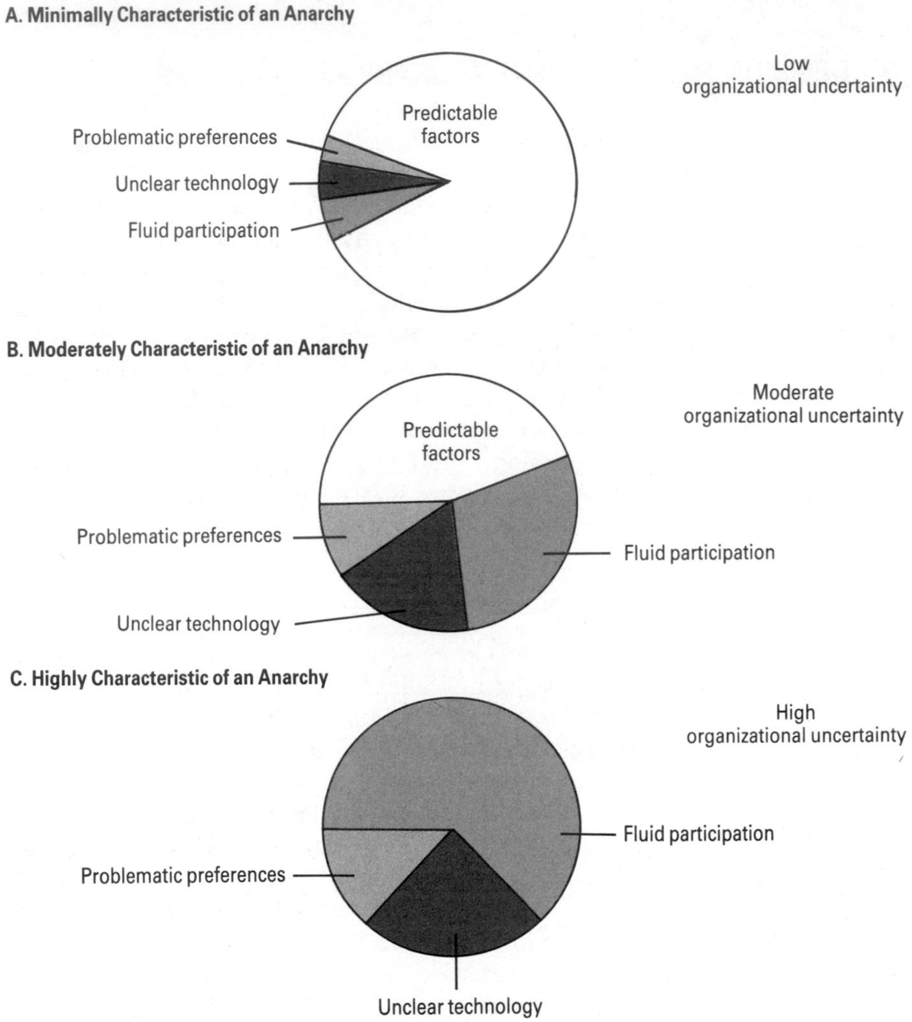

A. Minimally Characteristic of an Anarchy

Low
organizational uncertainty

Predictable
factors

Problematic preferences

Unclear technology

Fluid participation

B. Moderately Characteristic of an Anarchy

Moderate
organizational uncertainty

Predictable
factors

Problematic preferences

Fluid participation

Unclear technology

C. Highly Characteristic of an Anarchy

High
organizational uncertainty

Fluid participation

Problematic preferences

Unclear technology

more an organization possesses these characteristics, the more it qualifies as an organized anarchy (see Figure 14–3).

Uncertainty Varies.   No organization possesses extremes of the above characteristics all the time. Nevertheless, most organizations will regularly have to make decisions under uncertain and ambiguous circumstances. For example, Table 14–1 illustrates many uncertainties faced by General Motors in its attempts to automate its Hamtramck plant. Specific industries appear to go through cycles where decision makers are subject to extraordinary uncertainty. This is currently the situation facing the health care industry, particularly those firms involved with biotechnology.

Genentech and the other biotechnology companies face a number of issues that are clouding the industry's future. Just how well the early biotechnology patents will stand under challenge remains to be seen. . . .

Other uncertainties include product liability insurance, which is already slowing development of vaccines, contraceptives, and other risky drug categories. The industry also rails against export laws that prevent American drug companies from shipping products overseas that are not yet approved in the U.S.[17]

We will now examine a unique aspect of this model.

Not an Orderly Process. This approach is unique in that it assumes decision making does not follow an orderly series of steps. This contrasts sharply with the classical model, which proposed that decision makers follow a sequential series of steps beginning with a problem and ending with a solution. According to the present model, decisions result from a complex interaction between four independent streams of events: problems, solutions, participants, and choice opportunities. The interaction of these events creates "a collection of choices looking for problems, issues and feelings looking for decision situations in which they might be aired, solutions looking for issues to which they might be the answer, and decision makers looking for work."[18] The garbage can model attempts to explain how these events interact and lead to a decision. After discussing these streams of events and how they interact, this section highlights managerial implications of this model.

Streams of Events. The four streams of events—problems, solutions, participants, and choice opportunities—represent independent entities that flow into and out of organizational decision situations (see Figure 14–4). Because decisions are a function of the interaction among these independent events, the stages of problem identification and problem solution may be unrelated. For instance, a solution may be proposed for a problem that does not exist. This can be observed when students recommend that a test be curved, even though the average test score is a comparatively high 85 percent. On the other hand, some problems are never solved. Some professors, regardless of the average test score, refuse to curve exam results. Each of the four events in the garbage can model deserves a closer look.

- *Problems:* As defined earlier, problems represent a gap between an actual situation and a desired condition. But problems are independent from alternatives and solutions. The problem may or may not lead to a solution.
- *Solutions:* Solutions are answers looking for questions. They represent ideas constantly flowing through an organization. Contrary to the classical model, however, solutions are used to formulate problems rather than vice versa. This is predicted to occur because managers often do not know what they want until they have some idea of what they can get.
- *Participants:* Participants are the organizational members who come and go throughout the organization. They bring different values, attitudes,

---

[17] Joan O'C. Hamilton, "Biotech's First Superstar," *Business Week,* April 14, 1986, p. 72.
[18] Cohen, March, and Olsen, "A Garbage Can Model of Organizational Choice," p. 2.

and experience to a decision-making situation. Time pressures limit the extent to which participants are involved in decision making.

■ *Choice opportunities:* Choice opportunities are occasions in which an organization is expected to make a decision. While some opportunities, like hiring and promoting employees, occur regularly, others do not because they result from some type of crisis or unique situation. Union Carbide's response in 1984 to the Bhopal, India, gas leak, which resulted in the death of more than 3,000 people, is one such example.

Interactions among the Streams of Events.   Because of the independent nature of the streams of events, they interact in a random fashion. This implies decision making is more a function of random chance than a rational process. Thus, the organization is characterized as a "garbage can" in which problems, solutions, participants, and choice opportunities are all mixed together (see Figure 14–4). Only when the four streams of events happen to connect, like point A in Figure 14–4, is a decision made. Since these connections randomly occur among countless combinations of streams of events, decision quality generally depends on *timing*. (Some might use the term *luck*.) In other words, good decisions are made when these streams of events interact at the proper time. This explains why problems do not necessarily relate to solutions (point B in Figure 14–4) and why solutions do not always solve problems.

For example, computer manufacturers have been trying to convince all of us that computers are the solution for a host of business and personal problems. This is not necessarily true. Consider the comments from a management consultant hired by General Motors to help automate its plants.

> "New technologies haven't made any massive improvement in (the auto industry's) productivity," says James Harbour, an auto-industry consultant whom GM recently hired to help solve its technology problems. "So far, they have turned out to be more show than substance." Auto makers could make bigger gains, he says, by scrapping outmoded work rules, managing their work forces better and handling their parts more efficiently.[19]

As this example indicates, apparent solutions can create more problems than they solve. Hence, the garbage can is an appropriate metaphor of today's complex organizational decision making.

Managerial Implications.   The garbage can model of organizational decision making has four practical implications. First, many decisions will be made by oversight or the presence of a salient opportunity. Second, political motives frequently guide the process by which participants make decisions. Participants tend to make decisions that promise to increase their status. (Recall the discussion of organizational politics in Chapter 11.) Third, the process is sensitive to load. That is, as the number of problems increases, relative to the amount of time available to solve them, problems are less likely to be solved. Finally,

---

[19] Amal Nag, "Auto Makers Discover 'Factory of the Future' Is Headache Just Now," *The Wall Street Journal,* May 13, 1986, p. 1.

■ **FIGURE 14–4** Garbage Can Model of Organizational Decision Making

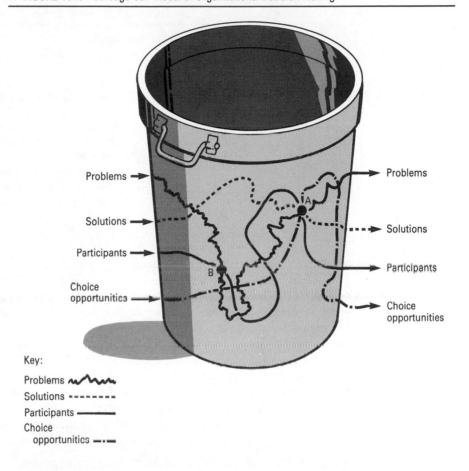

Key:

Problems ∿∿∿

Solutions ‑‑‑‑‑‑‑‑

Participants ————

Choice
  opportunities ‑•‑•

important problems are more likely to be solved than unimportant ones because they are more salient to organizational participants.[20]

Case Studies Identify New Decision Processes

A recent study attempted to investigate more thoroughly how managers make decisions. Decision-making processes were examined in 78 organizations. All the participating companies were from the service sector. The researcher, Paul Nutt, began the study by trying to identify the variety of decision-making processes used in these organizations. A technique called *process reconstruction* was employed.[21]

---

[20] These consequences were taken from James G. March and Roger Weissinger-Baylon, *Ambiguity and Command* (Marshfield, Mass.: Pitman Publishing, 1986), pp. 11–35.

[21] For details, see Paul C. Nutt, "Types of Organizational Decision Processes," *Administrative Science Quarterly,* September 1984, pp. 414–50.

■ **TABLE 14–4** Five Stages of Problem Solving Used to Analyze Case Studies in Nutt's Research

Stage	Description
Formulation	Consists of identifying the problem and setting objectives to solve it.
Concept development	Consists of generating alternative solutions to deal with the problem and meet the objectives.
Detailing	Consists of refining alternatives so they can be tested for their potential to solve the problem.
Evaluation	Consists of determining the costs and benefits of each alternative.
Implementation	Consists of installing the plan or solution.

SOURCE: Adapted from Paul C. Nutt, "Types of Organizational Decision Processes," *Administrative Science Quarterly*, September 1984, p. 416.

Two individuals from each organization who were familiar with a particular project were interviewed. Interviews were used to "reconstruct" the sequence of events that produced decisions during the project. Results were then analyzed to determine which stages of problem solving (see Table 14–4) were used and to identify the overall characteristics of the decision-making process. Five unique types of decision-making processes were identified: historical, off-the-shelf, appraisal, search, and nova. Each type incorporated some or all of the problem-solving stages listed in Table 14–4. Moreover, each type was provoked by either a problem, an opportunity, or a crisis. After we review each of the five decision-making processes identified by Nutt, we will turn our attention to the results of his study and some managerial implications.

Historical Processes.   This decision-making process incorporates the problem-solving stages of formulation, detailing, and implementation. The thrust of this style is to solve problems by looking to familiar sources for their ideas or solutions. For example, one hospital opened a renal dialysis center by copying the features used by a successful competitor.

Off-the-Shelf Processes.   This process focuses on identifying and comparing alternatives. For example, some managers solved problems by asking consultants to submit proposals regarding the project. These were then compared and evaluated. Solutions were likely to define problems, rather than vice versa, as a result of using this decision process. In other words, when a manager selected a proposal, the problem was defined in terms of the content of the proposal. This decision-making process contains the stages of formulation, detailing, evaluation, and implementation.

Appraisal Processes.   This method activates the formulation, evaluation, and implementation stages. The thrust of this decision-making process is to rigorously evaluate alternatives.

Search Processes. This approach is used when a manager senses a need, but lacks a workable solution. It is different from the historical and off-the-shelf processes because managers don't know where to look for solutions. The only stages of problem solving found during this process were formulation and implementation.

Nova Processes. Decision making in this fifth type of decision process is characterized by formulation, conceptualization, detailing, evaluation, and implementation. The thrust is to seek innovative solutions by creatively generating alternatives.

Research Findings. The historical model was the most frequently used decision-making process (see part A in Figure 14–5). This was followed in frequency of use by off-the-shelf and nova processes. Results further indicated that decision-making activities were caused more by problems (62 percent) than by either opportunities (25 percent) or crises (13 percent). When responding to problems, organizations tended to rely most heavily on the historical, off-the-shelf, and nova processes (see part B in Figure 14–5). In contrast, the decision-making processes of appraisal and search were predominant when organizations were responding to opportunities (see part B in Figure 14–5).

Managerial Implications. Decision making is a problem-oriented activity. Decision making, as mentioned earlier, ideally starts with a problem and ends with a solution. In addition, although managers use different stages of problem solving, they do not use them in a prescribed series of steps. This contradicts the classical model. Still, it is important to train managers in how to most effectively perform each stage of problem solving. This is exactly what Richard Jensen, a human factors specialist, did for the Federal Aviation Administration. In an attempt to reduce pilot errors, Jensen developed a training program to improve decision-making skills of airplane pilots (see Table 14–5). Further, since decision-making processes are activated by different organizational stimuli, it would be helpful for managers to know when a particular process is most effective. Organizations need to identify the decision-making processes they use on a regular basis. Managers can then be trained to use processes that are most effective for particular situations. This perspective meshes nicely with the contingency approach to management.

■ DYNAMICS OF DECISION MAKING

"Decision-making, like any other element of a manager's job, is partly science, partly art."[22] Accordingly, this section examines two dynamics of decision making—contingency considerations and group versus individual decision making—that affect the "science" component. We conclude by highlighting the practical implications of these dynamics.

---

[22] "Deciding about Decisions," *Management Review*, November 1985, p. 3.

■ **FIGURE 14–5**   Frequencies of Decision-Making Processes and the Organizational Event
Provoking Them

A. Frequency of Decision-Making Processes

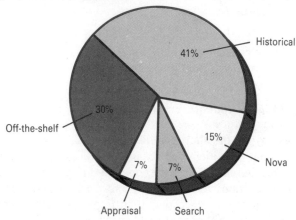

B. Frequency of Event Provoking Each Process

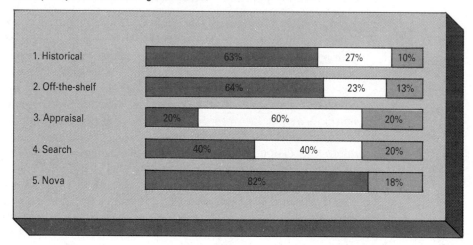

Key:

Problem

Opportunity

Crisis

SOURCE: Data from Paul C. Nutt, "Types of Organizational Decision Processes," *Administrative Science Quarterly*, September 1984, pp. 414–50.

■ **TABLE 14-5** Federal Aviation Administration Trains Pilots to Improve Their
Decision-Making Skills

> Researchers are currently writing training manuals based on earlier work by Jensen that
> determined pilots could be taught the decision-making skills central to good judgment. Such
> skills include assessment of the risks and hazards that arise; awareness of behavioral problems
> associated with accidents, such as an overeagerness to land; and knowledge that stress caused
> by factors unrelated to work, such as marital disputes, can affect performance.
>
> These manuals will be used to train individual and two-person teams of pilots. Both groups
> will learn decision-making skills.
>
> The teams also will learn communications skills in a program called cockpit resource manage-
> ment. This program teaches captains to welcome suggestions from other crew members and
> co-pilots to bring problems to the attention of the captain. Captains are also taught to delegate
> responsibility and recognize they cannot simultaneously communicate with air traffic control,
> spot and solve problems, and fly the plane.
>
> SOURCE: John Bales, "Human Factors Studies Help FAA to Make Skies Safer," *American Psychological Association Monitor*,
> February 1986, p. 10.

Selecting Solutions: A Contingency Perspective

The previous discussion of the classical model of problem solving noted
that managers either optimize, satisfice, or idealize when they select solutions.
However, we did not provide a framework to explain how managers actually
evaluate and select solutions. Figure 14–6 presents such a framework. We
now explore this model to better understand how individuals make decisions.

Strategies for Selecting a Solution.   What procedures do decision makers use
to evaluate the cost and benefits of alternative solutions? According to management experts Lee Roy Beach and Terence Mitchell, one of three approaches
is used: aided-analytic, unaided-analytic, and nonanalytic.[23] Decision makers
systematically use tools like mathematical equations, calculators, or computers
to analyze and evaluate alternatives within an **aided-analytic** approach. Technicians also may be commissioned to conduct a formal study. In contrast, decision
makers rely on the confines of their minds when using an **unaided-analytic**
strategy. In other words, the decision maker systematically compares alternatives, but the analysis is limited to evaluating information that can be directly
processed in his or her head. Decision-making tools such as a personal computer
are not used. Finally, a **nonanalytic** strategy consists of using a simple preformu-
lated rule to make a decision. Examples are flipping a coin, habit, normal con-
vention ("we've always done it that way"), using a conservative approach ("better safe than sorry"), or following procedures offered in instruction manuals.

---

[23] For a complete discussion, see Lee Roy Beach and Terence R. Mitchell, "A Contingency
Model for the Selection of Decision Strategies," *Academy of Management Review*, July 1978,
pp. 439–44.

■ **FIGURE 14–6**   A Contingency Model for Selecting a Solution

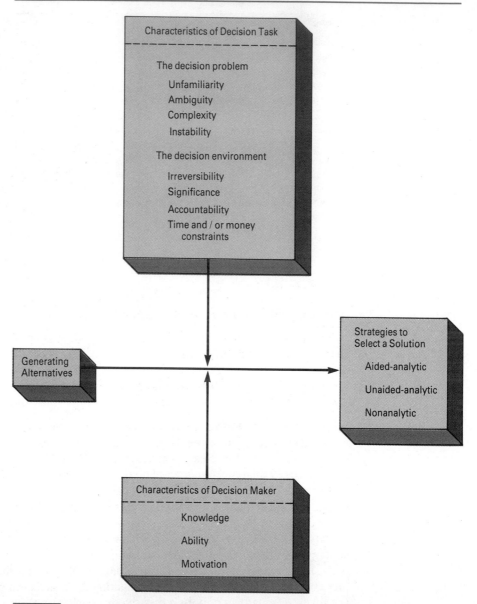

SOURCE: Based on Lee Roy Beach and Terence R. Mitchell, "A Contingency Model for the Selection of Decision Strategies," *Academy of Management Review,* July 1978, pp. 439–44.

Both the cost and level of sophistication decrease as one moves from an aided-analytic to a nonanalytic strategy.

Determining which approach to use depends on two contingency factors: characteristics of the decision task and characteristics of the decision maker (refer again to Figure 14–6).

Characteristics of the Decision Task.   This contingency factor reflects the demands and constraints a decision maker faces. In general, the greater these demands and constraints, the higher the probability that an aided-analytic approach will be used. These characteristics are divided into two components: those pertaining to the specific problem and those related to the general decision environment. Unfamiliar, ambiguous, complex, or unstable problems are more difficult to solve and typically require more sophisticated analysis. A recent study of 48 professionals in public accounting, financial analysis, and cost accounting demonstrated that the accuracy of a decision was inversely related to the complexity of the problem. In other words, more accurate decisions were made for easy problems and less accurate for difficult problems.[24]

The environment also restricts the type of analysis used.[25] For instance, managers experience increasing pressure to make good decisions when they are personally accountable for an irreversible decision or a significant problem. Moreover, time constraints affect selection of a solution. Consider the decision environment faced by Hamilton James, an investment banker at Donaldson Lufkin, while attempting to complete a merger between two companies.

> Mr. James was involved in early-evening talks in New York about the takeover of Children's Place Inc. by Federated Department Stores. He knew that at 8:30 the next morning he was expected to be the host at a meeting in Minneapolis on a different transaction. A Federated executive assured Mr. James that he could use Federated's company plane to fly to Minneapolis. But the offer was withdrawn when talks about Children's Place dragged on until 4 A.M.
>
> So in the dead of night, Mr. James began phoning charter services, eventually hiring a Learjet. At 5 A.M., he called the chief executive of Donaldson Lufkin to deliver the bad news: The jet would cost about $6,000. But there was good news, too: Donaldson Lufkin had earned about $10 million on the sale of Children's Place, in which the firm owned stock.[26]

Characteristics of the Decision Maker.   Chapter 3 highlighted a variety of individual differences that affect employee behavior and performance. In the present context, knowledge, ability, and motivation affect the type of analytical procedure used by a decision maker. In general, aided-analytic strategies require a more competent and motivated individual. David Lakhdhir, a corporate lawyer specializing in mergers and acquisitions represents a prime example (see Table 14–6).

Contingency Relationships.   There are many ways in which characteristics of the decision task and decision maker can interact to influence the strategy used to select a solution. In choosing a strategy, decision makers compromise between their desire to make correct decisions and the amount of time and

---

[24] For details, see Laurence Paquette and Thomas Kida, ''The Effect of Decision Strategy and Task Complexity on Decision Performance,'' *Organizational Behavior and Human Decision Processes,* February 1988, pp. 128–42.

[25] See Jay J. J. Christensen-Szalalski, ''A Further Examination of the Selection of Problem-Solving Strategies: The Effects of Deadlines and Analytic Aptitudes,'' *Organizational Behavior and Human Performance,* February 1980, pp. 107–22.

[26] George Anders, Paul Blustein, and Patricia Bellew Gray, ''Wall Street Prodigies Seek Money and Power as They Build Careers,'' *The Wall Street Journal,* June 2, 1986, p. 15.

■ **TABLE 14-6** Decision Making Requires Knowledge, Ability, and Motivation

His workday often runs from 9 A.M. to midnight, and even when he bought tickets recently to a popular play, . . . he had to miss the first act because legal papers had to be rushed to a client. . . .

"Transactions move at 150 miles per hour, and a single error can have extraordinary consequences." says Stuart Oran, a Paul Weiss partner. "You have to be extraordinarily bright and quick."

So far, Mr. Lakhdhir has met the test. Last spring [1985], for example, he was assigned to draft a $925 million loan accord involving Mesa Petroleum Co., which was starting an ultimately unsuccessful bid for Unocal Corp. In three days, he turned in a 180-page document that, much to his bosses' relief, was nearly perfect.

SOURCE: George Anders, Paul Blustein, and Patricia Bellew Gray, "Wall Street Prodigies Seek Money and Power as They Build Careers," *The Wall Street Journal,* June 2, 1986, p. 15.

■ **TABLE 14-7** Contingency Relationships in Decision Making

1. Analytic strategies are used when the decision problem is unfamiliar, ambiguous, complex, or unstable.
2. Nonanalytic methods are employed when the problem is familiar, straightforward, or stable.
3. Assuming there are no monetary or time constraints, analytic approaches are used when the solution is irreversible and significant, and the decision maker is accountable.
4. Nonanalytic strategies are used when the decision can be reversed and is not very significant, or the decision maker is not held accountable.
5. As the probability of making a correct decision goes down, analytic strategies are used.
6. As the probability of making a correct decision goes up, nonanalytic strategies are employed.
7. Time and money constraints automatically exclude some strategies from being used.
8. Analytic strategies are more frequently used by experienced and educated decision makers.
9. Nonanalytic approaches are used when the decision maker lacks knowledge, ability, or motivation to make a good decision.

SOURCE: Adapted from Lee Roy Beach and Terence R. Mitchell, "A Contingency Model for the Selection of Decision Strategies," *Academy of Management Review,* July 1978, pp. 439–44.

effort they put into the decision-making process. Table 14–7 lists contingency relationships that help reconcile these competing demands.[27]

Individual versus Group Decision Making

Chapter 10 examined the unique dynamics that arise when individuals work together in groups. Groups such as committees, task forces, or review panels often play a key role in the decision-making process. For example, August Busch III, chairman of Anheuser-Busch, brewer of Budweiser beer, uses a policy committee to help him make key decisions. He even created a special procedure to encourage group participation.

---

[27] For a review of related research, see John W. Payne, "Contingent Decision Behavior," *Psychological Bulletin,* September 1982, pp. 382–402.

Busch has encouraged openness with his policy committee, a nine-member executive forum that is the heart of Anheuser. He runs it Socratically, insisting that each member present an opinion on the topic at hand and back it up. To find the answer to what Busch calls "tough, meaty, complicated decisions," such as plant expansion, he stages formal debates, called "dialectics." Two executives take opposing sides and are given a small staff and several weeks to prepare their cases. "Once you set the facts on the table and take all the chaff off, you can get to the clean facts and make a clean-risk decision," declares Busch. "If the decision is wrong after that kind of homework, we never look back."[28]

Are two or more heads always better than one? Before involving groups in the decision-making process, managers need to consider the advantages and disadvantages of group-aided decision making and group versus individual performance.

Advantages and Disadvantages of Group-Aided Decision Making.   Including groups in the decision-making process has both pros and cons (see Table 14–8). To determine whether groups should be included, managers need to consider the extent to which the advantages and disadvantages apply to the decision situation. The following three guidelines may then be applied:

1. If additional information would increase the quality of the decision, managers should involve those people who can provide the needed information.

2. If acceptance is important, managers need to involve those individuals whose acceptance and commitment are important. As chairman of Corning Glass Works, James Houghton has formalized this second guideline.

Jamie has been reshaping the company with a remarkable show of consensus management, considering that the Houghtons still own 15% of Corning. His executive council of six men, which puts Corning's four operations managers atop the corporate pyramid for the first time, makes key decisions. At first, midlevel executives feared the new management by committee would stall decisions. But Houghton required the committee to respond in writing within 24 hours to middle-management presentations.[29]

3. If people can be developed through their participation, managers may want to involve those whose development is most important.[30]

Group versus Individual Performance.   Before recommending that managers involve groups in decision making, it is important to examine whether groups perform better or worse than individuals. After reviewing 61 years of relevant research (see Table 14–9), a decision-making expert concluded:

Group performance was generally qualitatively and quantitatively superior to the performance of the average individual. Group performance, however, was

---

[28] Ellyn E. Spragins and Marc Frons, "When You Say Busch You've Said It All," *Business Week,* February 17, 1986, p. 63.

[29] Barbara Buell, "Smashing the Country Club Image at Corning Glass," *Business Week,* May 5, 1986, p. 95.

[30] These guidelines were derived from Huber, *Managerial Decision Making,* p. 149.

■ **TABLE 14–8** Advantages and Disadvantages of Group-Aided Decision Making

Advantages	Disadvantages
1. **Greater pool of knowledge.** A group can bring much more information and experience to bear on a decision or problem than can an individual acting alone.	1. **Social pressure.** Unwillingness to "rock the boat" and pressure to conform may combine to stifle the creativity of individual contributors.
2. **Different perspectives.** Individuals with varied experience and interests help the group see decision situations and problems from different angles.	2. **Minority domination.** Sometimes the quality of group action is reduced when the group gives in to those who talk the loudest and longest.
3. **Greater comprehension.** Those who personally experience the give-and-take of group discussion about alternative courses of action tend to understand the rationale behind the final decision.	3. **Logrolling.** Political wheeling and dealing can displace sound thinking when an individual's pet project or vested interest is at stake.
4. **Increased acceptance.** Those who play an active role in group decision making and problem solving tend to view the outcome as "ours" rather than "theirs."	4. **Goal displacement.** Sometimes secondary considerations such as winning an argument, making a point, or getting back at a rival displace the primary task of making a sound decision or solving a problem.
5. **Training ground.** Less experienced participants in group action learn how to cope with group dynamics by actually being involved.	5. **"Groupthink."** Sometimes cohesive "in-groups" let the desire for unanimity override sound judgment when generating and evaluating alternative courses of action.

SOURCE: Robert Kreitner, *Management,* 3rd ed. (Boston: Houghton Mifflin, 1986), p. 211.

often inferior to that of the best individual in a statistical aggregate and often inferior to the potential suggested in a statistical pooling model. This research confirms the belief that the performance of one exceptional individual can be superior to that of a committee, . . . especially if the committee is trying to solve a complex problem and if the committee contains a number of low-ability members.[31]

In summary, managers have good reason to use a contingency approach when determining whether to include others in the decision-making process.

Practical Lessons from Research

Research on the dynamics of decision making offers the following practical implications for managers:

- If the decision occurs frequently, like deciding on promotions or who qualifies for a loan, a group will tend to produce more consistent decisions than will an individual.[32]
- Given time constraints, let the most competent individual, rather than a group, make the decision.

---

[31] Gayle W. Hill, "Group versus Individual Performance: Are N + 1 Heads Better Than One?" *Psychological Bulletin,* May 1982, p. 535.

[32] This finding was obtained by Peter Chalos and Sue Pickard, "Information Choice and Cue Use: An Experiment in Group Information Processing," *Journal of Applied Psychology,* November 1985, pp. 634–41.

■ **TABLE 14–9** Summary of 61 Years of Research on Group versus Individual Performance

Variable of Interest	Conclusion
Type of task:	
Learning task	Group performance was consistently superior to the performance of an individual.
Concept mastery and creative tasks	More unshared resources by high-ability group members.
	Contribution of medium-ability group members was greater when they were paired with partners who had high rather than low ability.
Problem solving	Groups took longer to complete the task, but made more accurate decisions.
	On difficult problems, groups pooled and integrated their resources.
	On easy tasks, group performance was determined by the contribution of one competent group member.
Brainstorming	Pooling individual responses resulted in a greater number of unique ideas than did group interaction.
Complex	Groups were superior to an individual, but inferior to pooling individual responses.
Training:	
In problem solving and group dynamics	Groups benefited more than individuals.
In brainstorming	Individuals benefited more than groups.
In ability to apply new skills in work environment	Individuals took less time to apply new knowledge than did groups.
Individual differences:	High-ability individuals performed better than did groups composed of mixed ability.
	Higher performance was obtained by groups whose members preferred to work in a group, rather than alone.
Decision-making processes:	Groups made riskier decisions.
	Group members did not put forth an equal amount of effort.

SOURCE: Conclusions were derived from Gayle W. Hill, "Group versus Individual Performance: Are N + 1 Heads Better Than One?" *Psychological Bulletin,* May 1982, pp. 517–39.

- Diversity among the characteristics of group members increases the quality of a decision.[33]
- In the face of environmental threats like time pressure and potential serious impact of a decision, groups use less information and fewer communication channels. This increases the probability of a bad decision.[34]

---

[33] See John P. Wanous and Margaret A. Youtz, "Solution Diversity and the Quality of Group Decisions," *Academy of Management Journal,* March 1986, pp. 149–58.

[34] See Deborah L. Gladstein and Nora P. Reilly, "Group Decision Making under Threat: The Tycoon Game," *Academy of Management Journal,* September 1985, pp. 613–27.

■ CREATIVITY

In light of today's fast-paced decisions, an organization's ability to stimulate the creativity and innovation of its employees is becoming increasingly important. As noted by Peter Drucker, the renowned management consultant, "Managing innovation will increasingly become a challenge to management, and especially to top management, and a touchstone of its competence."[35] For example, consider the difference between how Stephen Wozniak's creativity was managed at Hewlett-Packard and Arthur Fry's at 3M.

> In 1975 Stephen Wozniak, then a 25-year-old designer at Hewlett-Packard, went to his boss with the idea of a microcomputer that could be hooked up to a home television set. The firm was not interested. Wozniak therefore started his own company with Steven Jobs, a friend working at Atari. The company: Apple Computer. Sales last year [1984]: $1.5 billion. . . .
>
> Arthur Fry, 53, a 3M chemical engineer, used to get annoyed at how pieces of paper that marked his church hymnal always fell out when he stood up to sing. He knew that Spencer Silver, a scientist at 3M, had accidentally discovered an adhesive that had very low sticking power. . . . He figured that markers made with the adhesive might stick lightly to something and would come off easily. Since 3M allows employees to spend 15% of their office time on independent projects, he began working on the idea. Fry made samples and then distributed the small yellow pads to company secretaries. . . . 3M eventually began selling it under the name Post-It. Sales last year [1984]: more than $100 million.[36]

Mismanaging Wozniak cost Hewlett-Packard billions of dollars, while 3M's progressive managerial practices resulted in substantial profits. To gain further insight into managing the creative process, this section defines creativity, highlights the characteristics of creative people, summarizes creativity techniques, and discusses management of creative individuals.

Defining Creativity

Although many definitions have been proposed, the essence of **creativity** is creation of something new, something that has never existed before. It can be as simple as developing a new flavor of the month for an ice cream store or as complex as developing a pocket-size microcomputer.

Early approaches to explaining creativity were based on differences between the left and right hemispheres of the brain. Researchers thought the right side of the brain was responsible for creativity. In an attempt to test this hypothesis, one study examined the hemispheric dominance of a group of 22 CEOs. As expected, results indicated the CEOs relied predominantly on the right side

---

[35] Sharon Nelton, "How to Spark New Ideas," *Nation's Business,* June 1985, pp. 18–19.

[36] John S. DeMott, "Here Come the Intrapreneurs," *Time,* February 4, 1985, pp. 36–37. Copyright 1985 Time Inc. Reprinted by permission from Time.

of the brain.[37] More recently, however, researchers have questioned this explanation.

> "The left brain/right brain dichotomy is simplified and misleading," says Dr. John C. Mazziotta, a researcher at the University of California at Los Angeles School of Medicine.
>
> What scientists have found instead is that creativity is a feat of mental gymnastics engaging the conscious and subconscious parts of the brain. It draws on everything from knowledge, logic, imagination, and intuition to the ability to see connections and distinctions between ideas and things.[38]

Characteristics of Creative People

Creative people typically march to the beat of a different drummer. They are highly motivated individuals who spend many years mastering their chosen field or occupation. Contrary to stereotypes, however, creative people are not necessarily geniuses or introverted nerds. In addition, they are not *adaptors* (see Table 14–10). "Adaptors are those who seek to solve problems by 'doing things better.' They prefer to resolve difficulties or make decisions in such a way as to have the least impact upon the assumptions, procedures, and values of the organization. . . ."[39] In contrast, creative individuals are dissatisfied with the status quo. They look for new and exciting solutions to problems. Because of this, creative organizational members can be perceived as disruptive and hard to get along with. Further, research indicates that male and female managers do not differ in levels of creativity and creative people are more open to experiencing new and different activities.[40] Table 14–11 presents additional characteristics of creative individuals.

Creativity Techniques

Table 14–12 lists commonly used techniques for generating creative solutions. In choosing a technique, managers need to consider the nature of the problem or situation. Consistent with a contingency approach, different techniques are appropriate in certain situations. For example, brainstorming is useful when the problem is open-ended and well-defined. On the other hand, reverse brain-

---

[37] See Louis T. Coulson and Alison G. Strickland, "The Minds at the Top: An Analysis of the Thinking Style Preferences of Superintendents of Schools and Chief Executive Officers," *Journal of Creative Behavior,* Third Quarter 1983, pp. 163–74.

[38] Emily T. Smith, "Are You Creative?" *Business Week,* September 30, 1985, pp. 81–82. For a review of research about the left and right hemispheres of the brain, see Terence Hines, "Left Brain/Right Brain Mythology and Implications for Management and Training," *Academy of Management Review,* October 1987, pp. 600–606.

[39] Timothy A. Matherly and Ronald E. Goldsmith, "The Two Faces of Creativity," *Business Horizons,* September–October 1985, p. 9.

[40] Supporting findings are contained in Leonard H. Chusmir and Christine S. Koberg, "Creativity Differences among Managers," *Journal of Vocational Behavior,* October 1986, pp. 240–53; and Robert R. McCrae, "Creativity, Divergent Thinking, and Openness to Experience," *Journal of Personality and Social Psychology,* June 1987, pp. 1258–65.

■ **TABLE 14–10** From Adaptors to Creative Innovators: A Major Challenge for Japan

> If there is a single word that the Japanese find most challenging and perplexing, it is "creativity." Now that they have caught up with and surpassed many leading Western technologies, the Japanese face the task of exploring undreamed of frontiers.
>
> . . . True creative advances are a Japanese priority today, and in the past two years special emphasis has been placed on basic research.
>
> . . . But there are skeptics, including many Japanese, who say it will take more than money and facilities to meet the new challenge. Adapting, not creating, has been the Japanese strong point, the critics say, adding that Japan's educational system, which places a premium on rote learning, has ill-prepared its future researchers to take the lead in their fields. . . .
>
> Researchers say their principal creativity problem is managerial, not educational, and there is solid evidence suggesting that they are on the way to solving this key issue.
>
> SOURCE: Excerpted from Michael Berger, "Japan's Energetic New Search for Creativity," *International Management,* October 1987, pp. 71–72, 74, 77.

■ **TABLE 14–11** Characteristics of Creative People

1. Knowledge	Creative people spend a great number of years mastering their chosen field.
2. Education	Education does not increase creativity. Education that stresses logic tends to inhibit creativity.
3. Intelligence	Creative people do not necessarily have a high IQ. The threshold for IQ is around 130. After that, IQ does not really matter. Creative people have been found to possess the following intellectual abilities: sensitivity to problems, flexibility in forming fluid associations between objects, thinking in images rather than words, and synthesizing information.
4. Personality	Creative people are typically risk takers who are independent, persistent, highly motivated, skeptical, open to new ideas, able to tolerate ambiguity, self-confident, and able to tolerate isolation. They also have a strong sense of humor and are hard to get along with.
5. Childhood	Creative people have usually had a childhood marked by diversity. Experiences such as family strains, financial ups and downs, and divorces are common occurrences.
6. Social habits	Contrary to stereotypes, creative people are not introverted nerds. Creative people tend to be outgoing and enjoy exchanging ideas with colleagues.

SOURCE: Based in part on Robert G. Godfrey, "Tapping Employees' Creativity," *Supervisory Management,* February 1986, pp. 16–20; and "Mix Skepticism, Humor, a Rocky Childhood—and Presto! Creativity," *Business Week,* September 30, 1985, p. 81.

storming would be better suited for generating solutions for an open-ended and ill-defined problem.[41] In trying to stimulate employees to be more creative, managers also need to consider the mental locks that stifle creativity.

Roger von Oech, a creativity consultant in Silicon Valley, identified 10 mental locks or hang-ups that interfere with creativity. They are:

[41] For a review of the creativity techniques recommended by researchers, see Mark R. Edwards and J. Ruth Sproull, "Creativity: Productivity Gold Mine?" *Journal of Creative Behavior,* Third Quarter 1984, pp. 175–84. Also see Jack Gordon and Ron Zemke, "Making Them More Creative," *Training,* May 1986, pp. 30–45.

■ **TABLE 14–12** Techniques for Generating Creative Solutions

Technique	Description	Problem/Situation When Most Appropriate
Brainstorming	An uninhibited approach for generating new ideas. Solutions are generated in a nonjudgmental fashion.	Problem is open-ended; problem is well-defined; simple solution is sought; problem has more than one acceptable solution. Participants are able and willing to freewheel and emphasize the positive.
Free association	Symbols, like words or pictures, related to the problem are jotted down. These ideas are used to create additional symbols related to the problem.	Same as brainstorming.
Reverse brainstorming	Analysis is critical rather than nonjudgmental. The focus is to identify the components of a problem.	Problem is open-ended; problem is ill-defined; simple solution is sought; problem has more than one acceptable solution. Group members are initially unable to freewheel or emphasize positive aspects of a problem.
Edisonian (named after Thomas Edison)	Extensive trial-and-error experiments are conducted. Considered to be a last-ditch approach.	Same as reverse brainstorming.
Synectics	A two-stage approach that uses analogies and metaphors to make the familiar strange, and the strange familiar. An attempt is made to view the problem from different points of view.	Problem is open-ended; problem is fairly well-defined; a complex illogical solution is desired; problem has one best solution. Group members can emphasize the bizarre and take a positive outlook on the problem.
Attribute listing	Used to improve tangible objects. Properties or attributes of a product are listed, with a view toward improving each one.	Problem need not be open-ended; problem is well-defined; problem has several acceptable solutions, but one best solution. Attributes are well-defined, and group members can visualize combinations of attributes.
Morphological matrix analysis	A structured approach that examines all possible combinations to solve a problem. Problem variables are identified along two axes of a matrix, and interrelationships among each variable are examined within the body of the chart.	Same as attribute listing.
Collective notebook	Group members maintain a diary for a month that contains their ideas about a problem. A coordinator summarizes all notebooks, and these summaries are used to generate future discussions.	Problem may be either open- or closed-ended; problem is well-defined; simple, logical solution is desired. The technology being studied is well known and a logical process may be followed to reach a solution.
Scientific method	A problem-solving approach is used to test hypotheses about the causes of the problem.	Same as collective notebook.

SOURCE: Adapted from William E. Souder and Robert W. Ziegler, "A Review of Creativity and Problem Solving Techniques," *Research Management,* July 1977, p. 40.

1. Searching for the ''right'' answer.
2. Always trying to be logical.
3. Looking for solutions that ''follow the rules.''
4. Trying to be too practical.
5. Avoiding ambiguity.
6. Fearing failure.
7. Not playing or having fun at work.

■ FIGURE 14–7 Creativity Exercises

Exercise 1

In the line of letters listed below, cross out six letters so the remaining letters spell a familiar English word. You may not alter the sequence of the letters.

B S A I N X L E A T N T E A R S

Try to solve the exercise for a while before proceeding.

Exercise 2

What is this figure? Come up with as many interpretations as you can.

SOURCE: Reprinted by permission of Warner Books/New York, from *A Whack on the Side of the Head.* Copyright © 1983 by Roger von Oech, pp. 76–78.

8. Ignoring problems outside one's specialty.

9. Not wanting to look foolish.

10. Believing you are not creative.[42]

To demonstrate how these mental locks inhibit creativity, try the two exercises in Figure 14–7. After completing these exercises, look at the solutions provided in the footnote.[43] Which mental lock may have reduced your creativity? In

---

[42] A detailed discussion is provided by Roger von Oech, *A Whack on the Side of the Head,* (New York: Warner, 1983).

[43] Exercise 1: One way to solve this problem is to interpret the instructions in an ambiguous fashion. Instead of crossing out six letters, you can literally cross out the S, and the I, and the X, and the L, and the E, and so on until you have crossed out the words *six letters.* If you did this, you would have found the word *BANANA.* Another solution to this exercise would be to choose six different letters—say, B, S, A, I, N, and X—and cross them out every time they appear. You would end up with the word LETTER. Exercise 2: If you look at it one way, it's a bird; it could also be a question mark; if you turn it upside down, it's a seal juggling a ball on its nose.

■ **TABLE 14–13** Suggestions for Improving Employee Creativity

Develop an environment that supports creative behavior.

Try to avoid using an autocratic style of leadership.

Encourage employees to be more open to new ideas and experiences.

Keep in mind that people use different strategies, like walking around or listening to music, to foster their creativity.

Provide employees with stimulating work that creates a sense of personal growth.

Encourage employees to view problems as opportunities.

Don't let your decision-making style stifle those employees who have a different style.

Guard against employees being too involved with putting out fires and dealing with urgent short-term problems.

Make sure creative people are not bogged down with specific tasks all day long.

Allow employees to have fun and play around.

Encourage an open environment that is free from defensive behavior.

Treat errors and mistakes as opportunities for learning.

Let employees occasionally try out their pet ideas. Provide a margin of error.

Be a catalyst instead of an obstacle.

Avoid using a negative mind-set when an employee approaches you with a new idea.

Encourage creative people to communicate with one another.

Welcome diverse ideas and opinions.

Send yourself and your employees to creativity training.

Reward creative behavior.

SOURCE: Adapted from discussion in Eugene Raudsepp, "101 Ways to Spark Your Employees' Creative Potential," *Office Administration and Automation,* September 1985, pp. 38, 39–43, 56.

an organizational context, managers need to help employees identify and confront these mental locks. By doing so, the various creativity techniques can be used to their potential.

Managing Creative Employees

Managers are challenged by today's competitive pressures to develop an environment that supports creative behavior. As is the case at a leading ad agency, this can best be accomplished with top management's support.

> "Responsibility for creative excellence starts at the top," says Norman W. Brown, president and CEO of Foote, Cone & Belding, the world's eighth largest advertising agency. "It is my primary responsibility."
>
> Since creativity is central to the advertising business, Brown wanted to be sure that FCB was doing everything that could be done to support it. In late 1983, he set up a "creative strategy task force" representing the different disciplines and geographic areas of the Chicago-based company. . . .
>
> As a result of the task force findings, FCB adopted a set of principles called its "Strategic Creative Development Process."[44]

---

[44] Nelton, "How to Spark New Ideas," p. 19.

In a similar vein, Eastman Kodak Co. set up innovation centers, and Hallmark Cards Inc. is opening a $20 million Technology & Innovation Center. At W. L. Gore & Associates, a privately held firm, employees, who are called associates, are grouped into teams of 150 to 200 people to encourage creativity.[45] Table 14–13 lists some specific managerial recommendations to spark employee creativity.

After a supportive environment has been created, managers may want to consider creativity training for employees. Since each of us has the potential to be creative, training gives everyone a chance to participate in the creative process. In support of this idea, a meta-analysis of 46 research studies indicated that training led to significant increases in creativity.[46] Finally, managers will need to modify their own behavior and attitudes (the ideas in Table 14–13 point the way).

SUMMARY OF KEY CONCEPTS

A. There are two types of managerial decisions: programmed and nonprogrammed. Programmed decisions are repetitive and routine. Habit and standard operating procedures are most frequently used to make these decisions. Nonprogrammed decisions are novel, unstructured, and tend to have important consequences. To solve these decisions, managers rely on judgment, intuition, and creativity.

B. Decision making consists of identifying a problem, generating alternative solutions, and selecting a solution. The classical model of problem solving expands on these three steps by including implementation and evaluation of a solution. Research indicates that decision makers do not follow the series of steps outlined in the classical model.

C. A problem exists when there is a difference between an actual situation and a desired situation. Problems are identified through historical cues, planning, or other people's perceptions. In selecting solutions for problems, decision makers either optimize, satisfice, or idealize. Managers tend to satisfice.

D. The garbage can model of decision making describes decision making in organized anarchies. Organized anarchies represent any organization or decision situation characterized by problematic preferences, unclear technology, and fluid participation. In the garbage can process, decisions result from an interaction between four independent streams of events: problems, solutions, participants, and choice opportunities.

E. Five unique types of decision-making processes were identified in case

---

[45] See Smith, "Are You Creative?" pp. 80–84.

[46] For a review of training research, see Laura Hall Rose and Hsin-Tai Lin, "A Meta-Analysis of Long-Term Creativity Training Programs," *Journal of Creative Behavior*, First Quarter 1984, pp. 11–22. Sample problems that may be used to develop creativity are presented in C. Samuel Micklus, *Odyssey of the Mind: Problems to Develop Creativity* (Glassboro, N.J.: Creative Competitions, 1984).

studies of decision making: historical, off-the-shelf, appraisal, search, and nova. The historical approach was the most frequently used process. Either a problem, an opportunity, or a crisis was found to provoke these processes. Decision making was most frequently caused by a problem.

F. Decision makers use either an aided-analytic, unaided-analytic, or nonanalytic strategy when selecting a solution. The choice of a strategy depends on the characteristics of the decision task and the characteristics of the decision maker. Several contingency relationships have been identified.

G. There are both pros and cons of involving groups in the decision-making process. Research shows that groups typically outperform the average individual. However, group performance is usually lower than both the most competent individual and a statistical aggregate of each group member's performance.

H. Creativity is the creation of something new. It is not adequately explained by differences between the left and right hemispheres of the brain. Creativity involves an interaction between conscious and unconscious processes. Several characteristics differentiate creative people from average individuals. Decision makers need to consider the nature of the problem when selecting a technique to increase creativity. There are 10 mental locks that stifle an individual's creativity. Research shows that people can be trained to increase their creativity.

KEY TERMS

decision making
programmed decisions
nonprogrammed decisions
heuristics
problem solving
problem
scenario technique
optimizing

satisficing
idealizing
organized anarchies
aided-analytic
unaided-analytic
nonanalytic
creativity

DISCUSSION QUESTIONS

1. Identify both a programmed and a nonprogrammed decision you made recently. How did you arrive at a solution for each one?
2. Based on your experience, what is the most important step in problem solving? Why?
3. Do you think people are rational when they make decisions? Under what circumstances would an individual tend to follow a rational process?
4. Describe a situation in which you satisficed when making a decision. Why did you satisfice instead of optimize?

5. Do you think the garbage can model is a realistic representation of organizational decision making? Discuss your rationale.

6. How would you respond to someone who said, "Decisions are always made to solve problems"?

7. What is the most valuable lesson about selecting solutions through a contingency perspective? Explain.

8. Do you prefer to solve problems in groups or by yourself? Why?

9. Do you think you are creative? Why or why not?

10. What advice would you offer a manager who was attempting to improve the creativity of his or her employees? Explain.

BACK TO THE OPENING CASE

Now that you have read Chapter 14, you should be able to answer the following questions about decision making at Rolm Corp. and American Can Company:

1. What problem identification methods were used at Rolm Corp. and American Can Company? How can you tell?

2. Were the decision-making processes in these two companies more characteristic of the classical or garbage can model of decision making? Explain.

3. Which company, Rolm Corp. or American Can Co., relied more on group-aided decision making? Why do you think this occurred?

4. Who was more creative, Kenneth Oshman or William Woodside? Why?

EXERCISE 14

Objectives

1. To identify your level of creativity.
2. To explore how you might increase your level of creativity.

Introduction

A creativity expert named Eugene Raudsepp has examined the characteristics of creative individuals working in a variety of occupations. Through his research, he has been able to identify a unique set of traits, attitudes, values, motivations, and interests possessed by creative individuals. In order to determine how creative you are, we are going to assess the extent to which you possess these attributes.

Instructions

To assess your creativity, complete the 40-item instrument developed by Raudsepp. Be honest and do not try to guess how a creative person might respond to each question. For each item, indicate your answer by circling whether you agree (A), neither agree nor disagree (B), or disagree (C). After completing the instrument, use the scoring key to compute your total score.

Creativity Instrument[47]

1.	I always work with a great deal of certainty that I am following the correct procedure for solving a particular problem.	A	B	C
2.	It would be a waste of time for me to ask questions if I had no hope of obtaining answers.	A	B	C
3.	I concentrate harder on whatever interests me than do most people.	A	B	C
4.	I feel that a logical, step-by-step method is best for solving problems.	A	B	C
5.	In groups I occasionally voice opinions that seem to turn some people off.	A	B	C
6.	I spend a great deal of time thinking about what others think of me.	A	B	C
7.	It is more important for me to do what I believe to be right than to try to win the approval of others.	A	B	C
8.	People who seem uncertain about things lose my respect.	A	B	C
9.	More than other people, I need to have things interesting and exciting.	A	B	C
10.	I know how to keep my inner impulses in check.	A	B	C
11.	I am able to stick with difficult problems over extended periods of time.	A	B	C
12.	On occasion I get overly enthusiastic.	A	B	C
13.	I often get my best ideas when doing nothing in particular.	A	B	C
14.	I rely on intuitive hunches and the feeling of "rightness" or "wrongness" when moving toward the solution of a problem.	A	B	C
15.	When problem solving, I work faster when analyzing the problem and slower when synthesizing the information I have gathered.	A	B	C
16.	I sometimes get a kick out of breaking the rules and doing things I am not supposed to do.	A	B	C
17.	I like hobbies that involve collecting things.	A	B	C
18.	Daydreaming has provided the impetus for many of my more important projects.	A	B	C
19.	I like people who are objective and rational.	A	B	C
20.	If I had to choose from two occupations other than the one I now have, I would rather be a physician than an explorer.	A	B	C
21.	I can get along more easily with people if they belong to about the same social and business class as myself.	A	B	C
22.	I have a high degree of aesthetic sensitivity.	A	B	C
23.	I am driven to achieve high status and power in life.	A	B	C
24.	I like people who are most sure of their conclusions.	A	B	C
25.	Inspiration has nothing to do with the successful solution of problems.	A	B	C
26.	When I am in an argument, my greatest pleasure would be for the person who disagrees with me to become a friend, even at the price of sacrificing my point of view.	A	B	C

[47] This creativity instrument and scoring key were taken from Eugene Raudsepp, ''How Creative Are You?'' *Nation's Business*, June 1985, pp. 25–26. Used with author's permission.

27. I am much more interested in coming up with new ideas than in trying to sell them to others.   A B C

28. I would enjoy spending an entire day alone, just "chewing the mental cud."   A B C

29. I tend to avoid situations in which I might feel inferior.   A B C

30. In evaluating information, the source is more important to me than the content.   A B C

31. I resent things being uncertain and unpredictable.   A B C

32. I like people who follow the rule "business before pleasure."   A B C

33. Self-respect is much more important than the respect of others.   A B C

34. I feel that people who strive for perfection are unwise.   A B C

35. I prefer to work with others in a team effort rather than solo.   A B C

36. I like work in which I must influence others.   A B C

37. Many problems that I encounter in life cannot be resolved in terms of right or wrong solutions.   A B C

38. It is important for me to have a place for everything and everything in its place.   A B C

39. Writers who use strange and unusual words merely want to show off.   A B C

40. Below is a list of terms that describe people. Place a check mark next to 10 words that best characterize you.

_____ energetic	_____ factual	_____ courageous
_____ persuasive	_____ open-minded	_____ efficient
_____ observant	_____ tactful	_____ helpful
_____ fashionable	_____ inhibited	_____ perceptive
_____ self-confident	_____ enthusiastic	_____ quick
_____ persevering	_____ innovative	_____ good-natured
_____ original	_____ poised	_____ thorough
_____ cautious	_____ acquisitive	_____ impulsive
_____ habit-bound	_____ practical	_____ determined
_____ resourceful	_____ alert	_____ realistic
_____ egotistical	_____ curious	_____ modest
_____ independent	_____ organized	_____ involved
_____ stern	_____ unemotional	_____ absent-minded
_____ predictable	_____ clear-thinking	_____ flexible
_____ formal	_____ understanding	_____ sociable
_____ informal	_____ dynamic	_____ well-liked
_____ dedicated	_____ self-demanding	_____ restless
_____ forward-looking	_____ polished	_____ retiring

Scoring

For each question, there is a separate value associated with a response of A, B, or C. These values are given in the table below. To compute your total score, add the values assigned to each item.

SCORING KEY

QUESTION	A	B	C
		RESPONSE	
1.	0	1	2
2.	0	1	2
3.	4	1	0
4.	−2	0	3
5.	2	1	0
6.	−1	0	3
7.	3	0	−1
8.	0	1	2
9.	3	0	−1
10.	1	0	3
11.	4	1	0
12.	3	0	−1
13.	2	1	0
14.	4	0	−2
15.	−1	0	2
16.	2	1	0
17	0	1	2
18.	3	0	−1
19.	0	1	2
20.	0	1	2
21.	0	1	2
22.	3	0	−1
23.	0	1	2
24.	−1	0	2
25.	0	1	3
26.	−1	0	2
27.	2	1	0
28.	2	0	−1
29.	0	1	2
30.	−2	0	3
31.	0	1	2
32.	0	1	2
33.	3	0	−1
34.	−1	0	2
35.	0	1	2
36.	1	2	3
37.	2	1	0
38.	0	1	2
39.	−1	0	2

40. The following have values of 2:

energetic	dynamic	perceptive	dedicated
resourceful	flexible	innovative	courageous
original	observant	self-demanding	curious
enthusiastic	independent	persevering	involved

The following have values of 1:

self-confident	determined	informal	forward-looking
thorough	restless	alert	open-minded

The remaining characteristics have values of 0.

Questions for Consideration/Class Discussion

1. How creative are you?

95–116	Exceptionally creative
65–94	Very creative
40–64	Above average
20–39	Average
10–19	Below average
Below 10	Noncreative

2. Based on your scores for each question, how might you increase your level of creativity?

3. Will your present level of creativity help or hinder you as a manager of other people?

Chapter **15**

Job Design and Quality of Work Life Innovations

LEARNING OBJECTIVES

When you finish studying the material in this chapter,
you should be able to:

- Explain why job design is particularly important today.
- Explain how proponents of scientific management and job rotation would handle job design.
- Contrast job enlargement and job enrichment.
- Explain how internal work motivation is increased by using the job characteristics model.
- Discuss the practical significance of the sociotechnical and the social information-processing models of job design.
- Explain the relationship between participative management and job performance.
- Contrast flexitime and compressed workweeks.
- Demonstrate your familiarity with quality circles, gainsharing, and telecommuting.

Thorneburg Hosiery Experiments with Job Design

Just before Christmas in 1982, Jim Thorneburg called the first company-wide meeting in Thorneburg Hosiery Company's history and issued an ultimatum: Every employee had to be operating under what he called the "new system" in two years. He would go broke, if he had to, to bring about the change, but if they could not make it work, he would sell the company.

The problem was that things were going too well for the Statesville, N.C., firm. When it started manufacturing an innovative line of sports socks in 1980, sales jumped from $800,000 to $2.7 million in one year. As sales soared to more than $5 million the following year, Thorneburg realized that the little company his parents had founded nearly three decades before "was growing faster than was healthy."

Thorneburg had invented the new line. Called Thor-Lo PADDS Foot Equipment, it consists of eight types of socks, each engineered for a different sport. Averaging $6 a pair, they are the most expensive athletic socks made.

With the Thor-Lo line, Thorneburg believed his company could become a $50 million company. Except for the fact that it was not ready to take on that kind of growth. He was concerned about whether his employees would care enough to produce socks of the quality and quantity he knew were needed.

Thorneburg, 48, decided to revamp the corporate culture. "We've got every reason to believe that we can go to a $100 million or a $200 million company," he said at a meeting. He wanted to build "a great company for people to work in." And down the road, he said he envisioned sharing ownership of the company with its 140 employees.

But to make these things happen, he said, everybody—including himself—had to change. Under the new system, each employee would be held accountable for the quality and quantity of his own work. Thorneburg recalls saying, "The person that you work for is no longer responsible for your work. You are. Not your supervisor."

He predicted that the new system would be hardest on the company's 15 or so supervisors. In the past, they had been rewarded for exerting control and given credit when their subordinates were productive. Now he wanted them—and management—to become "servants to the worker."

"You are to teach, you are to coordinate, you are to move information to and from, you are to be a friend and counselor," he instructed them. "And when you do those things well, your people will produce." He said he would fire any supervisors who tried to make subordinates perform.

He offered $500 "exit bonuses" to employees who felt they would be unhappy with the changes (there were two takers). He threatened to sell if the new system did not work, because if it did not, he no longer wanted to run the company.

In the months that followed the Christmas meeting, quality circles were formed—not for the purpose of improving productivity or solving problems, Thorneburg says, but as a safe environment in which his employees, largely unskilled, could express their ideas without fear of ridicule and learn to cooperate with and trust one another. In addition, the quality circles were to be educational tools, involving employees in decisions about their work and helping them develop judgment.

Supervisors, too, went through an educational process. Instead of ordering subordinates to do something . . . they learned to ask, and to offer an explanation of why a certain job had to be done. That way, the subordinate would understand and become more knowledgeable.

In handling discipline problems, supervisors began to take more time counseling and coaching an employee, rather than jumping quickly to punitive solutions. The immediate supervisors still conduct performance reviews, but they do not set goals—the quality circles do that.

Early last year [1984], Thorneburg moved the company into a new $1.8 million plant, aimed at increasing productivity and improving working conditions.

He saw some signs of change. Employees began to pay more attention to how they looked when they came to work. The mill was kept cleaner. Some workers with drug problems began coming forward and asking for help. And some employees went back to get high school diplomas on their own time so they could participate more effectively in the quality circles.

Thorneburg's two years were up last December [1984]. He still owns the company, and he hasn't gone broke. Has the experiment met his expectations?

"Absolutely!" he responds. Sales have continued upward, reaching $7.5 million last year [1984]. . . .

His all-important knitters group has achieved 99.3 percent "first quality" production (meaning goods of high enough quality to be sent on to the retailers), against an industry average of about 90 percent.

SOURCE: Sharon Nelton, "Socking It to the Old Style." Reprinted by permission from *Nation's Business*, May 1985, p. 63. Copyright 1985, U.S. Chamber of Commerce.

■ Discussion questions linking this case with the following material appear at the end of this chapter.

There have been dramatic changes in America's economy and work force over the last two decades. As reviewed in Chapter 2, we now have a service economy that is increasingly creating relatively low-paying, partially low-tech jobs. To make matters worse, this change parallels the trend toward a more educated and older work force demanding jobs that offer challenge and personal fulfillment. The net result is a mismatch—leading to a lower quality of work life—between the types of jobs that people perform and the needs, desires, expectations, and values of a large and growing segment of the work force.

Commenting on this mismatch, Ronald Pilenzo, president of the American Society for Personnel Administration, noted:

Now we have a tremendous task ahead of us in retraining management to be more like consultants to their work force. This is because the workers of today are different. They have more education, are more self-directed or want to be, and want to control their working conditions. This requires a more participatory or nondirective approach for the manager who wants to get results.[1]

Companies are being challenged to design new organizational structures and jobs. W. L. Gore & Associates, Inc., cited as one of the 100 best companies to work for in America, has met this challenge.

> Gore makes a synthetic fiber called Gore-tex, used in camping equipment among dozens of other products. . . .
>
> Gore is a company without titles, hierarchy, or any of the conventional structures associated with enterprises of its size [sales of $150 million in 1983]. It has turned most forms of corporate life on their head.
>
> If you apply to work here, you may receive a letter that gives you fair warning of what to expect: "If you are a person who needs to be told what to do and how to do it, Dr. Gore says you will have trouble adjusting. . . . An associate [all employees are called associates] has to find his own place to a high degree. There's no job description, no slot to fit yourself into. You have to learn what you can do."
>
> Jack Dougherty discovered that the letter was more than a mere word of caution. He told *Inc.* that when he showed up for his first day of work at Gore, Bill Gore shook his hand and said, "Why don't you look around and find something you'd like to do." The startled 23-year-old business school graduate then spent the next several weeks wandering around. . . .[2]

In addition to Gore's radical solution, there are many other ways organizations can resolve the growing mismatch between jobs and people.

This chapter introduces and explores various approaches to designing work and improving the quality of work life. After reviewing historical approaches to job design, we focus on: (1) a job characteristics approach, (2) two social system approaches, (3) participative management, and (4) recent quality of work life innovations.

■ HISTORICAL APPROACHES

Job design, also referred to as job redesign, "refers to any set of activities that involve the alteration of specific jobs or interdependent systems of jobs with the intent of improving the quality of employee job experience and their on-the-job productivity."[3] There are two very different routes, one traditional and one modern, that can be taken when deciding how to design jobs. Each is based on a different assumption about people.[4]

[1] Harry Bacas, "Who's in Charge Here?" *Nation's Business,* May 1985, p. 57.

[2] Robert Levering, Milton Moskowitz, and Michael Katz, *The 100 Best Companies to Work for in America,* © 1984, Addison-Wesley Publishing Co., Inc., Reading, Massachusetts, pp. 128–129. Reprinted with permission.

[3] James L. Bowditch and Anthony F. Buono, *A Primer on Organizational Behavior* (New York: John Wiley & Sons, 1985), p. 210.

[4] For a complete discussion of each alternative, see J. Richard Hackman, "The Design of Work in the 1980s," *Organizational Dynamics,* Summer 1978, pp. 3–17.

■ **FIGURE 15–1** Historical Development of Job Design

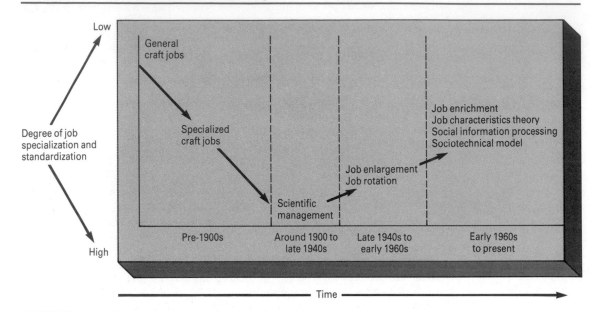

SOURCE: Adapted from *Task Design: An Integrative Approach* by Ricky W. Griffin. Copyright © 1982 by Scott, Foresman and Company. Reprinted by permission. After A. Filley, R. House, & S. Kerr. *Managerial Process and Organizational Behavior,* 2/E, 1976.

The first route entails *fitting people to jobs*. It is based on the assumption that people will gradually adjust and adapt to any work situation. Thus, employee attitudes toward the job are ignored, and jobs are designed to produce maximum economic and technological efficiency. This approach uses the principles of scientific management and work simplification (recall our discussion in Chapter 1). In contrast, the second route involves *fitting jobs to people*. It assumes that people are underutilized at work and that they desire more challenge and responsibility. Thus, employee attitudes play an important part in determining how jobs should be designed. Techniques such as job enlargement, job rotation, job enrichment, and job characteristics are used when designing jobs according to this second alternative.

The remainder of this section discusses the first four methods of job design to be widely used in industry (see Figure 15–1). They are scientific management, job enlargement, job rotation, and job enrichment. Subsequent sections explore the job characteristics, sociotechnical systems, and social information-processing approaches to job design.

Scientific Management

Developed by Frederick Taylor, scientific management relied on research and experimentation to determine the most efficient way to perform jobs. As shown in Figure 15–1, jobs are highly specialized and standardized when they are designed according to the principles of scientific management. Consider, for example, the application of scientific management at United Parcel Service (UPS).

> At UPS, more than 1,000 industrial engineers use time study to set standards for a myriad of closely supervised tasks. Drivers are instructed to walk to a customer's door at the brisk pace of three feet per second and to knock first lest seconds be lost searching for the doorbell. . . .
>
> UPS seeks maximum output from its drivers, as is shown by the time study Mrs. Cusack is conducting. On this day in suburban Whippany, she determines time allowances for each of Mr. Polise's 120 stops while watching for inefficiency in his methods. "What are you doing, Joe?" she asks as Mr. Polise wastes precious seconds handling packages more than once. She says that a mere 30 seconds wasted at each stop can snowball into big delays by day's end. . . .
>
> But not all UPS drivers enjoy the pace. For example, Michael Kipila, a driver in East Brunswick, N.J., says, "They squeeze every ounce out of you. You're always in a hurry, and you can't work relaxed." Some drivers say they cut their breaks in order to finish on time.[5]

As evident at UPS, scientific management produces both employee efficiency and dissatisfaction. Research revealed that simplified, repetitive jobs led to poor mental health and a low sense of accomplishment and personal growth.[6] These often-repeated scenarios paved the way for development of other job design techniques. These newer approaches attempt to design intrinsically satisfying jobs.

Job Enlargement

This technique was first used in the late 1940s in response to complaints about tedious and overspecialized jobs. **Job enlargement** involves putting more variety into a worker's job by combining specialized tasks of comparable difficulty. Some call this *horizontally loading* the job. For instance, the job of installing television picture tubes could be enlarged to include installation of the circuit boards.

Proponents of job enlargement claim it can improve employee satisfaction, motivation, and quality of production. To test these claims, an OB scholar summarized the available research evidence. His major conclusions were:

- Job enlargement increased training costs.
- Job enlargement was viewed as a managerial technique for getting employees to work harder.
- Job enlargement increased hiring qualifications.

---

[5] Daniel Machalaba, "United Parcel Service Gets Deliveries Done by Driving Its Workers," *The Wall Street Journal*, March 22, 1986, pp. 1, 26.

[6] Research on scientific management is reviewed by Toby D. Wall and Robin Martin, "Job and Work Design," in *International Review of Industrial and Organizational Psychology*, ed. Cary L. Cooper and Ivan T. Robertson (New York: John Wiley & Sons, 1987), pp. 61–91.

- There was no clear relationship between job enlargement and the *quantity* of production.[7]

Summarizing, job enlargement, by itself, does not appear to have a significant and lasting positive impact on job performance.

Job Rotation

As with job enlargement, job rotation's purpose is to give employees greater variety in their work. **Job rotation** calls for moving employees from one specialized job to another. Rather than performing only one job, workers are trained and given the opportunity to perform two or more separate jobs on a rotating basis. By rotating employees from job to job, managers believe they can stimulate interest and motivation, while providing employees with a broader perspective of the organization. An interesting variety of job rotation programs can be found in today's workplace (see Table 15–1).

Other proposed advantages of job rotation include increased worker flexibility and easier scheduling when employees are on vacation, absent, or quit because employees are cross-trained to perform different jobs. As used by Swissair, for example, job rotation also can be beneficial from a management development perspective.

> While there is no single key to Swissair's outstanding success [it has shown a profit for over 30 years], one of its more noteworthy innovations is a rotation program in which managers are periodically transferred to different departments, rather than spending an entire career handling the same duties. . . .
>
> The average Swissair manager will be rotated several times in the course of his or her career, often being exposed to totally unfamiliar areas.[8]

■ **TABLE 15–1**   Job Rotation Is Used in a Variety of Companies

Polaroid Corp. paid factory workers at a camera plant to demonstrate the SX-70 instant camera in Boston-area stores during Christmas. It says the move boosted sales.

Tony Lama Co., the El Paso, Texas, bootmaker, each year sends six workers in its customer-complaint department to work in a store. Also, its salespeople work a week a year in the shipping department. Every employee in his first year at Church's Fried Chicken is required to work at one of its fast-food outlets for two weeks, cutting chicken, scrubbing floors and frying food.

Ford Motor's "A Day in the Life" program a while back asked some white- and blue-collar workers to switch jobs for a day. . . .

SOURCE: "A Special News Report on People and Their Jobs in Offices, Fields and Factories," *The Wall Street Journal,* March 12, 1985, p. 1.

---

[7] Research on job enlargement was summarized by Ricky W. Griffin, *Task Design: An Integrative Approach* (Glenview, Ill.: Scott, Foresman, 1982).

[8] "Job Rotation Keeps Swissair Flying High," *Management Review,* August 1985, p. 10.

Unfortunately, the promised benefits associated with job rotation programs have not been adequately researched. Thus, it is impossible to draw any empirical conclusions about the effectiveness of this technique.[9]

Job Enrichment

Job enrichment is the practical application of Frederick Herzberg's motivator-hygiene theory of job satisfaction, discussed in Chapter 5. Herzberg proposed that people are motivated by "motivators"—achievement, recognition, stimulating work, responsibility, and advancement—in their jobs. These characteristics are incorporated into a job through vertical loading.

Rather than giving employees additional tasks of similar difficulty (horizontal loading), *vertical loading* consists of giving workers more responsibility. In other words, employees take on chores normally performed by their supervisors. Managers are advised to follow seven principles when vertically loading jobs (see Table 15–2). As an example, consider how Packard Electric used both job rotation and job enrichment to redesign jobs at one of its plants.

> In a sense, Antoinette Smith and Dominick P. Peters are their own bosses. They are part of a 22-member team that operates a "self-managed" assembly line at Packard Electric's Austintown (Ohio) plant. To avoid the tedium of working at the same station day after day, workers rotate line jobs and—most important— get to work off the line several times a month to handle material and repairs. The team members also perform many of the foreman's functions: setting the line speed, ordering material, establishing rules for handling disputes, checking quality, and doing paperwork.[10]

■ **TABLE 15–2** Principles of Vertically Loading a Job

Principle	Motivators Involved
A. Removing some controls while retaining accountability	Responsibility and personal achievement
B. Increasing the accountability of individuals for their own work	Responsibility and recognition
C. Giving a person a complete natural unit of work (module, division, area, and so on)	Responsibility, achievement, and recognition
D. Granting additional authority to an employee in his activity; job freedom	Responsibility, achievement, and recognition
E. Making periodic reports directly available to the worker himself rather than to the supervisor	Internal recognition
F. Introducing new and more difficult tasks not previously handled	Growth and learning
G. Assigning individuals specific or specialized tasks, enabling them to become experts	Responsibility, growth, and advancement

SOURCE: Reprinted by permission of the *Harvard Business Review.* An exhibit from "One More Time: How Do You Motivate Employees?" by Frederick Herzberg (January/February 1968). Copyright © 1968 by the President and Fellows of Harvard College; all rights reserved.

---

[9] Research on job rotation is reviewed in Griffin, *Task Design: An Integrative Approach.*

[10] "You Have to Bend and Stretch a Little to Keep Your Job," *Business Week,* August 29, 1983, p. 56.

Research on the effectiveness of job enrichment has uncovered mixed results. This is partly because job enrichment represents the application of Herzberg's motivator-hygiene theory, which has been severely criticized (see the related discussion in Chapter 5). Job enrichment also has been criticized because it does not explain why it works, making it hard for managers to determine specific situations in which job enrichment is best suited.

Another limitation is that job enrichment assumes that everyone wants enriched work. But we all know people who view work as a necessary evil. These people invest minimum effort and expect nothing more than a paycheck in return. Job enrichment proponents have failed to identify important individual differences revealing how people respond to job enrichment. Finally, the theory does not offer a set of specific actions managers can use to enrich a job. Because of these problems, job enrichment has fallen into disfavor among managers and researchers alike. Still, job enrichment provided a much-needed basis for the job characteristics approach, discussed next.

■ A JOB CHARACTERISTICS APPROACH TO JOB DESIGN

Two OB researchers, J. Richard Hackman and Greg Oldham, played a central role in developing the job characteristics approach. In devising their theory, they attempted to overcome some criticisms associated with job enrichment. An attempt was made to pinpoint those situations and those individuals for which job design is effective. In this regard, the job characteristics model represents a contingency approach. Building on their theory, Hackman and Oldham also provided a series of implementation steps managers can follow. After summarizing the major components of the job characteristics model, we discuss its application, relevant research, and managerial implications.

Overview of the Job Characteristics Model

Hackman and Oldham tried to determine how work can be structured so employees are internally (or intrinsically) motivated. **Internal motivation** occurs when an individual is "turned on to one's work because of the positive internal feelings that are generated by doing well, rather than being dependent on external factors (such as incentive pay or compliments from the boss) for the motivation to work effectively."[11] These positive feelings power a self-perpetuating cycle of motivation. As shown in Figure 15–2, internal work motivation is determined by three psychological states. In turn, these psychological states are fostered by the presence of five core job dimensions.[12] As you can see in Figure 15–2, the object of this approach is to promote high internal motivation

---

[11] J. Richard Hackman, Greg R. Oldham, Robert Janson, and Kenneth Purdy, "A New Strategy for Job Enrichment," *California Management Review,* Summer 1975, p. 58.

[12] For an expanded discussion of this approach, see J. Richard Hackman and Greg R. Oldham, *Work Redesign* (Reading, Mass.: Addison-Wesley Publishing, 1980).

■ **FIGURE 15–2** The Job Characteristics Model

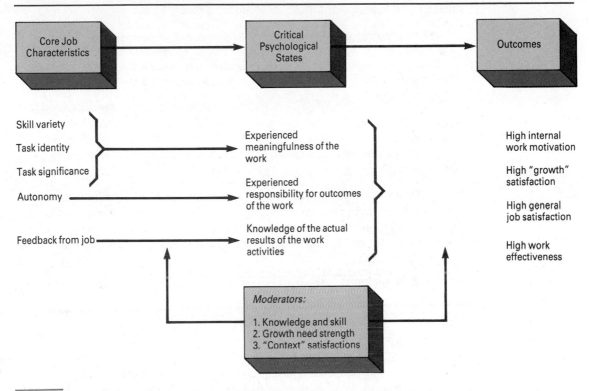

SOURCE: J. Richard Hackman and Greg R. Oldham, *Work Redesign,* © 1980, Addison-Wesley Publishing Co., Reading, Massachusetts. p. 90. Reprinted with permission.

by designing jobs that possess the five core job characteristics. Let us examine the major components of this model to see how it works.

Critical Psychological States.   A group of management experts described the conditions under which individuals experienced the three critical psychological states. They are:

1. **Experienced meaningfulness:** The individual must perceive his work as worthwhile or important by some system of values he accepts.
2. **Experienced responsibility:** He must believe that he personally is accountable for the outcomes of his efforts.
3. **Knowledge of results:** He must be able to determine, on some fairly regular basis, whether or not the outcomes of his work are satisfactory.[13]

These psychological states generate internal work motivation. Moreover, they encourage perseverance because they are self-reinforcing. Consider, for exam-

---

[13] Hackman, Oldham, Janson, and Purdy, "A New Strategy for Job Enrichment," p. 58. (Emphasis added.)

ple, the important role the three psychological states no doubt played in the superior performance of airline mechanics in recent years.

> Modern jets are designed to be able to fly despite even serious defects. Nevertheless, the role of the airline mechanic is critical to ensuring the safety of the nation's passenger jets. It is a job that demands precision work. It must be performed against the constant pressure of departure schedules and with the knowledge that even a single mistake could jeopardize life. . . .
>
> In 1985, accidents on scheduled airlines in the U.S. killed 528 people, the second largest one-year toll ever. But mechanical failure ranks behind pilot error and bad weather as a cause of fatal crashes. In fact, it has been six years since a major accident on a scheduled U.S. airline has been traced to an error by mechanics.[14]

If one of the three psychological states is shortchanged, motivation diminishes. For example, if an individual is completely responsible for outcomes associated with a meaningful job, but receives no feedback (knowledge of results) about performance, he or she will not experience the positive feelings that create internal motivation.

Core Job Dimensions.   In general terms, **core job dimensions** are common characteristics found to a varying degree in all jobs. Once again, five core job characteristics elicit the three psychological states (see Figure 15–2). Three of those job characteristics combine to determine experienced meaningfulness of work. They are:

- *Skill variety:* The extent to which the job requires an individual to perform a variety of tasks that require him or her to use different skills and abilities.
- *Task identity:* The extent to which the job requires an individual to perform a whole or completely identifiable piece of work. In other words, task identity is high when a person works on a product or project from beginning to end and sees a tangible result.
- *Task significance:* The extent to which the job affects the lives of other people within or outside the organization.

Experienced responsibility is elicited by the job characteristic of autonomy, defined as follows:

- *Autonomy:* The extent to which the job enables an individual to experience freedom, independence, and discretion in both scheduling and determining the procedures used in completing the job.

Finally, knowledge of results is fostered by the job characteristic of feedback, defined as follows:

---

[14] John Koten, "Timetables and Risks Put Constant Pressure on Jetliner Mechanics," *The Wall Street Journal,* January 3, 1986, p. 1.

- *Feedback:* The extent to which an individual receives direct and clear information about how effectively he or she is performing the job.[15]

Motivating Potential of a Job.   Hackman and Oldham devised a self-report instrument to assess the extent to which a specific job possesses the five core job characteristics. With this instrument, which is discussed in the next section, it is possible to calculate a motivating potential score for a job. The **motivating potential score** (MPS) is a summary index that represents the extent to which the job characteristics foster internal work motivation. Low scores indicate that an individual will not experience high internal work motivation from the job. Such a job is a prime candidate for job redesign. High scores reveal that the job is capable of stimulating internal motivation. The MPS is computed as follows:

$$\text{MPS} = \frac{\dfrac{\text{Skill}}{\text{variety}} + \dfrac{\text{Task}}{\text{identity}} + \dfrac{\text{Task}}{\text{significance}}}{3} \times \text{Autonomy} \times \text{Feedback}$$

Judging from this equation, which core job characteristic do you think is relatively more important in determining the motivational potential of a job? Since MPS equals zero when autonomy or feedback are zero, you are correct if you said both experienced autonomy and feedback.

The Theory Does Not Work for Everyone.   As previously discussed, not all people want enriched work. Hackman and Oldham incorporated this conclusion into their model by identifying three attributes that affect how individuals respond to jobs with a high MPS. These attributes are concerned with the individual's knowledge and skill, growth need strength (representing the desire to grow and develop as an individual), and context satisfactions (see Figure 15–2). Personal characteristics influence how individuals respond to their jobs at two points in the job characteristics model: initially at the linkage between the core job dimensions and the psychological states, and again at the linkage between the psychological states and work outcomes.

As shown in Figure 15–3, people respond positively to jobs with a high MPS when (1) they have the knowledge and skills necessary to do the job, (2) they have high growth needs, and (3) they are satisfied with various aspects of the work context, such as pay and co-workers. On the other hand, employees who score low on these attributes will be stretched by a job with a high MPS. Ultimately, these individuals will experience weaker psychological states and poorer work outcomes. For example, consider the response of an employee who has the necessary knowledge and skills and a strong desire to grow, but feels underpaid and does not get along with co-workers. Do you think this person would respond positively to having his or her job made more complex

---

[15] Definitions of the job characteristics were adapted from J. Richard Hackman and Greg R. Oldham, ''Motivation through the Design of Work: Test of a Theory,'' *Organizational Behavior and Human Performance,* August 1976, pp. 250–79.

■ **FIGURE 15–3**   Three Attributes Affect Who Will Respond Positively to Job Redesign

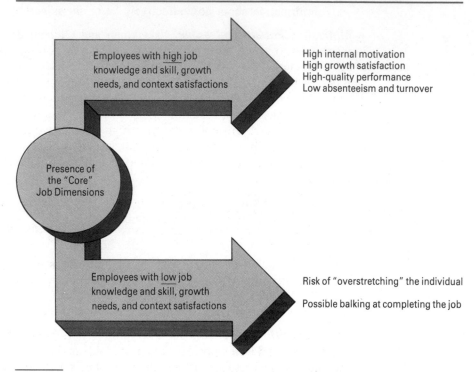

Employees with high job knowledge and skill, growth needs, and context satisfactions

High internal motivation
High growth satisfaction
High-quality performance
Low absenteeism and turnover

Presence of the "Core" Job Dimensions

Employees with low job knowledge and skill, growth needs, and context satisfactions

Risk of "overstretching" the individual

Possible balking at completing the job

SOURCE: Modified from J. Richard Hackman, Greg Oldham, Robert Janson, and Kenneth Purdy, "A New Strategy for Job Enrichment," *California Management Review,* Summer 1975, p. 60.

through enriched work? This dissatisfied employee would probably resent any attempts to make him or her work harder.

Applying the Job Characteristics Model

There are three major steps to follow when applying Hackman and Oldham's model. Since the model seeks to increase employee motivation and satisfaction, the first step consists of diagnosing the work environment to determine if a problem exists. Hackman and Oldham developed a self-report instrument for managers to use called the *Job Diagnostic Survey* (JDS).

Diagnosis begins by determining if motivation and satisfaction are lower than desired. If they are, a manager then assesses the MPS of the jobs being examined. National norms are used to determine whether the MPS is low or high.[16] If the MPS is low, an attempt is made to determine which of the core job characteristics is causing the problem. If the MPS is high, managers need to look for other factors eroding motivation and satisfaction. (You can

---

[16] The complete JDS and norms for the MPS are presented in Hackman and Oldham, *Work Redesign.*

■ FIGURE 15–4 Implementing Principles Effect Core Job Characteristics

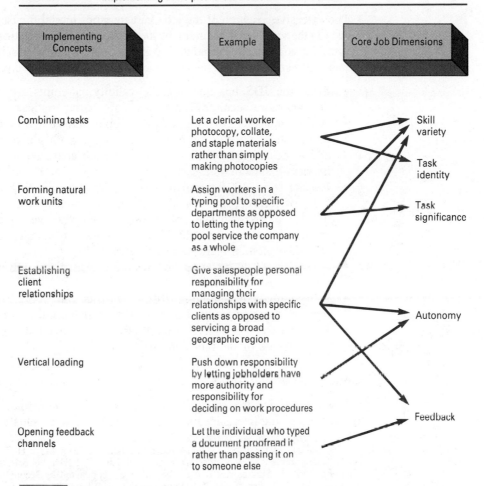

Implementing Concepts	Example	Core Job Dimensions

Combining tasks — Let a clerical worker photocopy, collate, and staple materials rather than simply making photocopies

Forming natural work units — Assign workers in a typing pool to specific departments as opposed to letting the typing pool service the company as a whole

Establishing client relationships — Give salespeople personal responsibility for managing their relationships with specific clients as opposed to servicing a broad geographic region

Vertical loading — Push down responsibility by letting jobholders have more authority and responsibility for deciding on work procedures

Opening feedback channels — Let the individual who typed a document proofread it rather than passing it on to someone else

Skill variety · Task identity · Task significance · Autonomy · Feedback

SOURCE: Modified from J. Richard Hackman, Greg Oldham, Robert Janson, and Kenneth Purdy, "A New Strategy for Job Enrichment," *California Management Review,* Summer 1975.

calculate your own MPS in the exercise at the end of this chapter.) Potential factors may be identified by considering other motivation theories discussed in this book.

Step two consists of determining whether job redesign is appropriate for a given group of employees. Job redesign is most likely to work for employees who have high knowledge and skills, strong growth needs, and context satisfactions.

In the third step, managers need to consider how to redesign the job. Hackman and Oldham suggest five implementing concepts. Each one, as shown in Figure 15–4, represents a specific action step aimed at bolstering one or more of the core job characteristics.

Summary of Research Findings

The extensive research of the job characteristics model focuses on two broad areas: (1) the validity or accuracy of the JDS, and (2) the relationships between the core job characteristics and the work outcomes of job satisfaction, productivity, absenteeism, and turnover. Some important findings are summarized below.

- Since the JDS has questionable validity, attempts are being made to develop more accurate measures of job characteristics.[17]
- A meta-analysis covering 15,542 people indicated a moderately strong relationship between job characteristics and both global job satisfaction and work satisfaction. Each of the five job characteristics had an equal impact on satisfaction.[18]
- Results from 30 experimental studies (some reporting more than one case) of job redesign revealed a median increase of 6.4 percent in the quantity of performance. Job redesign had a negative or near zero impact in 11 of these studies. In 21 cases, however, quality of performance showed a median increase of 28 percent.[19]
- A meta-analysis covering 961 people revealed that job redesign led to reduced absenteeism.[20]
- A meta-analysis involving 20 experiments and 6,492 people indicated that job redesign resulted in a 17 percent reduction in turnover.[21]
- Both the work context and employee growth need strength affected the effectiveness of job redesign programs.[22]

Managerial Implications

Since job design is strongly related to job satisfaction, managers may want to use the job characteristics model to increase employee satisfaction. Unfortu-

---

[17] The validity of the JDS is summarized by Ramon J. Aldag, Steve H. Barr, and Arthur P. Brief, "Measurement of Perceived Task Characteristics," *Psychological Bulletin,* November 1981, pp. 415–31. Studies that revised the JDS were conducted by Jacqueline R. Idaszak and Fritz Drasgow, "A Revision of the Job Diagnostic Survey: Elimination of a Measurement Artifact," *Journal of Applied Psychology,* February 1987, pp. 69–74; and Yitzhak Fried and Gerald R. Ferris, "The Dimensionality of Job Characteristics: Some Neglected Issues," *Journal of Applied Psychology,* August 1986, pp. 419–26.

[18] See Brian T. Loher, Raymond A. Noe, Nancy L. Moeller, and Michael P. Fitzgerald, "A Meta-Analysis of the Relation of Job Characteristics to Job Satisfaction," *Journal of Applied Psychology,* May 1985, pp. 280–89.

[19] These studies are reviewed in Richard E. Kopelman, *Managing Productivity in Organizations* (New York: McGraw-Hill, 1986).

[20] Results are discussed in Yitzhak Fried and Gerald R. Ferris, "The Validity of the Job Characteristics Model: A Review and Meta-Analysis," *Personnel Psychology,* Summer 1987, pp. 287–322.

[21] See Glenn M. McEvoy and Wayne F. Cascio, "Strategies for Reducing Turnover: A Meta-Analysis," *Journal of Applied Psychology,* May 1985, pp. 342–53.

[22] Results are presented in Gerald R. Ferris and David C. Gilmore, "The Moderating Role for Work Context in Job Design Research: A Test of Competing Models," *Academy of Management Journal,* December 1984, pp. 885–92. Findings for growth need strength are reviewed in Loher, Noe, Moeller, and Fitzgerald, "A Meta-Analysis of the Relation of Job Characteristics to Job Satisfaction."

nately, job design appears to reduce the quantity of output just as often as it has a positive impact. Caution and situational appropriateness are advised. Nonetheless, managers are likely to find noticeable increases in the *quality* of performance after a job redesign program. Moreover, designing jobs to include the core job characteristics can help managers reduce absenteeism and turnover. In conclusion, managers need to realize that job redesign is not a panacea for all their employee satisfaction and motivation problems. To enhance their chances of success with this approach, managers need to remember that a change in one job or department can create problems with perceived inequity in related areas or systems within the organization. Managers need to take an open systems perspective when implementing job design, as is suggested by social system approaches to job redesign.

■ SOCIAL SYSTEM APPROACHES TO JOB DESIGN

A social system perspective considers how job design is affected by interpersonal relationships both within and between organizational departments. Even though Hackman and Oldham proposed the job characteristics model, they now believe managers need to use a social systems approach when redesigning jobs. Accordingly, they wrote:

> Our observations of work redesign programs suggest that attempts to change jobs frequently run into—and sometimes get run over by—other organizational systems and practices, leading to a diminution (or even a reversal) of anticipated outcomes. . . .
> The "small change" effect, for example, often develops as managers begin to realize that radical changes in work design will necessitate major changes in other organizational systems as well.[23]

To gain further insight into this orientation, this section discusses the sociotechnical and social information-processing models. Knowledge of these models can help managers implement job design programs that are compatible with work group dynamics.

The Sociotechnical Model

The sociotechnical model is based on a stream of research conducted during the 1950s by the Tavistock Institute in London. Among other issues, this research focused on the relationships among technological changes, social processes, and productivity. For example, one study examined productivity changes associated with implementing an assembly-line method in a coal mine. The change was unsuccessful because management failed to recognize the social importance

---

[23] Greg R. Oldham and J. Richard Hackman, "Work Design in the Organizational Context," in *Research in Organizational Behavior*, ed. Barry M. Staw and Larry L. Cummings (Greenwich, Conn.: JAI Press, 1980), pp. 248–49.

■ **TABLE 15–3** The Sociotechnical Approach Shows Promise, but Is Not a Quick Fix

Semiautonomous work teams and other innovations enable some plants to be 30% to 50% more productive than conventional ones. Many leading companies have adopted the work-team approach, including Procter & Gamble, Cummins Engine, GM, GE, Westinghouse, IBM, Xerox, and Polaroid.

This burst in productivity is happening mainly in new plants, outfitted with advanced machinery and designed specifically with sociotechnical methods in mind. The semiautonomous team concept needs nurturing; quick-fix, cookie-cutter methods won't do. Nor is it applicable to all situations. But the use of teams and other work reforms in conjunction with technology can speed productivity growth in manufacturing.

SOURCE: John Hoerr, "Getting Man and Machine to Live Happily Ever After," *Business Week*, April 20, 1987, p. 61.

the miners attached to working in small, autonomous groups.[24] Findings such as these led researchers to conclude work environments represent an intertwined combination of technology—physical plant and equipment—and social system. The Tavistock researchers also concluded that these two subsystems influenced and shaped each other. Generalizing from these basic conclusions, the thrust of the **sociotechnical model** involves considering:

> The relationships both between people and technology and between the organization and its environments to suggest changes in work arrangements designed to improve the fit among the needs of individuals, groups, and technological processes in the pursuit of organizational goals.[25]

Thus, the sociotechnical model is a dynamic approach that takes a very broad perspective. This model has been criticized for being too general, which supposedly limits its practical application. Still, the sociotechnical approach made two important contributions. First, it led to increased use of participative management in a variety of organizations. (The next section discusses the effectiveness of participative management.) Second, it encouraged use of autonomous work groups. Since **autonomous work groups** provide the opportunity for employees to design and manage their own work, it is hypothesized that they will better satisfy social needs. Which, in turn, is said to enhance job satisfaction and work motivation[26] (see Table 15–3).

A group of researchers recently conducted a rigorous field experiment to assess the long-term effects of implementing autonomous work groups. Results revealed a long-lasting positive effect on intrinsic job satisfaction, a temporary increase in extrinsic satisfaction, and no effect on motivation and productivity.

---

[24] Results are found in E. Trist and K. Bamforth, "Social and Psychological Consequences of the Long-Wall Method of Coal-Getting," *Human Relations*, February 1951, pp. 3–38.

[25] William A. Pasmore, "Overcoming the Roadblocks in Work-Restructuring Efforts," *Organizational Dynamics*, Spring 1982, p. 55.

[26] A practical discussion of the application of sociotechnical systems is provided by Ron Zemke, "Sociotechnical Systems: Bringing People and Technology Together," *Training*, February 1987, pp. 47–57.

■ **TABLE 15–4** A. E. Staley Corporation's Sociotechnical Approach to Job Design

> The plant employs salaried technicians using computer-controlled machinery to convert corn into high-fructose syrup.
>
> Employees are divided into 16 teams of about 15 persons each, according to functions—production, maintenance and quality control—and according to shifts. Each team chooses two leaders from its ranks, one of them task-oriented, the other in charge of training, discussion and records. The teams make their own work assignments within the plant's overall schedules, and have a voice in hiring, promotion and discipline of team members. . . .
>
> The plant operates 365 days a year. The employees work three 12-hour days, take three days off and then work three nights.
>
> It was three years before production at the plant began to justify the experiment. . . . Operating costs are below those of other plants, absenteeism and turnover are under 1 percent, downtime in a 24-hour workday is less than 1 percent, and production runs at 115 percent of engineering specifications.

SOURCE: Excerpted from Harry Bacas, "Who's in Charge Here?" *Nation's Business,* May 1985, pp. 57–58.

While turnover increased, direct labor costs decreased because of the reduced demand for supervisory personnel.[27] Meanwhile, A. E. Staley, an agriproducts company, experienced significant benefits after designing its Lafayette, Indiana, plant according to sociotechnical principles (see Table 15–4). Although further research is needed to reconcile these discrepant results, findings from a recent study suggest that the effectiveness of autonomous work teams depends on how such teams are managed. For instance, autonomous work teams need to be *taught* to manage themselves. This entails special managerial or leadership behaviors aimed at guiding the work group through this process. The most important leader behaviors for improving the performance of autonomous work teams are those that encourage the group to evaluate and reinforce itself.[28]

The Social Information-Processing Model

The social information-processing model (SIPM) is the most recent approach to job design. It is based on research demonstrating that perceptions affect attitudes and behaviors (recall the discussion of perception in Chapter 4). Accordingly, the SIPM attempts to describe the process by which employees form perceptions about both the type and amount of job characteristics contained in their jobs, and how these perceptions affect work attitudes and behaviors.[29]

---

[27] See Toby D. Wall, Nigel J. Kemp, Paul R. Jackson, and Chris W. Clegg, "Outcomes of Autonomous Workgroups: A Long-Term Field Experiment," *Academy of Management Journal,* June 1986, pp. 280–304.

[28] For details, see Charles C. Manz and Henry P. Sims, Jr., "Leading Workers to Lead Themselves: The External Leadership of Self-Managing Work Teams," *Administrative Science Quarterly,* March 1987, pp. 106–28.

[29] A complete description of the model is presented in Gerald R. Salancik and Jeffrey Pfeffer, "A Social Information Processing Approach to Job Attitudes and Task Design," *Administrative Science Quarterly,* June 1978, pp. 224–53.

■ **FIGURE 15–5** A Social Information-Processing Approach to Job Design

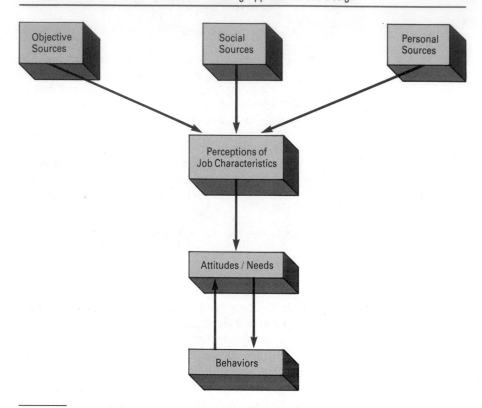

SOURCE: Adapted from Gerald R. Salancik and Jeffrey Pfeffer, "A Social Information Processing Approach to Job Attitudes and Task Design," *Administrative Science Quarterly,* June 1978, p. 227.

Three sources of information influence perceptions about job characteristics according to this model (see Figure 15–5). Objective sources include the physical working environment, the task itself, and formal policies and procedures. Social sources include other people in both the immediate work environment—such as co-workers and managers—and external to the organization, such as family and friends.[30] Past experience and background are sources of personal information. According to the **social information-processing model of job design,** social cues provided by co-workers and managers may have the strongest impact on perceptions of job characteristics. For example, an ambulance driver may believe he or she has a lot of skill variety, autonomy, and independence until sharing work experiences with a doctor. This comparison is likely to reveal that the doctor's job exhibits a richer variety of the core job characteristics. As this example illustrates, employees' perceptions of their own job characteris-

---

[30] See Joe G. Thomas, "Sources of Social Information: A Longitudinal Analysis," *Human Relations,* September 1986, pp. 855–70.

tics may be more a function of *subjective social cues* than of objective information.

Jeffrey Pfeffer, a respected OB researcher, summarized four major propositions that represent the basic philosophy of the SIPM.

> First, the individual's social environment may provide cues as to which dimensions might be used to characterize the work environment. . . . Second, the social environment may provide information concerning how the individual should weight the various dimensions—whether autonomy is more or less important than variety of skill, whether pay is more or less important than social usefulness or worth. Third, the social context provides cues concerning how others have come to evaluate the work environment on each of the selected dimensions. Whether a given job situation provides or does not provide autonomy, variety, or high pay is as much a matter of social perception as it is a function of the specific job. And fourth, it is possible that the social context provides direct evaluation of the work setting along positive or negative dimensions, leaving it to the individual to construct a rationale to make sense of the generally shared affective reactions.[31]

Let us turn to the relevant research and managerial implications of this model.

Research Findings.   A meta-analysis covering 10 studies and 1,698 individuals yielded the following three conclusions:

- Satisfaction and perceptions about job characteristics are affected by social cues in the work environment.
- There is no consistent relationship between social cues and performance.
- Laboratory research provided stronger support for the SIPM than field research.[32]

Other relevant research findings are:

- Contrary to predictions made by the SIPM, objective information had a stronger impact on perceptions of job characteristics than social cues.[33]
- Task experience was found to reduce the impact of social cues on employee attitudes.[34]

In summary, there is only moderate support for the proposition that social cues affect perceptions of job characteristics, satisfaction, and performance.

---

[31] Jeffrey Pfeffer, "Management as Symbolic Action: The Creation and Maintenance of Organizational Paradigms," in *Research in Organizational Behavior,* ed. Larry L. Cummings and Barry M. Staw (Greenwich, Conn.: JAI Press, 1981), p. 10.

[32] See Joe Thomas and Ricky Griffin, "The Social Information Processing Model of Task Design: A Review of the Literature," *Academy of Management Review,* October 1983, pp. 672–82.

[33] Results are found in Gary J. Blau, "Source-Related Determinants of Perceived Job Scope," *Human Communication Research,* Summer 1985, pp. 536–53.

[34] See Robert J. Vance and Thomas F. Biddle, "Task Experience and Social Cues: Interactive Effects on Attitudinal Reactions," *Organizational Behavior and Human Decision Processes,* April 1985, pp. 252–65.

However, social cues do not have a stronger influence on these criteria than do objective job characteristics.

Managerial Implications.   When implementing a job design program, social factors inevitably will come into play. Thus, it is important that managers not overlook the role of relevant social factors when redesigning jobs. Managers are encouraged to openly discuss and explain the rationale behind job design changes. Moreover, employee involvement in job design is likely to reduce the amount of inaccurate information from social sources as well as build employee commitment to the job redesign process.

These suggestions mesh well with the idea of participative management.

■ PARTICIPATIVE MANAGEMENT

Confusion exists about the exact meaning of participative management (PM). One management expert clarified this situation by defining **participative management** as the process whereby employees play a direct role in (1) setting goals, (2) making decisions, (3) solving problems, and (4) making changes in the organization.[35] Table 15–5 lists managerial behaviors that can increase an employee's involvement in these four activities.

Advocates of PM claim employee participation increases employee satisfaction, commitment, and performance. Practical experience at General Electric, Tandem Computers, and Du Pont, however, produced mixed results:

> Productivity at a General Electric Co. plant climbed 4% and absenteeism fell 33% when workers were allowed to determine how a new line was to be staffed. They decided they didn't need a foreman and all workers would be paid the same rate. Tandem Computers Inc. bids for workers' loyalty by giving them a voice in every new hire, including senior managers.
>
> But Du Pont Co. draws union flak for a program that lets some workers decide their own job responsibilities and work schedules, among other matters. . . . It's a "union-busting technique," contends Kenneth Henley, a union lawyer. He complains that the program restricts promotional opportunities, requires more work without higher pay and causes dissension in union ranks.[36]

To get a fuller understanding of how and when participative management works, we begin by discussing a model of participative management. After reviewing relevant research and practical suggestions for managers, a popular PM technique called quality circles is examined.

---

[35] See Marshal Sashkin, "Participative Management Is an Ethical Imperative," *Organizational Dynamics,* Spring 1984, pp. 4–22. Different forms of participation are thoroughly discussed by John L. Cotton, David A. Vollrath, Kirk L. Froggatt, Mark L. Lengnick-Hall, and Kenneth R. Jennings, "Employee Participation: Diverse Forms and Different Outcomes," *Academy of Management Review,* January 1988, pp. 8–22.

[36] "A Special News Report on People and Their Jobs in Offices, Fields and Factories," *The Wall Street Journal,* May 27, 1986, p. 1.

■ TABLE 15–5   Managerial Behaviors That Increase Employee Participation

1. Identify situations or decisions that provide opportunities for employee participation.
2. Actively encourage employees to participate.
3. Create an atmosphere of trust and openness.
4. Openly share information with employees.
5. Have more departmental meetings.
6. Develop teamwork within the work environment.
7. Solicit and use different points of view.
8. Make sure the group has enough resources to accomplish the task at hand.
9. Provide both positive and negative feedback with the intent of helping employees develop.
10. Train employees in problem-solving techniques.
11. Reinforce employees for participating.
12. Facilitate the process of getting group consensus.
13. Actively listen to employees.
14. Demonstrate those behaviors—like a lack of defensiveness—that build successful teamwork.

SOURCE: Adapted from Richard Hamlin, "Choosing between Directive and Participative Management," *Supervisory Management,* January 1986, pp. 14–16.

A Model of Participative Management

Consistent with both Maslow's need theory (see Chapter 5) and the job characteristics model of job design, participative management is predicted to increase motivation because it helps employees fulfill three basic needs: (1) autonomy, (2) meaningfulness of work, and (3) interpersonal contact. As shown in Figure 15–6, satisfaction of these needs enhances feelings of acceptance and commitment, security, challenge, and satisfaction. In turn, these positive feelings supposedly lead to increased innovation and performance.[37]

The model of participative management includes three contingency factors highlighting various situations in which PM is effective. Individual factors include employees' values, attitudes, and expectations that influence how they will respond to PM. As implied in the discussion of job enrichment, some people do not respond positively to participation. For example, a survey of 229 supervisor-subordinate pairs from a large retail drug company revealed that participative management was more successful for employees working on nonrepetitive tasks who had a high, rather than low, need for independence. Employees with a low need for independence did not respond favorably to participation.[38]

---

[37] For an expanded discussion of this model, see Sashkin, "Participative Management Is an Ethical Imperative."

[38] Results are found in Ahmed A. Abdel-Halim, "Effects of Task and Personality Characteristics on Subordinate Responses to Participative Decision Making," *Academy of Management Journal,* September 1983, pp. 477–84.

■ **FIGURE 15-6 A Model of Participative Management**

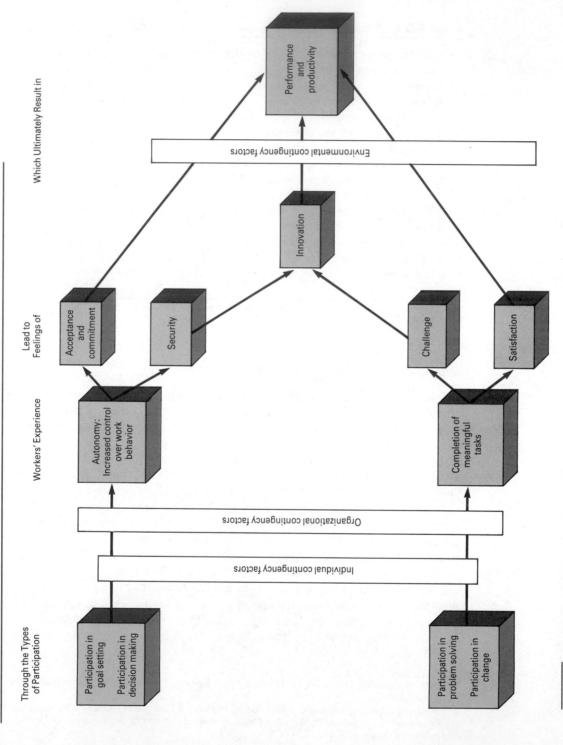

Through the Types
of Participation

Workers' Experience

Lead to
Feelings of

Which Ultimately Result in

SOURCE: Reprinted, by permission of the publisher, from "Participative Management Is an Ethical Imperative," by Marshall Sashkin, *Organizational Dynamics*, Spring 1984, p. 12, © 1984 American Management Association, New York. All rights reserved.

■ **TABLE 15–6** Korean-Style Participative Management

Lucky-Goldstar Group was the first large Korean company to put down U.S. roots: It opened a TV and microwave plant in Huntsville, Ala. . . . [in 1983]. Samsung followed in mid-1984. . . .

Don't confuse these immigrants with the Japanese, though. Yes, Koreans also espouse teamwork, employee participation, minimal hierarchies, and the corporation-as-family idea. But they tend to tailor their practices to the American style. "The Koreans are more flexible than we are," admits . . . [a Hitachi spokesman. According to] . . . a Samsung manager: "The Japanese are from a homogeneous society, so they are less accepting of anything that is not Japanese. Korea is a land of division, so the people are willing to listen and not get their feet stuck in concrete."

SOURCE: Laurie Baum, "Korea's Newest Export: Management Style," *Business Week,* January 19, 1987, p. 66.

The design of work and the level of trust between management and employees represent two organizational contingencies. With respect to the design of work, individual participation is counterproductive when employees are highly interdependent on each other, as on an assembly line. The problem with individual participation in this case is that interdependent employees generally do not have a broad understanding of the entire production process. Participative management also is less likely to succeed when employees do not trust management. Finally, PM is more effective when organizations face rapidly changing environmental contingencies, which include changes in technology, governmental regulations, and competition (see Table 15–6).

Research and Practical Suggestions for Managers

An analysis of 50 research studies revealed that employee participation in decision making and goal setting did not clearly result in higher productivity than authoritarian methods (see Table 15–7). These findings were supported by a recent meta-analysis of 25 studies. Participation had only a modest positive influence on productivity.[39] Similarly, participation did not enhance the impact of job enrichment when 76 receptionists participated in redesigning their jobs. On the positive side, however, participation significantly lowered employee role conflict and ambiguity over a period of six months.[40] Further, two recent

[39] Results are presented in Katherine I. Miller and Peter R. Monge, "Participation, Satisfaction, and Productivity: A Meta-Analytic Review," *Academy of Management Journal,* December 1986, pp. 727–53.

[40] These two studies were conducted by Rodger W. Griffeth, "Moderation of the Effects of Job Enrichment by Participation: A Longitudinal Field Experiment," *Organizational Behavior and Human Decision Processes,* February 1985, pp. 73–93; and Susan E. Jackson, "Participation in Decision Making as a Strategy for Reducing Job-Related Strain," *Journal of Applied Psychology,* February 1983, pp. 3–19.

■ **TABLE 15–7**   Summary of 50 Studies of Participative Management

	Participation Superior to Authoritarian Approach	Authoritarian Approach Superior to Participation	No Difference; Differences only in Certain Groups within the Study
Participation in decision making	9 (26%)	9 (26%)	17 (49%)
Participation in goal setting	1 (7%)	1 (7%)	13 (87%)
Total	10 (20%)	10 (20%)	30 (60%)

SOURCE: Reprinted, by permission of the publisher, from "Participation in Decision Making: When Should It Be Used?" by Edwin A. Locke, David M. Schweiger, Gary R. Latham, *Organizational Dynamics*, Winter 1986, p. 68, © 1986 American Management Association, New York. All rights reserved.

meta-analyses demonstrated that participation had a moderately strong impact on job satisfaction.[41]

These results indicate that PM is not a quick-fix solution for low productivity and motivation, as some enthusiastic supporters claim. Nonetheless, since participative management is effective in certain situations, managers can increase their chances of obtaining positive results by using once again a contingency approach. Experiences of companies implementing participative management programs suggest two additional practical recommendations.

First, supervisors and middle managers tend to resist participative management because it reduces their power and authority. For example, consider the following events at Boeing:

> The case of Boeing Aerospace's manufacturing division, with 300 managers spread through four organizational levels, has been fairly typical. The division's initial thrust at participation in 1980 was to put together trouble-shooting teams of workers, engineers, and managers to smooth bumps in production. Other middle managers often perceived the teams as intruders, and the idea flopped. "The only thing that remained was a negative attitude about employee involvement," notes Carl Hicks, head of quality improvement in the division. "We're still trying to undo that damage."[42]

When implementing PM programs, it is thus important to gain the support and commitment from employees who have managerial responsibility.

Second, as concluded by Richard J. Boyle, vice president and group executive at Honeywell's Defense and Marine Systems Group, the process of implementing participative management must be managed. Honeywell's PM program almost failed because the initial implementation stages were not monitored and managed by top management.[43]

---

[41] See Miller and Monge, "Participation, Satisfaction, and Productivity: A Meta-Analytic Review"; and John A. Wagner III and Richard Z. Gooding, "Shared Influence and Organizational Behavior: A Meta-Analysis of Situational Variables Expected to Moderate Participation-Outcome Relationships," *Academy of Management Journal*, September 1987, pp. 524–41.

[42] Bill Saporito, "The Revolt against 'Working Smarter,' " *Fortune*, July 21, 1986, p. 60.

[43] Honeywell's experience is discussed in Richard J. Boyle, "Wrestling with Jellyfish," *Harvard Business Review*, January–February 1984, pp. 74–83.

Participation through Quality Circles

Quality circles are small groups of people from the same work area who voluntarily get together to identify, analyze, and recommend solutions for problems related to quality and production. Quality circles, with an ideal size of 10 to 12 members, meet for about 60 to 90 minutes on a regular basis. Once a week or twice a month are typical. Primary objectives of quality circles, according to proponents, are to:

- Encourage employees to accept a sense of responsibility for improving product quality.
- Increase employees' awareness about production and production costs.
- Increase employee motivation.
- Help employees develop supervisory and managerial skills.[44]

Quality circles were introduced in Japan soon after World War II by a group of American productivity experts. Today, an estimated 8 million Japanese workers participate in quality circles, and about 200,000 U.S. workers in 6,200 companies belong to them.[45]

The effectiveness of quality circles is unclear because of a lack of rigorous research. Much of what exists amounts to testimonials from managers and consultants who have a vested interest in demonstrating the technique's success. Although documented failures are scarce, one expert recently concluded that quality circles have failed in more than 60 percent of the organizations that have tried them.[46] Poor implementation is probably more at fault than the quality circle concept itself. Table 15–8 illustrates what happened when General Motors tried to implement quality circles at its Adrian, Michigan, plant.

OB researchers are beginning to more thoroughly examine quality circles. To date, these studies are inconclusive. For example, results from a case study indicated that quality circles had little impact on attitudes and performance. In contrast, a longitudinal study spanning 24 months revealed that quality circles had only a marginal impact on employee attitudes, but led to a significant increase in productivity.[47] Overall, quality circles appear to be a promising

---

[44] These objectives were adapted from those given by James L. Bowditch and Anthony F. Buono, *A Primer on Organizational Behavior* (New York: John Wiley & Sons, 1985).

[45] The historical development of quality circles is discussed by Cynthia Stohl, "Bridging the Parallel Organization: A Study of Quality Circle Effectiveness," in *Organizational Communication*, ed. Margaret L. McLaughlin (Beverly Hills, Calif.: Sage Publications, 1987), pp. 416–30; and Thomas Li-Ping Tang, Peggy Smith Tollison, and Harold D. Whiteside, "The Effect of Quality Circle Initiation on Motivation to Attend Quality Circle Meetings and on Task Performance," *Personnel Psychology*, Winter 1987, pp. 799–814.

[46] See Mitchell L. Marks, "The Question of Quality Circles," *Psychology Today*, March 1986, pp. 36–38, 42, 44, 46.

[47] Results from the first study are found in Susan A. Mohrman and Luke Novelli, Jr., "Beyond Testimonials: Learning from a Quality Circles Programme," *Journal of Occupational Behavior*, April 1985, pp. 93–110. The second study is presented in Mitchell L. Marks, Philip H. Mirvis, Edward J. Hackett, and James F. Grady, Jr., "Employee Participation in a Quality Circle Program: Impact on Quality of Work Life, Productivity, and Absenteeism," *Journal of Applied Psychology*, February 1986, pp. 61–69.

■ **TABLE 15–8**   GM Takes Three Strikes at Implementing Quality Circles

Many American companies are discovering that, unlike a new piece of machinery, quality circles cannot simply be acquired, installed, and left to run on their own. This lesson was brought home repeatedly to managers and workers at General Motors' Chevrolet plant in Adrian, Michigan, southwest of Detroit, where they're now trying to make quality circles work for the third time. The factory supplies GM with plastic parts such as fan shrouds and dashboards.

GM first attempted to introduce quality circles at Adrian in 1977. In the process management broke most of the rules for how to get employees behind such a program. For starters, it failed to enlist the support of the local chapter of the United Auto Workers. It also neglected to train both workers and supervisors in how the circles were supposed to work. According to Charles Sower, president of the union local, workers soon quit the circles in disgust.

A second attempt to get the circles running began somewhat more auspiciously in 1979, with meetings for all employees at the local Holiday Inn. Meals and, on the last night, an open bar were inducements to a good turnout. However, this time management focused the circles on what might, to dignify them, be called human resources issues. Union official Sower describes the problem: "You might understand why your foreman was in a bad temper, but what were you supposed to do about it?" The circle meetings, to quote Sower, became "bitch sessions that discussed garbage like how far it was to walk to the parking lot." Predictably, this round of circles petered out too.

It wasn't until 1981 that management and the UAW jointly presented a well-planned program with solid training for managers and workers in how to make employee participation groups, as they are known throughout GM, achieve practical results. Circle members were taught how to raise issues, how to discuss them amicably, and how to implement their ideas. Sower admits that he initially "thought it was a bunch of crap," and the new plant manager, Fred Meissinger, says he was more comfortable with the old-style, more adversarial approach, but both men decided to give this try a chance. Instead of complaining about parking, workers sat down to discuss things like how to improve a troublesome conveyor belt. Two years later many of the original groups are still talking productively.

The only problem now is that the union is split over whether the circles should continue. While Sower wholeheartedly backs the experiment, two of the five members of the union's shop committee won office recently on a platform of old-style hostility to management. Sower now says he feels reluctant to show his face in the union office. The future of quality circles at the Adrian plant is by no means guaranteed.

SOURCE: Jeremy Main, "The Trouble with Managing Japanese-Style," *Fortune,* April 2, 1984, pp. 50–51. Used with permission.

participative management tool, *if they are carefully implemented and supported by all levels of management.*

■ QUALITY OF WORK LIFE INNOVATIONS

In Chapter 5, we defined *quality of work life* (QWL) as the overall quality of an individual's experiences at work. Accordingly, QWL innovations refer to a host of managerial techniques that focus on increasing employee well-being.[48] As implied in the discussions of job design and participative management—both considered QWL innovations—quality of work life programs have the twin objectives of increasing productivity and satisfaction by creating work conditions that foster:

- Personal dignity and respect.
- Self-control or autonomy.
- Personal recognition.
- Rewarding people commensurate with performance.
- Pride in doing a good job.
- Job security.[49]

This section provides a brief overview of five additional types of QWL programs: union-management cooperative projects, alternative work schedules, physical environment enhancements, gainsharing, and telecommuting. Each has exciting potential.

Union-Management Cooperative Projects

The United States has a long-standing tradition of an adversarial relationship between unions and management. Mistrust and poor communication have been the norm. During the last decade, however, there has been a growing awareness that a more cooperative relationship is needed if American industry is to successfully meet the challenge of foreign competition. Industrywide QWL programs involving the United Auto Workers, the Communications Workers of America, and the United Steelworkers of America foreshadow a new era in American labor-management relations (see Table 15–9). These programs give employees more input in actually running the business. Going one step further, Chrysler and Eastern Airlines, among others, now have union officials on their corporate boards of directors.

The success of these programs is heavily dependent on creating positive attitudes between the union and management.[50] This is not easy. Human relations training for first-line supervisors or managers is another critical component of a successful union-management cooperative program. Ford Motor Co. followed this bit of advice by training its first-line supervisors on the assembly line to shift from an authoritarian style to a more participative one.

---

[48] A broad overview of quality of work life innovations is provided by Susan A. Mohrman and Edward E. Lawler III, "Quality of Work Life," in *Research in Personnel and Human Resources Management*, ed. Kendrith M. Rowland and Gerald R. Ferris (Greenwich, Conn.: JAI Press, 1984).

[49] See Herman Gadon, "Making Sense of Quality of Work Life Programs," *Business Horizons*, January–February 1984, pp. 42–46; and Walter J. Gershenfeld, "Employee Participation in Firm Decisions," in *Human Resources and the Performance of the Firm*, ed. Barbara D. Dennis (Madison, Wis.: Industrial Relations Research Association, 1987), pp. 123–58.

[50] Results are found in Martin D. Hanlon and David A. Nadler, "Unionists' Attitudes toward Joint Union-Management Quality of Work Life Programmes," *Journal of Occupational Behavior*, January 1986, pp. 53–59; and James W. Thacker and Mitchell W. Fields, "Union Involvement in Quality-of-Worklife Efforts: A Longitudinal Investigation," *Personnel Psychology*, Spring 1987, pp. 97–111.

■ **TABLE 15–9**   Slow but Steady Progress in Labor-Management Cooperation at General Motors

For three decades, General Motors Corp. and its workers have made mostly automatic transmissions at the Alexis Road factory . . . [in Toledo, Ohio.] But now, they also spend substantial time working on working together.

In the past year, GM and United Auto Workers Local 14 have set up a 22-acre "jointness" park, a 13-room "joint-education" wing, a plantwide "joint communications network" with 44 TV monitors, a "joint" newsletter, and 200-plus "joint employee involvement groups."

Labor-management cooperation has long been hailed as a key to Japan's competitive edge—and to restoring U.S. industrial power. But the traditional hostility between labor and management in the U.S. makes cooperation difficult. Thus, the simple Japanese ideal of labor-management cooperation, when translated into an American setting, has become highly formalized and bureaucratic. As American labor and management face their greatest competitive challenge, they are pushing a slew of costly new programs, many of which have little to do with building cars but much to do with building mutual trust. . . .

But in some places, the elaborate network is yielding dividends. GM's Toledo transmission factory already has shaved $20 million in production costs over the past year, and quality has improved so much that the number of transmissions rejected by assembly facilities has dropped 90%, John D. Crabtree, the plant manager, says. He attributes part of the gains to the joint programs, although he acknowledges that he can't say how much.

SOURCE: Excerpted from Jacob M. Schlesinger, "Auto Firms and UAW Find That Cooperation Can Get Complicated." Reprinted by permission of *The Wall Street Journal,* Dow Jones & Company, Inc., September 25, 1987. All rights reserved.

Foreman Donald R. Hennion . . . was a "hard-nosed, loudmouthed disciplinarian," he says of himself. But now he chats with the workers, solicits their ideas, and even encourages them to use recently installed buttons to stop the line if a defect prevents them from correctly doing their job. . . . But the "stop concept" is one aspect of a worker participation program that has improved quality, reduced absenteeism, and lessened hostility between bosses and workers at Ford's Edison plant. Its success depends on first-line supervisors: They must listen to what workers have to say, use the workers' ideas, and focus on problem-solving rather than meting out discipline.[51]

Alternative Work Schedules

Flexitime and compressed workweeks are two of the most popular alternative work schedules. **Flexitime** provides employees with greater autonomy by allowing them to choose their daily starting and finishing times within a given period called a bandwidth (see Figure 15–7). The only other stipulation is that all employees must be present during a *core period* of time. According to recent estimates, more than 4 million workers in the United States are using flexitime. Although the majority of research on flexitime is anecdotal, two studies rigorously examined its effectiveness. With a sample of 219 hourly employees, flexitime enhanced employee flexibility and work group and supervi-

[51] "The Old Foreman Is on the Way Out, and the New One Will Be More Important," *Business Week,* April 25, 1983, p. 74.

■ **FIGURE 15–7** A Flexitime Program

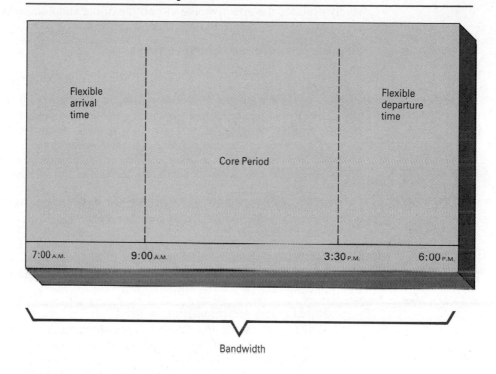

Bandwidth

sory relations. But it had no impact on productivity or job satisfaction. Absenteeism also declined. The second study demonstrated that flexitime increased the productivity of computer programmers by 24 percent over a two-year period. However, it did not affect the performance of data entry operators, suggesting that flexitime is not appropriate for all types of jobs.[52]

Under a **compressed workweek** plan, employees work approximately 40 hours in less than five days. The two typical patterns are to work 40 hours in four days (4/40) or 38 in three (3/38). Research on the 4/40 schedule indicated inconsistent effects on productivity, absenteeism, turnover, and job satisfaction. However, an 18-month test of the 3/38 schedule, with a sample of computer operations personnel, revealed reductions in overtime, sick time costs, and personal time off. Productivity increased with no effect on job satisfaction.[53]

[52] See V. K. Narayanan and Raghu Nath, "A Field Test of some Attitudinal and Behavioral Consequences of Flexitime," *Journal of Applied Psychology,* April 1982, pp. 214–18; David A. Ralston, William P. Anthony, and David J. Gustafson, "Employees May Love Flexitime, but What Does It Do to the Organization's Productivity?" *Journal of Applied Psychology,* May 1985, pp. 272–79.

[53] The effectiveness of compressed workweeks was reviewed and tested by Janina C. Latack and Lawrence W. Foster, "Implementation of Compressed Work Schedules: Participation and Job Redesign as Critical Factors for Employee Acceptance," *Personnel Psychology,* Spring 1985, pp. 75–92; and Randall B. Dunham, Jon L. Pierce, and Maria B. Castaneda, "Alternative Work Schedules: Two Field Quasi-Experiments," *Personnel Psychology,* Summer 1987, pp. 215–42.

In summary, additional high-quality research is needed before we can conclusively evaluate the effectiveness of both flexitime and compressed workweeks.

Physical Environment Enhancements

Physical design of the work environment can dramatically affect employee behavior. Consider TRW's experience.

> TRW Inc. started an experiment in 1981 to boost the productivity of 40 computer-program designers in Redondo Beach, Calif. Each TRW designer was given a separate office, and a choice of a chair. Many offices had windows and views. Workers could also adjust their own lighting and computer terminals. The design process was automated and designers got an advanced computer network to work with.
>
> After two years, the designers figured that their output of software jumped an average of 45% a year. There was also a reduction in sick days taken and in employee turnover.[54]

From a QWL perspective, it is important to consider how people respond to physical characteristics within the work environment. Research findings identify the following patterns:

- Bright colors are stimulating.
- Office locations have a strong impact on patterns of communication.
- Open office designs are not preferred over conventional closed office arrangements.
- Physical stimuli can be used to cue desired behavior.
- Comfortable chairs reduce back strain and relieve stress.
- Managers are constantly bombarded by distracting stimuli.
- Work space characteristics moderately influence turnover and job satisfaction.[55]

So it appears that managers should add a specialist in organizational behavior to the architectural committee when planning a new facility.

Gainsharing

Profit-sharing plans of various kinds are increasing. By using a profit-sharing formula, these plans provide for workers to receive a certain percentage of the profits. Although sometimes paid in cash, these benefits are often deferred until retirement. In 1983, for example, it was estimated that there were about

---

[54] "A Special News Report on People and Their Jobs in Offices, Fields and Factories," *The Wall Street Journal*, July 30, 1985, p. 1.

[55] The impact of the physical environment on employee behavior is reviewed by Tim R. V. Davis, "The Influence of the Physical Environment in Offices," *Academy of Management Review*, April 1984, pp. 271–83. The relationship between work space characteristics and employee turnover and satisfaction was examined by Greg R. Oldham and Yitzhak Fried, "Employee Reactions to Workspace Characteristics," *Journal of Applied Psychology*, February 1987, pp. 75–80.

■ TABLE 15–10 The Trials and Tribulations of Telecommuting

Hartford Insurance Group last year thought that allowing employees to work from home, using computers, might boost productivity and morale.

But even this unit of telecommunications giant ITT Corp. found "telecommuting" wasn't that simple.

Some managers protested they couldn't supervise—much less get to know—employees they couldn't see. Telephone lines linking home terminals to the company's central computer weren't always reliable. "We'd lose a line in the middle of transmission, and many times have to redo the work," says Raymond Howell, who helped oversee Hartford's yearlong experiment.

In the end, Hartford decided that although it might allow employees on sick leave or maternity leave to telecommute, most workers would remain office-bound.

Since the advent of the personal computer, technology buffs have been predicting the end of the daily nine-to-five grind at the office. Telecommuting—working at home on a terminal hooked to a central computer—not only was supposed to make huge company headquarters obsolete, but also was expected to solve several personnel problems. Companies would be able to hire disabled people and others who wanted to work but couldn't easily leave home. And the costs of leasing and furnishing a comfortable workplace would be sharply reduced.

Still an Anomaly

Yet, telecommuting remains an anomaly for corporate America. Just one major U.S. company—Pacific Telesis Group's Pacific Bell unit—has a large-scale formal program allowing salaried employees to telecommute full time. Other businesses have tried the practice on a smaller scale, only to reject it after managers complained that they were unable to manage workers from a distance. And many employers worry about liability issues stemming from telecommuting, such as who's responsible if an employee trips walking into a room used as an office at home. . . .

Dealing with telecommuting employees may actually add to a manager's workload. Susan Tracey, an assistant manager in Hartford's information-management department, found that she had to work around her telecommuting employee's schedule in setting up meetings and had to spend more time monitoring the telecommuter's work.

"I don't think I'd feel comfortable with the whole staff telecommuting," she says. "Just having one required additional effort."

Telecommuting can also deprive a company of the in-office contributions of experienced employees. Ms. Tracey says the productivity of her entire division slipped when the telecommuter, who had tended to go out of his way to help colleagues, was no longer present. In the office "he was a problem solver," she says. . . .

Managers may find it difficult to accept some of the more relaxed work habits that telecommuting promotes. Computer Central Corp. of St. Charles, Mo., found that its telecommuters were more likely than other workers to take a day off on the spur of the moment.

At Hartford, the telecommuter in Ms. Tracey's department became so used to working at his leisure that he carried those habits over when he came into the office. He started showing up at the office without a tie, causing his colleagues to think he was getting special treatment. Ms. Tracey says some co-workers "began joking about him coming to work in a bathrobe."

Since telecommuting turns an employee's home into an extension of the office, managers also must deal with the lack of control they have over what happens in the workplace. Sometimes the risks are rather peculiar. When a Computer Central employee's husband decided he didn't want his wife to work, he took a hammer to the equipment in the couple's home, says Ilene Neal, the company's president. Computer Central sued the man in small-claims court to recover the $550 in equipment damages.

SOURCE: Excerpted from Clare Ansberry, "When Employees Work at Home, Management Problems Often Rise." Reprinted by permission of *The Wall Street Journal*, Dow Jones & Company, Inc., April 20, 1987. All rights reserved.

350,000 U.S. companies using some sort of profit sharing. In contrast to the traditional profit-sharing approach, which does not involve workers in managing the company, **gainsharing** plans share both managerial responsibility and profits. The Scanlon Plan and Improshare are two commonly used gainsharing plans. The U.S. General Accounting Office estimates that about 1,000 companies were using these plans in 1983.[56] Evidence of the positive impacts of gainsharing are anecdotal. Solid research evidence is not yet available.

Telecommuting

Telecommuting involves receiving and sending work from home by using a modem to link a home computer to an office computer. Electronic Services Unlimited, a research company, estimates that there were about 300,000 telecommuters in the United States in 1984. However, only 50,000 of these people were involved in a formal corporate program. An estimated 5 million people will be telecommuting by 1990.[57] Proposed benefits of telecommuting include: (1) increased flexibility and autonomy for workers, (2) ability to retain qualified and trained personnel who are either unwilling or unable to work in an office, (3) ability to recruit from a larger geographic area, and (4) lower office expenses.[58]

Although telecommuting represents an attempt to accommodate employee needs and desires, it requires adjustments and is not for everybody (see Table 15–10). According to John Naisbitt, the futurist who wrote the best-selling *Megatrends,* "not very many of us will be willing to work at home. People want to be with people; people want to go to the office."[59] It thus appears that the growth of telecommuting will depend more on behavioral than technical limitations. Given the prevalence of dual-career couples, working mothers, and an information-based economy, it is likely that more organizations will experiment with telecommuting.

SUMMARY OF KEY CONCEPTS

A.   Job design is one possible solution for the mismatch between jobs that people perform and the needs, expectations, and values of the work force.

---

[56] Statistics on the frequency of profit-sharing plans drawn from Joani Nelson-Horchler, "Paying for Productivity," *Industry Week,* April 4, 1983, pp. 35–38.

[57] See Doug Garr, "Home Is Where the Work Is," *Omni,* December 1984, pp. 132–34, 136, 166; and "Quality and Productivity Management," *BNA Bulletin to Management,* July 3, 1986, pp. 2–6.

[58] These are discussed by Dorothy Kroll, "Telecommuting: A Revealing Peek inside Some of Industry's First Electronic Cottages," *Management Review,* November 1984, pp. 18–23.

[59] John Naisbitt, *Megatrends: Ten New Directions Transforming Our Lives* (New York: Warner Books, 1982), p. 36.

Job design involves altering jobs with the intent of increasing both employee quality of work life and productivity.

B.   Scientific management designs jobs by using research and experimentation to identify the most efficient way to perform tasks. Jobs are horizontally loaded in job enlargement by giving workers more than one specialized task to complete. Job rotation increases workplace variety by moving employees from one specialized job to another. Job enrichment vertically loads jobs by giving employees administrative duties normally performed by their superiors.

C.   The psychological states of experienced meaningfulness, experienced responsibility, and knowledge of results produce internal work motivation. These psychological states are fostered by the presence of five core job characteristics. People respond positively to jobs containing these core job characteristics when they have the knowledge and skills necessary to perform the job, high growth needs, and high context satisfactions.

D.   Social system perspectives of job design advocate an open systems approach to redesigning jobs. The sociotechnical model divides work environments into a technical system and a social system. When jobs are redesigned, these systems interact and influence each other. According to the social information-processing model, social cues play an important role in determining employee perceptions about job characteristics.

E.   Participative management reflects the extent to which employees participate in setting goals, making decisions, solving problems, and making changes in the organization. Research revealed that participative management does not consistently increase productivity, but does increase satisfaction.

F.   Quality circles entail using groups of workers to identify, analyze, and recommend solutions for improving the quality of production. Due to a lack of rigorous research, it is not possible to evaluate conclusively the effectiveness of quality circles.

G.   Quality of work life innovations increase employee well-being. Union-management cooperative projects accomplish this by giving nonmanagerial employees more input in running the company. Success of these programs depends on creating positive attitudes between union members and management and instituting specialized training for first-level supervision. Flexitime and compressed workweeks are popular alternative work schedules. Flexitime increases employee autonomy by allowing workers to select their own starting and finishing times. Employees work 38 to 40 hours in less than five days under compressed workweek plans.

H.   The physical design of the work environment affects employee attitudes and behavior. Companies are increasingly using profit-sharing plans. Gainsharing plans call for the sharing of managerial responsibilities along with profits. Telecommuting involves using a computer to receive and send work from home. This practice is still in its infancy in the United States.

KEY TERMS ———————————————————————————————————

job design

job enlargement

job rotation

internal motivation

experienced meaningfulness

experienced responsibility

knowledge of results

core job dimensions

motivating potential score

sociotechnical model

autonomous work groups

social information-processing
  model of job design

participative management

quality circles

flexitime

compressed workweeks

gainsharing

telecommuting

DISCUSSION QUESTIONS ——————————————————————————————

1. If you were redesigning a job, would you use one or more of the methods of job design we discussed? Explain your rationale.

2. How might the implementing concepts of the job characteristics model be used to increase your internal motivation to study?

3. What does the job characteristics approach really contribute to our knowledge about job enrichment?

4. Do you know anyone who would not respond positively to an enriched job? Describe this person.

5. Do you agree with the statement that the sociotechnical model is too complex to apply? Explain.

6. Have social cues ever influenced your choice of what professor to take for a course? Describe how these cues affected your decision.

7. Given the intuitive appeal of participative management, why do you think it fails as often as it succeeds? Explain.

8. Have you ever been involved in a quality circle? Describe your experience.

9. Do you think companies really care about quality of work life? Why or why not?

10. What is the most valuable lesson you have learned about quality of work life from this chapter?

BACK TO THE OPENING CASE

Now that you have read Chapter 15, you should be able to answer the following questions about the Thorneburg Hosiery case:

1. How did Jim Thorneburg use the principles of job enrichment?
2. Which of the implementing concepts for the job characteristics approach were used by the company?
3. What quality of work life innovations did the company use?
4. Can you identify any social cues that may have increased the effectiveness of Thorneburg Hosiery's ''new system''?

EXERCISE 15 ———————————————————————————

Objectives

1. To assess the motivating potential score (MPS) of your current or former job.
2. To determine which core job characteristics need to be changed.
3. To explore how you might redesign the job.

Introduction

The first step in calculating the MPS of a job is to complete the job diagnostic survey (JDS). Since the JDS is a long questionnaire, we would like you to complete a subset of the instrument. This will enable you to calculate the MPS, identify deficient job characteristics, and begin thinking about redesigning the job.

Instructions

Indicate whether each of the following statements in the JDS is an accurate or inaccurate description of your present or most recent job. Please select one number from the following scale for each statement. After completing the instrument, use the scoring key to compute a total score for each of the core job characteristics.

1 = Very inaccurate
2 = Mostly inaccurate
3 = Slightly inaccurate
4 = Uncertain
5 = Slightly accurate
6 = Mostly accurate
7 = Very accurate

_____ 1. The job requires me to use a number of complex or high-level skills.

_____ 2. The job is arranged so that I have the chance to do an entire piece of work from beginning to end.

_____ 3. Just doing the work required by the job provides many chances for me to figure out how well I am doing.

_____ 4. The job is not simple and repetitive.

_____ 5. This job is one where a lot of other people can be affected by how well the work gets done.

_____ 6. The job does not deny me the chance to use my personal initiative or judgment in carrying out the work.

_____ 7. The job provides me the chance to completely finish the pieces of work I begin.

_____ 8. The job itself provides plenty of clues about whether or not I am performing well.

_____ 9. The job gives me considerable opportunity for independence and freedom in how I do the work.

_____10. The job itself is very significant or important in the broader scheme of things.

Scoring Key

Compute the **average** of the two items that measure each job characteristic.

Skill variety (#1 and #4)   _____
Task identity (#2 and #7)   _____
Task significance (#5 and #10)   _____
Autonomy (#6 and #9)   _____
Feedback from job itself (#3 and #8) _____

Now you are ready to calculate the MPS. Use the MPS formula presented earlier in this chapter. Norms are provided below to help you interpret the relative status of the MPS and each individual job characteristic.[60]

Norms

	TYPE OF JOB			
	PROFESSIONAL/ TECHNICAL	CLERICAL	SALES	SERVICE
Skill variety	5.4	4.0	4.8	5.0
Task identity	5.1	4.7	4.4	4.7
Task significance	5.6	5.3	5.5	5.7
Autonomy	5.4	4.5	4.8	5.0
Feedback from job itself	5.1	4.6	5.4	5.1
MPS	154	106	146	152

[60] The JDS and its norms were adapted from J. Richard Hackman and Greg R. Oldham, *Work Redesign* (Reading, Mass.: Addison-Wesley Publishing, 1980), pp. 280–81, 317.

Questions for Consideration/Class Discussion

1. What is the MPS of your job? Is it high, average, or low?
2. Using the norms, which job characteristics are high, average, or low?
3. Which job characteristics would you change? Why?
4. How might you use the implementing concepts to redesign your job?

Chapter **16**

Managing Occupational Stress

LEARNING OBJECTIVES

When you finish studying the material in this chapter,
you should be able to:

- Define the term *stress.*
- Describe Matteson and Ivancevich's model of occupational stress.
- Discuss four reasons why it is important for managers to understand the causes and consequences of stress.
- Explain how stressful life events create stress.
- Specify three managerial solutions for both burnout and substance abuse.
- Explain the mechanisms of social support.
- Describe the coping process.
- Contrast the four dominant stress-reduction techniques.

OPENING CASE 16

The Stressful Life of a Paramedic

New York—Certain things drive paramedics up the wall.

1:19 P.M. Richard Awe and Joseph Pessolano are cruising midtown Manhattan. "Smith's Bar & Grill, 701 Eighth Ave.," the dispatcher's voice says. "Forty-year old female going in and out of consciousness."

Sounding the siren, Mr. Awe weaves through heavy traffic to Smith's. The medical emergency is at a booth in the rear, with a half-eaten noodle dish on the table and a bulging canvas carryall on the seat beside her.

"They gave me food and then I fell on the floor," she explains. She is fairly alert. Her chief problem seems to be that she lost her room in a welfare hotel. She refuses to go to a hospital. Why—or whether—she fainted remains a mystery. The paramedics leave.

Unnecessary Calls

"I hope we get someone who is legitimately sick today," Mr. Awe says.

The fact is that most of the more than 750,000 ambulance calls handled yearly by New York City's Emergency Medical Services [EMS] are unnecessary.

More than 40% are false alarms. The ambulance arrives, nobody is there. "You never know if it was a real false alarm," says James Kerr, the EMS executive director. "You're all revved up to treat somebody, and you can't find them."

Maybe another third turn out to be bogus in other ways. Poor people with no doctors call the medics instead. People with minor injuries call an ambulance instead of hailing a cab. It all contributes to the paramedic's big occupational hazard, getting "fried"—burnout.

Time was, not so long ago, when ambulance drivers tended to be hot-doggers who screamed the sirens as they went for coffee, and didn't have much medical training. That has changed. New York's EMS, like those in other cities, began to put the dramatic lessons of Vietnam in emergency life-saving into civilian use in the mid-1970s. . . .

Meager Benefits

Working in pairs, with radio contact to a physician if they need it, the city's medics handle everything from cardiac cases to burns and bullet wounds. They are proud of their ability to operate independently and take responsibility. But the paramedic system is plagued by bureaucratic hitches, by meager benefits and pay (much lower than that of garbage collectors), and by the lack of an attractive career path.

Richard Gutwirth, 35, has been a city paramedic for six years. "I saw a show about it on TV," he recalls. "I thought, 'I'd love to do that.' It looked exciting." He did, and it was. But now he is frustrated and is active in the paramedics' union agitating for parity with police and firemen.

Turnover in the city EMS is 14% a year—one in seven. Many trained, experienced people simply move to the Police Department—

four paramedics did that in July—or become firemen. Alexander Keuhl, the city health official who heads EMS, says, "It's very hard to develop a career ladder for paramedics unless they go into administration."

Top pay for city medics, in the mid-$20,000s, is reached in three years. Medics at voluntary hospitals do a little better. Overtime adds a little. But police, firemen and sanitation men still get maybe $8,000 more. "That's a mortgage right there," Mr. Gutwirth says.

Nevertheless, paramedics "hunger for the good job, the good save," says Richard Westphal, the director of ambulance services at St. Vincent's. But at a price. "People curse them, throw things at them," says Dr. Westphal. One patient tried to strangle Mr. Gutwirth. The nastiness comes especially from heroin addicts jolted back to reality by the drug Narcan.

Stress comes in many forms. Ambulance sirens are hard on hearing. The tension of emergencies raises blood pressure. Meals are grabbed on the run; a rush call then produces indigestion.

"You're always dealing with death," says John Clappin, paramedic instructor at St. Vincent's. Or with failure. "You work on them for an hour and then they die," he remarks. "It has to affect you."

"I love it when we save a life," says Joe Pessolano. He is 25. "We saved one man in full cardiac arrest," he recalls proudly. He also gets a charge out of delivering babies; he did that once in the bathroom of a McDonald's on 34th Street.

For Discussion

Does the stress that paramedics experience have both good and bad aspects? Explain.

■ Additional discussion questions linking this case with the following material appear at the end of this chapter.

Have you ever felt like you didn't fit in when attempting to work with others? If so, you were probably uncomfortable. Unfortunately, as pointed out in Part One, many employees experience a lack of fit between their needs and values and the demands of their workplace. Consider the recent wave of corporate mergers. Mergers too often result in a lack of fit between a manager's orientation and that of the acquiring company.

After Masonite Corp. was acquired by U.S. Gypsum Co. . . . [in 1985], Donald Slocum, Masonite's vice president of advanced technology, tried to adapt to his new employer's corporate practices.

But in seeking support for his projects and staff, Mr. Slocum found that he had to fight through several tiers of management and thought that the parent company was wary of spending in uncharted technical areas.

After nine months, he resigned. "I gave it a shot, but I felt there was a

■ **FIGURE 16-1** Poor Individual-Organization Fit Produces Stress

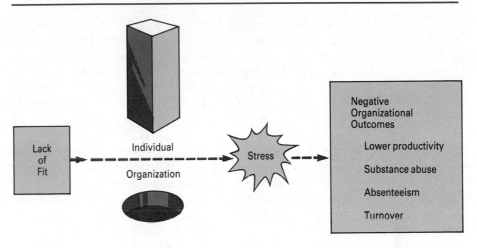

climate change,'' says Mr. Slocum, who now works with companies to develop new products.[1]

Imagine the personal stress experienced by Mr. Slocum as he tried to adapt to U.S. Gypsum's unfamiliar methods. Given that he eventually quit his job, the lack of fit must have been overwhelming. But such did not have to be the case. Whether due to the trauma of a merger or a variety of other situations, the stressful consequences of poor individual-organization fit are manageable problems. Hence, this chapter helps you understand and manage occupational stress.

Trying to insert a square peg into a round hole can be a frustrating and fruitless experience. Similarly, the poor fit between a progressive manager and a stodgy bureaucratic organization, as in Mr. Slocum's case, can create stress (see Figure 16-1). In work settings, stress has been linked to lower productivity, substance abuse, absenteeism, and intention to quit.[2] On the other hand, a good individual-organization fit can reduce stress and lead to positive work outcomes. With this end in mind, this chapter discusses the foundations of stress, examines stressors and two important outcomes of stress, highlights three moderators of occupational stress, and explores a variety of stress-reduction techniques.

[1] Larry Reibstein, ''After a Takeover: More Managers Run, or Are Pushed, Out the Door,'' *The Wall Street Journal*, November 15, 1986, p. 29.

[2] See results presented in Paul E. Spector, Daniel J. Dwyer, and Steve M. Jex, ''Relation of Job Stressors to Affective, Health, and Performance Outcomes: A Comparison of Multiple Data Sources,'' *Journal of Applied Psychology*, February 1988, pp. 11–19.

■ FOUNDATIONS OF STRESS

We all experience stress on a daily basis. Although stress is caused by many factors, researchers conclude that stress triggers one of two basic reactions: active fighting or passive flight (running away or acceptance). Thus, the so-called **fight-or-flight response.**[3] Physiologically, this stress response is a bio-chemical "passing gear" involving hormonal changes that mobilize the body for extraordinary demands. Imagine how our prehistoric ancestors responded to the stress associated with a charging saber-toothed tiger. To avoid being eaten, they could stand their ground and fight the beast or run away. In either case, their bodies would have been energized by an identical hormonal change, involving the release of adrenaline into the bloodstream.

In today's hectic urbanized and industrialized society, charging beasts have been replaced by problems such as deadlines, role conflict and ambiguity, financial responsibilities, traffic congestion, noise and air pollution, and work overload. As with our ancestors, our response to stress may or may not trigger negative side effects including headaches, ulcers, insomnia, heart attacks, high blood pressure, and strokes. The same stress response that helped our prehistoric ancestors survive has too often become a life-threatening factor in modern life. Take Edward Mulcahey, for example. Mulcahey, a sports editor, died of a cerebral hemorrhage after covering a football game. His doctor indicated the hemorrhage was caused by job stress that aggravated his high blood pressure and diabetes.[4] Since stress and its consequences are manageable, it is important for managers to learn as much as they can about occupational stress. This section provides a conceptual foundation by defining stress, presenting a model of occupational stress, and highlighting related organizational costs.

Defining Stress

To an orchestra violinist, stress may stem from giving a solo performance before a big audience. While heat, smoke, and flames may represent stress to a firefighter, talking on the phone, delivering a speech, or presenting a lecture may be stressful for those who talk fast (see Table 16–1). In short, stress means different things to different people. Managers need a working definition.

Formally defined, **stress** is "an adaptive response, mediated by individual characteristics and/or psychological processes, that is a consequence of any external action, situation, or event that places special physical and/or psychological demands upon a person."[5] This definition is not as difficult as it seems

---

[3] The stress response is thoroughly discussed by Hans Selye, *Stress without Distress* (New York: J. B. Lippincott Co., 1974).

[4] The specifics of this case are discussed in "Deadline Pressure Aggravates Stress: Court Orders Money for Widow," *Monthly News on Human Resource Management,* May 1985, p. 1.

[5] John M. Ivancevich and Michael T. Matteson, *Stress and Work: A Managerial Perspective* (Glenview, Ill.: Scott, Foresman, 1980), pp. 8–9.

■ **TABLE 16–1** Talking Can Be Stressful

> Orlando, Fla.—Talking may be hazardous to your health, especially if you talk fast, a researcher says.
>
> When people speak, they hold their breath, and that causes their blood pressure to rise, says Dr. James Lynch, professor of psychiatry at the University of Maryland. . . .
>
> Studies have shown the highest fluctuations in blood-pressure readings occur during telephone conversations at work, especially if the dialogue is stressful, according to Lynch.
>
> "Patients have no idea what's happening," he said. "The more reactive your blood pressure is when you speak, the less likely you are to feel it."

SOURCE: Excerpted from "Motor Mouths Drive Up Their Blood Pressure," *The Arizona Republic,* March 21, 1985, pp. 1, 4.

when we reduce it to three interrelated dimensions of stress: (1) environmental demands, referred to as stressors, that produce (2) an adaptive response that is influenced by (3) individual differences.

Hans Selye, considered the father of the modern concept of stress, pioneered the distinction between stressors and the stress response. Moreover, Selye emphasized that both positive and negative events can trigger an identical stress response that can be beneficial or harmful (see Table 16–2). He also noted:

- Stress is not merely nervous tension.
- Stress can have positive consequences.
- Stress is not something to be avoided.
- The complete absence of stress is death.[6]

These points make it clear that stress is inevitable. Efforts need to be directed at managing stress, not at somehow escaping it altogether.

A Model of Occupational Stress

OB researchers Michael Matteson and John Ivancevich proposed an instructive model of occupational stress. As illustrated in Figure 16–2, stressors lead to stress, which in turn produces a variety of outcomes. The model also specifies several individual differences that *moderate* the stressor-stress-outcome relationship. A moderator is a variable that causes the relationship between two variables—like stress and outcomes—to be stronger for some people and weaker for others. For example, a field study of 341 employees from the U.S. Department of Defense and 29 from a hospital revealed that people who were overweight and older, smoked, and did not exercise had higher than desirable levels of cholesterol in their blood.[7] As indicated in Figure 16–2, high cholesterol is

---

[6] See Selye, *Stress without Distress.*

[7] Results can be found in William H. Hendrix, Nestor K. Ovalle II, and R. George Troxler, "Behavioral and Physiological Consequences of Stress and Its Antecedent Factors," *Journal of Applied Psychology,* February 1985, pp. 188–201.

■ **TABLE 16–2** Hans Selye Defines Stress and the Stress Response

Stress is the nonspecific response of the body to any demands made upon it. To understand this definition we must first explain what we mean by nonspecific. Each demand made upon our body is in a sense unique, that is specific. When exposed to cold, we shiver to produce more heat, and blood vessels in our skin contract to diminish the loss of heat from the body surfaces. When exposed to heat, we sweat because the evaporation of perspiration from the surface of our skin has a cooling effect. . . .

From the point of its stress-producing or stressor activity, it is immaterial whether the agent or situation we face is pleasant or unpleasant; all that counts is the intensity of the demand for readjustment or adaptation. The mother who is suddenly told that her only son died in battle suffers a terrible mental shock; if years later it turns out that the news was false and the son unexpectedly walks into her room alive and well, she experiences extreme joy. The specific results of the two events, sorrow and joy, are completely different, in fact, opposite to each other, yet their stressor effect—the nonspecific demand to readjust herself to an entirely new situation—may be the same.

SOURCE: Hans Selye, *Stress without Distress* (New York: J.B. Lippincott Co., 1974), pp. 27–29.

one of the physiological outcomes of stress. The major components of this stress model require a closer look.

Stressors.   **Stressors** are environmental factors that produce stress. Stated differently, stressors are a prerequisite or antecedent to experiencing the stress response. There are four major types of stressors. Individual-level stressors are those directly associated with a person's job duties. A survey of more than 40,000 women across the United States found that the five most frequently mentioned occupational stressors were: (1) having responsibility without authority, (2) not being able to provide input on how the work is completed, (3) performing work that is not interesting or challenging, (4) performing repetitious and monotonous work, and (5) having an excessive work load. Another survey of 532 managers from organizations in Western Australia supported these findings. In that sample, a lack of autonomy and an excessive work load were strongly related to stress.[8]

Group and organizational-level stressors are broader in focus and include factors such as group cohesiveness, intragroup conflict, organizational climate, and organizational design. Finally, extraorganizational stressors are those caused by factors outside the organization. For instance, changing family values are creating stress for Japanese workers (see Table 16–3).

Outcomes.   Theorists contend that stress has behavioral, cognitive, and physiological consequences or outcomes. A large body of research supports the conclu-

---

[8] Data are reported in R. Chris Knight, ''Can Stress Make You Sick?'' *Working Women*, April 1984, pp. 142–50; and Kenneth Hall and Lawson K. Savery, ''Tight Rein, More Stress,'' *Harvard Business Review*, January–February 1986, pp. 160–62, 164.

■ **FIGURE 16–2**   A Model of Occupational Stress

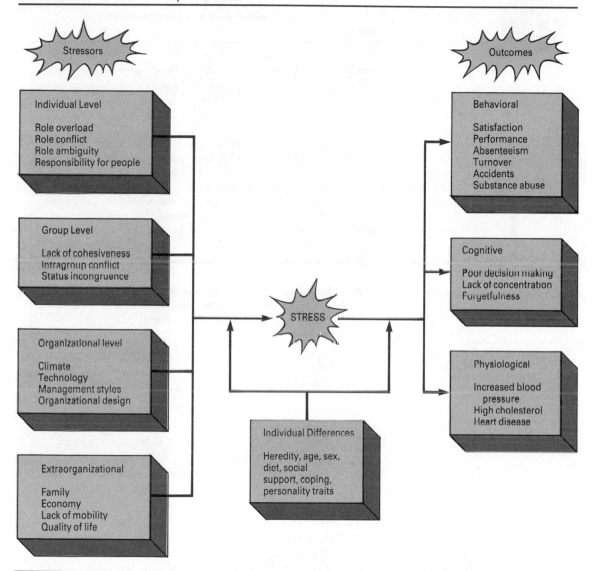

SOURCE: Adapted from Michael T. Matteson and John M. Ivancevich, "Organizational Stressors and Heart Disease: A Research Model," *Academy of Management Review*, July 1979, p. 350. Used with permission.

sion that stress produces harmful physiological outcomes.[9] But researchers have only recently begun to examine the relationship between stress and work-related behavioral and cognitive outcomes. For instance, results from a field

_____

[9] A variety of evidence is presented in the readings contained in Hans Selye, *Selye's Guide to Stress Research* (New York: Van Nostrand, 1980).

■ **TABLE 16–3** A Conflict between Work Orientation and Family Life Creates Stress for
Japanese Workers

"Thank God it's Monday" is a fitting motto for accountant Takechi Uehara. Every Friday he feels a sharp pain spreading from his shoulders across the back of his neck. He then spends the entire weekend in bed. But when Monday comes along, he feels fine. Uehara, who is too embarrassed to give his real name, is a victim of the "holiday syndrome." He can't bear to be away from the office.

"It is a uniquely Japanese disease," says psychiatrist Tooru Sekiya, who treats many such men. He takes some patients in overnight, and they go to work directly from his clinic after a morning counseling session.

The families of such men have built separate lives without them. Wives, rather than cater to their husbands' every need, focus on the children and ignore their spouses. One businessman tells of being ordered by his wife to leave the house on a Sunday because his son was having a birthday party.

It may take more than counseling to put these men's families back together. An informal survey conducted by a weekly magazine concluded that Japanese couples communicate for an average of only six minutes a day.

"Women used to accept that relationship, acting as the all-forgiving mother," says Michiko Fukazawa, a Tokyo psychiatrist. Now, she says, "women are getting bored with their husbands." As a result, an increasing number of women are divorcing their spouses as soon as the men receive their retirement bonuses.

SOURCE: "All Work and No Play Is Tearing the Family Apart." Reprinted from April 7, 1986, issue of *Business Week* by special permission, copyright © 1986 by McGraw-Hill, Inc.

study of 217 people employed at a food processing company revealed that stress had both direct and indirect impacts on the behavioral outcomes of performance and turnover, respectively.[10] Nonetheless, the exact nature of the relationship between stress and performance is still open to question.

Historically, researchers generally have believed there was an *inverted U-shaped relationship* between stress and performance (see dashed line in Figure 16–3). Low levels of stress were thought to lead to low performance because individuals were not "charged up" to perform. At the other extreme, high levels of stress were predicted to force an individual into an energy-sapping fight-or-flight response, thereby resulting in low performance. This hypothesized relationship proposes that optimal performance is achieved when people are subjected to moderate levels of stress.

Although several laboratory studies supported this relationship, three more recent field studies did not. For samples of 440 nurses, 227 managers, and 283 hourly workers, results demonstrated a negative relationship between stress

---

[10] Behavioral outcomes were examined by, Saroj Parasuraman and Joseph A. Alutto, "Sources and Outcomes of Stress in Organizational Settings: Toward the Development of a Structural Model," *Academy of Management Journal*, June 1984, pp. 330–50.

Reprinted from *The Wall Street Journal;* permission Cartoon Features Syndicate.

■ **FIGURE 16–3**   The Relationship between Stress and Performance

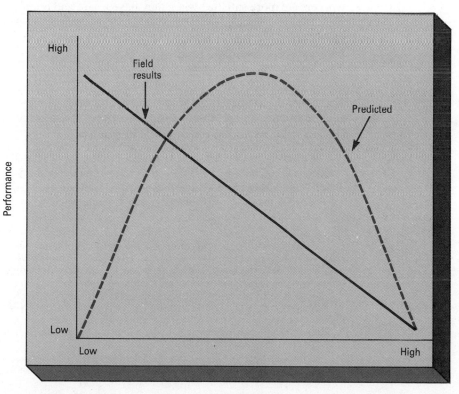

and performance (solid line in Figure 16–3).[11] In other words, performance declined as stress increased. Despite differing evidence from laboratory and field studies, it is clear that high levels of stress diminish human performance. More research is needed to identify the optimum stress-performance relationship.

Individual Differences.   People do not experience the same level of stress or exhibit similar outcomes for a given type of stressor. As discussed later, stressors are less apt to produce stress for people with a strong social support network and those who employ a variety of coping strategies. *Perception* of a stressor is another important moderator. If a stressor is perceived as threatening, an individual tends to experience greater stress and more negative outcomes. According to Harvard Medical School research, the type of job an individual performs is another potential moderator. Research found that employees paid by the hour had a 40 percent higher risk of developing coronary heart disease than salaried employees (after controlling for risk factors like smoking and weight).[12] Even though researchers have been able to identify several important moderators, a large gap still exists in identifying relevant individual differences.

Economic Costs and Legal Liabilities of Stress

Managers need to understand the causes and consequences of stress for at least four compelling reasons. First, from a quality-of-work-life perspective, workers are more satisfied when they have a safe and comfortable work environment. Second, a moral imperative suggests that managers should reduce occupational stress because it leads to negative outcomes. A third reason centers on the staggering economic costs of stress.

The U.S. Office of Technology Assessment estimates that stress-related illnesses cost American businesses between $50 billion and $70 billion a year.[13] These figures do not tell the whole story, however. Stress-related costs multiply when substance abuse, absenteeism, and turnover are factored into the equation. Consider, for example, the costs of drug abuse.

> According to the Research Triangle Institute, . . . drug abuse cost the U.S. economy $60 billion in 1983, or nearly 30% more than the $47 billion estimated for 1980. Other studies have found that employees who use drugs are far less productive than their co-workers and miss ten or more times as many workdays.

[11] See Muhammad Jamal, "Job Stress and Job Performance Controversy: An Empirical Assessment," *Organizational Behavior and Human Performance,* February 1984, pp. 1–21; and Muhammad Jamal, "Relationship of Job Stress to Job Performance: A Study of Managers and Blue-Collar Workers," *Human Relations,* May 1985, pp. 409–24.

[12] Research about the perception of stressors is reviewed by Randolph J. Paterson and Richard W. J. Neufeld, "Clear Danger: Situational Determinants of the Appraisal of Threat," *Psychological Bulletin,* May 1987, pp. 404–16. Results from the Harvard study are discussed in "Labor Letter: A Special News Report on People and Their Jobs in Offices, Fields, and Factories," *The Wall Street Journal,* December 3, 1985, p. 1.

[13] Statistics are provided in "Health and Safety Review: Stress-Related Illnesses Cost Business $50 Billion to $70 Billion Annually, Office of Technology Assessment Reports," *Monthly News on Human Resource Management,* November 1984, p. 3.

Drug abusers are three times as likely as nonusers to injure themselves or someone else. . . .

Concern is greatest, of course, in industries where mistakes can cost lives. Since 1975, about 50 train accidents have been attributed to drug- or alcohol-impaired workers. In those mishaps, 37 people were killed, 80 were injured, and more than $34 million worth of property was destroyed.[14]

A fourth and final reason revolves around recent court cases where employees sued their employers for worker compensation benefits resulting from stress-related problems. Although the courts have not consistently ruled in favor of compensating people for psychological injury due to stress, the trend is in that direction. The following cases illustrate this trend:

Helen J. Kelly, a Raytheon Co. employee with 22 years' seniority, suffered a nervous breakdown when told she would be transferred to another department. The Massachusetts Supreme Judicial Court ruled 4 to 3 that she was entitled to worker's comp benefits. . . .

Harry A. McGarrah, an Oregon deputy sheriff, blamed his depression on the belief that his supervisor was persecuting him. . . .

Kelly collected $40,000 and McGarrah, $20,000.[15]

In summary, managers cannot afford to ignore the many implications of occupational stress.

■ IMPORTANT STRESSORS AND STRESS OUTCOMES

As we have seen, stressors trigger stress, which in turn leads to a variety of outcomes. This section explores an important category of *extraorganizational* stressors, stressful life events. Two especially troublesome stress-related outcomes, burnout and substance abuse, also are examined.

Stressful Life Events

Events such as experiencing the death of a family member, being assaulted, moving, ending an intimate relationship, being seriously ill, or taking a big test can create stress. These events are stressful because they involve significant changes that require adaptation and often social readjustment. Accordingly, **stressful life events** are defined as nonwork-related changes that disrupt an individual's lifestyle and social relationships. They have been the most extensively investigated extraorganizational stressors.

Thomas Holmes and Richard Rahe conducted pioneering research on the relationship between stressful life events and subsequent illness. During their research, they developed a widely used questionnaire to assess life stress.[16]

---

[14] Janice Castro, "Battling the Enemy Within," *Time,* March 17, 1986, p. 53.

[15] Resa W. King and Irene Pave, "Stress Claims Are Making Business Jumpy," *Business Week,* October 14, 1985, p. 152.

[16] This landmark study was conducted by Thomas H. Holmes and Richard H. Rahe, "The Social Readjustment Rating Scale," *Journal of Psychosomatic Research,* August 1967, pp. 213–18.

Assessing Stressful Life Events.   The *Schedule of Recent Experiences* (SRE), developed by Holmes and Rahe, is the dominant method for assessing an individual's cumulative stressful life events. As shown in Table 16–4, the SRE consists of 43 life events. Each event has a corresponding value, called a life change unit, representing the degree of social readjustment necessary to cope with the event. The larger the value, the more stressful the event. These values were obtained from a convenience sample of 394 people who evaluated the stressfulness of each event. (Please take a moment to complete the SRE and calculate your total life stress score.)

Research revealed a positive relationship between the total score on the SRE and subsequent illness. For example, the odds are you will experience good health next year if you scored below 150. But there is a 50 percent chance of illness for those scoring between 150 and 300. Finally, a score above 300 suggests a 70 percent chance of illness.[17] A word of caution is in order, however. If you scored above 150, don't head for a sterile cocoon. High scores on the SRE do not guarantee you will become ill. Rather, a high score simply increases one's statistical risk of illness.

Research and Practical Implications.   Numerous studies have examined the relationship between life stress and both illness and job performance. Subjects with higher SRE scores had significantly more problems with sudden cardiac death, pregnancy and birth complications, tuberculosis, diabetes, anxiety, depression, and a host of minor physical ailments. Meanwhile, academic and work performance declined as SRE scores increased.[18] Negative, as opposed to positive, personal life changes were found to be more strongly correlated with lower levels of job satisfaction, organizational commitment, and job stress, and greater levels of depression and anxiety.[19] Finally, but importantly, life events that were uncontrollable (for example, death of spouse), rather than controllable (such as marriage), were more strongly associated with subsequent illness.[20]

The key implication is that employee illness and job performance are affected

---

[17] Normative predictions are discussed in Orlando Behling and Arthur L. Darrow, "Managing Work-Related Stress," in *Modules in Management* ed. James E. Rosenzweig and Fremont E. Kast (Chicago: Science Research Associates, 1984).

[18] For a review of this research, see Rabi S. Bhagat, "Effects of Stressful Life Events on Individual Performance Effectiveness and Work Adjustment Processes within Organizational Settings: A Research Model," *Academy of Management Review,* October 1983, pp. 660–71; and David Dooley, Karen Rook, and Ralph Catalano, "Job and Non-Job Stressors and Their Moderators," *Journal of Occupational Psychology,* June 1987, pp. 115–32.

[19] See Rabi S. Bhagat, Sara J. McQuaid, Hal Lindholm, and James Segovis, "Total Life Stress: A Multimethod Validation of the Construct and Its Effects on Organizationally Valued Outcomes and Withdrawal Behaviors," *Journal of Applied Psychology,* February 1985, pp. 202–14; and Arthur M. Nezu, Christine M. Nezu, and Sonia E. Blissett, "Sense of Humor as a Moderator of the Relations between Stressful Events and Psychological Distress: A Prospective Analysis," *Journal of Personality and Social Psychology,* March 1988, pp. 520–25.

[20] The influence of perceived control over stressors on stress outcomes is thoroughly discussed by David A. Brenders, "Perceived Control: Foundations and Directions for Communication Research," in *Communication Yearbook,* ed. Margaret L. McLaughlin (Beverly Hills, Calif.: Sage Publications, 1987), pp. 86–116.

■ **TABLE 16–4**   The Holmes and Rahe Schedule of Recent Experiences

Instructions: Place a check mark next to each event you experienced within the past year. Then add the life change units associated with the various events to derive your total life stress score.

Life Event	Life Change Unit
_____ Death of spouse	100
_____ Divorce	73
_____ Marital separation	65
_____ Jail term	63
_____ Death of close family member	63
_____ Personal injury or illness	53
_____ Marriage	50
_____ Fired at work	47
_____ Marital reconciliation	45
_____ Retirement	45
_____ Change in health of family member	44
_____ Pregnancy	40
_____ Sex difficulties	39
_____ Gain of new family member	39
_____ Business readjustment	39
_____ Change in financial state	38
_____ Death of close friend	37
_____ Change to different line of work	36
_____ Change in number of arguments with spouse	35
_____ Mortgage over $10,000	31
_____ Foreclosure of mortgage or loan	30
_____ Change in responsibilities at work	29
_____ Son or daughter leaving home	29
Trouble with in-laws	29
_____ Outstanding personal achievement	28
_____ Wife begin or stop work	26
_____ Begin or end school	26
_____ Change in living conditions	25
_____ Revision of personal habits	24
_____ Trouble with boss	23
_____ Change in work hours or conditions	20
_____ Change in residence	20
_____ Change in schools	20
_____ Change in recreation	19
_____ Change in church activities	19
_____ Change in social activities	18
_____ Mortgage or loan less than $10,000	17
_____ Change in sleeping habits	16
_____ Change in number of family get-togethers	15
_____ Change in eating habits	15
_____ Vacation	13
_____ Christmas	12
_____ Minor violations of the law	11

Total Score = _____

SOURCE: Adapted from Thomas H. Holmes and Richard H. Rahe, "The Social Readjustment Rating Scale," *Journal of Psychosomatic Research*, August 1967, p. 216. Used with permission.

■ **TABLE 16–5** More People Rely on Counseling to Reduce Stress

By one government estimate, five million people this year [1986]—up from half a million three decades ago—will consult psychiatrists, psychologists and psychiatric social workers for help in relieving anxiety, depression or other emotional distress. A federal study released in 1984 found that one in five Americans had had some type of mental-health treatment, compared with one in eight in 1960. . . .

The use of psychotherapy by adolescents also has soared, say employers and insurers who pay for much of the treatment. Ciba-Geigy Corp. reports that nearly 60% of its psychiatric insurance bill is for care to teen-age children of employees. GTE says its costs for adolescent care more than doubled last year [1985], to $15 million.

SOURCE: Excerpted from Michael Waldholz, "Treating the Mind: Use of Psychotherapy Surges, and Employers Blanch at the Costs," *The Wall Street Journal*, October 20, 1986, pp. 1, 21.

by extraorganizational stressors, particularly those that are negative and uncontrollable. Because employees do not leave their personal problems at the office door or factory gate, management needs to be aware of external sources of employee stress. Once identified, training programs or counseling (see Table 16–5) can be used to help employees cope with these stressors. This not only may reduce costs associated with illnesses and absenteeism, but also may lead to positive work attitudes and better job behaviors. In addition, by acknowledging that work outcomes are caused by extraorganizational stressors, managers may avoid the trap of automatically attributing poor performance to low motivation or lack of ability. Such awareness is likely to engender positive reactions from employees and lead to resolution of problems, not just symptoms. For individuals with a high score on the SRE, it would be best to defer controllable stressors, such as moving or buying a new car, until things settle down.

Burnout

Burnout is a stress-induced problem common among members of "helping" professions such as teaching, social work, employee relations, nursing, and law enforcement. It does not involve a specific feeling, attitude, or physiological outcome anchored to a specific point in time. Rather, **burnout** is a condition that occurs over time and is characterized by emotional exhaustion and a combination of negative attitudes. Table 16–6 describes 10 attitudinal characteristics of burnout. Experts say a substantial number of people suffer from this problem. The director of New York's Survey Information Research Center estimated in 1984 that about 20 percent of the owners, managers, professionals, and technical workers in the United States were suffering from burnout.[21]

---

[21] The frequency of burnout is discussed by Donald P. Rogers, "Helping Employees Cope with Burnout," *Business*, October–December 1984, pp. 3–7.

■ **TABLE 16–6**   Attitudinal Characteristics of Burnout

Attitude	Description
Fatalism	A feeling that you lack control over your work
Boredom	A lack of interest in doing your job
Discontent	A sense of being unhappy with your job
Cynicism	A tendency to undervalue the content of your job and the rewards received
Inadequacy	A feeling of not being able to meet your objectives
Failure	A tendency to discredit your performance and conclude that you are ineffective
Overwork	A feeling of having too much to do and not enough time to complete it
Nastiness	A tendency to be rude or unpleasant to your co-workers
Dissatisfaction	A feeling that you are not being justly rewarded for your efforts
Escape	A desire to give up and get away from it all

SOURCE: Adapted from Donald P. Rogers, "Helping Employees Cope with Burnout," *Business*, October–December 1984, p. 4.

This percentage is likely higher today. To promote better understanding of this important stress outcome, we turn our attention to a model of the burnout process and highlight relevant research and techniques for its prevention.

A Model of Burnout.   There are two paths to burnout. As Figure 16–4 illustrates, these two paths have a cumulative effect. The first route is a direct outgrowth of the model of occupational stress we just discussed. That is, traditional work-related stressors produce stress, which leads to attitudinal and behavioral symptoms that may culminate in burnout. Burnout does not automatically occur as a result of stress and occasional symptoms of burnout. Instead, burnout develops in phases and ultimately takes place when symptoms become so severe that an individual gives up trying to perform effectively. Consider the case of a teacher named Martha.

> "When I started as a teacher," says Martha, "I felt the mark I was making on every child was significant. But year in and year out, you go through the same hassles, and you begin to say to yourself, 'Nothing ever changes.' You struggle so hard with every kid, and there are so many of them every year. Eventually you realize, 'If it weren't me, somebody else would do it.' A kind of work-weariness overtakes you, like a big 'So What?' "
>
> Martha is typical of many people in the helping professions . . . who have overblown expectations. The very idealism that motivates them eventually burns them out. Anxious to make an impact, they undervalue their small successes, don't savor the struggle itself, and so never derive the satisfaction they crave.[22]

As in Martha's case, burnout is also caused by three unique stressors (path 2 in Figure 16–4): unrealistic expectations or goals, high-pressure working conditions, and a lack of positive feedback or rewards.

Research Findings and Prevention.   Research on burnout produced the following insights:

---

[22] Robert Karen, "Beware of Career Burnout!" *Cosmopolitan*, May 1986, p. 120.

■ **FIGURE 16–4** A Model of Burnout

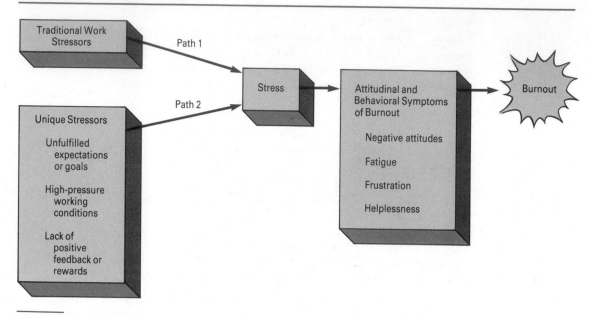

SOURCE: Based in part on Donald P. Rogers, "Helping Employees Cope with Burnout," *Business,* October–December 1984, p. 5.

- Burnout develops in phases. (Three likely phases have been identified: from depersonalization, to feeling a lack of personal accomplishment, to emotional exhaustion.)[23]
- Burnout can be accurately measured.
- The extent to which a job requires an individual to intensely work with others is highly related to burnout.
- Burnout is significantly associated with a lack of feedback, low job satisfaction, desire to quit one's job, impairment of interpersonal relationships with family and friends, insomnia, absenteeism, and taking more rest breaks at work.[24]
- Burnout significantly predicted individuals' thoughts about quitting and actual job leaving.[25]

---

[23] Phases of burnout were examined by Ronald J. Burke, Jon Shearer, and Eugene Deszca, "Correlates of Burnout Phases among Police Officers," *Group & Organization Studies,* December 1984, pp. 451–66.

[24] A review of research on burnout and the development of a burnout survey are provided by Christina Maslach and Susan E. Jackson, "The Measurement of Experienced Burnout," *Journal of Occupational Behavior,* April 1981, pp. 99–113. The validity of burnout scales was examined by Michael J. Fimian and Linda P. Blanton, "Stress, Burnout, and Role Problems among Teacher Trainees and First-Year Teachers," *Journal of Occupational Behaviour,* April 1987, pp. 157–65.

[25] Results are found in Susan E. Jackson, Richard L. Schwab, and Randall S. Schuler, "Toward an Understanding of the Burnout Phenomenon," *Journal of Applied Psychology,* November 1986, pp. 630–40.

Removing stressors that cause burnout is the most straightforward way to prevent it. Thus, one solution is for managers to create down-to-earth job expectations, possibly through the use of realistic job previews discussed in Chapter 9. Managers also can reduce burnout by buffering its effects. **Buffers** are resources or administrative changes that alleviate the symptoms of burnout. Potential buffers include extra staff or equipment at peak work periods, support from top management, increased freedom to make decisions, recognition for accomplishments, time off for personal development or rest, and equitable rewards. Decreasing the quantity and increasing the *quality* of communications is another possible buffer. Finally, managers can change the content of an individual's job by adding or eliminating responsibilities, increasing the amount of participation in decision making, altering the pattern of interpersonal contacts, or assigning the person to a new position.[26]

Substance Abuse

Employee substance abuse occurs when the use of alcohol or drugs hurts one's job performance. Although people drink alcohol and take drugs for a variety of reasons, many people reportedly rely on these mood-altering substances to relieve stress. For individuals with pressure-packed, fast-paced jobs, alcohol and barbiturates may be used to calm frayed nerves. Drugs like cocaine or amphetamines may offer routine-task personnel needed stimulation. Employee substance abuse is a costly problem of epidemic proportions. It critically affects product quality and job safety.

U.S. government experts estimate that 10 to 23 percent of the American work force uses dangerous drugs at work. Substance abuse is found at all organizational levels. Some experts estimate the problem might be more severe in the managerial ranks because managers are in a better position to hide alcohol and drug habits. Managers can close their office doors, delegate work to others, and travel more frequently.[27] Although no single symptom is indicative of substance abuse, behavioral changes such as increased absenteeism, radical mood swings, sleeping at work, or working in frantic, spasmodic bursts are suggestive of substance abuse.[28] Corporations have attacked the substance abuse problem in three ways.

The first, and most controversial, involves sting operations to identify employees involved with the sale and use of illegal drugs. Both Pennzoil and General Motors have used this approach. The second program involves drug testing—commonly through urinalysis—when screening job applicants and/or on a random basis. Workplace drug testing has increased dramatically in recent years, with about 35 percent of American companies doing so by 1988. Finally, companies use rehabilitation programs—called employee assistance programs

---

[26] These recommendations were derived from Donald P. Rogers, "Helping Employees Cope with Burnout."

[27] See Castro, "Battling the Enemy Within."

[28] Warning signs are presented in Steven Flax, "The Executive Addict," *Fortune*, June 24, 1985, pp. 24–31.

■ **TABLE 16–7** Drug-Treatment Professionals Offer Advice for Reducing Substance Abuse

Tackle the problem early, when recovery is still possible.

Get professional help from a counselor who has experience with the problem at hand.

Don't try to counsel the employee by yourself. Employees may believe you are providing all the help that is needed.

Document the employee's deterioration in performance.

Confront the employee with factual information about his or her performance. Don't be overly sympathetic during this confrontation.

Let the employee's family deal with off-the-job behavior.

Pay for treatment and assure the employee of complete confidentiality of his or her participation.

If the employee resists treatment, deliver an ultimatum that continued employment is contingent on receiving treatment.

SOURCE: Adapted from Steven Flax, "The Executive Addict," *Fortune*, June 24, 1985, p. 26.

(EAPs)—to counter the problem. Approximately 5,000 corporate EAPs are operating in the United States today.[29] These three interventions have important OB implications.

Sting operations and drug testing may erode organizational trust and job satisfaction because they are likely to be viewed as punitive or "heavy-handed" methods. On the other hand, employee assistance programs are likely to enhance labor-management relations and improve job commitment/satisfaction because they focus on helping rather than punishing employees. In conclusion, although there are no easy solutions to the problem of employee substance abuse, managers might consider the advice offered by drug-treatment professionals (see Table 16–7).

■ MODERATORS OF OCCUPATIONAL STRESS

Moderators are variables that cause the relationships between stressors, stress, and outcomes to be weaker for some people and stronger for others. Managers with a working knowledge of important stress moderators can confront employee stress in the following ways.

First, awareness of moderators helps identify those most likely to experience stress and its negative outcomes. Stress reduction programs then can be formulated for high-risk employees. Second, moderators, in and of themselves, suggest possible solutions for reducing negative outcomes of occupational stress. Keeping these objectives in mind, we will examine three important moderators. They are social support, coping, and hardiness.

---

[29] See Castro, "Battling the Enemy Within"; Katie Hafner, "Testing for Drug Use: Handle with Care," *Business Week*, March 28, 1988, p. 65; Theodore H. Rosen, "Identification of Substance Abusers in the Workplace," *Public Personnel Management*, Fall 1987, pp. 197–207; and Paul V. Lyons, "EAPs: The Only Real Cure for Substance Abuse," *Management Review*, March 1987, pp. 38–41.

Social Support

Talking with a friend or taking part in a bull session can be comforting during times of fear, stress, or loneliness. For a variety of reasons, meaningful social relationships help people do a better job of handling stress. **Social support** is the amount of perceived helpfulness derived from social relationships. Importantly, social support is determined by both the quantity and quality of an individual's social relationships.[30] Figure 16–5 illustrates the mechanisms of social support.

A Model of Social Support.   As Figure 16–5 shows, one's support network must be perceived before it can be used. Support networks evolve from four sources: cultural norms, social institutions, groups, or individuals. For example, there is more cultural emphasis on caring for the elderly in Japan than in America. Japanese culture is thus a strong source of social support for older Japanese people. Alternatively, individuals may fall back on social institutions such as social security or welfare, religious groups, or family and friends for support. In turn, these various sources provide four *types* of support:

- *Esteem support:* providing information that a person is accepted and respected despite any problems or inadequacies.
- *Informational support:* providing help in defining, understanding, and coping with problems.
- *Social companionship:* spending time with others in leisure and recreational activities.
- *Instrumental support:* providing financial aid, material resources, or needed services.[31]

If social support is perceived as available, an individual then decides whether or not to use it. Generally, support is used for one or both of two purposes. The first purpose is very broad in scope. **Global social support,** encompassing the total amount of support available from the four sources, is applicable to any situation at any time. The narrower **functional social support** buffers the effects of stressors or stress in specific situations. When relied on in the wrong situation, functional social support is not very helpful. For example, if you lost your job, unemployment compensation (instrumental support) would be a better buffer than sympathy from a bartender. On the other hand, social companionship would be more helpful than instrumental support in coping with loneliness. After social support is engaged for one or both of these purposes, its effectiveness can be determined. If consolation or relief is not experienced, it may be that the type of support was inappropriate. The feedback loop in

---

[30] Social support is defined and described by John G. Brunn and Billy U. Philips, "Measuring Social Support: A Synthesis of Current Approaches," *Journal of Behavioral Medicine,* June 1984, pp. 151–69.

[31] Types of support are discussed by Sheldon Cohen and Thomas Ashby Wills, "Stress, Social Support, and the Buffering Hypothesis," *Psychological Bulletin,* September 1985, pp. 310–57.

■ **FIGURE 16–5**   A Flow Model of the Mechanisms of Social Support

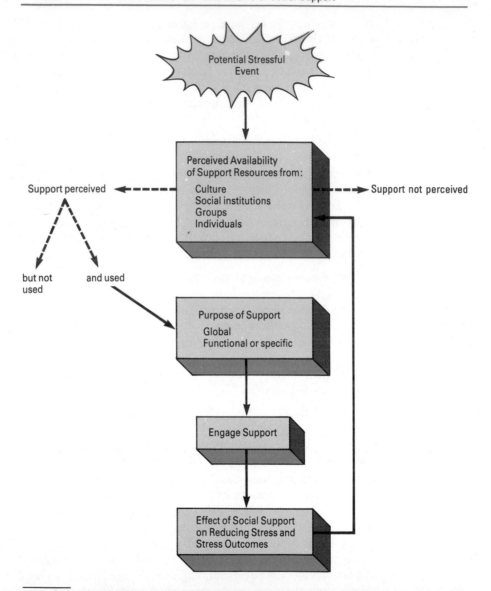

SOURCE: Portions adapted from Sheldon Cohen and Thomas Ashby Wills, "Stress, Social Support, and the Buffering Hypothesis," *Psychological Bulletin,* September 1985, pp. 310–57; and John G. Bruhn and Billy U. Philips, "Measuring Social Support: A Synthesis of Current Approaches," *Journal of Behavioral Medicine,* June 1984, pp. 151–69.

Figure 16–5, from effect of social support back to perceived availability, reflects the need to fall back on other sources of support when necessary.

Research Findings and Managerial Lessons.   Research shows that global social support is negatively related to mortality. In other words, people with low social support tend to die earlier than those with strong social support networks. Further, global support protects against depression, mental illness, pregnancy complications, and a variety of other ailments. In contrast, functional social support buffers stress only when a match exists between the type of support and the situation.[32] As suggested by the model of social support, global social support is positively related to the availability of support resources. That is, people who interact with a greater number of friends, family, or co-workers have a wider base of social support to draw upon during stressful periods.[33] Finally, gender does not influence the receipt of social support.[34]

One practical recommendation is to keep employees informed about external and internal social support systems. Internally, managers can use esteem and informational support while administering daily feedback and coaching. Further, participative management programs and company-sponsored activities that make employees feel they are an important part of an "extended family" can be rich sources of social support. Consider, for example, how Genentech Inc. launched its first major product in 1985:

> The fireworks bursting above San Francisco Bay were so brilliant that officials at nearby San Francisco International Airport suspended air traffic. Below, in tents pitched in Genentech Inc.'s bayside parking lot, 800 employees danced to a Dixieland band. The Food & Drug Administration had just approved Genentech's gene-spliced version of a vital human growth hormone, the first drug taken from discovery to market by a biotechnology company. The revelers whooped and cheered as the first shipment of Protropin was handed to a uniformed Federal Express driver.[35]

Employees need time and energy to adequately maintain their social relationships. If organizational demands are excessive, employees' social relationships and support networks will suffer, resulting in stress-related illness and decreased performance. Also, the positive effects of social support are enhanced when functional support is targeted precisely.

Coping

Coping is "the process of managing demands (external or internal) that are appraised as taxing or exceeding the resources of the person."[36] Because

---

[32] For a review of research findings, see both Cohen and Wills, "Stress, Social Support, and the Buffering Hypothesis"; and Ronald C. Kessler, Richard H. Price, and Camille B. Wortman, "Social Factors in Psychopathology: Stress, Social Support, and Coping Processes," in *Annual Review of Psychology*, ed. Mark R. Rosenzweig and Lyman W. Porter (Palo Alto, Calif.: Annual Reviews, Inc., 1985), pp. 531–72.

[33] For details, see Carolyn E. Cutrona, "Objective Determinants of Perceived Social Support," *Journal of Personality and Social Psychology*, February 1986, pp. 349–55; and Sandra L. Kirmeyer and Thung-Rung Lin, "Social Support: Its Relationship to Observed Communication with Peers and Superiors," *Academy of Management Journal*, March 1987, pp. 138–51.

[34] Gender differences in social support were examined by Marcelline R. Fusilier, Daniel C. Ganster, and Bronston T. Mayes, "The Social Support and Health Relationship: Is There a Gender Difference?" *Journal of Occupational Psychology*, June 1986, pp. 145–53; and Christine Dunkel-Schetter, Susan Folkman, and Richard S. Lazarus, "Correlates of Social Support Receipt," *Journal of Personality and Social Psychology*, July 1987, pp. 71–80.

[35] Joan O'C. Hamilton, "Biotech's First Superstar," *Business Week*, April 14, 1986, p. 68.

[36] Richard S. Lazarus and Susan Folkman, "Coping and Adaptation," in *Handbook of Behavioral Medicine*, ed. W. Doyle Gentry (New York: The Guilford Press, 1984), p. 283.

■ **FIGURE 16–6** A Model of the Coping Process

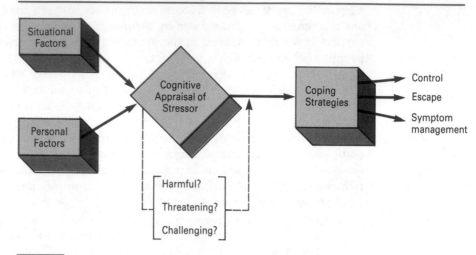

SOURCE: Based in part on Richard S. Lazarus and Susan Folkman, "Coping and Adaptation," in *Handbook of Behavioral Medicine*, ed. W. Doyle Gentry (New York: The Guilford Press, 1984), pp. 282–325.

effective coping helps reduce the impact of stressors and stress, your personal life and managerial skills can be enhanced by better understanding this process. Figure 16–6 depicts an instructive model of coping.

The coping process has three major components: (1) situational and personal factors, (2) cognitive appraisal of the stressor, and (3) coping strategies. As shown in Figure 16–6, both situational and personal factors influence appraisal of stressors. In turn, appraisal directly influences choice of coping strategy. Each of the major components of this model deserves a closer look.

Situational and Personal Factors.   Situational factors are environmental characteristics that affect how people interpret (appraise) stressors. For example, the ambiguity of a situation—such as walking down a dark street at night in an unfamiliar area—makes it difficult to determine whether a potentially dangerous situation exists. Ambiguity creates differences in how people appraise and subsequently cope with stressors. Other situational factors are the frequency of exposure to a stressor and social support networks.

Personal factors are personality traits and personal resources that affect the appraisal of stressors. For instance, because being tired or sick can distort the interpretation of stressors, an extremely tired individual may appraise an innocent question as a threat or challenge. Traits such as locus of control and Type A (recall the discussion in Chapter 3) have been found to affect the appraisal of stressors as have the personal resources of skills, energy, and stamina.[37]

---

[37] Ibid., pp. 282–325.

Cognitive Appraisal of Stressors. Cognitive appraisal reflects an individual's overall evaluation of a situation or stressor. This appraisal results in a categorization of the situation as either harmful, threatening, or challenging. It is important to understand the differences among these appraisals because they influence how people cope. " 'Harm' (including loss) represents damage already done; 'threat' involves the potential for harm; and 'challenge' means the potential for significant gain under difficult odds."[38] Coping with harm usually entails undoing or reinterpreting something that occurred in the past because the damage is already done. In contrast, threatening situations engage anticipatory coping. That is, people cope with threat by preparing for harm that may occur in the future. Challenge also activates anticipatory coping. In contrast with threat, an appraisal of challenge results in coping that focuses on what can be gained rather than what may be lost.[39]

Coping Strategies. Coping strategies are characterized by the specific behaviors and cognitions used to cope with a situation. People use three approaches to cope with stressors and stress (see Figure 16–6). The first, called a *control strategy*, consists of using behaviors and cognitions to directly anticipate or solve problems. A control strategy has a take-charge tone. A managerial example is to devote more time and energy to planning and scheduling. In contrast to tackling the problem head-on, an *escape strategy* amounts to running away. Behaviors and cognitions are used to avoid or escape situations. Individuals use this strategy when they passively accept stressful situations or avoid them by failing to confront the cause of stress (an obnoxious co-worker, for instance). Finally, a *symptom management strategy* consists of using methods such as relaxation, meditation, or medication (see Table 16–8) to manage the symptoms of occupational stress.[40]

Research Findings and Managerial Recommendations. A recent study of 109 managers and professionals examined the relationships among situational and personal factors, coping strategies, and organizational outcomes. The following findings emerged:

- A control strategy was less likely to be used when the work situation was characterized by role ambiguity.
- Symptom management strategies were used to cope with personal life changes.
- Type A's and people with a higher level of social support used a control strategy.
- The use of a control strategy led to lower anxiety, lower chances of quitting, and increased job satisfaction.

---

[38] Ibid., p. 289.

[39] Ibid., pp. 282–325.

[40] Descriptions of coping strategies are provided by Janina C. Latack, "Coping with Job Stress: Measures and Future Directions for Scale Development," *Journal of Applied Psychology,* August 1986, pp. 377–85.

■ **TABLE 16–8**   Performers Use a Drug to Cope with Anxiety of Stage Fright

Trembling hands, pounding heart, labored breathing and nausea are all in a day's work for performers who suffer from stage fright. So during the past few years, many of them have quietly begun popping a pill called propranolol.

The drug suppresses the symptoms of stage fright, but unlike such anti-anxiety aids as alcohol and tranquilizers, it rarely has side effects that can impair a performance. It isn't addictive and it is easy to get. . . .

"I've tried it and there's no question that it works," says Ivan Shulman, a surgeon and occasional oboist with the Los Angeles Philharmonic Orchestra. . . .

But Dr. Shulman and others familiar with the drug say its use among performers may be getting out of hand. Though no one knows how many people use it for stage fright, performers and doctors who treat performers estimate that between 20% and 50% of stage artists have tried the drug. . . .

For people with certain conditions, such as asthma, diabetes and heart problems, the drug can be dangerous or even fatal without a physician's care. Some physicians fret that those who use the drug often to lessen anxiety may become psychologically dependent on it.

SOURCE: Excerpted from David Stipp, "Heart Pill Used to Ease Anxiety of Stage Fright." Reprinted by the permission of *The Wall Street Journal,* Dow Jones & Company, Inc., October 2, 1985. All rights reserved.

- Both escape and symptom management strategies were related to psycho-somatic symptoms.[41]

In partial support of the coping model illustrated in Figure 16–6, several studies revealed that personal factors, appraisal, and coping all significantly predicted psychological symptoms of stress.[42]

The above results suggest that a control strategy is more likely to produce positive outcomes. Employees should be encouraged to use a control strategy when coping with occupational stress. Moreover, the coping model also can be used to help managers detect the reasons employees adopt an escape or symptom management strategy. The causes may be due to cognitive appraisals or situational and personal factors. Once identified, individualized training programs can be designed to help employees adopt an appropriate control strategy. The final section of this chapter discusses specific control techniques.

Hardiness

Suzanne Kobasa, a behavioral scientist, identified a collection of personality characteristics that neutralizes occupational stress. This collection of characteristics, referred to as **hardiness,** involves the ability to perceptually or behaviorally

---

[41] Ibid.

[42] See Susan Folkman and Richard S. Lazarus, "Coping as a Mediator of Emotion," *Journal of Personality and Social Psychology*, March 1988, pp. 466–75; and Carolyn M. Aldwin and Tracey A. Revenson, "Does Coping Help? A Reexamination of the Relation between Coping and Mental Health," *Journal of Personality and Social Psychology*, August 1987, pp. 337–48.

transform negative stressors into positive challenges. Hardiness embraces the personality dimensions of commitment, locus of control, and challenge.[43]

Personality Characteristics of Hardiness. *Commitment* reflects the extent to which an individual is involved in whatever he or she is doing. Committed people have a sense of purpose and do not give up under pressure because they tend to invest themselves in the situation.

As discussed in Chapter 3, individuals with an *internal locus of control* believe they can influence the events that affect their lives. People possessing this trait are more likely to foresee stressful events, thus reducing their exposure to anxiety-producing situations. Moreover, their perception of being in control leads "internals" to use proactive coping strategies.

Challenge is represented by the belief that change is a normal part of life. Thus, change is seen as an opportunity for growth and development rather than a threat to security.

Hardiness Research and Application. A five-year study of 259 managers from a public utility revealed that hardiness—commitment, locus of control, and challenge—reduced the probability of illness following exposure to stress.[44] Hardy undergraduate students were similarly found to display lower psychological distress than their less hardy counterparts. Hardy students also were more likely to interpret stressors as positive and controllable, supporting the idea that hardy individuals perceive situations in less stressful ways.[45]

One practical offshoot of this research is organizational training and development programs that strengthen the characteristics of commitment, personal control, and challenge. Because of cost limitations, however, it likely would be necessary to target key employees or those most susceptible to stress (e.g., air traffic controllers). The hardiness concept also meshes nicely with job design. Jobs can be redesigned to take fuller advantage of hardiness characteristics. As is true of orchestra conductors, for example, there appears to be a positive linkage between interesting and challenging jobs and longevity.

> Arturo Toscanini lived to be 90. Bruno Walter lived to the age of 85. Walter Damrosch lived to 88. And Leopold Stokowski married for the third time at the age of 63 to a woman 42 years younger than he was, and then went on to live to 95. One of the last things he did was sign a contract for work that he would have concluded on his 100th birthday. . . .

---

[43] This pioneering research is presented in Suzanne C. Kobasa, "Stressful Life Events, Personality, and Health: An Inquiry into Hardiness," *Journal of Personality and Social Psychology,* January 1979, pp. 1–11.

[44] See Suzanne C. Kobasa, Salvatore R. Maddi, and Stephen Kahn, "Hardiness and Health: A Prospective Study," *Journal of Personality and Social Psychology,* January 1982, pp. 168–77.

[45] Results are contained in Frederick Rhodewalt and Sjofn Agustsdottir, "On the Relationship of Hardiness to the Type A Behavior Pattern: Perception of Life Events versus Coping with Life Events," *Journal of Research in Personality,* June 1984, pp. 212–23. A review of research on hardiness is provided by Jay G. Hull, Ronald R. Van Treuren, and Suzanne Virnelli, "Hardiness and Health: A Critique and Alternative Approach," *Journal of Personality and Social Psychology,* September 1987, pp. 518–30.

[A professor of medicine named Donald] Atlas believed that the enviable longevity of conductors may be linked to their sense of work fulfillment. They enjoy a challenging profession in which they exercise almost complete control over their co-workers, and they often receive worldwide recognition and acclaim.[46]

A final application of the hardiness concept is as a diagnostic tool. Employees scoring low on hardiness would be good candidates for stress-reduction programs.

■ STRESS-REDUCTION TECHNIQUES

Organizations are increasingly implementing a variety of stress-reduction programs to help employees cope with stress. John Hancock, Texas Instruments, PepsiCo, and Adolph Coors Co. offer such programs.

John Hancock Mutual Life Insurance Co. holds three-hour sessions that teach deep muscle relaxation, among other things. More advanced sessions teach breathing exercises and prepare workers to devise a "coping plan." Texas Instruments' Project Recharge teaches relaxation, perception and coping skills. Several companies also have built gyms and wellness centers.

PepsiCo Inc.'s program includes a worker incentive that offers rebates on program fees for losing weight and keeping it off. It also offers discounts on sporting goods for workers who complete stress management courses. Adolph Coors Co. holds several stress classes, including one dealing with the stress of child-rearing.[47]

As these programs suggest, many stress-reduction techniques are available. The four most frequently used approaches are muscle relaxation, biofeedback, meditation, and cognitive restructuring. Each method involves a somewhat different way of coping with stress (see Table 16–9).

Muscle Relaxation

The common denominators of various muscle relaxation techniques are slow and deep breathing, a conscious effort to relieve muscle tension, and an altered state of consciousness. Among the variety of techniques available, progressive relaxation is probably most frequently used. It consists of repeatedly tensing and relaxing muscles beginning at the feet and progressing to the face. Relaxation is achieved by concentrating on the warmth and calmness associated with relaxed muscles. Take a few moments now to try this technique, as described below.

Sitting in a chair, start by taking slow, deep breaths. Inhale through your nose and exhale through your mouth. Continue until you feel calm. Begin

---

[46] "The Stokowski Advantage," *University of California, Berkeley Wellness Letter,* January 1985, p. 1.

[47] "Labor Letter: A Special News Report on People and Their Jobs in Offices, Fields and Factories," *The Wall Street Journal,* July 30, 1985, p. 1.

■ **TABLE 16–9** Stress-Reduction Techniques

Technique	Descriptions	Assessment
Muscle relaxation	Uses slow deep breathing, systematic muscle tension reduction, and an altered state of consciousness to reduce stress.	Inexpensive and easy to use. May require a trained professional to implement.
Biofeedback	A machine is used to train people to detect muscular tension. Muscle relaxation is then used to alleviate this symptom of stress.	Expensive due to costs of equipment. However, equipment can be used to evaluate effectiveness of other stress-reduction programs.
Meditation	The relaxation response is activated by redirecting one's thoughts away from oneself. A four-step procedure is used.	Least expensive, simple to implement, and can be practiced almost anywhere.
Cognitive restructuring	Irrational or maladaptive thoughts are identified and replaced with those that are rational or logical.	Expensive because it requires a trained psychologist or counselor.
Holistic wellness	A broad, interdisciplinary approach that goes beyond stress reduction by advocating that people strive for personal wellness in all aspects of their lives.	Involves inexpensive but often behaviorally-difficult lifestyle changes.

progressive relaxation by pointing your toes toward the ceiling for 10 seconds. Concentrate on the tension within your calves and feet. Now return your toes to a normal position and focus on the relaxed state of your legs and feet. (Your goal is to experience this feeling all over your body.) Tense and relax your feet for 10 seconds one more time. Moving to your calves, and continuing all the way to the muscles in your face, tense one major muscle at a time for 10 seconds, and then let it relax. Do this twice for each muscle before moving to another one. You should feel totally relaxed upon completing this routine.

Biofeedback

A biofeedback machine is used to train people to detect and control stress-related symptoms such as tense muscles and elevated blood pressure. The machine translates unconscious bodily signs into a recognizable cue (flashing light or beeper). Muscle relaxation and meditative techniques are then used to alleviate the underlying stress. The person learns to recognize bodily tension without the aid of the machine. In turn, according to the advocates of biofeedback, this awareness helps the person proactively cope with stress.

Meditation

Meditation activates a relaxation response by redirecting one's thoughts away from oneself. The **relaxation response** is the physiological and psychological opposite of the fight-or-flight stress response. Importantly, however, the relaxation response must be learned and consciously activated, whereas the stress response is automatically engaged. Herbert Benson, a Harvard medical doctor, analyzed many meditation programs and derived a four-step relaxation response. The four steps are (1) find a *quiet environment,* (2) use a *mental device* like a peaceful word or pleasant image to shift the mind from externally oriented thoughts, (3) disregard distracting thoughts by relying on a *passive attitude*, and (4) assume a *comfortable position*—preferably sitting erect—to avoid undue muscular tension or going to sleep. Benson emphasizes that the most important factor is a passive attitude. Maximum benefits supposedly are obtained by following this procedure once or twice a day for 10 to 20 minutes, preferably just before breakfast and dinner.[48]

Cognitive Restructuring

A two-step procedure is followed. First, irrational or maladaptive thought processes that create stress are identified. For example, Type A individuals may believe they must be successful at everything they do. The second step consists of replacing these irrational thoughts with more rational or reasonable ones. Perceived failure would create stress for the Type A person. Cognitive restructuring would alleviate stress by encouraging the person to adopt a more reasonable belief about the outcomes associated with failure. For instance, the person might be encouraged to adopt the belief that isolated failure does not mean he or she is a bad person or a loser.

Effectiveness of Stress-Reduction Techniques

An OB researcher reviewed 13 field studies and concluded that muscle relaxation, biofeedback, meditation, and cognitive restructuring all helped employees cope with occupational stress. Unfortunately, stress reductions did not appear to last long.[49] Two additional studies examined the ability of muscle relaxation and cognitive restructuring to reduce either emotional exhaustion, personal strain, absenteeism, or anxiety. The following results were obtained:

- Emotional exhaustion, personal strain, and anxiety were reduced.
- Both techniques were equally effective.
- Absenteeism was not affected.
- Reductions in anxiety persisted for at least a month after the intervention.[50]

Some researchers advise organizations not to implement these stress-reduction programs despite their positive outcomes. They rationalize that these techniques relieve *symptoms* of stress rather than eliminate stressors themselves.[51] Thus,

---

[48] See Herbert Benson, *The Relaxation Response* (New York: William Morrow and Co., 1975).

[49] These studies are summarized by Lawrence R. Murphy, "Occupational Stress Management: A Review and Appraisal," *Journal of Occupational Psychology*, March 1984, pp. 1–15.

[50] See Nancy C. Higgins, "Occupational Stress and Working Women: The Effectiveness of Two Stress Reduction Programs," *Journal of Vocational Behavior*, August 1986, pp. 66–78; and Robin L. Rose and John F. Veiga, "Assessing the Sustained Effects of a Stress Management Intervention on Anxiety and Locus of Control," *Academy of Management Journal*, March 1984, pp. 190–98.

[51] Criticisms of stress-reduction programs are summarized by Daniel C. Ganster, Bronston T. Mayes, Wesley E. Sime, and Gerald D. Tharp, "Managing Organizational Stress: A Field Experiment," *Journal of Applied Psychology*, October 1982, pp. 533–42.

■ **TABLE 16–10** Tenneco Develops a Successful Fitness Program

The two-story, 100,000-square-foot facility in Houston, where Tenneco . . . is headquartered, is open exclusively to Tenneco employes—everyone from mailroom clerk to board chairman. The center, which cost $11 million, includes indoor gardens drip-watered from above to simulate rainfall, employe and executive dining areas, four racquetball courts, dressing rooms, Nautilus exercise equipment, a sauna and whirlpool bath, and a conference and training center for 264 people. A five-mile, glass arcade jogging track belts the entire facility. There is an executive chef and a health staff that includes a doctor, nurse, physiologist and eight fitness trainers.

And there is the computer. Entering the center, a Tenneco employe inserts a metal card into a computer. When the employe finishes a workout, he reinserts the card and punches a description of what has been done. The computer prepares a "fitness profile" that includes how many calories have been burned off in exercise and how far the employe has to go in his own specially designed program. Every month the employe receives a printout of progress to date. If there is too little use of the fitness center, workout privileges may be lifted.

SOURCE: Excerpted from Bob Gatty, "How Fitness Works Out." Reprinted by permission from *Nation's Business*, July 1985. Copyright 1985, U.S. Chamber of Commerce.

they conclude that organizations are using a "Band-Aid" approach to stress reduction. A holistic approach has subsequently been offered as a more proactive and enduring solution.

A Holistic Wellness Model

A **holistic wellness approach** encompasses but goes beyond stress reduction by advocating that individuals strive for "a harmonious and productive balance of physical, mental, and social well-being brought about by the acceptance of one's personal responsibility for developing and adhering to a health promotion program."[52] Five dimensions of a holistic wellness approach are:

1. *Self-responsibility:* Take personal responsibility for your wellness (e.g., quit smoking, moderate your intake of alcohol, wear your seat belt, and so on).

2. *Nutritional awareness:* Because we are what we eat, try to increase your consumption of foods high in fiber, vitamins, and nutrients—such as fresh fruits and vegetables, poultry, and fish—while decreasing those high in sugar and fat.

3. *Stress reduction and relaxation:* Use the techniques just discussed to relax and reduce the symptoms of stress.

---

[52] Robert Kreitner, "Personal Wellness: It's Just Good Business," *Business Horizons*, May–June 1982, p. 28.

■ **TABLE 16–11** Lifestyle Activities Leading to Personal Wellness

Monitor your stress symptoms.

Identify and neutralize or limit your exposure to major stressors.

Capitalize on your strengths and work on your limitations.

Establish and periodically review your priorities.

Cultivate a social support network.

Adopt a philosophical outlook to put things into proper perspective (be able to laugh at yourself).

Build flexibility and harmony into your work and lifestyle.

Make time for exercise and hobbies.

Learn to relax.

Eat nutritionally.

Avoid alcohol and substance abuse.

Don't smoke.

4. *Physical fitness:* Exercise to maintain strength, flexibility, endurance, and a healthy body weight. More than 50,000 U.S. companies have established fitness programs for employees (see Table 16–10).[53]

5. *Environmental sensitivity:* Be aware of your environment and use a "control" coping strategy to identify and eliminate stressors and stress.[54]

In conclusion, advocates say that both your personal and professional life can be enriched by adopting a holistic approach to wellness. Table 16–11 lists practical tips to get headed in the right direction.

SUMMARY OF KEY CONCEPTS

A. Stress is an adaptive response to environmental demands or stressors that involves a fight-or-flight response. This response creates hormonal changes that mobilize the body for extraordinary demands.

B. Matteson and Ivancevich's model of occupational stress indicates that stress is caused by four sets of stressors: individual level, group level, organizational level, and extraorganizational. In turn, stress has behavioral, cognitive, and physiological outcomes. Several individual differences moderate relationships between stressors, stress, and outcomes.

C. Stressful life events are changes that disrupt an individual's lifestyle and social relationships. Holmes and Rahe developed the Schedule of Recent Experiences (SRE) to assess an individual's cumulative stressful life

---

[53] An informative overview of these programs is provided in Loren E. Falkenberg, "Employee Fitness Programs: Their Impact on the Employee and the Organization," *Academy of Management Review,* July 1987, pp. 511–22; and Peter Conrad, "Who Comes to Work-Site Wellness Programs? A Preliminary Review," *Journal of Occupational Medicine,* April 1987, pp. 317–20.

[54] See the discussion by Judith A. Webster and Vicki A. Moss, "To Your Health," *Nation's Business,* March 1986, p. 65.

events. A positive relationship exists between the SRE and illness. Uncontrollable events that are negative create the most stress.

D. Burnout and employee substance abuse are troublesome stress-related outcomes. Burnout is common among members of helping professions and is characterized by emotional exhaustion and negative attitudes. Employee substance abuse occurs when the use of alcohol or drugs hurts an individual's job performance. Corporations attack the problem through sting operations, drug testing, and rehabilitation programs.

E. Social support, an important moderator of relationships between stressors, stress, and outcomes, represents the amount of perceived helpfulness derived from social relationships. Cultural norms, social institutions, groups, and individuals are sources of social support. These sources provide four types of support: esteem, informational, social companionship, and instrumental.

F. Coping is the managing of stressors and stress. Coping is directly affected by the cognitive appraisal of stressors, which in turn is influenced by situational and personal factors. People cope by using control, escape, or symptom management strategies. A control strategy appears to produce the most beneficial results.

G. Hardiness is a collection of personality characteristics that neutralizes stress. It includes the characteristics of commitment, locus of control, and challenge.

H. Muscle relaxation, biofeedback, meditation, and cognitive restructuring are predominant stress-reduction techniques. Slow and deep breathing, a conscious effort to relieve muscle tension, and altered consciousness are common denominators of muscle relaxation. Biofeedback relies on a machine to train people to detect bodily signs of stress. This awareness facilitates proactive coping with stressors. Meditation activates the relaxation response by redirecting one's thoughts away from oneself. Cognitive restructuring entails identifying irrational or maladaptive thoughts and replacing them with rational or logical thoughts.

I. A holistic wellness approach to stress reduction advocates that people accept personal responsibility for their physical, mental, and social well-being.

KEY TERMS

fight-or-flight response	social support
stress	global social support
stressors	functional social support
stressful life events	coping
burnout	hardiness
buffers	relaxation response
employee substance abuse	holistic wellness approach

DISCUSSION QUESTIONS

1. What are the key stressors in your life? Which ones are under your control?

2. Describe the behavioral and physiological symptoms you typically experience when under stress?

3. Why do uncontrollable events lead to more stress than controllable events? How can the SRE be used to identify uncontrollable stressors?

4. Have you ever felt burned out? Describe your feelings during this period and explain the events that culminated in this stress outcome.

5. How would you respond to a president of a small firm who asked you to recommend a method for reducing employee substance abuse?

6. From what sources do you derive social support? What type of social support do you find most useful in your role as a student?

7. Which coping strategies have you used over the last three months? How did you happen to choose one strategy over the others?

8. Do you think you have a hardy personality? Explain.

9. Do you currently follow a holistic wellness approach to stress reduction? What improvements in your lifestyle do you need to make?

10. What is the most valuable lesson you learned from this chapter about stress? Explain.

BACK TO THE OPENING CASE

Now that you have read Chapter 16, you should be able to answer the following questions about the paramedic case:

1. What individual level, group level, organizational level, and extra-organizational stressors are paramedics exposed to?

2. Which types of stress outcomes do paramedics experience?

3. Which unique stressors are instrumental in causing burnout among paramedics? Explain.

4. How might a paramedic use a control coping strategy to reduce occupational stress?

EXERCISE 16

Objectives

1. To determine the extent to which you are burned out.
2. To determine if your burnout scores are predictive of burnout outcomes.
3. To identify specific stressors that affect your level of burnout.

Introduction

An OB researcher named Christina Maslach developed a self-report scale measuring burnout. This scale assesses burnout in terms of three phases: depersonalization, personal accomplishment, and emotional exhaustion. To determine if you suffer from burnout in any of these phases, we would like you to complete an abbreviated version of this scale. Moreover, because burnout has been found to influence a variety of behavioral outcomes, we also want to determine how well burnout predicts three important outcomes.

Instructions

To assess your level of burnout, complete the following 18 questions developed by Maslach.[55] Each question asks you to indicate how frequently you experience a particular feeling or attitude. If you are presently working, use your job as the frame of reference for answering the questions. If you are a full-time student, use your role as a student as your frame of reference. After you have completed the 18 questions, refer to the scoring key and follow its directions. Remember, there are no right or wrong answers. Indicate your answer by circling one number from the following scale:

1 = A few times a year
2 = Monthly
3 = A few times a month
4 = Every week
5 = A few times a week
6 = Every day

Burnout Inventory

1. I've become more callous toward people since I took this job	1 2 3 4 5 6
2. I worry that this job is hardening me emotionally	1 2 3 4 5 6
3. I don't really care what happens to some of the people who need my help	1 2 3 4 5 6
4. I feel that people who need my help blame me for some of their problems	1 2 3 4 5 6
5. I deal very effectively with the problems of those people who need my help	1 2 3 4 5 6
6. I feel I'm positively influencing other people's lives through my work	1 2 3 4 5 6
7. I feel very energetic	1 2 3 4 5 6
8. I can easily create a relaxed atmosphere with those people who need my help	1 2 3 4 5 6
9. I feel exhilarated after working closely with those who need my help	1 2 3 4 5 6
10. I have accomplished many worthwhile things in this job	1 2 3 4 5 6
11. In my work, I deal with emotional problems very calmly	1 2 3 4 5 6
12. I feel emotionally drained from my work	1 2 3 4 5 6
13. I feel used up at the end of the workday	1 2 3 4 5 6
14. I feel fatigued when I get up in the morning	1 2 3 4 5 6
15. I feel frustrated by my job	1 2 3 4 5 6
16. I feel I'm working too hard on my job	1 2 3 4 5 6
17. Working with people directly puts too much stress on me	1 2 3 4 5 6
18. I feel like I'm at the end of my rope	1 2 3 4 5 6

[55] Adapted from Maslach and Jackson, "The Measurement of Experienced Burnout."

Scoring

Compute the average of those items measuring each phase of burnout.

Depersonalization (questions 1–4)   _____
Personal Accomplishment (questions 5–11)   _____
Emotional Exhaustion (questions 12–18)   _____

Assessing Burnout Outcomes

1. How many times were you absent from work over the last three months (indicate the number of absences from classes last semester if using the student role)?
   _____ absences
2. How satisfied are you with your job (or role as a student)? Circle one.
   Very dissatisfied   Dissatisfied   Neutral   Satisfied   Very Satisfied
3. Do you have trouble sleeping? Circle one.
   Yes   No

Questions for Consideration/Class Discussion

1. To what extent are you burned out in terms of depersonalization and emotional exhaustion?
   Low = 1–2.99   Moderate = 3–4.99   High = 5 or above
2. To what extent are you burned out in terms of personal accomplishment?
   Low = 5 or above   Moderate = 3–4.99   High = 1–2.99
3. How well do your burnout scores predict your burnout outcomes?
4. Do your burnout scores suggest that burnout follows a sequence going from depersonalization, to feeling a lack of personal accomplishment, to emotional exhaustion? Explain.
5. Which of the unique burnout stressors illustrated in Figure 16–4 are affecting your level of burnout?

PART FIVE

Understanding and Managing the Evolving Organization

EXTERNAL ENVIRONMENT

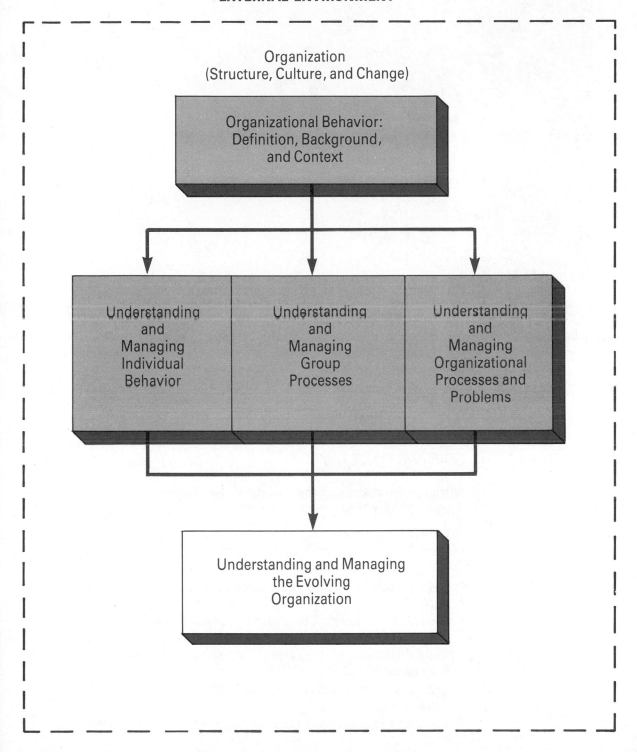

Organization
(Structure, Culture, and Change)

Organizational Behavior:
Definition, Background,
and Context

Understanding
and
Managing
Individual
Behavior

Understanding
and
Managing
Group
Processes

Understanding
and
Managing
Organizational
Processes and
Problems

Understanding and Managing
the Evolving
Organization

Chapter **17**

Organizations: Life Cycles, Effectiveness, and Design

LEARNING OBJECTIVES

When you finish studying the material in this chapter,
you should be able to:

- Describe the four characteristics common to all organizations.
- Contrast the following organizational metaphors: military/mechanical, biological, and cognitive systems.
- Identify and briefly explain the three stages of the organizational life cycle.
- Describe the four generic organizational effectiveness criteria and explain why a multidimensional approach is recommended.
- Explain the relationship between differentiation and integration in effective organizations.
- Discuss Burns and Stalker's findings regarding mechanistic and organic organizations.
- Explain the relationship between strategic choice and organization structure.
- Identify and briefly describe the five organization design configurations in Mintzberg's typology.

How the U.S. Air Force's Tactical Air Command Dethroned Its Hangar Queens

One of the Air Force's Red Flag training exercises . . . [is] a mock war that rages year-round over several million acres of Nevada desert. On one side are the men and planes of the Tactical Air Command (TAC), which is charged with defending American interests in the skies anywhere in the world. On the other, squadrons of F-5 Tigers sporting Warsaw Pact paint jobs, flown by American pilots who have been specially trained in Soviet air tactics.

On this day, the good guys win. But it wasn't always that way. A decade ago, when Red Flag was just beginning, the Tactical Air Command was in a sorry state. At any one time, half of the planes in its $25 billion fleet were not battle ready and more than 220 airplanes were classified as "hangar queens"—grounded at least three weeks for lack of spare parts or maintenance. Because of equipment problems, TAC pilots—trained at a cost of $1 million each—lacked the flying time necessary to keep their skills sharp, and the best of them were deserting the Air Force in droves. So, too, were mechanics and technicians, frustrated in their jobs and disappointed by the deplorable living conditions at almost every TAC installation. Perhaps worst of all was the soaring accident rate that resulted in tragic deaths, unnecessary loss of expensive airplanes, and embarrassment for the service.

Into this mess in 1978 stepped General W. L. (Bill) Creech. As the new commander sized up his domain from TAC headquarters at Langley Air Force Base, in Virginia, it looked to him like a potential national security disaster. "The U.S. military was coming apart," is how he remembers it. "It was worse than you think."

This is the remarkable story of how, in six and a half years, Creech turned his command into one of the bright stars of the defense firmament. TAC fighters today are in superb condition, its pilots fully trained, its installations sparkling. The number of hangar queens has declined from 200 to just a handful. Reenlistment rates are way up. And a dramatic reduction in the crash rate has saved dozens of lives and billions of dollars' worth of airplanes.

Perhaps most remarkable, Creech was able to work his magic with no more money, no more planes, and no more personnel than were available when he started. Creech's strategy was to force a bottoms-up management style on an organization that had always been strictly top-down—pushing responsibility and authority down into the tiniest crevices of his command. And so stunning was his execution that the Pentagon has now begun to apply his techniques throughout the U.S. military. . . .

Any chief executive officer would have been daunted by the challenge of simply running so sprawling an operation, let alone reviving it. At the time that Creech settled into his post, he was in charge of 115,000 full-time employees working at 150 installations around the world—plus another 65,000 men and women trained and on call. The assets under his control were valued at more than $40 billion, including some 3,800 aircraft—more than twice as many as all U.S. airlines combined. He had a discretionary budget of $1.4 billion, with billions more reserved for fuel and spare parts. . . .

By the time Creech put on his fourth star and took command of TAC, Robert McNamara was long gone from Defense, but his dogma of centralized management and command had become inviolate within the Pentagon. Only it wasn't working—not at TAC anyway. Granted, some duplication had been eliminated, along with some jobs. But the cost had been high: the American military command had been robbed of much of its vigor. Innovation and initiative were discouraged, and people were dehumanized, thought of as mere costs of production, like so many bullets or mess kits.

It was not that Creech was unwilling to use quantitative means by which to judge TAC's performance. On the contrary, taking stock of the crucial measurement of production—the number of training sorties flown—Creech found that TAC had been losing ground at the rate of 8% each year since 1969. And to deal with the problem, he proposed nothing less than a radical restructuring of his command, one that would send authority down the ranks along with responsibility for meeting clear and simple goals. . . .

It all added up to a lackluster fighter force, beset with apathy, sagging morale, and horrifying statistics. Only 20% of "broken" planes were getting repaired in a typical eight-hour shift. Pilots who needed a minimum of 15 hours of flying time a month were getting 10 or less. The average plane, which had flown 23 sorties a month in 1969, was flying only 11 by 1978. And for every 100,000 hours flown, seven planes were crashing. Investigators blamed many of the crashes on faulty maintenance.

"One reason we were doing so poorly is because we were so good at centralization," says Creech. "It was a highly matrixed system, where the functional specialists only loosely worked for the person in charge of getting the job done. The supervisor was just a voice on the radio. Nobody really cared."

Creech's first move was to structure his command around a smaller and more manageable unit of organization—the squadron, which consists of 24 planes, rather than the wing, which is three times the size. Starting on a trial basis at a few installations, he created squadron repair teams, drawing technicians from each of the maintenance disciplines. The team would work only on their own squadron's aircraft. And instead of operating out of rear-area dispatching locations, Creech ordered them to move right down to the flight lines. . . .

The idea was to give each operational squadron and its companion maintenance team a common identity, purpose, and spirit. The maintenance people, who had been faceless cogs in a 2,000-person wing operation, found themselves sporting the prestigious flight squadron patches on their fatigues. They now belonged to the Buccaneers or the Black Falcons. They began wearing squadron baseball caps.

With the crew chiefs, the general practitioners of the maintenance staffs, this sense of identity was further reinforced. Where before they had worked on any jet in the wing, now they were assigned airplanes of their very own. They painted their names on the sides, just as pilots did. And all of a sudden, a 23-year-old buck sergeant making $15,000 a year was in charge—yes, in charge—of a $27 million jet. . . .

In Creech's decentralized TAC, squadron commanders were given a sortie goal and set free to design their own flying schedules. And they were given some added incentive to meet their targets: if a squadron met its monthly goal early, Creech decreed, then the entire squadron, from pilots to maintenance techs, could take an extra three-day weekend.

Mind you, meeting these goals wasn't easy. These were highly sophisticated jets with hundreds of components that often require repair or replacement. And the training hops were no snaps for fliers, either. An F-16 pilot, for instance, had to master precision bombing, air-to-air combat with complicated missiles systems, and the delicate maneuvers required for tactical nuclear strikes, should they ever be required. Still, the incentive plan worked splendidly. Virtually every squadron in TAC now averages 10 extra three-day weekends a year. . . .

By the time General Creech left TAC, 85% of his airplanes were rated as mission capable, and jets were averaging 21 sorties a month, with 29 hours in the air. In wartime, TAC was capable of launching 6,000 sorties a day, double what it had been when he arrived at Langley. In peacetime, the crash rate had dropped from one for every 13,000 flying hours to one for every 50,000—and crashes traced to faulty maintenance nearly vanished.

TAC, under Creech, had gone from the Air Force's worst command to its best. For much of the time, it had been a battle, and heads had rolled. The lazy and the incompetent, who had found numerous hiding places in a centralized structure, were smoked out when maintenance operations moved to the flight line and squadrons were held accountable for their performance. Some had to leave. But many more decided to stay. In 1983, two-thirds of the first-term mechanics decided to reenlist, or nearly double the rate of 1977, the year before Creech took command. Second-termer retention rates went from 68% to 85% over the same period. And some of the older technicians found they liked Creech's program so much that they recalled retirement papers to see it through.

For Discussion

What was the key to Creech's successful reorganization of TAC?

SOURCE: Excerpted from Jay Finegan, "Four-Star Management," pp. 42–44, 46, 48, 50–51. Reprinted with permission, INC. magazine, January 1987. Copyright © 1987 by INC. Publishing Company, 38 Commercial Wharf, Boston, MA 02110.

■ Additional discussion questions linking this case with the following material appear at the end of this chapter.

Virtually every aspect of life is affected at least indirectly by some type of organization. We look to organizations to feed, clothe, house, educate, and employ us. Organizations attend to our needs for entertainment, police and fire protection, insurance, recreation, national security, transportation, news and information, legal assistance, and health care. Many of these organizations seek a profit, others do not. Some are extremely large, others are tiny "mom-and-pop" operations. Despite this mind-boggling diversity, modern organizations have much in common. Organization theorists have categorized and analyzed organizations and their environments into meaningful patterns and contingencies. Since organizations are the primary context for organizational behavior, present and future managers need to be familiar with the basics of organization theory, research, and design.

This chapter explores the structural determinants and consequences of modern organizations. We begin by defining the term *organization,* discussing organization charts, and reviewing the evolution of organizational metaphors. Contemporary ideas about organizational life cycles and organizational effectiveness are then examined. Finally, the contingency approach to organization design is introduced and discussed as a context for examining specific design configurations.

■ DEFINING AND CHARTING ORGANIZATIONS

As a necessary background for this chapter, we need to formally define the term *organization* and clarify the meaning of organization charts.

What Is an Organization?

According to Chester I. Barnard's classic definition, an **organization** is "a system of consciously coordinated activities or forces of two or more persons."[1] Embodied in the *conscious coordination* aspect of this definition are four common denominators of all organizations: coordination of effort, a common goal, division of labor, and a hierarchy of authority[2] (see Figure 17–1). Organization theorists refer to these factors as the organization's *structure.*

Coordination of effort is achieved through formulation and enforcement of policies, rules, and regulations. Division of labor occurs when the common goal is pursued by individuals performing separate but related tasks. The hierarchy of authority, also called the chain of command, is a control mechanism dedicated to making sure the right people do the right things at the right time. Historically, managers have maintained the integrity of the hierarchy of authority by adhering to the unity of command principle. The **unity of command principle** specifies that each employee should report to only one manager. Otherwise, the argument goes, inefficiency would prevail because of conflicting orders and lack of personal accountability. Managers in the hierarchy of authority also administer rewards and punishments. When the four factors in Figure 17–1 operate in concert, the dynamic entity called an organization exists.

Organization Charts

An **organization chart** is a graphic representation of formal authority and division of labor relationships. To the casual observer, the term *organization chart* means the family tree-like pattern of boxes and lines posted on workplace walls. Within each box one usually finds the names and titles of current position holders. To organization theorists, however, organization charts reveal much more. The partial organization chart in Figure 17–2 reveals four basic dimensions

---

[1] Chester I. Barnard, *The Functions of the Executive* (Cambridge, Mass.: Harvard University Press, 1938), p. 73.

[2] Drawn from Edgar H. Schein, *Organizational Psychology,* 3rd ed. (Englewood Cliffs, N.J.: Prentice-Hall, 1980), pp. 12–15.

■ **FIGURE 17–1** Four Characteristics Common to All Organizations

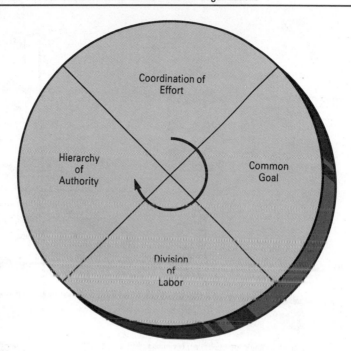

of organizational structure: (1) hierarchy of authority (who reports to whom), (2) division of labor, (3) spans of control, and (4) line and staff positions.

Hierarchy of Authority.   As Figure 17–2 illustrates, there is an unmistakable hierarchy of authority. Working from bottom to top, the nine directors report to the two executive directors who report to the president who reports to the chief executive officer. Ultimately, the chief executive officer answers to the hospital's board of directors. The chart in Figure 17–2 shows strict unity of command up and down the line. A formal hierarchy of authority also delineates the official communication network.

Division of Labor.   In addition to showing the chain of command, the sample organization chart indicates extensive division of labor. Immediately below the hospital's president, one executive director is responsible for general administration while another is responsible for medical affairs. Each of these two specialties is further subdivided as indicated by the next layer of positions. At each successively lower level in the organization, jobs become more specialized.

Spans of Control.   The term **span of control** refers to the number of people reporting directly to a given manager.[3] Spans of control can range from narrow to wide. For example, the president in Figure 17–2 has a narrow span of

---

[3] For an excellent overview of the span of control concept, see David D. Van Fleet and Arthur G. Bedeian, "A History of the Span of Management," *Academy of Management Review,* July 1977, pp. 356–72.

■ **FIGURE 17-2** Sample Organization Chart for a Hospital (Executive and director levels only)

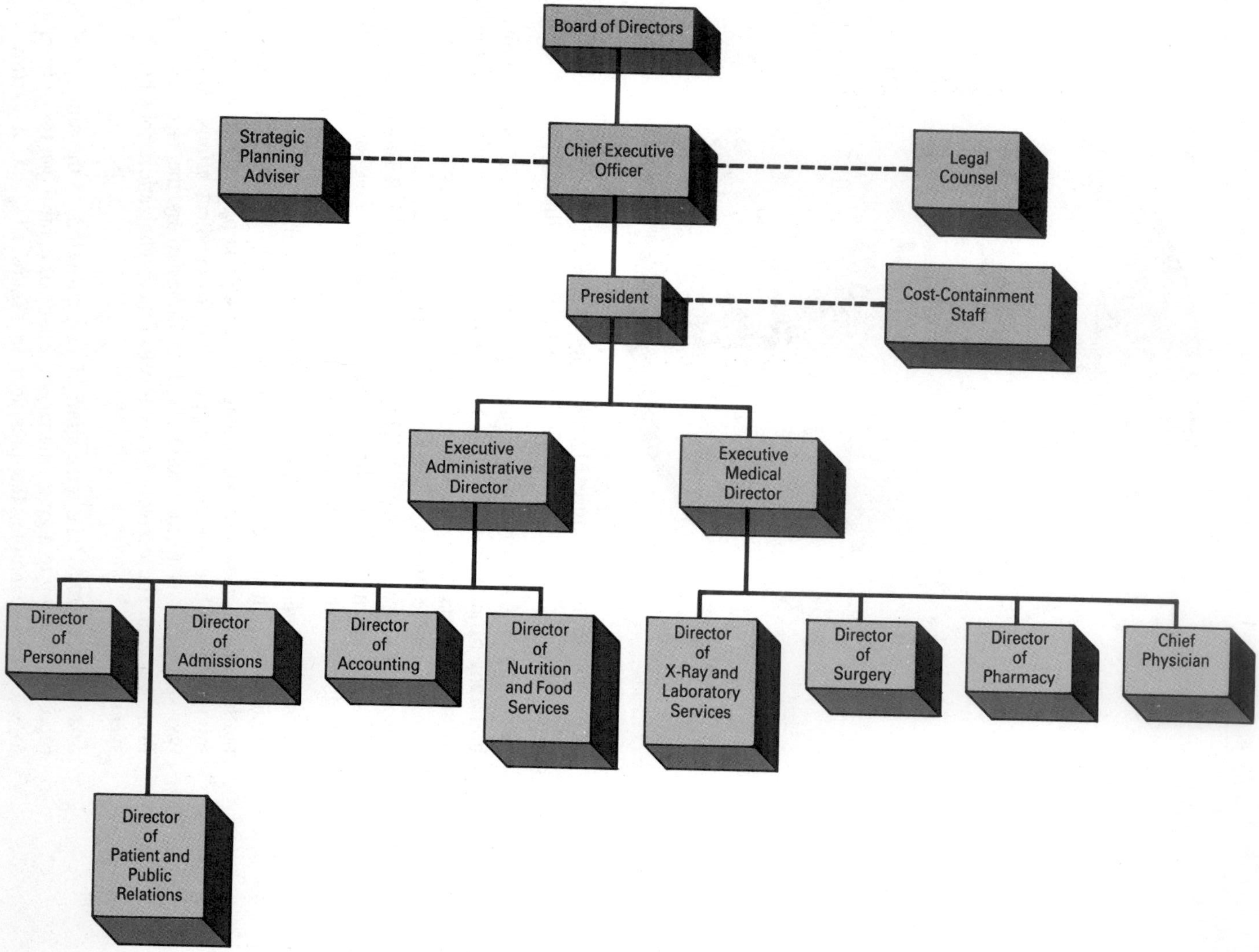

control of two. (Staff assistants usually are not included in a manager's span of control.) The executive administrative director in Figure 17–2 has a wider span of control of five. Spans of control exceeding 30 can be found in assembly-line operations where machine-paced and repetitive work substitutes for close supervision. Historically, spans of five to six were considered best. Despite years of debate, organization theorists have not arrived at a consensus regarding the ideal span of control.

Generally, the narrower the span of control, the closer the supervision and the higher the administrative costs due to a higher manager-to-worker ratio. Recent emphasis on leanness and administrative efficiency dictates spans of control as wide as possible but guarding against inadequate supervision and lack of coordination. Wider spans also complement the trend toward greater worker autonomy.

Line and Staff Positions.   The organization chart in Figure 17–2 also distinguishes between line and staff positions. Line managers such as the president, the two executive directors, and the various directors occupy formal decision-making positions within the chain of command. Line positions generally are connected by solid lines on organization charts. Dotted lines indicate staff relationships. Staff personnel do background research and provide technical advice and recommendations to their line managers who have the authority to make decisions. For example, the cost-containment specialists in the sample organization chart merely advise the president on relevant matters. Apart from supervising the work of their own staff assistants, they have no line authority over other organizational members.

■ THE EVOLUTION OF ORGANIZATIONAL METAPHORS

The complexity of modern organizations makes them somewhat difficult to describe. Consequently, organization theorists have resorted to the use of metaphors. A metaphor is a figure of speech that characterizes one object in terms of another object. For example, when we hear that someone has "put down roots" we know they have found a place to stay, like a tree taking root in fertile ground. Good metaphors help us comprehend complicated things by describing them in everyday terms. OB scholar Kim Cameron sums up the value of organizational metaphors as follows: "Each time a new metaphor is used, certain aspects of organizational phenomena are uncovered that were not evident with other metaphors. In fact, the usefulness of metaphors lies in their possession of some degree of falsehood so that new images and associations emerge."[4]

Three organizational metaphors that have evolved over the years characterize organizations alternatively as military/mechanical systems, biological systems, and cognitive systems. These three metaphors can be plotted on a continuum

---

[4] Kim S. Cameron, "Effectiveness as Paradox: Consensus and Conflict in Conceptions of Organizational Effectiveness," *Management Science*, May 1986, pp. 540–41.

■ **FIGURE 17–3** Three Contrasting Organizational Metaphors

	Closed Systems		Open Systems	
	Military/Mechanical Model (bureaucracy)	**Biological Model (resource transformation system)**	**Cognitive Model (interpretation and meaning system)**	
Metaphorical comparison:	Precision military unit/well-oiled machine	Human body	Human mind	
Assumption about organization's environment:	Predictable (controllable impacts)	Uncertain (filled with surprises)	Uncertain and ambiguous	
Organization's primary goal:	Maximum economic efficiency through rigorous planning and control	Survival through adaptation to environmental constraints and opportunities	Growth and survival through environmental scanning, interpretation, and learning	

ranging from simple closed systems to complex open systems (see Figure 17–3). We need to clarify the important distinction between closed and open systems before exploring the metaphors.

Closed versus Open Systems

A **closed system** is said to be a self-sufficient entity. It is "closed" to the surrounding environment. In contrast, an **open system** depends on constant interaction with the environment for survival. The distinction between closed and open systems is a matter of degree. Since every worldly system is partly closed and partly open, the key question is: How great a role does the environment play in the functioning of the system? For instance, a battery-powered clock is a relatively closed system. Once the battery is inserted, the clock performs its time-keeping function hour after hour until the battery goes dead. The human body, on the other hand, is a highly open system because it requires a constant supply of life-sustaining oxygen from the environment. Nutrients also are imported from the environment. Open systems are capable of self-correction, adaptation, and growth thanks to characteristics such as homeostasis and feedback control, as discussed in Chapters 5 and 7.

The traditional military/mechanical metaphor is a closed system model because it largely ignores environmental influences. It gives the impression that organizations are self-sufficient entities. Conversely, the biological and cognitive metaphors emphasize interaction between organizations and their environments. These newer models are based on open-system assumptions. A closer look at the three organizational metaphors reveals instructive insights about organizations and how they work. Each perspective offers something useful.

Organizations as Military/Mechanical Bureaucracies

A major by-product of the Industrial Revolution was the factory system of production. People left their farms and cottage industries to operate steam-powered machines in centralized factories. The social unit of production evolved from the family to formally managed organizations encompassing hundreds or even thousands of people. Managers sought to maximize the economic efficiency of large factories and offices by structuring them according to military principles. At the turn of the century, German sociologist Max Weber formulated what he termed the most rationally efficient form of organization. He patterned his ideal organization after the vaunted Prussian army and called it **bureaucracy.**

Weber's Bureaucracy.   According to Weber's theory, the following four factors should make bureaucracies the epitome of efficiency:

1. Division of labor (people become proficient when they perform standardized tasks over and over again).

2. A hierarchy of authority (a formal chain of command ensures coordination and accountability).

3. A framework of rules (carefully formulated and strictly enforced rules ensure predictable behavior).

4. Administrative impersonality (personnel decisions such as hiring and promoting should be based on competence, not favoritism).[5]

How the Term Bureaucracy *Became a Synonym for Inefficiency.*   All organizations possess varying degrees of these characteristics. Thus, every organization is a bureaucracy to some extent. In terms of the ideal metaphor, a bureaucracy should run like a well-oiled machine, and its members should perform with the precision of a polished military unit. But problems arise when bureaucratic characteristics become extreme or dysfunctional. For example, as explained in Table 17–1, extreme expressions of specialization, rule following, and imper-

■ **TABLE 17–1** Dysfunctional Bureaucracy Can Make Employees Insensitive

> The bureaucrat . . . is restricted to those actions that his work rules permit him and that fall within the scope of his jurisdiction. He, as bureaucrat, is not allowed to tune in to the subjective meanings and needs that a client of the bureaucracy is trying to convey; he must tune in only to those meanings and needs that have officially recognizable standing. For example, a welfare investigator is not officially permitted to take cognizance of the psychological stress that a mother on welfare experiences because welfare rules forbid her husband to live with her. Or a consumer advocate in a consumer protection agency cannot consider the intensity of poverty or the severity of psychic agony of a client who wishes to file a complaint but fails to produce the necessary sales receipt.
>
> SOURCE: Ralph P. Hummel, *The Bureaucratic Experience* (New York: St. Martin's Press, 1977), pp. 4–5.

---

[5] Based on Max Weber, *The Theory of Social and Economic Organization,* translated by A. M. Henderson and Talcott Parsons (New York: Oxford University Press, 1947). An instructive analysis of the mistranslation of Weber's work may be found in Richard M. Weiss, "Weber on Bureaucracy: Management Consultant or Political Theorist?" *Academy of Management Review,* April 1983, pp. 242–48.

sonality can cause a bureaucrat to treat a client as a number rather than as a person.[6]

Weber probably would be surprised and dismayed that his model of rational efficiency has become a synonym for inefficiency. Today, bureaucracy stands for being put on hold, waiting in long lines, and getting shuffled from one office to the next. This irony can be explained largely by the fact that organizations with excessive or dysfunctional bureaucratic tendencies become rigid, inflexible, and resistant to environmental demands and influences.

Organizations as Biological Systems

Drawing upon the field of general systems theory that emerged during the 1950s,[7] organization theorists suggested a more dynamic model for modern organizations. As noted in Figure 17–3, this metaphor likens organizations to the human body. Hence, it has been labeled the *biological model*. In his often-cited organization theory text, *Organizations in Action,* James D. Thompson explained the biological model of organizations in the following terms:

> Approached as a natural system, the complex organization is a set of interdependent parts which together make up a whole because each contributes something and receives something from the whole, which in turn is interdependent with some larger environment. Survival of the system is taken to be the goal, and the parts and their relationships presumably are determined through evolutionary processes. . . .
>
> Central to the natural-system approach is the concept of homeostasis, or self-stabilization, which spontaneously, or naturally, governs the necessary relationships among parts and activities and thereby keeps the system viable in the face of disturbances stemming from the environment.[8]

Unlike the traditional military/mechanical theorists who downplayed the environment, advocates of the biological model stress organization-environment interaction. As Figure 17–4 illustrates, the biological model characterizes the organization as an open system that transforms inputs into various outputs. The outer boundary of the organization is represented by a broken line to emphasize that the organization's boundary is permeable. People, information, capital, and goods and services move back and forth across this boundary. Moreover, each of the five organizational subsystems—goals and values, technical, psychosocial, structural, and managerial—is dependent on the others. Feedback about such things as sales and customer satisfaction or dissatisfaction

---

[6] For a critical appraisal of bureaucracy, see Ralph P. Hummel, *The Bureaucratic Experience,* 3rd ed. (New York: St. Martin's Press, 1987). The positive side of bureaucracy is presented in Charles T. Goodsell, *The Case for Bureaucracy: A Public Administration Polemic* (Chatham, N.J.: Chatham House Publishers, 1983).

[7] A management-oriented discussion of general systems theory—an interdisciplinary attempt to integrate the various fragmented sciences—may be found in Kenneth E. Boulding, "General Systems Theory—The Skeleton of Science," *Management Science,* April 1956, pp. 197–208.

[8] James D. Thompson, *Organizations in Action* (New York: McGraw-Hill, 1967), pp. 6–7.

■ **FIGURE 17–4** The Organization as an Open System: The Biological Model

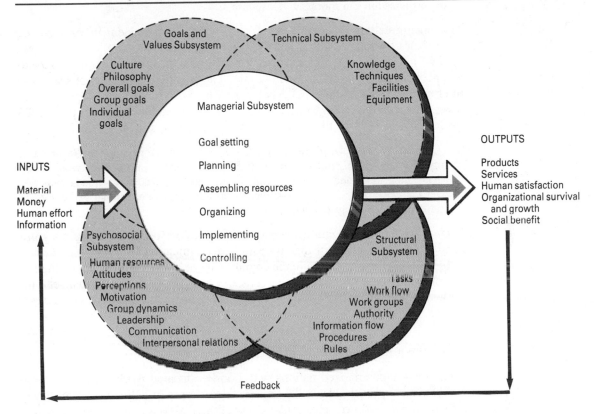

SOURCE: This model is a combination of Figures 5–2 and 5–3 in Fremont E. Kast and James E. Rosenzweig, *Organization and Management: A Systems and Contingency Approach*, 4th ed. (New York: McGraw-Hill, 1985), pp. 112, 114. Used with permission.

enables the organization to self-adjust and survive despite uncertainty and change.

Organizations as Cognitive Systems

A more recent metaphor characterizes organizations in terms of mental functions. According to respected organization theorists Richard Daft and Karl Weick:

> This perspective represents a move away from mechanical and biological metaphors of organizations. Organizations are more than transformation processes or control systems. To survive, organizations must have mechanisms to interpret ambiguous events and to provide meaning and direction for participants. Organizations are meaning systems, and this distinguishes them from lower level systems. . . .

Almost all outcomes in terms of organization structure and design, whether caused by the environment, technology, or size, depend on the interpretation of problems or opportunities by key decision makers. Once interpretation occurs, the organization can formulate a response.[9]

This interpretation process, carried out at the top-management or strategic level, leads to organizational *learning* and adaptation.

U.S. tobacco companies exemplify how organizational strategists adapt to an uncertain and ambiguous environment. The cognitive processes of scanning, interpreting, and learning have led narrowly focused tobacco companies to diversify recently. Philip Morris's acquisition of General Foods Corp. in 1985 made sense in light of the following environmental realities:

> The business has weathered past years of bad news, from Surgeon General's reports to tax hikes. But the forces that turned tobacco into a dirty word are accelerating more and more as social, legal, and financial storm clouds gather over the industry. . . . For the survivors, cost-cutting, international expansion, and diversification are the new battle cries.[10]

Each of the five organizational subsystems at Philip Morris has changed significantly as a direct result of the company's diversification strategy.

In sum, the flow of events in the cognitive model is: environmental ambiguity → interpretation → strategy → structure → organizational performance. This sequence is expanded on later in this chapter under the heading of strategic choice.

Organizational Metaphors in Perspective

In newly industrialized nations with poorly educated workers, the military/mechanical approach was widely applicable. Narrowly defined jobs, military-like discipline, and strict chains of command enabled factory and office managers to control their employees and meet production quotas. As things grew more complex, however, the military/mechanical model was found lacking. Thanks to modern open-system thinking, we now see organizations as more than internally focused control mechanisms.

A useful model of modern organizations emerges when we integrate the biological and cognitive metaphors. Conceptually, the organization's *body* and *head* need to be connected. One cannot function without the other. Managers of today's productive organizations are responsible for transforming factors of production into needed goods and services (the body). Yet they can remain competitive only if they wisely *interpret* environmental opportunities and obstacles (the head). By combining the biological and cognitive models, we gain a realistic organizational context for theory and practice.

---

[9] Richard L. Daft and Karl E. Weick, "Toward a Model of Organizations as Interpretation Systems," *Academy of Management Review*, April 1984, p. 293.

[10] Scott Ticer, "Big Tobacco's Fortunes Are Withering in the Heat," *Business Week*, July 27, 1987, p. 47.

■ ORGANIZATIONAL LIFE CYCLES AND EFFECTIVENESS

Like the people who make up organizations, organizations themselves go through life cycles. Organizations are born and, barring early decline, eventually grow and mature. If periods of decline are not reversed, the organization dies. Just as you will face new problems and challenges during different phases of your lifetime, so do organizations. Thus, managers need a working knowledge of organizational life cycles and the closely related topic of organizational effectiveness. According to a pair of experts on the subject: A consistent pattern of development seems to occur in organizations over time, and organizational activities and structures in one stage are not the same as the activities and structures present in another stage. This implies that the criteria used to evaluate an organization's success in one stage of development also may be different from criteria used to evaluate success in another stage of development.[11] This section examines stages of the organizational life cycle concept and discusses alternative ways of assessing organizational effectiveness.

Organizational Life Cycle Stages

Although the organizational life cycle concept has been around for a long time, it has enjoyed renewed interest among respected researchers in recent years. Many life cycle models have been proposed.[12] One point of agreement among the competing models is that organizations evolve in a predictable sequence of identifiable stages. Table 17–2 presents a basic organizational life cycle model. Stages 1 through 3 of the model are inception, high-growth, and maturity. Changes during these three stages can be summed up in the following rule: *As organizations mature, they tend to become larger, more formalized, and more differentiated (fragmented).* Differentiation increases because of added levels in the hierarchy, further division of labor, and formation of political coalitions.

Life Cycle Timing and Type of Change. Two key features of this life cycle model address the timing and type of changes experienced by the organization. Relative to timing, the duration of each phase is highly variable, depending on a host of organizational and environmental factors. This explains why there is no time frame in Table 17–2. Regarding the type of change organizations undergo from one stage to the next, Indiana University researchers noted, "The very nature of the firm changes as a business grows in size and matures. These are not changes in degree; rather, they are fundamental changes in kind."[13] This sort of *qualitative* change helps explain the unexpected departure

---

[11] Robert E. Quinn and Kim Cameron, "Organizational Life Cycles and Shifting Criteria of Effectiveness: Some Preliminary Evidence," *Management Science,* January 1983, p. 40.

[12] Ten organizational life cycle models are reviewed in Ibid., pp. 34–41.

[13] Richard A. Cosier and Dan R. Dalton, "Search for Excellence, Learn from Japan—Are These Panaceas or Problems?" *Business Horizons,* November–December 1986, p. 67.

■ **TABLE 17–2**   Stages of the Organizational Life Cycle

Characteristics	Stage 1: Inception	Stage 2: High-growth	Stage 3: Maturity — — — — — — — Decline	
Type of organizational structure	No formal structure	Centralized Formal	Decentralized Formal	Rigid, top-heavy, overly complex
Communication process and planning	Informal Face-to-face Little planning	Moderately formal Budgets	Very formal Five-year plans Rules and regulations	Communication breakdowns Blind adherence to "success formula"
Method of decision making	Individual judgment Entrepreneurial	Professional management Analytical tools	Professional management Bargaining	Emphasis on form rather than substance Self-serving politics
Organizational growth rate	Inconsistent but improving	Rapid positive growth	Growth slowing or declining	Declining
Organizational age and size	Young and small	Larger and older	Largest or once large and oldest	Variable age and shrinking

SOURCES: Characteristics and first three stages excerpted from Ken G. Smith, Terence R. Mitchell, and Charles E. Summer, "Top Level Management Priorities in Different Stages of the Organizational Life Cycle," *Academy of Management Journal*, December 1985, p. 802. Organizational decline portion adapted from discussion in Peter Lorange and Robert T. Nelson, "How to Recognize—and Avoid—Organizational Decline," *Sloan Management Review*, Spring 1987, pp. 41–48.

of founder Mitchell D. Kapor from Lotus Development Corp., maker of the highly successful 1–2–3® computer spreadsheet program (see Table 17–3).

The Ever-Present Threat of Decline.   While decline is included in the model, it is not a distinct stage with predictable sequencing (hence the broken line

■ **TABLE 17–3**   Why the Founder of Lotus Development Corp. Walked Away from It All

> Why would the founder and head of one of the most successful computer software companies in history give up the reins[*] and return to college? *Inc.* magazine's interview with Mitch Kapor uncovered the answer. Kapor is the classic entrepreneur and he became disenchanted when his company matured beyond the inception stage of its life cycle. Here is an excerpt from that interview:
>
> INC.: You founded a tremendously successful company in a growing industry and, after only five years, you decided to walk away from it. Why?
>
> KAPOR: If you look at Lotus as it started and as it is today, I think you'll see more differences than similarities. In the beginning, it was classically entrepreneurial: a small group of people trying to break into a market with a new product around which they hoped to build a company and achieve market share for the company and financial success for themselves and their investors. Today, Lotus is a company of 1,350 people with diversified, worldwide operations, with the organizational structure and challenges of a $275 million company. And so the nature of the challenges facing the company, and facing the people in it—and, to your question, facing me—is radically different.
>
> ---
> [*] Kapor retained a seat on Lotus's board of directors and 1.6 million shares of the firm's stock.
> SOURCE: Interview portion excerpted from Robert A. Mamis and Steven Pearlstein, " '1–2–3' Creator Mitch Kapor," *Inc.*, January 1987, p. 31.

between maturity and decline in Table 17–2). Organizational decline is a *potential,* rather than automatic, outcome that can occur any time during the life cycle. Stage 1 and stage 2 organizations are as readily victimized by the forces of decline as mature stage 3 organizations. Experts report 50 percent of all new businesses in the United States fail within seven years.[14] Most of the failed businesses experience decline after an extended inception stage or an abbreviated high-growth stage. While noting "decline is almost unavoidable unless deliberate steps are taken to prevent it,"[15] specialists on the subject have alerted managers to 14 early warning signs of organizational decline:

1. Excess personnel.
2. Tolerance of incompetence.
3. Cumbersome administrative procedures.
4. Disproportionate staff power (for example, technical staff specialists politically overpower line managers whom they view as unsophisticated and too conventional).
5. Replacement of substance with form (for example, the planning process becomes more important than the results achieved).
6. Scarcity of clear goals and decision benchmarks.
7. Fear of embarrassment and conflict (for example, formerly successful executives may resist new ideas for fear of revealing past mistakes).
8. Loss of effective communication.
9. Outdated organizational structure.[16]
10. Increased scapegoating by leaders.
11. Resistance to change.
12. Low morale.
13. Special interest groups are more vocal.
14. Decreased innovation.[17]

Managers who monitor these early warning signs of organizational decline are better able to reorganize in a timely and effective manner.[18]

Organizational Life Cycle Research and Practical Implications. The best available evidence in this area comes from the combination of a field study and a laboratory simulation. Both studies led researchers to the same conclusions. In the field study, 38 top-level electronics industry managers from 27 randomly

---

[14] See "The Disenchantment of the Middle Class," *Business Week,* April 25, 1983, p. 86.

[15] Peter Lorange and Robert T. Nelson, "How to Recognize—and Avoid—Organizational Decline," *Sloan Management Review,* Spring 1987, p. 47.

[16] Excerpted from Ibid., pp. 43–45.

[17] For details, see Kim S. Cameron, Myung U. Kim, and David A. Whetten, "Organizational Effects of Decline and Turbulence," *Administrative Science Quarterly,* June 1987, pp. 222–40.

[18] Twelve dysfunctional consequences of decline are discussed and empirically tested in Kim S. Cameron, David A. Whetten, and Myung U. Kim, "Organizational Dysfunctions of Decline," *Academy of Management Journal,* March 1987, pp. 126–38.

selected companies were presented with a decision-making scenario. They then were asked to complete a questionnaire about priorities. It was found that priorities shifted across the three life cycle stages introduced in Table 17–2. As the organization matured from stage 1 to stages 2 and 3, top management's priorities shifted as follows:

- A strong emphasis on technical efficiency grew even stronger.
- The desire for personal power and commitment from subordinates increased significantly.
- The desire for organizational integration (coordination and cooperation) decreased significantly.[19]

In a separate but related study, researchers examined the relationship between life cycle stages and effectiveness criteria. This five-year case study of a New York State mental health agency revealed that top management's effectiveness criteria changed during the organization's life cycle. Early emphasis on flexibility, resource acquisition, and employee development/satisfaction gave way to formalization as the agency matured. Formalization criteria encompassed increased attention to factors such as goal setting, information management, communication, control, productivity, and efficiency.[20]

This research reveals that different stages of the organizational life cycle are associated with distinctly different managerial responses. It must be noted, however, that management's priorities and effectiveness criteria in the foregoing studies were not necessarily the *right* ones. Much research remains to be done to identify specific contingencies. Still, the point remains that managers need to be flexible and adaptive as their organizations evolve through the various life cycle stages.[21] As learned the hard way by the U.S. steel industry during the 1980s, yesterday's formula for success can be today's formula for noncompetitiveness and decline.[22]

Four Generic Organizational Effectiveness Criteria

How effective are you? If someone asked you this apparently simple question, you would likely ask for clarification before answering. For instance, you might want to know if they were referring to your grade point average, annual income, actual accomplishments, ability to get along with others, public service,

---

[19] Based on Ken G. Smith, Terence R. Mitchell, and Charles E. Summer, "Top Level Management Priorities in Different Stages of the Organizational Life Cycle," *Academy of Management Journal*, December 1985, pp. 799–820.

[20] Additional details may be found in Quinn and Cameron, "Organizational Life Cycles and Shifting Criteria of Effectiveness: Some Preliminary Evidence," pp. 33–51.

[21] For an instructive conceptual model of the relationship between organizational politics, strategy, and organizational life cycles, see Barbara Gray and Sonny S. Ariss, "Politics and Strategic Change across Organizational Life Cycles," *Academy of Management Review*, October 1985, pp. 707–23. Practical advice regarding the organizational life cycle can be found in Jim Mayers, "How to Withstand a Merger," *Management Review*, October 1986, pp. 39–42.

[22] See Gregory L. Miles, "Cancel the Funeral—Steel Is on the Mend," *Business Week*, October 5, 1987, pp. 74, 76.

or perhaps something else entirely. So it is with modern organizations. There is no quick answer about how to gauge organizational effectiveness because organizations vary so widely in purpose, size, and social and economic impacts. Self-interest also clouds the picture. For example, Ford Motor Company became the world's most profitable car maker in 1986 and 1987 (a sure sign of effectiveness to some). But the owners of the 4.3 million Ford cars and trucks recalled in 1987 to repair fuel systems that could catch fire might be reluctant to call the company effective.[23] Assessing organizational effectiveness is an important topic for an array of people, including managers, stockholders, government economists, and researchers.

A good way to better understand this complex subject is to consider four generic approaches to assessing an organization's effectiveness (see Figure 17–5). These effectiveness criteria apply equally well to all life cycle stages of large or small and profit or not-for-profit organizations. Moreover, as denoted by the overlapping circles in Figure 17–5, the four effectiveness criteria can be used in various combinations. The key thing to remember is "no single approach to the evaluation of effectiveness is appropriate in all circumstances or for all organizational types."[24] Because a multidimensional approach is required, we need to look more closely at each of the four generic effectiveness criteria.

Goal Accomplishment. This is the most widely used effectiveness criterion for organizations. Key organizational results or outputs—such as refrigerators manufactured, lunches served, or students graduated—are compared with established goals. Goals also may be set for intangibles such as minority hiring, quality of service, or community service programs. Effectiveness is gauged by how well the organization meets or exceeds its goals.

Resource Acquisition. This second criterion relates to inputs rather than outputs. An organization is deemed effective in this regard if it acquires necessary factors of production such as raw materials, labor, capital, and managerial and technical expertise.

Internal Processes. Some refer to this third effectiveness criterion as the "healthy systems" approach. An organization is said to be a healthy system if information flows smoothly and employee loyalty, commitment, and trust prevail. Healthy systems also tend to have a minimum of dysfunctional conflict and destructive political maneuvering.

Strategic Constituencies Satisfaction. Organizations both depend on people and affect the lives of people. Consequently, many consider the satisfaction of various strategic constituencies to be an important criterion of organizational effectiveness.

---

[23] See James B. Treece, "Can Ford Stay on Top?" *Business Week,* September 28, 1987, pp. 78–86.

[24] Kim Cameron, "Critical Questions in Assessing Organizational Effectiveness," *Organizational Dynamics,* Autumn 1980, p. 70.

■ **FIGURE 17–5** Four Ways to Assess Organizational Effectiveness

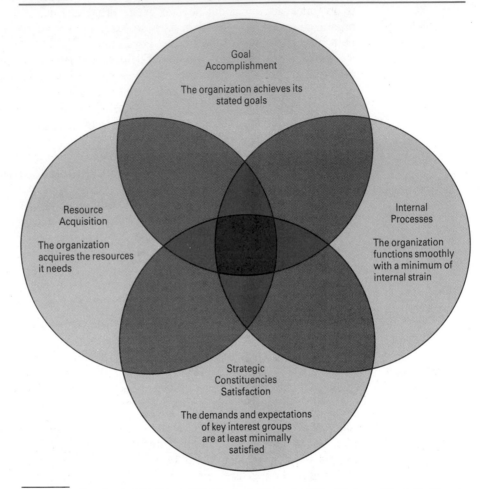

SOURCE: Adapted from discussion in Kim Cameron, "Critical Questions in Assessing Organizational Effectiveness," *Organizational Dynamics,* Autumn 1980, pp. 66–80; and Kim S. Cameron, "Effectiveness as Paradox: Consensus and Conflict in Conceptions of Organizational Effectiveness," *Management Science,* May 1986, pp. 539–53.

A **strategic constituency** is any group of individuals who have some stake in the organization—for example, resource providers, users of the organization's products or services, producers of the organization's output, groups whose cooperation is essential for the organization's survival, or those whose lives are significantly affected by the organization.[25]

Strategic constituencies generally have competing or conflicting interests. For instance, stockholders who want higher dividends and consumers who seek low prices would likely disagree with a union's demand for a wage increase.

[25] Ibid., p. 67. (Emphasis added.)

■ **TABLE 17–4**   Balancing Strategic Constituencies at West Germany's Volkswagen

"Profits are not the goal, but a means of reaching your goals," [Karl-Heinz] Briam [VW's personnel director] explains. "A company has numerous goals, which include protecting the interests of the workers; protecting the interests of the Federal Republic (the government still holds 20 percent of VW's stock); to pay taxes—and naturally, to produce a good product at a good price."

This package of goals, according to Briam, puts a priority on reaching readily understood and well-balanced decisions that will be backed by the workforce. For example, this February VW decided to take over Spain's troubled SEAT (Sociedad Espanola de Automoviles de Turismo, S.A.). The new subsidiary will strengthen VW's position in the subcompact market. The company's Works Council fully supported the SEAT purchase, once they were assured it would not mean losing any jobs in West Germany. (Actually, about 2,000 jobs are expected to be *added* to VW's design section here because of the SEAT acquisition, says Briam.)

A never-ending challenge for management is to strike a workable balance among strategic constituencies so as to achieve at least minimal satisfaction on all fronts. For example, as described in Table 17–4, Volkswagen's management must balance the demands of at least four strategic constituencies: employees, the West German government, taxpayers, and customers.

Multiple Effectiveness Criteria: Some Practical Guidelines

Experts on the subject recommend a multidimensional approach to assessing the effectiveness of modern organizations. This means no single criterion is appropriate for all stages of the organization's life cycle. Nor will a single criterion satisfy competing constituencies. Well-managed organizations mix and match effectiveness criteria to fit the situation. Managers need to identify and seek input from strategic constituencies. This information, when merged with the organization's stated mission and philosophy, enables management to derive an appropriate *combination* of effectiveness criteria. The following guidelines are helpful:

- The *goal accomplishment* approach is appropriate when "goals are clear, consensual, time-bound, measurable."[26]
- The *resource acquisition* approach is appropriate when inputs have a traceable impact on results or output.
- The *internal processes* approach is appropriate when organizational performance is strongly influenced by specific processes.

---

[26] Kim S. Cameron, "Effectiveness as Paradox: Consensus and Conflict in Conceptions of Organizational Effectiveness," *Management Science*, May 1986, p. 542.

The *strategic constituencies* approach is appropriate when powerful constituencies can significantly benefit or harm the organization.[27]

Keeping the discussion of organizational life cycles and effectiveness in mind, let us turn our attention to the design of effective organizations.

■ THE CONTINGENCY APPROACH TO ORGANIZATION DESIGN

According to the **contingency approach to organization design,** organizations tend to be more effective when they are structured to fit the demands of the situation. A contingency approach can be put into practice by first assessing the degree of environmental uncertainty.[28] Next, the contingency model calls for using various organization design configurations to achieve an effective organization-environment fit. This section presents an environmental uncertainty model along with two classic contingency design studies.

Assessing Environmental Uncertainty

Robert Duncan proposed a two-dimensional model for classifying environmental demands on the organization (see Figure 17–6). On the horizontal axis is the simple → complex dimension. This dimension "focuses on whether the factors in the environment considered for decision making are few in number and similar or many in number and different."[29] On the vertical axis of Duncan's model is the static → dynamic dimension. "The static-dynamic dimension of the environment is concerned with whether the factors of the environment remain the same over time or change."[30] When combined, these two dimensions characterize four situations that represent increasing uncertainty for organizations. According to Duncan, the complex-dynamic situation of highest uncertainty is the most common organizational environment today.

Amid these fast-paced times, nothing stands still. Not even in the simple-static quadrant. For example, during the first 94 years of Coca-Cola's history (through 1980), only one soft drink bore the company's name. Just six years later, Coke had its famous name on seven soft drinks, including Coca-Cola Classic, Coke, and Cherry Coke. Despite operating in an environment character-

---

[27] Alternative effectiveness criteria are discussed in Ibid.; Arthur G. Bedeian, "Organization Theory: Current Controversies, Issues, and Directions," in *International Review of Industrial and Organizational Psychology,* ed. Cary L. Cooper and Ivan T. Robertson (New York: John Wiley & Sons, 1987), pp. 1–33; and Michael Keeley, "Impartiality and Participant-Interest Theories of Organizational Effectiveness," *Administrative Science Quarterly,* March 1984, pp. 1–25.

[28] An interesting distinction between three types of environmental uncertainty can be found in Frances J. Milliken, "Three Types of Perceived Uncertainty about the Environment: State, Effect, and Response Uncertainty," *Academy of Management Review,* January 1987, pp. 133–43.

[29] Robert Duncan, "What Is the Right Organization Structure?" *Organizational Dynamics,* Winter 1979, p. 63.

[30] Ibid.

■ **FIGURE 17–6** A Four-Way Classification of Organizational Environments

	Simple	Complex
Static	*Low perceived uncertainty* Small number of factors and components in the environment Factors and components are somewhat similar to one another Factors and components remain basically the same and are not changing Example: Soft drink industry	*Moderately low perceived uncertainty* Large number of factors and components in the environment Factors and components are not similar to one another Factors and components remain basically the same Example: Food products
Dynamic	*Moderately high perceived uncertainty* Small number of factors and components in the environment Factors and components are somewhat similar to one another Factors and components of the environment are in continual process of change Example: Fast-food industry	*High perceived uncertainty* Large number of factors and components in the environment Factors and components are not similar to one another Factors and components of environment are in a continual process of change Examples: Commercial airline industry Telephone communications (AT&T)

(quadrant labels between cells: 1 | 2 / 3 | 4)

SOURCE: Reprinted, by permission of the publisher, from "What Is the Right Organization Structure?" by Robert Duncan, *Organizational Dynamics,* Winter 1979, p. 63. © 1979 American Management Association, New York. All rights reserved.

ized as simple and static, Coca-Cola has had to become a more risk-taking, entrepreneurial company.[31] This means organizations facing moderate to high uncertainty (quadrants 3 and 4 in Figure 17–6) have to be highly flexible, responsive, and adaptive today. Contingency organization design is more important than ever because it helps managers structure their organizations to fit the key situational factors discussed next.

Differentiation and Integration: The Lawrence and Lorsch Study

In their 1967 classic, *Organization and Environment,* Harvard researchers Paul Lawrence and Jay Lorsch explained how two structural forces simultaneously fragment the organization and bind it together. They cautioned that

---

[31] See Thomas Moore, "He Put the Kick Back into Coke," *Fortune,* October 26, 1987, pp. 46–56.

■ **FIGURE 17-7**   Differentiation and Integration Are Opposing Structural Forces

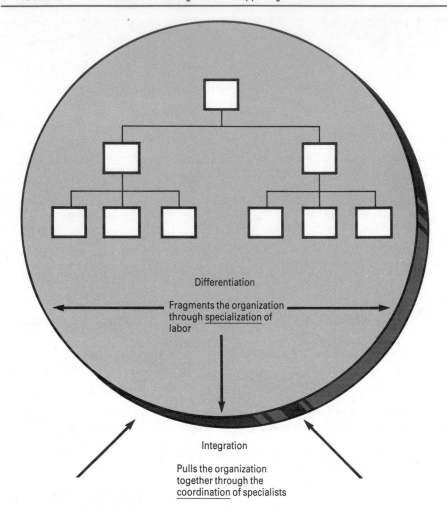

an imbalance between these two forces—labeled differentiation and integration—could hinder organizational effectiveness.

Differentiation Splits the Organization Apart. **Differentiation** occurs through division of labor and technical specialization. A behavioral outcome of differentiation is that technical specialists such as computer programmers tend to think and act differently than specialists in, say, accounting or marketing. Excessive differentiation can cause the organization to bog down in miscommunication, conflict, and politics. Thus, differentiation needs to be offset by an opposing structural force to ensure needed *coordination*. This is where integration enters the picture (see Figure 17–7).

Integration Binds the Organization Together. **Integration** occurs when specialists cooperate to achieve a common goal. According to the Lawrence and

Lorsch model, integration can be achieved through various combinations of the following six mechanisms: (1) a formal hierarchy; (2) standardized policies, rules, and procedures; (3) departmentalization; (4) committees and cross-function teams; (5) human relations training; and (6) individuals and groups acting as liaisons between specialists.

Achieving the Proper Balance. When Lawrence and Lorsch studied successful and unsuccessful companies in three industries, they concluded the following: *As environmental complexity increased, successful organizations exhibited higher degrees of both differentiation and integration.* In other words, an effective balance was achieved. Unsuccessful organizations, in contrast, tended to suffer from an imbalance of too much differentiation and not enough offsetting integration. This outcome was confirmed by the life cycle research discussed earlier. As the organization matured, management's desire for integration became a significantly less important priority. Managers need to fight this tendency if their growing and increasingly differentiated organizations are to be coordinated.

Lawrence and Lorsch also discovered that "the more differentiated an organization, the more difficult it is to achieve integration."[32] Managers of today's complex organizations need to strive constantly and creatively to achieve greater integration.[33] For example, Hardee's found an unusual way to promote hierarchical integration: "Once a year, each of the top 60 executives of Hardee's Food Systems Inc. has to spend a week behind the counter in one of the company's restaurants."[34] Consequently, Hardee's executives probably are more responsive to the needs and problems of their restaurant managers and employees. Meanwhile, Compaq Computer Corp. strives for hierarchical and cross-function integration through consensus management (see Table 17–5). The success of Compaq's consensus management program depends a great deal on well-trained human relations skills.

Mechanistic versus Organic Organizations

A second classic contingency design study was reported in 1961 by a pair of British behavioral scientists, Tom Burns and G. M. Stalker. In the course of their research, they drew a very instructive distinction between what they called mechanistic and organic organizations. **Mechanistic organizations** are rigid bureaucracies with strict rules, narrowly defined tasks, and top-down communication.

In contrast, **organic organizations** are flexible networks of multitalented individuals who perform a variety of tasks. W. L. Gore & Associates, as

---

[32] Paul R. Lawrence and Jay W. Lorsch, *Organization and Environment* (Homewood, Ill.: Richard D. Irwin, 1967), p. 157.

[33] Pooled, sequential, and reciprocal integration are discussed in Jay W. Lorsch, "Organization Design: A Situational Perspective," *Organizational Dynamics,* Autumn 1977, pp. 2–14.

[34] Dean Foust, "Hardee's: The Bigger It Grows, the Hungrier It Gets," *Business Week,* May 4, 1987, p. 106.

■ **TABLE 17–5** Management by Consensus Helps Compaq Computer Achieve
Organizational Integration

Known simply as "the process," it involves informal team meetings where members discuss a problem or policy. Every department involved gives its view. Then the group attempts to separate fact from instinct, examines the trade-offs, and arrives at a decision. At a new-product meeting recently, representatives from Compaq's international group argued against the date the domestic division had chosen for a launch. And sales department staffers worried about the product's effect on dealer inventories. It is rare that a single member or group will dominate.

SOURCE: Excerpted from Jo Ellen Davis, "Who's Afraid of IBM?" *Business Week,* June 29, 1987, p. 72.

discussed in Chapter 15, is a highly organic organization because it lacks job descriptions, titles, and a formalized hierarchy.

Decision making tends to be centralized in mechanistic organizations and decentralized in organic organizations. **Centralized decision making** occurs when key decisions are made by top management. **Decentralized decision making** occurs when important decisions are made by middle- and lower-level managers. Generally, centralized organizations are more tightly controlled while decentralized organizations are more adaptive to changing situations.

Importantly, as illustrated in Figure 17–8, each of the mechanistic-organic characteristics is a matter of degree. Organizations tend to be *relatively* mechanistic or *relatively* organic. Pure types are rare because divisions, departments, or units in the same organization may be more or less mechanistic or organic. From an employee's standpoint, which organization structure would you prefer?

■ **FIGURE 17–8** Characteristics of Mechanistic and Organic Organizations

Characteristic	Mechanistic Organization	Organic Organization
1. Task definition and knowledge required	Narrow; technical	Broad; general
2. Linkage between individual's contribution and organization's purpose	Vague or indirect	Clear or direct
3. Task flexibility	Rigid; routine	Flexible; varied
4. Specification of techniques, obligations, and rights	Specific	General
5. Degree of hierarchical control	High	Low (self-control emphasized)
6. Primary communication pattern	Top-down	Lateral (between peers)
7. Primary decision-making style	Authoritarian	Democratic; participative
8. Emphasis on obedience and loyalty	High	Low

SOURCE: Adapted from discussion in Tom Burns and G. M. Stalker, *The Management of Innovation* (London: Tavistock, 1961), pp 119–25.

Relevant Research Findings.   When they classified a sample of actual companies as either mechanistic or organic, Burns and Stalker discovered one type was not superior to the other. Each type had its appropriate place, depending on the environment. When the environment was relatively *stable and certain,* the successful organizations tended to be *mechanistic. Organic* organizations tended to be the successful ones when the environment was *unstable and uncertain.*[35]

In a more recent study of 103 department managers from eight manufacturing firms and two aerospace organizations, managerial skill was found to have a greater impact on a global measure of department effectiveness in organic departments than in mechanistic departments. This led the researchers to recommend the following contingencies for management staffing and training:

> If we have two units, one organic and one mechanistic, and two potential applicants differing in overall managerial ability, we might want to assign the more competent to the organic unit since in that situation there are few structural aids available to the manager in performing required responsibilities. It is also possible that managerial training is especially needed by managers being groomed to take over units that are more organic in structure.[36]

Another interesting finding comes from a study of 42 voluntary church organizations. As the organizations became more mechanistic (more bureaucratic) the intrinsic motivation of their members decreased. Mechanistic organizations apparently undermined the volunteers' sense of freedom and self-determination. This conforms to Deci's cognitive evaluation theory that extrinsic rewards tend to erode intrinsic motivation (recall the discussion in Chapter 7). Moreover, the researchers believe their findings help explain why bureaucracy tends to feed on itself: "A mechanistic organizational structure may breed the need for a more extremely mechanistic system because of the reduction in intrinsically motivated behavior."[37] Thus, bureaucracy begets greater bureaucracy.

Both Mechanistic and Organic Structures Are Needed.   Although achievement-oriented students of OB typically express a distaste for mechanistic organizations, not all organizations or subunits can or should be organic. For example, McDonald's could not achieve its admired quality and service standards without extremely mechanistic restaurant operations. Imagine the food and service you would get if McDonald's employees used their own favorite ways of doing things! On the other hand, as indicated in Table 17–6 and the foregoing research, mechanistic structure alienates some employees because it erodes their sense of self-control.

---

[35] Details of this study can be found in Tom Burns and G. M. Stalker, *The Management of Innovation* (London: Tavistock, 1961).

[36] Dennis J. Gillen and Stephen J. Carroll, "Relationship of Managerial Ability to Unit Effectiveness in More Organic versus More Mechanistic Departments," *Journal of Management Studies,* November 1985, pp. 674–75.

[37] J. Daniel Sherman and Howard L. Smith, "The Influence of Organizational Structure on Intrinsic versus Extrinsic Motivation," *Academy of Management Journal,* December 1984, p. 883.

■ **TABLE 17–6**   The Mechanistic World of McDonald's

To find out how a McDonald's restaurant works, Correspondent Kathleen Deveny spent a lunch hour behind the counter. Her report:

On my way down Chicago's Magnificent Mile, past Tiffany's and Gucci, to the McDonald's restaurant, I keep thinking back to the Tastee Treet in Minneapolis. That was my first job, making ice cream cones and flipping burgers for the high school students who swarmed into the converted gas station during the short summers.

McDonald's is nothing like Tastee Treet. Here every job is broken down into the smallest of steps, and the whole process is automated. The videotape that introduces new employees to French fries, for example, starts with boxes of frozen fries rolling off a delivery truck. Stack them in the freezer six boxes high. Leave one inch between the stacks, two inches between the stacks and the wall. Cooking and bagging the fries is explained in even greater detail: 19 steps.

Out of Sync

Anyone could do this, I think. But McDonald's restaurants operate like Swiss watches, and the minute I step behind the counter I am a loose part in the works. By noon the place is mobbed. I keep thinking of the McDonald's commercial that shows former Raiders Coach John Madden diagramming the precision moves of a McDonald's crew in action. I imagine a diagram of my own jerky movements, zigzagging wildly behind the counter because I keep forgetting the order.

I bag French fries for a few minutes, but I'm much too slow. Worse, I can't seem to keep my station clean enough. Failing at French fries is a fluke, I tell myself.

Condiment detail sounds made to order. First comes the mustard, one shot of the gun, five perfect drops centered on the bun. Next, the ketchup: One big shot. Quite a difference from Tastee Treet, where I used to measure out the ketchup by writing my boyfriend's initials on each hamburger bun.

I try to speed up. Now a quarter ounce of onions and two pickles—three, if they're small. Cover them with a slice of cheese, slap on the burger. Another slice of cheese.

I am happy with the tidy piles I am making, but the grillman is not as pleased. I move too slowly, and he could cook the patties and dress the buns a lot faster without my help.

Disheartened, I move on to Filet-O-Fish. I put six frozen fish patties into the fryer basket and drop them into the hot grease. When the red light flashes, I put the buns in to steam. After a few minutes, the square patties are done. I line them up in neat rows and center the cheese on each. I try to move faster, but my co-workers are playing at 45 rpm, and I'm stuck at 33 ⅓.

Debbie, the crew member who rescued my French fries earlier, comes back to see how I'm doing. It's my last chance to shine. I pull out more cooked fish, slap on the cheese, burn my hands on the buns, and pinch my finger in the tartar sauce gun. "You're doing O.K.," she somehow says. That's all I wanted to hear. The regimented work is wearing on my nerves. The strict rules, which go so far as to prescribe what color nail polish to wear, are bringing out the rebel in me. I can't wait to get back to my cluttered office, where it smells like paper and stale coffee and the only noise is the gentle hum of my personal computer.

SOURCE: Kathleen Deveny, "Bag Those Fries, Squirt That Ketchup, Fry That Fish." Reprinted from October 13, 1986, issue of *Business Week* by special permission, copyright © 1986 by McGraw-Hill, Inc.

■ THREE IMPORTANT CONTINGENCY VARIABLES: TECHNOLOGY, SIZE, AND STRATEGIC CHOICE

Both contingency theories just discussed have one important thing in common. Each is based on an "environmental imperative," meaning the environment is said to be the primary determinant of effective organizational structure. Other organization theorists disagree. They contend that factors such as the organization's core technology, organization and subunit size, and corporate strategy hold the key to organizational structure. This section examines the significance of these three additional contingency variables.

The Impact of Technology on Structure

Joan Woodward proposed a *technological imperative* in 1965 after studying 100 small manufacturing firms in southern England. She found distinctly different structural patterns for effective and ineffective companies based on technologies of low, medium, or high *complexity*. Effective organizations with either low- or high complexity technology tended to have an organic structure. Effective organizations based on a technology of medium complexity tended to have a mechanistic structure. Woodward concluded that technology was the overriding determinant of organizational structure.[38]

Since Woodward's landmark work, many studies of the relationship between technology and structure have been conducted. Unfortunately, disagreement and confusion have prevailed. For example, a comprehensive review of 50 studies conducted between 1965 and 1980 found six technology concepts and 140 technology-structure relationships.[39] A statistical analysis of those studies prompted the following conclusions:

- The more the technology requires *interdependence* between individuals and/or groups, the greater the need for integration (coordination).
- "As technology moves from routine to nonroutine, subunits adopt less formalized and [less] centralized structures."[40]

Additional insights can be expected in this area as researchers coordinate their definitions of technology and refine their methodologies.

Organizational Size and Performance

Size is an important structural variable subject to two schools of thought. According to the first school, economists have long extolled the virtues of

---

[38] See Joan Woodward, *Industrial Organization: Theory and Practice* (London: Oxford University Press, 1965); and Paul D. Collins and Frank Hull, "Technology and Span of Control: Woodward Revisited," *Journal of Management Studies*, March 1986, pp. 143–64.

[39] See Louis W. Fry, "Technology-Structure Research: Three Critical Issues," *Academy of Management Journal*, September 1982, pp. 532–52.

[40] Ibid., p. 548.

economies of scale. This approach, often called the "bigger is better" model, assumes the per-unit cost of production decreases as the organization grows. In effect, bigger is said to be more efficient. For example, on an annual basis, General Motors supposedly can produce its 100,000th car less expensively than its 10th car.

The second school of thought pivots on the law of diminishing returns. Called the "small is beautiful" model,[41] this approach contends that oversized organizations and subunits tend to be plagued by costly behavioral problems. Large and impersonal organizations are said to breed apathy and alienation with resulting problems such as turnover and absenteeism. Two strong advocates of this second approach are the authors of the best-selling *In Search of Excellence:*

> In the excellent companies, small *in almost every case* is beautiful. The small facility turns out to be the most efficient; its turned-on, motivated, highly productive worker, in communication (and competition) with his peers, outproduces the worker in the big facilities time and again. It holds for plants, for project teams, for divisions—for the entire company.[42]

Recent research suggests that when designing their organizations, managers should follow a middle ground between "bigger is better" and "small is beautiful" because both models have been oversold.

Recent Research Evidence. Researchers measure the size of organizations and organizational subunits in different ways. Some focus on financial indicators such as total sales or total asset value. Others look at the number of employees, transactions (such as the number of students in a school district), or capacity (such as the number of beds in a hospital). A meta-analysis[43] of 31 studies conducted between 1931 and 1985 that related organizational size to performance found:

- Larger organizations (in terms of assets) tended to be more productive (in terms of sales and profits).
- There were "no positive relationships between organizational size and efficiency, suggesting the absence of net economy of scale effects."[44]
- There were zero to slightly negative relationships between *subunit* size and productivity and efficiency.
- A more recent study examined the relationship between organizational

---

[41] The phrase "small is beautiful" was coined by the late British economist E. F. Schumacher. See E. F. Schumacher, *Small Is Beautiful: Economics as If People Mattered* (New York: Harper & Row, 1973).

[42] Thomas J. Peters and Robert H. Waterman, Jr., *In Search of Excellence* (New York: Harper & Row, 1982), p. 321.

[43] Richard Z. Gooding and John A Wagner III, "A Meta-Analytic Review of the Relationship between Size and Performance: The Productivity and Efficiency of Organizations and Their Subunits," *Administrative Science Quarterly,* December 1985, pp. 462–81.

[44] Ibid., p. 477.

■ **TABLE 17-7** Organizational Size: Management Consultants Address the Question of "How Big Is Too Big?"

Peter F. Drucker, well-known management consultant:

> The real growth and innovation in this country has been in medium-size companies that employ between 200 and 4,000 workers. If you are in a small company, you are running all out. You have neither the time nor the energy to devote to anything but yesterday's crisis.
>
> A medium-size company has the resources to devote to new products and markets, and it's still small enough to be flexible and move fast. And these companies now have what they once lacked—they've learned how to manage.

Thomas J. Peters and Robert H. Waterman, Jr., best-selling authors and management consultants:

> A rule of thumb starts to emerge. We find that the lion's share of the top performers keep their division size between $50 and $100 million, with a maximum of 1,000 or so employees each. Moreover, they grant their divisions extraordinary independence—and give them the functions and resources to exploit it.

SOURCES: Excerpted from John A. Byrne, "Advice from the Dr. Spock of Business," *Business Week,* September 28, 1987, p. 61; and Thomas J. Peters and Robert H. Waterman, Jr., *In Search of Excellence* (New York: Harper & Row, 1982), pp. 272-73.

size and employee turnover over a period of 65 months. Turnover was unrelated to organizational size.[45]

Striving for Small Units in Big Organizations. In summary, bigger is not necessarily better and small is not necessarily beautiful. Hard-and-fast numbers regarding exactly how big is too big or too small are difficult to come by. Management consultants offer some rough estimates (see Table 17–7). Until better evidence is available, the best managers can do is monitor the productivity and efficiency of divisions, departments, and profit centers. Unwieldy units need to be broken promptly into ones of more manageable size. The trick is to *create smallness within bigness.* For example, the health care products giant, Johnson & Johnson, has more than 150 divisions. Technology leader 3M Company has more than 40 divisions.

Strategic Choice and Organizational Structure

In 1972, British sociologist John Child rejected the environmental imperative approach to organizational structure. He proposed a *strategic choice* model

---

[45] Results are presented in Philip G. Benson, Terry L. Dickinson, and Charles O. Neidt, "The Relationship between Organizational Size and Turnover: A Longitudinal Investigation," *Human Relations,* January 1987, pp. 15–30.

based on behavioral rather than rational economic principles.[46] Child believed structure resulted from a political process involving organizational power holders. According to the strategic choice model that has evolved from Child's work,[47] an organization's structure is determined largely by a dominant coalition of top-management strategists.

A Strategic Choice Model.   As Figure 17–9 illustrates, specific strategic choices or decisions reflect how the dominant coalition perceives environmental constraints and the organization's objectives. These strategic choices are tempered by the decision makers' personal beliefs, attitudes, and values. For example, Sam Bronfman, longtime head of Seagram, had a personal distaste for vodka and kept Seagram from seriously pursuing the vodka market. By the 1980s, when vodka had become the top-selling liquor in the United States, Seagram was lagging.[48] Directing our attention once again to Figure 17–9, the organization is structured to accommodate its mix of strategies. Ultimately, corrective action is taken if organizational effectiveness criteria are not met.

Recent Research and Practical Lessons.   In a recent study of 97 small and mid-size companies in Quebec, Canada, strategy and organizational structure were found to be highly interdependent. Strategy influenced structure and structure influenced strategy. This was particularly true for larger, more innovative, and more successful firms.[49]

Strategic choice theory and research teaches managers at least two practical lessons. First, the environment is just one of many codeterminants of structure. Second, like any other administrative process, organization design is subject to the byplays of interpersonal power and politics.

■ ALTERNATIVE ORGANIZATION DESIGN CONFIGURATIONS: MINTZBERG'S TYPOLOGY

Henry Mintzberg, whose work on managerial roles was discussed in Chapter 1, believes most organizations fall into five natural structure-situation configurations. He urges managers not to make the common mistake of haphazardly mixing and matching design components, based on whim, convenience, or fashion. According to Mintzberg:

---

[46] See John Child, "Organizational Structure, Environment and Performance: The Role of Strategic Choice," *Sociology,* January 1972, pp. 1–22.

[47] See Jay Galbraith, *Organization Design* (Reading, Mass.: Addison-Wesley Publishing, 1977); John R. Montanari, "Managerial Discretion: An Expanded Model of Organization Choice," *Academy of Management Review,* April 1978, pp. 231–41; and H. Randolph Bobbitt, Jr., and Jeffrey D. Ford, "Decision-Maker Choice as a Determinant of Organizational Structure," *Academy of Management Review,* January 1980, pp. 13–23.

[48] Example drawn from "What Edgar Bronfman Wants at Seagram," *Business Week,* April 27, 1981, pp. 135–42.

[49] Details may be found in Danny Miller, "Strategy Making and Structure: Analysis and Implications for Performance," *Academy of Management Journal,* March 1987, pp. 7–32.

■ **FIGURE 17–9**   The Relationship between Strategic Choice and Organizational Structure

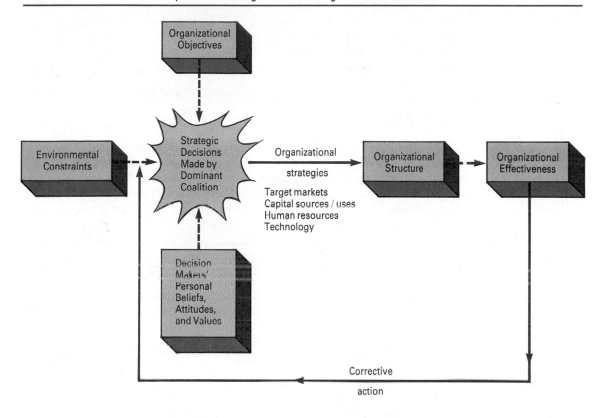

Spans of control, degrees of job enlargement, forms of decentralization, planning systems, and matrix structure should not be picked and chosen at random. Rather, they should be selected according to internally consistent groupings. And these groupings should be consistent with the situation of the organization— its age and size, the conditions of the industry in which it operates, and its production technology. In essence, my argument is that—like all phenomena from atoms to stars—the characteristics of organizations fall into natural clusters, or *configurations*. When these configurations are mismatched—when the wrong ones are put together—the organization does not function effectively, does not achieve a natural harmony. If managers are to design effective organizations, they need to pay attention to the fit.[50]

Mintzberg's instructive typology includes the *simple structure*, the *machine bureaucracy*, the *professional bureaucracy*, the *divisionalized form*, and *adhocracy*. Each has its own distinct pattern of coordination, structural elements, and situational elements (see Table 17–8).

----

[50] Henry Mintzberg, "Organization Design: Fashion or Fit?" *Harvard Business Review*, January–February 1981, pp. 103–4.

Simple Structure

This configuration is found typically in small entrepreneurial companies. Nearly all organizations start as simple structures. Simple structure organizations are organic because standardization, formalization, and administrative layers are minimal. Operations are flexible and adaptive because top managers/owners directly supervise operating personnel.

Machine Bureaucracy

An offshoot of the Industrial Revolution, machine bureaucracies are built around narrowly defined, repetitive, low-skill jobs. Communication and authority flow through the formal chain of command. Machine bureaucracies are highly mechanistic. Decision making is centralized. There is an obsession with control to eliminate uncertainty and to contain inevitable alienation and conflict. This configuration is found in large mass production companies in the automobile industry, for example. Mass service organizations such as McDonald's are machine bureaucracies, as are most large government agencies. Employee alienation, lack of flexibility, and poor adaptability are overriding problems for machine bureaucracies. Nonetheless, "machine bureaucracy remains indispensable—and probably the most prevalent of the five configurations today."[51]

Professional Bureaucracy

The distinguishing difference between machine bureaucracy and professional bureaucracy is the means of coordination or control. Machine bureaucracies rely on standardized tasks for coordination. Professional bureaucracies rely on highly trained professionals to exercise *self-control*. College professors, accountants, lawyers, and hospital physicians prefer to work independently in decentralized organizations. Thus, universities, accounting and law firms, and hospitals tend to be configured as professional bureaucracies. While skilled professionals enjoy the characteristic autonomy and democracy of professional bureaucracies, this configuration is not very adaptable. Professional bureaucracies are most effective in a stable or static environment.

Divisionalized Form

"Divisionalization refers to a structure of semiautonomous market-based units."[52] Typically, a headquarters unit has loose administrative control over several machine bureaucracies. For example, before a recent reorganization, General Motors grew into a world leader by having its Chevrolet, Buick, Pontiac, Oldsmobile, and Cadillac divisions compete with each other as if they were independent companies.

---

[51] Ibid., p. 109.
[52] Ibid., p. 110.

■ **TABLE 17–8**   Selected Characteristics of Mintzberg's Five Organization Design Configurations

	Simple Structure	Machine Bureaucracy	Professional Bureaucracy	Divisionalized Form	Adhocracy
Key means of coordination	Direct supervision	Standardization of work	Standardization of skills	Standardization of outputs	Mutual adjustment
Structural elements					
Specialization of jobs	Little specialization	Much horizontal and vertical specialization	Much horizontal specialization	Some horizontal and vertical specialization (between divisions and headquarters)	Much horizontal specialization
Formalization of behavior—bureaucratic/organic	Little formalization—organic	Much formalization—bureaucratic	Little formalization—bureaucratic	Much formalization (within divisions)—bureaucratic	Little formalization—organic
Decentralization	Centralization	Limited horizontal decentralization	Horizontal and vertical decentralization	Limited vertical decentralization	Selective decentralization
Situational elements					
Age and size	Typically young and small	Typically old and large	Varies	Typically old and very large	Typically young (operating adhocracy)
Technical system	Simple, not regulating	Regulating but not automated, not very complex	Not regulating or complex	Divisible, otherwise like machine bureaucracy	Very complex, often automated (in administrative adhocracy), not regulating or complex (in operating adhocracy)
Environment	Simple and dynamic; sometimes hostile	Simple and stable	Complex and stable	Relatively simple and stable; diversified markets (esp. products and services)	Complex and dynamic; sometimes disparate (in administrative adhocracy)
Power	Chief executive control; often owner managed; not fashionable	Technocratic and external control; not fashionable	Professional operator control; fashionable	Middle-line control; fashionable (esp. in industry)	Expert control; very fashionable

Although this configuration appears to be highly decentralized, the opposite is generally true. Division heads often exercise highly centralized control over their respective units. Headquarters maintains overall control through financial and performance reporting mechanisms, thus ensuring that the divisions' outputs are standardized. Other divisional affairs are constrained by headquarters policies and directives. For instance, "Dana Corp., an automotive-parts maker in Toledo, Ohio, gives its divisions broad latitude on such matters as hiring and firing, though within limits specified by the company."[53] Divisionalization

---

[53] Amanda Bennett, "Airline's Ills Point Out Weaknesses of Unorthodox Management Style," *The Wall Street Journal*, August 11, 1986, p. 15.

enables machine bureaucracies to be more adaptable. Divisions can be added or expanded and sold or cut back as business conditions dictate.

Adhocracy

Mintzberg borrowed the term **adhocracy** from Alvin Toffler's book *Future Shock* to describe highly organic structures based on temporary project teams. Organizations such as NASA, Boeing Company, and Intel rely on flexible adhocracy to remain innovative and responsive to fast-changing conditions. According to Mintzberg:

> Of all the configurations, Adhocracy shows the least reverence for the classical principles of management, especially unity of command. The regulated system does not matter much either. In this configuration, information and decision processes flow flexibly and informally, wherever they must, to promote innovation. And that means overriding the chain of authority if need be.[54]

The most widely known and used form of adhocracy is the matrix organization.

Matrix Organization.

A **matrix organization** is a project-oriented approach to organization design that combines vertical and horizontal authority. It often is referred to simply as project management. Notice the gridlike pattern in Figure 17–10. In flagrant violation of the traditional unity of command principle (each employee should report to only one boss), the functional specialists in Figure 17–10 have two bosses. Each functional manager is responsible for general administrative duties such as hiring, training, performance appraisal, and project assignments. Meanwhile, the project managers have temporary authority over varying numbers of functional specialists, depending on project requirements. For example, the manager of project X may need the services of three design specialists early in the project, one during the manufacturing phase, and none when the product goes to market.

Matrix Advantages and Disadvantages.

Proponents of matrix organizations list among its advantages flexibility, enhanced coordination, better communication, and improved motivation and commitment. Detractors point to power and authority struggles, increased conflict, slow decision making, and the expense of double management.[55] A recent field study of the implementation of a matrix structure in the engineering division of an aircraft manufacturer uncovered the following consequences:

- A greater *quantity* of communication.
- Lower *quality* communication.
- A negative impact on work attitudes and coordination.[56]

---

[54] Henry Mintzberg, *Structure in Fives: Designing Effective Organizations* (Englewood Cliffs, N.J.: Prentice-Hall, 1983), p. 255.

[55] An excellent analysis of matrix organization may be found in Erik W. Larson and David H. Gobeli, "Matrix Management: Contradictions and Insights," *California Management Review*, Summer 1987, pp. 126–38.

[56] See William F. Joyce, "Matrix Organization: A Social Experiment," *Academy of Management Journal*, September 1986, pp. 536–61.

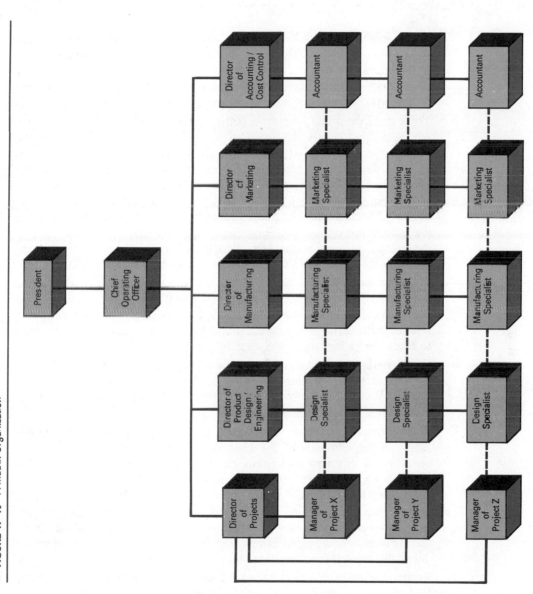

■ FIGURE 17–10   A Matrix Organization

As with each of the other structural configurations, matrix organization is not a cure-all. It needs to fit the circumstances (see the lower-right portion of Table 17–8) and be refined as structural problems arise.[57]

SUMMARY OF KEY CONCEPTS

A. An organization is a system of consciously coordinated activities or forces of two or more persons. The four common denominators of all organizations are coordination of effort, a common goal, division of labor, and a hierarchy of authority. Among other things, organization charts reveal the hierarchy of authority, division of labor, and line-staff distinctions.

B. Three metaphors that help us to better understand complex organizations are the military/mechanical, biological, and cognitive models. While the military/mechanical model views organizations as self-sufficient closed systems, the biological and cognitive models view organizations as environment-dependent open systems. Max Weber's concept of bureaucracy exemplifies the military/mechanical model. All organizations possess some degree of bureaucracy. Extreme or dysfunctional bureaucracy has made the term synonymous with inefficiency and red tape. A combination of the biological (resource transformation) and cognitive (interpretation) metaphors paints a realistic picture of modern complex organizations.

C. The three stages of the organizational life cycle are inception, high growth, and maturity. Decline is an ever-present threat during the organizational life cycle. Research shows that managerial priorities and effectiveness criteria shift during the organizational life cycle. Thus, managers need to adjust and adapt from one stage to the next.

D. Four generic organizational effectiveness criteria are goal accomplishment, resource acquisition, internal processes, and strategic constituencies satisfaction. Because there is no single best effectiveness criterion, a multidimensional approach is suggested.

E. The contingency approach to organization design calls for fitting the organization to the demands of the situation. Environmental uncertainty can be assessed in terms of various combinations of two dimensions: (1) simple or complex and (2) static or dynamic. Harvard researchers Lawrence and Lorsch found that successful organizations achieved a proper balance between the two opposing structural forces of differentiation and integration. Differentiation forces the organization apart. Through a variety of mechanisms—including hierarchy, rules, teams, and liaisons—integration draws the organization together.

F. British researchers Burns and Stalker found that mechanistic (bureaucratic, centralized) organizations tended to be effective in stable situations. In unstable situations, organic (flexible, decentralized) organizations were

---

[57] Problems with Texas Instruments' widely acclaimed matrix structure are discussed in "Texas Instruments Cleans Up Its Act," *Business Week,* September 19, 1983, pp. 56–64.

more effective. These findings underscored the need for a contingency approach to organization design.

G. Technology, organization and subunit size, and strategic choice are important contingency design variables. Regarding the optimum size for organizations, the challenge for today's managers is to achieve smallness within bigness. The strategic choice model emphasizes how environmental and personal factors affect the dominant coalition, which in turn formulates strategies that shape the organization's structure.

H. Henry Mintzberg contends that organizations naturally fall into five structure-situation configurations. They are: simple structure, machine bureaucracy, professional bureaucracy, divisionalized form, and adhocracy. Machine bureaucracies are both the most mechanistic and most common configuration today. Adhocracies, typically in the form of matrix organizations, are the most organic configuration.

KEY TERMS

organization

unity of command principle

organization chart

span of control

closed system

open system

bureaucracy

strategic constituency

contingency approach to organization design

differentiation

integration

mechanistic organizations

organic organizations

centralized decision making

decentralized decision making

adhocracy

matrix organization

DISCUSSION QUESTIONS

1. How many organizations directly affect your life today? List as many as you can.

2. What would an organization chart of your present (or last) place of employment look like? Does the chart you have drawn reveal the hierarchy (chain of command), division of labor, and line-staff distinctions? Does it reveal anything else? Explain.

3. How would you respond to a person who said, "All bureaucracies are useless"?

4. Why is it instructive to characterize today's complex organizations as cognitive (interpretation) systems?

5. What role does decline play in the organizational life cycle?

6. How would you respond to a manager who claimed the only way to

measure a business's effectiveness is in terms of how much profit it makes?

7. What evidence of integration can you find in your present (or last) place of employment?

8. If organic organizations are popular with most employees, why can't all organizations be structured in an organic fashion?

9. How can you tell if an organization (or subunit) is too big?

10. Why would early management writers who promoted the military/mechanical model of organizations probably dislike the matrix configuration?

BACK TO THE OPENING CASE

Now that you have read Chapter 17, you should be able to answer the following questions about the Tactical Air Command (TAC) case:

1. How can the effectiveness of TAC be assessed? Is one of the criteria you have specified superior to the others? Explain.

2. Did General Creech strive to make TAC more mechanistic or more organic? Explain your evidence.

3. What evidence of organizational integration can you find in this case? Why is integration important in such a large organization?

4. How important was the three-day weekend incentive plan to General Creech's turnaround program? Explain.

EXERCISE 17

Objectives

1. To get out into the field and talk to a practicing manager about organizational structure.
2. To increase your understanding of the important distinction between mechanistic and organic organizations.
3. To broaden your knowledge of contingency design, in terms of organization-environment fit.

Introduction

As with the manager interview in exercise 1, a good way to test the validity of what you have just read about organizational structure is to interview a practicing manager.

Instructions

Your objective is to interview a manager about aspects of organizational structure, environmental uncertainty, and organizational effectiveness. A *manager* is defined as anyone who supervises other people in an organizational setting. The organization may be small or large and profit or not-for-profit. Higher-level managers are preferred, but middle managers and first-line supervisors are acceptable. If you interview a lower-level manager, be sure to remind him or her that you want a description of the overall organization, not just an isolated subunit. Your interview will center on the adaptation of Figure 17–8, as discussed below.

When conducting your interview, be sure to explain to the manager what you are trying to accomplish. But assure the manager that his or her name will not be mentioned in class discussion or any written projects. Try to keep side notes during the interview for later reference.

Questionnaire

The following questionnaire, adapted from Figure 17–8, will help you determine if the manager's organization is relatively mechanistic or relatively organic in structure. Note: For items 1 and 2 on the following questionnaire, have the manager respond in terms of the *average* nonmanagerial employee. (Circle one number for each item.)

Characteristic

1. Task definition and knowledge required — Narrow; technical 1—2—3 4 5 6 7 Broad; general
2. Linkage between individual's contribution and organization's purpose — Vague or indirect 1—2—3—4—5—6 7 Clear or direct
3. Task flexibility — Rigid; routine 1—2—3—4—5—6—7 Flexible; varied
4. Specification of techniques, obligations, and rights — Specific 1—2—3—4—5—6—7 General
5. Degree of hierarchical control — High 1—2—3—4—5—6—7 Low (self-control emphasized)
6. Primary communication pattern — Top-down 1—2—3—4—5—6—7 Lateral (between peers)
7. Primary decision-making style — Authoritarian 1—2—3—4—5—6—7 Democratic; participative
8. Emphasis on obedience and loyalty — High 1—2—3—4—5—6—7 Low

Total score = _____

Additional question about the organization's environment:

This organization faces an environment that is (circle one number):
Stable and certain 1—2—3—4—5—6—7—8—9—10 Unstable and uncertain

Additional questions about the organization's effectiveness:

a. Profitability (if a profit-seeking business):
    Low   1—2—3—4—5—6—7—8—9—10   High
b. Degree of organizational goal accomplishment:
    Low   1—2—3—4—5—6—7—8—9—10   High
c. Customer or client satisfaction:
    Low   1—2—3—4—5—6—7—8—9—10   High
d. Employee satisfaction:
    Low   1—2—3—4—5—6—7—8—9—10   High

Total effectiveness score = _____
(Add responses from above)

Questions for Consideration/Class Discussion

1. Using the following norms, was the manager's organization relatively mechanistic or organic?

     8–24 = Relatively mechanistic

    25–39 = Mixed

    40–56 = Relatively organic

2. In terms of Burns and Stalker's contingency theory, does the manager's organization seem to fit its environment? Explain.

3. Does the organization's degree of effectiveness reflect how well it fits its environment? Explain.

Chapter **18**

Organizational Cultures:
Change and Development

LEARNING OBJECTIVES

When you finish studying the material in this chapter,
you should be able to:

- Define the term *organizational culture.*
- Describe four functions of organizational culture and explain how culture can become a competitive advantage.
- Explain how the two main modes of Nutt's transactional model of change interact.
- Discuss what research has taught us about participation as a change tactic.
- List at least five reasons why employees resist change.
- Describe the identifying characteristics of organization development (OD).
- Discuss the overriding practical lesson from OD research.

Hershey: A Company Driven by Values

At no other time in business history was the term "friendly takeover" more appropriate than when Hershey Foods Corporation, in 1981, acquired the Massachusetts-based Friendly Restaurant chain for $166 million as part of its strategy to become a major diversified foods company. Friendly was evidently pleased with what it considered a fitting match—during a speech to executives and their spouses, the wife of Friendly's president even blessed Hershey with a wish for all their "kisses" to be "friendly."

This "Friendly" saga is cited frequently at Hershey as an example of the parent company's emphasis on *values* as a central criterion in acquisition decisions. "It's like a marriage," Chairman and CEO Richard Zimmerman explains. "If the core values of two individuals or companies don't mesh, then the match should never take place—no matter how attractive it might seem from other angles."

It's hard to see how the core values at Hershey could do anything *but* mesh with any other socially conscious company—to refute them would be like scorning motherhood and apple pie. "Have honesty and integrity," Hershey preaches. "Be people-oriented. Be quality- and consumer-conscious. Be results-oriented."

But the point is, Hershey also spends a great amount of time *practicing* what it preaches—both in acquisition strategy and in-house standard operating procedure. The company has recently completed an intensive "values study" to identify and vocalize core beliefs. It is using the results to further Hershey's sense of self, and cohere its various decentralized divisions and growing list of subsidiaries into a harmonious whole.

Just how, one might ask, did Hershey decide the time was ripe to sit back and do this corporate soul-searching? William P. Noyes, vice-president of human resources for Hershey, can list a host of reasons. "The old Hershey of kisses-and-cocoa fame had strong values and culture—an all-American quality that grew out of a strong work ethic, a southwestern Pennsylvania heritage. Then, suddenly, we diversified and grew—and the new companies brought in their heritages, some very similar, some different. Also, retirements of key personnel left open holes, and new division presidents and leaders were brought in. The question was, what did *they* stand for? And in the 1970s, we hired many new technical people and created new divisions—legal, corporate planning, public relations. We'd never had these before.

"At that time, we delved into strategic planning more aggressively and formulated many new plans. The question was, were they realistic? Could our culture and values support these plans for growth?

"With so many changes," Noyes concludes, "it was difficult to determine what Hershey meant. We initiated the values study so that we could pinpoint our beliefs and communicate them, so that employees would be sure to understand the culture and rich history of Hershey.''

The Hershey Chronicle

It's an interesting history. Hershey Chocolate Company was founded in 1903 by Milton Snavely Hershey, a quiet Pennsylvanian entrepreneur. In 1909, he and his wife, being childless, decided to donate part of their chocolate fortune toward a school for deprived boys—it today has evolved into the coeducational Milton Hershey School, and is, with 50.1 percent of shares, the major stockholder of Hershey Foods Corporation.

In addition to this special *raison d'etre,* Milton Hershey also gave his company values synonymous with his own lifestyle: high moral and religious principles; truth, honesty, and integrity; thrift, economy, and industry; the golden ''do unto others'' rule; the value of education; very high quality standards; the rewards of doing good and benefiting others; and an emphasis on the family and the community.

All this sounds awfully downhome, solid, and cozy. But as Hershey continues on its way toward becoming a major diversified foods company, it will be more and more difficult to preserve the specifically ''Hershey'' feelings that come from lunching with the schoolkids or walking down Chocolate Avenue, its sidewalks lit with streetlights in the shape of Hershey kisses. Plant managers in Fresno, California, now work for Hershey who have never laid eyes on Chocolate Town, U.S.A. What do they know of its values?

Anchor to Windward

In order to find out, Richard Zimmerman in 1985 mandated the organization of a task force, headed by Noyes and with each Hershey division represented, to study the situation. ''What was needed,'' says Zimmerman, ''was an anchor to windward—an identity, inspired by our founder, reflected in our sharing common values and goals.''

And so, in an early communication to values task force members, the objectives of the values study were defined as follows:

''To identify a common set of corporate-wide values that we, as a corporation, wish to publicize and emphasize to our various publics, including employees, customers, investors, and the communities in which we are located.

''To identify how we can best communicate these values, and how we can gain acceptance and commitment from our employees to them.

''To identify any internal issues that might hamper success in this area, and how we successfully can deal with them.''

How to go about attaining these objectives was another story. ''What we decided,'' says Noyes, ''was that we had to go out and talk to people. We worked out the general structure of an interview, with questions such as 'What do you think is important to this company?' and 'What values do you have to identify with in order to succeed at Hershey?' ''

Interview rules were not hard and fast; each team member adopted his or her own style to the task at hand. John Rawley, director of corporate planning, distributed handouts from a book on corporate culture, as well as some ''feeler'' questions to prime his participants. All task force members, however, conducted their interviews one-on-one with interviewees, who were taken from all areas and many levels of the company. Most interviews lasted about an hour. The entire interviewing process lasted about six months. . . .

Survey Results

The main players—Zimmerman, Noyes, Rawley, president and COO [chief operating officer] Ken Wolfe, and vice-president for corporate communications Ken Bowers—all agree that the survey results were surprisingly unsurprising. Participants identified 12 basic values, with a ring to them vaguely reminiscent of the corporate philosophy Hershey had

Concluded:

committed to a few years before. These 12 values subsequently boiled down to four; people orientation, consumer- and quality-consciousness, honesty and integrity, and results-orientation. The 20,000-odd Hershey employees now carry a copy of these values printed on a card in their wallets.

Zimmerman explains why the values are couched in such general terms. "We don't want to orient values talk just to Hershey Chocolate Company, whence we came. We have to have values which can be identified, accepted, and utilized by people in Dayton, Ohio, or Abilene, Texas, or Wilbraham, Massachusetts." The little card is just a start, of course. New management training seminars at Hershey also will talk about these four values. An orientation film is now being reworked to incorporate the subject of values at Hershey. House newsletters are communicating the project and its central issues to employees.

But most importantly, says Zimmerman, "We must *demonstrate,* over a long period of time, that we are serious. You can't preach ethics and integrity and be a little sloppy in your own habits. Each manager must have a grip on those clearly defined values and be able to demonstrate them—through their own behavior—to employee groups."

John Rawley concurs: "You can have a little piece of plastic in your wallet that says what you are. But it's really what you *do*—how you demonstrate care for each and every employee. Management has to think about

this all the time—it must seep down throughout the company."

Zimmerman feels the values emphasis of Hershey's management training programs will be vitally important to the company's future managers. "As time goes by," he predicts, "talking about values will be regarded as absolutely essential. Just as essential as marketing, or logistics, or strategic planning, or thinking or decision making—as any of those great subjects that they teach in the Harvards and the Stanfords. So this is a very important step for us."

The values must also be demonstrated to subsidiaries and potential acquisitions. "The only way these groups can buy into what you're doing," says Zimmerman, "is over a period of time during which you demonstrate that you're serious. But you have to start off by telling them what you intend to do and how you intend to do it, opening communication and establishing credibility. To those who accept this, we are a caring company. Not everyone will buy into it, I know. We do our best to try and sell it."

For Discussion

Why was Hershey's value survey important considering the company's strategic direction?

SOURCE: Excerpted, by permission of the publisher, from "Hershey: A Company Driven by Values," by Sally J. Blank, from *Management Review*, November 1986, © 1986 American Management Association, New York. All rights reserved.

■ Additional discussion questions linking this case with the following material appear at the end of this chapter.

We live in an age of mergers and acquisitions. Hardly a day passes without news of a complicated corporate takeover. A less publicized fact, however, is that an estimated 90 percent of corporate mergers are disappointments for those involved. Moreover, nearly one third of acquired companies are sold within five years.[1] Observers attribute this poor showing mainly to incompatible corporate values and management's inability to handle large-scale change.[2] Steps can and should be taken to remedy both pitfalls because wrenching organizational changes—including mergers, strategic redirection, and new technology—are common. This final chapter explores the concept of organizational culture. This provides a backdrop for examining the mechanics of organizational change and discussing systematic change through a collection of techniques called organization development.

■ UNDERSTANDING ORGANIZATIONAL CULTURES

Much has been written and said about organizational, or corporate, cultures in recent years. The results of this activity can be arranged on a continuum of academic rigor. At the low end of the continuum are simplistic typologies and exaggerated claims about the benefits of imitating Japanese-style corporate cultures. Here the term *corporate culture* is little more than a pop psychology buzzword. At the other end of the continuum is a growing body of theory and research with valuable insights but plagued by definitional and measurement inconsistencies. By systematically sifting this diverse collection of material, we find that an understanding of organizational culture is central to learning how to manage organizational change.

What Is Organizational Culture?

While noting that cultures exist in social units of all sizes (from civilizations to countries to ethnic groups to organizations to work groups), Edgar Schein defined **culture** as:

> A pattern of basic assumptions—invented, discovered, or developed by a given group as it learns to cope with its problems of external adaptation and internal integration—that has worked well enough to be considered valid and, therefore, to be taught to new members as the correct way to perceive, think, and feel in relation to those problems.[3]

The word *taught* needs to be interpreted carefully because it implies formal education or training. While formal culture training does occur on the job, such as in orientation sessions for new employees, it is secondary. Most cultural lessons are learned by observing and imitating role models as they conduct their daily affairs. Culture generally remains below the threshold of conscious

---

[1] Data from Morty Lefkoe, "Why So Many Mergers Fail," *Fortune,* July 20, 1987, pp. 113–14.

[2] See Mitchell Lee Marks and Philip Harold Mirvis, "The Merger Syndrome," *Psychology Today,* October 1986, pp. 36–42.

[3] Edgar H. Schein, *Organizational Culture and Leadership* (San Francisco: Jossey-Bass, 1985), p. 9.

■ **TABLE 18-1** General Motors' Strong, Change-Resistant Culture Is Holding the Giant Automaker Back

In the early 1980s GM looked like the company that could do no wrong. It had beaten Ford and Chrysler to market with a lineup of fuel-efficient front-wheel-drive cars. And when oil prices fell it continued to outshine its competition because it had more big cars still in production.

As GM's earnings picked up in 1983 and soared to record highs in 1984 and 1985, [chairman Roger B.] Smith threw the company into hyperdrive with a visionary plan to transform it into a 21st-century corporation. . . .

He shook up the company with broad and frequent reorganizations, continuing a consolidation drive that began in the 1970s. He combined engineering groups, shucked off such marginally profitable businesses as heavy trucks and earthmoving equipment, and in 1984 lumped the five car divisions and Canadian activities into a small-car group (Chevrolet-Pontiac-GM of Canada) and a big-car group (Buick-Oldsmobile-Cadillac). Smith was widely hailed as a management visionary. . . .

But he lost track of the short run. GM attempted so much so fast—new models, new plants, and new organizations—that it soon lost control of what it used to do well: building good cars for every pocketbook at comparatively cheap prices. Quality began to slip, styling stagnated, costs rose, and new models ran into delays. . . .

Confusion from the reorganization undoubtedly contributed to the problems. But Smith grossly underestimated the inertia within his company and failed to provide the leadership and clear goals that might have galvanized its 100,000-odd managers. In the best of circumstances, GM's bureaucratic structure and culture have ensured that change comes only glacially. During the profitable mid-eighties, there especially seemed no reason to shift course. Managers lulled by success discounted the mounting evidence of trouble and dug in their heels.

SOURCE: Excerpted from Thomas Moore, "Make-or-Break Time for General Motors," *Fortune*, February 15, 1988, p. 34. Used with permission.

awareness because it involves *taken-for-granted assumptions* about how one should perceive, think, and feel.

Organizational culture is the social glue that binds members of the organization together through shared values, symbolic devices, and social ideals.[4] An organization's culture may be strong or weak, depending on variables such as cohesiveness, value consensus, and individual commitment to collective goals. Contrary to what one might suspect, a strong culture is not necessarily a good thing. The nature of the culture's central values is more important than its strength. For example, a strong but change-resistant culture (see Table 18–1) may be worse, from the standpoint of profitability and competitiveness, than a weak but innovative culture. Thus, when evaluating an organization's culture, we need to consider the strategic appropriateness of its central values as well as its strength.

---

[4] Adapted from Linda Smircich, "Concepts of Culture and Organizational Analysis," *Administrative Science Quarterly*, September 1983, pp. 339–58.

Manifestations of Organizational Culture

When is an organization's culture most apparent? According to one observer, cultural assumptions assert themselves through socialization of new employees, subculture clashes, and top management behavior.[5] Consider these three situations, for example. A newcomer who shows up late for an important meeting is told a story about someone who was fired for repeated tardiness. Conflict between product design engineers who emphasize a product's function and marketing specialists who demand a more stylish product reveals an underlying clash of subculture values. Top managers, through the behavior they model and the administrative and reward systems they create, prompt a significant improvement in the quality of a company's products.

A Model for Interpreting Organizational Culture.   A useful model for observing and interpreting organizational culture was developed by a Harvard researcher (see Figure 18–1). Four general manifestations or evidence of culture in his model are shared things (objects), shared sayings (talk), shared doings (behavior), and shared feelings (emotion). One can begin collecting cultural information by asking, observing, reading, and feeling. However, a more detailed analysis is required to capture the essence of an organization's culture. We need to supplement the foregoing model with a more extensive list of cultural manifestations.

A Closer Look.   Organizational culture expresses itself in a rich variety of ways. For example, a comprehensive list of cultural manifestations and definitions is presented in Table 18–2. We now see why Schein has called organizational culture ''a deep phenomenon.''[6] Missing from the list in Table 18–2 are values and organizational heroes, both worthy of mention. The instrumental and terminal values discussed in Chapter 3 become culturally embedded through group or organizational consensus. Apple Computer, for example, published a detailed list of nine ''Apple Values'' identified a few years ago by a task force of employees. Among those Apple values, imparted during the socialization process for new employees, are empathy for customers/users, positive social contribution, team spirit, and good management.

Organizational Heroes.   Heroes are those individuals who personify the organization's highest ideals. At IBM, for example, corporate heroes primarily are marketing representatives from the computer giant's 10,000-person sales force.

> ''Reps'' are first among equals in IBM. Every man who ever ran the company
> rose through their ranks, beginning with [IBM's founder] Thomas Watson, Sr.
> They are the main reason for the company's tight hold on the computer market.
> IBM treats them accordingly, motivating this army of politely aggressive blue

---

[5] Based on Alan L. Wilkins, ''The Culture Audit: A Tool for Understanding Organizations,'' *Organizational Dynamics,* Autumn 1983, pp. 24–38.

[6] Edgar H. Schein, ''What You Need to Know about Organizational Culture,'' *Training and Development Journal,* January 1986, p. 30.

■ **FIGURE 18–1** A Model for Observing and Interpreting General Manifestations of Organizational Culture

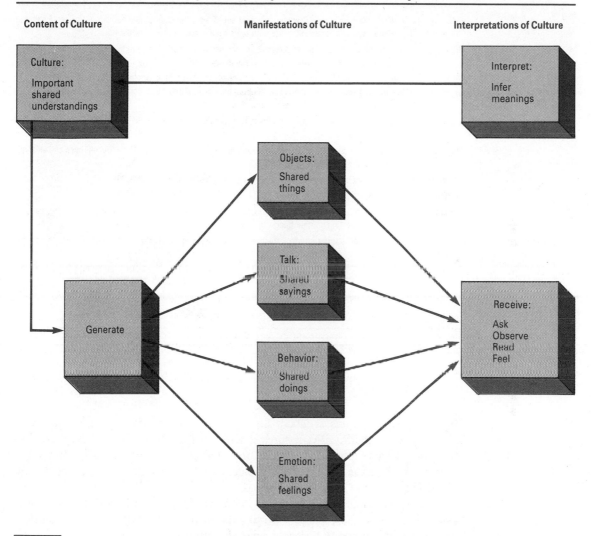

Content of Culture	Manifestations of Culture	Interpretations of Culture

Culture: Important shared understandings

Interpret: Infer meanings

Objects: Shared things

Talk: Shared sayings

Generate

Behavior: Shared doings

Emotion: Shared feelings

Receive: Ask Observe Read Feel

suits with tons of cash [some make over $100,000 a year], intense peer pressure and enough rah-rah rallies to rival a college fraternity. The rewards begin in IBM's 250 U.S. sales branches, where size is limited to 100 or 200 people to instill a small-team spirit.

Each January, branches stage glitzy "kickoff" meetings replete with slogans, skits and mascots. Monthly meetings often close with a dramatic tale about an unnamed rep; finally, the person is named and comes forward to accept an award amid crackling applause. "It takes your breath away, it really does,"

■ **TABLE 18–2**   Specific Manifestations of Organizational Culture

Rite	A relatively elaborate, dramatic, planned set of activities that combines various forms of cultural expressions and that often has both practical and expressive consequences.
Ritual	A standardized, detailed set of techniques and behaviors that manages anxieties but seldom produces intended, practical consequences of any importance.
Myth	A dramatic narrative of imagined events, usually used to explain origins or transformations of something. Also, an unquestioned belief about the practical benefits of certain techniques and behaviors that is not supported by demonstrated facts.
Saga	A historical narrative describing (usually in heroic terms) the unique accomplishments of a group and its leaders.
Legend	A handed-down narrative of some wonderful event that has a historical basis but has been embellished with fictional details.
Story	A narrative based on true events—often a combination of truth and fiction.
Folktale	A completely fictional narrative.
Symbol	Any object, act, event, quality, or relation that serves as a vehicle for conveying meaning, usually by representing another thing.
Language	A particular manner in which members of a group use vocal sounds and written signs to convey meanings to each other.
Gesture	Movements of parts of the body used to express meanings.
Physical setting	Those things that physically surround people and provide them with immediate sensory stimuli as they carry out culturally expressive activities.
Artifact	Material objects manufactured by people to facilitate culturally expressive activities.

SOURCE: Excerpted, by permission of the publisher, from "How an Organization's Rites Reveal Its Culture," by Janice M. Beyer and Harrison M. Trice, from *Organizational Dynamics*, Spring 1987, © 1987 American Management Association, New York. All rights reserved.

says Diana Ingram, a Chicago rep who has received four awards in less than four years at IBM.[7]

By setting sales quotas so about 80 percent of the marketing representatives meet or exceed them, IBM ensures it will not run out of heroes. At Sikorsky Aircraft, an innovation-driven company, the heroes are inventors. Sikorsky employees who have been awarded a patent wear special name tags emblazoned with a U.S. Patent Office logo.[8]

When management makes heroes of outstanding employees, the message is clear: "Look at these people. Be like them. It pays." Often-repeated stories and legends of company heroes deepen the culture.

Four Functions of Organizational Culture

As illustrated in Figure 18–2, an organization's culture fulfills four functions.[9] To help bring these four functions to life, let us consider how each of them has taken shape at United Parcel Service (UPS), the company with the familiar

[7] Dennis Kneale, "Working at IBM: Intense Loyalty in a Rigid Culture," *The Wall Street Journal*, April 7, 1986, p. 21.

[8] See Allan Halcrow, "A Symbolic Gesture at Sikorsky," *Personnel Journal*, March 1986, p. 11.

[9] Adapted from Smircich, "Concepts of Culture and Organizational Analysis."

■ **FIGURE 18–2**   Four Functions of Organizational Culture

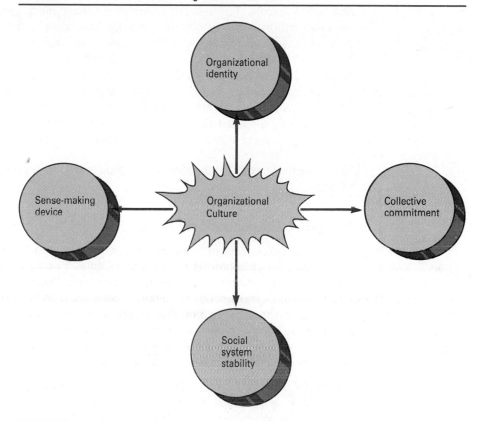

SOURCE: Adapted from discussion in Linda Smircich, "Concepts of Culture and Organizational Analysis," *Administrative Science Quarterly*, September 1983, pp. 339–58.

brown delivery vans. UPS is a particularly instructive example because it is the most profitable company in its industry and has a very strong and distinctive culture.

1. *Gives members an organizational identity:* According to *Fortune* magazine: "What makes UPS stand out is its ability to attract, develop, and keep talented people. Top managers, most of whom have come up through the ranks, instill a spirit of winning so pervasive that people who fail are ranked as least best, not losers. Workers, in turn, have almost a Japanese-like identification with the company."[10]

2. *Facilitates collective commitment:* UPS managers own almost all of the firm's stock. Many managers who began their careers with UPS as drivers and clerks have retired as multimillionaires. Compensation throughout the company is high by industry standards, with delivery truck drivers averaging $16 per hour. Middle managers receive generous stock bonuses and dividend checks.

---

[10] Kenneth Labich, "Big Changes at Big Brown," *Fortune*, January 18, 1988, p. 56.

3. *Promotes social system stability:* UPS is known for its strict standards and tight controls. For instance, employees must meet grooming standards and task performance is specified down to the finest detail. "Longtime UPSers—most of the work force due to a 4% turnover rate—talk about their company's 'mystique,' an aura that generates an unusual mixture of passionate commitment to hard work and a strong identification with the company."[11]

4. *Shapes behavior by helping members make sense of their surroundings:* UPS recruits primarily from its 40,000-person part-time work force of college students. Only the most promising are offered full-time positions. Even those with college degrees start at bottom-rung jobs to learn the basics of the business.

This example shows that the term *social glue* is indeed appropriate in reference to organizational culture.

Research on Organizational Cultures

Because the concept of organizational culture is a relatively recent addition to OB, the research base is incomplete. Studies to date are characterized by inconsistent definitions and varied methodologies. Quantitative treatments are rare since there is no agreement on how to measure cultural variables. Anecdotal accounts, in the form of practical examples drawn from interviews, are the norm. As a matter of convenience, we will review two streams of organizational culture research in this section. One stream has been reported in best-selling books and the other in research journal articles.

Anecdotal Evidence from Best-Selling Books about Organizational Culture.
Initial widespread interest in organizational cultures was stirred by William Ouchi's 1981 best-seller, *Theory Z: How American Business Can Meet the Japanese Challenge*. Interviews with representatives from 20 large American corporations doing business in both the United States and Japan led Ouchi to formulate his Theory Z model. Ouchi applied the Theory Z label to a few highly successful American organizations—including IBM, Eli Lilly, Intel, Eastman Kodak, and Hewlett-Packard—that exhibited Japanese-like qualities. Primary among those qualities was a participative, consensual decision-making style (see Figure 18–3). Ouchi found the internal cultures of these hybrid companies so consistent that he called them *clans*.

Ouchi noted, however, that clannish Theory Z organizations can become socially inbred to the point of rejecting unfamiliar ideas and people. Theory Z characteristics, when taken to extreme, can stifle creativity and foster unintentional sexism and racism. For instance, Ouchi described top management in one Theory Z company as "wholesome, disciplined, hard-working, and honest, but unremittingly white, male, and middle class."[12] From a research standpoint, Ouchi's two main contributions were: (1) focusing attention on internal culture

---

[11] Ibid., p. 58.

[12] William G. Ouchi, *Theory Z: How American Business Can Meet the Japanese Challenge* (Reading, Mass.: Addison-Wesley Publishing, 1981), p. 91.

■   **FIGURE 18-3**   Ouchi's Theory Z Model of Organization

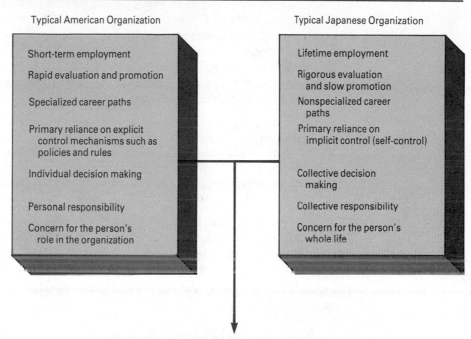

Typical American Organization

- Short-term employment
- Rapid evaluation and promotion
- Specialized career paths
- Primary reliance on explicit control mechanisms such as policies and rules
- Individual decision making
- Personal responsibility
- Concern for the person's role in the organization

Typical Japanese Organization

- Lifetime employment
- Rigorous evaluation and slow promotion
- Nonspecialized career paths
- Primary reliance on implicit control (self-control)
- Collective decision making
- Collective responsibility
- Concern for the person's whole life

Theory Z Organization

- *Long-term employment:* Recycling of human talent through retraining
- *Relatively slow evaluation and promotion:* Promotability determined by skills rather than seniority
- *Cross-functional career paths:* Wide-ranging skills acquired through job rotation
- *Combination of explicit and implicit control:* Self-control guided by policies and rules
- *Participative, consensual decision making:* All affected employees are involved in key decisions
- *Personal responsibility:* Individual managers are held accountable for their decisions
- *Wholistic concern for employees:* Employees' work and nonwork lives are important to organization

SOURCE: Adapted from discussion in William G. Ouchi, *Theory Z: How American Business Can Meet the Japanese Challenge* (Reading, Mass.: Addison-Wesley Publishing, 1981).

as a key determinant of organizational effectiveness and (2) developing an instructive typology of organizations based in part on cultural variables.

Close on the heels of Ouchi's book came two 1982 best-sellers: Deal and Kennedy's *Corporate Cultures: The Rites and Rituals of Corporate Life*[13] and Peters and Waterman's *In Search of Excellence*.[14] Both books drew upon interviews and the authors' consulting experience. Each team of authors relied on abundant anecdotal evidence to make the point that successful companies tend to have strong cultures. For example, Peters and Waterman observed:

> Without exception, the dominance and coherence of culture proved to be an essential quality of the excellent companies. Moreover, the stronger the culture and the more it was directed toward the marketplace, the less need was there for policy manuals, organization charts, or detailed procedures and rules. In these companies, people way down the line know what they are supposed to do in most situations because the handful of guiding values is crystal clear.[15]

These best-sellers generated excitement about cultural factors such as heroes and stories. But they failed to break new ground in the measurement and evaluation of organizational cultures.[16] Their main contribution was the vivid portrayal of the rich cultural texture of today's organizations.

Evidence from Research Articles.   Three very different studies yielded the following insights:

- A survey of 1,498 American managers (13 percent female) suggested that greater congruence between individual and organizational values can enhance personal fulfillment and organizational effectiveness.[17]
- According to a case study of a merger between two banks, the blending of different but functional organizational cultures can cause major difficulties. Poor communication, resistance to change, and even sabotage were observed before, during, and after the merger.[18]
- Seventy-five interviews with human resource executives from 14 large U.S. companies revealed two distinct reward systems: hierarchy-based and performance-based. Companies with hierarchy-based reward systems were found to have cultures characterized as clans (following Ouchi's use of the term). On the other hand, organizations with performance-

---

[13] See Terrence E. Deal and Allan A. Kennedy, *Corporate Cultures: The Rites and Rituals of Corporate Life* (Reading, Mass.: Addison-Wesley Publishing, 1982).

[14] See Thomas J. Peters and Robert H. Waterman, Jr., *In Search of Excellence* (New York: Harper & Row, 1982).

[15] Ibid., pp. 75–76.

[16] Critical reviews of these two popular books can be found in William I. Gorden, "Corporate Cultures," *Academy of Management Review*, April 1984, pp. 365–66; and Daniel T. Carroll, "A Disappointing Search for Excellence," *Harvard Business Review*, November–December 1983, pp. 78–88.

[17] Details may be found in Barry Z. Posner, James M. Kouzes, and Warren H. Schmidt, "Shared Values Make a Difference: An Empirical Test of Corporate Culture," *Human Resources Management*, Fall 1985, pp. 293–309.

[18] See Anthony F. Buono, James L. Bowditch, and John W. Lewis III, "When Cultures Collide: The Anatomy of a Merger," *Human Relations*, May 1985, pp. 477–500.

based reward systems tended to have "market" cultures. In a market culture, the individual-organization relationship is driven by a negotiated contract rather than mutual loyalty, as in a clannish organization. While noting that the different reward systems and cultures are not necessarily good or bad, the researchers emphasized the importance of reward systems in shaping organizational cultures.

> Reward systems express and reinforce the values and norms that comprise corporate culture. A careful consideration of reward system design can help decision makers successfully modify the organization's culture. Reward systems are, in effect, powerful mechanisms that can be used by managers to communicate desired attitudes and behaviors to organization members. We believe that, over time, cultures are amenable to change through the clear communication of performance criteria and the consistent application of rewards.[19]

With this background of theory and research in mind, let us turn our attention to the development of organizational cultures.

DEVELOPING ORGANIZATIONAL CULTURES

Imagine yourself in the position of a manager at Atari a few years ago when the following conditions prevailed:

> A marketing manager who worked at Atari before it got new management recalls: "You can't imagine how much time and energy around here went into politics. You had to determine who was on first base this month in order to figure out what you needed in order to get the job done. There were no rules. There were no clear values. Two of the men at the top stood for diametrically opposite things. Your bosses were constantly changing. All this meant that you never had time to develop a routine way for getting things done at the interface between your job and the next guy's. Without rules for working with one another, a lot of people got hurt, got burned out, and were never taught the 'Atari way' of doing things because there wasn't an Atari way."[20]

Atari's new management has since turned the company around. But what could you, as a manager at Atari, have done to develop the company's culture? This section suggests some workable answers by discussing how culture can become a competitive advantage and introducing a practical model for developing an organization's culture.

Organizational Culture as a Competitive Advantage

It is possible for the four cultural functions listed in Figure 18–2 to be so well fulfilled that they give the organization a competitive advantage. One

---

[19] Jeffrey Kerr and John W. Slocum, Jr., "Managing Corporate Culture through Reward Systems," *Academy of Management Executive,* May 1987, p. 106.

[20] Richard Pascal, "Fitting New Employees into the Company Culture," *Fortune,* May 28, 1984, p. 40.

scholar cited three criteria of an organizational culture capable of providing a sustained competitive advantage. The culture must be *valuable, rare,* and *impossible to imitate.*[21] While many organizations achieve valuable and rare cultures, it requires great diligence to build one that is impossible to imitate. Of course, from a competitive standpoint, *impossible* does not necessarily mean physically impossible; it can mean doing more than others are *willing* to do.

A prime example of building a culture around things that competitors are unwilling to do is Stew Leonard's, the world's largest dairy store, in Norwalk, Connecticut. Picture a single 100,000-square-foot store with 100,000 customers which sells $100 million worth of groceries annually! That's Stew Leonard's. At the front door of the store is a huge 3-ton rock with the following inscription:

OUR POLICY

Rule 1—The customer is always right!

Rule 2—If the customer is ever wrong, reread Rule 1.[22]

To casual observers, it is just a big rock with an interesting inscription. To Stew Leonard's employees, however, it is a tangible symbol of a deep-seated commitment to serving customers better than anyone else. Supporting that symbol are a rigorous hiring program and a promote-from-within policy ensuring that outstanding people are hired and retained. Stew Leonard's competitors could put all kinds of inscribed boulders in front of their stores, but they would have great difficulty imitating the cultural commitment to excellent day-to-day customer service. Stew Leonard's culture gives the company a competitive advantage.

A Practical Model for Developing an Organization's Culture

Judging from the foregoing discussion, imitation of another organization's culture is unsatisfactory. (Careful study of successful organizations' cultures and skillful *adaptation,* however, is a good idea.) This is true not only from a competitive standpoint but also because management has imperfect control over culture. According to Schein, every culture is unique because:

> The culture that eventually evolves in a particular organization is . . . a complex outcome of external pressures, internal potentials, responses to critical events, and, probably, to some unknown degree, chance factors that could not be predicted from a knowledge of either the environment or the members.[23]

The best alternative for management is to influence and develop the organization's unique culture as it evolves naturally. The model in Figure 18–4 is a practical road map for this endeavor.

---

[21] Drawn from discussion in Jay B. Barney, "Organizational Culture: Can It Be a Source of Sustained Competitive Advantage?" *Academy of Management Review,* July 1986, pp. 656–65.

[22] Stew Leonard, "Love That Customer!" *Management Review,* October 1987, p. 36.

[23] Schein, *Organizational Culture and Leadership,* pp. 83–84.

■ **FIGURE 18–4** How to Develop an Organization's Culture

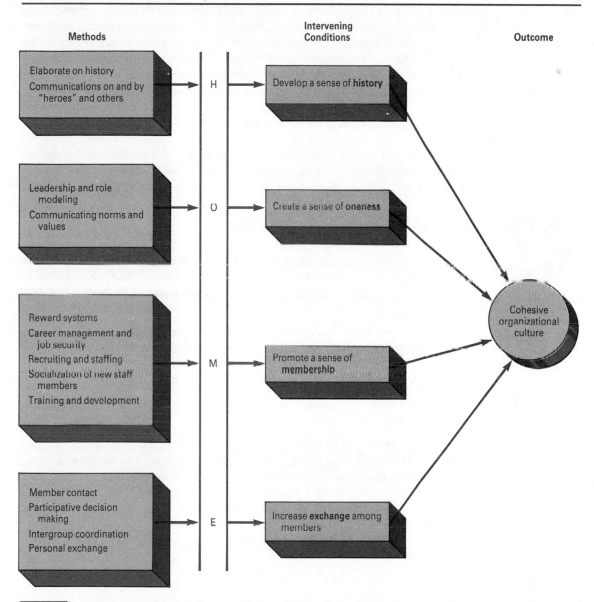

Because the authors of this model view a strong organizational culture as being analogous to a well-functioning family, the word HOME is a particularly appropriate acronym.[24] H stands for *history,* O stands for *oneness,* M stands for *membership,* and E stands for *exchange.* Each of these intervening conditions can foster the desired outcome, a cohesive organizational culture, if management makes a concerted and coordinated effort to implement the methods listed in Figure 18–4. Recall from our opening case, for example, how history plays a big part in Hershey's culture.[25] Also, as discussed earlier, reward systems (in the M portion of the model) are a potent cultural force subject to managerial control.

Having examined organizational cultures as the behavioral context for all organizational change, we now need a better understanding of the change process itself.

■ BASIC CONCEPTS OF ORGANIZATIONAL CHANGE

The only certainty in modern organizational life is constant change. This statement may be a well-worn cliché, but it remains a fact of life. Managers are challenged to either prepare for change and manage it or be bowled over by it. According to a pair of consulting psychologists:

> Today's business environment produces change in the workplace more suddenly and frequently than ever before. Mergers, acquisitions, hostile takeovers, deregulation, new technology, and organizations going through cycles of centralization and decentralization are all factors that contribute to a growing climate of uncertainty. Jobs, health, even marriages can be placed at risk, jeopardizing productivity and profitability. Now, more than ever, organizations must find ways to manage and master change.[26]

A significant emotional/attitudinal consequence of the present era of rapid and complex change is greater insecurity among managers. In repeat surveys of 500 U.S. managers, the proportion of middle managers who said they were "very secure" in their positions dropped from 43 percent in 1982 to 27 percent in 1986.[27] Growing insecurity among managers mirrors an erosion of perceived job security, commitment, loyalty, trust, and motivation among all employees. Management can help curb these negative outcomes by better managing change.

---

[24] See Warren Gross and Shula Shichman, "How to Grow an Organizational Culture," *Personnel,* September 1987, pp. 52–56.

[25] The role of history in organizational culture is discussed in Alan L. Wilkins and Nigel J. Bristow, "For Successful Organization Culture, Honor Your Past," *Academy of Management Executive,* August 1987, pp. 221–29.

[26] Cynthia D. Scott and Dennis T. Jaffe, "Survive and Thrive in Times of Change," *Training and Development Journal,* April 1988, p. 25.

[27] Data from Kirkland Ropp, "Restructuring: Survival of the Fittest," *Personnel Administrator,* February 1987, pp. 44–47.

■ **FIGURE 18–5** A Generic Typology of Organizational Change

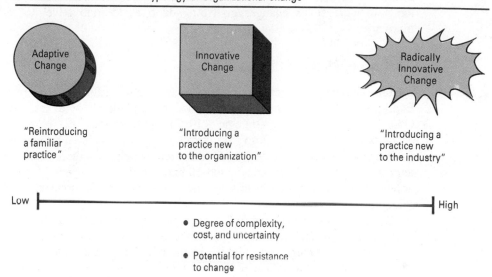

"Reintroducing a familiar practice"

"Introducing a practice new to the organization"

"Introducing a practice new to the industry"

Low ├──┤ High

- Degree of complexity, cost, and uncertainty
- Potential for resistance to change

Types of Change

A useful three-way typology of change is displayed in Figure 18–5.[28] This typology is generic because it relates to all sorts of change, including both administrative and technological changes. Adaptive change is lowest in complexity, cost, and uncertainty.[29] It involves reimplementation of a change in the same organizational unit at a later time or imitation of a similar change by a different unit. For example, an adaptive change for a department store would be to rely on 12-hour days during the annual inventory week. The store's accounting department could imitate the same change in work hours during tax preparation time. Adaptive changes are not particularly threatening to employees because they are familiar.

Innovative changes fall midway on the continuum of complexity, cost, and uncertainty. An experiment with flexitime, as discussed in Chapter 15, by a farm supply warehouse company qualifies as an innovative change if other firms in the industry already use it. Unfamiliarity, and hence greater uncertainty, make fear of change a problem with innovative changes.

At the high end of the continuum of complexity, cost, and uncertainty are radically innovative changes. Changes of this sort are the most difficult to implement and tend to be the most threatening to managerial confidence and employee job security. They can tear the fabric of an organization's culture. For example, organized labor was very resentful when robots were introduced

---

[28] This three-way typology of change is adapted from discussion in Paul C. Nutt, "Tactics of Implementation," *Academy of Management Journal*, June 1986, pp. 230–61.

[29] These variables come from Manuel London and John Paul MacDuffie, "Technological Innovations: Case Examples and Guidelines," *Personnel*, November 1987, pp. 26–38.

in the automobile industry. As indicated in Figure 18–5, resistance to change tends to increase as changes go from adaptive, to innovative, to radically innovative.

A Model of Planned Change

Some changes are forced upon the organization by unforeseen circumstances. Examples include wildcat strikes, accidents, and death of a key executive. Other changes, including strategic shifts, reorganizations, personnel changes, or adoption of new technology, are purposefully implemented by management. Contingency plans and crisis management teams help managers deal with unintentional change.[30] A systematic and planned approach is needed for the intentional variety. Our focus in this section is on the general concept of planned change.

Most models of organizational change portray the process in unrealistically static terms. Changes and the organizational and decisional contexts in which they occur are dynamic and highly interactive. Paul Nutt, whose research on decision making was discussed in Chapter 14, has synthesized a dynamic and realistic model of planned organizational change (see Figure 18–6). It is appropriately labeled a *transactional* model. Five stages of change form the skeleton of Nutt's model. Those stages are formulation, concept development, detailing, evaluation, and installation. Let us explore the primary components of this model.

Decision and Developmental Modes.   Nutt's model makes an important distinction between the decision-making and developmental portions of the change process. Within the circle, in the decision mode portion of the model, is the manager who has formal authority and ultimate responsibility for the proposed change. As we know from previous chapters, however, organizational problem solving, creativity, and decision making generally are *group* activities. This is where the developmental mode enters the picture. Committees and project teams normally are responsible for assisting line managers as they translate a change from an idea into an accomplished fact. The decision-making manager may or may not play a full role in the developmental team. Regardless, as indicated by the arrows in Figure 18–6, critical transactions occur between the manager and developmental team during each stage.

A Series of Transactions.   Each set of transactions brings the proposed change closer to reality. The manager can contribute to the change process by specifying needs in stage I and premises (assumptions about how to proceed) in stage II. He or she can further assist the developmental team by pointing out misconceptions in stage III and specifying criteria for weighing options in stage IV.

[30] See, for example, Dale D. McConkey, ''Planning for Uncertainty,'' *Business Horizons*, January–February 1987, pp. 40–45; and Ian I. Mitroff, Paul Shrivastava, and Firdaus E. Udwadia, ''Effective Crisis Management,'' *The Academy of Management Executive*, November 1987, pp. 283–92.

■ **FIGURE 18–6** Nutt's Transactional Model of Planned Organizational Change

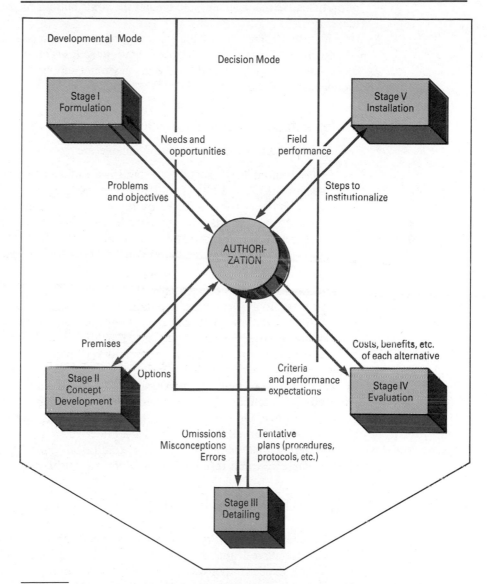

SOURCE: Paul C. Nutt, "Tactics of Implementation," *Academy of Management Journal,* June 1986, p. 235. Used with permission.

Before installation of the change, in stage V, the manager needs to do some administrative housekeeping. Skilled people, resources, incentives, and delegation mechanisms must be in place. For its part, the committee or project team defines problems and suggests objectives. It also recommends options and tentative plans, considers costs and benefits, and gathers feedback information once the change has been installed.[31] Of course, the greater the degree of participative management, the greater the contributions by the developmental team.

Within the framework of this general process of planned change one (or a combination) of the following implementation tactics is employed. These tactics determine how much relative say the manager and support team have in shaping the change.

Implementation Tactics: Research Insights

Four basic tactics for implementing change are:

- *Intervention:* Key executives establish a rationale for the change, build support for it, and influence the change process.
- *Participation:* Those affected by the proposed change help design it.
- *Persuasion:* Experts such as consultants and staff specialists attempt to sell the change to those likely to be affected by it.
- *Edict:* Managers direct subordinates to adopt the change.[32]

A study of major changes in 91 government and private service organizations in the United States and Canada provided evidence about the use and effectiveness of these four implementation tactics. The changes were reconstructed via multiple interviews with key executives. Persuasion turned out to be the most frequently used tactic (42 percent). Edict was next (23 percent), followed by intervention (19 percent) and participation (17 percent). The most effective implementation tactic was intervention (100 percent success rate), followed by participation (84 percent), persuasion (73 percent), and edict (43 percent). Ironically, intervention and participation, the *least frequently used* tactics, were the *most effective*. On the other hand, the most frequently used tactics—persuasion and edict—turned out to be the least effective.[33]

Considering that participation is the traditional remedy for resistance to change, these research results take on added significance.

■ UNDERSTANDING AND MANAGING RESISTANCE TO CHANGE

In an interview with *Business Week,* ReBecca K. Roloff, the 32-year-old Pillsbury executive featured in the Chapter 1 opening case, said: "This generation doesn't expect tomorrow to be a lot like yesterday. . . . It doesn't hold the view that change is unfair."[34] Unfortunately, the typical employee does

---

[31] For excellent reading on large-scale organizational change, see Jeffrey K. Liker, David B. Roitman, and Ethel Roskies, "Changing Everything All at Once: Work Life and Technological Change," *Sloan Management Review,* Summer 1987, pp. 29–47; and Gloria Barczak, Charles Smith, and David Wilemon, "Managing Large-Scale Organizational Change," *Organizational Dynamics,* Autumn 1987, pp. 22–35.

[32] Adapted from Nutt, "Tactics of Implementation," p. 242.

[33] Ibid., pp. 242, 252.

[34] Teresa Carson, "Fast-Track Kids," *Business Week,* November 10, 1986, p. 91.

■ **TABLE 18–3** Resistance to Change in Action

> Sophisticated computer technology allows the central office of a large company to begin monitoring electronic telecommunications switching equipment in remote locations. This may eventually allow for fewer and less skilled employees at local sites. But the local technicians resist the central monitoring centers. They fear forced relocation, job loss, the inability to keep up their skills, and loss of control over their work while they nevertheless remain accountable for the local operation. When a central monitoring center is implemented by management fiat, it fails. Technicians resist working in the center and taking orders from it. When, however, the technicians later become involved in the center's implementation (e.g., deciding who staffs it and when it has control over the local site), the concept succeeds.
>
> SOURCE: Manuel London and John Paul MacDuffie, "Technological Innovations: Case Examples and Guidelines," *Personnel,* November 1987, p. 26.

not share this fast-track executive's enthusiasm for change in the workplace. Rare is the manager who does not have several stories about carefully cultivated changes that died on the vine because of resistance to change (see Table 18–3). This section examines why employees resist change, relevant research, and practical ways of dealing with the problem.

Why People Resist Changes in the Workplace

No matter how technically or administratively perfect a proposed change may be, *people* will make or break it. **Resistance to change** is an emotional/behavioral response to real or imagined threats to an established work routine. It can take many forms, ranging from foot-dragging and lack of cooperation, to vocal opposition, to sabotage. Eight leading reasons why employees resist change are:[35]

1. *Surprise and fear of the unknown:* When innovative or radically innovative changes are introduced without warning, affected employees become fearful of the implications. Grapevine rumors fill the void created by a lack of official announcements. Harvard's Rosabeth Moss Kanter recommends appointing a transition manager charged with keeping all relevant parties adequately informed.[36]

2. *Climate of mistrust:* Trust, as discussed in Chapter 10, involves reciprocal faith in others' intentions and behavior. Mutual mistrust can doom an otherwise well-conceived change to failure. Mistrust encourages secrecy, which begets deeper mistrust. Managers who trust their employees make the change process an open, honest, and participative affair. Employees who in turn trust manage-

---

[35] Adapted in part from Joseph Stanislao and Bettie C. Stanislao, "Dealing with Resistance to Change," *Business Horizons,* July–August 1983, pp. 74–78.

[36] See Rosabeth Moss Kanter, "Managing Traumatic Change: Avoiding the 'Unlucky 13,'" *Management Review,* May 1987, pp. 23–24.

ment are more willing to expend extra effort and take chances with something different.

3. *Fear of failure:* Intimidating changes on the job can cause employees to doubt their capabilities. Self-doubt erodes self-confidence and cripples personal growth and development.

4. *Loss of status and/or job security:* Administrative and technological changes that threaten to alter power bases or eliminate jobs generally trigger strong resistance. For example, participative management programs often run into stubborn resistance from middle managers and supervisors who fear a loss of status (see Table 18–4).

5. *Peer pressure:* Someone who is not directly affected by a change may actively resist it to protect the interest of his or her friends and co-workers.

6. *Disruption of cultural traditions and/or group relationships:* Whenever individuals are transferred, promoted, or reassigned, cultural and group dynamics are thrown into disequilibrium.

7. *Personality conflicts:* Just as a friend can get away with telling us something we would resent hearing from an adversary, the personalities of change agents can breed resistance.

8. *Lack of tact and/or poor timing:* Undue resistance can occur because changes are introduced in an insensitive manner or at an awkward time. One of J. C. Penney Company's nine principles of managing change advises: "Determine if there is a 'natural' point in time to end the old and begin the new."[37]

Research on Resistance to Change

The classic study of resistance to change was reported in 1948 by Lester Coch and John R. P. French. They observed the introduction of a new work procedure in a garment factory. The change was introduced in three different ways to four separate groups of workers. In the "no participation" group, the garment makers were simply told about the new procedure. Members of a second group, called the "representative" group, were introduced to the change by a trained co-worker. Employees in the "total participation" groups learned of the new work procedure through a graphic presentation of its cost-saving potential. Mixed results were recorded for the representative group. The no participation and total participation groups, meanwhile, went in opposite directions. Output dropped sharply for the no participation group, while grievances and turnover climbed. After a small dip in performance, the total participation groups achieved record-high output levels while experiencing no turnover.[38] Since the Coch and French study, participation has been the recommended approach for overcoming resistance to change.

Two recent studies of attitudes toward computers have implications for those concerned with resistance to change. Computers are an appropriate subject

---

[37] J. Alan Ofner, "Managing Change," *Personnel Administrator*, September 1984, p. 20.

[38] See Lester Coch and John R. P. French, Jr., "Overcoming Resistance to Change," *Human Relations*, 1948, pp. 512–32.

■ TABLE 18–4 Middle-Manager and Supervisory Resistance to Participative Management

Corning, N.Y.—When senior management at *Corning Glass Works* here began a program last year to foster a more participatory style of management, some supervisors were dubious. Now they're believers.

What turned them around were experiences like one at the company's plant in nearby Erwin, N.Y., where a die-manufacturing problem needed to be solved. Supervisors put five machinists in a room and gave them whatever information they needed. Five hours later, the team had a solution costing less than $200.

Under the old management style, says Bob Pierce, a department head, supervisors and engineers would have huddled, "and it would have come out as an edict" with uncertain results. Now, by getting workers involved, the people who actually have to carry out a decision "have a personal obligation to make it happen."

Corning has been fortunate. Getting plant supervisors and middle managers to give it a serious try is the essential first step in establishing a more participatory management style. But to hear executives tell it, that isn't an easy task at many companies. In fact, says Mark Andrews Jr., president of Mark Andy Inc., a small printing-press maker in Chesterfield, Mo., "It's like pulling teeth."

Eager Troops

The aim of participatory management is to get first-line supervisors and plant managers to elicit ways of doing a better job from workers on the shop floor. Hourly workers who have been ignored for years, usually like the idea of being listened to, and top executives who launched the program are eager for it to happen.

But mid-level employees, like the Corning supervisors in Erwin, are sandwiched in between. They worked hard to get into management and tend to guard their old-style authority jealously. They grew up in a system in which "management has all the answers"—even if it didn't—and they have long been taught that their job is to keep the hourly employees in the dark and the production lines humming.

Now, their bosses tell them, "We want more participation" from the workers, as well as better management and a steady flow of quality products, says Joseph Propersi, Corning's manufacturing-education manager. Managers in the middle are left wondering, "How do I do both?"

Faced with that dilemma, many managers and supervisors dig in to oppose the change. When one big telecommunications company started its program, middle managers boycotted an orientation meeting. At S.C. Johnson & Son, Inc., in Racine, Wis., Phillip Ricco, the productivity director, says he once watched a hard-bitten manager bluntly tell a boss: "I've been here longer than you, and I'll be here after you've gone, so don't tell me what really counts at this company."

Because of the central role middle managers and supervisors play in implementing a more participatory management style, attitudes like that obviously jeopardize the entire program. "People in the middle are the ones who make it go or don't go," says Mark Arnold, consulting services director of Organizational Dynamics Inc. in Burlington, Mass.

The problem of getting middle managers to make the transition to managing worker teams from the more traditional, autocratic management of individuals "is huge," says Mr. Ricco of S.C. Johnson. "It's *the* problem." Johnson, he says, has made more progress than most companies. Among other things, it holds working sessions three or four times a year to help middle managers focus on the company's overall strategy and goals, and it publishes a quarterly managers' newsletter.

SOURCE: Excerpted from Leonard M. Apcar, "Middle Managers and Supervisors Resist Moves to More Participatory Management." Reprinted by permission of *The Wall Street Journal*, Dow Jones & Company, Inc., September 16, 1985, p. 25. All rights reserved.

matter because they are a significant technological change encumbered by a great deal of resistance.

1. A survey of 284 nonmanagerial office personnel (43 percent male) employed by three California manufacturers examined preconditions for willingness to use computers. Regarding the use of computers, female employees tended to have more experience, stronger favorable attitudes, and fewer negative attitudes than their male counterparts. There were no significant relationships between education, age, or tenure and positive or negative attitudes toward computers. Employees who actually used computers in their work had more positive attitudes toward computers than co-workers who had little or no experience with computers. Those reporting high job involvement had significantly fewer concerns about working with computers than co-workers with low job involvement. These results suggest that hands-on experience with computers, whether through training or on-the-job practice, can foster positive attitudes toward working with computers.[39]

2. A pair of studies relying on university psychology students as subjects revealed a significant positive correlation between personal efficacy and the use of a number of advanced technology products. People with high personal efficacy scores believe they can handle nonsocial situations such as solving puzzles and building things. The researchers concluded that "only through changes in perceived efficacy does experience with computer technology lead to a higher likelihood of technology adoption."[40] A practical implication springing from this study involves the need to accompany computer skills training with personal efficacy development. For example, computer trainees could be exposed to persuasive evidence about the many *personal* benefits of learning how to use computers.

Alternative Strategies for Overcoming Resistance to Change

Organizational change experts have criticized the tendency to treat participation as a cure-all for resistance to change. They prefer a contingency approach because resistance can take many forms and, furthermore, because situational factors vary (see Table 18–5). Participation + Involvement does have its place, but it takes time that is not always available. Similarly, as indicated in Table 18–5, each of the other five methods has its situational niche, advantages, and drawbacks. In short, there is no universal strategy for overcoming resistance to change. Managers need a complete repertoire of change strategies.[41]

---

[39] Complete details may be found in Anat Rafaeli, "Employee Attitudes toward Working with Computers," *Journal of Occupational Behavior,* April 1986, pp. 89–106.

[40] Thomas Hill, Nancy D. Smith, and Millard F. Mann, "Role of Efficacy Expectations in Predicting the Decision to Use Advanced Technologies: The Case of Computers," *Journal of Applied Psychology,* May 1987, p. 313.

[41] Excellent advice on building political support for change can be found in David A. Nadler, "The Effective Management of Organizational Change," in *Handbook of Organizational Behavior,* ed. Jay W. Lorsch (Englewood Cliffs, N.J.: Prentice-Hall, 1987), pp. 358–69.

■ **TABLE 18–5** Six Strategies for Overcoming Resistance to Change

Approach	Commonly Used in Situations	Advantages	Drawbacks
Education + Communication	Where there is a lack of information or inaccurate information and analysis.	Once persuaded, people will often help with the implementation of the change.	Can be very time-consuming if lots of people are involved.
Participation + Involvement	Where the initiators do not have all the information they need to design the change, and where others have considerable power to resist.	People who participate will be committed to implementing change, and any relevant information they have will be integrated into the change plan.	Can be very time-consuming if participators design an inappropriate change.
Facilitation + Support	Where people are resisting because of adjustment problems.	No other approach works as well with adjustment problems.	Can be time-consuming, expensive, and still fail.
Negotiation + Agreement	Where someone or some group will clearly lose out in a change, and where that group has considerable power to resist.	Sometimes it is a relatively easy way to avoid major resistance.	Can be too expensive in many cases if it alerts others to negotiate for compliance.
Manipulation + Co-optation	Where other tactics will not work, or are too expensive.	It can be a relatively quick and inexpensive solution to resistance problems.	Can lead to future problems if people feel manipulated.
Explicit + Implicit coercion	Where speed is essential, and the change initiators possess considerable power.	It is speedy, and can overcome any kind of resistance.	Can be risky if it leaves people mad at the initiators.

SOURCE: Reprinted by permission of the *Harvard Business Review.* An exhibit from "Choosing Strategies for Change" by John P. Kotter and Leonard A. Schlesinger (March/April 1979). Copyright © 1979 by the President and Fellows of Harvard College; all rights reserved.

■ MANAGING CHANGE THROUGH ORGANIZATION DEVELOPMENT

Organization development (OD) is a branch of applied behavioral science that has a short but colorful history. Its roots trace back to the mid-1940s and such practices as laboratory training (also known as T-groups and sensitivity training) and survey feedback.[42] T-groups originally were used to develop self-awareness and interpersonal skills in structured laboratory settings.[43] Later, the practice was extended to the workplace, with enhancements such as flip-chart data collection and feedback. But abuses by inadequately trained facilitators caused T-groups to fall out of favor. Survey feedback, meanwhile, was developed by Rensis Likert (father of the five-point Likert scale commonly found on questionnaires) and his University of Michigan colleagues. They discovered that a positive climate for change could be created by having employees complete an attitude survey and then discuss the cumulative results. Unlike T-groups, survey feedback is alive and well today. From this mixed beginning grew a

---

[42] Adapted from Wendell L. French, "The Emergence and Early History of Organization Development: With Reference to Influences on and Interaction among Some of the Key Actors," *Group & Organization Studies,* September 1982, pp. 261–77.

[43] For a recent perspective of T-groups, see Robert E. Kaplan, "Is Openness Passé?" *Human Relations,* March 1986, pp. 229–43.

loosely knit collection of practices based on the assumption that behavioral science techniques can help employees and organizations function properly.

In this final section, we define organization development and examine how it can facilitate organizational change.

OD: Definition and Identifying Characteristics

The authors of a recent review of the field of OD defined **organization development** as follows:

> Applying theory from psychology and organizational behavior, organization development (OD) comprises a set of actions undertaken to improve organizational effectiveness and employee well-being. These actions, or "interventions," are typically designed and sequenced by an OD consultant following his/her diagnosis of an organization's needs and shortcomings. The tool kit these practitioners draw on ranges broadly from organization-wide changes in structure to psychotherapeutic counseling sessions with groups and individuals.[44]

The sheer diversity of practitioners and techniques wearing the label OD make precise definition difficult. Lack of a unifying theory does not help. Consequently, it is instructive to expand on the above definition with a brief overview of four identifying characteristics of OD.

OD Involves Profound Change.   Change agents using OD generally desire deep and long-lasting improvement. OD consultant Warner Burke, for example, who strives for fundamental *cultural* change, wrote: "By fundamental change, as opposed to fixing a problem or improving a procedure, I mean that some significant aspect of an organization's culture will never be the same."[45]

OD Is Value-Loaded.   Owing to the fact that OD is rooted partially in humanistic psychology, many OD consultants carry certain values or biases into the client organization. They prefer cooperation over conflict, self-control over institutional control, and democratic and participative management over autocratic management. Not surprisingly, these values are not eagerly embraced by managers with a Theory X view of employees. (Recall the discussion of McGregor's Theories X and Y in Chapter 1.)

OD Is a Diagnosis/Prescription Cycle.   OD theorists and practitioners have long adhered to a medical model of organizations. Like medical doctors, internal and external OD consultants approach the "sick" organization, "diagnose" its ills, "prescribe" and "administer" a treatment, and "monitor" progress (see Figure 18–7). Four basic diagnostic tools include direct observation, study of internal documents, interviews, and surveys.

---

[44] Michael Beer and Anna Elise Walton, "Organization Change and Development," in *Annual Review of Psychology*, ed. Mark Rosenzweig and Lyman W. Porter (Palo Alto, Calif.: Annual Reviews Inc., 1987), pp. 339–40.

[45] W. Warner Burke, *Organization Development: A Normative View* (Reading, Mass.: Addison-Wesley Publishing, 1987), p. 9. Also see William G. Dyer and W. Gibb Dyer, Jr., "Organization Development: System Change or Culture Change?" *Personnel*, February 1986, pp. 14–22.

■ **FIGURE 18–7**   OD as a Diagnosis/Prescription Cycle

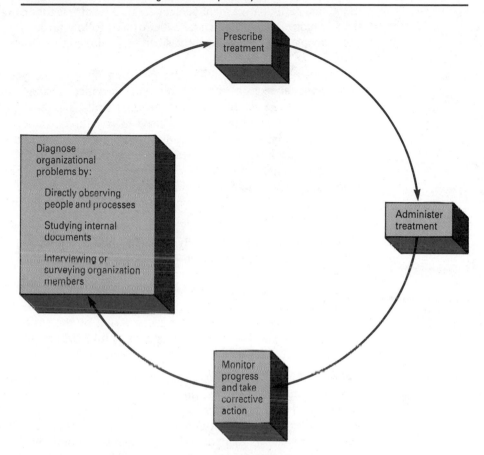

OD Is Process-Oriented.   Ideally, OD consultants focus on the form and not the content of behavioral and administrative dealings. For example, product design engineers and market researchers might be coached on how to communicate more effectively with one another without the consultant knowing the technical details of their conversations. In addition to communication, OD specialists focus on other processes, including problem solving, decision making, conflict handling, trust, power sharing, and career development.

OD Interventions

OD interventions involve different methods of introducing planned change. They should not occur in isolation. Constructive actions need to be taken before and after intervention to ensure that the desired changes take hold. A useful metaphor for this entire process was suggested by OD pioneer Kurt Lewin. He advised change agents to ''unfreeze, change, and refreeze'' the situation.[46] Tactics such as announcements, symbolic support from top management, and participative management create a readiness for change by unfreezing the situation. Refreezing can take the form of follow-up support for the change. For example, group pay incentives can be instituted to encourage greater teamwork.

Dozens of OD interventions have sprung up over the years.[47] They carry such exotic labels as action research, sociotechnical systems, grid organization (named for Blake and Mouton's Managerial Grid), and third-party consultation. Our focus here is on three widely used interventions. Importantly, each seeks to facilitate improvement of organizational processes without selling a specific "product" such as an ideal leadership style, management by objectives, or transactional analysis. These three interventions, in effect, are pure OD. Consultants using them help organizations probe for new frontiers instead of predetermined objectives. Our discussion is intended to be an illustrative rather than exhaustive exposure to OD offerings.

Role Analysis.   The **role analysis technique** strives to enhance cooperation among work group members by getting them to discuss their mutual expectations.[48] Ambiguity and misconceptions about one's own role and the roles of one's co-workers are targeted. Role analysis is typically facilitated by a consultant in a workshop setting. Each team member writes his or her role expectations on a flip-chart for discussion by the entire work group. This can be time-consuming, but the investment of time can pay off in better communication, less conflict, and improved performance (see Table 18–6).

Survey Research and Feedback.   As mentioned earlier, a stimulus for improvement can be generated by surveying employees and then feeding back the results of the survey. This widely used practice is called **survey research and feedback.** To prevent defensiveness or embarrassment, only cumulative, anonymous data is shared with respondents. Future behavior is influenced through the feedback mechanisms discussed in Chapter 7. While warning against information overload, feedback expert David Nadler recommends that feedback data be relevant, understandable, illustrative of real problems, valid and accurate, and controllable by those involved.[49]

Team Building.   **Team building** is a catchall term for a whole host of techniques aimed at improving the functioning of work groups. The extensive use of team building appears to be justified. In a recent survey of human resource

---

[46] See Kurt Lewin, "Group Decisions and Social Change," in *Readings in Social Psychology,* ed. J. E. Maccoby, T. W. Newcomb, and E. Harley (New York: Holt, Rinehart & Winston, 1947), pp. 459–93.

[47] See Marshall Sashkin, Ronald J. Burke, Paul R. Lawrence, and William Pasmore, "OD Approaches: Analysis and Application," *Training and Development Journal,* February 1985, pp. 44–50.

[48] Role analysis is discussed in detail in Wendell L. French and Cecil H. Bell, Jr., *Organization Development* (Englewood Cliffs, N.J.: Prentice-Hall, 1984).

[49] See David A. Nadler, *Feedback and Organization Development: Using Data-Based Methods* (Reading, Mass.: Addison-Wesley Publishing, 1977), pp. 147–48.

■ **TABLE 18–6** A Case Study of Role Analysis in Action

About 80 laborers and 12 salaried workers are employed at a small mine in northeastern Washington. The management team consists of the mine manager; the mine, mill, and maintenance superintendents; the production supervisor; the engineer; and the geologist and administrative staff. Gold is the primary product mined; mining excavation occurs through several shafts and tunnels, and ores are processed by using a cynadization mill.

The mine manager observed that, despite his team's high degree of technical expertise, many projects were not being completed successfully. There was a great deal of missed communication; team members complained about general uncertainty over who was supposed to do which tasks. The manager suspected that these problems evolved because the mine was growing rapidly, requiring each person to perform many tasks that were not usually associated with their positions.

The manager considered rewriting everyone's job description, but finally decided on role analysis as the best way to help the team resolve these problems. With the help of a corporate OD (organization development) facilitator, the manager conducted a series of role-analysis meetings. . . . Eight positions were analyzed, including those of first-line supervisor, production superintendent, geologist, engineer, office manager, maintenance superintendent, safety foreman, and mill superintendent. Some of the results are described below.

Most of the first-line supervisors attained their positions by working up through the ranks. Many of them perceived their role to be that of a helper, running down supply parts, extra tools, and so forth. In the role-analysis meeting, the mine manager explained that he wanted supervisors to *manage* their areas of responsibilities. If supervisors had to chase down spare parts, they weren't planning the work well enough in advance. The supervisors accepted this clarification and have since increased their emphasis on managerial functions.

Three superintendents are responsible, respectively, for mine production, milling, and maintenance. In the past, they usually took coordination problems to the mine manager. In the role-analysis meeting the mine manager explained that he wanted the superintendents to resolve coordination issues at their level. They were surprised to learn this, thinking the manager wanted to be actively involved in these discussions. The three superintendents now resolve coordination issues at their own level, freeing up several hours a week for the mine manager to do other things.

During the role-analysis meetings, the mine geologist and the engineer were able to identify several tasks they could help each other with. In addition, each was assigned the task of heading specific projects so that accountability could be identified.

There had been several complaints about all the paperwork demanded by the office manager. By the same token, the office manager frequently complained about incorrect entries on records and forms by other people. During the role-analysis meetings, production supervisors learned why accurate and timely paperwork is important to payroll and other administrative systems. In addition, the team identified reports requiring the same information, and with a little reconfiguration, several of these were eliminated.

Since the mine is small, a full-time safety foreman is not warranted. Safety inspection services are provided by a corporate safety professional. Before role analysis, team members believed that the corporate safety professional was a spy and an auditor. In the role-analysis meetings, he explained that he sees his role as that of a resource person for each supervisor and superintendent. The safety man explained that he does not make reports to corporate officials about the results of his inspections. Because of this clarifying discussion, he is now perceived by mine team members as a team member himself and is frequently sought out for advice.

SOURCE: Excerpted, by permission of the publisher, from "Applying Role Analysis in the Workplace," by Robert H. Buckham, from *Personnel*, February 1987, © 1987 American Management Association, New York. All rights reserved.

development managers from 179 Fortune 500 companies, team building reportedly was the most successful management technique.[50]

Team building specialist William Dyer recommends a six-phase cycle: (1) recognition of a current *problem;* (2) *data gathering* via interviews and/or discussion sessions; (3) *data evaluation;* (4) *problem solving and planning;* (5) *implementation;* and (6) *evaluation.*[51] Most of the work is completed by group members with needed structure and support from a facilitator. Communication and conflict exercises and simulations often are used to heighten awareness of flawed interpersonal processes (see Table 18–7).

OD Research and Practical Implications

Research on OD effectiveness has been hampered by a number of problems. For example, consultants' clients want concrete action for their expenditures of time and money, not experimental setups complete with control groups.[52] However, one review of 65 laboratory and field studies involving OD-related interventions produced the following insights:

- Job design, job enlargement, job enrichment, and sociotechnical systems design yielded better results at the work-group level than other interventions.
- When both white-collar and blue-collar employees were involved, multifaceted interventions—including worker participation, team building, and structural reorganization—were the most effective.
- Interventions aimed strictly at blue-collar employees generally failed.

The reviewer concluded his analysis by noting: "The single most apparent finding of this research is that no one change technique or class of techniques works well in all situations."[53]

One practical implication derived from this research is that a contingency approach to OD is required. Until researchers are able to more precisely specify the situational appropriateness of the various OD interventions, managers are advised to rely on multifaceted interventions. As indicated elsewhere in this book, goal setting, feedback, modeling, training, participation, and challenging job design have good track records relative to improving performance and satisfaction. OD's unique contribution to effective management can be to combine as many of these potent tactics as possible into well-integrated programs for planned and systematic change.

---

[50] Data from Eric Stephan, Gordon E. Mills, R. Wayne Pace, and Lenny Ralphs, "HRD in the Fortune 500: A Survey," *Training and Development Journal,* January 1988, pp. 26–32.

[51] Complete discussion can be found in William G. Dyer, *Team Building: Issues and Alternatives,* 2nd ed. (Reading, Mass.: Addison-Wesley Publishing, 1987).

[52] Three additional research problems are discussed in Beer and Walton, "Organization Change and Development," pp. 343–44.

[53] John M. Nicholas, "The Comparative Impact of Organization Development Interventions on Hard Criteria Measures," *Academy of Management Review,* October 1982, p. 540.

■ **TABLE 18–7** Team Building for the Cockpit Crews of Trans Australia Airlines

Trans Australia Airlines was alarmed by aviation statistics that indicate that no matter how technically sophisticated airplanes become, they will still be vulnerable to human error, causing incidents and accidents. The airline invited us to work with aircrews and design a management development initiative that would help them improve cockpit team work. The airline began by conducting a survey in various countries to see what was being done to help aircrew members manage their cockpit and flight operations effectively. Surprisingly it was found that very little had been done, particularly in the area of team management.

We conducted various interviews with captains, first officers, and flight engineers and with union representatives, senior managers, and check pilots and engineers who are accountable for examining their colleagues and licensing them to fly. Initially the aircrews expressed skepticism about the relevance of management principles to their work. They emphasized the high technical requirements of their jobs.

We listened carefully to the issues outlined by the members of the aircrews. We asked them what they felt were the major issues that they had to confront when they were flying. Interestingly, after voicing little interest in managerial matters, they went on to relate, chapter and verse, a number of incidents which indicated major management problems. . . .

Developing the Program

It became clear that pilots and flight engineers *did* recognize management problems in the cockpit but could not see how these could be rectified other than through a technical approach. We agreed to work with them to produce a prototype management development workshop focusing on team management.

This was proposed not as a cure-all but as one way in which crew members could assess their own skills and examine a wider context within which they did their technical work. This led to the formation of a steering group involving members of our own team, management, and union representatives of the airline, which outlined policies and principles. Then technical advisory groups were formed consisting of pilots and flight engineers. These groups collaborated to produce the detailed materials required for the team management intervention. We acted as designers.

Over the next year we produced a wide range of resources. We were able to create a learning design covering key aspects of the management of flight operations. The program uses a variety of techniques, including the following:

Specially designed videos illustrating incidents and examples cited by the aircrews.
Role play situations simulating specific incidents that the crews had to manage.
Group decision-making exercises forcing aircrews to reach decisions under pressure
   and learn the principles involved.
Group discussion relating key managerial principles and ideas to the technical aspects
   of flying.
A team management index specially adapted for the airline that allows the aircrews
   to gather personal feedback on their own team management style.

The result has been the production of an intensive cockpit management development workshop under the name Aircrew Team Management. During the workshop the pilots and flight engineers deal with issues common to normal management courses: group decision making, planning and priority setting, delegation, communication, and a variety of other similar topics. However, the nature of the program concentrates specifically on the high-tech aspects of these managerial functions in the cockpit.

SOURCE: Excerpted from Charles Margerison, Rod Davies, and Dick McCann, "High-Flying Management Development," *Training and Development Journal*, February 1987, pp. 40–41. Copyright 1987, *Training and Development Journal*, American Society for Training and Development. Reprinted with permission. All rights reserved.

SUMMARY OF KEY CONCEPTS

A. Organizational culture is the social glue that binds organizational members together through shared values, symbolic devices, and social ideals. Most of the assumptions underlying an organization's culture are taken for granted. A culture's central values are more important than its strength.

B. General manifestations of an organization's culture are shared objects, talk, behavior, and emotion. Specific manifestations of culture include rituals, legends, stories, values, and heroes. Four functions of organizational culture are organizational identity, collective commitment, social system stability, and sense-making device. Ouchi's Theory Z, which described a hybrid type of American company with Japanese-like qualities, prompted much early managerial interest in organizational cultures.

C. Culture can become a competitive advantage if it is valuable, rare, and impossible to imitate. Given that successful organizations evolve their own unique cultures, passive imitation needs to be replaced by active development. The HOME model—history, oneness, membership, exchange—can help.

D. Three types of change are adaptive, innovative, and radically innovative. They are listed in increasing order of complexity, cost, and uncertainty. Nutt's transactional model of planned organizational change demonstrates the interdependence of two modes, the decision-making manager and the developmental team. Research indicates that the two least used change implementation tactics, intervention and participation, tend to be the most effective.

E. Eight reasons employees resist change are: (1) surprise and fear of the unknown, (2) climate of mistrust, (3) fear of failure, (4) loss of status and/or job security, (5) peer pressure, (6) disruption of cultural traditions and/or group relationships, (7) personality conflicts, and (8) lack of trust and/or poor timing. Because of the classic Coch and French study of change in a garment factory, participation has long been considered the best tool for overcoming resistance to change.

F. Research suggests that resistance to computers can be reduced through a combination of hands-on training and personal efficacy development. Alternative strategies for overcoming resistance to change are education + communication, participation + involvement, facilitation + support, negotiation + agreement, manipulation + co-optation, and explicit + implicit coercion. Each has its situational appropriateness and advantages and drawbacks.

G. Modern organization development (OD) grew out of laboratory training and survey feedback. The identifying characteristics of OD are: (1) involves profound change; (2) value-loaded; (3) a diagnosis/prescription cycle; and (4) process-oriented. Kurt Lewin recommended that change agents unfreeze, change, and refreeze complex organizational situations.

H. Three pure OD interventions are role analysis, survey research and feedback, and team building. A review of OD research studies found no single best intervention. Multifaceted interventions are recommended for effective planned change.

KEY TERMS

culture

organizational culture

resistance to change

organization development (OD)

role analysis technique

survey research and feedback

team building

DISCUSSION QUESTIONS

1. How would you respond to someone who made the following statement? "Organizational cultures are not important, as far as managers are concerned."

2. What taken-for-granted assumptions do you have about the organization where you presently work or go to school? How did you learn those assumptions?

3. Can you think of any organizational heroes who have influenced your work behavior? Describe them and explain how they affected your behavior.

4. Why is it inappropriate for a manager to read a book like Peters and Waterman's best-seller, *In Search of Excellence,* and attempt to imitate the culture of an excellent company such as IBM?

5. What kinds of innovative or radically innovative changes have you experienced in the workplace?

6. Have you ever resisted a change at work? Explain the circumstances and your thinking at the time.

7. Which source of resistance to change do you think is the most common? Which is the most difficult for management to deal with?

8. In what situations would participation be an inappropriate tool for attempting to overcome resistance to change?

9. What distinguishes organization development (OD) from common management techniques such as participative decision making, job enrichment, or goal setting?

10. What would you say to a manager who insists that role analysis, for example, is the best overall OD technique?

BACK TO THE OPENING CASE

Now that you have read Chapter 18, you should be able to answer the following questions about the Hershey case:

1. What specific manifestations of organizational culture can you detect in this case?
2. From a cultural standpoint, what is the practical significance of Hershey's value survey?
3. Using OD terminology, how did Hershey's managers unfreeze, change, and refreeze the company?

EXERCISE 18

Objectives

1. To help you better understand the components of teamwork.
2. To give you a practical diagnostic tool to assess the need for team building.

Introduction

As discussed earlier in this text, teamwork is essential in modern organizations. Virtually all administrative activity is group-oriented. The more present and future managers know about effective teamwork the better.

Instructions

If you currently have a full-time or part-time job, think of your immediate work group and circle an appropriate response for each of the following five questions. If you are not currently employed, think of your work group in your last job. Alternatively, you might want to evaluate a class project team, sorority, fraternity or club to which you belong. Compute a total score and use the scoring key for interpretation.

Questionnaire[54]

1. To what extent do I feel "under wraps," that is, have private thoughts, unspoken reservations, or unexpressed feelings and opinions that I have not felt comfortable bringing out into the open?

1	2	3	4	5
Almost completely under wraps	Under wraps many times	Slightly more free and expressive than under wraps	Quite free and expressive much of the time	Almost completely free and expressive

---

[54] Excerpted from Dyer, *Team Building: Issues and Alternatives*, 2nd ed., © 1987, Addison-Wesley Publishing Company, Inc., Reading, Massachusetts. Pgs. 69–71. Reprinted with permission.

2. How effective are we, in our team, in getting out and using the ideas, opinions, and information of all team members in making decisions?

1	2	3	4	5
We don't really encourage everyone to share their ideas, opinions, and information with the team in making decisions.	Only the ideas, opinions, and information of a few members are really known and used in making decisions.	Sometimes we hear the views of most members before making decisions and sometimes we disregard most members.	A few are sometimes hesitant about sharing their opinions, but we generally have good participation in making decisions.	Everyone feels his or her ideas, opinions, and information are given a fair hearing before decisions are made.

3. How well does the team work at its tasks?

1	2	3	4	5
Coasts, loafs, makes no progress	Makes a little progress, most members loaf	Progress is slow, spurts of effective work	Above average in progress and pace of work	Works well, achieves definite progress

4. How are differences or conflicts handled in our team?

1	2	3	4	5
Differences or conflicts are denied, suppressed, or avoided at all cost.	Differences or conflicts are recognized, but remain unresolved mostly.	Differences or conflicts are recognized and some attempts are made to work them through by some members, often outside the team meetings.	Differences and conflicts are recognized and some attempts are made to deal with them in our team.	Differences and conflicts are recognized and the team usually is working them through satisfactorily.

5. How do people relate to the team leader, chairman, or "boss"?

1	2	3	4	5
The leader dominates the team and people are often fearful or passive.	The leader tends to control the team, although people generally agree with the leader's direction.	There is some give and take between the leader and the team members.	Team members relate easily to the leader and usually are able to influence leader decisions.	Team members respect the leader, but they work together as a unified team with everyone participating and no one dominant.

Total score = _____

Scoring key:

  5–9   "Get out the boxing gloves!"
 10–14   "You call this a team?"
 15–19   "Almost there; go team, Go!"
 20–25   "A real team! Line up for a team picture!"

Questions for Consideration/Class Discussion

1. Having analyzed your work group, is it a stronger or weaker team than you originally thought? Explain.
2. Which factor is your work group's biggest barrier to cooperative and productive teamwork?
3. What sort of OD intervention would be appropriate for your work group? Give details.

Index

Collecting Art
on a Shoestring

ALICIA CRAIG FAXON

Collecting Art on a Shoestring

BARRE PUBLISHERS

Barre, Massachusetts 1969

Contents

Acknowledgments

I WOULD LIKE to acknowledge first the role of Vassar College in my education, where the joy of scholarship and the zest of intellectual search became an actuality. My gratitude to the Prints and Drawings Department of the Boston Museum of Fine Arts also must be expressed. Its members have introduced me to much reference material and have demonstrated masterly research in tracing down mystery prints and drawings.

I would like to thank the DeCordova Museum in Lincoln, Massachusetts, for stimulating my interest in prints through their print club and fine exhibits. I am also grateful to Sinclair Hitchings, Keeper of Prints at the Boston Public Library, for his work in this field and his comments on the manuscript. It is seldom that scholarship goes with such an outgoing temperament and interest in sharing information. My thanks go to the friends who have read the manuscript and made suggestions, particularly Mr. Craig Wylie, Mrs. Mary Bradley, Mr. and Mrs. Daniel Schiff, Miss Anne Swearingen and Mrs. Marley Watton. My publishers also have been most helpful with ideas and criticism. Lastly, gratitude must go to my patient family who have encouraged me on this venture: Richard, Paul and Tommy.

Alicia Craig Faxon

Introduction

*"The artist must prophesy not in the sense
that he foretells things to come, but in the sense
that he tells his audience, at the risk of their dis-
pleasure, the secrets of their own hearts."*
                           R. G. Collingwood
                      THE PRINCIPLES OF ART

THIS BOOK IS WRITTEN for the average person who is interested in art, who loves beautiful and creative things
but does not have a great deal of money to spend on
collecting. It is for the lady who recently wrote to her
local newspaper saying, "I have thirty dollars to spend for a
piece of art. What should I buy?"

This book is not for art majors, experts, professionals in the
field, teachers or art dealers. They already know far more than
it includes. Neither is it for the wealthy collector with plenty
of money to spend and with dealers and experts to advise him,
nor for one who specializes in certain areas such as sets of
etchings or chessmen. It is not for a person with such hobbies
as collecting toy soldiers, dolls, fans, china, period furniture
and the like.

It is for the person of modest means who enjoys looking at
art and who wants to buy original prints, paintings, sculptures,
and artifacts for reasonable prices. It is for those who like to
explore new interests or get to know old ones more thoroughly.
It is for the young of heart who will embark on a treasure
hunt with me, filled with the spirit of adventure and possessing
strong legs!

This will be a general aid to collecting on a shoestring, not a
guide to any specific areas. If you become interested in a par-

ticular form of art, there are many good books, catalogues, museums and people to help you. I will be talking about original art for the most part, not color reproductions of famous paintings or museum reproductions of well-known pieces of sculpture. Such copies are easy to find in museums and bookstores, and there are catalogues of them available. A good quality reproduction, however, often costs as much or more than an original piece, is equally expensive to frame or mount, and does not have completely the "feel" of the original. I have no quarrel with people who want reproductions, but that is not what this book is about.

What, then, is an original? Precisely, it is something made by an artist or craftsman and by him alone. An original painting, one would think, would be unique, and this is usually the case. Artists have, however, often duplicated their most successful works, sometimes at the request of a patron who wanted to give his friends copies, or on the artist's own initiative. The thorny question of which is the original and which is the copy has caused centuries of controversy between museums and collectors, but for our purposes, they are all "originals."

The works done by a master and his studio assistants are more difficult to classify. How much was done by him, how much by his assistants? And what of works by pupils, much in the style of the master? Or the ubiquitous works "attributed to" artists? Naturally, the work of a pupil or studio assistant is not as valuable as that of the master's own hand, but it can often be attractive and interesting in its own right, pleasant to own and a great deal less expensive than the master's work. Many of the works by pupils are not copies, but pictures done under the tutelage and in the style of the master. This is something to consider when acquiring art on a shoestring. And the copy, or version, by one master of another's work has a special interest—for example, Van Gogh's copy of Delacroix or Fragonard's etching based on a painting by Tintoretto. Often a fine artist puts his own interpretation into such work and makes it doubly rewarding.

As for sculpture, a work that is an original may be produced in multiples. A bronze which is cast in a mold may result in an edition of a dozen identical statues. If there is only one of a bronze it is called "unique" but a limited number of identical casts are considered originals. Of course this does not occur in stone or wood carving. In whatever medium a piece of sculpture may be done, however, it is likely to be the most expensive type of art to buy, because of the complicated technique employed, the length of time sculpture takes and the high cost of the material. It is a very rewarding sort of art to collect, but not one into which the shoestring collector can enter lightly.

In the case of ancient artifacts, terracotta statuettes, African tribal scultpure and antique pottery there is still a certain ambiguity about the word "original." Until recently, many of these works which followed tribal or local archetypes very closely were considered archeological or anthropological material only, and were hidden away in ethnological museums. Now, more and more, they are seen as works of art in their own right and whole galleries specialize in them. More and more too, museums are upgrading them and displaying them in new, well-lit galleries. Artifacts of the past, votive offerings, grave relics and the like have a certain fascination and, in addition to their appeal to the modern eye, carry with them associations of whole cultures and civilizations, even though some in their time were considered humble utensils or representations and were produced in considerable quantity.

Fine prints—that is, etchings, engravings, lithographs, woodcuts and serigraphs—like cast bronzes, appear in multiple originals. In printmaking, the artist makes his own plate, stone, screen or woodblock and either prints the set himself or supervises the work. Modern prints are usually produced in a limited, numbered and signed edition. After the desired quantity is made, the plate or stone is destroyed or "cancelled" so that it cannot be used in its original state to print again. This is not always the case, and "restrikes" are sometimes made from a plate after the artist's death, or from a cancelled plate, with the marks of cancellation on it (such as bored holes or X's). This has been done with some plates of Berthe Morisot, Degas, and others. In the 1790's Basan made impressions from some of Rembrandt's plates, and well into the twentieth century the Italian and Spanish governments made new prints from the plates of Piranesi and Goya. Reputable dealers will always tell you when they know that a print is from a later printing or cancelled plate. In purchasing a later printing of a work you must take into account its quality: is the detail still fine, and is it faithful to the first printing, or has it degenerated into a blur or a mutilated fragment that does not convey the artist's intention? Later printings or restrikes are, of course, less valuable than the early ones and can often be picked up on your shoestring, but they also have less resale value. In the past, etchings, engravings and woodcuts were usually not limited, numbered and signed by the artist. Often he signed the work on the plate itself, but not always.

The printing of books began in the fifteenth century, when printing types were invented and paper came into general use in Europe as a cheap medium for mass reproduction. In preparations for printing these books, metal printing types were placed side by side with woodcuts of the same height; text and illustrations were printed together. Early printed books such as the *Nuremberg Chronicle* of 1493 and the Parisian Books of Hours of the late fifteenth and early sixteenth century imitated the script and illumination techniques of the handwritten manuscripts in a charming fashion.

Individual religious engravings and woodcuts for pilgrimage shrines and playing cards divorced the print from its solely bookish base, and then Martin Schongauer, Albrecht Dürer and other artists used prints to carry their personal styles and ideas to a wider audience. You may be surprised to learn how many of the old masters and great painters from the sixteenth century to the present have expressed themselves in etchings, engravings, woodcuts and lithographs. These are still available to the collector of small means, as are the works of fine printmakers through the ages who did not paint or sculpt, men like Raimondi, Callot, Piranesi, Peterdi and many others.

One final word. Your author is not an expert on anything. I have had several history of art courses in and out of college, have read a number of books on art and have haunted museums and galleries for many years. I collect on a shoestring because that's what I have available, and I do not pretend to have any special knowledge or inside tips. I am happy if in my wanderings I have found out a few things which may be of interest to a collector starting out with a small budget, and can share them with you.

ONE

Why Collect Art?

*"Art is the work of a person, a human being,
who is free to take into himself what he sees outside and from his free center put his human
stamp on it."*

               Sister Corita
               FOOTNOTES AND HEADLINES

W HY COLLECT ART? The most important reason is that you love art and enjoy living with the creative expression of others. It could be pointed out, as husbands, wives or children *do* point out, that art can be enjoyed in a museum or in galleries without acquiring it. This is quite true, and if you live in a city with adequate museums and galleries you are very fortunate. It is also true that you can enjoy good art through reproductions in art books that you or your local library own. However, you will find it a unique privilege to be surrounded by art works, to see them every day in many moods and seasons, not only in a special gallery or at a special exhibit. This experience enlightens your existence.

Collecting art, like collecting anything, is a form of acquisition, and we do live in an acquisitive society. Collecting seems to bring out that primitive instinct for the hunt in some of its devotees, who stalk their prey with skill. The delight of finding something valuable is part of the collecting game, and has been from the lost coin on down through the ages.

Sometimes art collecting is a matter of inheritance and family tradition, a "greatness thrust upon" one. Usually collectors inheriting objects of art move into a collecting realm of their own, but often they add to valuable holdings in one field.

Collecting art can, of course, be a matter of conspicuous consumption. In an affluent society especially, when the material needs are met—the car, furniture, and hi-fi set installed—esthetic and spiritual needs remain which can be met in part by art collecting. The shoestring collector is probably not affluent, but he too may feel that art on his walls testifies to his character and cultural aspirations.

For the affluent collector, social status and press notice may be a part of collecting, but this is not likely to befall the collector on small means. A wealthy collector may enjoy seeing himself in the role of patron of the arts in commissioning young or established artists; although the small collector cannot do this on a grand scale, he can encourage and sometimes modestly commission the beginning artist. There can be great rewards in communicating with creative and often dedicated people.

Sheer decoration alone may be the beginning of an art collecting career. The walls look bare, so let's find something to put on them. When they are filled, the art collecting career may have only begun. The adventure may have proved so exciting that one becomes addicted to it.

Of course, art collecting can be a very delightful recreation, and often is less expensive than, say, skiing, boat-owning or scuba-diving. It can be done solo, or it can be sociably engaged in with friends on museum trips and gallery going. Your children can become involved in the pursuit occasionally—though often not without protest! It can be a cooperative venture between husband and wife. One wife told me she started collecting in self-defense as her husband-to-be was always at art exhibits or museums! It can be a very happy form of sharing an esthetic adventure. And the amount of walking you do in the pursuit of art should qualify collecting as an appropriate activity for physical fitness enthusiasts!

Sometimes what starts out as a recreation or hobby becomes an occupation (see Peggy Guggenheim's *Confessions of an Art Addict* for a humorous description of this). It occupies a good deal of one's waking time and interest. When the Sunday paper arrives, the Art section is the first one read, and news of the art world is followed avidly.

Most of us don't get to quite that stage, but collecting art can at least provide a balance to everyday humdrum activities at home or in the business world. The creative powers of art can be a refreshment of spirit, a defense against the routine, a transcendence of the ordinary, a help in "moving through things temporal that we lose not the things eternal."

Some people see an interest in art almost as a form of therapy, a way of recovering wholeness in a fragmented world. In responding to a great work of art, you gather together the scattered parts of your life—the business appointments, office trivia, errands to run, dinner to get, diapers to wash—in an affirmation of the creative spirit. In such a way art can provide an escape from emptiness, boredom or meaninglessness, or the constant demands of other people. Art demands nothing: you only look and affirm the beauty or depth of a piece; or, if it does make demands on the understanding of the viewer, the search for its meaning yields great satisfactions.

The resurgence of interest in art in America in the 1960's can be seen as part of the New Frontier, not only the Kennedy New Frontier (although the art life of Washington was certainly influenced by that) but also a new frontier as opposed to the old, in the closing of the West and the admission of Alaska to statehood. Culturally and psychologically speaking, the closing of the frontier has had a subconscious effect on the American people, and they are looking for a way to move out, to move beyond. As Alvin Toffler points out in *The Culture Consumers*, art may be the one unbounded creative area left.

At the same time, paradoxically enough, collecting art from all periods of history brings the records of time into our lives. In this way there is a recovery of the past to enrich the present. As with old furniture and old books, we achieve a sense of history in the remembrance of things past. It adds a dimension in a world of prefabricated houses, premixed cakes, computer-living and "instant" everything.

The appeal of the esthetic is an important motive for most art collectors. Color, texture and line evoke a response, and one wishes to own the picture and look at it often. This need is felt even by corporations and banks like the Chase Manhattan Bank, which has collected a sizeable amount of art from all ages to distribute among its offices—not to impress the clients so much as to refresh the workers!

In the economy of today the satisfying of taste and desire is more possible for many people. We enjoy more leisure today and turn to the arts for stimulation. At the same time, the capacity to enjoy fine art is growing hand in hand with the possibility of possessing works of art. Not only can we look, but we can "taste, touch and see" in a very satisfying form.

Marshall McLuhan says that "the medium is the message": where better to see this than in the impact of art? Here the response of the eye, and in sculpture, touch, is paramount and immediate.

You may find the meanings and priorities of your life revealed to you in your collecting, even on a shoestring, and this might be even more significant than the collected objects themselves. You may start in an open-minded way, ready for an adventure in enrichment of spirit. You will gain discrimination as you go along and find your esthetic and spiritual home. Then again, you may start in a small field of art interest and find that one thing leads to another, that your involvement is covering more and more fields in the art world. Many people lack a creative outlet, and, while they may not have the talent and ability to create art themselves, they do have the ability to appreciate it and thereby enter into an alliance with the artist and maker. Collecting art is a form of self-expression and a uniquely satisfying one.

One word of warning could be given, though. You can get "hooked" on art. Don't let it devour you, even on a shoestring. Then again, you could get hooked on many lesser pursuits. It's a great adventure, and one in which you use your eyes, ears, hands and feet, intellect and even your "guts response." Collecting on a shoestring helps keep the acquisition of art from becoming a consuming obsession, sharpens your judgment and provides a great deal of enjoyment in life. Even if all your collecting is only in your imagination, you will still be rich in spirit.

TWO

Collecting on a Shoestring

*"To love painting is, above all, to feel that this
presence is radically different from that of the most
beautiful piece of furniture of the same period;
it is to know that a painting—the* Mona Lisa,
the Avignon Pietà, *or Vermeer's* Young Girl with
a Turban*—is not an object but a voice."*
                    André Malraux
                    MUSEUM WITHOUT WALLS

IT WAS ONLY RECENTLY that I realized that you could own works of art even though you were not wealthy. I made my first purchase, a watercolor, during my senior year in college, and told my father it was to be my graduation present. (He responded very well, especially as it was only $25 framed.)

The world of fine prints opened up more recently, when I became aware that it was possible to buy etchings, woodcuts and lithographs of great artists reasonably, and even to find some very inexpensive ones if you were fortunate. Once you become aware of the possibilities of acquiring old master prints, you can find some beautiful things, even in unlikely places. To give you some examples of what I mean, let me take you on a few treasure hunts.

One of the most spectacular was the discovery of three framed Piranesi prints at the White Elephant table at a church fair. I had been told that there were some old frames there, which is why I was poking around in the first place. In the dim light the etchings did not look very prepossessing, but I had read about the work of Piranesi, and his style was easy to identify. I purchased one for $8.50, and had it verified by the Boston Museum of Fine Arts Print Department as the fourth state of an early printing, done in 1775. It was an exciting find. The print now hangs as a treasured possession with an interesting story to accompany it.

I am told that the Morgan Memorial in Boston (Goodwill Industries) is a fine hunting ground; a friend once purchased a Rembrandt etching there for the immense sum of $1.50. Of course, in this and all treasure hunting, it helps to have the knowledge of your quarry which will enable you to recognize the real thing.

Secondhand bookstores can be treasure troves, although often dusty ones. Knowing that Winslow Homer had done his woodcut illustrations in *Harper's Weekly* between 1861 and 1877, I reasoned that instead of buying expensive cullings at the galleries, I might be able to find them in the old magazines themselves. After some searching, I did discover four lovely examples for the grand total of $4.50!

Of course, luck plays a part in many finds. Looking for more Homer woodcuts for a friend, and finding none, I idly asked the bookstore owner whether he had any Japanese woodcut prints. "Oh, yes," he said, and came up with an assortment of tattered little books. I purchased a couple, as they interested me, and because one looked vaguely like a copy of the great Japanese artist Hokusai's little men. Imagine my delight when the Asiatic department of the Boston Museum of Fine Arts told me that I had two books of Hokusai's original woodblock prints, one of them from the famous Manga series.

One of the happy by-products of collecting is the chance to browse—not only in museums, galleries, and bookstores, but also in libraries, particularly museum libraries—finding out about your treasures and their creators. For collecting is a continuous education and a means of communication with the spirits of the past. It is a very personal thing too, as you pick what suits your fancy (within your financial reach) and it becomes part of your way of expressing yourself. It may range from a hobby to a consuming passion and a disease, but true collecting should be an enlargement of the spirit. Collecting on a shoestring is a good discipline as well because it makes you ask yourself if you truly want the object, and it makes you seek for your treasures.

Ideally, art collecting should be a process of exploration. Following your natural taste and inclination can be only the start. To enrich your understanding of the object which he produced, you may learn about the individual artist, his background and influences, and the school to which he belongs. Sometimes whole periods or areas of art previously unknown to you open up. What a treat lies in store for someone just discovering Japanese woodcuts! Here is a field where works can still be acquired inexpensively, since they are produced in fairly numerous quantity. They can introduce you to new color techniques and forms. You can become acquainted with the Japanese spirit in leafing through landscape prints and portraits, studying the subtle color harmonies, the rhythms of line and the abstract spacings in composition. And these woodcut prints are available to the beginning collector—even the works of the great masters such as Moronobu, Hokusai and Hiroshige—for as little as $7.50, $12, $15, $25 or $30.

Another area in which discovery is a delight is the field of primitive art. Some of this art, like the artifacts of Pre-Columbian Mexico, may be over 2,000 years old; it comes to you with the history of a vanished culture behind it. Other primitive art, like the wood carvings, masks and metal work of Africa, may be more recent but equally fascinating. On encountering some majestic heads and masks I discovered the whole story of Benin bronzes, produced by the sophisticated *cire perdue* or "lost wax" casting process, a courtly art in a kingdom sealed from the European world.

One of the things I am suggesting here is the wide range of art interest—the endless forms of man's imagination and their influence on one another. I myself am fascinated by the juxtaposition of different centuries and cultures, the influence of, say, the Japanese on the Impressionists or primitive art on such moderns as Picasso, Vlaminck, Modigliani or Henry Moore. Practically speaking, it is of advantage to a modest collector to look in new fields, or in ones presently neglected, as objects from these periods do not have inflated prices and may be procured reasonably. The pendulum of taste often swings back to them and you may find you have a masterpiece that you discovered yourself. The history of art is, after all, not a static thing, and new areas are constantly being discovered. Good examples of this are the new appreciation of Pre-Columbian sculpture and the present vogue for seventeenth century Italian Mannerist painting and Art Nouveau, particularly the work of Aubrey Beardsley.

It isn't a good idea to buy something just because it seems to be in a rising trend, though, because after all you may be wrong and be stuck with something you do not like. One thing is always true: if you buy something that really means something to you, whether it's "in" or "out," you will have gotten your money's worth. Don't just go by the current. Do some exploring yourself, in museums, galleries and books. You may find you are becoming a trendsetter yourself when others see what you have appreciated.

For bold souls, dare to buy some "difficult pictures" rather than just comfortable, easily-appreciated ones. You will probably find that these are the ones that take longer to understand but will yield rich dividends in long-term enjoyment. In a recent *New York Times* article, Sidney Janis, the art dealer and collector who gave his collection to the Museum of Modern Art in New York, said that in many cases he had been stuck with the difficult, hard-to-sell pictures in his collection, but that these had turned out, in the long run, to be the best. Alfred Barr, Jr., commenting on the collection, said, "There isn't a dull picture in it." Wouldn't that be a wonderful compliment to your collection?

One thing I would like to emphasize strongly. Collecting art on a shoestring does not mean looking for bargains in the art world to the exclusion of all other motives for buying. If you barge into a gallery screeching "Where is your bin of dollar items?" you may never find it. Collecting art on a small budget is not an excuse to harry gallery owners, museum personnel and busy auctioneers. These people may become your most willing allies and sources if they respond to your genuine interest in art. But art dealers, after all, are in the business to make money, and they must receive a legitimate profit for their labors in research, display, ferreting out treasures, gallery upkeep, and publicity. A person will not endear himself to dealers by hunting only bargains, and what is more, he will not find them that way.

What is a bargain anyway? Certainly it is not the soiled or torn print, watercolor or drawing, because proper repair and restoration of such an item costs a good deal more than the item itself. It is not a work poorly rendered or with such a gruesome or depressing subject that you don't want to hang it on your walls. A bargain may be a work from a period currently out of style, or a piece by a talented student just beginning his art career, or an item in an area that has not come very far into the commercial trade. These may be legitimate bargains. But you usually get what you pay for, and very seldom do you get something for nothing unless it is in that intangible area of esthetic satisfaction.

The important thing is to be seized by the work of art itself —not to go looking for a "find." It is a find if you respond to it instantly and can fit it into your budget. When a piece hits me this way I start telling myself, "I really didn't need that spring coat, matching shoes are a ridiculous idea, good-bye Easter hat . . ."

(By the way, I am not suggesting that you say "good-bye mortgage," "no more charity giving," or "shoot the food budget." For your peace of mind and in the interests of family unity, I would tactfully hint that your shoestring should come out of excess funds, pin money, or savings set aside for that purpose.)

In the long run, your most important acquisition doesn't cost even a shoestring. It is the pleasure of seeing beautiful works of art in museums, galleries, art associations and books. It is the training of your eye to appreciate and respond to the creativity of artists of many periods and civilizations. It is the thrill when you catch the meaning of an artist as he speaks to you through his work. Even the memory of fine art becomes your constant companion after the experience of seeing it is over. This is a kind of ownership you do not pay for; you are only grateful for sharing with creators and appreciators through history.

THREE

How to Hunt Treasures

*"To create is to relate. We trust in the artist in
everybody to make his own connections, his own
juxtapositions."*

Sister Corita
FOOTNOTES AND HEADLINES

WHAT ARE SOME OF THE TECHNIQUES of acquisition
open to the buyer on a shoestring?

First, many galleries have a rental service,
whereby you can rent a work of art for a certain
number of months and, if you decide to buy it, apply the rental
price towards the ultimate purchase price. Even some museums
—such as the Corcoran Gallery in Washington, D.C., the
Museum of Modern Art in New York, and the Institute of
Contemporary Art in Boston—have such rental services.

Or, you may place a deposit on an article that you really want
but which may be beyond your means at the time. If you wait
until you have all the money for it, it may be gone. If you put
a small deposit on the piece and get a receipt for it, this holds
the object for you and assures the dealer of your real interest
in it.

One method of acquiring art is to make saving for an art
work a regular item in the budget. Some couples, for example,
know that they will always buy at least one painting a year as
a Christmas or anniversary present, and they save for the purchase throughout the whole year. Others like to have a regular
art fund so that if at any time they encounter a work they really
love, they will be able to buy it and not just dream about it.

Many gallery owners are also willing to have a young collector buy works of art on time. This is a great help to those who can save a small sum monthly but cannot put out a large sum at once.

It pays the collector on a shoestring to look in "the bin" in a gallery, art association or art store. Sometimes all prints are displayed in bins specially built for that purpose and it is fun to browse through them. Sometimes works in the bins are things that the artist has not had time or inclination to frame: water-colors, drawings, preliminary sketches, prints. Occasionally there are works that the dealer has bought in a lot at an auction. Along with the bad or mediocre, the sloppy or marred, you may be fortunate to pick up some really handsome drawings or prints, which you can frame yourself and enjoy greatly. It is extremely unlikely that you will find a lost masterpiece or even, in older prints and drawings, discover who the artist was. But your local museum can be of great help in tracking down the origins of your find, either artist or period. If you think this is a myth, let me give you the following example. I went rum-maging through the bin of a gallery in Cambridge, Massachu-setts, and came forth with five items that seemed to me desirable: three drawings and two engravings, for the grand total of five dol-lars or one dollar each. One good-sized engraving, slightly foxed in the margins and with a certain rakish charm, was inscribed as being by Houbrouken after the portrait of Henry Bennett, Earl of Arlington, by Sir Peter Lely, done in London in 1739. Another was identified in the Boston Museum Print and Draw-ings department as an engraving by Cornelis Boel done in 1610 from a series on the life of St. Thomas Aquinas. One of the drawings was identified by the Museum through tracing the paper watermark—a Dutch paper most current in Europe at the end of the eighteenth century; one was a wash study of a Guercino drawing of a saint; and the third was tentatively identified by style as probably French of the Empire period in the Neo-classic style popularized by David. The framing cost me a total of $7.50 and some hard work in mat cutting, rubbing the wood with silver paint, and so on, but it seemed quite an acquisition for $12.50 altogether!

Another important place to look is in the print and drawing boxes or cabinets to be found in galleries. Most galleries are short on wall space and so store their unframed prints and drawings in flat black boxes or cabinets to protect them—and also, incidentally, to save the dealer the cost of framing. Some dealers like the Associated American Artists and F.A.R. Gallery in New York have their boxes labelled by artists alphabetically. Others, like the Gropper Gallery in Cambridge, Mass., have their cabinet drawers labelled by era and field as well as by artist. Most gallery owners are happy to have you browse through them, provided that, after being shown how, you use the proper technique in handling the prints and drawings, which includes never touching the print or drawing itself, only the mat, and stacking the items correctly right side up.

Still another hiding place in galleries is the racks. Framed watercolors, oils, gouaches, drawings and prints are stored in galleries, and again, if you are careful, you usually are allowed to go through them at your leisure. In some places, like the rental gallery of the Institute of Contemporary Art in Boston and the Bader Gallery in Washington, D.C., the racks are in the gallery and open to public browsing. In others, they are in the background and the gallery owner may prefer to show you their contents himself. (The Bader Gallery, by the way, has a marvelous combination of upper large exhibition room, several smaller rooms chock-full of art books in all languages and at all prices, and downstairs several bins for prints and a room of smaller pictures, with open racks. It is an experience to go there.)

One more bit of advice. If you are seeking a particular artist, medium or period, be sure to *ask* the art dealer. Often he has other work stowed away at home or out of sight and may be able to supply you with just what you want. Tell him what you need, indicate what you can pay, and you will be pleasantly surprised at the interest he will take. You will find, too, that if art dealers know you are interested in a certain thing, they will go out of their way to let you know when they have it—even if you are only a shoestring collector!

Contemporary art you can often buy directly from the artist himself. It may not save you money, as he may charge just what his dealer would (if he has a dealer), but it will afford you the opportunity to see a wider range of his output and the pleasure of meeting a creative person whose work you admire. Not only that, but he may be willing to charge you less than you would pay in a gallery, as the dealer markups can be anywhere from 15% to 100% of the artist's price.

Trading with dealers or with other collectors can be an enjoyable and profitable technique of acquisition. Sometimes no cash changes hands—it is an even exchange. Sometimes you may trade back a picture to the dealer from whom you bought it, using it as part-payment for a more expensive item. One of the advantages of owning prints or paintings by established artists is that art dealers know they have a certain resale value and are more willing to trade with you. This is also true of trading with other collectors, but here you may have more latitude, and personal taste may be a larger factor.

Art clubs or print clubs provide another good way of acquiring art. Often a series may be commissioned by the club for less than such prints would cost commercially because a ready market is supplied.

Another possibility is acquiring art by ordering from catalogues. Certain art suppliers do all their business that way, while others, like Associated American Artists in New York, Craddock and Barnard in London, and Ferdinand Roten Gallery of Baltimore, do some of their selling through the mail and some in their galleries. Recently some of these organizations have started to hold exhibitions and sales of moderately-priced original prints in schools and universities across the country. These firms deal with prints from the fifteenth century to the present and, because of the volume of their business and their commissioning of contemporary artists, can be relatively moderate in their prices.

The disadvantages of catalogue buying are twofold: first, you cannot see the actual object itself, though there may be a reproduction of it in the catalogue; and second, you cannot know whether your bid will get in soon enough to secure the item you want. The prices in Craddock and Barnard and Folio Fine Arts, Ltd., London catalogues are so reasonable that many dealers buy from them. Sale day procedures begin to resemble plans for D-Day. At Folio's, for example, *nothing* may be sold before 9:30 a.m. of the sale day. There is only one telephone extension into the store to prevent the same item's being sold several times in the frenzy of buying. All written orders are shuffled, opened and processed while a member of the staff stands by at the telephone. For those wishing to cable (a night letter to London costs $2.53 from Boston, a cable 23 cents a word) there is a simplified cable address plus a marvelous code name like PEARL which means "Please send from catalogue 52 item number . . ." which cuts down wordage considerably. Whether or not you get what you bid on, the excitement of it all is as stimulating as being in the midst of a good espionage adventure.

Some bookstores also deal in original prints and small works of art on the side. Brentano's is the best known of these bookstores, and you can pick up things reasonably there, but still greater bargains may be found in musty print bins in Greenwich Village if you don't mind taking the bad with the good. Books themselves may be a fine source of art treasures, as some books have been illustrated with lithographs, etchings, or woodcuts by famous artists like Picasso, Braque, Leger, Miró, Matisse, Chagall, or artists of the past such as Blake, who published his own exquisite books. These books usually appreciate greatly in value. A few years ago you could buy Chagall's *Drawings for the Bible* with 24 original lithographs in it for $30. Recently I saw each of these 24 lithographs selling for $55 to $65 framed, and they are probably worth more now.

Gifts are a good technique of acquisition. If someone wants

to give you a gift certificate, have him purchase it at a gallery or a bookstore like Brentano's. If a friend or relative is travelling to or living in a place which has interesting art work, ask him for artifacts or art which he can get more reasonably on the spot. If you want a big item in, say, German prints or Pre-Columbian pottery, offer to reimburse him. Most of the time you will acquire the item for a good deal less than it would cost you through a gallery, which must pay export and transportation costs and gallery upkeep and also make a profit.

Several times to my surprise when I recognized and admired a work that a friend or relative had, it was given to me! My appreciation brought me three prints by Thomas Rowlandson from my father-in-law and a matching one from the series from another friend. I received a lovely oil from an artist friend, a charming small abstract "baby present" from an acquaintance who had gone to museums with me, and even an exquisite Russian cross from benevolent neighbors. Enthusiasm and appreciation often seem to bring out real generosity in people who like to know that someone else loves beautiful things too. I know, because I have given away prints and drawings to people who really liked them.

FOUR

Some Buys on a Shoestring

"Collecting at its best is very far from mere
acquisitiveness; it may become one of the most
humanistic of occupations, seeking to illustrate,
by the assembling of significant reliques, the
march of the human spirit in its quest for beauty
and the aspirations that were its guide. To
discover, preserve, relate and criticize these
memorials is the rational aim of the collector.
The joy of pursuit which he experiences is a crude
but delightful one, and discovery has the tri-
umphant sweetness of all successful effort."

Arthur Davison Ficke
CHATS ON JAPANESE PRINTS

WHAT THINGS ARE AVAILABLE to an art buyer for an investment of $25 to $35? There are quite a few possibilities, depending on your interests. You might want to shoot it all on one of the many beautiful illustrated art books in the field, if you have nothing like it. Or you might want to put some of it into a subscription to an art magazine like *Art News, Art in America,* or *Apollo* and spend some on a less expensive general art book or one which covers a field of your special interest.

A museum membership, if you don't already have one, might be a most rewarding investment of a shoestring. The benefits are innumerable, including attendance at delightful teas, the use of excellent lunchrooms and members' rooms and receiving the museum bulletins.

If you really enjoy treasure hunting, you might like to spend some of the amount on old books with good prints, out of style paintings or other dusty relics. Don't depend on this source of supply, though, because while it is possible to make finds in secondhand, antique or junk shops, a collection, no matter how small, cannot be put together or shaped in that way.

What might be obtainable in the area of art objects themselves? In the field of original prints, there are several possibilities. Prints under $25 are available through the IGAS (International Graphic Arts Society) series, the Ferdinand Roten Gallery Catalogue and many others. One excellent source of catalogue buying is Craddock and Barnard in London, which has some well-authenticated, moderately-priced offerings.

The gallery of the Associated American Artists in New York City has a wide selection of signed and numbered original prints of contemporary American artists, both in color and black and white. European Old Master prints from the fifteenth century to the recent past (from Jacques Callot and Wenzel Hollar to modern masters) are also available there for less than $25.

The Gropper Gallery in Cambridge, Massachusetts, has a wide range of graphics in this price range: lithographs by Honoré Daumier and Winslow Homer woodcuts; small Thomas Rowlandson, William Hogarth and James Gillray etchings; animal prints by Karel Du Jardin; small landscapes by Charles François Daubigny and Frederick Kobell; woodcut illustrations of Aristide Maillol; linocuts by Ossip Zadkine; Japanese prints and wash drawings; and many other original prints.

This is just a small sampling of where inexpensive original prints may be located. Original prints by beginning contemporary artists, and by some established ones, are available at this price in most galleries and are a very good buy. Especially delightful are the vibrant serigraphs of Sister Mary Corita.

Exquisite Japanese color woodcut prints by such nineteenth century masters as Hiroshige, Kunisada, Eisen, Toyokuni, Kuniyoshi and others are available at Childs Gallery and Origins in Boston and Bernheimer Antique Arts in Cambridge, Mass.

For a wider variety of art forms, Origins Gallery presents modestly priced small Pre-Columbian terracotta figures in Tlatilco, Colima, Jalisco and other Mexican styles; Costa Rican pots; Aztec artifacts; jewelry of many cultures; illustrated pages from Persian manuscripts; antique Chinese seals; and even a small Graeco-Roman Hellenistic head from Alexandria. What riches!

A small drawing or watercolor by a young artist or student might be available at this price at a local gallery or an auction that handles this kind of material. It would be very unusual to find an oil or sculpture at this price, even by an amateur or student, as $50 is about the very lowest price.

If you could spend as much as $100, you might be fortunate enough to find a small oil which pleased you. You might also find drawings by less well-known artists of the past. Small sculpture models and pieces by young artists might be available, although material and casting costs usually put their price much higher. Such possibilities exist mainly in local galleries and art associations, not in the prestigious, expensive New York galleries which are in the business of making reputations.

Sometimes people feel that if they pay a great deal for an article, it must be good. This is not always true. This attitude represents a need for cultural reassurance and a desire to be in on the latest trends. In other words, price does not determine esthetic quality.

I once made the exciting discovery of a small terracotta figurine of high esthetic quality for the modest price of $18. It is a fragment mounted on a pedestal, three and a half inches high from the waist up, with one arm raised in command. She wears the elaborate headdress of a goddess or priestess, and flakes of the original red paint are still visible after at least 2,500 years. The figure looks as modern as one of Picasso's ladies, but it is actually a Pre-Columbian artifact from Mexico. She was discovered in a brickyard outside Mexico City named Tlatilco, meaning "Where things are hidden" in the Nahuatl Indian language. The objects found here were all of the purest Zacatenco style, the oldest known culture in the Valley of Mexico, dating from 1500 to 500 B.C. This figurine was probably buried with the dead, a charming testimonial to a lady of commanding personality. The tiny figure is of very high quality, yet a collector on a shoestring could afford to buy her. Besides giving me great esthetic satisfaction, my purchase opened up the whole field of Pre-Columbian art for me.

With this I conclude a very sketchy account of a small corner of the field. You will find your own favorite galleries, museums, art associations, clothesline exhibits and auctions if you become interested in art. So "not farewell, but fare forward, voyager."

FIVE

A Passion for Prints

*"The essence of engraving resides in line, how
and where it is placed; but its life-blood is the ink
which joins the incised lines of the plate or raised
surfaces of the woodblock in a mysterious marriage
with the paper. Any engraver worthy of the
name knows that it is in this union of ink and
paper that the peculiar beauty of his art consists."*
Claude Roger-Marx
GRAPHIC ART OF THE 19TH CENTURY

A S ANYONE MAY HAVE GUESSED from reading this far, I have
a passion for original prints. They are the medium
which can be most easily purchased on a shoestring,
yet make one acquainted with the great artists. By
original or fine prints I mean etchings, engravings, woodcuts,
lithographs, aquatints and serigraphs produced by the artist himself. They may range in price from less than $5 to more than
$5,000, but most are relatively inexpensive, certainly when they
are compared to the paintings or sculptures of the same artists.

My eyes were first opened to the rich field of prints at the
Vincent Price collection at Sears, Roebuck, where I saw exquisite prints by Corot, Whistler, Goya, Millet, Piranesi, Picasso,
Léger, Matisse and many others selling for less than $100. I
started investigating and found that most of the Old Masters
from the fifteenth century onward had produced beautiful
woodcuts, etchings, engravings, aquatints and lithographs which,
because they were produced in quantity, were available to the
collector of small means. The roster of outstanding printmakers
is extraordinary: Schongauer, Dürer, Lucas van Leyden, Brueghel, Mantegna, Van Dyck, Callot, Holbein, Piranesi, Canaletto,

Goya, Tiepolo, Hogarth, Rembrandt, Fragonard, Blake, Daumier, Delacroix, Degas, Mary Cassatt, Klee, Kollwitz, Toulouse-Lautrec, Maillol, Whistler, Corot, Matisse, Picasso, Renoir, Villon, Pisarro, Cézanne, Rowlandson, Homer, Kandinsky, Bonnard, Braque, Chagall, Redon, Dali, Miró, Rouault, Beckmann, Giacometti, Shahn and many others.

Seeing, studying and living with Old Master prints can train your eye to recognize the subtlety of great art. It will also develop in the viewer a taste for quality. After looking at a Dürer woodcut or a Rembrandt etching for some time, you will be able to detect many of the false gestures or sloppy techniques that can charm momentarily. The viewer learns much about the quality of line, texture, placement, and possibilities in the use of space. He sees how both deep emotion and fleeting grace can be portrayed by economy of line. This is a great education and a marvelous revelation.

One of the things that never ceases to amaze is the great difference between the reproduction of an etching or other fine print and the actual print itself. Why this should be so is somewhat of a mystery to me, but one factor is certainly the care the artist took in the making of the plate and the individual prints. Another is that fine prints are produced on special kinds of paper which show ink very differently from a photographic reproduction. This is true for black and white prints and for color prints also, particularly for those like the Japanese woodblock prints which are done on a rice paper. You can see, too, the bite or pressure of a woodcut, copperplate or lithographic stone into the paper. There is a very different feeling of flatness in a reproduction, in contrast to "the bite of the print," due to the original's having been filtered through a camera, the reproducing eye.

Certain clues that tell the viewer right away that this is an original print are the indentation of the plate mark on the paper that is left around the print in making an etching or engraving, or the slight relief of a lithograph on the surface of the paper. Original prints seem to have a feeling of a life of their own, not like a copy of a work in another medium.

Many good books describe the techniques of production of the various forms of etching, aquatint, drypoint, mezzotint, engraving, woodcut, wood engraving, lithograph, and serigraph. I do not propose to go into them here at any length, as I am not sure they are of interest to the general reader or casual collector. I will just indicate their history very briefly so as to familiarize the beginning collector with the forms and their appearance.

The woodcut is the oldest form of print, used in Europe in the fifteenth century. It is made by cutting into a wooden plank or board with a knife; the wood is then inked and damp paper is pressed onto it. The impression does not require a heavy press as does etching, lithography or engraving, but may be made by rubbing the paper with so humble an instrument as a wooden spoon. Of course, many woodcuts were printed by a press, as, for example, in the early woodcut books. Linoleum cuts and cardboard relief prints are variations of the woodcut. Wood engraving is done with a graver on the hard end or cross-grain of a block of wood such as boxwood. In a woodcut the wood is cut away to form the white area, and the area in relief is black; just the reverse is true for wood engraving. There the background is the black-inked block of the wood.

Metal engraving is also a product of the fifteenth century and, because of the difficulty of incising the hard metal plate, it often became the specialist work of engravers by trade. Many engravings reproduced paintings or drawings of others, after the easier process of etching was discovered and before photographic techniques of reproduction were invented.

Etching was popularized by Dürer in the sixteenth century in Germany. An etching is made from a copper or zinc plate coated with wax and drawn on by an etching needle which exposes the metal. The plate is then submerged in an acid bath which eats into the exposed lines. Next, the plate is inked and wiped, the ink remaining only in the inked lines. Damp paper is placed over the inked plate in the press. When the plate and paper are run through the press, the inked areas adhere to the paper. The inking and wiping must be done for each print. This process, as in all original prints except the serigraph, gives a reverse image of the design on the plate. Aquatint, mezzotint and drypoint are variations on this technique, with different preparations of the ground of the plate. In the aquatint technique which both Goya and Rouault used to such effect, the cleaned plate has cherry rosin or other granular coating placed on it and is then put through a series of bitings, or immersions in an acid bath. The shades and tones on the finished print are produced by different amounts and kinds of coatings on the aquatint plate and also by the amount of exposure of the plate to the acid bath. Frequently the techniques of etching, engraving and aquatint are combined in making one plate. Any of these techniques in which the incised line makes the impression may be called intaglios.

The collograph is a contemporary variation of the intaglio process. The plate is usually made of masonite, though metal can be used. To form the composition, material is built up on the plate. This material is various: acrylic modeling paste, polymer medium, collage elements such as fabric, sandpaper, labels, coins, etc. When the plate is finished, it is inked with oil paint and printing medium, wiped, and then run through an etching press.

The lithograph, one of the more recent techniques of printmaking, was invented in Bavaria in 1796 by Aloys Senefelder, allegedly while he was trying to make a laundry list and had no paper available. The technique is based on the premise that oil and water do not mix; in the process the artist draws with a greasy crayon directly on a slab of prepared limestone. The ink accretes only to the crayoned surface after the stone has been "washed" by a chemical process, and the print is "pulled" (that is, taken off after being run through the press). The lithograph came into its own in the 19th century, particularly with the inspired use of the technique by Daumier and Toulouse-Lautrec. Modern artists are very partial to this form because the drawing can be made spontaneously, and there are now a number of workshops producing editions of lithographs of high quality. A great deal of interesting lithographic experimentation has been done recently on the West Coast and in Long Island workshops by well known contemporary artists such as Robert Rauschenberg, Jasper Johns, Robert Motherwell and Helen Frankenthaler.

Photolithography, often used commercially, is not considered a technique of producing original prints when it uses totally photographic means of reproduction. However, it has been used creatively, combining photo images with images drawn on the lithographic stone in printed collages with exciting effects.

The serigraph is considered suspect in certain quarters because it has been used so much commercially. Another name for this process is silk screen because it is made by stretching a piece of silk on a screen and drawing the print form directly on the stretched silk. The colors are then squeezed in series through the screen. A separate screen is needed for each color. Some very attractive prints are made by this process and they are often most appealing in their bright colors. Sister Mary Corita uses this technique to great advantage.

What are the techniques for producing original prints in color? I have never seen them enumerated in one book, so I shall try to do so here. There are several different ways of making woodblock color prints. The earliest ones, as in the *Nuremberg Chronicle* of 1493, were colored by hand—presumably the "deluxe edition." In the sixteenth century the Italians produced the chiaroscuro print, which used several blocks for tonal variations with a black key block. The Japanese made many color prints in the eighteenth and nineteenth centuries by using a different block for setting down each of the colors used in the print. Such artists as Utamaro, Hokusai, and Hiroshige achieved some unbelievably beautiful and vivid prints this way. A modern woodcut artist sometimes uses this technique of a series of blocks or sometimes plans his block so that different areas may be inked with different colors at the same time and the whole work printed at once.

Many color etchings were also hand colored. London publishers in 1800 had their own "coloring tables" at which assistants sat, each adding a single color as prints were passed along the table. Rowlandson's prints were colored in this way. Modern printmakers have experimented effectively with a color etching process, using different colored inks on the plate. Relief etchings in color are printed with several colors on one plate at once by employing inks that do not blend into each other. Sometimes different colored inks are superimposed one over the other in intaglio prints for a dense effect, and occasionally color is stencilled on intaglio prints for a luminous result.

Lithographs may be made with colored inks in a wide variety of hues. For each color a different stone must be drawn and inked, which makes this quite a complicated process. It is usually done in a workshop of experienced craftsmen, such as those at Mourlot's print shop in Paris. Color lithographs often have unusual brilliance, directness and verve, especially when artists are expressing themselves in terms of this medium alone and not in imitation of a painting.

With the colored serigraph a different screen (or the same one with the stencil-making fluid, or tusche, washed out) must be used for each color. In this technique, as with all those using successive separate color applications, the print must be "registered" or marked at the corners to ensure correct placement for each color being applied.

In the buying of fine prints, particularly Old Master prints, the condition of the print is very important. A weak, soiled or blurry impression is not desirable. An exhibit several years ago at the Boston Museum of Fine Arts, "Good and Bad Impressions," tellingly pointed out the difference between crisp and poor impressions of the same print. Price in print selling is often based on the fineness of the impression and this is noted in catalogues of sale. Always look for neat, clean edges on the lines and the images in the print and on its periphery—the mark of good craftsmanship and mastery of technique. And if the prints taken off the press at the end of an edition are inferior to the earlier ones, due to deterioration of the plate or stone, or carelessness of the printer, you should be aware of this.

Are posters, particularly those made by recognized artists, to be considered art or not? There is a difference of opinion about this, although posters can often be extremely good decoration. Certainly ever since Toulouse-Lautrec made his striking posters, they have assumed artistic importance and are collected as art. Art Nouveau posters are much in vogue, and at the Museum of Modern Art in New York the January 1968 exhibit of posters from the 1880's to the present pointed up their artistic qualities.

What advice, if any, might be given on buying original prints? They are an ideal field for the collector on a shoestring because nowhere else can he get such quality and such variety for such a small outlay. Somewhere in this vast field almost any collector should find an area, artist or school that pleases him and that he can afford to buy. Some collectors like to buy the work of only one artist, others prefer a period in time, still others like to take examples from different artists and schools of printmaking. This is obviously up to you and to what gives you satisfaction in collecting.

If you were to ask where to get the best value for money spent on prints, I think most dealers would say the works of established artists, old or modern, because they have a better resale value and trading counter. This may not be particularly important to a person who buys to please only his own eye and taste. In my own experience, however, while my first purchase was a woodcut of a contemporary unknown artist, I have been drawn further and further back in time to the works of the Old Masters, and I am now an avid Dürer fan!

Prints of the sixteenth century and of the eighteenth century (particularly English ones) are the best buys at present. For instance, there are good examples of Dürer's woodcut *Small Passion* series available reasonably, also some of the smaller works of Lucas van Leyden, Goltzius, and much of the work of the so-called "Little Masters" of the sixteenth century in Germany. This is true too of the works of eighteenth century English artists like Hogarth, Rowlandson, Gillray and Blake. Though the first three tend to be satiric and broad in their humor, their prints can be very attractive decorations in a casual corner. (I am not suggesting any areas of art speculation, as some books on collecting do, because I do not have the expertise for this sort of gamble, and inside-dopestering is not the purpose of this book. I believe the important reason for buying art is to enjoy it, not because you expect it to appreciate in value, even though it may do so.)

Another bit of common sense advice I might pass on: if you hear of a certain exhibit or sale of prints with something especially desirable, get there early! Good things reasonably priced are snapped up quickly, particularly prints. One of my few disappointments in print collecting was arriving at a sale of Old Master prints at Associated American Artists in New York and finding an exquisite Aldegrever engraving sold to the Detroit Institute of Art! It was particularly hard to lose the engraving as I could have afforded to buy it, but I comfort myself with the thought that many more people will see it at the museum.

SIX

Where to Look for Art

"If there were dreams to sell
What would you buy?"
    Thomas Lovell Beddoes
    DREAM PEDLARY

THIS BRINGS US to the question of where to look, if you are interested in acquiring a painting or sculpture or fine print.

If your community has an Art Center, this may be a good place to see continuing exhibitions in various fields. There, too, you may buy at a fairly reasonable price a work by a local artist who has not yet acquired a reputation, gallery or dealer. Of course, some artists may never persuade galleries or dealers to sell their work and will remain relatively unknown. Some may be amateurs in the arts. That need not keep you from acquiring some of their work, because it is always possible that your interest may help spark a career, but in terms of resale value or trading there is not as much of a counter.

Outdoor or indoor art festivals may also serve to acquaint a prospective buyer with art possibilities, and he may find something which he would like to own. Most of these festivals, if they are not juried or invited, tend to be uneven in quality and have a good deal of amateur work, but they can be good fun.

In the long run, of course, the best sources for purchasing art are the art galleries or dealers. This is, after all, what they are in business for, whether they serve as an outlet for student work or whether they deal only in accredited masterpieces.

There are all sorts of galleries. Most recent are those which are attached to a department store or large merchandising concern, such as the Vincent Price Collection at Sears Roebuck or galleries of Lord & Taylor's, Brentano's or E. J. Korvette.

There are a few galleries which have student work at relatively modest prices, particularly in areas near art schools or universities with strong art programs. Other galleries usually specialize in one area or another: prints and drawings (although some that have the major works of certain contemporary artists also carry their prints and drawings), contemporary work, Old Masters, antique art and artifacts, primitive art, or the art of a certain country or century. It may be an adventure to visit any of these, although possibly a beginner should start with the more modest galleries first, which are more likely to carry work within his purchase range. You will find in most cases that the dealers are glad to help you, and if you mention a certain interest or artist to them, they will be happy to show you what they have. One word of caution, though. Most dealers are reputable, and will gladly give you information and authentication of the purchase. However, in some of the slightly shady antique-junk type of shops the owner may try to mislead a buyer as to the desirability of the piece. It is always better to come back and look a second time than to decide too fast. One of the hardest things to gauge in an object of art is durability. How will it wear? Will you love it in December as you did in May? Will it go with anything in your house? Will the family like it? One of the best ways to determine this is to rent it or take it on approval and return it if it doesn't really suit you.

One other suggestion about dealing with galleries. Sometimes it is wise to do a little comparison shopping, especially on prints. Occasionally one dealer's price may be inflated, or possibly another dealer will have had a lucky bid at an auction and he can pass the low price along to you. One dealer's source of supply for a certain type of painting or print may be better than another's, allowing him to offer a picture or print at a more reasonable rate. Or his rent or overhead costs may be lower. In any case, there is often a considerable difference in pricing, and it pays to be aware of it.

If an art explorer likes to mix a little treasure hunting with his art hunting, he can always haunt secondhand bookstores or junk-to-antique shops. Don't expect too much, and if something is expensive, investigate it fully. Often old pictures turn out to be copies or downright fakes. If you find something which you think may be good, you can always have it appraised by a specialist or reputable dealer. Your museum may be willing to give you an opinion on the origin and genuineness of an old painting or print. Also your museum may have a well-stocked library with art specialists' reference works, and you may be able to look up some things yourself.

Another good source for collecting on a shoestring is the local auction. Here I am not speaking of the big international society auction which is televised on three continents and where bids run into the millions. I mean rather the auctions by local art associations, museums and charitable organizations, where money is being raised to help the organization and the works are donated by interested artists or patrons. Some of these auctions are silent auctions, that is, bids are placed anonymously on a slip of paper under the picture or in an envelope at the desk, and there is often great suspense as to who wins a choice treasure. Others are regular bid auctions, usually of the works of local artists. Generally speaking, many of the things offered go for less than the original price the artist put on the object, and so you may get quite a bargain. However, here again, most of this work is contemporary, often by unknown artists, although there are usually some established artists included. If you buy something you like and can live with it happily, your purchase is well justified. Certainly I have seen paintings priced at $50 to $100 bought for $5 to $10, so it is possible to experience the fun and excitement of an auction without spending too much money.

The best way to buy at an auction is to arrive early and look at what is offered. Determine which things you would like to buy and the top price you wish to pay for them beforehand. Then you will have had a more adequate look at the painting and will not have to judge on a brief glance. Before the auction starts, try to find out more about the artist who created the object you are interested in. Is he an amateur or a professional? Does he have a gallery affiliation? What are his training and qualifications? This technique will help you to bid sensibly and not spend too much for an item.

SEVEN

Galleries for the Collector on a Shoestring

"Spend all you have for loveliness,
Buy it, and never count the cost;
For one white singing hour of peace
Count many a year of strife well lost."

Sara Teasdale

BARTER

ANY LIST OF GALLERIES becomes dated very soon, as art galleries go out of business very rapidly or change their names and locations. *Art Collecting for Pleasure and Profit* by Ted Farah contains a good list of galleries all over the country. Most lists do not include much on print galleries or those with primitive art or ancient artifacts, so I will try to fill in from my own experience. Some good galleries will inevitably be left out as I have included only those I have visited myself where I have found prices moderate, and the examples of art interesting and of fine quality. At the end of the book is a supplementary list of galleries all over the United States and in London and Paris.

In New York City

1. Associated American Artists, 663 Fifth Avenue

This gallery is very fine for modern American, European and Oriental prints and Old Master prints modestly priced. It is a pleasure to browse through their numerous bins and boxes.

2. Brentano's Galerie Moderne, 586 Fifth Avenue

Carries some moderately priced Oriental and modern prints.

3. Croquis Gallery, 19 West 55th Street

Carries drawings by unknown artists from $10 to $80—lively wall decoration.

4. F.A.R. Gallery, 746 Madison Avenue

An established gallery with a very wide selection of original prints and drawings. A few things like Rouault woodcuts done by Aubert are moderately priced although most are fairly expensive.

5. IGAS, 410 62nd Street

The International Graphic Arts Society commissions series of original prints which it distributes to galleries around the country as well as to its members.

6. Galerie Felix Vercel, 710 Madison Avenue

This gallery has some modestly-priced prints as well as more expensive oils by contemporary French artists.

7. Marlborough Graphics Gallery, 41 East 57th Street

Graphics start here at $45 and go much higher. This gallery mostly handles work of British artists such as Sutherland and Kitaj, and some contemporary Americans.

8. Phyllis Lucas Old Print Center, 981 Second Avenue

Here you will find many old and quaint prints as well as the graphic work of Salvador Dali.

9. The Picture Decorator, 740 Madison Avenue, at 65th Street

Has old Winslow Homer woodcuts from *Harper's Weekly,* also modern color lithographs.

10. John Torson, 340 East 63rd Street

Operates by appointment only, but it is well worth going to see original drawings and watercolors by famous and unknown artists, many very moderately priced.

11. Pratt Center for Contemporary Printmaking, 831 Broadway

Excellent experimental program with modestly-priced prints by contemporary artists.

12. Walter Schatzki Gallery, 153 East 57th Street

A pure delight for the browser, with prints and drawings starting at 50¢. Especially rich in book illustrations from the fifteenth century on, also a massive supply of very reasonable

Daumier lithographs; and woodcuts, etchings and engravings from many sources.

In Boston

1. Botolph Gallery, 161 Newbury Street

The Botolph Group handles a good deal of contemporary religious art and sells the work of Sister Mary Corita and her students very reasonably. It has religious prints in files by artists of many denominations.

2. Childs Gallery, 169 Newbury Street

Has Old Master prints and paintings—some, like the lovely Japanese prints, moderately priced—as well as much Americana.

3. Copley Society, 158 Newbury Street

Carries the work of contemporary artists of the area and has a Christmas sale where small paintings and prints may be picked up for $25 or under.

4. Harcus Krakow Gallery, 167 Newbury Street

Mainly contemporary prints at contemporary prices. Some very stimulating work.

5. Obelisk Gallery, 130 Newbury Street

Contemporary artists, mostly paintings and drawings, some moderately priced.

6. Origins Gallery, 136 Newbury Street

Marvelous mélange of ancient artifacts, textiles, and jewelry, from Mexican and South American Pre-Columbian to Greek, Roman and Oriental finds—many in the range of the small collector. The owner, Mrs. Shulman, is always willing to tell you about the various things and enlarge your knowledge greatly.

7. Pucker-Safrai Gallery, 171 Newbury Street

Israeli artists—some handsome lithographs and etchings modestly priced.

8. Institute of Contemporary Art Rental Gallery, 1175 Soldiers Field Road, Brighton

This gallery rents and sells the work of contemporary artists both well known and obscure. Prices start as low as $30 and go up to well over $300. You will find here sculpture, drawings, watercolors, oils and original prints, mostly in an abstract vein.

9. The Alpha Gallery Inc., 121 Newbury Street

Here you will find the work of contemporary artists, both in and out of the area. Some prints are fairly moderately priced.

10. Thomas Ford Gallery, 159 Newbury Street

Varieties of antique art and artifacts, including icons, usually fairly expensive.

11. Weeden Gallery, 35 Lewis Wharf

Encourages the work of young artists. It is in a fascinating location in the building that once housed the Dutch East India Company.

In Cambridge, Mass.

1. Bernheimer Antique Arts, 44 Brattle Street

Carries African, Pre-Columbian, Oriental, Greek, Roman, Egyptian, Medieval, etc., works of art and artifacts, and some fine Japanese prints, many moderately priced. A good browsing place.

2. Cambridge Art Association, 23 Garden Street

Has the work of local artists, much modestly priced, also rental gallery and many prints.

3. Gropper Gallery, 1768 Massachusetts Avenue

One of the best. Mr. Gropper deals mainly in original prints and has some beginning as low as $10. Has a wide stock of Daumier, Hogarth, Rowlandson and others. Go see.

4. Roten Gallery, 26 Dunster Street

A branch of the Baltimore firm, has excellent range of prints.

5. Paul Schuster Gallery, 134 Mt. Auburn Street

Old Master prints reasonably priced, also young artists' work.

6. Swetzoff Gallery, Mt. Auburn Street

Contemporary artists mainly and some old drawings.

7. Off-The-Square Gallery, 52 Boylston Street
Modestly priced work of young artists, with a wide variety of graphics.

In the suburban Boston area

1. Galleri III, Boston Post Road, Sudbury
Beautifully set up small gallery with reasonably priced work of contemporary artists in both realistic and abstract styles. Many fine graphics.
2. Sudbury Art Association, 435 Concord Road, Sudbury
Carries work of local artists as well as annual Christmas craft show. You will find some good work here at reasonable prices.
3. Intrepid Gallery, Wellesley
Some attractive work of local artists, quite reasonably priced.
4. Concord Art Association, 15 Lexington Street, Concord
Open April-October with frequent shows and some pleasant work.
5. Westwood Gallery, 36 Hartford St., Westwood
Mainly the work of local artists, with some attractive prints, reasonably priced.
6. Berman-Medalie Gallery, 10 Austin Street, Newton
Dealing mainly in prints, with a wide variety of contemporary artists. Fairly moderately priced.

Be sure to look for art galleries wherever you go. Cape Cod, Maine, the Berkshires, and Rockport, Mass., swarm with galleries in the summer. Some have good work moderately priced and finding them should add great zest to your travelling.

In Washington, D.C.

1. The Artists' Mart, Wisconsin Ave., N.W. (Georgetown)
Has work of local artists including painting, sculpture, drawings and prints. Drawings and prints in bin are moderately priced.
2. Bader Gallery, 2124 Pennsylvania Avenue, N.W.
This delightful gallery has already been described. Some

moderate buys may be had, particularly in contemporary and Old Master prints.

3. Corcoran Gallery of Art, Rental Gallery, 17th and D Sts., N.W.

Carries the works of local and New York artists in specially decorated rooms. Very attractive to see, with some reasonably priced works.

4. Georgetown Graphics, O St. off Wisconsin Ave., N.W.

Variety of modestly priced original prints from many sources.

5. I.F.A., 2623 Connecticut Avenue, N.W.

Some moderately priced graphic work, attractive sculpture.

6. Mickelson Gallery, 707 G Street, N.W.

Moderately priced original prints.

In Baltimore

Ferdinand Roten Galleries, 123 W. Mulberry St.

Does a large catalogue and student business with mostly graphic work, moderately priced.

In Lakeside, Michigan

John Wilson, Lakeside Studio, 150 S. Lakeshore Rd.

John Wilson is a printseller formerly associated with Roten galleries, who travels around the country selling a variety of original prints. He gravitates mainly to museum and university centers and has many reasonably priced lithographs, woodcuts, etchings and engravings.

In London

1. Craddock & Barnard, 23 Museum Street, London W.C. 1

Has a large stock of Old Master prints at very reasonable prices. It sends out catalogues of sales items which are quickly snapped up. It pays to enquire about specific interests, as they often have prints by an artist you like.

2. Folio Fine Arts, Ltd., 6 Stratford Place, London W. 1

This firm deals in Old Master and modern prints, drawings, watercolors, rare books, antiquities and manuscripts. They issue quarterly illustrated catalogues which have many items at very reasonable prices.

EIGHT

What Should You Buy?

*"He attempts always to acquire the best, and his
knowledge of what is best is always widening.
His is the task of judging between degrees of
perfection. It differs not so very widely from that
desperate search for an ideal which is the curse,
the inspiration and the one abiding joy of the
artist."*

Arthur Davison Ficke
CHATS ON JAPANESE PRINTS

HOW DOES A PERSON JUDGE ART? In buying art as in
buying anything, your own taste is most important.
You should never buy anything that you don't want
to live with, no matter how valuable or how much
of a bargain you think it is. But how do you judge good art
from bad? Here gallery owners, collectors, and experts all say:
look. Become familiar with the standards of good art, both in
the contemporary field and in art of the past.

One of the best places to start making this discovery is in a
museum. Here is a vast treasure house of various types of art
spanning the centuries, the best examples of various art forms.
Here a person can educate his eye and taste. He may also be
able to hear about art, as many museums have guided tours,
lectures on collections, or whole seminars on art history. If a
collector has a particular interest, the museum may be able to
advise on a gallery which specializes in it.

Books are another good source for forming judgment in art,
particularly if a person is far away from any museums. Read
about the major styles of art and the criteria for excellence in
each. In this way you will come to recognize quality—and will

enjoy the experience! There are now many paperback histories of art and surveys on particular eras or types of art available. The local library may have a good collection of art books, or be able to get them for you. Keep an open mind: sometimes the very styles you don't "see" at first will reveal themselves to you with their particular charm. If you have discovered a picture or sculpture that interests you, tracing down its history can be like reading a detective story: finding suspense, surprises, and rewards.

Visit the galleries and art associations near you to get a general idea of what different kinds of art are available and at what prices. You can evaluate your responses to lithographs, etchings, watercolors, drawings, oils, sculpture and artifacts and see how the artist works in each medium and what effects he achieves in each.

The impact that a work of art makes on you determines, in the last analysis, whether you buy it. Taste and preference affect this impact. You may prefer abstract works to realistic ones because they seem modern and express your feeling of the importance of the present. You may, on the other hand, prefer representational works because they hark back to a more ordered past or bring pleasant scenes to mind. One style or another may particularly intrigue you because it goes with your furnishings or represents an elegance you admire. Or your taste may develop along very catholic lines, and you may respond more to each individual work of art regardless of style or associations. The important thing to cultivate is a sense of quality. An educated eye and an appreciation of the best artists of the past and present should form your sense of quality. Although you probably will not be able to buy the finest work of an artist on the small budget you have, you may be able to select fine small prints, drawings or watercolors or artifacts which exemplify the best of his style.

What are some of the esthetic factors to look for? Most important, I think, is a sense of wholeness in the work. It makes a statement in itself. It has a character of its own to proclaim, an identity. Though it may come out of a tradition, such as the tribal sculpture of Africa or icons strictly prescribed by a Byzantine pattern, it has nonetheless a life of its own. It speaks both for the culture which produced it and for itself.

A work of quality has a sense of organization and discipline; it does not fall apart nor is it diffuse or vague. The artist has considered lines and movement, balance, the sense of space; he has executed all with an economy of means. If he is experimenting, he knows what he is doing. If there is distortion, it is done on purpose to achieve certain effects. The relationship of line, shape and color produces a harmonious whole or an exciting forceful statement. The composition shows a mastery of scale, design and movement, or monumentality. In other words, a work of quality shows that the artist has achieved his end and has produced a piece which proclaims this with vigor.

In selecting a work of art, one thing which you should consider is its lasting quality. I do not mean just physical durability, but rather continuing appeal. This is often a very difficult matter to judge, as works which appear to have most exciting qualities at first sometimes do not wear well. As you continue to look at art objects, you become more aware of the artist's mastery that makes the initial appeal grow rather than diminish.

Another consideration you should take into account as your collection increases is the relationship of new acquisitions to the rest of your collection. Will it round out a certain period or grouping? Does it fill a gap in the collection or add balance to the whole?

It is important to ask the question, do I have a place for it? It isn't only whether you like or admire something objectively but also whether it will fit in with the style of what you have already. Where will it go on your walls? This, strangely enough, is often the acid test, as I have found that if you really respond to the quality of a work, you can always find a place for it. Perhaps this is the ultimate compliment and concern: that you are willing to let something enter your everyday field of perception and let yourself be changed by its interpretation of the world.

When you actually select an object, the question of price must arise. Is the price asked in line with that of other pieces on the market? Can you afford it, no matter how much you admire it? Is it really worth that amount to you?

Finally, I think you should ask, is it genuine? If the piece is spurious it is not worth anything to you.

NINE

Prices

"The real value of art is not always revealed
by the price set upon it."
> Jeffrey Loria
> COLLECTING ORIGINAL ART

WHAT FACTORS DETERMINE THE PRICES for works of art? In many cases only experts can say why one painting was more valuable than another, but there are some general guidelines one can follow. First and most important is quality.

If you buy a work of art of the highest quality, whether great or small, you have gotten something worthwhile, something which is valuable in itself. It will educate your eye, give you great pleasure, and ultimately ride out the tides of taste. It will give you an idea of the best of one school or time or style or artist, and it will satisfy you esthetically. Sometimes it is very hard to obtain quality on a shoestring budget, but if you buy prints and drawings and are willing to explore new territory or eras currently out of favor, it is possible.

Another more prosaic factor is size. Generally speaking, a larger painting, print, drawing, sculpture or *objet d'art* is more expensive, but there are exceptions to this rule. A famous work that is small, but whose quality, appeal and rarity are the highest —Leonardo's Mona Lisa, or the Liechtenstein portrait of Ginevra de Benci sold to the National Gallery of Art in Washington for between five and six million dollars, or Rembrandt's portrait of Titus as a child, bought by Norton Simon—is beyond this form of calculation. Then again, if a work is too large, like some of Rubens' huge canvasses and the works of many lesser-known artists, the demand dwindles because no normal dwelling place has room for it.

A factor which influences price greatly is appeal, which also depends on contemporary taste. The landscapes with cows or stags dear to one generation's heart may be anathema to the next. Generally speaking, nothing is so out of favor as the immediately preceding era, as, for instance, the Victorians to us. However, appeal goes further than that, and certain subjects such as the mother and child, handsome still lifes, beautiful children or ladies, and attractive landscapes and seascapes seem always to be salable. In our times other subjects are completely out of favor: pictures of dead game or anything suggesting death (except fine crucifixions and martyrdoms), anecdotal pictures, and so forth, tend to bring low prices or to be totally unsalable.

Color as well as subject matter may play a determining factor in the pricing of pictures, since, generally speaking, people tend to prefer the light and bright colors of the impressionist range rather than more somber tones. There are, of course, exceptions to this also, as proved by the value placed on Rouault's dark *Miserère* series and on the black and white or somber palettes of certain contemporary painters, but generally it holds true.

Promotion by dealers and current fads seem to have a great deal to do with pricing. A certain artist or school tends to be regarded as "in" and can command high prices while others are neglected. Some people feel that they must have the latest style on the contemporary art scene, or the appropriate Old Master. This situation gives the more modest collector of an independent mind an opportunity to investigate less publicized areas and find treasures more appropriately priced.

Condition is an important factor in pricing a picture, sculpture or print. If the work is damaged, even if it can be repaired, it is worth much less than if it is in perfect condition. If something is torn, spotted, or the colors have faded, or if it has lost a part, it is naturally less valuable than it would be if whole. If something is rare enough, however, and the damage can be repaired, people will be willing to buy it. Check carefully in strong light from front and back to see if it has been repaired. A "restored" oil painting may be quite changed from the artist's original conception.

Rarity of the object or of the artist's work is a very important factor in determining price. The paintings of artists like Leonardo da Vinci and Vermeer command astronomical prices because there is so little of their known work. Certain ancient artifacts are also very expensive as there are so few of them.

Fragility of a work is another consideration in determining price. Glass is often broken, gold and silver melted down, stone chipped, frescoes damaged by the weather, textiles and wood decayed, and so forth. It is fascinating to think that the humblest material of all, terracotta, a form of baked clay, is often the one that survives best, as witnessed by Greek, Roman and Egyptian finds, and of course, the vast mass of Pre-Columbian remains.

Ownership and provenance are also factors in making an object rare, desirable, and therefore expensive. What is provenance? It is the pedigree or history of a work of art which adds value and authenticity to the work. It may trace the picture or sculpture back to a certain owner or the artifact to a certain archeological "dig" in a precise area. A comb which would be otherwise ignored assumes great allure if it belonged to an Egyptian queen, Roman empress or famous actress. The provenance bestowed by such documented royal or famous ownership makes the object rare and interesting, as it enhances, for example, a picture, sculpture or possession from a well-known collection of a person of great taste, connoisseurship and knowledge. A person acquiring an object from such a collection feels he is getting an ironbound guarantee of genuineness and quality as well as a glamorous background. Of course, the history as well as the objects themselves can be faked. Also, many objects found on archeological expeditions cannot, by very nature, have a long pedigree of ownership, as they have been stored in the earth for many centuries.

This brings us to the matter of objects forbidden to leave

their country of origin. In some cases this occurs in European countries which, feeling that masterpieces should enrich the culture of their own land, refuse export passes. In other cases —and this is happening more and more frequently on archeological digs—the country will not allow any objects excavated to be exported. This is particularly true now in the Middle East and also recently in Mexico and South America. Naturally the desirability and price of the objects are thus enhanced.

Another example of rarity, which affects prices in prints such as etchings, lithographs, or woodcuts, is a limited issue after which the plate is destroyed. Purposely destroying the stone, block or plate is a relatively modern idea to ensure rarity, but it happened in the past when only a few copies were printed for one reason or another, or where several "states" of a print were made, the plate being altered after each one, therefore resulting in a limited number of "first states," "second states," etc. This kind of rarity attracts certain collectors who may acquire, for instance, only "first states" and who collect more because of the rarity of an object than because of its esthetic merit. The final, finished state is usually more esthetically satisfying. Rarity in old prints is often simply the outcome of the fragility of paper and its disposability.

TEN

Fakes, Frauds and Forgeries

"The buyer needs a hundred eyes, the seller not one."

> *George Herbert*
> JACULA PRUDENTUM

WITH THE GREAT AMOUNT OF PUBLICITY of late given to fakes, frauds and forgeries in the art world, the collector on a shoestring may well wonder whether the *caveat emptor* or "let the buyer beware" doctrine may not do him in when serious collectors and even experts have been fooled. The *New York Times* has reported lately such items as the insertion of a fraudulent Kline painting into a legitimate auction, the arrests of several dealers for selling fake paintings purporting to be the work of artists like Picasso and Chagall, and the discovery of a forged bronze Greek horse at the Metropolitan Museum of New York. I frankly do not think the collector on a real shoestring need fear this, simply because such items are out of his reach. If someone offered you a Picasso oil painting for $100, surely your common sense would tell you that it was a fake!

A faked painting or sculpture often looks very well, as it is a pastiche of the elements of the master or period and in the style of the master or era. An out-and-out forgery is usually a copy of an actual painting in a museum or a private collection. There are many books of fakes and forgeries, if you are interested, which discuss famous forgers such as Van Meegeren, the Dutch painter who produced fraudulent "Vermeers." The one element, they point out, that can't be faked, is the spirit of the age in which the work was done: its values, its presuppositions, its esthetic canon.

The collector on a shoestring might run into fakes or forgeries among original prints and artifacts and possibly drawings and watercolors. If you buy from an established, reputable dealer, however, you are not likely to run into this difficulty, even if you are buying on a shoestring. The most important thing is to develop your eye in all areas, to look for spontaneity and technical mastery in a drawing or watercolor, and to become aware of the total work of an artist. For the great masters of prints this can be done by consulting a book of their complete graphic *oeuvre* illustrated, which museum and other libraries may have, or which you may be interested in buying for yourself. There are works on Hogarth, several on Picasso, and complete illustrated books on the graphic work of Dürer (by Karl-Adolf Knappe, New York: Harry Abrams 1965), Goya (by Enrique LaFuente Ferrari, New York: Harry Abrams), Rembrandt (by K.G. Boon, New York: Harry Abrams 1963), Toulouse-Lautrec (by Jean Adhémar, New York: Harry Abrams 1965) and Pieter Brueghel the Elder and Lucas van Leyden (by Jacques Lavalleye, New York: Harry Abrams 1967)—to mention a few readily available.

In the area of artifacts, such as Pre-Columbian, not only the look but the actual "feel" of the object is important. By handling you grow to sense the characteristic surface, curves, and line as well as see its style. There are legitimate reproductions available, like those at Brentano's, but they have a veneer of newness and of the machine, attractive though they be. Of course you may not care about genuineness, but to me the appeal of an object actually made over two thousand years ago is very great.

In the area of prints where a new collector on a small budget could start, you might not expect forgeries, as the amount of money involved is not large. However, prints have been forged. The most famous forgeries of prints are sometimes hard to detect, as they were done in the artist's time. Marcantonio Raimondi's copies of Dürer's woodcuts and etchings in the sixteenth century and the contemporary borrowings of Hogarth's engravings in eighteenth century England are in this category. Both artists were so enraged that they sought legal redress, and Dürer did get some satisfaction, while Hogarth actually obtained an act of Parliament to protect artists' productions! Some copies or apparent copies of famous prints were made later, such as Captain Baillie's reworking of Rembrandt's plates and Durand's nineteenth century reproductions of Rembrandt's etchings. Often these are done with no intention to defraud, but of course may be sold fraudulently or unwittingly afterwards.

Sometimes restrikes or later printings of a plate are made; the gallery or catalogue (as well as the price) should indicate this clearly. Some knowledge of the current market is helpful: the fact, for example, that there are later printings from some of the plates of Kaethe Kollwitz, Cézanne, Renoir, Rembrandt, Mary Cassatt, Manet, Goya and Piranesi, and the cancelled plates of Degas, Millet and Berthe Morisot, among others. Another thing to remember is that the execution of a work based on a drawing or painting of a master is not usually as valuable as a plate by the master's hand. There is a great difference, for example, in price between works done by Rouault alone and the wood engravings of Rouault's work done by Aubert.

A problem the art buyer with a small budget does run into is that of "attributed" drawings. Many drawings are unsigned but may be confidently attributed to certain artists by the dealer. The attributions often are wrong, although the period of the drawing may be right. After all, there are a great many 17th and 18th century drawings around and many more from the 19th century. People who buy a drawing attributed to Corot or Renoir are going to have to pay a high price for that name. When the drawing or sketch is priced at $50 or $100 and is attributed to some less-known artist, the question of attribution bears on the subject of this book. The same drawing, with a candid note, "By an unidentified artist," might be priced at $10 or $25.

Your best guarantee of genuineness is a reputable dealer. After all, his reputation is at stake and not to be forfeited lightly. In the art world honor and fairness are among the principal assets of a dealer. Of course, a dealer may have been fooled himself on an item, but then he should return your money willingly. Many galleries do give certificates of authenticity with purchases, although in a few cases I have found that their accuracy, in such details as exact titles of series, can be improved by your own research.

In my own buying on a shoestring I have very seldom been offered anything not genuine. Things I felt were too good to be true were verified for me by consulting books and by the most helpful Print Department of the Boston Museum of Fine Arts. I have only been pleasantly surprised in this respect, but then I have tried to cultivate a small knowledge of the subject, and that helps. In the area of original prints, there is a code of ethics published by the Print Council of America, 527 Madison Avenue, New York, N.Y., which gives the criteria for an original print, and many dealers display this in their galleries.

Why does someone forge art at all? There are many reasons, simple profit probably being the main one. However, there is disappointed ambition, too, as was alleged of Van Meegeren, a painter who could not make good on his own, but felt that people bought established names only. Why not put an established name on a work to sell it? This is, after all, what a dealer might do in displaying a picture of the same period as a desirable Old Master. Sometimes it might be revenge on a society which appears to buy works on the basis of the name alone and not on the quality of the work. Sometimes it could be a desire to prove one's own cleverness or craftsmanship, as the young Michelangelo did in producing a pseudo-antique sleeping Cupid statue. Sometimes a talented art student turns out a number of faked paintings, either copies or in the style of a master, at the behest of a fraudulent art operator. It does seem a waste of artistic talent, but of course what is missing is originality, the real dividing line between the master and the follower. If the forger had that, he could not be content with producing mere copies or pastiches.

ELEVEN

How and Where
to Learn About Art

*"Education is not just working algebra problems
or listening to lectures on Greek history. It is
doing anything that changes you."*

George B. Leonard
LOOK SENIOR EDITOR

L ET'S SAY YOU FIND YOURSELF becoming interested in art
and are in need of more general information before
you plunge into any sort of buying. How and where
do you educate your eye and learn about the different
fields of art?

Part of this depends on where you live. If you are in a large
city, there is usually a good museum where you may look
through the various galleries, go to guided tours and lectures,
and perhaps attend history of art classes or seminars. If you
live near a university or college, try their art gallery and look
into evening or day courses on the history of art or special fields
of art.

Your local library, art association or high school may give
art education programs. If not, why not give them a prod? After
all, it's your civic duty to beautify America these days, and this
would surely help no end. And if you can't get any of these
going, how about starting a group in your own neighborhood
and paying an art teacher or expert to give you a general
course?

All sorts of slide courses are available and the Metropolitan
Museum of Art has produced a New York Portfolio written
by critic John Canaday and distributed through the Book-of-

the-Month Club. You are not bound to accept any particular point of view with these courses, but they can help you learn to see quality in different kinds of art in a variety of styles. You will probably find yourself drawn to a certain type of expression, a certain field or era, and will want to learn more about it.

Many books are available to the beginner—too many to enumerate fully, but I can suggest a few general ones which I have found interesting and helpful, which give a general coverage of the subject, are easily available and not too expensive. They tend to be well-illustrated but are not just "show books."

First, in paperbacks:

Apollonio, Argen, Brion, Hunter, Read, etc. editors, *Art Since 1945*
Barnes & Noble series on individual artists
Christensen, Erwin, *The History of Western Art*
Farah, Ted, *Art Collecting for Pleasure and Profit*
Haas, Irvin, *A Treasury of Great Prints*
Hunter, Sam, *Modern American Painting and Sculpture*
Janson, H. W., and Dora Jane Janson, *The Story of Painting*
Lumsden, E. S., *The Art of Etching*
Murray, Peter and Linda, *Penguin Dictionary of Art and Artists*
Newmeyer, Sarah, *Enjoying Modern Art*
Newton, Eric, *European Painting and Sculpture*
Observer books of art. London: Frederick Warne & Co., Ltd.
Pocket Library of Great Art series
Praeger Art Books. New York: Frederick Praeger, Inc.
Sachs, Paul J., *A Pocket Book of Great Drawings*
Seuphor, Michel, *Abstract Painting*
Tudor Publishing Company art series
Wechsler, Herman, ed., *The Pocket Book of Old Masters*
Wingert, Paul S., *Primitive Art*

In hard cover books I would suggest the following as a preliminary list:

For advice on collecting

Loria, Jeffrey H., *Collecting Original Art*
Reitlinger, G., *The Economics of Taste*
Rush, Richard, *Art as an Investment*
Seddon, Richard, *Art Collecting for Amateurs*
Solomon, Irwin W., *How to Start and Build an Art Collection*

For a general sampling

Arnau, Frank, *The Art of the Faker*
Canaday, John, *Mainstreams of Modern Art*
Covarrubias, Miguel, *Indian Art of Mexico and Central America*
Garvey, Eleanor, *The Artist and the Book 1860-1960*
Getlein, Frank and Dorothy, *The Bite of the Print*
Janson, H. W., *History of Art*
Lake, Carlton, and Robert Maillard, eds., *Dictionary of Modern Painting*
Lane, Richard, *Masters of the Japanese Print*
Leight, Hermann, *History of the World's Art*
Longstreet, Stephen, *Treasury of the World's Great Prints*
Peterdi, Gabor, *Printmaking*
Runes, Dagobert, and Harry Schrickel, eds., *Encyclopedia of the Arts*
Taylor, Francis Henry, *Fifty Centuries of Art*
Zigrosser, Carl, *The Book of Fine Prints*
Zigrosser, Carl, and Christa A. Gaehde, *A Guide to the Collecting and Care of Original Prints*
(This book is somewhat specialized, but a great help to the interested print collector.)

For museum and gallery guides

Faison, S. Lane, Jr., *A Guide to the Art Museums of New England*
Spaeth, Eloise, *American Art Museums and Galleries*
(This is especially good as a guide to galleries in different areas, including the price range and media carried in each gallery reviewed.)

A fuller list of books on art, with complete bibliographical data, appears at the end of this book, for readers wishing to pursue the subject further. For those who would like additional information on art periodicals or would like to learn more about terms for the different art media, appendices are provided.

TWELVE

The Art Detective

"Every work of art has a structure, or at least,
a shape, and that shape permits it to be labeled
a species. And it is well to categorize it as such,
for it is indeed a thing alive, a living thing
presuming to vanquish inexorable time."
> Aldo Pellegrini
> NEW TENDENCIES IN ART

THE COLLECTOR ON A SHOESTRING needs a lively curiosity, a willingness to research finds and the instincts of a detective, as well as an informed eye. What happens when you find an attractive painting or etching that has no attribution attached to it? This is a constant problem of the museum, art dealer, and auctioneer, and you pay for their research quite legitimately, but you may find it more rewarding to uncover the evidence yourself.

Sometimes your best bet is to go to the specialists in the field: the museum, the dealer or the appraiser. These are busy people, however, and you can do some of the work and have some of the fun yourself. First, of course, a signature, initials, title or inscription on the work will give you a start, as will an informed guess on the period and country of the object. With this, or possibly knowing the name of the artist but not the title or date of the work, you can go to work in books of reference to find out more about the probable creator or period and place.

You may also wish to know more about an item described in a catalogue of sale. Often catalogues of sale come from firms far away, such as Craddock and Barnard in London or Associated American Artists in New York. They may list a print, sometimes even give the appropriate catalogue number, but how do you, in your living room, know what it looks like and whether you would like it?

You can consult reference books at your local library or museum, such as E. Bénézit, *Dictionnaire des peintres, sculpteurs, dessinateurs et graveurs,* which gives brief biographies of almost all known artists, together with an account of their major works and signatures. Another fine book of this nature is Bryan's *Dictionary of Painters and Engravers.* For a description of the graphic work of artists there is a variety of detailed catalogues such as Adam Bartsch, *Le Peintre-graveur;* Loÿs Delteil, *Le Peintre-graveur illustré (XIX & XX Siècles)*; Arthur M. Hind, catalogues of Rembrandt, Dürer, Goya, Hogarth and Piranesi; F. W. H. Hollstein, *German Engravings, Etchings and Woodcuts ca. 1400-1700,* and *Dutch and Flemish Etchings, Engravings and Woodcuts ca. 1450-1700* (15 volumes, to be completed); and catalogues of the graphic work of one artist, such as Edward G. Kennedy, *The Etched Work of Whistler;* Way on Whistler lithographs; DeVesme, Meaune, Lieure, Meder (in German); Mourlot catalogues on Picasso and Braque; Wildenstein on Fragonard; and Zigrosser on Kaethe Kollwitz. A little more general and very helpful are Arthur M. Hind, *An Introduction to a History of Woodcut* in two volumes, and his *A History of Engraving and Etching from the Fifteenth Century to the Year 1914,* both now in paperback. Most of these are technical books known to professionals in the field and they will help you find the appropriate references.

For home research you can obtain books which do not come in a multitude of expensive volumes; some of them, like Hind, are in paperback. In the print area, which I know best, books like Carl Zigrosser, *The Book of Fine Prints,* Irvin Haas, *A Treasury of Great Prints,* Frank and Dorothy Getlein, *The Bite of the Print,* and Stephen Longstreet, *A Treasury of the World's Great Prints,* are good for general information and many illustrated prints. For even more general coverage, books like the Praeger Encyclopedia of Art series (in paperback) or the *Dictionary of Modern Painting* (Lake and Maillard, eds.) or the *Encyclopedia of the Arts* (Runes and Schrickel, eds.) can be very helpful for orientation in style, period, nationality, and so on. If you become interested in a certain field, your museum, college art department, library or art dealer in that field can usually tell you the books most likely to be available and to be of most help to you. In reading these books you can learn more about the medium that interests you, the period and conditions under which a work was produced, and the artist or craftsman that worked on it.

Inscriptions and titles on a work can be a great help to the art detective. They are like clues in solving a mystery. Sometimes they will refer to the maker of the object followed by the word *fecit* ("made it," in Latin) or *pinxit* ("painted it") or *sc.* or *sculpt.* ("made the plate for it," in prints) or *del.* ("drew it") or *inv.* ("designed" or "invented" the picture). The inscription after *Imp.* is the printer's name; after *ex.* or *excudit* is the name of the publisher. "After Van Dyck" means a copy or representation of the original painting or drawing. Other inscriptions may refer to the place where something was made, or they may give a clue to the meaning, title or content of an article. The inscription may give the date or time of making, or refer to its patron or commissioner. In identifying allegorical figures, gods and goddesses from Greek mythology or the numerous saints, a knowledge of the characteristic symbols of each is helpful. Books of Christian iconography and pagan symbols are available in libraries and museums and may be consulted on such problems. One such book is George Ferguson, *Signs and Symbols in Christian Art,* in hardback and paperback.

Other clues may be found on the side of a print, such as a collector's mark or a museum identification, as museums do dispose of duplicates in their collections. Look at the back of a painting or print also. Inscriptions may be written giving the artist's name, the title of the work, an indication of whether it is a copy of a work or *ad vivem* ("from life"), a collection notation or even the original price.

Finding out more about a piece through inscriptions can be a fascinating adventure and can add much meaning to the work. For example, I recently picked up a small page of something identified by the dealer as "Fifteenth Century Manuscript," and on such an inexpensive item he wasn't going to do any more research. It was up to me. What was it? It looked as if it might have come from a small book and had charming woodcut illustrations on the borders and illuminated capitals on the verses. The first clue I found was in the subject matter—obviously religious, no surprise for that period. The illustrations showed what I took to be Veronica's veil shown to the people, possibly a Resurrection scene, and other harder-to-identify subjects. Was this a book of prayers?

The next clue was presented in the inscription on the page. Even my rusty Latin could pick out *Psalmus*. And how did the psalm go? It started out, as luck would have it, *De profundis*. It didn't take me long to find a crib—the Bible—and discover that this was Psalm 130 ("Out of the depths have I called thee, O Lord . . ."), one of my favorites, which greatly enhanced the value of the little page to me.

Then I read in Douglas Percy Bliss's book *A History of Wood Engraving* and thumbed through its illustrations. Sure enough, there was something very close to what I had: The Book of Hours published in Paris in the early 1500's by Pierre Pigouchet for Simon Vostris. With this information, I made an appointment with the long-suffering Print Department of the Boston Museum of Fine Arts and came in, page in hand.

They immediately confirmed my guess on The Book of Hours but thought it was by Thielman Kerver rather than Pigouchet. It turned out we were both wrong—it was from Gillet Hardouyn who published several editions of Books of Hours from 1504 to 1529. In the process of researching I had the added pleasure of looking at three of their beautiful Books of Hours, pages of which were hand-illuminated and fresh as the day they were made. I learned that the Books of Hours had been part of a transition from the hand-done manuscripts to the printed word, and therefore imitated their originals as closely as possible in hand-illumined capitals and other details. The psalm was one of the Seven Penitential Psalms included in these books of prayer and meditation. In further reading I was cheered by Zigrosser's description of these books on page 31 of *The Book of Fine Prints*: "Among the most beautiful and touching productions in the whole history of prints were the "Horae" or Books of Hours printed in Paris in the two decades just preceding and succeeding the turn of the sixteenth century"—but I had found that out for myself!

Other helps to the thrill of discovery can be more general, clues given by style or manner of painting, and also by the style of clothing, architecture or furniture represented. They help place a work in a period and nationality and give the searcher more hints on just where to look further for his identifications. You might call them the fingerprints of time, for they can be just as helpful. An artist's style can be as distinctive and personal as a fingerprint to one who knows his period.

Science has produced many aids for the art detective in the museum or the wealthy collector. Who has not heard of the use of X-rays on pictures or the investigation of cracks and layers of paint? In the field of archeology and antique artifacts the recent discovery of the radiocarbon test to establish dating has been a great help. This test is based on the rate of decay of organic material and gives indications as to how long the object has been decaying, therefore when it was made. In the field of Pre-Columbian art, where so many of the written records of the culture have been destroyed, it has revised the whole notion of the length of time of the civilization and its stages.

One of the jobs of the art detective may be to establish the provenance of an article. Everything you know or can learn about a piece helps you place it in time and in the period of the artist's development and may tell you more about his meaning and orientation. It also adds value to a piece, however small it may be. If you are buying something, try to get as much information as you can about the artist, its former owner (if any), place of origin, and catalogue number if it is recorded.

Naturally, if you buy the work of a contemporary artist either directly from him or are the first buyer of a work from his gallery, this question of provenance will not occur, but you should record this fact and the purchase price in your book of records, along with any information about the artist's training, his work in other collections, prizes won, and other details.

Why go to all this trouble? It enhances the value of a piece to know what it is, but, more important to me, it lets the searcher in on a great adventure of discovery. In the end he or she has added greatly to his knowledge of the opinions, outlook and orientation of a particular artist or period in history. It can be very helpful to a collector to keep a written account of his finds, together with his research on a subject. He should include a record of where he got the object, what he paid for it, what its date or catalogue number is, if these are available, as well as the artist, period or nationality of the piece. Should he wish to dispose of a piece, he has an account of its history and value which can help set the price. If he is giving it to an institution or passing it on to heirs, documentation enhances it greatly. There is nothing more infuriating than inheriting a mass of undifferentiated "junk" with no more than an apocryphal family legend to go on, if that. Tracking down information may take years and the impatient heirs usually give it to an auctioneer for a pittance, or they may hire an appraiser, only to find it wasn't worth the expense. Also, human nature being what it is, although a person is willing to research his own find, and back his own taste or hunch, he is much less willing to do so for accumulations of someone else which so often represent the taste of a different era.

Under just such care and research your "shoestring" may stretch and stretch; you may find a particular field of interest, give special scope or balance to your collection, and see it taking on the personality of its collector.

THIRTEEN

Framing and Displaying Your Treasures

"There assuredly exists a supreme value for modern painters, but it is painting itself."
André Malraux
MUSEUM WITHOUT WALLS

AS IS WELL KNOWN, it is always less expensive to buy a print or picture unframed. Occasionally you can save money on an already framed print or picture, when the store has custom-framed a number of works at a less expensive rate than you would have to pay were you to custom-frame the print individually. You often pay more, however, for an over-elaborate frame than for the print itself, and this seems extravagant to me. In certain cases you will want to specially frame a work, but usually you can find a good and helpful framer who will not charge you exorbitant prices. It is worthwhile finding someone like this and studying techniques of framing properly, particularly in the preservation of old prints, because if you don't, you may be spending all your money on the framing and not on the works themselves. When you frame or have framed works of art on paper—drawings, pastels, watercolors, or prints—you should be sure to insist that the mat and backing are made of one hundred percent rag content, as otherwise the work may deteriorate. All such works must, of course, be framed under glass for their protection, although oil paintings should not be behind glass.

It is economical to learn to mat and frame the pictures yourself. You may not be able to make the frames from scratch, by carpentering the moldings, but you can purchase good standard frames, and spray, paint, or rub them to suit your fancy. If you cannot find frames with glass in them when you need them, hardware stores will cut the glass to fit your frame and you can painstakingly fit the nails into the back of the frame. Good sources of interesting old frames are antique stores or church fairs, though some of these are getting increasingly wise to the charm of old frames and pricing them accordingly!

Another project is the mounting of sculpture, artifacts or prize treasures you feel worthy of notice. From lumber yards you can get good blocks of wood that may be oiled, stained or painted most attractively. If you have any carpentry or wood-working done in your house, save the cut-off ends, which make handy instant pedestals. They can be sprayed or painted black, or waxed and then rubbed with an oil paint, such as burnt sienna, most effectively. For standing a small figure upright, piano wire doubled in half and inserted in a drilled hole in the center of the block will support the object from behind, embracing it in the middle. Actually, your best bet on mounting is to ask the owner of the establishment where you buy the object about the best way of mounting it. You will usually find him most helpful. If you are going to have a piece of sculpture or an artifact mounted, you must add this into the total price of the work when you are buying.

One more word about framing and mounts. Often it will pay you to have frames and pedestals which are not firmly fastened to their objects so that you can rotate objects. For example, for prints, you may use braquettes and two sheets of glass which are easily removable. Associated American Artists in New York makes a slide-out frame for such a purpose, and an 11" x 14" one with transparent plastic front and solid back, either vertical or horizontal, is put out by Marboro Books and other book stores. Pedestals may be used for various objects in succession, or interchangeably if you do not mount your piece on a pipe or attached wires, but just place it free standing on the block. In this way you can try an object at different heights in different places in the room until you find the one that suits it best.

It is difficult if not impossible to give advice on the many ways to display or hang your treasures. This is a matter of personal taste, of harmonizing with your other furnishings, of available space and many other factors. However, I will be happy to share a few of my prejudices with you.

The first is: never let the setting overwhelm the object. That is, don't over-frame or make your mounting so elegant nobody notices what is mounted. Beware of the dealer who calls your attention to the framing of a painting or print. Surely *what* is framed is the most important thing. Good framing can greatly enhance a work but it should do so unobtrusively. In the same way, a clever base for a statue or artifact should complement the article, not compete with it or distract from it. And, in a larger sense, the furnishings and wall decoration should not be so vibrant as to drown out any works of art placed near them. White, cream or grey walls are often the most effective for prints, paintings and sculpture, as you may have noticed in galleries and museums.

Another preference I have is for interesting groupings. Pictures placed in juxtaposition can be very effective and bring out the good qualities in each. However, I do not think you can place too disparate types of mediums together. A heavy oil, for example, may tend to drown out a delicate drawing or etching.

I enjoy the mingling of different styles and periods, as they can set off interesting sparks or suggest unthought-of relationships to one another. African art, for example, goes very well with contemporary art; historically speaking, contemporary art was influenced by it, in just the same way that Japanese woodcuts influenced the Impressionists. Pre-Columbian artifacts tend to go better with the moderns than with eighteenth century art, which in turn does well with Greek and Roman works whose classicism inspired it.

A prejudice on my part is the idea of a balanced collection—prints, for instance, representing different artists, schools and times. I think this makes for a lively interplay of forces and a broad scope for the viewer. I don't deny that if I had the means, I might like all the etchings of Rembrandt—but then what a world he included! Balance also might be between fine prints and other forms of art—watercolors, drawings, oils or sculpture. This can make for a very pleasant or exciting diversity if you choose.

Rooms have certain moods, some informal and gay, some more classical, severe or reposeful. Art works can greatly contribute to their character and enhance your feeling for the room. I am one who believes that a dining room should be furnished more formally than a bedroom, and that more *intime* and meaningful small works of art are more at home in informal rooms, such as a bedroom or small study or library.

In the display of sculpture or artifacts, bookcases, cabinets and mantels are very suitable and tend to blend better with a room than do isolated pedestals. However, if you have a dramatic, stark modern setting, go in for pedestals and spotlights, by all means. On the whole, though, I think they tend to disrupt and overdramatize the average living room. If you want ideas for the display of art, go to your local museums and galleries, as well as to interior decorators and model rooms. Galleries and museums spend days in planning exhibits: what will go well with what, which spot will bring out which picture, and so forth. You could get some exciting ideas.

While I do not believe the best motivation for choosing a picture is that it should blend in with the colors of a room, if you buy a good picture it will enhance the original motive for buying it. We bought a "blue picture" a few years ago and still enjoy it—probably because it is a strong work of art in its own right and because it suggests the water which we both love. After all, a preference for a certain color or subject matter reflects your personality and taste in art, which is a most important element in your collecting. In the last analysis, after

informing your eye and taste, what appeals to you is fundamental, since you are the one who will live with and cherish a
particular work of art.

I suggest, however, that you do not necessarily stick with
your first preference in art buying. Many people start out wanting a nice restful seascape, and while it is wonderful to acquire
a nice restful seascape, a whole house of them might be a bit
boring. Explore further afield, mix realistic and abstract styles,
and go beyond period style or subject matter. It will make
both you and your house more interesting.

FOURTEEN

Some Extra Dividends
to Collecting

*"Without art the view of the world would be
incomplete."*
        Conrad Fiedler
        ON JUDGING WORKS OF VISUAL ART

THERE ARE EXTRA DIVIDENDS to getting interested in art.
You begin to enter the events of the art world: openings, special museum and gallery happenings, art
films, broadcasts and periodicals which are stimulating
and often enlarge your knowledge of the subject considerably.

For example, museums and galleries sponsor many events
which are of interest to the average person as well as to the art
student and scholar. Openings of shows are fascinating events,
not a particularly good time to see the pictures themselves, perhaps, but often a glittering gathering of interesting people.
Artists-at-work days, such as those sponsored by the DeCordova
Museum in Lincoln, Massachusetts, and by the Boston Museum
of Fine Arts, offer a wonderful opportunity to see the processes
of construction in many areas of endeavor: casting and welding
sculpture, painting with oil, acrylic, and watercolor, making
woodcuts and serigraphs, stained glass, enamelling on copper,
silversmithing, making pottery and ceramics, painting murals
—a vast panorama of art activity. It is exciting to actually see
the steps of creating in a medium. Or take the Gallery-Go-
Round sponsored by the Institute of Contemporary Art in
Boston: here, on a mild spring day, four blocks on Newbury
Street are roped off for the public and all the galleries are
open. Extra activity is provided in do-it-yourself swirl and

sponge painting, singing groups and bands, "happenings," wine tasting, painting demonstrations—all a great deal of fun. Then there may be such events as an open house I attended, where rooms professionally furnished with art were shown, "underground cinema" was provided, and there were psychedelic displays with an intriguing demonstration of the refraction of light.

Many museums run programs of associated arts such as film series, dance programs and concerts. Art tours offer the viewing of private collections.

The variety of periodicals that serve the field and the many art bookstores to browse in can provide great delight as well as enlightenment to the "art bug." The art addict also discovers his own walking tours—up and down Madison Avenue or 57th Street in New York City, a stroll on Newbury Street in Boston or on Wisconsin Avenue, Georgetown, in Washington, D.C.— where he can see the galleries' new shows, browse through art books in the bookstores and generally do pleasant esthetic window-shopping.

When you become interested in art, you frequently get to meet practising artists at the local art association or gallery. Learning about the experiments in different fields is stimulating. You may talk to a young artist who grinds his own colors, perhaps mixing bronze or silver powder to achieve great luminosity; meet sculptors casting in epoxy or fiberglass; or hear about the use of commercial techniques in both painting and sculpture. If you admire a particular artist's work or wish to purchase it, you may even be invited to his studio to see other paintings, prints or sculpture that he is doing. Getting to know artists is being in touch with talented, creative people and this in itself is a marvelous happening.

You yourself may enter classes in painting, sculpture or crafts. The local museums, art association, art school or high school often gives these courses at many levels, from the beginner on up. Learning the different techniques and disciplines can be a rewarding experience. Your discovery of your own limitations in a field, or learning the complicated steps to creating a work of art may lead you to a greater appreciation of the works of professionals. Then again you may discover your own talent in a field which can be very satisfying.

Finally, an extra dividend to art collecting may be the financial appreciation of your collection, if you have been fortunate and have chosen with an informed eye and mind. Along with the general inflation of the economy, art prices have inflated recently in many fields from primitive art to Impressionist masterpieces. While I do not suggest collecting with only financial gain in mind, (especially as such appreciation is almost as uncertain as the stock market), increase in the value of art does occur, and sometimes in an astounding amount. Shifting contemporary taste plays an important part in this, though, and the "masterpieces" of today are sometimes the duds of tomorrow. Your own appreciation of a work of art is your best dividend in collecting it.

Art Periodicals

A VERY PLEASANT WAY to learn about art is through periodicals in the field. Most art magazines are beautifully illustrated, so that reading them is like taking a quick visit to a gallery or museum, with a knowledgeable commentary on what you are seeing. Some of these periodicals are published for a strictly professional group in a limited area, but many are for the reader interested in art in general. The following is a list of some art magazines, with brief comments on the main interest of each periodical and the price of a yearly subscription.

Apollo, The International Magazine of Art and Antiques 720 Fifth Avenue, New York, N.Y. 10019
    12 issues $24.00
    A beautiful magazine written mainly for the connoisseur and collector of Old Master paintings, prints and antiques.
Archaeology 100 Washington Square, New York, N.Y. 10003
    4 issues $6.00
    This magazine has a wide variety of articles in many areas for the general reader. It would be of particular value to the person interested in antique artifacts and pottery.
the ART gallery Ivoryton, Conn. 06442
    10 issues $9.00
    Extremely useful for information on current shows in galleries in New York and around the country, with good illustrations and articles. It is usually available in most galleries.
Art in America 635 Madison Avenue, New York, N.Y. 10022
    6 issues $15.00
    A hardbound, informative periodical, published bi-monthly

with a fine layout; well worth keeping. It deals mainly with contemporary American art, though it does include articles on earlier American painters also.

Art Journal (College Art Association of America) 432 Park Ave. South, New York, N.Y.

4 issues $3.00

This is mainly concerned with college collections and exhibits, and has very informative articles.

Art News 444 Madison Avenue, New York, N.Y. 10022

12 issues $11.50

One of the oldest magazines in the field, *Art News* is well diversified and includes the latest art as well as Old Master paintings, drawings and prints. It is well illustrated and has good articles on museum collections around the country.

Art Scene 925 Michigan Avenue, Chicago, Ill.

12 issues $5.00

This periodical is concerned mainly with the Midwest, and covers exhibits in Illinois, Indiana, Michigan, etc.

Arts International Via Maraina 17-A, 6900 Lugano, Switzerland

10 issues $15.00

This is an attractive magazine, and especially useful for anyone going abroad, but less helpful if you are interested in the American scene.

arts magazine 60 Madison Avenue, New York, N.Y.

8 issues $9.50

Not as lavishly illustrated as some of the others, but worthwhile.

Boston Arts 270 Summer Street, Boston, Mass.

12 issues $5.00

Covers the arts in Boston including theatre, radio programs, dance, art exhibits, and concerts, with articles on leading artists.

Bulletin of the Metropolitan Museum of Art Metropolitan Museum of Art, Fifth Avenue at 82nd Street, New York, N.Y.

Museum bulletins are fine dividends of museum membership. This is probably the best as a combination of scholarship and popular appeal.

The Connoisseur 250 West 55th Street, New York 19, N.Y.

12 issues $16.00

Mainly for the connoisseur of antique furniture, china, pottery, and other fields of collecting, but has good articles of art of the Old Masters and occasional pieces on contemporaries, with excellent illustrations.

Horizon 551 Fifth Avenue, New York 17, N.Y.

6 issues $18.00

This is not strictly an art periodical as it has articles on the theatre, archaeology, history, and literature, but it also has excellent illustrations of art, is bound in hard cover and is well worth saving for your library.

Studio International 155 West 15th Street, New York, N.Y. 10011

11 issues $15.00

Published in London, this periodical deals mainly with modern European art and reviews the London galleries and a few Continental exhibits. It occasionally has a Christmas bonus of an original print in the magazine.

Some Art Terms

IT CAN BE A HELP to know some of the terms for techniques in the different media. There is a variety of techniques in painting. The fresco (painting directly on wet lime or plaster) and the mosaic (a composition of small stone or glass fragments) are among the oldest. In medieval times tempera was used, usually with an egg yolk base, applied on a wood panel to create a painting or icon. This technique is still employed, notably by such meticulous contemporary painters as Andrew Wyeth. Illumination of manuscripts was another mode of painting in the Middle Ages. There were also enamelled pictures, relic cases and triptychs.

Oil painting was first used in the fifteenth century and is the most popular form of painting today. However, acrylic, a product of research in plastics, is now used by many contemporary artists. Acrylic is a waterbase medium which is fast drying and can be used either as an oil paint or as a watercolor. Other modern techniques in painting include collage, initiated by the Surrealists in the 1920's, and the *papiers collés* made of newspaper, tickets and other paper scraps, by Picasso and Braque around 1910. Another innovation is the shaped canvas, where the canvas, instead of being flat and rectangular, is three dimensional and usually curved in unusual ways.

Pastel was a medium developed in the eighteenth century, using chalk on paper. The paper now used is often tinted. Pastels should be displayed under glass to keep the color from fading or flaking off.

Since men first drew on cave walls, drawings have been done on all sorts of surfaces with all sorts of implements. They are usually executed with pen or pencil or charcoal. A wash of brownish ink is sometimes added to enhance the picture. The Old Masters often made many studies for a painting, drawing with silverpoint or red chalk as well as with ink or pencil.

Watercolors were used as early as Dürer's time, and he produced some unusually delicate pictures in this medium. The technique is particularly apt to catch quick impressions of subjects, as the artist usually works on dampened paper, and when the paint dries, it is hard to change the first impression.

Gouache is much like watercolor but is opaque and can produce heavier effects, as in an oil. The term "mixed media" refers to a combination of techniques, such as drawing in crayon, with gouache and chalk added.

In sculpture there is also a variety of techniques. The use of terracotta or baked clay is the oldest. Ceramic sculpture is made from baking a hollowed piece of clay in a kiln. Plaster, cast stone and bronze pieces are formed by casting the material in a mold, which in turn has been made around the original model in plasticene or other material. Casting must be very carefully done in several stages to avoid bubbles or cracking. The "lost wax" or *cire perdue* technique of casting uses a coating of clay around a wax model; the wax melts under heat as the liquid bronze is poured in. This results in a unique piece and is a technique used in many lands, as it was in the Benin kingdom in Africa.

Contemporary technique of sculpture includes casting aluminum, epoxy and fiberglass, as well as the unusual technique of encasing living models in plaster-wetted bandages that is employed by George Segal.

Welded steel is a modern way of creating sculpture. Here steel rods are welded into figures or abstract shapes using regular welder's equipment: acetylene torch, helmet with shield, etc. Sometimes, as in so-called "junk sculpture" of such material as chrome bumpers and car equipment, the torch is also used to dismantle the car.

In the carving techniques of sculpture, a variety of materials may be used: marble, limestone, jade, ivory, volcanic rock, "featherstone" (a light, porous, easy to carve stone), granite, found rock, wood of all types from mahogany to pear wood. Here the sculptor must carve his figure or shape from the block with a chisel and mallet or drills. Carving is a very time-consuming process, in which one wrong stroke may spell ruin, or total destruction of the piece.

Contemporary techniques of sculpture have recently gone rather far from this classic base. The mobiles of Alexander Calder are moving sculpture. Light sculptures are made from neon tubing, as in the works of Chryssa. A challenging new school has arisen producing stark pieces called "primary structures," made by artists such as Anthony Caro and Anthony Smith. Even such material as vinyl has been used by such sculptors as Claes Oldenberg, who has given the world his giant Hamburger, Ghost Telephone and other inventions.

Some technical terms for prints not discussed before are *relief process*, which includes woodcuts, wood engraving, linoleum cuts and Japanese prints; *intaglio process*, in which the line making the impression is cut into the plate and which includes engraving on metal, etching, aquatint and mezzotint; and *planographic process*, where the design is drawn on the area and the ink retained chemically as in the lithograph drawn on stone. *Edition* means the number of prints issued, and in modern printmaking the artist numbers each print of the edition in the left hand lower corner, such as 5/75: the number five out of an edition of seventy-five. He signs the print on the right hand side. *Proof* is a trial check while the artist is working on the plate. An *artist's proof* or *a.p.* is an unnumbered impression which the artist keeps. *State* refers to each printing of a plate before the final one when all the changes have been made.

Sometimes in a sales catalogue or a book on prints you will see a capital letter and a number after the title of a print, such as "Dürer, Albrecht, Christ appearing to Magdalen B. 47." This refers to the catalogue number of the woodcut and means that it is number 47 in Adam Bartsch's catalogue of the complete graphic works of Dürer. Here the print with its date of issue and number of states is described in detail, and it is an excellent way to verify the etching, engraving, woodcut or lithograph.

The most common notations of this sort are B (followed by a number) for Adam Bartsch's *Le Peintre-graveur,* which describes the main graphic works from the fifteenth to the eighteenth centuries in 22 volumes, and D or L.D. which stands for Loÿs Delteil, *Le Peintre-graveur illustré* in 31 volumes for the nineteenth and early twentieth century graphics, published in Paris 1906-1930. Both of these are in French, but are easy to read if you know a smattering of the language. Other initials or names are for more specialized graphic catalogues like Hind and Bredius on Rembrandt; Lieure and Meaune on Callot; Meder on Dürer; Klipstein on Kollwitz; Mellerio on Redon; Kennedy on Whistler etchings; Way on Whistler lithographs; Mourlot on Chagall, Picasso and Braque; Roger-Marx on Vuillard and Bonnard; Hind on Piranesi and Hogarth; Hollstein on Northern European etchings in a work now in progress; Basteler on Brueghel, Breeskin on Cassatt; Guerin on Gauguin and Manet. Some graphic artists are not completely catalogued as yet, particularly recent or contemporary ones.

More Galleries Here and Abroad

THE FOLLOWING IS A LIST of galleries in various cities not covered in Chapter 7. It is based on information from current art periodicals and directories. Not all of these galleries will be of the shoestring variety, but they will be able to put the searcher on the track of good exhibitions in the area. The most complete current guide to all commercial galleries in the United States is the 9th edition (1967-68) of the *International Directory of the Arts,* published in Berlin in 1968 and costing approximately $25.00. Your local museum library may have a copy of this for reference.

ALABAMA

BIRMINGHAM

Art Originals Gallery, 1922 12th S. Crafts and paintings of local artists, reasonably priced.

Littlehouse on Linden, 2911 Linden. Good shows and selections of graphics.

ALASKA

ANCHORAGE

The Gilded Cage, 225 E St. Paintings, graphics, sculpture and artifacts.

M.K.I., 608 4th Ave. Paintings, graphics.

ARIZONA

TUCSON

America West, 81 North Park. Oceanic, African, Pre-Columbian antiquities.

Rosequist Galleries, 18 South Convent St. Regional artists and some European prints and drawings.

Swihart International Art, Ltd., 122 S. Country Club, Broadway Village.

ARKANSAS

LITTLE ROCK

The Gallery, Lakewood House, North Little Rock.

CALIFORNIA

BEVERLY HILLS

Frank Perls, 9777 Wilshire Blvd.

LOS ANGELES

Ankrum, 657 North La Cienega Blvd. Contemporary California art.

David Stuart Galleries, 807 North LaCienega Blvd. Contemporary painting and sculpture, Pre-Columbian, ancient and primitive art.

Dwan, 1091 Broxton Ave, Westwood. All media.

Dalzell Hatfield Gallery 3400 Wilshire Blvd., Ambassador Hotel. Prices fairly high, but give excellent exhibits.

Frank Perls Gallery, 350 North Camden Dr., Beverly Hills. All media, prices from moderate up.

Esther Robles Galleries, 665 N. La Cienega Blvd.

SAN FRANCISCO

Conacher, 134 Maiden Lane. Twentieth century art.

John Bolles, 729 Sansome St. All media, fairly high prices.

Gump's, 250 Post St. Oriental, European and West Coast artists. Prints and drawings reasonable.

The R.E. Lewis Gallery, 555 Sutter St. Japanese, Old Master and established modern prints, prices very reasonable. Mr. Lewis is a scholar and a gentleman, and he and his assistants can tell you a great deal about prints and drawings.

Eric Locke Gallery, 2557 California Street. Good graphics, sculpture.

Arleigh Gallery, 1812 Pacific Ave. Paintings and prints.

Britten Fine Arts and Original Prints Gallery, 2801 Leavenworth St. Contemporary prints.

Poor Man's Gallery, 1300 Polk St. Contemporary artists.

SANTA BARBARA

Austin Gallery, 539 San Ysidoro Rd. Graphics by Sister Mary Corita, Étienne Ret and others.

COLORADO

ASPEN

Aspen Art Gallery. Paintings and graphics.

Bethune and Moore, Old Railway Station. Graphics, paintings.

DENVER

The Gallery, 314 Detroit St. Contemporary artists including Meeker, Altmann and Amen.

Saks Gallery, 3019 2nd Ave.

CONNECTICUT

HARTFORD

Verle Gallery, 707 Farmington Ave. Contemporary art and graphics.

NEW CANAAN

Silvermine Guild, Silvermine Rd. Contemporary prints and paintings.

NEW HAVEN

Athena Gallery, 278 Orange St. Graphics by Levine, Marsh, Sloan.

FLORIDA

MIAMI

Bacardi, 2100 Biscayne Blvd.

Berenson, 1128 Kane Con., Bay Harbor Islands.

Gallery 3007, 3007 Grand, Coconut Grove. Has Pre-Columbian art, batiks, etchings and paintings very reasonably priced.

Mirell, 3421 Main Highway, Coconut Grove. Great range of art, including works of Old Masters.

JACKSONVILLE

Cummer Gallery of Art, 829 Riverside. Drawings, prints, Pre-Columbian pieces moderately priced.

PALM BEACH

Society of the Four Arts, Four Arts Plaza. Has collectors' sales.

SARASOTA

Sarasota Art Association. Shows local artists whose work is for sale.

GEORGIA

ATLANTA

Artists Association Inc., 1105 Peachtree St. N.E. Work by local artists.

Fine Arts Gallery, 935 W. Peachtree St. N.E. Contemporary art.

Eugene Okarma's Gallery, 1050 Spring St. N.W. Traditional art.

Gavant Gallery, 3889 Peachtree N.E. European contemporary artists. Prices start under $10.

Signature Shop, 3267 Roswell. Interesting crafts, sculpture, hangings.

ILLINOIS

CHICAGO

Fairweather-Hardin Gallery, 101 East Ontario. Area artists, all media, prints reasonable.

Richard Feigen Gallery, 226 E. Ontario St. 20th century European artists.

Allen Frumkin Gallery, 620 N. Michigan Ave. Especially good for prints and sculpture; also includes painting and primitive artifacts.

Distelheim Gallery, 113 E. Oak St. Oils, watercolors and graphics.

Sears Vincent Price Gallery, 140 E. Ontario St. Vast variety from prints and drawings to oils. Changing exhibits.

B. C. Holland Gallery, 224 E. Ontario St. 20th century painting, drawings, and sculpture.

Main Street Galleries, 642-646 N. Michigan Ave. 19th and 20th century American and French paintings, graphics, ethnic art.

Welna Gallery, 936 N. Michigan Ave. Young artists of promise.

Merrill Chase, 540 N. Michigan Ave., also Oakbrook Center and River Oaks Center. Oils, drawings, etchings, lithographs.

IOWA
DES MOINES

Grand Gallery, 4715 Grand Ave. Contemporary, international, representative art.

KENTUCKY
LOUISVILLE

Merida Gallery, 315 W. Broadway. Contemporary.

Port O' Call, 517 Zane St. Painting, graphics, artifacts.

The Thor Gallery, 734 South First St. 17th-19th century Old Masters, contemporary art, sculpture.

LOUISIANA
NEW ORLEANS

Lansford Gallery, 632 St. Peter St. Regional folk art.

Marc Antony 331, 331 Chartres St. Prints and oils, prices good.

The Orleans Gallery, 527 Royal St. Cooperative artists' gallery.

MASSACHUSETTS
WORCESTER

Casdin Gallery, 93 Elm St. Good modern prints at reasonable prices and modestly priced oils and watercolors of local artists.

MICHIGAN

DETROIT

Detroit Artists' Market, 1452 Randolph St. Local artists, prices modest.

Arwin Gallery, 222 Grand River West, Detroit. Michigan artists, except for wide range of prints.

J. L. Hudson Gallery, 1206 Woodward Ave. Fine shows.

Gertrud Kasle, 310 Fisher Bldg. Graphics, painting, sculpture by American contemporaries.

London Grafica Arts, 321 Fisher Bldg. Many prints, some high priced.

Donald Morris Gallery, 20082 Livernois. 20th century American and European.

Franklin Siden Gallery, 213 David Whitney Bldg., Washington Blvd. Excellent contemporary prints.

MINNESOTA

MINNEAPOLIS

Dayton's Gallery 12, 700 on the Mall. American and European modern artists, fairly high priced.

Kilbride-Bradley Gallery, 68 South Tenth St. Regional art. Mostly local artists, prints, pottery, art rental.

MISSOURI

ST. LOUIS

St. Louis Artists' Guild, 812 North Union Blvd.

Harry Mark Gallery, 5608 Pershing Ave. By appointment. Continental 19th century and contemporary.

KANSAS CITY

Little Gallery Frame Shop, 5002 State Line. Painting, graphics, art books.

Palmer Gallery, 6330 Brookside Plaza. Painting, graphics.

NEW JERSEY

ATLANTIC CITY

Atlantic City Art Center, Garden Pier, Boardwalk. Contemporary.

Claire Fox Art Gallery, Hotel Traymore, Illinois Ave. at Boardwalk.

MADISON

Argus Gallery, 2 Green Village Rd. Contemporary work by 150 artists.

MONTCLAIR

Piggins Art Gallery, 403 Bloomfield Ave. Contemporary.

NEW MEXICO

ALBUQUERQUE

Art Center, 8202 Menaul Blvd. N.E. Has graphics, painting.

Fisher at College Inn Book Store, 1910 E. Central. Includes artifacts, prints, as well as painting and sculpture.

Stone Gallery, 105 Amherst S.E.

Symbol Gallery, 2049 Plaza N.W.

TAOS

Blair Galleries. Early Western, representational American art.

Manchester Gallery, Ledoux St. Contemporary art.

NEW YORK

BUFFALO

James Goodman Gallery, The Park Lane, 33 Gates Circle. 20th century American and European drawing, watercolors, sculpture.

D'Arcangelo Fine Arts, 1740 Main St. Artifacts, paintings.

Moffatt, John D. Ltd., 822 Elmwood Ave. Graphics, primitive art.

Tilon Gallery, 417 Franklin St. Artifacts, graphics, painting.

NEW YORK CITY

Kennedy, 20 East 56 St. American and European prints, good catalogue.

Weyhe Gallery, 794 Lexington Ave. Good prints, drawings.

Peter H. Deitsch, 24 East 81 St. Quality prints, some inexpensive.

Lucien Goldschmidt, 1117 Madison Ave. A few moderately priced prints.

Martha Jackson, 32 East 69 St. Is starting a section of lower priced contemporary graphics.

Multiples, Inc., 929 Madison Ave. Contemporary graphics and mass produced objects.

NEW ROCHELLE

Greene Gallery, 368 North Ave.

NYACK

Market Fair, 152 Main St.

Tappan Zee Art Center, 107 S. Broadway. Contemporary art.

KATONAH

Katonah Gallery, Katonah Library. Draws on New York City galleries as well as local artists; has prints, drawings, oils and a rental service.

OHIO

CINCINNATI

Closson's, 421 Race St. Local painters and others, many prints.

Flair House, 113 W. 4th St. Good prints, N.Y. and European.

CLEVELAND

Circle Gallery, 11322 Euclid Ave. Contemporary, mostly local.

International Gallery, 13218 Superior at Euclid Ave. Contemporary.

Kaufman's Gallery, 2799 Euclid Heights Blvd., Cleveland Heights.

Linden-Kicklighter Gallery, 10608 Carnegie Ave.

Ross Widen Gallery, 11320 Euclid Ave. Contemporary, primitive, Oceanic and Pre-Columbian art.

Vixseboxse Art Galleries, 2258 Euclid Ave. 18th-20th century representational art by English, French, Dutch and American artists.

OREGON

PORTLAND

The Fountain Gallery of Art, 115 South West 4th Ave. Has work by Gabor Peterdi, Hayter, Callahan and others.

Image Gallery, 2483 N.W. Overton St. Contemporary.
Window Gallery, 1225 Commercial St. S.E. All periods and styles.

PENNSYLVANIA
PHILADELPHIA
The Print Club, 1614 Latimer St. Contemporary prints.
Makler Gallery, 1716 Locust St. Contemporary European and American Asian and African sculpture.
Newman Contemporary Art Gallery, 1625 Walnut St.
Fisherman-Weiner Gallery, 1715 Spruce St.
Vanderlip Gallery, 1823 Sansom St.

SOUTH CAROLINA
CHARLESTON
Gibbes Art Gallery, 135 Meeting St. This association has a permanent collection and monthly exhibits. Original art is sold at the annual state show and a few of the exhibits.

TENNESSEE
MEMPHIS
International Gallery, 4646 Poplar St. Local artists and ship paintings.

TEXAS
DALLAS
W. R. Fine Galleries, 2524 Cedar Springs.
Haydon Calhoun Galleries, 3030 Sale at Cedar Springs. Contemporary.
Valley House Gallery, 6616 Spring Valley Rd. 19th and 20th century painting and sculpture.

HOUSTON
Cushman Gallery, 419 Lowett Blvd. Regional, Eastern and European artists, some Old Masters.
New Arts Gallery, 3106 Bragas St. Pre-Columbian, Eastern, European and regional artists.

David Gallery, 2243 San Felipe Rd.

Houston Galleries, 2323 San Felipe Rd. Has paintings, sculpture, graphics and Oriental art.

James Bute Gallery, 711 William St.

VERMONT

MANCHESTER VILLAGE

Deely Gallery, 19th and 20th century American art.

VIRGINIA

RICHMOND

Eric Schindler, 2305 East Broad St. Contemporary artists, except in prints which have a greater range and start at $10.

WILLIAMSBURG

House of Eight Winds, Duke of Gloucester St. Good American Indian crafts and art, moderate prices.

Twentieth Century, Nicholson St. Work by Eastern contemporary artists.

WASHINGTON STATE

BELLEVUE

The Collectors' Gallery, Crossroads. Contemporary art, especially Northwest painters, sculptors and printmakers.

SEATTLE

Otto Seligman Gallery, 4727 University Way N.E. Mark Tobey and other contemporaries.

Dolorese Gallery, 4002 University N.E. Contemporary.

WISCONSIN

MILWAUKEE

Bradley Galleries, 2107 N. Prospect Ave. Pre-Columbian, African, primitive and contemporary art.

Irving Galleries, 400 E. Wisconsin Ave. Contemporary painting, sculpture and graphics.

LONDON

Alecto Gallery, 38 Albemarle St. W1. Contemporary prints.

Colnaghi, P. & D. & Co. Ltd., 14 Old Bond St. W1. Although known as purveyors of masterpieces, has some moderately priced items, especially in old prints.

Curwen Gallery, 1 Colville Pl., Whitfield St. W1. Young printmakers.

Drian, 5-7 Porchester Pl. W2. International art.

Lisson Gallery, 68 Bell St., Marylebone NW1. Large editions of prints to bring price down to under $10.00.

Redfern Gallery, 20 Cork St. W1. Has largest stock of 20th century prints.

PARIS

Sagot-Le Garrec et Cie, 24 Rue du Four, Paris VI. Drawings and prints.

Yvon Lambert, 15 Rue de l'Echaude. Young artists, many drawings

LaGravure, 41 Rue de Seine. 20th century graphics.

Denise René, Rive Droite, 124 Rue La Boétie. Contemporary art, especially kinetics.

Denise René, Rive Gauche, 196 Boulevard St. Germain. Multiple graphics and other objects.

Creuzevault, 9 Avenue Matignon. Modern masters such as Picasso, Dufy, Ernst, Viera da Silva. (Not a shoestring gallery, but fine shows.)

Berggruen, 70 Rue de l'Université. Excellent graphics.

Prouté, Paul, 74 Rue de Seine. Many old and modern prints and drawings; catalogue (in French) may be sent for, although it is better to browse through.

Michel, R. G., 17 Quai St. Michel. Now run by son; has some moderately priced art.

Selected Bibliography
for *Collecting Art on a Shoestring*

THE BOOKS SELECTED have been chosen for their general interest and availability to the amateur collector. Except for some reference works they do not represent the more technical or esoteric works on the subject, nor are some of the older classic works included, as many of these are out of print or very difficult to find. Books on individual artists are not shown for the most part as these can be looked up easily in library card catalogues, and their inclusion would swell the list to unmanageable proportions. If a work is available in a paperback edition this is also indicated.

COLLECTING AND COLLECTORS

BEHRMAN, S. N. *Duveen.* New York: Random House 1952 (paper)

CABANNE, PIERRE. *The Great Collectors.* New York: Farrar, Straus 1963

CONSTABLE, WILLIAM G. *Art Collecting in the United States of America.* New York: Macmillan 1964

COOPER, DOUGLAS. *Great Family Collections.* New York: Macmillan 1965

COOPER, DOUGLAS. *Great Private Collections.* New York: Macmillan 1963

DUVEEN, JAMES HENRY. *Art Treasures and Intrigue.* Garden City, N.Y.: Doubleday, Doran and Co. 1935

DUVEEN, JAMES HENRY. *Secrets of an Art Dealer.* New York: E. P. Dutton 1938

FARAH, TED. *Art Collecting for Pleasure and Profit.* New York: Pocket Books 1964

GIMPEL, RENÉ. *Diary of an Art Dealer.* New York: Farrar, Straus and Giroux 1966

GUGGENHEIM, MARGUERITE. *Confessions of an Art Addict.* New York: Macmillan 1960

LORIA, JEFFREY H. *Collecting Original Art.* New York: Harper & Row 1965

REITLINGER, GERALD. *The Economics of Taste.* New York: Holt, Rinehart and Winston 1964

RHEIMS, MAURICE. *The Strange Life of Objects.* New York: Atheneum 1961

RIGBY, DOUGLAS AND ELIZABETH. *Lock, Stock and Barrel: The Story of Collecting.* Philadelphia: J. P. Lippincott Co. 1944

RUSH, RICHARD. *Art as an Investment.* Englewood, N.J.: Prentice-Hall 1961

SAARINEN, ALINE B. *The Proud Possessors.* New York: Random House 1958

SCHACK, WILLIAM. *Art and Argyrol.* New York: T. Yoseloff 1960

SEDDON, RICHARD. *Art Collecting for Amateurs.* London: Frederick Muller, Ltd. 1965

SELIGMAN, GERMAIN. *Merchants of Art 1880-1960: Eighty Years of Professional Collecting.* New York: Appleton-Century-Crofts 1961

SOLOMON, IRWIN W. *How to Start and Build an Art Collection.* Philadelphia: Chilton Press 1961

TOFFLER, ALVIN. *The Culture Consumers: A Study of Art and Affluence in America.* New York: St. Martin's Press 1964 (also in paper)

VON HOLST, NIELS. *Creators, Collectors and Connoisseurs.* New York: G. P. Putnam's Sons 1967

CONTEMPORARY ART AND TECHNIQUE

APOLLONIO, ARGEN, BRION, HUNTER, READ, ETC., EDS. *Art Since 1945.* New York: Washington Square Press 1962 (paper)

BARR, ALFRED H., JR., ED. *Masters of Modern Art.* New York: Simon & Schuster 1954

BAUER, JOHN, ED. *New Art in America and Fifty Painters of the 20th Century.* New York: Frederick A. Praeger 1957

CANADAY, JOHN. *The Embattled Critic.* New York: Farrar, Straus and Cudahy 1962 (paper)

CANADAY, JOHN. *Mainstreams of Modern Art.* New York: Simon & Schuster 1959

CHAET, BERNARD. *Artists at Work.* Cambridge, Mass.: Webb Books, Inc. 1960 (paper)

CHENEY, SHELDON. *The Story of Modern Art.* New York: Viking Press 1941

DIEHL, GASTON. *The Moderns.* New York: Crown Publishing Co. n.d.

GELDZAHLER, HENRY. *American Painting in the Twentieth Century.* New York: Metropolitan Museum of Art 1965

HAFTMAN, WERNER. *Painting in the Twentieth Century.* Vols. 1 and 2. London: Lund Humphries 1965 (also in paper)

HESS, THOMAS B. *Abstract Painting.* New York: Viking Press 1951

HUNTER, SAM. *Modern American Painting and Sculpture.* New York: Dell Publishing Co. 1962 (paper)

HUNTER, SAM. *Modern French Painting 1855-1956.* New York: Dell Publishing Co. 1956 (paper)

HUNTER, SAM; ALAIN JOUFFROY; ALAN BOWNESS, ETC. *New Art Around the World.* New York: Harry N. Abrams, Inc. 1966 (paper)

KUH, KATHARINE. *The Artist's Voice.* New York: Harper & Row 1962

KUH, KATHARINE. *Break-up: The Core of Modern Art.* Greenwich, Conn.: New York Graphic Society 1965

LIPPARD, LUCY. *Pop Art.* New York: Frederick A. Praeger 1966

NEWMEYER, SARAH. *Enjoying Modern Art.* New York: Reinhold 1955 (paper)

PELLEGRINI, ALDO. *New Tendencies in Art.* New York: Crown Publishing Co. 1966

READ, HERBERT. *A Concise History of Modern Painting.* New York: Frederick A. Praeger 1959 (paper)

READ, HERBERT. *A Concise History of Modern Sculpture.* New York: Frederick A. Praeger 1964 (paper)

ROBERTSON, BRYAN; JOHN RUSSELL; AND LORD SNOWDON. *Private View.* London: Thomas Nelson, Ltd. 1965

ROSE, BARBARA. *American Art Since 1900.* New York: Frederick A. Praeger 1967 (paper)

RUBLOWSKY, JOHN. *Pop Art.* New York: Basic Books 1965

SEGHERS, PIERRE, ED. *The Art of Painting in the Twentieth Century.* New York: Hawthorn Books, Inc. 1965

SELZ, PETER. *New Images of Man.* New York: Museum of Modern Art 1960

SEUPHOR, MICHEL. *Abstract Painting.* New York: Dell Publishing Co. 1964 (paper)

CRITICISM AND CONNOISSEURSHIP

ASHTON, DORÉ. *The Unknown Shore: A View of Contemporary Art.* Boston: Little, Brown & Co. 1962

BERENSON, BERNARD. *Essays in Appreciation.* London: Chapman & Hall 1958

BERENSON, BERNARD. *Rudiments of Connoisseurship.* New York: Schocken Books 1962 (paper)

FOCILLON, HENRI. *The Life of Forms in Art.* New York: Wittenborn 1957

FRIEDLANDER, MAX J. *On Art and Connoisseurship.* Boston: Beacon Press 1960 (paper)

FRY, ROGER. *Transformations: Critical and Speculative Essays on Art.* Garden City, N.Y.: Doubleday & Co. 1956 (paper)

GOMBRICH, ERNST H. *Art and Illusion.* 2d ed. New York: Pantheon Books 1965

GREENBERG, CLEMENT. *Art and Culture.* Boston: Beacon Press 1961 (paper)

GROSSER, MAURICE. *The Painter's Eye.* New York: New American Library 1963 (paper)

LOWRY, BATES. *The Visual Experience, an Introduction to Art.* Englewood Cliffs, N.J.: Prentice Hall 1963

LYNES, RUSSELL. *Confessions of a Dilettante*. New York: Harper & Row 1966

LYNES, RUSSELL. *The Tastemakers*. New York: Harper & Bros. 1954

READ, HERBERT. *The Meaning of Art*. Baltimore, Md.: Penguin Books 1964 (paper)

ROSENBERG, HAROLD. *The Anxious Object: Art Today and its Audience*. New York: Horizon Press 1964

DICTIONARIES & REFERENCE

AMSTUTZ, WALTER. *Who's Who in Graphic Art*. Zurich: Amstutz and Herdeg Graphic Press 1962

Art Index. January 1929 to the present. New York: H. W. Wilson & Co.

Art Prices Current. London: The Art Trade Press Ltd. Published annually since 1907 (except none 1917-20)

BARTSCH, ADAM VON. *Le Peintre-graveur*. 20 vols. Vienna: Pierre Mechetti 1803-1821 (other later editions, such as Leipzig 1870)

BÉNÉZIT, F. *Dictionnaire des peintres, sculptres, dessinateurs et graveurs*. 8 vols. Paris: Librairie Gründ 1960

BROUGH, JAMES. *Auction!* New York: Bobbs-Merrill Co., Inc. 1963

BRYAN'S *Dictionary of Painters and Engravers*. 5 vols. London: G. Bell and Sons 1930

CARRICK, NEVILLE. *How to Find Out About the Arts*. New York: Pergamon Press 1965

CUMMINGS, PAUL. *Dictionary of Contemporary American Artists*. New York: St. Martin's Press 1966

DAVIS, FRANK (INTRO). *Art at Auction: The Year at Sotheby's and Parke-Bernet 1966-67*. New York: Viking Press 1967

DELTEIL, LOŸS. *Le Peintre-graveur illustré (XIX et XX Siècles)*. Paris 1906-1930

Encyclopedia of World Art. New York: McGraw Hill Co. 1959

FERGUSON, GEORGE. *Signs and Symbols in Christian Art.* New York: Oxford University Press 1961 (paper)

FIELDING, MANTLE. *Dictionary of American Painters, Sculptors and Engravers.* New York: Struck 1945

GILBERT, DOROTHY B., ED. *American Art Dictionary 1967.* Rev. ed. New York: R. R. Bowker Co. 1967

GILBERT, DOROTHY B., ED. *Who's Who in American Art.* New York: R. R. Bowker Co. 1962

HAGGAR, REGINALD GEORGE. *A Dictionary of Art Terms.* New York: Hawthorn Books 1962

HIND, ARTHUR M. *A History of Engraving and Etching from the 15th Century to the Year 1914.* New York: Dover Publications 1963 (paper)

HIND, ARTHUR M. *An Introduction to a History of Woodcut.* 2 vols. New York: Dover Publications 1963 (paper)

HIND, ARTHUR M. *Albrecht Dürer, His Engravings and Woodcuts.* New York: Stokes 1911

HIND, ARTHUR M. *Francisco Goya.* New York: Stokes 1911

HIND, ARTHUR M. *Giovanni Battista Piranesi.* London: Cotswold Gallery 1922

HIND, ARTHUR M. *Rembrandt's Etchings.* London: Methuen and Co. 1920

HIND, ARTHUR M. *William Hogarth, His Original Engravings and Etchings.* New York: Stokes 1912

HOLLSTEIN, F. W. H. *Dutch and Flemish Etchings, Engravings and Woodcuts ca. 1450-1700* (15 vols, to be completed) Amsterdam 1953-

HOLLSTEIN, F. W. H. *German Engravings, Etchings and Woodcuts ca. 1400-1700.* Amsterdam 1954

KECK, CAROLINE K. *How to Take Care of Your Pictures.* New York: Brooklyn Museum 1954

KENNEDY, EDWARD G. *The Etched Work of Whistler.* New York: Grolier Club 1910

KLIPSTEIN, AUGUST. *Graphic Work of Kaethe Kollwitz.* New York: Galerie St. Étienne 1955

LAKE, CARLTON, AND ROBERT MAILLARD, EDS. *Dictionary of Modern Painting.* New York: Tudor Publishing Co. 1964

LAKE, CARLTON, AND ROBERT MAILLARD, EDS. *Dictionary of Modern Sculpture.* New York: Tudor Publishing Co. n.d.

LEHNER, ERNST. *Symbols, Signs and Signets.* New York: World 1950

LEVY, MERVYN. *The Pocket Dictionary of Art Terms.* Greenwich, Conn.: N.Y. Graphic Society 1964

LUGT, FRITS. *Les Marques de Collections.* Amsterdam: Vereenigde Drukkerijen 1921, supplement 1956

MOURLOT, FERNAND. *Braque Lithographe.* Monte Carlo: Sauret 1963

MOURLOT, FERNAND. *Picasso Lithographe.* 4 vols. Monte Carlo: Sauret 1949-

MURRAY, PETER AND LINDA. *Penguin Dictionary of Art and Artists.* Baltimore: Penguin 1967 (paper)

MYERS, BERNARD. *Great Art and Artists of our World: How to Look at Art.* New York: Frederick Watts and Grolier, Inc. 1965

NAGLER, GEORG KASPAR. *Neues Allgemeines Künstler-Lexikon.* 24 vols. Linz 1835-52 and Leipzig 1904-14

The Praeger Picture Encyclopedia of Art. New York: Frederick A. Praeger 1958

RAUSCHENBUSCH, HELMUT, ED. *International Directory of Arts.* 9th edition. 2 vols. Berlin: Deutsche Zentraldruckerei 1967-69

RUNES, DAGOBERT, AND HARRY SCHRICKEL, EDS. *Encyclopedia of the Arts.* New York: Philosophical Library 1946

STAUFFER, DAVID MCNEELEY. *American Engravers Upon Copper and Steel.* 2 vols. New York: Grolier Club 1907

THIEME, ULRICH, AND FELIX BECKER. *Künstler-Lexikon.* 37 vols. Leipzig 1907-50

VOLLMER, HANS. *Allgemeines Lexikon der bildenden Künstler des XX Jahrhunderts.* 6 vols. (20th century supplement to Thieme-Becker) Leipzig 1935-62

WATERS, CLARA CLEMENT. *A Handbook of Legendary and Mythological Art.* New York: Hurd and Houghton 1871

Who's Who in Art. 11th ed. Eastbourne 1962

WRAIGHT, ROBERT. *The Art Game.* New York: Simon & Schuster 1966

DRAWINGS

ALTENA, J. Q. VAN REGTEREN. *Dutch Drawings: Masterpieces of Five Centuries.* Washington, D.C.: National Gallery of Art 1958

BEAN, JACOB. *100 European Drawings in the Metropolitan Museum of Art.* New York: Metropolitan Museum of Art 1964

HOLME, BRYAN, ED. *Master Drawings.* New York: The Studio Publications, Inc. 1943

KENT, NORMAN. *Drawings by American Artists.* New York: Watson-Guptill 1947

MONGAN, AGNES. *One Hundred Master Drawings.* Cambridge, Mass.: Harvard University Press 1949

REITLINGER, HENRY SCIPIO. *Old Master Drawings: A Handbook for Amateurs and Collectors.* London: Constable & Co., Ltd. 1922

SACHS, PAUL J. *Modern Prints and Drawings.* New York: Alfred A. Knopf 1954

SACHS, PAUL J. *A Pocket Book of Great Drawings.* New York: Washington Square Press 1961 (paper)

Shorewood Publishers, New York 1965, series including: HILLIER, J. R. *Japanese Drawings from the 17th through the 19th Century, French Drawings, Italian Drawings, Flemish and Dutch Drawings, German Drawings, Spanish Drawings, Twentieth Century Drawings* (Part I 1900-1940, Part II 1940-1964), *American Drawings, Persian Drawings, From Cave to Renaissance*

TIETZE, HANS. *European Master Drawings in the United States.* New York: Augustin 1947

TONEY, ANTHONY. *150 Masterpieces of Drawing.* New York: Dover Publications 1963 (paper)

HISTORY OF ART AND CULTURAL BACKGROUND

ARNAU, FRANK. *The Art of the Faker.* Boston: Little, Brown & Co. 1961

ASHMOLE, BERNARD, AND H. A. GROENEWEGEN-FRANKFORT. *The Ancient World.* Vol. 1. The Library of Art History. New York: New American Library (Mentor) 1967 (paper; see others in series also)

BACON, EDWARD, ED. *Vanished Civilizations of the Ancient World.* New York: McGraw-Hill 1963

BARKER, VIRGIL. *American Painting.* New York: Macmillan 1951

BECKWITH, JOHN. *The Art of Constantinople: An Introduction to Byzantine Art 330-1453.* New York: Phaidon 1961

BERENSON, BERNARD. *Italian Painters of the Renaissance.* London: Oxford University Press 1952

BINYON, LAURENCE. *Painting in the Far East.* 3d rev. ed. New York: Dover Publications 1959 (paper)

BOAS, FRANZ. *Primitive Art.* New York: Dover Publications 1955 (paper)

CANADAY, JOHN. *Keys to Art.* New York: Tudor 1962

CHRISTENSEN, ERWIN. *The History of Western Art.* New York: New American Library (Mentor) 1959 (paper)

COTTRELL, LEONARD. *The Horizon Book of Lost Worlds.* New York: American Heritage Publishing Co. 1962

COVARRUBIAS, MIGUEL. *Indian Art of Mexico and Central America.* New York: Alfred A. Knopf 1957

CRAVEN, THOMAS, ED. *A Treasury of Art Masterpieces.* New York: Simon & Schuster 1939

Editors of *Art in America. The Artist in America.* New York: W. W. Norton & Co. 1967

ESPEZEL, PIERRE D', AND FRANÇOIS FOSCA. *A Concise Illustrated History of European Painting.* New York: Washington Square Press 1961 (paper)

FLEXNER, JAMES T. *A Short History of American Painting.* Boston: Houghton Mifflin Co. 1950 (also in paper)

GOMBRICH, E. H. *The Story of Art.* New York: Phaidon Press 1950

HARE, RICHARD. *The Art and Artists of Russia.* Greenwich, Conn.: New York Graphic Society 1966

HUYGHE, RENÉ, ED. *Larousse Encyclopedia of Byzantine and Medieval Art.* New York: Prometheus Press 1963

HUYGHE, RENÉ, ED. *Larousse Encyclopedia of Modern Art from 1800 to the Present Day.* New York: Prometheus Press 1965

HUYGHE, RENÉ, ED. *Larousse Encyclopedia of Prehistoric and Ancient Art.* New York: Prometheus Press 1962

HUYGHE, RENÉ, ED. *Larousse Encyclopedia of Renaissance and Baroque Art.* New York: Prometheus Press 1964

JANSON, H. W. *History of Art.* Englewood Cliffs, New Jersey, and New York: Harry N. Abrams, Inc. 1962

JANSON, H. W., AND DORA JANE JANSON. The Story of Painting. New York: Harry N. Abrams, Inc. 1968 (paper)

LACROIX, PAUL. *The Arts in the Middle Ages.* New York: Frederick Ungar Publishing Co. 1964

LARKIN, OLIVER W. *Art and Life in America.* Rev. ed. New York: Holt, Rinehart and Winston 1964

LASAREFF, VICTOR. *Russian Icons from the 12th to the 15th Century.* New York: New American Library (Mentor) 1962 (paper)

LEIGHT, HERMANN. *History of the World's Art.* London: Spring Books 1963

LEUZINGER, ELSY. *Africa: the Art of the Negro Peoples.* New York: McGraw-Hill 1960

LIPMAN, JEAN, ED. *What is American in American Art?* New York: McGraw-Hill 1963

MALRAUX, ANDRÉ. *Museum without Walls.* London: Martin, Secker & Warburg 1967 (paper)

MC COUBREY, JOHN W. *American Tradition in Painting.* New York: George Braziller 1963

MEDLEY, MARGARET. *A Handbook of Chinese Art for Collectors and Students.* New York: Horizon Press 1965

MENDELOWITZ, DANIEL M. *A History of American Art.* New York: Holt, Rinehart and Winston 1967

METZL, ERVINE. *The Poster: Its History and Its Art*. New York: Watson-Guptill 1963

MYERS, BERNARD S., AND TREWIN COPPLESTONE, EDS. Landmarks of *the World's Art* series. New York: McGraw-Hill 1965. Titles include:
  LOMMEL, ANDREAS. *Prehistoric and Primitive Man*
  GARBINI, GIOVANNI. *The Ancient World*
  STRONG, DONALD. *The Classical World*
  LASSUS, JEAN. *The Early Christian and Byzantine World*
  GRUBE, ERNST. *The World of Islam*
  AUBOYER, JEAN, AND ROGER GOEPPER. *The Oriental World*
  KIDSON, PETER. *The Medieval World*
  MARTINDALE, ANDREW. *Man and the Renaissance*
  KITSON, MARTIN. *The Age of the Baroque*
  LYNTON, NORBERT. *The Modern World*

NEWTON, ERIC. *The Arts of Man*. Greenwich, Conn.: New York Graphic Society 1960

NEWTON, ERIC. *European Painting and Sculpture*. Baltimore, Md.: Penguin Books Inc. 1962 (paper)

OUSPENSKY, LEONID, AND VLADIMIR LOSSKY. *The Meaning of Icons*. Boston: Boston Book and Art Shop 1952

PANOFSKY, ERWIN. *Meaning in the Visual Arts*. Garden City, N.Y.: Doubleday 1955 (paper)

Praeger Art Books series in hard cover and paperback. New York: Frederick A. Praeger Inc.

REWALD, JOHN. *The History of Impressionism*. 2d ed. New York: Museum of Modern Art 1955

REWALD, JOHN. *Post-Impressionism from Van Gogh to Gauguin*. New York: Museum of Modern Art 1956

RICHARDSON, E. P. *Painting in America*. New York: Thomas Y. Crowell 1956

SAVAGE, GEORGE. *Forgeries, Fakes and Reproductions: A Handbook for the Art Dealer and Collector*. New York: Frederick A. Praeger 1964

TAYLOR, FRANCIS HENRY. *Fifty Centuries of Art*. New York: Harper & Bros. 1954

THOMPSON, JAMES W. *Masterpieces of Italian Painting.* New York: Harry N. Abrams, Inc. 1953

WATERHOUSE, ELLIS K. *Italian Baroque Painting.* London: Phaidon 1962

WATERHOUSE, ELLIS K. *Painting in Britain 1530-1790.* Baltimore, Md.: Penguin Books 1953 (paper)

WECHSLER, HERMAN J., ED. *The Pocket Book of Old Masters.* New York: Pocket Books, Inc. 1949

WILENSKI, R.H. *An Introduction to Dutch Art.* London: Faber & Faber 1937

WILENSKI, R.H. *French Painting.* Boston: Charles T. Branford 1950

WILLIAMS, HERMANN WARNER, JR. *The Civil War: The Artists' Record.* Boston: Beacon Press 1961

WINGERT, PAUL. *Primitive Art.* New York: Meridian Books 1965 (paper)

WÖFFLIN, HEINRICH. *Principles of Art History.* New York: Dover Publications 1950 (paper)

ZUCKER, PAUL. *Styles in Painting.* New York: Dover Publications 1963 (paper)

ILLUSTRATIONS IN BOOKS AND PERIODICALS

BREWER, REGINALD. *The Delightful Diversion.* New York: Macmillan 1935

CRANE, WALTER. *Of the Decorative Illustration of Books Old and New.* London: George Bell & Sons 1896

ELLIS, RICHARD WILLIAMSON. *Book Illustration: A Survey of Its History and Development, Shown by the Work of Various Artists.* Kingsport, Tenn.: Kingsport Press 1952

GARVEY, ELEANOR. *The Artist and the Book 1860-1960.* Cambridge: Harvard University Press 1961

HORODISCH, ABRAHAM. *Picasso as a Book Artist.* Cleveland, Ohio: World Publishing Co. 1962

IVINS, WILLIAM M., JR. *Prints and Books.* Cambridge, Mass.: Harvard University Press 1926

KELLER, MORTON. *The Art and Politics of Thomas Nast.* New York: Oxford University Press 1968

MCMURTRIE, DOUGLAS C. *The Golden Book.* New York: Covici Friede 1927

MICHENER, JAMES. *The Hokusai Sketchbooks.* 7th printing. Rutland, Vt.: Charles E. Tuttle Co. 1965

SIMON, HOWARD. *500 Years of Art in Illustration.* Cleveland, Ohio: World Publishing Co. 1945

STORM, COLTON, AND HOWARD PECKHAM. *Invitation to Book Collecting.* New York: R. R. Bowker Co. 1947

MUSEUM AND GALLERY GUIDES

Art in the U.S.A. and Where to Find It. New York: *Art Digest* 1965

The Curatorial Staff of the Metropolitan Museum. *Art Treasures of the Metropolitan.* New York: Harry N. Abrams, Inc. 1952

BRAIDER, DONALD. *Putnam's Guide to the Art Centers of Europe.* New York: G. P. Putnam's Sons 1965

BROWN, BLANCHE R. *Five Cities: An Art Guide to Athens, Rome, Florence, Paris and London.* New York: Doubleday and Co., Inc. 1964

CHARMET, RAYMOND. *The Museums of Paris (Great Galleries* series—see others also). New York: Meredith Press 1967

FAISON, S. LANE, JR. *Art Tours and Detours in New York State.* New York: Random House 1964

FAISON, S. LANE, JR. *A Guide to the Art Museums of New England.* New York: Harcourt Brace & Co. 1958

The Handbook of American Museums. Washington, D.C.: American Association of Museums, Smithsonian Institution 1932

HENDY, PHILIP. *Art Treasures of the National Gallery, London.* New York: Harry N. Abrams, Inc. 1955

HUYGHE, RENÉ. *Art Treasures of the Louvre.* New York: Dell 1962 (paper)

KATZ, HERBERT AND MARJORIE. *Museums U.S.A.: A History and a Guide.* New York: Doubleday 1965

NORMAN, JANE AND THEODORE. *Traveler's Guide to America's Art.* New York: Meredith Press 1968

NORMAN, JANE AND THEODORE. *Traveler's Guide to Europe's Art.* Rev. ed. New York: Meredith Press 1968

POLLEY, ROBERT L., ED. *Great Art Treasures in America's Smaller Museums.* New York: G. P. Putnam's Sons 1967

ROBERTS, LAURANCE P. *The Connoisseur's Guide to Japanese Museums.* Rutland, Vt.: Charles E. Tuttle Co. 1967

SPAETH, ELOISE. *American Art Museums and Galleries.* New York: Harper & Bros. 1960

WALKER, JOHN. *Art Treasures of the National Gallery (Great Paintings of the World* series—see others). New York: Harry N. Abrams, Inc. 1956

ORIGINAL PRINTS (including engravings, etchings, woodcuts, wood engravings and lithographs)

ADHÉMAR, J. *Graphic Art of the 18th Century.* New York: McGraw Hill Co. 1964 (paper and hard cover)

ARMS, JOHN TAYLOR. *Handbook of Printmaking and Print Makers.* New York: Macmillan 1934

BINYON, LAWRENCE, AND J. J. O'BRIEN SEXTON. *Japanese Colour Prints.* Frederick Publications 1954 (Originally printed London 1923; more recent edition London 1960)

BLAND, JANE COOPER. *Currier & Ives: A Manual for Collectors.* Garden City: Doubleday, Doran & Co. 1931

BLISS, DOUGLAS PERCY. *A History of Wood Engraving.* London: Spring Books 1964

BRIGHAM, CLARENCE S. *Paul Revere's Engravings.* Worcester, Mass.: American Antiquarian Society 1954

BURGESS, FRED W. *Old Prints and Engravings.* New York: G. P. Putnam's Sons 1925

CRAVEN, THOMAS, ED. *A Treasury of American Prints.* New York: Simon & Schuster 1939

DREPPARD, CARL W. *Early American Prints.* New York: Century Co. 1930

EICHENBERG, FRITZ, ED. *Artists' Proof: The Annual of Prints and Printmaking.* Vols. VII, VIII and IX (and earlier volumes; each includes an original print). Barre, Mass.: Barre Publishers 1967, 1968, 1969

FICKE, ARTHUR DAVISON. *Chats on Japanese Prints.* Rutland, Vt.: Charles E. Tuttle Co. 1958

FIELD, RICHARD S. *Fifteenth Century Woodcuts and Metalcuts.* Washington, D.C.: National Gallery of Art 1965

GETLEIN, FRANK AND DOROTHY. *The Bite of the Print.* New York: Clarkson N. Potter, Inc. 1963

HAAS, IRVIN. *A Treasury of Great Prints.* New York: A. S. Barnes & Co. 1956 (paper)

HAYDEN, ARTHUR, AND CYRIL G. E. BUNT. *Old Prints.* London: Ernst Benn Ltd 1956

HAYTER, S. W. *About Prints.* London: Oxford University Press 1962

HILLIER, J. R. *Japanese Masters of the Colour Print.* London: Phaidon 1954.

HIND, ARTHUR M. *A History of Engraving and Etching from the 15th Century to the Year 1914.* New York: Dover Publications 1963 (paper)

HIND, ARTHUR M. *An Introduction to a History of Woodcut.* 2 vols. New York: Dover Publications 1963

HOUSTON, JAMES. *Eskimo Prints.* Barre, Mass.: Barre Publishers 1967

IVINS, WILLIAM M., JR. *How Prints Look.* Boston: Beacon Press 1958 (paper)

IVINS, WILLIAM M., JR. *Notes on Prints.* New York: Da Capo Press 1967

KARSHAN, DONALD H. "American Printmaking, 1670-1968." *Art in America* 4, July-August 1968, pp. 22-54

KRISTLER, ALINE. *Understanding Prints.* New York: Associated American Artists 1936

LANE, RICHARD. *Masters of the Japanese Print*. Garden City, N.Y.: Doubleday 1962

LAVER, JAMES. *A History of British and American Etching*. New York: Dodd, Mead & Co. 1929

LEVIS, HOWARD C. *A Descriptive Bibliography of the Most Important Books in the English Language relating to the Art and History of Engraving and the Collecting of Prints*. London: Chiswick Press 1912

LONGSTREET, STEPHEN. *A Treasury of the World's Great Prints*. New York: Simon & Schuster 1961

LUMSDEN, E. S. *The Art of Etching*. New York: Dover Publications 1962 (paper)

MABERLY, J. *The Print Collector*. New York: Dodd, Mead & Co. 1880

MAYOR, A. HYATT. *Prints*. New York: Metropolitan Museum of Art 1964 (paper)

MICHENER, JAMES A. *The Floating World*. New York: Random House 1954

MICHENER, JAMES A. *The Modern Japanese Print*. Rutland, Vt.: Charles E. Tuttle Co. 1968

PENNELL, JOSEPH. *The Graphic Arts*. Chicago: University of Chicago Press 1921

PETERDI, GABOR. *Printmaking*. New York: Macmillan 1959

ROGER-MARX, CLAUDE. *Graphic Art of the 19th Century*. London: Thames & Hudson 1962 (paper)

SACHS, PAUL J. *A Loan Exhibition of Early Italian Engravings, Fogg Art Museum*. Cambridge, Mass.: Harvard University Press 1915

SHESTACK, ALAN. *Fifteenth Century Engravings of Northern Europe*. Washington, D.C.: National Gallery of Art 1967 (paper)

STEWART, BASIL. *Subjects Portrayed in Japanese Colour-Prints: A Collector's Guide to All the Subjects Illustrated*. London: K. Paul, Trench, Trubner and Co., Ltd. 1922

WECHSLER, HERMAN J. *Great Prints and Printmakers*. New York: Harry N. Abrams, Inc. 1967

WEITENKAMPF, FRANK. *How to Appreciate Prints.* New York: Moffat, Yard & Co. 1909

ZIGROSSER, CARL. *The Book of Fine Prints.* New York: Crown Publishers, Inc. 1956

ZIGROSSER, CARL, AND CHRISTA A. GAEHDE. *A Guide to the Collecting and Care of Original Prints.* New York: Crown Publishers, Inc. 1965

SCULPTURE AND ARTIFACTS

BECKER-DONNER, E. *Ancient American Painting.* New York: Crown Publishers, Inc. 1963 (for artifacts)

BUSHNELL, G. H. S. *Ancient Arts of the Americas.* New York: Frederick A. Praeger 1965 (paper and hard cover)

COE, MICHAEL D. *The Jaguar's Children: Pre-Classic Central Mexico.* Greenwich, Conn.: New York Graphic Society 1967

D'HARCOURT, RAOUL. *Primitive Art of the Americas.* New York: Tudor 1950

DOUGLAS, FREDERICK H., AND RENÉ D'HARNONCOURT. *Indian Art of the United States.* New York: Museum of Modern Art 1941

FAGG, WILLIAM, AND MARGARET PLASS. *African Sculpture.* Rev. ed. New York: E. P. Dutton & Co. 1966

GOLDWATER, ROBERT. *Senufo Sculpture from West Africa.* Greenwich, Conn.: New York Graphic Society 1967

HANFMANN, GEORGE M. A. *Classical Sculpture.* Greenwich, Conn.: New York Graphic Society 1967

LEHMANN, HENRI. *Pre-Columbian Ceramics.* New York: Viking Press 1962

LICHT, FRED. *Sculpture of the 19th and 20th Centuries.* Greenwich, Conn.: New York Graphic Society 1967

LOTHROP, S. K.; W. F. FOSHAG; AND JOY MAHLER. *Pre-Columbian Art.* New York: Phaidon 1957

Masterpieces in the Museum of Primitive Art: Handbook #1. Greenwich, Conn.: New York Graphic Society 1967

MYERS, BERNARD. *Sculpture: Form and Method.* New York: Reinhold Publishing Corporation 1965 (paper)

NICHOLSON, FELICITY. *Greek, Etruscan and Roman Pottery and Small Terracottas.* London: Cory, Adams & MacKay, Ltd. 1965

RACHELWITZ, BORIS DE. *Introduction to African Art.* New York: New American Library 1966

READ, HERBERT. *The Art of Sculpture.* New York: Pantheon Books 1956

READ, HERBERT. *A Concise History of Modern Sculpture.* New York: Frederick A. Praeger 1964 (paper)

SAWYER, ALAN R. *Ancient Peruvian Ceramics.* New York: Metropolitan Museum of Art 1966 (paper and hard cover)

SOUSTELLE, JACQUES. *The Arts of Ancient Mexico.* New York: Viking Press 1967

TUCHMAN, MAURICE. *American Sculpture of the Sixties.* Greenwich, Conn.: New York Graphic Society 1967

VAILLANT, GEORGE C. *Aztecs of Mexico.* Rev. ed. Garden City, N.Y.: Doubleday & Co. 1962

WESTHEIM, PAUL. *The Art of Ancient Mexico.* Garden City, N.Y.: Doubleday & Co. 1965 (paper)